D1604195

The Collected Works of Hugh Nibley: Volume 8
The Book of Mormon

THE PROPHETIC
BOOK OF MORMON

Hugh Nibley

John W. Welch
Editor

Deseret Book Company
Salt Lake City, Utah
and
Foundation for Ancient Research and Mormon Studies
Provo, Utah

The Collected Works of Hugh Nibley

The Collected Works of Hugh Nibley
includes volumes on the following subjects:

The Old Testament and Related Studies
Ancient History
The Pearl of Great Price
Early Christianity
The Book of Mormon
The Doctrine and Covenants and Mormonism
Education, Politics, and Society

Other volumes in this series:

Old Testament and Related Studies
Enoch the Prophet
The World and the Prophets
Mormonism and Early Christianity
Lehi in the Desert/The World of the Jaredites/There Were Jaredites
An Approach to the Book of Mormon
Since Cumorah

Library of Congress Cataloging-in-Publication Data

Nibley, Hugh, 1910–
    The prophetic Book of Mormon.
        (The Collected works of Hugh Nibley ; v. 8)
    Includes bibliographies and index.
        1. Book of Mormon—Criticism, interpretation, etc.   I. Welch, John W. (John Woodland)   II. Title.   III. Series: Nibley, Hugh, 1910–   .   Works. 1986 ; v. 8.

BX8627 .N483   1988   289.3'22   88-30986
ISBN 0-87579-179-4

Printed in the United States of America   18961-2963
R. R. Donnelley and Sons, Crawfordsville, IN

10   9   8   7   6

Contents

Key to Abbreviations

ARW	Archiv für Religionswissenschaft
CJ	Classical Journal
CWHN	Collected Works of Hugh Nibley
JAOS	Journal of the American Oriental Society
JBL	Journal of Biblical Literature
PEFQ	Palestine Exploration Fund Quarterly
PG	J.-P. Migne, Patrologiae Cursus Completus . . . Series Graeca (Paris: Migne, 1857–66), 161 vols.
PL	J.-P. Migne, Patrologiae Cursus Completus . . . Series Latina (Paris: Migne, 1844–64), 221 vols.
PO	R. Graffin and F. Nau, eds., Patrologia Orientalis (Paris: Firmin-Didot, 1907–)
RE	Pauly-Wissowa, Paulys Realencyclopädie der classischen Altertumswissenschaft (Stuttgart: Metzler, 1893–)
WPQ	Western Political Quarterly
ZDMG	Zeitschrift der deutschen morgenländischen Gesellschaft
ZDPV	Zeitschrift des Deutschen Palästina-Vereins

Foreword

For Hugh Nibley, the Book of Mormon is prophetic in every sense of the word. It is written by prophets and about prophets. It was foreseen by prophets and foresees our day. It is a book brought forth by prophetic gifts for prophetic purposes. It speaks forth in a clarion voice of warning with words of counsel to those who would survive the last days.

The articles in this volume, brought together under one cover for the first time, approach the Book of Mormon through a variety of prophetic themes. These essays speak out incisively on themes ranging from the prophecies of Ezekiel 37, and Nephi's vision of Columbus, to internal and external evidences of the divine origins of the Book of Mormon, and jolting messages of things as they really are in the world around us and of things that must soon come to pass.

Many of these themes are familiar to readers of Nibley's three main volumes on the Book of Mormon: *Lehi in the Desert* (1952), *An Approach to the Book of Mormon* (1957), and *Since Cumorah* (1967), appearing in volumes 5, 6, and 7 in these *Collected Works*. The essays in this volume are the remaining Book of Mormon articles and talks written by Nibley from 1953 to the present. These materials are presented in this volume in the order in which they were written, to give the reader a sense of Nibley's consistent but diverse work on the Book of Mormon over the forty years since he joined the faculty at Brigham Young University. Most of these chapters have been previously published in scattered locations, but some appear here for the first time. Some are carefully developed papers; others are transcripts of talks; in some places they include unpolished exploratory notes.

Although these articles were not originally written to appear in a single volume, they cluster together naturally and without difficulty. Thus, while there is a bit of duplication among some of the chapters, each case approaches its subject matter from a distinctive, informative angle. Moreover, while each article was addressed to a different audience and was written for its own particular purpose, the entire volume is conceptually unified by the important methodological comments developed in chapter 3, "New Approaches to Book of Mormon Study." The points raised there sensitize the reader to the fact that different kinds of evidence exist—internal, external, circumstantial—and that each kind must be accurately assessed and soundly employed. Furthermore, the assorted tasks, specific purposes, and challenges undertaken in these essays also justify the various approaches employed from one chapter to the next.

Nibley's points are as relevant today as they were the day they were written. The topics he discusses, like forgery, or facile attempts to attribute Book of Mormon authorship to Joseph Smith, sound as current as this morning's newspaper.

In 1948, Nibley wrote his first published statement on the Book of Mormon. It was a book review of Sidney Sperry's *Our Book of Mormon*.[1] This short review reveals more about Nibley than the book being reviewed. More than he or anyone else in 1948 could have known, his comments presage his own work on the Book of Mormon over the next forty years; for the virtues he saw in Sperry's book, and the standards by which he judged it, are the ideals Nibley himself has consistently strived to attain in his own

works. They are the standards by which it is fair to judge
Nibley himself.

Nibley admired Sperry's book for being "forthright,
methodical," one "that hues to the line and never
flinches." He praised a "refreshing directness" in an author
who "raises and answers searching but simple questions
one after another that surprise the reader by their obviousness and almost alarm him with the sense of his own
ignorance." He delighted in seeing "long-neglected
lore . . . put on display, much of it for the first time." He
extolled the writer who does not "go overboard for any
one theory, . . . [who] never temporises and never quib-
bles." He admired one who avoids "the tricks and pitfalls
of rhetoric . . . like the plague." Above all, he found that
a book about the Book of Mormon exercises its greatest
fascination on the reader by drawing the reader "again and
again" back into the Book of Mormon itself, for it is "a
mighty revelation which we neglect at our peril."

Nibley saw these things as strengths in the work of
another. In the present volume, readers will unmistakably
see Nibley at work on his own terms: forthright, methodical, refreshingly direct, searching but simple, surprising
the reader with an obviousness that instills a sense of one's
own ignorance, utilizing many theories, speaking honestly
and in search of truth, not of rhetoric, and, above all,
drawing the reader again and again back into lengthy nar-
ratives of the Book of Mormon, a book we have still only
begun to understand and must not neglect. It is a matter
of great seriousness, one that we neglect at our peril.

As Nibley has said in a variety of ways, "The Book of
Mormon should take priority. We need to make the Book
of Mormon the object of serious study—superficiality is
quite offensive to the Lord. We have not paid enough
attention to this important book. The Book of Mormon is
a witness of God's concern for all his children, and the
intimate proximity of Jesus Christ to all who will receive

him. It is a wonderful guide in the present world situation. Learning is of immense value, and careful study of the Book of Mormon is of eternal value. Rather than wasting valuable time reading so much empty drivel, we should be studying things of the eternities."

The present volume of essays takes all readers in this direction. Though one may revise, refine, challenge, reexamine, and rethink points from time to time in these essays, their lasting contribution is powerful. This is basically because Nibley takes the Book of Mormon seriously: textually, historically, doctrinally, and practically. For him, the Book of Mormon surely means what it says, and thus his pursuit of its meaning, in word and in deed, has been not a casual curiosity but a lifetime pilgrimage.

Nibley praised Sperry for his persistent campaign in behalf of the Book of Mormon as deserving "nothing but praise." It is now fitting to return that compliment to Nibley himself. No one has made the Book of Mormon more an object of persistent, serious, and extensive study than he has. And no one sees more clearly than he does the need for this ongoing endeavor to continue.

This volume concludes the Book of Mormon component of *The Collected Works of Hugh Nibley*. The four Book of Mormon volumes in this series should be seen as a unit in order to understand the interrelated Book of Mormon insights of Nibley's mind and spirit. These four volumes could not have been collected, checked, edited, and published without the dedicated work of Fran Clark, Stephen Callister, Gary Gillum, John Gee, Darryl Hague, Richard Hiltbrunn, Jack Lyon, Cie Mason, Darrell Matthews, Brent McNeely, Brenda Miles, Mari Miles, Phyllis Nibley, Don Norton, Stephen Ricks, and Jim Tredway. Funding to facilitate these publications has been generously donated by John S. and Unita Welch, Wallace E. and Patricia Hunt, Jr., Randall and Jann Paul, and others. Their dedicated efforts and support is gratefully acknowledged and appreciated.

JOHN W. WELCH
EDITOR

Notes

1. *Improvement Era* 51 (January 1948): 42.

1

The Stick of Judah

The word of the Lord came again unto me, saying,
Moreover, thou son of man, take thee one stick, and
write upon it, For Judah, and for the children of Israel
his companions: then take another stick, and write upon
it, For Joseph, the stick of Ephraim, and for all the house
of Israel his companions: and join them one to another
into one stick; and they shall become one in thine hand.

And when the children of thy people shall speak
unto thee, saying, Wilt thou not shew us what thou
meanest by these? Say unto them, Thus saith the Lord
God; Behold, I will take the stick of Joseph, which is in
the hand of Ephraim, and the tribes of Israel his fellows,
and will put them with him, even with the stick of Judah,
and make them one stick, and they shall be one in mine
hand.

And the sticks whereon thou writest shall be in thine
hand before their eyes. And say unto them, Thus saith
the Lord God; Behold, I will take the children of Israel
from among the heathen, whither they be gone, and will
gather them on every side, and bring them into their
own land (Ezekiel 37:15-21).

This article first appeared in five parts in the Improvement Era *(January
1953–May 1953). It draws heavily on an earlier article by the author,* "The
Arrow, the Hunter, and the State," *Western Political Quarterly 2/3
(1949): 328-44. It was also summarized in chapter 24 of* An Approach
to the Book of Mormon *(Salt Lake City: Deseret Book, 1957 and 1964);
reprinted in CWHN, 6:311-28.*

The Doctors Disagree

In maintaining that Ezekiel in his account of the sticks of Judah and Joseph (Ezekiel 37:15-21) was actually referring in prophetic language to the Bible and the Book of Mormon, the Latter-day Saints may invoke the prerogative of any pious reader of the scriptures to interpret any symbolic passage in whatever way carries the most conviction. But the more aggressive use of the passage to support the claims of the Book of Mormon cannot but elicit loud protests and challenges from the outside world. To answer these, it is necessary to demonstrate not only that our interpretation of the passage is a possible one—for there are many possibilities—but that it is also the one most likely intended by the Prophet Ezekiel. The one way to do this is to show (1) that Ezekiel's strange conception and manipulation of the sticks was not a bizarre or original conceit, but that it was strictly in accordance with ancient practices perfectly familiar to the Jews of that time though lost to the modern world, and (2) that the prophet put a definite interpretation on the stick ritual according to which it can hardly have represented anything but the two books in question.

In explaining this remarkable scripture we are not bound by the opinions of even the most learned so long as there is no consensus among them. Fortunately, we find ourselves in perfect agreement with them in all those points on which they agree among themselves. But for the rest we need not and cannot follow them, for they all rush in different directions. Nor do we expect others to follow our opinions in the matter, but only to view the evidence and form their own. The distinguishing mark of biblical commentaries in general is a dignified unconcern for anything that might be called evidence on the subject. The sheer momentum of a heavy theological phraseology, sustained by an occasional (often irrelevant) passage of scripture, is thought quite sufficient to override any "saucy doubts and fears" of the layman.

Two sticks are mentioned. What were they actually? Simply sticks or small pieces of wood, according to some writers,[1] the two parts of a broken scepter,[2] "two pieces of what was probably a broken, scepter-shaped stick,"[3] "sticks — probably shaped like scepters,"[4] according to others. "Tribal rods" is another interpretation, based on Numbers 17,[5] and even "pilgrim rods" has been suggested.[6] Shepherds' staves,[7] branches cut from a common trunk,[8] and boards for writing[9] have also been considered. Against all of these one of the weightiest authorities, Keil, insists that there is not the slightest proof that ʿetz, "wood," the Hebrew word here so lyrically interpreted, means "staff" or "rod" at all, and that if any kind of staff had been intended a different word would have been used. "Nor have we even to think of flat boards, but simply of pieces of wood upon which a few words could be written," adds Dr. Keil, thus denying the wood any form at all.[10] But since the Septuagint renders Ezekiel's "wood" as *rhabdos*, "staff," "rod," and the Bible itself offers convincing parallels (especially Numbers 17), the commentators overwhelmingly favor some form of staff, and in this we gladly concur. As to Ezekiel's refusal to call a staff a staff, upon which Keil lays so much stress, we shall see that that is significant when we come to deciding what the "woods" actually were.

Next we are told that the two sticks are joined together to make one. How was that done? According to the broken-staff theory, by joining together the two broken ends; according to the pilgrim-staff theory, by simply carrying the two sticks together in one hand;[11] they were *tied* together according to some — and the Septuagint would bear this out;[12] but still other methods have been suggested, such as "by a notch, dovetail, glue, or some such method."[13] Skinner says the prophet "put them end to end, and made

them look like one," but also suggests the possibility that
"when the rods are put together they miraculously grow
into one."[14] Is it necessary to suppose that Ezekiel did
anything at all with sticks? "It is a little difficult to decide,"
says the authority just cited, "whether this was a sign that
was actually performed before the people, or one that is
only imagined. It depends on what we take to be meant
by the joining of the two pieces. . . . If the meaning
is . . . that when the rods are put together, they miraculously grow into one, . . . it is no longer necessary to assume that the action was really performed."[15] "This
symbolical action," writes Davidson in the Cambridge
Bible, "may have been actually performed, though the
supposition is scarcely necessary."[16]

So all the experts have to offer us is a vague admission
that there were sticks and that they were joined: *What* the
sticks were and *how* they were joined remains a mystery.
As to *why* they were joined, Ezekiel himself gives an adequate explanation, only to encumber it, in the view of the
critics, by a needlessly complex description of what was
done. "The purpose of the sign is not merely to suggest
the idea of political unity," writes Skinner, speaking of the
joining of the two sticks, "which is too simple to require
any such illustration, but rather to indicate the complete-
ness of the union and the divine force needed to bring it
about."[17] But is this not also "too simple to require an
illustration" that has the sticks united now in one bundle,
now in another, and variously brought together in the
hands of Ezekiel, Joseph, Ephraim, Judah, David, and the
Lord? The passage "seems to be filled out with explanatory
notes which spoil the balance and harmony of the clauses,"
according to Cooke, who to restore balance and harmony
will strike out whatever seems clumsy.[18] Yet as Housman
so emphatically observes, it is just such clumsiness that is
the surest sign of genuineness in an ancient text. Even the
great Bentley, says Housman, "forgot that counterfeit

verses are not wont to be meaningless . . . and that the aim of interpolators is not to make difficulties but to remove them,"[19] i.e., that if an ancient text displays that "balance and harmony" which our critics crave, it is probably because earlier critics have tidied it up. When all the manuscripts at our disposal display signs of confusion, "those MSS are to be preferred," Housman reminds us, "which give the worst nonsense, because they are likely to be the least interpolated."[20]

Let the nineteenth verse of the thirty-seventh chapter illustrate the real complexity of Ezekiel's account, upon which scholars have sought to impose simplicity by altering the text. Rendered literally, the verse reads: "Verily I am taking the wood of Joseph which is in the hand of Ephraim and the *shivte* of Israel his associates, and I shall place them upon it along with [*eth*] the wood of Judah, and I shall make them for one wood, and they shall be one in my hand." Three things here complicate the picture.

First, there are the *shivte* of Israel. Now, *shivte* means simply staff or rod: it is cognate with the Latin *scipio*, probably with our own "staff," and certainly with the Greek *skeptron*, whence our word "scepter." Since tribes were anciently identified by rods (Numbers 17:2), *shevet* can be read "tribe" in certain contexts. But since in this verse the *shivte* of Israel are to be placed upon or fitted against the stick of Joseph, this is one place where the rendering of *shevet* in its proper sense of rod is particularly appropriate, as Migne observes,[21] since tribes cannot be placed upon another rod, while other rods can. One has the authority of the Septuagint for reading *shivte* here as "tribes," but it is clear that the Septuagint has distorted the whole passage, for every time "staff" or "wood" appears in the verse, it is uniformly rendered "tribe," so that the whole ritual of the sticks is completely obliterated. As the passage stands, it describes Ephraim as possessing a number of documents relating to Joseph and members of the house of Israel associated with him; these are to be fitted together with a like collection of documents relating to Judah and "his companions" (Ezekiel 37:16). This complexity renders the passage "incomprehensible" (*unverständlich*) to Guthe,[22] while Jamieson would escape it by changing "them" to read "it."[23] To leave the passage as it stands opens up a number of disturbing possibilities which must be removed at all cost, even if it means rewriting the text or declaring it nonsense.

An annoying confirmation of this seemingly needless complexity is the Hebrew *eth*, which we have rendered "along with" and which implies that the stick of Joseph, having first been compounded in the hand of Ephraim of a number of "rods," will then be joined to the (compound) stick of Judah. Read this way, the *eth* makes perfectly good sense, but if one wants a simpler reading "the construction is rather unnatural," as the Cambridge Bible observes.[24] "Jack and Jill went up the hill," etc., is an "unnatural construction" if an editor is convinced that water is found only at the bottom of hills, and so "up" should be emended to read "down." Just so, some editors faced by this *eth* have calmly changed it to *el* and thus removed the offensive word from their sight.[25]

The third rock of offense in this one verse is the statement "they shall become one in *my* hand." There have always been scholars favoring the Septuagint reading, "in the hand of Judah."[26] Yet as the Cambridge Bible points out, such an emendation is not permissible, since "there is no trace in the passage of any preeminence of Judah over Israel of the north" — which should be obvious to any reader, since the equality of the two nations is strongly emphasized in the chapter.[27] Why then do the scholars prefer a reading that is poorly supported by text and context to one that is well supported? Because "in the hand of Judah" sounds more like history, while "in my hand" is the stuff of prophecy — always more suspect and baffling.

Modern scholars, like ancient Targumists, have not hesitated "to modify the language of the prophet . . . and even, in certain cases, to reverse the plain meaning of the text," when it has served their purpose to do so.[28]

And so our appeal to the experts brings little reward, since their work is little more than speculation rather than searching for evidence. Such a search, however, may turn out to be quite profitable, and if the least be said we cannot well avoid undertaking it.

What Were the Sticks?

The theme of the whole thirty-seventh chapter of Ezekiel is clear to all: it is the great final gathering of the Lord's people into a holy nation, united forever under the scepter of the rightful king, God's anointed, with the sanctuary of the Lord forever in their midst (Ezekiel 37:21-28).[29] The dry bones of the first half of the chapter represent an Israel that has lost hope of ever becoming a nation again, and as Professor Driver observes, Ezekiel shows that "God can endow the seemingly dead nation with fresh life, and plant it again in its old land."[30] Driver further points out what most scholars overlook, that the uniting of the sticks to represent (as the prophet explains, Ezekiel 37:20-22) the reuniting of the nation is a necessary part of the picture. More recently, Rabbi Fisch has confirmed this basic interpretation.[31] Now the bringing together of tribal rods or staffs marked with the names of tribes was actually practiced in Israel when the nation assembled, and indeed commentators have not failed to note the probable identity of the "sticks" of Ezekiel with the tribal rods described in the seventeenth chapter of Numbers. But since the experts have failed to look into the remarkable institution of the tribal rods, it will be necessary here for us to consider the subject briefly, referring the reader, as much out of necessity as vanity, to studies of our own on the topic.

The great national assemblies of the Israelites, such as

that one idealized in Ezekiel 37, had their counterpart in every nation of the ancient world. For thousands of years and "at hundreds of holy shrines, each believed to mark the exact center of the universe, . . . one might have seen assembled at the New Year—the moment of creation, the beginning and ending of time—vast concourses of people, each thought to represent the entire human race in the presence of all its ancestors and gods."[32] The concept of a great and perfect assembly of the whole human race at the throne of a heavenly king is thus the dream and ideal of every nation of the ancient world, and that not by virtue of independent invention or evolutionary development, but rather as the common, though often denatured, heritage from a single lost pattern of church and priesthood.[33]

All who came to these assemblies were represented individually and collectively by rods or sticks. Consider first the individual identification rod:

> Throughout the northern steppe it was the custom to require all who came to the king's assembly to bring arrows with them, and to present these personally to the king. From these arrows a census was taken, each man submitting but a single shaft, which represented him and bore his mark, for "both the Old World and the New, the arrow came to stand as the token and symbol of a man." To the arrows thus used may be applied, for want of a better term, the name "census-arrow." The census-arrow is found among the Scythians, Tartars, Persians, Georgians, Norsemen, and American Indians, and it survived in recognizable form in India, Egypt, and the Far East.[34]

The Greeks and Romans preserved the census-arrows as a simple rod or staff, such as the marked rods that had to be presented by the jurors for admission to the heliastic courts, and the "sections of reed" submitted by all who would participate in the great public feasts in the Eastern Empire. The Arabs always "employed reed arrow-shafts, devoid alike of feathers and heads, but bearing some marks of individual ownership, 'to make division' at their tribal feasts,"[35] a custom which Freeman refers directly to the "sticks" of Ezekiel, chapter 37.[36] The use of such identification-sticks on the occasion of the great assembly of Israel is clear from Numbers 17, while in the oldest Christian literary composition, "the Pastor of Hermas (*Similitudes* viii, 1-6), all who come to the assembly of the Lord present sections of willow-reed for admission, each receiving his proper place as designated by certain cuts (*schismata*) on his rod."[37]

The rods or arrows submitted by all who came to the feast were often bound together in a ritual bundle to signify the unity of the nation. "Bundles of fifty-two rods, bearing individual and tribal markings, . . . represented the full membership of Indian tribes in assembly," as of the Tartar tribes of Asia.[38] Equally common are tribal bundles of seven arrows, such as the holy bundle of the Osage, which "represented the Seven Chiefs, who held the tribe together in peaceful unity."[39] Such tribal bundles are found in the Old World among "the Scythians, Alans, Slavs, and ancient Germans (who also chose their leaders by drawing willow lots), and these have been compared with the Persian Baresma."[40] The Persian king would sit with the Baresma spread out before him at the New Year, telling the fortunes of the year as he gave away unlimited wealth to all the tribes who came to answer the summons to present themselves before him on that day—the only day of the year on which the veil between him and the outer world was removed. This recalls the king of Babylon "shaking out the arrows" before him in divination at the New Year,[41] and Hoenir in the Far North, holding his holy lottery in the Golden Age.[42] It most vividly reminds one of the ritual feasts of certain Indians of the northwest coast.[43]

The most famous of all tribal bundles, with one exception, was the Roman *fasces*, symbol of the unity and au-

thority of the nation—originally twelve sticks bound together to represent twelve Etruscan tribes.[44] The one
exception is, of course, that bundle of twelve rods which,
according to the Talmud, were all cut from a single stick
and bound together when Moses laid them up in the ark.[45]
What may be the earliest Christian writing after the New
Testament thus elaborates on the account in Numbers 17:

> And he took them and bound them together, and
> sealed [them] with the rings of the leaders of the tribes,
> and he laid them up in the Ark of the Covenant before
> the altar of God. And he closed the Ark and sealed the
> locks, just as he had the rods. Then he said unto them:
> Men and brethren, that tribe whose rod shall blossom
> has been chosen of God to be priests and ministers to
> Him. And when it was morning, he summoned together
> all Israel, the 600,000 men, showed the seals to the lead-
> ers of the tribe, opened the Ark of the Covenant, and
> brought out the rods.[46]

A variation on this theme is the very ancient story of
"how all the men of Israel were required to attend a great
assembly, bringing each his staff, to be handed over to the
high priest and used in a lottery for the distribution of
brides," which has close parallels among the Bedouins,
Scythians, the ancient Turkish, Finnish, Mongolian, and
Ossetian tribes.[47] There is a remarkable expression found
in the colophon of the oldest known Hebrew text of the
Pentateuch (the Aleppo Codex, cir. A.D. 930), in which the
author of the text is designated as "Mar Rab Ahron Ben
Mar Rab Sher, may his soul be bound in the Bundle of Life
with the righteous and wise prophets."[48] Farther on, the
colophon speaks of a group of other venerable doctors:
"May their souls be bound in the Bundle of Life in the
Garden of Eden beneath the Tree of Life."[49] From these
expressions it is apparent that the tribal bundle was actually
an ancient Hebrew institution.

It is quite obvious that these customs, found throughout the entire world (we have but skimmed the surface here), are no local inventions, but all go back to a single prototype. When Fowkes compares the holiest possession of the Cheyennes, a ritual arrow-bundle, with the Jewish Ark of the Covenant,[50] we are faced with a challenge that cannot easily be brushed aside — whence this amazing uniformity in the ways of ancient men the world over? We cannot investigate the problem here: *Why* the ancients chose to be represented individually and collectively by marked rods when they came together at their great national assemblies is a subject I have treated elsewhere;[51] what concerns us here is simply the fact that they did practice such a strange economy, and that the tribal rods of which Ezekiel is speaking are no fanciful invention of his own but something quite familiar to the people to whom he is speaking. The ruin of Moab is represented by Jeremiah as the breaking of his rod: "And all ye that know [or recognize] his name, say, How is the strong staff broken, and the beautiful rod!" (Jeremiah 48:17). Here the name is recognized written on the rod. Ezekiel himself (Ezekiel 19:10-14) depicts the fall of the nation by the breaking of its rods: "Her strong rods were broken and withered" (Ezekiel 19:12), the rods being "strong rods for the sceptres of them that bare rule" (Ezekiel 19:11).

It is only natural that an identification-staff should serve as a rod of office or authority. As such it commonly served in ancient times as a message-staff or "summons-arrow":

> Throughout the ancient world a ruler was thought to command everything his arrow could touch. Thus whenever a ruler of the North would summon all his subjects to his presence, he would order an arrow, usually called a "war-arrow" (*herör*) to be "cut up" and sent out among them. Upon being touched by this arrow, every man had immediately to "follow the arrow" (*fylga örum*) to the royal presence or suffer banishment from

the kingdom. . . . The "cutting" of the arrow was the placing of the royal mark upon it, giving it the form of the king's seal. As often as not the arrow *took the form of a simple rod (stefni),* bearing marks of authorization, while the message was delivered by word of mouth.[52]

Such a use of the message-stick is found everywhere in antiquity—we need not go through the list again but should point out that the institution was also found among the Jews. Thus "the Lord, calling upon a city to declare its allegiance to him, sends his rod to it, and a herald (a man of *tushiah),* seeing the name on the rod, calls out to the people: 'Hear ye the rod and the one who hath appointed it' "[53] (see also Micah 6:9). In Ezekiel 37:18 it is evident that the inscribed sticks are to serve as messenger-staves. The prophet is to show them to all the people, and when they ask him what the message is, he is to repeat the words summoning them all to the great assembly: "The Lord Jehovah . . . will take the sons of Israel out of the nations among whom they walk, and will gather them from round about, and lead them into their land." The prophet is God's herald, sent to gather in the hosts for the last time. Jane Harrison has noted that the herald's staff "is in intent a king's sceptre held by the herald as deputy,"[54] and few have failed to observe that the sticks in Ezekiel 37 are, among other things, scepters.

How thoroughly familiar the Jews of old were with the use and significance of various types of symbolic rods may be seen from the wealth of tradition built up around the wonderful Rod of Aaron. This was "the rod that the Holy One . . . created in the twilight of the first Sabbath eve and gave to Adam. He transmitted it to Enoch," from whom it passed down in succession to Noah, Shem, Abraham, and Joseph, from whom it was stolen by servants of Pharaoh, only to be stolen back again by the man whose daughter married Moses who alone of all her suitors was able to grasp the rod without being consumed.[55] According to another account, "Jacob wrested the rod from Esau, and . . . he always kept it with him. . . . At his death he bequeathed it to his favorite son Joseph."[56] We are assured that "Aaron's rod is identical with the rod of Judah," and that the same rod was in David's hand when he went to fight Goliath, and that it will come from hiding in the time of the Messiah.[57] It is this very rod "that the Judean kings used until the time of the destruction of the Temple, when, in miraculous fashion, it disappeared. Elijah will in the future fetch it forth and hand it to the Messiah."[58] For when the Messiah comes, it is by this rod, which bears his name, that he will establish his *identity* before the people: first of all, we are told, will come Elijah, and to make sure of the identity of the Messiah, "the Jews will demand that he perform the miracle of resurrection before their eyes," instead of which he will "wave the sceptre given him by God. . . . Then the Jews will believe that Elijah is the Elijah promised to them and the Messiah."[59] The Book of the Bee brings this same staff into the Christian system by claiming that "it belonged to Joseph [the carpenter] . . . at the moment of the birth of the Saviour, and it served afterwards as one of the planks in the Cross of Christ."[60]

Note that this staff in the hand of a prophet or patriarch is a true herald's staff, "in intent a king's sceptre held by the herald as deputy." Thus God is represented as promising to Moses in the hereafter: "One of my many sceptres upon which is engraved the Ineffable Name, one that I had employed in the creation of the world, shall I give to thee, the image of which I had already given thee in this world."[61] And thus Moses speaks to the Red Sea: "For a whole day I spoke to thee at the bidding of the Holy One, . . . but thou didst refuse to heed my words; *even when I showed thee my rod*, thou didst remain obdurate."[62] When Pharaoh asked Moses and Aaron, "Who will believe you when you say that you are ambassadors of God, as you pretend to be?" the credentials they produced were the rod and its miracles.[63] This aspect of the rod as a sign to the world that God has given his authority to the holder is very significant, since it represents the power of priesthood: Indeed, the early Christian Fathers insist that the rod is simply a symbolic representation of the power of priesthood: "The rod of Aaron," says Justin Martyr, "bearing blossoms showed him to be the High Priest. A rod from the root of Jesse became the Christ. . . . By the wood God showed himself to Abraham."[64] It is exceedingly convenient to have such a message-stick to confirm one's claim to have been sent by some king or by God himself. There are many instances of the usage in the ancient world, and they all seem to go back to the divine pattern. Thus, "the Herald of Zeus goes forth to summon his subjects armed with a golden wand that subdues all creatures with its touch." This is the civilizing and governing rod of Hermes that makes its holder ruler of the world; the golden wand of the two entwined serpents, the caduceus; the arrow of Zeus in whose name all things are compelled to do obeisance.[65] It was this same caduceus with which Aesculapius presumed to raise the dead—an office reserved to God alone, and to this day the life-giving staff of Aesculapius with its two serpents is the symbol of the medical profession. Strangest of all, the episcopal staves borne by the heads of various ancient Christian churches are still adorned by the two serpents that clearly betray the pagan origin and descent of their emblems of priesthood.[66] Innocent III tells us that the pontifical staff signifies the power of Christ and quotes Psalms 2 and 44 to prove it.[67] Yet there are few better-known traditions in the Roman Church than that which reports that the Pope has no rod, because the rod of Peter, the only one he could have, was given by Peter to Eucherius, Bishop of Trier, when he was sent on his mission to the Germans; this rod is said to have raised Eucherius' successor, Maternus, from the dead,[68] just as the rod of Elijah was said to have raised the dead.

The various aspects of ancient rods of office are given here not by way of picturesque diversion, but because we cannot understand the sticks of Ezekiel until we know what such sticks could and did represent. At this point some general observations are in order:

1. The ancients used marked staves for identification. The staff and ring of the Babylonians[69] recall the staff and ring by which Tamar identified Judah.

2. A king's staff in the hand of another showed that the other was a delegate of the king, with authority to act in his name. The royal staff is thus a sign of power, a scepter.

3. In referring to the sticks of Joseph and Judah, Ezekiel is using a familiar custom (not inventing fantastic imagery) to illustrate a lesson. The lesson has to do with the establishing of identity and the exercise of divine power, or priesthood, in the days of the restoration of Israel. An important clue to the situation is the peculiar way in which the two sticks "become one."

How Do the Sticks Become One?

The prophet is very emphatic on one point: No matter how many sticks there were originally, they become *one* in the hand of the Lord — "And bring them together to thee for one stick . . . and they shall become one stick, and shall be one in my hand." What is the strange manipulation by which one and one make one? We are reminded of the miraculous rod of Aaron that ate up the wooden rods of Pharaoh's priests and still became no larger,[70] but a far more practical explanation is at hand. First of all, there is, of course, the binding of the sticks into a ritual bundle, by which the many become one: Ezekiel duly explains that as the sticks become one so "I will make them one nation" (Ezekiel 37:22). The Septuagint of Ezekiel 17:7 reads, "And thou shalt fit them together for thyself, into a single staff of tying themselves, and they shall be one in thy hand."

The Greek is as bad as the English, but it is clear that the staves become one by being fitted together first (*synapseis*), and then held fast by tying (*tou desai*). We have already had occasion to note the ritual tying of the bundle; what interests us here is the *fitting together*, on which Ezekiel lays peculiar stress. We have noted the Jewish tradition that all the tribal rods were originally cut from a single staff, and that ancient commentators remind us that the rods naturally belong together because they were all shoots from a single stock.[71] Both in the Old World and the New, divination and identification rods "in their original form consist of *split* arrow shaftments, and are marked both inside and out with bands or ribbonings."[72] What is behind this splitting and rejoining of the stick may be best explained by the example of the ancient institution of *tally-sticks*. A tally, to follow the definition of the principal authority on the subject, is "a stick notched and split through the notches, so that both parties to a transaction may have a part of the record."[73] In the ancient world, according to the same source, "the tally-stick, split or unsplit, is widely used: instances of it have been noted all over England and Europe, indeed all over the world, and in all kinds of trades."[74] In England, where tallies may best be studied, their use was required in all business transactions with the royal exchequer from the twelfth century (though they are much older) to the nineteenth, when their place was taken by paper bills and indentures, though the word "bill," meaning a stick of wood, still recalls their use,[75] as does *indenture*, meaning a dent in the wood. A rod of hazelwood or willow was cut according to strictly prescribed rules into two parts, one with a notch on the end called a *stock*, the smaller piece being the *foil*. "The stock went with the payer, the accountant; the Exchequer kept the foil."[76] Being cut with scratches and notches *before* the parts of the stick were separated, the tally furnished a foolproof control over both parties, for no two pieces of wood in the world would fit

Tally-sticks 600 years old with their original bag and labels. The shorter sticks are the "stocks," the larger ones the "foils" to which the "stocks" were fitted to "become one stick" in the hand of the king's representative upon the completion of payment by either party and the settlement of the account.

together perfectly to match mark for mark and grain for grain unless at their original marking they were *one stick.* When in 1297 one William de Brochose tried to cheat the king's treasury by adding a notch to his half of the wood, he was promptly detected and sent to prison.[77] The fact that both parties held parts of the tally is fundamental, "implying a check on both rather than a debit on one."[78] Thus while the king held his half as a *foil* on any attempt to cheat him, the other party held the *stock* (stick) by which he could prove his exact status in the contract: from this the word *stock* is still retained in the business world, while the old expression "lot and scot" betrays the original role of the arrow shaft in the transmission of property.[79] The great advantage of the tally-stick was that it gave parties to a contract a sure means of identification and an authoritative claim upon each other no matter how many miles or how many years might separate them. When, however, the final payment was made and all the terms of the contract fulfilled, the two pieces were joined together at the exchequer, tied as one, and laid up forever in the vaults of the royal building—becoming as it were "one in the king's hand."[80] So great was the heap of such sticks in the basement of the old Houses of Parliament, that when they were ordered burned the ensuing conflagration, "according to the well-known story, . . . caused the fire which destroyed the Houses of Parliament in 1834."[81] At any rate "the exchequer exacted a return of the [stock] at audit," and only when the sticks had been united as one was the standing of the debtor cleared.[82] The analogy with Ezekiel's story of the sticks is at once apparent. But was the system of tallies really ancient, and did the Jews have them? It is interesting in this regard to note that all exchequer tallies had to be written on in Latin, the official language of the state, with the notable exception of an important class of tallies in which the names, dates, places, etc., are noted down in *Hebrew*, while the Jewish Plea Roll furnishes the best evidence for the use of private tallies.[83] Now though a great deal of tally-business was carried on between the king and foreign parties (e.g., the great Flemish merchant Henry Cade), the only foreign language found on the tallies is Hebrew. Not even English is allowed.[84] Had the Jews adopted tallies for the first time when the government did, they would like everybody else have been required to adopt the official method of marking them, so the remarkable

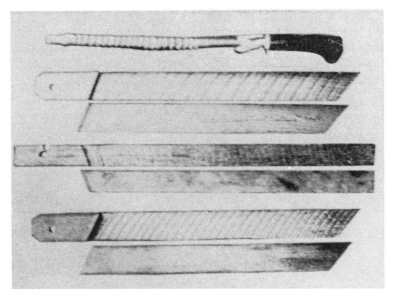

Modern English tally-sticks, showing how the sticks fit together to "become one," as well as the manner in which simple rods of willow or other wood could be used to cut primitive tallies.

exception made in their case, persecuted and unpopular as they were, certainly implies that they had their own tradition of tally marking, which they were allowed to retain. In this respect, it is strange that the commentators, while consistently identifying the sticks of Ezekiel 37 with tribal rods, never refer to the cutting of the rods in Zechariah 11.[85] We have noted that the *breaking* of a rod signifies in Jerusalem and Ezekiel the destruction of a nation; but the *cutting* of a rod has quite another symbolism. Thus Zechariah 11:10, 14: "And I took my staff, even Beauty, and *cut* it asunder, *that I might break my covenant* which I had made with all the people. Then I cut asunder mine other staff, even Bands, *that I might break the brotherhood between Judah and Israel*" (emphasis added). When the rod is *cut* in two, instead of being broken, Judah and Israel are not destroyed but separated; the bond that binds them together (and that is the meaning of the strange name

Bands) is loosened, and the two go their separate ways. As the tie between the nations is broken, so the mightier bond between God and men, the staff Beauty, is broken when the staff is "cut in two." This is the obvious reversal of the process of bringing the two divided sticks together, as described by Ezekiel, to renew the very covenants here broken—those between Judah and Israel, and those between God and "all the people." The technique of the tally-stick as a means of establishing a covenant and bringing parties together in normal contract is here plainly indicated.

We need not establish the antiquity of the tally-stick by working back through the records of the Middle Ages, for the institution is met fully developed in the earliest records of antiquity. This may be illustrated by the archaic feasting-tickets of the Greeks and Romans. Originally little rods, these tokens, which everyone had to present for admission to the great public feasts, took various forms and went by the name of *tesserae*. In the Roman usage, the guest who came into the banquet would be stopped by an official or servant and asked to show his token; this would be fitted against a like token kept at the house of the host, and if the two pieces matched perfectly the guest would be recognized as one who had entered into a contract of *hospitium* with the host and duly admitted to the feast.[86] One is strongly reminded of the "white stone" that is borne by those who "eat of the hidden manna" in Revelation 2:17. The act of placing the two tokens side by side (on which Ezekiel is so insistent) gave the feasting-token among the Greeks its name of *symbolon*, meaning to place (or shoot) two things together. From it comes our word *symbol*. A *symbolon* is by definition something that has value only when placed beside something else to show just what is "symbolized." It is simply a very ancient tally-stick— how ancient may be judged from the use of wooden divining-sticks at the prehistoric Italian shrine of Praeneste

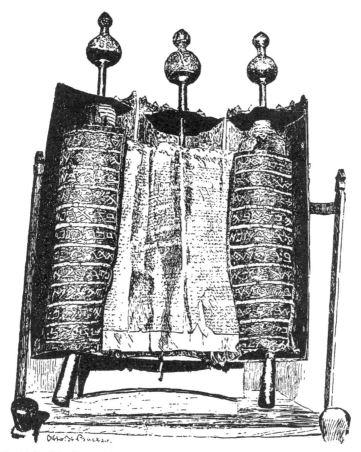

The Roll of the Law. Palestine.

and the Greek Delphi.[87] The tribal rod, herald's staff, or scepter is a glorified tally-stick that appears in its nature as an exact copy of God's own staff and in the provision that it is only on earth as a temporary loan, to be taken back in due time into the hand of God, where it rightfully belongs.[88] Ezekiel, then, is talking sense when he speaks of the two sticks that become one. Not merely did the ancients have such sticks, but they used them specifically in the situation described by Ezekiel for a summoning and gathering of the nation and for the establishment of identity and the renewing of contracts. The scattered tribes of Israel are described as apparently lost for good, smashed, dispersed, forgotten, nay, dead—dry bones. This all looks to a *far future* time, for the *dry* bones show us not a sick nation, not a dying one, nor even one now dead, but one that has been dead for a long, long time. That the nations are depicted as scattered far and wide, having lost their identity and disappeared from history, is noted by the commentators—hence the need for a miracle of resurrection, hence the need for a sure means of identification, symbolized by the identification of sticks. The "extinct" nations are summoned to the Great Assembly by the Lord's herald, who takes their marked rods and places them side by side; they fit together perfectly to become *one stick* as the herald performs the joining before the eyes of all the people (cf. Numbers 17:9). Judah and Joseph are thereby recognized beyond a doubt as parties to the original covenant long after separation and the original unity of the Covenant people is thereby restored. The united scepter is then returned to the hand of the king (Ezekiel 37:19, 22-24), where it is to remain forever, all outstanding debts, the price of sin and transgression, having at last been paid off and all old scores settled.

Were the Sticks Books?

But now we come to the crux of the matter for Latterday Saints. Can the sticks of Ezekiel, along with everything else they represent, be understood to be *books?* Strictly speaking, they were nothing else. A book, says Webster, is "specifically: A formal written document; esp., a deed of conveyance of land; a charter." The tribal rods were just that, no matter how brief the writing on them, while the whole Old Testament, in spite of its length and complexity, is a "book" in exactly the same sense: a "testament," a single binding legal document. But the identity of rods and books goes much further than this.

Books and Sticks. From the very first, the significance of message-staffs and tribal rods lay in what was written on them — signs that had to be read and recognized. This cutting and divining of marks led to the reading and writing of books.[89] To this day the word *book* recalls the box- or beech-wood staves (cf. Ger. *Buchstabe,* Oldslav. *buky, bukva,* "letter") or sticks scratched with runes which were the first books in the North.[90] Even the Latin word *codex,* now venerated for its association with books of the law everywhere, means simply a slip of wood, while the classic *liber* means *wood-pulp.*[91] The oldest laws of the Greeks and Romans were kept on tablets and sticks (*axones*), which Freeman actually compares with the sticks mentioned in Ezekiel.[92] "It is noteworthy," says Ginzberg, "that the tablets and the rod of Moses were not only of the same weight (60 *seah*), but also of the same material."[93] The equating of sticks with tablets is, as we have seen, found among early Jewish commentators on Ezekiel 37, and is explained by Keil as a natural result of the emphasis which Ezekiel places on the *writing* on his sticks. The celebrated rod of Moses might well be taken for a writing tablet, for it had engraved on it "in plain letters the great exalted name, the names of the ten plagues inflicted upon the Egyptians, and the names of the three Fathers, the six Mothers, and the Twelve Tribes of Jacob," in other words, for every function it performed, it had to bear a specific writing, making a total of no less than thirty-two separate inscriptions in all.[94] How many words does it take to make a book? In the ancient world, length was no object, and a single word could contain a whole sermon in itself. This is seen in the early use of the words *logos* and *logographoi,* which refer to a writing of *any* length as a separate opus or book. Many commentators are convinced that the text of Ezekiel contains the actual words that the prophet was ordered to write on the sticks. Thus Kautzsch translates in his critical editions: "Take for thyself a staff of wood and write upon it: 'Judah and the Israelites that are Associated with Him,' "[95] the last phrase being the actual words put upon the staff. Cooke simplifies this to the bare names of "Judah" and "Joseph."[96] But such a rendering completely ignores the preposition *l-*, "to" or "for," which precedes the names of Joseph and Judah every time the writing is mentioned: "Take a staff of wood and write on it *for* Judah," etc.[97] The *l-* means that Ezekiel was not to write simply "Joseph" or "Judah" on the stick, but that he was to write something to or for them. It was to be a writing that somehow concerned them. No more obvious means of connecting Joseph and Judah with the sticks could be imagined, of course, than that of simply putting their names on the wood. But that is just the point: why in such an obvious situation does Ezekiel not do the obvious thing and put the names on the sticks? That is the way it was normally done: "Write thou every man's name upon his rod," "Write the Ineffable name upon it," "Write thy name upon it," and so on.[98] But what Ezekiel writes on the rods is not "Joseph" or "Judah," but "for Joseph" and "for Judah," or, according to some interpreters, "Joseph's" and "Judah's." The wide variety of translations shows that we are not concerned here with a mere writing of names. Property is not marked this way: Names found on ancient seals are in the nominative case, not in the genitive. When Kautzsch wants to make it appear that the names of Joseph and the others were actually written on the rods, he must render the inscription in the nominative, which Ezekiel conspicuously avoids. Hebrew uses no quotation marks, and so when the text reads "write on the wood for Joseph," it should be left as it stands, for when we introduce our own punctuation and translate, "write on wood, 'For Joseph' " we are employing a type of inscription that was used to dedicate votive offerings to deities but not to denote possession.[99] Ezekiel tells us of a writing *for* Judah and another *for* Joseph, both writings to perform certain important functions; but he does not, as some suppose, give us the text of the writings. However eloquent or informative the single rod or staff may have been, it presented serious limitations of space when a lengthy communication was in order. The obvious solution to this problem was simply to add more rods, and it is in this multiplication of sticks to form a ritual bundle that Culin sees the origin of the book in some parts of the world. "The ancestry of the book in Eastern Asia," he says, "may be traced, not only to the engraved strips of bamboo (Chinese *ch'ak*), but, in the opinion of the writer, to the bundle of engraved or painted arrow-derived slips used in divination. . . . The folding fan of China and Japan is not unlikely to have originated from these *tanzaku* or writing slips, which the nobles carried in order to make memoranda when in the presence of the sovereign."[100] The Orientals would cut a piece of wood into strips notched on the sides like tally-sticks, which could be "fanned out" to present a larger writing surface, and when not in use folded together perfectly to make "one stick" in the hand of the nobleman who inscribed upon them the words of majesty. The method recalls the legendary cutting of the twelve rods of Israel from a single stock, but more important is the use of the bundle of twelve rods to determine the fortunes of the nations. These tribal bundles, of which we spoke above, were always used as books of divination from which the past and present and future history of the people was determined. As census-books they made up a "Book of Life opened at the foundation of the world" to tell the history of the coming age; if one's name were missing from this book, he was "cut off from among the people" and had no part in the life of the race.[101] The modern card deck is derived from a bundle of tribal rods, fifty-two in number, used in divination all over the world. Individually each token has a message; together they make

up a book which is read by the adept with as much confidence as if it were in writing.[102] It is thus quite possible
for the staves of Judah and his associates, as well as those
of Joseph and his associates, to represent books containing
the census and history of these nations.

Sticks and Scrolls. When a rod or staff serves as a token
of authority and identification, it is important that no copy
or duplicate of it be allowed to circulate.[103] In that case the
multiplication of message-staffs is impossible. What is to
be done if a longer message is to be sent? This problem
and its solution are actually met in the ancient North,
where only *one* royal summons-arrow was legal, and no
others could be cut.[104] To make room for a long message,
a piece of parchment was attached to the staff and was
rolled around it.[105] To this day in Tibet the summons-arrow
is sent out exactly as it once was among our northern
ancestors: "A mobilization order is sent on a piece of red
cloth attached to an arrow. The arrow is dispatched by a
special rider who gallops to the nearest headman and
hands it over to him. The headman takes notice of the
contents of the order and immediately dispatches a fresh
rider to another headman."[106] On festival assembly days
the ancient Japanese warriors would bind strips of holy
paper bearing written texts on their arrows, "inscribed
sacred paper for the gods."[107] The Ojibwa may substitute
for the painted rod or arrow shaft, which serves as an
invitation-stick, "a piece of birch bark bearing characters."[108] Here we have a natural scroll, as anyone who has
tried to write on tough, curling birch-bark can attest, and
we are reminded that the word *birch* is closely related to
beech, box, and *book,* and also that *liber* originally meant *bast*
or *bark.* Whether the ancient scroll originated in one or
many places, its attachment to a *stick*[109] certainly betrays
its origin; for the stick is by no means necessary to a scroll —
it is in fact an inconvenience, used by the ancients only in

ritual and very valuable literary text, a quaint, old-fashioned survival.

Latter-day Saints often interpret the word *stick* in Ezekiel 37 to refer to the stick or rod around which a scroll was wrapped. The interpretation is perfectly possible. As Gregory the Great observed long ago, the Hebrew word ʿetz (wood) can mean almost anything in the Old Testament depending entirely on the context in which it is used.[110] Sometimes ʿetz must be translated as *tree*, sometimes as *branch, image, musical instrument, framework, idol, house, ax, plow, spear, beam, stalk of flax* (!), *rod, gallows,* and so on.[111] When one tills with wood, it is rendered not *wood* but *plow*; when one plays music on it, it is no longer mere wood, but an *instrument*; when one worships, it is an *idol*; and so forth. Now what is the specific use to which the wood is put in Ezekiel 37? It is used, as Keil insists, to be written on, and for that purpose only. It is hence not surprising that the early Jewish commentators on the passage rendered *wood* here as *tablet*, but Keil cannot accept this because the sticks in Ezekiel are not treated at all as tablets would be. On the other hand Keil finds it very significant that the prophet deliberately avoids calling the sticks *rods* or *staffs*, as if that, too, would give the wrong impression.[112] How can a *stick* be a book?

Sticks and the Law

The sticks around which the scrolls of the law were rolled were always regarded as holy and treated as *scepters*.[113] It will be recalled that nearly all commentators point out that the sticks of Ezekiel are in some way or other scepters. The scrolls of the law were used by the kings of Judah as other kings used scepters, being "kept near his throne and carried into battle." "The scroll itself," we are told, "is girded with a strip of silk, and robed in a Mantle of the Law," while the wooden rod had a crown on its upper end, like the mace or scepter of a king. "Some scrolls," says the *Jewish Encyclopedia*, "have two crowns, one for each upper end."[114] These honors shown the Jewish scrolls of the law are the same given to the royal herald's-staff or scepter in other parts of the world. "At the feast of the Oschophoria at Athens," for example, "the herald's staff was crowned with garlands, but not the herald himself."[115] As in the ancient North, the staff was "a willow bough . . . always cut from a living tree, and was never allowed to wither or dry up"[116] — which exactly recalls the blossoming rod of Aaron, which withered when Israel fell from grace. Among our Norse ancestors this rod was taken from place to place, and at each place to which it went, a roll-call was taken and a notch cut on the rod, which was the king's own staff. "The king was represented by the bailiff of the Hundred carrying a ward-staff. *It was the staff* [not the bailiff] *which represented majesty and received the honours.*"[117]

The peculiar honors bestowed upon the *sticks* of the Jewish law-scrolls show by their nature that the sticks themselves were regarded originally as the bearers of the law. But once parchment had been rolled around these sticks (and the antiquity of this custom may be surmised from the fact that all official scrolls of the law should be on the skin of *wild* beasts),[118] could they still be brought together like tallies to make one stick? The accompanying illustration shows an actual application of this idea: to an edict of the Empress Wu, the Emperor Tai Tsung (A.D. 763-779), her successor, wished to add a supplement of his own, incorporating it in the original law. The two rolls, each with one stick in it, are here seen placed side by side and bound together as one by a silken cloth, just as the roll of the Jewish law with its two sticks is "girded with a strip of silk" when it is rolled up to be put into the tabernacle. There are two rolls having different designs on them and of different colors, showing that originally the scrolls do not have two sticks to them, but only one

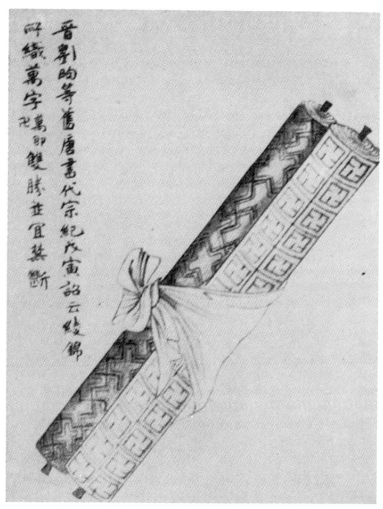

晋劉昫等舊唐書代宗紀戊寅詔云陵錦

研織萬字卍即雙勝並宜禁斷

An edict of the Empress Wu, to which her successor, the Emperor Tai Tsung (A.D. 763-779), has appended an amplification by having the new scroll placed beside the old and bound to it with a silken cloth. Here the two sticks that are joined into one in the emperor's hand are actually scrolls. From *Improvement Era* (Nov. 1953).

apiece.[119] This suggests the origin of the scroll in the single message-stick with the message-scroll wrapped around it, as well as the probability that in Ezekiel's day the scrolls were still of the primitive, one-shaft variety. That the scroll-sticks of the Greeks and Romans were derived from message-arrows is indicated by a number of things. Instead of having convenient handles at the bottom and smooth knobs at the top, the roll-sticks had points at both ends which made them resemble the well-known double-headed thunderbolt, the scepter of Zeus and the best known of all rods of office. That the resemblance is not accidental appears not only in the impractical arrangement of the thing and the identification of scroll-rods with scepters, but likewise in the name given to the points, *koronis*, Latin *cornua*, usually explained as referring to the shape of the sharpened ends. But these do *not* resemble horns, and the name probably has the same origin as that of the little arrow-marks often used in the marking of scrolls by their makers, called *ceraunia*, "little thunderbolts."[120]

We have seen that the heroes of Israel identified themselves as emissaries of the Most High by bearing his rod before the eyes of those to whom they were sent, Jew or Gentile. In this connection the rod is also interchangeable with the scroll, for in the Middle Ages every Jew was required by Jewish law to carry a scroll of the law with him at all times as his identification and passport.[121] The connection between staff and book is here not far to seek — the staff is a mark and token, symbolizing that by which the Jew is known to the world; the scroll is a step closer to home — it is almost the thing itself. The scripture, says Clement of Alexandria in an eloquent discourse on the subject, is the rod by which God teaches his people.[122] The double function of the rod, said Gregory of Nyssen, is that of consolation and direction, which are the offices of the scripture for all believers.[123] If the rod is the symbolic means by which Judah is identified and set apart from the rest of the world (and the use of such a symbol was regarded by the early Christians as a thing of great significance and secrecy), what is the means by which Judah is actually thus distinguished, that is, what is the real equivalent of the rod? It is the Bible, of course. In figurative language the Jews will recognize the Messiah by examining the rod: "Search the scriptures," said the Lord, for "they are they which testify of me" (John 5:34).

The identity of staff and scripture was noted by the earliest and best informed of the Christian historians. For the great Eusebius the sticks of Ezekiel represent the Old Testament and the New Testament.[124] A century and a half earlier Irenaeus speaks of the (hidden) meanings of the sticks as "hidden from us, for," he says, "since by the wood we rejected him, by the wood his greatness shall be made visible to everyone, and as one of our predecessors has said, by the holy reaching out of the hands the two people are led to one God. For there are two hands and two nations scattered to the ends of the earth."[125] There is every indication that the Saints of the *early* Church regarded the teaching of the sticks and the gathering as of great secrecy and great significance, the meaning of the whole thing being later lost.[126] The later Fathers took the usual allegorical liberties in dealing with Ezekiel 37.

Conclusion

Cyril of Alexandria notes that "everywhere life is by the wood" — as sin came by the wood, so also redemption comes by the wood, and he cites the rod of Moses and the cross of Christ.[127]

Jerome says the two rods of Ezekiel are the church and the synagogue,[128] while the two rods of which Isaiah speaks are the congregations of the Jews on the one hand and the Gentiles on the other;[129] and again, "the two rods are the covenant of God with men twice entered upon," in other words, the Old and New Testaments;[130] the joining of the two to make one scepter signifies that which is joined together in the baptism of Christ, united "to make one new man."[131]

Why are not these interpretations accepted by the Christian commentators of our day? Because while the Old Testament conspicuously satisfies all qualifications for the stick of Judah, the New Testament is not a whit less the property of Judah, having on the other hand no special affinity for Joseph, with whom in fact neither the Gentile congregation nor the Christian Church have any direct connection. The license of allegory, all but unlimited throughout most of the scriptures, is peculiarly checked in Ezekiel 37, and the scholar or churchman who would make an arbitrary "spiritual" interpretation of the chapter finds his usual liberty severely curtailed, for Ezekiel employs concrete symbols to illustrate an historical event. The terms he uses are specific; the names of Israel, Joseph, and Judah are not mysterious, and the great events to which he refers are those to which the chosen people have been instructed to look forward for centuries, and for which the Christians have yearned no less. In Ezekiel's prophecy Joseph does not absorb Judah, as the church is supposed to have absorbed the synagogue; Joseph is not a Gentile, but as authentically of Israel as Judah is; it is Israel that triumphs, not the Gentiles; the sticks represent covenants between two nations that are contemporary, not, as Jerome suggests, the making of a single covenant with the same nations at two different times; both nations are to be brought back home again after having been scattered from a common center, and hence no Gentile nation qualifies for the promise—"God hath not cast away his people which he foreknew."[132] The whole situation is clearly set forth in Ezekiel 37: The chapter is speaking of the scattering and gathering of Israel and the resurrection;[133] there cannot be the slightest doubt as to what is meant by Joseph and Judah, and while the *New* Testament might conceivably be described as the stick of Judah, by no effort of the imagination can it be interpreted as the stick of Joseph. It is on the stick of Joseph that every attempt to interpret the passage breaks down hopelessly.

It is as if we were completing a jigsaw puzzle. There is a peculiarly shaped blank which calls for a missing piece designated as the stick of Judah. The Old Testament fits easily into the gap. Then there remains an adjacent blank space to be filled by a missing "stick of Joseph." Naturally the first thing we do is to try to slip the New Testament into it. But turn it and push it and force it as we will, the New Testament simply does not belong there, for it is not the story of Joseph and his associates in contradistinction to that of Judah and his associates, which makes up the Bible — if anything it belongs to the latter class, to the stick of Judah. Since the missing piece refuses to be found, the skillful jigsaw artist simply goes ahead and completes the rest of the picture; and then if the missing piece is still lost, he can infer from the shape of the last empty space and from the design and color of the surrounding areas almost exactly what the missing piece should be. This is what we are attempting here. When the Bible commentators failed to supply the missing piece or to agree on what it should look like, we simply continued to work out the puzzle, putting into position every piece we could find that had to do with sticks and covenants. As a result we are now in a position to make some pretty near guesses as to the shape, size, and color of the missing piece to our puzzle — the baffling "stick of Joseph."

Let us read the text again, sticking as closely to the Hebrew as possible:

> And the word of the Lord came to me, saying, And thou, son of man, take to thyself, one (piece of) wood and write upon it for Judah and for the children of Israel his associates, and take one wood and write upon it for Joseph wood of Ephraim and all the house of Israel his associates, and approach them one to (the) other for thee

for one wood so they shall become for single ones in thy hand. And when they say to thee the sons of thy people, wilt thou not show us what thou meanest by this? (lit.: what these are to thee?) Say to them, Thus saith the Lord Jehovah, Behold I will take the wood of Joseph, which is in the hand of Ephraim and the staves (or scepters) of Israel his associates and I shall place them upon it along with (or alongside) the wood of Judah and I shall make them for one wood, and they shall be one in my hand. And the woods which thou hast written upon (shall be) in thy hand before their eyes. So say to them, Thus saith the Lord Jehovah, Behold I will take the sons of Israel out of the nations among whom they walk, and will gather them from round about and lead them into their land (Ezekiel 37:16-21).

In connection with this must be taken the previous episode in verses 11-12: "And he said to me the Son of man, these bones *are the whole house of Israel*; behold, they say, our bones are dried, and our hope has perished; we are destroyed! Therefore prophesy, and say to them, Thus saith the Lord Jehovah, Behold I will open your graves, and cause you to come out of your graves, my people, and bring you to the land of Israel." Here, as Rabbi Fisch notes, "the prediction of national resurrection, as symbolized in the vision of the dry bones, is followed by the symbolic action of the reunion of the two Kingdoms."[134] That the prophet was referring to the resurrection of the flesh, as well as indicating that such was recognized by the ancients, of course, has been too much for the scholars, who, even in Tertullian's time, were determined to see in this a purely symbolic resurrection. But what specifically is the "wood of Judah"—why does the prophet choose this particular symbol? Because it symbolizes both a writing and a covenant, and—the unique means by which Judah is to be recognized and distinguished in the world—it is Judah's tribal staff. All of which says as plain as day—it is the scripture. What, then, is the stick or wood of Joseph? Likewise a writing and a covenant, something written for Joseph and those associated with Joseph. It is a compound document, like the Bible, but it is not the Bible, for it deals with that branch of Israel concerned with Joseph, not Judah, as the Bible does, and it will be held in the hand of Ephraim. After it has been brought together, it will be placed by the side of the wood of Judah and his associates that has been compiled in a like manner. When this is done, the two will match perfectly, thereby proving the identity and the claims of parties long separated and thought dead and vindicating their former common covenant with God. This will be a great miracle of recognition of a piece (as Rabbi Fisch observes)[135] with the supreme miracle of restoring the dead nations to life in the fulness of times. The long and complete separation of the two nations is an important part of the story (*dudum separata,* says Jerome).[136] But there was no such separation between the Jews of the Old Testament and those of the New: the people, like their book, represent, as they proclaim and Jesus admits, an unbroken continuation of tradition and blood from the days of the Old Covenant; no identification is needed here—"Ye are indeed Abraham's children," etc.

To fill the qualifications of the stick of Joseph:

(1) it must be a writing;

(2) it must be compounded of the doings of the descendants and associates of *Joseph* (not Judah);

(3) it must be held in the hand of Ephraim, who is of Joseph, not Judah;

(4) it must be much like the Bible, the stick of Judah, so much so that the two will fit together perfectly like two parts of a single tally-stick;

(5) it must be brought forth *long* after the scattering of Israel, at a time when "the whole house of Israel" shall say "our bones are dried, and our hope has perished; we are destroyed!"

(6) It must go forth as a summons "before their eyes" at that time when the Lord sets his hand to "take the children of Israel from among the heathen, whither they be gone."

(7) The bringing together of the two documents will reverse the process described in Zechariah, by which covenants between these two nations and God were broken when two rods were "cut in two," for as all commentators agree, the joining of the sticks means the reestablishment of the old covenants between them.

In the Book of Mormon we have a document that fulfills all these qualifications, and even the Doctrine and Covenants and Pearl of Great Price may enter into the picture, for they are all of Joseph, are all given into the hand of Ephraim to propagate and defend, and are all bound together as "one stick" with the Book of Mormon, all of which would plead strongly for the claims of the Book of Mormon even in a field of competitors. But where are the competitors? We have seen that the doctors do not agree for a minute on what the sticks of Ezekiel were or how they were joined together; we have further seen that they try to whittle away Ezekiel's full account by diligently altering the text. They might save themselves the trouble, for the Book of Mormon offers an explanation which (1) leaves the text *almost* as it stands, (2) offers literal fulfillment of a prophecy which all will admit Ezekiel meant should be literally fulfilled, and (3) sees in the "mystery" performed by the prophet with the sticks a familiar and established institution and not a wild and unbridled fantasy of the prophet which would have meant nothing to his hearers.

Against the Book of Mormon explanation there is just one objection. It assumes that Ezekiel actually was a prophet. For the scholars, that spoils everything. In criticizing historical texts it is essential to recognize that a man cannot possibly talk about events that occur after his death.

But this fundamental principle of historical criticism cannot
be applied to prophetic writings: When the purpose of an
investigation is to test the validity of a revelation, we can
hardly take as our basic rule of criticism the proposition
that revelation is impossible! Yet this is exactly what the
scholars have done. Thus the celebrated Eduard Meyer can
report of Ezekiel: "That the visions and symbols are literary
fictions is obvious; and the same goes for all the other
accounts."[137] By what gift of divination is this obvious?
"The prophetic apparatus," he continues, "has sunk to the
most literal forms. Ezekiel is a literary grind, he does not
work through the living word, struggling for expression
from the depths of the soul as with Isaiah and Jeremiah, . . . but he simply gives us the contents of a book
which he is supposed to have swallowed in a vision. . . .
Ezekiel is narrow minded, limited, without sweep or
power, completely devoid of creative imagination [Phan-
tasie] and hence marked by unendurable pedantry and
monotony."[138]

Interestingly enough, these are the same charges that
the same Eduard Meyer brings against Joseph Smith and
the Book of Mormon. Whereas, he tells us, Mohammed,
like a true religious hero, sweated blood to produce the
Koran, and went through those long and terrible periods
of doubt and inner struggle through which every proper
religious founder should fight his way to growing self-
realization, etc. Joseph Smith showed the unpardonably
bad taste never to have betrayed the slightest doubt as to
his calling: "It is very significant in the case of Joseph
Smith," we are told, "that the question of such doubting
never arises, however readily he questions the vision and
inspirations of others when they do not please
him. . . . Thus Mohammed's revelations are higher than
Joseph Smith's because in them we feel, at least in the
earliest Suras, something of the power of a conviction won
by a truly strenuous spiritual struggle, and at times we

sense even a poetical exhilaration."[139] Neither Joseph Smith
nor Ezekiel is the kind of prophet (as Mohammed is) to
please a German professor; both are guilty of the "crassest
literalism." While Mohammed's book remains decently in-
visible in the hand of the angel, Joseph Smith, without the
slightest feeling for drama, mystery, or the usual religious amenities, actually copies out the characters of his
holy book for circulation![140] Poetry, "Phantasie," inner
struggle—such are the stuff of prophetic experience for
Eduard Meyer and the lesser pedants, and any thought
that a prophet might really be a prophet and not merely
a poet, thinker, or moralist is quite out of the question.
And so in criticizing the modern Joseph and the ancient
Ezekiel in identical terms, one of the greatest modern scholars bears unintentional witness to the existence of a class
of prophetic experience totally beyond the ken of the aca-
demician. Needless to say, when such prophets speak, the
doctors are not equipped to judge them. Whether Ezekiel
was really prophesying or not does not depend on whether
this or that scholar thinks prophecy is possible. The whole
account of the stick of Judah and the stick of Joseph should
serve to admonish us that there are many things hidden
from the wise and prudent which are known to the prophets of the Lord and shared by them with his people. In
due time these things come one by one to the knowledge
of the outside world, but in the meantime we may rest
assured that the Saints are under no obligation to accept
every conjecture that engages the fancy of the Scribes and
Pharisees.

Notes

1. Matthew Henry and Thomas Scott, *Commentary on the Holy
Bible*, 6 vols. (London: Religious Tract Society, 1850), 4:346; Carl F.
Keil, *Biblical Commentary on the Prophecies of Ezekiel*, 2 vols. (Edinburgh: Clark, 1885), 2:130; John R. Dummelow, *A Commentary on
the Holy Bible* (New York: Macmillan, 1927), 515.

2. W. L. Wardle, "Ezekiel," *The Abingdon Bible Commentary*, ed.
Frederick C. Eiselen (New York: Abingdon, 1929), 740.

3. Herbert C. Alleman and Elmer E. Flack, *Old Testament Commentary* (Philadelphia: Muhlenberg, 1948), 770.

4. Wardle, "Ezekiel," 740.

5. Robert Jamieson, et al., *A Commentary, Critical and Explanatory, on the Old and New Testaments*, 2 vols. (Hartford: Scranton, n.d.), 1:611.

6. Henry A. Ironside, *Expository Notes on Ezekiel the Prophet* (New York: Loizeaux, 1949), 261.

7. Emil Kautzsch, tr., *Die Heilige Schrift des alten Testaments*, 2 vols., 4th ed. (Tübingen: Mohr, 1922), 1:975.

8. Thus Origen, *Commentaria in Evangelium Joannis* (*Commentary on John*) 23, in *PG* 14:64; Raban Maurus, *Commentaria in Ezechielem* (*Commentary on Ezekiel*) XIII, 37, in *PL* 110:863; cf. Jerome, *Commentarius in Ezechielem* (*Commentary on Ezekiel*) XI, in *PL* 25:352.

9. Jacques-Paul Migne, ed., *Scripturae Sacrae Cursus Completus*, 25 vols. (Paris: Migne, 1839-40), 19:925.

10. Keil, *Biblical Commentary on the Prophecies of Ezekiel*, 2:130-31.

11. Ironside, *Expository Notes on Ezekiel the Prophet*, 261; "The two sticks are to be joined lengthwise in the hand," George A. Cooke, *A Critical and Exegetical Commentary on the Book of Ezekiel*, International Critical Commentary, 2 vols. (New York: Scribner, 1937), 2:401.

12. See Hugh W. Nibley, "The Arrow, the Hunter, and the State," *WPQ* 2 (1949): 336.

13. Adam Clarke, *The Holy Bible, a Commentary and Notes*, 6 vols. (New York: Abingdon), 4:524-25, n. 3.

14. John Skinner, *The Book of Ezekiel* (London: Hodder and Stoughton, 1895), 352.

15. Ibid.

16. Andrew B. Davidson, *The Book of the Prophet Ezekiel* (Cambridge: Cambridge University Press, 1892), 271, note on Ezekiel 37:20.

17. Skinner, *The Book of Ezekiel*, 353.

18. Cooke, *A Critical and Exegetical Commentary on the Book of Ezekiel*, 2:400.

19. A. E. Housman, *M. Manilii Astronomicon*, 5 vols. (London: Cambridge University Press, 1937), 1:xviii.

20. Ibid., 1:lxv.

21. Migne, *Scripturae Sacrae Cursus Completus*, 19:926.

22. Kautzsch, *Die Heilige Schrift des alten Testaments*, 1:975, n. 19.

23. Jamieson, et al., *A Commentary, Critical and Explanatory, on the Old and New Testaments*, 1:611.

24. Davidson, *The Book of the Prophet Ezekiel*, 271, note on Ezekiel 37:19. Cases in which *eth* is to be rendered *una cum* (along with) are given in Franz Zorell, *Lexicon Hebraicum et Aramaicum Veteris Testamenti* (Rome: Pontifical Biblical Institute, 1946), 90. Raban Maurus renders this *eth* as *pariter cum*, Raban Maurus, *Commentary on Ezekiel* XIII, 37, in *PL* 110:862.

25. Davidson, *The Book of the Prophet Ezekiel*, 271, note on Ezekiel 37:19.

26. Kautzsch, *Die Heilige Schrift des alten Testaments*, 1:975, v. 19, and the Abingdon commentator, Wardle, "Ezekiel," 741, both favor it, as do Dummelow, *A Commentary on the Holy Bible*, 515-16; and Rabbi S. Fisch, *Ezekiel* (London: Soncino, 1950), 249.

27. Davidson, *The Book of the Prophet Ezekiel*, 271, note on Ezekiel 37:19; Cooke, *A Critical and Exegetical Commentary on the Book of Ezekiel*, 2:401, also favors this reading, which, though "it sounds surprising, . . . is no more than what the preceding part of the verse affirms."

28. For an excellent treatment of the liberties taken by scholars at all periods with the texts of the prophets, see John F. Stenning, *The Targum of Isaiah* (Oxford: Clarendon, 1949), viii-xvi; quote is from xiv.

29. "This is the chief passage in which Ezekiel reaffirms the social ideal characteristic of the prophets: an age of peace under the government of a righteous ruler." Cooke, *A Critical and Exegetical Commentary on the Book of Ezekiel*, 2:400.

30. Samuel R. Driver, *Einleitung in die Literatur des Alten Testaments* (Berlin: Reuther and Reichard, 1896), 311. For the English version, see Samuel R. Driver, *An Introduction to the Literature of the Old Testament* (Edinburgh: Clark, 1897), 291.

31. Fisch, *Ezekiel*, 249: "The prediction of national resurrection, as symbolized in the vision of the dry bones, is followed by the symbolic action of the reunion of the two kingdoms to indicate that unity is an essential factor in preserving the life of the nation."

32. Hugh W. Nibley, "The Hierocentric State," *WPQ* 4 (1951): 226.

33. For a general treatment of this subject, Lord Fitz Roy Raglan, *The Origins of Religion* (London: Watts, 1945).

34. Nibley, "The Arrow, the Hunter, and the State," 333-34.

35. Ibid., 335-36.

36. James M. Freeman, *Hand-book of Bible Manners and Customs* (New York: Nelson and Phillips, 1877), 305-6, 309.

37. Nibley, "The Arrow, the Hunter, and the State," 335.

38. Ibid., 336.

39. Alice C. Fletcher and Francis La Flesche, "The Omaha Tribe," in *The Twenty-seventh Annual Report of the Bureau of Ethnology to the Secretary of the Smithsonian Institution 1905-06* (Washington: Government Printing Office, 1911), 242, 228.

40. Nibley, "The Arrow, the Hunter, and the State," 336.

41. Ibid., esp. n. 55.

42. *Poetic Edda, Völuspa,* 63 (numbering of stanzas varies slightly in the different editions).

43. Like the kings of Persia and Babylon, the host among the Kwakiutis gives away all his wealth at the New Year, as he sits with the staves or arrows of all his guests spread out before him; Franz Boas, "The Social Organization and the Secret Societies of the Kwakiuti Indians," in *Report of the U. S. National Museum 1895* (Washington: Government Printing Office, 1897), 503-4.

44. Nibley, "The Arrow, the Hunter, and the State," 336.

45. Louis Ginzberg, *The Legends of the Jews,* 7 vols. (Philadelphia: Jewish Publication Society, 1909-38), 3:306.

46. Clement, *Epistola I ad Corinthios (First Epistle to the Corinthians)* 43, in *PG* 1:295-96.

47. Nibley, "The Arrow, the Hunter, and the State," 334.

48. Paul Kahle, *Masoreten des Westens,* 2 vols. (Stuttgart: Kohlhammer, 1927-30), 1:3-5.

49. Ibid., 6.

50. Gerard Fowke, "Stone Art," in *The Thirteenth Annual Report of the Bureau of Ethnology to the Secretary of the Smithsonian Institution 1891-92* (Washington: Government Printing Office, 1896), 116.

51. Nibley, "The Arrow, the Hunter, and the State," 334.

52. Ibid., 330-31 (emphasis added).

53. Ibid., 332.

54. Jane E. Harrison, *Prolegomena to the Study of Greek Religion* (Cambridge: Cambridge University Press, 1922), 44.

55. Ginzberg, *The Legends of the Jews,* 2:291-92.

56. Ibid., 5:412.

57. Ibid., 6:106.

58. Ibid., 3:307.

59. Ibid., 4:234.

60. Quoted in Angelo S. Rappoport, *Myth and Legend of Ancient Israel,* 3 vols. (London: Gresham, 1928), 2:366: "When Adam was driven out of Paradise, he cut a branch from the fig tree which was the tree of knowledge, and this branch served him as a staff all his life. This staff he left to his son, and it was transmitted from gen-

eration to generation till it came into the possession of Abraham. It was with this staff that the Patriarch smashed the idols of his father Terah. Jacob used the staff as he tended the flocks, . . . and his son Judah gave it as a pledge to his daughter-in-law Tamar." Later it was hidden by an angel and found by Jethro, who gave it to Moses. "The staff then came into the possession of Phinehas, who buried it in the desert. It belonged to Joseph . . . at the moment of the birth of the Saviour, and it served afterwards as one of the planks in the Cross of Christ."

61. Ginzberg, *The Legends of the Jews*, 3:430-31.

62. Ibid., 3:19 (emphasis added).

63. Ibid., 2:335.

64. Justin Martyr, *Dialogus cum Tryphone* (*Dialogue with Trypho*) 86, in *PG* 6:680-81: "The cross is the symbol of the wood of Life in Paradise. Moses with a rod was sent to liberate the people, and holding this rod in his hand, as commander of the nation he divided the Red Sea. By its power he struck water from the rock and by throwing it into the waters of Merra he made them sweet. . . . Jacob boasts that he passed through the river on this staff," etc.

65. Nibley, "The Arrow, the Hunter, and the State," 331, with special reference to the notes.

66. Usually the staff of authority is thought to represent the thunderbolt by which the enemies of God are smitten: for extensive identifications see Christian S. Blinkenberg, *The Thunder Weapon in Religion and Folklore* (Cambridge: Cambridge University Press, 1911); Arthur B. Cook, *Zeus*, 3 vols. (Cambridge: Cambridge University Press, 1914-40), 2:1045-46, 473, 775, 780, 786-89 (the trident is the lightning). Thunderbolt, caduceus, plant of immortality, and the lance of St. George are identified by Benjamin W. Bacon, "Eagle and Basket on the Antioch Chalice," *Annual of the American Schools of Oriental Research* 5 (1923): 6-8, 10, 19; scepter, "rods" of Israel, and the staff of the inspired poet are identified by Ludwig Deubner, "Die Bedeutung des Kranzes im klassischen Altertum," *ARW* 30 (1932): 82-84; extensive comparisons are given by Edward D. Clarke, "On the Lituus of the Ancient Romans," *Archaeologia* 19 (1821): 386-404. On the trident and fleur-de-lis (found on early Christian bishops' staves), see William M. Wylie, "Remarks on the Angon, or Barbed Javelin of the Franks, Described by Agathias," *Archaeologia* 35 (1853): 48-55; and Henry B. Walters, "Poseidon's Trident," *Journal of Hellenic Studies* 13 (1892-93): 13-20. "In the archaic period, . . . Poseidon has . . . instead of a trident a lotos sceptre," as does Zeus, ibid., 19. Significantly, early bishops' staves were topped

with the lotus sign; Frederick G. Lee, "Episcopal Staves," *Archaeologia* 51 (1888): 374, the "Finger of God," ibid., 372, or the hunter's sign of St. Hubert, and bore such formidable inscription as "Strike-Spare," ibid., 360. The earliest bishops' staves resemble the caduceus, crowned with double serpents, as can be seen from the photographs in Maynard O. Williams, "Color Records from the Changing Life of the Holy City," *National Geographic* 52 (1927): 383-89, and the oldest such staff from the north, reproduced in J.J.A. Worsaae, *Nordiske Oldsager i det Kongelige Museum i Kjöbenhavn* (Copenhagen: Kittendorff and Aagaards, 1859), 150, pl. 542; cf. Charles H. Read, "On Morse Ivory Tau Cross Head of English Work of the Eleventh Century," *Archaeologia* 58 (1903): 409, fig. 2; 412, fig. 5. In the oldest pictures Hermes' caduceus is topped by the serpent or the fleur de lis; Eduard Gerhard, *Etruskische Spiegel*, 5 vols. (Berlin: Reimer, 1840-97; reprinted Rome: Bretschneider, 1966), vol. 5, taf. 8, nos. 1, 2. In these and many other cases the rods of office borne by Christian bishops can be traced back to the pagan priesthoods of antiquity. Their use in the Christian churches is *first* met with in the seventh century, and is not general until the eleventh century; Louis M. O. Duchesne, *Origines du Culte Chrétien*, 5th ed. (Paris: Ancienne Librairie Fontemoing, 1920), 417; English translation of the 4th French edition by M. L. McClure, *Christian Worship: Its Origin and Evolution*, 3rd English ed. (London: Society for Promoting Christian Knowledge, 1910), 397.

67. Innocent III, *De Sacro Altaris Mysterio* (*On the Sacred Mystery of the Altar*) I, 45, in *PL* 217:790.

68. Index CCXXVII, *De Vestitus Sacerdotalibus Monasticis et Laicalibus, quorum fit Mentio in Patrologia, Exponeus Mysticam illorum Significationem* (*On Sacred Vestments*), in *PL* 221:600.

69. Herodotus, *History* I, 195.

70. Ginzberg, *The Legends of the Jews*, 2:335-36.

71. Medieval commentators unite everything in the rod of Aaron: Mary is the rod of Aaron, Peter Damian, *Sermones* (*Sermons*) 40, in *PL* 144:721, *Sermons* 46, in *PL* 144:760; Bruno Astensis, *Sentertiae* I, 3, in *PL* 165:884, the flowering rod from the root of Jesse, Tertullian, *Adversus Mareionem* V, 8, 4, in *PL* 2:521; Christ is also the rod of Aaron, Peter Damian, *Sermons* 42, in *PL* 144:730; as well as the rod of Moses, Hildebert, *Sermones de Sanctis* (*Sermons on Holy Things*) 72 (77), in *PL* 171:686; Wolberus, *Commentaria in Canticum Canticorum* (*Commentary on the Song of Solomon*) 1:9, in *PL* 195:1061. The rod of Moses represents the Cross of Christ and his power; Rupert, *De Trinitate et Operibus Ejus* (*On the Trinity and Its Operations*) XLII, 33,

in *PL* 167:641-42. It represents also the congregation of the righteous, Raban Maurus, *Allegoriae in Universam Sacram Scripturam* (*Allegories on All the Scriptures*), s.v. "Vigra," in *PL* 112:1081, and even the whole human race, see Peter Lombard, *Commentarium in Psalmos* (*Commentary on the Psalms*) 73:3, in *PL* 191:684. The blossoming rod is the humanity of Christ, who is the blossom on the rod from the root of Jesse; Rupert, *On the Trinity and Its Operations* XLII, 17, in *PL* 167:584. The rod is naturally the symbol of divine judgment, Rupert, *De Incendio Oppidi Tuitii* 7, in *PL* 170:339, and of dominion, Eucherius, *Formularum Spiritalis Intelligentiae* (*The Forms of Spiritual Intelligence*) 2, in *PL* 50:738.

72. Stewart Culin, "Games of the North American Indians," in *The Twenty fourth Annual Report of the Bureau of American Ethnology to the Secretary of the Smithsonian Institution* (Washington: Government Printing Office, 1907), 46.

73. Hilary Jenkinson, "Exchequer Tallies," *Archaeologia* 62 (1911): 367. See illustration, plate xlviii.

74. Ibid., 368.

75. Hilary Jenkinson, "Medieval Tallies, Public and Private," *Archaeologia* 74 (1924): 305. See illustration, plate lxv.

76. Jenkinson, "Exchequer Tallies," 373-74. The foil is sometimes called the *contratallia*, the counter-tally, 374.

77. Ibid., 374.

78. Jenkinson, "Medieval Tallies, Public and Private," 318.

79. Ibid., 292; on "lot and scot," see Nibley, "The Arrow, the Hunter, and the State," 331-32, 334, where the technical term for marking an *arrow* (*skera ör upp*) is the same as that for marking tallies. Jenkinson, "Medieval Tallies, Public and Private," 318. The length of the tallies is determined exactly as the Indians determine the length of gaming sticks cut from arrow shafts, by measuring from the tip of the forefinger to the tip of the extended thumb.

80. Jenkinson, "Exchequer Tallies," 374; Jenkinson, "Medieval Tallies, Public and Private," 315.

81. Jenkinson, "Exchequer Tallies," 369. So complete was the destruction that all knowledge of the institution of tally cutting was completely lost in England after the fire; ibid., 371.

82. Jenkinson, "Medieval Tallies, Public and Private," 315.

83. Jenkinson, "Exchequer Tallies," 378; Jenkinson, "Medieval Tallies, Public and Private," 313-14, 293.

84. Of all the surviving tallies, only two bear writing in English; Jenkinson, "Medieval Tallies, Public and Private," 314.

85. The one exception is Cooke, *A Critical and Exegetical Com-*

mentary on the Book of Ezekiel, 2:400: "The symbol evidently made a lasting impression, for it is imitated in Zechariah 11:7, where, however, the two *staves* (a different word) are given names but not inscribed."

86. The operation has been studied by Theodor Mommsen, *Römische Forschungen,* 2 vols. (Berlin: Weidmann, 1864), 1:338-48; and in Theodor Mommsen, "Das römische Gastrecht und die römische Clientel," *Historische Zeitschrift* 1 (1859): 339-42, cited by Hugh W. Nibley, "Sparsiones," *CJ* 40 (1945): 538.

87. Nibley, "Sparsiones," 537-38. The oldest known *symbolon* was the messenger staff given by Apollo to his missionary Abarus; Abarus used it as a feasting ticket and sign of authority wherever he went; Nibley, "The Arrow, the Hunter, and the State," 331.

88. "It is the arrow of the *summus deus,* held on loan by an earthly king as a gage of divine support, that everywhere gives the latter his earthly power and authority." Nibley, "The Arrow, the Hunter, and the State," 333.

89. Ibid., 337-38.

90. *The Oxford English Dictionary,* 12 vols. (Oxford: Clarendon, 1933), 1:988-89, s.v. "book."

91. Friedrich W. Blass, "Palaeographie, Buchwesen und Handschriftenkunde," in Ivan von Müller, *Handbuch der klassischen Altertumswissenschaft,* 12 vols. (Munich: Beck, 1892), 1:308: "In Italien muss in alter Zeit vielfach auf Bast geschrieben sein, da das Wort *liber* noch bei Vergil dies bedeutet; . . . der Gebrauch des Holzes aber ist in beiden Ländern alt. Im Lateinischen stammt daher das Wort *codex* = *caudex.*"

92. Freeman, *Hand-book of Bible Manners and Customs,* 309, no. 583.

93. Ginzberg, *The Legends of the Jews,* 6:54.

94. Ibid., 3:19.

95. Kautzsch, *Die Heilige Schrift des alten Testaments,* 1:975.

96. Cooke, *A Critical and Exegetical Commentary on the Book of Ezekiel,* 2:401; "The prophet is . . . to inscribe one with the name *Judah,* and the other with the name *Joseph.*"

97. *"For Judah . . . his companions.* The stick, emblem of the royal sceptre, was to be inscribed with those words." Fisch, *Ezekiel,* 249.

98. See generally, Nibley, "The Arrow, the Hunter, and the State."

99. Numerous examples of seal inscriptions and dedications may be found in Anton Deimel, *Sumerische Grammatik* (Rome: Pontifical Biblical Institute, 1924); and in Henri Frankfort, *Cylinder Seals* (Lon-

don: Macmillan, 1939). Publications of collected Oriental seals are very numerous.

100. Stewart Culin, "Chess and Playing Cards," in *Report of the U. S. National Museum for 1896* (Washington: Government Printing Office, 1898), 887-88.

101. Nibley, "Sparsiones," 536-39; quotes are from 539, n. 155.

102. Nibley, "The Arrow, the Hunter, and the State," 336. Even in Egypt the 52 arrow shafts of divination "drifted down into the vulgarisation of gaming cards," according to W. M. Flinders Petrie, *Scarabs and Cylinders with Names* (London: University College, 1917), 4.

103. William H. Ward, *The Seal Cylinders of Western Asia* (Washington: Carnegie Institute of Washington, 1910), 3-5.

104. The only time that *two* arrows were sent was when one (a wooden shaft) went by land and the other (of iron) by sea, according to Karl Weinhold, "Beiträge zu den deutschen Kriegsalterthümern," *Sitzungsbericht der Akademie der Wissenschaft zu Berlin* 29 (1891): 536.

105. Ibid., 548.

106. George N. Roerich, *Trails to Inmost Asia* (New Haven: Yale University Press, 1931), 352.

107. Fritz Rumpf, tr., *Japanische Volksmärchen* (Jena: Diederich, 1938), 43; see note on documents of this type, in Nibley, "The Arrow, the Hunter, and the State," 341, n. 80.

108. Garrick Mallery, "Picture writing of the American Indians," in *The Tenth Annual Report of the Bureau of Ethnology to the Secretary of the Smithsonian Institution 1888-89* (Washington: Government Printing Office, 1893), 367, fig. 475.

109. Blass, "Palaeographie, Buchwesen und Handschriftenkunde," 1:335-36. The first genuine ancient scrolls ever to be discovered intact are the Dead Sea Scrolls, none of which have sticks attached to them.

110. Gregorius Magnus (Gregory the Great), *S. Gregori Magni Vita, Ex Ejus Scriptis Adornata (The Life of Gregory the Great, Embellished from His Own Words)* III, 9, in *PL* 75:394.

111. Zorell, *Lexicon Hebraicum et Aramaicum Veteris Testamenti*, 618.

112. Keil, *Biblical Commentary on the Prophecies of Ezekiel*, 2:130.

113. *Jewish Encyclopedia* (New York: Funk and Wagnalls, 1905), 11:126, s.v. "Scroll of the Law."

114. Ibid., 11:126.

115. F. S. Burnell, "Staves and Sceptres," *Folklore* 59 (1948): 164.

116. Ibid.

117. Ibid.

118. *Jewish Encyclopedia*, "Scroll of the Law," 11:126.

119. Jörg Lechler, *Vom Hakenkreuz* (Leipzig: Kabitz, 1934), 74, fig. 6.

120. Fernand Cabrol and Henri Leclerq, *Dictionnaire d'archéologie chrétienne et de liturgie*, 15 vols. (Paris: Letouzey et Ané, 1907-52).

121. *Jewish Encyclopedia*, "Scroll of the Law," 11:134.

122. Clement of Alexandria, *Paedagogus* (*The Tutor*) I, 7, 1, in *PG* 8:321-25.

123. Gregorius Nyssen (Gregory of Nyssen), *Commentarius in Canticum Canticorum* (*Commentary on the Song of Songs*) 12, in *PG* 44:1031; and *Contra Apollinaris* (*Against Apollinaris*) 52, in *PG* 45:1250.

124. Eusebius, *Demonstratio Evangelica* (*Proof for the Gospel*) X, 479-82, in *PG* 22:741-48.

125. Irenaeus, *Contra Haereses* (*Against Heresies*) V, 17, in *PG* 7:1171.

126. Though modern critics fail to detect anything of great importance or mystery in the rods of identification, for the earliest writers of the Church they were regarded as objects of great symbolic significance, conveying a message of real, if hidden, importance; Justin, *Dialogue with Trypho*, in *PG* 6:682, n. 43.

127. Cyril of Alexandria, *Commentarius in Oseam Prophetam* (*Commentary on Hosea*) 3, 12, in *PG* 71:129.

128. Jerome, *Epistolae* (*Letters*) 74, in *PL* 22:683-84.

129. Rupert, *Commentarii in Duodecim Prophetas Minores* (*Commentary on the Twelve Minor Prophets, On Zechariah*) IV, 11, in *PL* 168:786.

130. Ibid. The first was made with Noah and all mankind; the second was made with Abraham and his seed.

131. Jerome, *Commentary on Ezekiel* XI, in *PL* 25:353-54.

132. Romans 11:2.

133. Tertullian, *De Resurrectione* (*On the Resurrection*) 29, in *PL* 2:882-83, cites Ezekiel 37 as proof of an ancient belief in the resurrection, and notes ch. 30, that whereas heretics say it refers to the restoration of the Jews to their land, it nonetheless shows that the resurrection had been revealed earlier to the Jews; ibid., 30, in *PL* 2:884. What settles the argument in favor of a real resurrection is the very frequent reference to the resurrection of the flesh in early Jewish apocryphal writings. Thus in the very early Life of Adam and Eve 51:2, Michael appears to Seth and says: "Man of God, mourn not for thy dead more than six days, for on the seventh day is the sign of the resurrection, and the rest of the age to come." Such expressions are common in the *earliest* Christian fragments. The ancient Jewish belief in the resurrection of the flesh is a subject

deserving of special treatment, but since there undoubtedly was
such a belief, the remarks of Ezekiel regarding dead bones would
have been referred before everything else to it.

134. Fisch, *Ezekiel*, 249.

135. Ibid.

136. "Vere enim in adventu Domini Salvatoris, *duae virgae,* et ut
in Hebraico positum est, *duo ligna* in unum juncta sunt sceptrum,
et in baptismate Christi dudum separata sociantur: ut fiant in unum
novum hominen." Jerome, *Commentary on Ezekiel* XI, in *PL* 25:353.

137. Eduard Meyer, *Geschichte des Altertums,* 4th ed. (Stuttgart:
Cotta, 1944), vol. 4, pt. 1, p. 167, n. 1.

138. Ibid., 168, 170-71.

139. Eduard Meyer, *Ursprung und Geschichte der Mormonen* (Halle:
Niemeyer, 1912), 80-83; published also as *Origin and History of the
Mormons,* tr. H. Rahde and E. Seaich (Salt Lake City: University of
Utah Press, 1961), 54-56.

140. Ibid., 81-82; 55 in English translation.

2

Columbus and Revelation

> And it came to pass that the angel said unto me: Behold the wrath of God is upon the seed of thy brethren. And I looked and beheld a man among the Gentiles, . . . and I beheld the Spirit of God, that it came down and wrought upon the man; and he went forth upon the many waters (1 Nephi 13:11-12).

Why does the Book of Mormon devote a whole verse to Columbus? America was bound to be discovered, at any rate. What was so wonderful about its discovery? Everything!

There is a class of men of high academic attainment known as "Columbists." They devote their lives to finding out things about Columbus. Four standard works written by contemporaries of Columbus plus the extensive writings of Columbus himself, preserved and transmitted in various states of perfection, form the nucleus of all studies of Columbus. Among the accepted data on Columbus there is more than enough evidence to make an exciting commentary on the words of Nephi.

First of all, the mere existence of the Columbists after 400 years of controversy and research justifies the assertions of his contemporaries and himself that he was a man of mystery. The experts still disagree not only on minor details but on every major point of his vital statistics: the place and date of his birth, his name, his nationality, his

---

This article appeared in the Instructor, *88 (October 1953): 319-20.*

race, his education, his religion, his plans, and his accomplishments.

No man knows his history, though his is one of the most richly documented careers on record. Why should this be? The parallel case of Joseph Smith at once springs to mind, and the explanation of the mystery may well be the same. For as Madariaga points out, most of what is mysterious and contradictory in the story of Columbus comes from the refusal of the experts to believe what he tells them. They say he was an outrageous liar when he was actually telling the truth!

All are agreed that Columbus was an imaginative and a visionary man, often carried away by his own enthusiasm. But on one thing he was clear and specific—he was called for a definite mission. Let us quote two of the latest studies on Columbus, by men who take opposite points of view and refute each other on almost everything else:

> Three features stand out from the glimpses which his contemporaries have let us catch. . . . Mystery surrounds him. Pride stiffens him up. A sense of a mission entrusted to him from on high drives and illumines him. No one knows who he is, where he comes from, what he actually wishes to do. No one can browbeat him, pin him down, make him accept one inch less than the whole of what he demands. No one can fail to feel that he is possessed of an idea, bent on action, bearer of a message, entrusted with a mission. Can we wonder at his success?[1]

Thus Madariaga. And Samuel Eliot Morison:

> For he was not, like a Washington, a Cromwell or a Bolivar, an instrument chosen by multitudes to express their wills and lead a cause; Columbus was a Man with a Mission. . . . He was Man alone with God against human stupidity and depravity, against greedy conquistadors, cowardly seamen, even against nature and the sea. Always with God, though. . . . Men may doubt this, but there can be no doubt that the faith of Columbus

was genuine and sincere, and that his frequent com-
munion with forces unseen was a vital element in his
achievement.[2]

Specifically, Columbus believed that if he would sail a
certain specific distance in a certain specific direction (and
there was nothing vague about the distance and the direction) he would discover land. In this he was right; yet
he was not right in calling this land the Indies—still, the
Indies it had to be if the project was ever to be successfully
promoted.

His contemporary and friend, Las Casas, in an oft-
quoted passage says he was as certain of finding what he
said he would as if he had it already locked up in his trunk.
Las Casas tells how "from all sides and in many ways did
God give Columbus motives and causes that he should
not doubt to undertake so great a deed," and that "God
seemed to move him on by constant pushes."[3] Everything
else in Columbus' life is subservient to the carrying out of
that one mission. The aim and purpose of all his work and
suffering was what happened at 2 A.M. on the morning of
October 12, 1492, and must not be judged by what happened after (it was "the wrath of God upon the seed of
my brethren," says Nephi), or by any other quirks or mis-
adventures. In retrospect we see that this is so—but Columbus himself *always* knew it was: God had chosen him
to do this one great deed.

Two facts about Columbus here claim our respectful
attention:

1. He claimed that his discovery of the Indies was the
result of revelation: "I have said," he wrote to Ferdinand
and Isabella, "that in the carrying out of this enterprise of
the Indies neither reason nor mathematics nor maps were
any use to me: fully accomplished were the words of Isaiah."[4]

2. His performance was magnificent and unparalleled:

a crackpot or a charlatan would have collapsed a thousand times in the painful and humiliating promotion, the arduous and hard-headed preparation, and the dangerous and strenuous execution of his project.

Sailing into a perfect blank on the map, Columbus infallibly did the right thing: "He did not make a single false move in the entire voyage!" says the geographer Professor Nunn. He maintains that Columbus must have been the discoverer of the Trade and prevailing Westerly Winds since it was only by taking fullest advantage of both that his journey was possible—yet his subsequent voyages show that Columbus knew nothing about the wind system.[5] This was not Columbus' doing. Neither was the flight of birds that appeared just in time to keep the ships from turning back, nor the sudden rising of the sea that at another time inspired the expedition to continue. Call it what you will, Columbus was convinced he was being helped.

Finally a day came when he was forced to give the whole fleet his solemn word that he would turn back within two days if land was not discovered—and on the morning of the second day land *was* discovered. About eight or nine hours before the discovery, at sunset on October 11, Columbus gave a strange and sudden order for a marked change of course. "Why he did this, nobody explained," writes Professor Morison, a very sober historian and a nautical expert.[6] But he assures us that if he had *not* done it, the great discovery of October 12, 1492, would have been a tragic discovery of deadly reefs that lay but a short distance dead ahead of the little fleet on its original course.

To the King and Queen, Columbus boldly declared: "I say that the Holy Ghost works in Christians, Jews, Moors and all men of any other sect and not merely in the learned, but in the ignorant."[7] It is remarks like this that raise serious controversies as to just what Columbus' religion was. Those who have never had a revelation can easily enough deny that Columbus ever did, but is his own sober and repeated declaration to be brushed lightly aside? "No man alive," says Morison, speaking as a mariner, "limited to the instruments and means at Columbus's disposal, could obtain anything near the accuracy of his results."[8]

Hamlet in a rage denounced the sophisticated Guildenstern for presuming to play on him when he could not do anything so simple as play on a little flute. If a man is going to tell us what made Columbus tick, he had better first show that he can do the equivalent in the way of honest brainwork to handling those crude instruments of navigation with a tenth the knowledge and skill of a Columbus. This man was no impostor and no hysterical neurotic—and no man would have said "Amen" to the words of Nephi more fervidly than he.

Notes

1. Salvador de Madariaga, *Christopher Columbus* (London: Hollis and Carter, 1949), 16. Discussing the same theme recently is Pauline Moffitt Watts, "Prophecy and Discovery: On the Spiritual Origins of Christopher Columbus's 'Enterprise of the Indies,' " *American Historical Review* (February 1985): 73-102.

2. Samuel Eliot Morison, *Admiral of the Ocean Sea* (Boston: Little, Brown, 1942), 46-47.

3. This theme is discussed at some length in Bartolome de las Casas, *Historia de las Indias* (Mexico City: Fondo de Cultura Economica, 1951), 27-34.

4. Quoted in Madariaga, *Christopher Columbus,* 100.

5. As quoted in Morison, *Admiral of the Ocean Sea,* 198. See George E. Nunn, *The Geographical Conceptions of Columbus* (New York: American Geographical Society, 1924).

6. Morison, *Admiral of the Ocean Sea,* 223.

7. Madariaga, *Christopher Columbus,* 360.

8. Morison, *Admiral of the Ocean Sea,* 195.

3

New Approaches to Book of Mormon Study

In the short time since the appearance of two series of articles in the *Era* under the titles *Lehi in the Desert* (1950) and *The World of the Jaredites* (1951-52),[1] a number of important discoveries and significant studies have come forth, bringing new and surprising light to the study of the authenticity of the Book of Mormon. By a fortunate coincidence, the new materials are particularly pertinent to answering the objections of those critics of the Book of Mormon who have found the above-named studies hard to accept. But before we take the cover off, we must remind the doubters of certain responsibilities.

It seems that those who would attack the Book of Mormon are now forsaking the dangerous ground of tangible and objective evidence to set up their artillery on the eminence of moral and philosophical superiority. Their arguments are sweeping and general, and they suffer from the fatal weakness of overlooking entirely the well-established rules of textual criticism. Since these rules seem to be virtually unknown to many, yet have a vital bearing on the problem of the Book of Mormon, a few words illustrating their application are not only in order but also long overdue. So the discoveries must wait until we have settled some preliminary points.

This article first appeared as a nine-part series in the Improvement Era, *from November 1953 to July 1954.*

One of the best-established disciplines in the world is the critical examination of written texts to detect what in them is spurious and what is genuine. The revival of learning came with the discovery of quantities of ancient documents resurrecting the glories of classical antiquity, but not one of these manuscripts was an original; all without exception were copies of copies. For four hundred years the main business of "scholarship" has been to produce from the materials at hand texts which would most closely correspond to the lost originals, sifting the true from the false by a strenuous and exacting discipline.[2] With the accumulated wisdom and technical experience of centuries it should be possible in our day—as it should have been in Joseph Smith's—to give the Book of Mormon the full treatment. It seems strange that such a controversial book should never have been subjected to a systematic application of the rules of textual criticism. That may be because critics are very few in number and have always thought they have had more important work at hand. But whatever the reason, the fact is that all criticism of the Book of Mormon in the past has been suspiciously superficial.

To illustrate this claim and not to undertake a thorough investigation at this time, let us briefly apply to the Book of Mormon the main rules put forth by Friedrich Blass in his classic work on hermeneutics and criticism, which remains the "standard work" on the subject.[3] The rules given by Blass are all obvious enough to experience and reflection, but every one of them is a stumbling block to the superficial critic, and they have all been scrupulously avoided by those attacking the Book of Mormon.

To begin with, says Blass, "We have the document, and the name of its author; we must begin our examination by assuming that the author indicated really wrote it." You always begin by assuming that a text is genuine.[4] What critic of the Book of Mormon has ever done that? One can hear the screams of protest: "How unscientific! How naive!

How hopelessly biased!" Yet to the experience of the centuries Blass adds perfectly convincing reasons for his
shocking rule. It is equally biased to accept or reject a text
at first glance, but still one must assume at the outset that
it is either spurious or genuine if one is to make any progress.

Jacoby, the foremost authority on Greek historical writing, observes that no great historical writing was ever produced "*sine ira et studio*"⁵ — in other words, without par-
tiality — one must take a stand on something if one is to
lift or move anything. An open mind is not a mind devoid
of opinions, but one that is willing to change opinions in
the face of new evidence. If we must assume something
about the authenticity of the Book of Mormon at the outset,
why not assume that it is false, as its critics regularly do?
Because, says Friedrich Blass, once you assume that a document is a fake, no arguments and no evidence to the end
of time can ever vindicate it, even if it is absolutely genuine.
Why is that? Because "there can be no such thing as an
absolutely positive proof."⁶ The only possible certainty lies
in the negative; for example, if we know *for sure* that a
crime has been committed by a woman, the negative fact
that a suspect is *not* a woman completely exonerates him;
but on the other hand the fact that one *is* a woman proves
neither guilt nor innocence. Thus, while we can never
prove absolutely that the Book of Mormon is what it claims
to be, we are justified at the outset in assuming that it is
what it claims to be. If one assumes that it is true, its
features at least become testable.

Whoever refuses to accept the original claim of a document's origin "is under obligation," says Blass, "to supply
in its place a credible explanation" of its origin. In doing
so, he warns us, we must be on our guard against "assuming the existence of forgers who are at one moment
so clever and adroit as to imitate the writing of Plato or
Demosthenes with deceptive skill, and in the next moment

are so idiotic and stupid as to let themselves get caught red-handed in the most colossal blunders. Nor is the existence of forgers of genius believable, nor of highly gifted writers who are at the same time completely uninformed, such as those to whom the *Phaedo* and the Gospel of John have been attributed. All this sort of thing represents no true cause, and any explanation that requires such an hypothesis is to be put aside without hesitation in favor of the simple appeal to the preserved writings of the writer."[7]

Even in explaining mistakes and blunders in a document, we are told, fraud is always the last theory to turn to, for forgery "must always be based on the assumption that we are dealing with vicious jugglers and coiners, to whom the critic, whenever it suits his interest, imputes a degree of cunning equal to his own. In reality such a breed of forger is simply a product of fantasy, a race of spooks with which the critic peoples his world, and which are at his disposal when and as he wants them, taking every form, like Proteus, which occasion demands appearing now as stupid idiots and now as incredibly sly deceivers. Before the sober eye these ghosts vanish."[8]

Now is not this sly but ignorant forger who never existed the very image of the "Joseph Smith" who is now being put forward as the only possible explanation for the Book of Mormon?

The critics who think they have at last found a plausible explanation for the book have simply fallen into the oldest booby trap of all, the one which the critic, according to Blass, must avoid before all others as the easiest but silliest solution of the problem.

But how can we be certain about anything in criticizing the Book of Mormon? To this Blass gives us the answer: the nearest we can get to certainty, he says, is when we have before us a *long, historical* document, for it is "improbable in the highest degree, and therefore to be regarded at all times as inadmissible that any forger coming later [than the pretended date of authorship] can have the knowledge and diligence necessary to present any *quantity* of *historical* data without running into contradictions." In this, the one sure way of detecting a falsifier, according to our guide, is by those things which he cannot well have succeeded in imitating because they were too trifling, too inconspicuous, and too troublesome to reproduce.[9]

In *Lehi in the Desert* we said: The test of an historical document lies, as we have so often insisted, not in the story it tells, but in the casual details that only an eye-witness can have seen.[10] It is in such incidental and inconspicuous details that the Book of Mormon shines. Blass, then, notes that when these details occur in considerable numbers (as they certainly do in the Book of Mormon), we can confidently assume a genuine text; and, above all, when the large numbers of details fit together and prove each other, we have the strongest proof of all, for difficulties increase not mathematically with the length of a document, but geometrically.[11]

Speaking of the Jaredites, the author has said: "Individually, I find the parallels between the Jaredites and the early Asiatics very impressive, but taken together their value increases as the cube of their number. In the Book of Ether they are woven into a perfect organic whole, a consistent picture of a type of society the very existence of which has come to be known only in recent years."[12] For Blass this is the final test.

A principle on which Blass lays great emphasis is that "whatever lies outside the usual and familiar" is to be regarded as "incredible."[13] Hence the sly, stupid forger must go out the window. But what about Joseph Smith's story? Does that lie in the province of the usual and familiar? If it is totally "outside the usual and familiar" course of events for an ignorant rustic to produce a huge and elaborate book, that proves that he didn't write it; but then we are "under obligation to supply a credible explanation" of who did. Recently clergymen have been making much of the claim that Sidney Rigdon was the man. The claim is ridiculous—Rigdon himself would have shouted it from the housetops, after he left Nauvoo, were it true—but even if that were so, where does it get us? The fabulous forger has merely changed his name. As if one were to say, "They claim that a man named Jones dug the Grand Canyon. Preposterous! It was a man named Brown!" In a word, *who* in 1830 could have written the Book of Mormon?

Joseph Smith's own story of the book's authorship certainly lies far "outside the usual and familiar," and we have every right to ask for special proof of it. This he obligingly supplies when he puts the book in our hands and asks us how *we* explain it. Books of Mormon do not occur at all "in the usual course of events." Therefore, we have every right to doubt the book's existence, except for one thing: We have the book. The only alternative to Joseph Smith's explanation is to assume, paraphrasing Blass, the existence of a forger who at one moment is so clever and adroit as to imitate the archaic poetry of the desert to perfection and supply us with genuine Egyptian names, and yet so incredibly stupid as to think that the best way to fool people and get money out of them is to write an exceedingly difficult historical epic of six hundred pages.[14] Endowed with the brains, perseverance, and superhuman cunning necessary to produce this monumental forgery, the incredibly sly genius did not have the wit to know, after years of experience in the arts of deception, that there are ten thousand safer and easier ways of fooling people than by undertaking a work of infinite toil and danger which, as he could see from the first, only made him immensely unpopular. This is the forger who never existed.

According to Blass, there has never been a clever forgery. Some forgeries have been very successful, but that always required the willing cooperation of dupes and salutary neglect of critics.[15] A classic illustration of the prin-

ciple is furnished by an experience of the Arab poet Khalaf
al-Ahmar, by whom, according to Nicholson, "this art of
forgery was brought to perfection" in the eighth century
A.D. After the scholars of Basra and Kufa had accepted his
work as genuine for many years, the impostor, grown old
and penitent, confessed to them that the verses he had
palmed off on them as genuine writings of the ancients
were really his own compositions. To this honest but be-
lated admission, the scholars gave the astonishing reply
that they preferred to regard the documents as genuine,
pompously declaring, "What you said then seems to us
more trustworthy than your present assertion."[16] They believed the forgery because they were determined to, and
from many other cases it is clear that the numerous forgeries of the Arab poets were successful not because they
were cleverly done, but because of the ignorance, gulli-
bility, and above all the eagerness of the schoolmen to
accept them. As late as the nineteenth century, German
scholars were still studying as the genuine work of a Greek
poet an adroit imitation composed by the celebrated Joseph
Scaliger: and yet the document that fooled them was not
even a forgery, for Scaliger had actually signed his name
to it! If no forgery can stand without the will to believe it,
on the other hand, once that will is present, no forgery is
too clumsy to be acceptable to the experts.

This point is further illustrated in recent studies on the
false Isidorian Decretals, the most famous and influential
of all forgeries. It is agreed among experts that whoever
produced this celebrated cornerstone of papal power could
have succeeded in the ruse only by being "strong enough
to *prevent* any investigation of its origin and hence the
discovery of the fraud."[17]

There has been some disagreement as to who the guilty
parties were, but none as to their methods. Haller has
argued that it was Pope Nicholas I who, finding the new
document useful to his purposes, insisted that it had re-

According to Blass, there has never been a clever forgery. Much energy and ingenuity went into the production of these copper rolls, purportedly found in a cave near Lunton, Arizona, yet it was instantly apparent upon examination that they are modern fabrications. The rolls were strips of modern roofing copper of standard composition and width. There was no sign of aging or patination, though clumsy attempts had been made to achieve the effect with acid. By introducing a confusion of symbols from a number of ancient alphabets, the forger only made his trickery more apparent. Every slip required a dozen tricks to cover it up, and every one of those tricks produced a dozen more slips.

posed in the Roman archives since early Christian times.[18] The celebrated Hincmar accepted the document as genuine, and "when we remember how often clever specialists have let themselves be fooled, it is not surprising" that Hincmar was one of the first to accept the Isidorian fraud in spite of its sudden appearance out of nowhere. The point to notice, however, is that Hincmar, sympathetic though he was with the document, could not be fooled for long: He soon began to doubt, and as he studied the text, his doubts increased until finally within a few years he had proved to himself and others that it was beyond a doubt a forged document.[19] Yet though the Decretals were held in suspicion all over France, the pope was able to check criticism by a shrewd appeal to self-interest, showing the irreverent clergy that they had made full use of the forgery when it suited their interests.[20] In the seventeenth century the Jesuits were still defending the pseudo-Isidorian Decretals, but their only argument was that it was a sin of supreme presumption to question or lay irreverent hands on a holy document, that it is sacrilegious to question what the Church has accepted—a claim to immunity which has become fundamental to the modern Catholic defense. Forgers cannot afford to risk examination. But Joseph Smith to the day of his death placed the Book of Mormon in the hands of all who could do him the most harm if anything about it could be in any way suspected.

It might be objected that there may be any number of forgeries so clever that they have entirely escaped detection and so are ignorantly accepted by us as genuine. This may be so—and we will never know the answer; but the fact that all known forgeries have turned out to be clumsy ones that succeeded only because their public wanted them to succeed makes the super-forgery hypothesis exceedingly improbable. The Book of Mormon cannot be attacked on that ground, since it was never, to say the least, a popular book, and thousands of cunning people would have given a great deal to be able to discredit it with unanswerable proofs; considering the circumstances of its production and publication it must be, if a fraud, one of the clumsiest and most obvious of frauds ever produced.

But is *forgery* the proper word to use at all? Might not the author of the Book of Mormon have been weak and foolish rather than vicious; might he not have written a long book simply because he was too naive to know how dangerous that sort of thing was? Geniuses are often quite naive and combine immense ability with hopeless irresponsibility. After all, no one would accuse Chatterton of being depraved—yet he did fool people. To which the answer is that Chatterton's forgeries were very obvious and fooled only romantic critics who were very ignorant

Much study and care went into the preparation of this "ancient Hebrew inscription" near Los Lunas, New Mexico, yet a cursory glance was enough to
reveal the crisp freshness of the newly-cut letters. Numerous other flaws appeared upon closer inspection. To anyone not determined to accept this inscription as genuine, it furnishes an interesting illustration of the pains to which
people will go to produce a convincing-looking antique, and the impossibility
of doing so without immense and laborious preparation. Yet such a forgery as
this would be infinitely easier to get away with than one of Book of Mormon
proportions.

of early English or determined to accept the wonderful
new finds. The author of the Book of Mormon was not
naive: he could not have written such a long book without
having given it much thought, and that he dares then to
put it into our hands shows that he is very sure of himself.
To follow Blass, a forger can be sure of himself for two
reasons only: either because he is too utterly silly to know
what he is up against or because he is immensely clever.[21]
As to the Prophet, the man who was clever enough to
overcome the difficulties presented in writing the Book of
Mormon was certainly capable of recognizing that those
difficulties existed. He cannot have overcome them un-

consciously without a slip in book after book, no matter how foolishly confident he may have been; there are some things which even irresponsible geniuses cannot do. The author of the Book of Mormon was neither shallow nor naive. But an intelligent forger is not going to risk a long forgery at all when a short one will do just as well, nor is he going to publish and circulate permanent evidence of his crime among the general public, who would be far more willing to accept him without it! A silly man *could* not have composed the Book of Mormon, and a clever man absolutely *would* not have!

Are there then no skillful but innocent forgeries? Must we take a hard, uncompromising stand? Cannot Joseph Smith have been a religiously sincere quack? Willrich, noting that it has been popular practice to designate forgeries as "inventions" or "free compositions" to avoid the ugly word, assures us that if the *purpose* of any writing is to deceive, it is a forgery. Thus for all their pious purpose, the letters attributed to Hellenistic rulers in Josephus are forgeries, dishonest documents invented to furnish proof that the Jews had formerly been honored by the great ones of the earth.[22] "We must designate as a forgery any document that claims, without justification, to be genuine, even though the claim may be a comparatively harmless one."[23] In discussing the forgeries of the famous Lanfranc of Canterbury, Bohmer writes: "Is it possible and permissible to consider such a high official and such a devoted priest as a sly forger?" The answer is yes! "It can be proven that the Archbishop when it suited his purpose had not the slightest scruple against taking crooked paths when it appeared that he could not reach his goal by straight ones.

"Whoever knows and understands the men of the Middle Ages, how many of them, though excellent bishops, abbots, clerics, and monks by the standards of the time, practised falsification of documents—Hincmar of Rheims, Adaldag of Mamburg-Bremen, Frederick of Salzburg, Pilgrim of Passau, Thietmar of Merseburg, Pope Calixtus II, Wibald of Stablo, Abbot Giselber of Laach— will answer with an unqualified affirmitive" the question, "Could Lanfranc have been a common forger?"[24]

Joseph Smith was either telling the truth or he was a criminal—not just a fool—and no sentimental compromises will settle anything. It is base subterfuge to refuse to apply the fair tests which the Prophet himself freely invited and which will just as surely condemn him if he is lying as they will vindicate him if he is telling the truth.

Three Types of Evidence

Evidence for the authenticity of documents falls into three categories: internal, external, and circumstantial.[25]

To summarize, let us list some of the most tangible evidences for the Book of Mormon

Internal Evidence. Imagine that a Book of Mormon has been dropped from a helicopter to a man stranded on a desert island, with instructions to decide on its reliability. On the first page the man would find a clear statement of what the book claims to be, on the following pages a story of how it came into existence, and finally the testimonies of certain witnesses. Here are three astonishing claims— all supernatural. Has the man on the island enough evidence in the contents of the book alone—no other books or materials being available to him—to reach a satisfactory decision? By all means. Internal evidence is almost the only type ever used in testing questioned documents; it is rarely necessary to go any further than the document itself to find enough clues to condemn it, and if the text is a long one, and an historical document in the bargain, the absolute certainty of inner contradictions is enough to assure adequate testing.[26] This makes the Book of Mormon preeminently testable, and we may list the following points on which certainty is obtainable.

1. The mere existence of the book, to follow Blass, is

a powerful argument in favor of its authenticity.[27] Without knowing a thing about LDS Church history, our stranded islander can immediately see that someone has gone to an enormous amount of trouble to make this book. Why? If the author wishes to deceive, he has chosen a strange and difficult way to do it. He has made the first move; he has magnanimously put into our hands a large and laborious text; in the introductory pages of that text, he gives us a clear and circumstantial account of what it is supposed to be and invites us to put it to any possible test. This is not the method of a man out to deceive. We must credit him with being honest until he is proved otherwise.

2. Before he has read a word, our islander notes that the book in his hand is a big one. This is another strong argument in its favor. A forger knows that he runs a risk with every word he writes; for him brevity is the soul of success and, as we have seen, the author of such a long book could not have failed to discover what he was up against before he proceeded very far. In giving us a long book, the author forces us to concede that he is not playing tricks.

3. Almost immediately the castaway discovers that the Book of Mormon is both a religious book *and* a history. This is another point in its favor, for the author could have produced a religious book claiming divine revelation without the slightest risk had he produced a *Summa Theologica* or a *Key to the Scriptures*. If one searches through the entire religious literature of the Christian ages from the time of the Apostles to the time of Joseph Smith, not one of these productions can be found to profess divine revelation aside from that derived through the reading of the scriptures. This is equally true whether one inspects the writings of the apostolic fathers, of the doctors of the Middle Ages — even the greatest of whom claim only to be making commentaries on the scriptures — or more modern religious leaders who, though they claimed enlightenment, spoke

only as the Scribes and Pharisees of old, who, though they could quote and comment on scripture on every occasion, never dared to speak as one having authority. This writer never falls back on the accepted immunities of double meaning and religious interpretations in the manner of the Swedenborgians or the schoolmen. This refusal to claim any special privileges is an evidence of good faith.

4. Examining the book more closely, the islander is next struck by its great complexity. Doesn't the author know how risky this sort of thing is? If anyone should know, he certainly does, for he handles the intricate stuff with great understanding. Shysters may be diligent enough, in their way, but the object of their trickery is to avoid hard work, and this is not the sort of laborious task they give themselves.

5. In its complexity and length lies the key to the problem of the book, for our islander, having once read Blass, remembers that *no* man on earth can falsify a history of any length without contradicting himself continually.[28] Upon close examination all the many apparent contradictions in the Book of Mormon disappear. It passes the sure test of authenticity with flying colors.

6. Since the author must in view of all this be something of a genius, the lonely critic begins to study his work as creative writing.[29] Here it breaks down dismally. The style is *not* that of anyone trying to write well. There is skill of a sort, but even the unscholarly would know that the frequent use of "it came to pass" does not delight the reader, and it is not biblical. Never was writing less "creative" as judged by present standards: there is no central episode, no artistic development of a plot; one event follows another with equal emphasis in the even flow of a chronicle; the author does not "milk" dramatic situations, as every creative writer must; he takes no advantage of any of his artistic opportunities; he has no favorite characters; there is no gain in confidence or skill as the work progresses,

nor on the other hand does he show any sign of getting tired or of becoming bored, as every creative writer does in a long composition: the first and last books of the Book of Mormon are among the best, and the author is going just as strong at the end as at the beginning. The claim of the "translator" is that this book is no literary creation, and the internal evidence bears out the claim. Our critic looks at the date of the book again—1830. Where are the rich sentimentality, the incurable romanticism, and the lush but mealy rhetoric of "fine writing" in the early 1800s? Where are the fantastic imagery, the romantic descriptions, and the unfailing exaggerations that everyone expected in the literature of the time? Here is a book with all the elements of an intensely romantic adventure tale of far away and long ago, and the author turns down innumerable chances to please his public!

7. For the professional religionist, what John Chrysostom called "the wise economy of a useful deception," i.e., religious double-talk, has been ever since his day a condition of survival and success.[30] But there is little of this in the Book of Mormon. There are few plays on words, few rhetorical subtleties, no reveling in abstract terms, no excess of esoteric language or doctrine to require the trained interpreter. This is not a "mystic" text, though mysticism is the surest refuge for any religious quack who thinks he might be running a risk. The lone investigator feels the direct impact of the concrete terms; he is never in doubt as to what they mean. This is not the language of one trying to fool others or who has ever had any experiences in fooling others.

8. Our examiner is struck by the limited vocabulary of the Book of Mormon. Taken in connection with the size and nature of the book, this is very significant. Whoever wrote the book must have been a very intelligent and experienced person; yet such people in 1830 did not produce books with rudimentary vocabularies. This cannot be the

work of any simple clown, but neither can it be that of an able and educated contemporary.

9. The extremely limited vocabulary suggests another piece of internal evidence to the reader. The Book of Mormon never makes any attempt to be clever. This, says Blass,[31] is a test *no* forger can pass. The Achilles' heel of the smart impostor is vanity. The man who practices fraud to gain an ascendancy and assert his superiority over others cannot forego the pleasure of enjoying that superiority. The islander does not know it, but recent attempts to account for Joseph Smith claim to discover the key to his character in an overpowering ambition to outsmart people. Why then doesn't he ever try to show how clever he is? Where are the big words and the deep mysteries? There is no cleverness in the Book of Mormon. It was not written by a deceiver.

10. Since it claims to be translated by divine power, the Book of Mormon also claims all the authority—and responsibility—of the original text. The author leaves himself no philological loopholes, though the book, stemming from a number of nations and languages, offers opportunity for many of them. It is a humble document of intensely moral tone, but it does not flinch at reporting unsavory incidents not calculated to please people who think that any mention of horror or bloodshed should be deleted from religious writing.

External Evidence. Our islander has been rescued by a British tramp steamer. Burning with curiosity, he jumps ship in London, rushes to Great Russell Street, and bounds up the steps of the British Museum three at a time. He is now after *external* proofs for the Book of Mormon. He may spend the next forty years in the great library, but whatever external evidence he finds must fulfill three conditions:

1. The Book of Mormon must make clear and specific statements about certain concrete, objective things.

2. Other sources, ancient and modern, must make

equally clear and objective statements about the same
things, agreeing substantially with what the Book of Mormon says about them.

3. There must be clear proof that there has been no
collusion between the two reports, i.e., that Joseph Smith
could not possibly have knowledge of the source by which
his account is being "controlled" or of any other source
that could give him the information contained in the Book
of Mormon.

The purpose of our studies on Lehi and the Jaredites
was to supply information that fulfilled these three conditions, and the purpose of the present articles is to supply
yet more evidence of the same type. In criticizing such
information one might classify the various items as (a)
positive, (b) possible, and (c) doubtful evidence of authenticity. As positive proof, we might accept the evidence
of such authentically Egyptian names as Paanchi, Manti,
and Hem, or such freakish Jaredite customs as keeping
kings in comfortable imprisonment all their days, for these
things are clearly described in the Book of Mormon, well
established in the secular world, yet known to no one at
the time the Book of Mormon came forth. As possible but
not positive proof we have a good deal of evidence from
the New World; the hesitation to accept this proof as final
comes from the inability or reluctance of our secular experts
to come to an agreement regarding just what they have
found. Until they reach a consensus, our condition number
two above remains unsatisfied and the issue unsettled.
Finally there are doubtful bits of evidence put forth as
proof, but which were better left alone. Thus while the
Book of Mormon says that mountains rose and fell during
the great earthquakes, the presence of the Rocky Mountains does not prove a thing, since the Book of Mormon
does not pretend for a moment that mountains were never
formed at any other time or in any other way. Such "evidence" only does harm.

Circumstantial Evidence. Entirely apart from the contents of the Book of Mormon and the external evidences that might support it, there are certain circumstances attending its production which cannot be explained on grounds other than those given by Joseph Smith. These may be listed briefly:

1. There is the testimony of the witnesses.

2. The youth and inexperience of Joseph Smith at the time when he took full responsibility for the publication of the book—proof (a) that he could not have produced it himself and (b) that he was not acting for someone else, for his behavior at all times displayed astounding independence.

3. The absence of notes and sources.

4. The short time of production.

5. The fact that there was only one version of the book ever published (with minor changes in each printing). This is most significant. It is now known that the Koran, the only book claiming an equal amount of divine inspiration and accuracy, was completely re-edited at least three times during the lifetime of Mohammed. This brings up:

6. The unhesitating and unchanging position of Joseph Smith regarding his revelations, a position that amazed Eduard Meyer more than anything else.[32] From the day the Book of Mormon came from the press, Joseph Smith never ceased to spread it abroad, and he never changed his attitude toward it. What creative writer would not blush for the production of such youth and inexperience twenty years after? What impostor would not lie awake nights worrying about the slips and errors of this massive and pretentious product of his youthful indiscretion and roguery? Yet, since the Prophet was having revelations all along, nothing would have been easier, had he the slightest shadow of a misgiving, than to issue a new, revised, and improved edition, or to recall the book altogether, limit its circulation, claim it consisted of mysteries to be grasped

by the uninitiated alone, say it was to be interpreted only in a "religious" sense, or supersede it by something else. The Saints who believed the Prophet were the only ones who took the book seriously anyway.

7. There has never been any air of mystery about the Book of Mormon; there is no secrecy connected with it at the time of its publication or today; there is a complete lack of sophistry or policy in discussions of the Book of Mormon; it plays absolutely no role in the history of the Church as a pawn; there is never dispute about its nature or contents among the leaders of the Church; there is never any manipulating, explaining, or compromise. The book has enjoyed unlimited sale at all times.

8. Finally, though the success of the book is not proof of its divinity, the type of people it has appealed to — sincere, simple, direct, highly unhysterical, and non-mystical — is circumstantial evidence for its honesty. It has very solid supporters.

The reader using Franklin S. Harris, Jr.'s[33] excellent new collection of materials might add to these lists at his leisure. When one considers that any one of the above arguments makes it very hard to explain the Book of Mormon as a fraud, one wonders if a corresponding list of arguments against the book might not be produced. For such a list one waits with interest but in vain. At present the higher critics are scolding the Book of Mormon for not talking like the dean of a divinity school. We might as well admit it, the Victorian platitudes are simply not there.

New Discoveries

Sealed Up to Come Forth. Until the year 1947, all ancient texts in the possession of our schools and libraries were such documents as had survived by accident. Ancient writers knew and hoped their words would be copied, as we learn from the Roman poets, but no one expected that the very paper or leather on which he was writing would survive the ages. Perhaps the most remarkable type of accidental preservation in modern times has been that of the *genizas*. *Genizas* were windowless rooms or bins connected with ancient synagogues; into these bins were thrown all old worn-out books of scripture to await a time when they could be burned with proper reverence, for since such texts contained the name of God they could not be thrown into common trash heaps or burnt with ordinary junk. Being windowless, and having little or no ventilation, the *genizas* were occasionally walled up and forgotten, and so their precious contents — Hebrew biblical texts of many centuries ago — were preserved in safe obscurity while the Bible texts in continued use were altered again and again by various learned committees through the centuries.[34] The rediscovery of some of these *genizas* has shown to just what extent our Hebrew Bible has been corrupted through the years; scholar Paul Kahle, who has made the study of the old *geniza* texts his life work, has been at particular pains to emphasize certain points of textual criticism which other scholars habitually overlook. One of these is the principle, which should be apparent enough, that there is only one way in which the purity of a text can possibly be preserved through long periods of time, and that is to conceal the text completely from the eyes of men. For years the experts have thought their rules could resurrect ancient texts in their purity, and to this day Westcott and Hort's *New Testament in the Original Greek* is still widely used, though we now know that we shall probably never get a text of the New Testament "in the original Greek," and it is being seriously questioned whether the original language of the New Testament was Greek at all. Only within the past few years has the true force of 1 Nephi 14:26 become apparent: "They are *sealed up* to come forth in their purity, according to the truth which is in the Lamb, in the own due time of the Lord, unto the house of Israel." Unless documents are actually thus "sealed up," they invariably suffer the fate of the Apocrypha as described in Doctrine and Covenants 91 (1833): "There are many things contained therein that are true, and it is mostly translated correctly; there are many things contained therein that are not true, which are interpolations by the hands of men. And whoso is enlightened by the Spirit shall obtain benefit therefrom" (D&C 91:1-2, 5). The habit of scholars right down to the present has been to accept or reject apocryphal works completely, and only since the momentous discoveries beginning in 1947 has the correctness of the Lord's evaluation in section 91 become fully apparent. The new documents have shown, for example, that such apocrypha as *Jubilees* and the *Testament of the Twelve Patriarchs*, while full of interpolations, are nonetheless among the most valuable and authentic sources we have for the understanding of early Christianity.

To return to our original theme, the texts that have turned up with such dramatic suddenness in the past few years,[35] as if a signal had been given, are the first ancient documents which have survived not by accident but by design. They were hidden away on purpose, to be dug up at a later date. It is naturally assumed that during a time of danger for the sect that produced the texts, certain members in authority stored the scrolls away secretly for safekeeping until they could be used again. The intention of the hiders may become known when some of the missing scrolls (which are still being held back by people who took them secretly from the caves) are examined, but for the present we are left to speculation.[36] In this, however, we may enlist the aid of a document related to the Scrolls, the apocryphal Assumption of Moses (as preserved in a Latin copy of the sixth century) in which Moses before being taken up to heaven is instructed by the Lord to "seal up" the covenant: "Receive thou this writing that thou mayest know how to preserve the books which I shall deliver unto thee: and thou shalt set these in order and anoint them with oil of cedar and put them away in earthen vessels in the place which He made from the beginning of the creation of the world." The purpose of this hiding, we are told, is to preserve the books through a period of darkness when men shall have fallen away from the true covenant and would pervert the truth.[37] In Eusebius' *Chronicon*, in which the author often displays a really remarkable intimacy with genuine ancient sources (such as Berossus and Sanchthoniathon), we learn that Noah was ordered in his day "to inscribe in writing the beginning, middle, and end of everything, and to bury the records in the city of Sippar."[38]

Here we see that there was actually an ancient tradition in Israel, according to which one dispensation would hide up records to come forth in another. Now the newly found Dead Sea Scrolls not only show marked affinities with the Assumption of Moses, but the peculiar manner of their preservation is also exactly that prescribed to Moses: they were found in specially made earthen jars, wrapped in linen which was "coated with wax or pitch or asphalt which proves that the scrolls were hidden in the cave for safe preservation, to be recovered and used again later."[39] By whom? The peculiar method of storage also indicates very plainly that the documents were meant for a long seclusion, for the purpose of such treatment of documents is explained in the Moses text; and to lay a roll away with scrupulous care and after the very manner of entombing an Egyptian mummy certainly indicates a long and solemn farewell and no mere temporary storage of convenience.

At any rate, we now have proof both of the tradition and practice in Israel of hiding up holy documents as the only means of conveying them in their purity to the men of another and a distant age. With this, one of the great stumbling blocks of Joseph Smith's story is removed, and the Book of Mormon appears as an established type of document.

Metal Plates. One of the most interesting things about

the Book of Mormon, however, was not its hiding but its metallic format. By now the discovery of writings on plates of precious metal, once the hardest thing to swallow in Joseph Smith's story, has become almost commonplace in the Near East.[40] In 1950 was announced the discovery, in a greatly eroded bronze (or "brass") vessel found in the Beritz Valley, of some silver-lead plates, rectangular, 4.5 by 5 centimeters, quite thin, and entirely covered with Semitic characters, twenty-two lines of them, pressed into the metal with a hard, sharp object. The plates are thought to be from the late Hittite period, that is, from about Lehi's time.[41] At the same time this find was announced, Dupont-Sommer described two newly discovered sheets of gold and silver, bearing a Hebrew-Aramaic inscription of curious nature and mentioning the God of Israel. The script dates the documents from about 200 A.D. So the fabulous plates that were buried by an ancient prophet are beginning to find themselves in respectable company, and just where they should—in ancient Israel.[42]

Pre-Christian Christianity. The great argument of those who have steadfastly refused, in the face of a rising flood of evidence, to accept the antiquity and authenticity of the new scrolls has been that the language they contain is totally out of keeping with the language that should have been used by Jews of such an early period. Here we have pre-Christian Jews talking like the New Testament: "Echoes of New Testament thought and phraseology are clear in the Scrolls; especially those having apocalyptic associations," says B. J. Roberts.[43] But "New Testament thought and phraseology" have always been supposed at divinity schools to be the product of a gradual and rather late evolution of the Christian community, and have no business at all appearing in pre-Christian Jewish texts! Christian language is familiar enough in old Jewish apocalypses and other texts, but "hitherto perplexed exegetes faced with such texts have usually found in them the interpolations of Christian copyists. But now, . . . thanks to the *Habakkuk Commentary* (one of the Scrolls), such excisions which could formerly be understood are now no longer to be tolerated; these 'Christological' passages, taken as a whole, henceforth seem to be of the greatest worth, and to continue to reject them *a priori* as being of Christian origin would appear to be contrary to all sound method."[44] The author of these words notes that "it is now certain — and this is one of the most important revelations of the Dead Sea discoveries — that Judaism in the first century B.C. saw a whole theology of the suffering Messiah, of a Messiah who should be the redeemer of the world." We even find in the Scrolls clear indication of three persons in the Godhead.[45]

Years ago Hermann Gunkel pointed out that a full-blown gospel of redemption and atonement was in existence among the preexilic Jews, but this claim, so jarring to the prevailing schools of theology, which would only accept an evolutionary pattern of slow and gradual development, was strenuously resisted by the experts.[46] The discovery of the Scrolls has changed all that: "Now that the warning has been given," writes Dupont-Sommer, "many passages of the Old Testament itself must be examined with a fresh eye. Everywhere where there is a more or less explicit question of an Anointed One or of a Prophet carried off by a violent death, how is it possible to avoid asking whether the person indicated is not precisely our Master of Justice?"[47] It is that scholar's theory that a certain Master of Justice, mentioned in the Scrolls as the head of a sect of the Essenes in the first century B.C., was the original pre-Christian inspiration for the Messiah idea. Yet the numerous and ubiquitous references to the Messiah in the Old Testament as in the Apocrypha claim to go back not only to pre-Christian times, but far beyond the first century B.C. as well. So if Dupont-Sommer will not tolerate the business of glibly attributing whatever in those writings

betrays a Christological tone to "the interpolations of Christian copyists," neither may he attribute the same passages
to interpolations of men living after the Master of Justice.
The Messianic theme belongs to the oldest traditions in
the world.[48]

The bearing of this on the Book of Mormon should be
at once apparent. The words of an Alma, a Nephi, or a
Helaman are replete with "echoes of New Testament
thought and phraseology," just as the Scrolls are; yet those
prophets are all supposed to have lived long before Christ.
The New Testament flavor of so much of the Book of Mormon has been until now the strongest single argument
against its authenticity. Men trained in sectarian seminaries
have leaned back in their armchairs and pointed to Book
of Mormon phrases that according to them could have
come only from a Christian — and a late Christian — environment: *ergo*, Joseph Smith had simply worked his own
religious conceptions into the book, grossly ignorant as he
was of the crass anachronisms they represented. An excellent example of this type of criticism appeared quite
recently in the leading Jewish newspaper, *Vorwärts*. Speaking of the Book of Mormon, a critic wrote:

> It is full of citations from the Old and New Testa-
> ments. . . . The small number of people who have tried
> to read the book declare that it is dreadfully dull; in it
> are found quotations from Shakespeare and other Eng-
> lish poets. That is one of the very comical things about
> the book. According to the book itself, it is written in
> the Egyptian language of some thousands of years ago;
> yet in it are cited excerpts from the New Testment, a
> much later document, or from wholly modern poets.[49]

We shall deal with Shakespeare presently. As for the
"other English poets," their identity remains a secret
locked in the bosom of the editors of *Vorwärts*. Since "reformed Egyptian" was being written long after New Testament times, the charges of anachronism on linguistic

grounds are worthless. But the basic issue is one which is being fought out furiously today, and the apple of discord is not the Book of Mormon but the Scrolls.

That New Testament language and thought cannot possibly have been familiar to the ancient Jews is a fiercely defended axiom in some schools. Less than a year ago Solomon Zeitlin declared of the Scrolls, "The entire story of the discovery may be a *hoax*," and even if it were not, still the Scrolls "have no value for the history of the Jewish people, or the development of their ideas, or literature, or language. The so-called Manual of Discipline is a conglomeration of words. The Hebrew text makes no sense. . . . It undoubtedly was written by an uneducated Jew of the Middle Ages."[50] How strangely like the conventional criticism of the Book of Mormon this reads! Yet here we have to do with texts which the ablest scholars of our time have declared to be not only genuine, but also the most important discovery ever made in biblical archaeology! How is such disagreement possible among the doctors in the face of so much evidence? Paul Kahle has discoursed at length on the incredible stubbornness and self-will of the best religious scholars when they make up their minds on a subject.[51] One expert now decides that the Scrolls are a Kurdish production of the twelfth century A.D.[52] On what does he base this remarkable deduction? On certain details of literary style! But what of the other evidence, such as the fact that "not a single medieval manuscript exhibits the same script as that of the Scrolls"?[53] That is simply ignored. The scholars who maintain that the Scrolls are medieval "accord preferential treatment to the evidence supplied by the . . . literary and linguistic relations between the Scrolls" and other medieval documents, according to Teicher, while on the other hand "the archaeologists and paleographers . . . set *their* feet on what they consider to be the firm ground of their paleographic and archaeological evidence and reject airily the literary and linguistic evidence."[54] As an illustration, "to maintain, as Dr. Weis does, that 'the examinations of the [Habakkuk] Scroll suggest that it was written about the year 1096 by an Isawite or a Judganite,' is, in view of the archaeological and paleological evidence alone, simply impossible."[55]

It is because it has been judged in the light of certain fundamental preconceptions about the nature of Jewish and Christian history that the Book of Mormon has been held to be a mass of crude anachronisms. Today the finding of the Scrolls shows these fundamental preconceptions to have been quite false: "Everything is now changed," writes Dupont-Sommer, "and all the problems relative to primitive Christianity—problems earnestly examined for so many centuries—all these problems henceforth find themselves placed in a new light, which forces us to reconsider them completely. . . . It is not a *single* revolution in the study of biblical exegesis which the Dead Sea documents have brought about; it is, one already feels, a whole cascade of revolutions."[56] Recently a leading English liberal clergyman has declared that in order to support the accepted viewpoints, he and his fellows have been under constant strain "of having to contort [Christ's] message, ignoring a considerable portion of it and making unwarranted deductions from other parts, to suit our preconceptions"; the confession of this folly and the acceptance of literal interpretations in place of what he calls the liberal, ameliorist, social-gospel view "gives a sense of relief, of illumination, of enlargement."[57]

Such changing points of view, largely the result of the new discoveries, are very significant for Book of Mormon study. Their immediate result is to show for the first time on what extremely flimsy groundwork criticism of the Book of Mormon has rested in the past. Recently the writer has been taken to task for dealing somewhat roughly with the conventional commentators on Ezekiel. It is therefore with considerable complacency that he can now point to W. A.

Irwin's very recent study on Ezekiel research between 1943 and 1953, in which that scholar after a thorough investigation can announce that in spite of the diligence and number of the researchers, "not a single scholar has succeeded in convincing his colleagues of the finality of *his* analysis of so much as *one* passage!"[58] Though the experts propound wildly varying views—some having Ezekiel flourishing in Palestine in 400 B.C., while Messel dates his call, with great exactness, at 593 B.C.—none of them bothers to submit the evidence for his claims: "It is unfortunate," says Irwin, after a careful survey of the whole field, "that none of these scholars argued his position. We concede readily that they had weighty reasons for their views, but as matters stand, they have given only opinions, when the situation cries aloud for assembling of evidence and for close-knit argument."[59] Every Ezekiel scholar, according to Irwin, follows "the method that is far too frequent in Old Testament criticism, that of presenting a plausible story as final evidence in a case, when in reality it is not evidence at all."[60] The result of this is that "as soon as one pushes beyond the general admission of spurious matter in the book, and seeks to identify it, he is at once plunged into confusion and chaos not one whit relieved through these years. Still worse, there is no clearly emerging recognition of a sound method by which to assault this prime problem. Every scholar goes his own way, and according to his private predilection chooses what is genuine and what is secondary in the book; and the figure and work of Ezekiel still dwell in thick darkness."[61] Can we expect the Book of Mormon to enjoy unprejudiced and objective criticism when such treatment is accorded the Bible?

Any "Christological" elements in the Book of Mormon must have taken their rise not merely in pre-Christian times but in that world to which the Nephites must ultimately trace all their Israelitish traditions, the Jerusalem of 600

B.C. Now there is much to indicate that that period was
one of those times when great emphasis was being laid on
the Messianic doctrine.[62] One leaving Jerusalem at that time
would take with him a powerfully prophetic religion, un-
damaged by the centuries of learned exposition and ra-
tionalization which were to make the Jewish religion a
product of schools and committees.[63] The whole treatment
of the Messianic tradition and the mission of Israel in the
Book of Mormon is of a piece not with the demonstrations
and *sententiae* of the doctors nor with the flights of the
mystics, but with the systematic and traditional exposition
which we find in the Scrolls and Apocrypha. Both in the
Old World and the New we are led into a pool of common
ideas and terms centering about the Messianic concept.

"In every age," writes Guerrier, discussing parallels in
early Christian papyri, "and especially where religious
matter is concerned, there has circulated in a more or less
extensive area [of the Near East] a certain fund of ideas
and formulas, exact or inexact, which have been employed
everywhere, and it is not always easy to discover their
origin." As a result, he says, we find parallels everywhere
without being able to trace them to any single doctrine or
document as a source; for example, the *Testament of the
Twelve Patriarchs*, though pre-Christian and non-Christian,
is thoroughly typical of genuine early Christian writing.[64]
We need not be surprised if striking but common ideas
cannot be traced to their sources, for from the very beginning borrowing has been general and universal in the East:
"As soon as a book was completed, its life was
ended. . . . There was no idea in those times of authorship. . . . A book was nobody's property. It belonged to
everyone."[65] Texts far more ancient than the Scrolls, now
read with a new understanding, show us how all through
the ages the same ideas and even the same expressions
have been current with regard to an expected Messiah.[66]
But in particular there have always been special groups of

pious people, separating themselves from the main body of Israel to prepare in a most particular way for the coming of the Lord, and thereby incurring the mockery, wrath, and persecution of the society as a whole, under the leadership of conservative priests.[67] This situation is indicated in the Scrolls and also in the Lachish letters, which are contemporaneous with Lehi.[68] It is tersely and finely described in the Book of Mormon as well: "Our father Lehi was driven out of Jerusalem because he testified of these things. Nephi also testified of these things, and also almost all of our fathers, even down to this time; yea, they have testified of the coming of Christ, and have looked forward, and have rejoiced in his day which is to come" (Helaman 8:22). Here we are told that the situation in the Old World persisted in the New World, and what the Book of Mormon describes—pious separatist groups living in a religion of expectation, suffering persecution, and moving into the "wilderness" from time to time under inspired leaders, who often visit royal courts and cities on dangerous missionary assignments—is precisely the picture that is beginning to emerge in the Old World.

Literary Criticism. With the finding of the Scrolls it becomes apparent that large sections of the Book of Mormon (for example, in Jacob, Alma, Helaman, and so on) are actually specimens of a very peculiar literary style that would be exceedingly difficult to forge at any time. It is still too early for a definitive study of the problem, and the whole question of ancient *nonbiblical* literary types in the Book of Mormon has hardly been scratched. But the first step in such an investigation has already been made by capable researchers who have attempted to expose the Book of Mormon as a typical modern American fabrication. Now it takes no great genius to discover that the Book of Mormon first appeared in western New York in the early nineteenth century: that is a given quantity. What the literary savant must show us is that it is a *typical* production of its environment—that there were many, many other writings just like the Book of Mormon being produced in the world of Joseph Smith. If that is asking too much, let the experts furnish but *one* other example of such a book. It will not do merely to point to any text using "thee" and "thou," or to any work that mentions the lost tribes or a possible Hebrew origin for the Indians or ancient war and migrations—what we must have is a book that is something like the Book of Mormon, which resembles it in form and structure, and not merely in casual and far-fetched parallels of detail such as abound in all literature. It is not enough to observe that "Lehi" sounds like "Lehigh" or that a man was murdered on the shores of Lake Erie in Joseph Smith's day—nothing is proved by such silly parallels. The Bible will not do, either, for the Bible was not written in western New York in the early nineteenth century. If we can find a book written in imitation of the Bible, that will do for our point of departure—but even for such a book we search in vain.

The Book of Mormon, like the Bible, is an organic whole. We are asking the literary experts to produce just one modern work which resembles it as such.

There are, we believe, plenty of *ancient* parallels, but if the Book of Mormon is a fraud, a cheat, a copy, a theft, and so on, as people have said it is, we have every right to ask for a sampling of the abundant and obvious sources from which it was taken. Smith's *View of the Hebrews* is no more like the Book of Mormon than a telephone directory.[69] All attempts to find contemporary works which the Book of Mormon even remotely resembles have been conspicuous failures. So it has been necessary to explain the book as a work of pure and absolute fiction, a nonreligious, money-making romance. But one need only read a page of the book at random to see that it is a religious book through and through, and one need only read the title page of the first edition to see that it is given to the world as holy scripture, no less. Here we come to the crux of the whole matter.

The whole force and meaning of the Book of Mormon rests on one proposition: that it is true. It was written and published to be believed.

People who believe the Book of Mormon (and this writer is one of them) think it is the most wonderful document in the world. But if it were not true, the writer could not imagine a more dismal performance. There is nothing paradoxical in this. As Aristotle noted, the better a thing is, the more depraved is a spurious imitation of it. An imitation nursery rhyme may be almost as good as an original, but a knowingly faked mathematical equation would be the abomination of desolation. Curves and equations derive all their value not from the hard work they represent or the neatness with which they are presented on paper, but from one fact alone — the fact that they speak the truth and communicate valid knowledge. Without that they are less than nothing. To those who understand and believe Einstein's equation that $E = mc^2$, that statement is a revelation of power; to those who do not understand or believe it (and there are many!), it is nothing short of an insolent and blasphemous fraud. So it is with the Book of Mormon, which if believed is a revelation of power but otherwise is a nonsensical jumble. "Surely," wrote Sir Richard Burton, "there never was a book so thoroughly dull and heavy; it is as monotonous as a sage-prairie."[70]

It will be said that this merely proves that the greatness of the Book of Mormon lies entirely in the mind of the reader. Not entirely! There are people who loathe Bach and can't stand Beethoven; it was once as popular among clever and educated people to disdain Homer and Shakespeare as barbaric as it is now proper to rhapsodize about them in great-book clubs. Different readers react differently to these things — but they must have something valid to work on. We are not laying down rules for taste or saying that the Book of Mormon is good because some people like it or bad because others do not. What we are saying is that the Book of Mormon, whatever one may think of it, is one of the great realities of our time, and what makes it so is that certain people believe it. Its literary or artistic qualities do not enter into the discussion: it was written to be believed. Its one and only merit is truth. Without that merit, it is all that nonbelievers say it is. With that merit, it is all that believers say it is. And we must insist on this truism because it supplies a valuable clue to the authorship of the book.

Joseph Smith wanted only one thing of the Book of Mormon — that people should believe it. The story never sold well and only made trouble for the "author." Those who believed he was a prophet would have believed him just as much without the Book of Mormon. His enemies would have had far less against him — the Book of Mormon might even be called his undoing. From the day he received the plates it gave him only trouble and pain.

But leave Joseph Smith out of it. Whoever wrote the Book of Mormon wanted before all else that people should believe in it. But what could any impostor gain by that? A deceiver would want people to buy the book, and would write a book that would sell — what concern of his whether anyone *believed* it or not? That rules out anyone but Joseph Smith as the author, for his case only was strengthened by such belief. As for a minister such as Spaulding or Sidney Rigdon producing it, that is completely out of the question once we appreciate the immense emphasis laid by the Book of Mormon itself on being believed, for what greater outrage or deadlier risk could a minister of the gospel run than that of forging scripture? Did Spaulding's heirs ever think of the terrible crime with which they were charging him? They asked the world to imagine the venerable divine in the presence of his attentive loved one reeling off a recitation of his own composition which, if not genuine, could only be the grossest blasphemy!

Again, we are forced back onto the old dilemma. Joseph Smith was either the fantastic, preposterous, implausible genie his enemies describe—perpetrating the most monstrous crimes ever conceived by man with a clear countenance and sunny disposition, performing prodigies of labor for no reward but danger and contempt, engineering the most fiendishly cunning, criminal operations completely without motive—or else he was telling the truth. There is no middle way, for the Book of Mormon was given to the world as scripture, to be believed in the most literal sense. It is that aspect of it which gives us the key to the book's authorship. One can imagine all sorts of things, but one cannot imagine any inhabitant of this planet composing just this type of book in the nineteenth century. It is to other ages that we must turn for the prototypes of the Book of Mormon.

Among the Scrolls is a great "Hymn of Thanksgiving," a literary composition of real merit yet one which contains hardly a single original line! "These songs are as if woven from quotations from the Old Testament. . . . The style closely imitates that of the *Psalms* and other poetic writings of the Old Testament. Biblical reminiscences abound, . . . quotations shine out at every moment."[71] This poetry illustrates the use of set and hallowed expressions in religious writing to convey ancient and eternal ideas: the employment of stereotyped phrases is not a sign of mental weakness here, but actually of artistic skill. If the Book of Mormon actually comes from the Old World religious milieu with which it identifies itself, it should also resort often to set and accepted forms of expression, and the last thing we should expect to find in it would be gropings for original means of expression. And the former situation is what, to the distress of modern literary critics, we do find.

An interesting phenomenon, announced by D. W.

Thomas in 1950, supplies an important commentary on the
Old World background to the Book of Mormon. It can be
shown from the Lachish *ostraca* (discovered in 1935 and,
up until the finding of the Scrolls, "the most valuable discovery ever made in . . . biblical archaeology"), "that our
Hebrew Bible bears upon it the stamp of the dialect of
Judah current round about the sixth century B.C."[72] This
can only mean that *our* text of the Old Testament comes
from about the time of Lehi and closely resembles the Bible
he used—for otherwise the details of the particular dialect
of his time and place could not possibly predominate in
the text. That being the case, the close—though not
slavish—adherence of Old Testament quotations in the
Book of Mormon to the style of our own Bible need not
be regarded as a suspicious circumstance. If the least be
said for it, this is a fortunate coincidence for the Book of
Mormon, for though of course it does not prove the correctness of the book, it does prove that the Nephite scripture is not guilty of anachronism when it quotes the prophets in the words that seem to be taken from our own version
of the Bible.

Paul and Moroni. The Book of Mormon passage most
often attacked as evidence of fraud is the statement in Ether
that "faith is things which are hoped for and not seen"
(Ether 12:6). The natural impulse is to detect in the verse
an obvious distortion of Hebrews 11:1, but wouldn't Joseph
Smith while translating the Book of Mormon have had the
same idea? A basic principle of textual criticism is that
impostors always avoid *obvious* pitfalls, and when they
make crude blunders, it is because of ignorance and over-
sight—but the Prophet was not ignorant of the scriptural
parallel, nor can he have overlooked it. "There is nothing
easier," says Blass, "than to argue from contacts and resemblances that a text is spurious," and he reminds us
that, since parallel passages are *extremely* common in literature, to view even close parallels as a proof of fraud is

a very uncritical practice.[73] In the present case, however, it is hard to see how Moroni could have avoided speaking like Paul, since they are both discussing the same limited concept from the same traditional point of view. In the chapter in which the passage occurs, the word *faith* is used no fewer than twenty-six times, for this is Moroni's great treatise on faith. What word did he use? Surely the classic *amn* was the root, for it is used in all Semitic languages as in Egyptian to express the basic ideas of "faith," (1) loyalty or firmness, and (2) expectation. Both these ideas are clearly expressed in the best-known of all Semitic words, our own "Amen." [74] This is rendered in the Septuagint by *genoito*, a simple optative expressing hope: "May it come to pass!" Faith, in the direct and concrete language of the Semites, is *something* hoped for: the Arab has no abstract word for "faith" as we do but instead uses a number of terms all meaning "*something* in the mind," "something imagined or wished."[75] What else could Moroni have said if he used any Semitic (or Egyptian) word for *faith*, except that it was the things we hope for?

If faith is the keynote of Moroni's whole commentary on the Book of Ether, it is also the keynote of the Messianic religion, which was before all things a religion of hope. We have noted above that the Scrolls, the Apocrypha, and the New Testament speak a common language wherever they have "apocalyptic associations." The Book of Hebrews, aside from being the most baffling and mysterious piece in all the scriptures, is also the most apocalyptic, and the eleventh chapter is the nucleus of the whole thing; it runs, in the Apocryphal tradition, through the last of the "elders" of each of the ancient dispensations—Abel, Enoch, Noah, Abraham, Joseph, Moses, and Christ, showing how each lived by faith and so received things from heaven. In the same way, Moroni reviews the world's history in terms of faith, showing that men must live by faith in the hope for things to come. And in the same way all the Apocrypha, a huge and very ancient literature—far older than Paul or Moroni—treat this as their standard theme.[76] Since all these writers have the same conception of history, religion, and politics, is it surprising that they should have the same ideas about faith, the cornerstone of the whole doctrine? The Scrolls and Apocrypha are just beginning to show us what the Book of Mormon describes so fully and so well—the complete engrossment of the righteous folk of Israel in a religion of expectation.

Lehi and Shakespeare. The only rival of the "faith-is-things-which-are-hoped-for" passage as a target for critics is Lehi's description of himself as one "whose limbs ye must soon lay down in the cold and silent grave, from whence no traveler can return" (2 Nephi 1:14). This is the passage—the lone passage—that has inspired those scathing descriptions of the Book of Mormon as a mass of stolen quotations from "Shakespeare and other English poets." Lehi does not quote Hamlet directly, to be sure, for he does not talk of "that undiscovered country, from whose bourne no traveler returns," but simply speaks of "the cold and silent *grave*, from whence no traveler can return." In mentioning the grave, the eloquent old man cannot resist the inevitable "cold and silent," nor the equally inevitable tag about the traveler—a tag so inevitable that not only Shakespeare but also Lehi's own contemporaries made constant use of it!

Long ago Friedrich Delitzsch wrote a classic work on the Babylonian and Assyrian, i.e., the common Near Eastern, ideas about death and the beyond. And what was the title of his book? *Das Land ohne Heimkehr*—"the Land of No Return."[77] In the story of Ishtar's descent to the underworld, the lady goes to the *irsit la tari*, "the land of no return" (where *tari* may be the same root as that used in our own "re-turn"). She visits "the dark house from which no one ever comes out again" and travels along "the road on which there is no turning back."[78] Someone is plagiarizing like mad, for these are the most obvious variations on the Hamlet theme—even more obvious than Lehi's! Recently Tallquist has made a thorough study of Sumerian and Akkadian names for the world of the dead; conspicuous among these are "the hole," "the earth," "the land of no return," "the city of no return," "the path of no turning back," "the road whose course never turns back," "the distant land," "the steppe," "the desert," and so on.[79] Shakespeare should sue. In *Lehi in the Desert* we had occasion to note more than once that Lehi loved poetic discourse and high-flown speech, was proud of his sound literary education, and was much given to recitation.[80] Since custom sanctioned and expected the use of such terms as he employed in speaking of the grave, it is hard to deny him the luxury of speaking as he was supposed to speak. Especially significant is the fact that the ideas to which the aged Lehi here gives such moving expression by no means reflect either his own (or Mormon's or Joseph Smith's!) ideas as to what the afterlife is really like. That shows that he is indulging in a strictly conventional and normal bit of educated eloquence, as old men are wont to. If he had a weakness for paraphrasing Hamlet's soliloquy when speaking about death, so did all his contemporaries!

Lehi's Poetry and Imagery. Speaking of Lehi's poetry, we should not overlook the latest study on the *qaṣida*, that of Alfred Bloch, who distinguishes four types of verse in the earliest desert poetry: (1) the *ragaz*-utterances to accompany any rhythmical work, (2) verses for instruction or information, (3) elegies, specializing in sage reflections on the meaning of life, and (4) *Reiselieder*, recited on a journey to make the experience more pleasant and edifying.[81] Lehi's *qaṣida* (1 Nephi 2:9-10), as we described it in *Lehi in the Desert*, conforms neatly to any of the last three of these types, thus vindicating its claims to be genuine.[82] The same verses may also be described as *sajᶜ*, a type of "rhymed prose," according to Nicholson, "which . . . originally . . .

had a deeper, almost religious, significance as the special form adopted by poets, soothsayers, and the like in their supernatural revelations and for conveying to the vulgar every kind of mysterious and esoteric lore."[83]

The most characteristic mark of apocryphal literature is the constant use of stereotyped imagery — the tower, the vineyard, the kingdom, and so on — to convey familiar and venerable ideas. This same characteristic is conspicuous in Book of Mormon writers of the early period, that is, those who were educated in the Old World or were brought up by those who were. Lehi himself is much given to allegorical discourse, and his dreams are full of striking imagery; but in the book of his son Jacob is the longest and most involved parable in the book. It has to do with repeated visits of the lord of an estate to his vineyard and reminds us that Deissmann showed that the *Parousia* of a governor or estate-owner, a term employed in New Testament times and in the Apocrypha to describe the visits of the Lord to this earth, is not of Christian origin at all. Both the word and the institution are a conspicuous part of the economy of the Near East throughout ancient times,[84] but this was not known until Deissmann's studies in the present century.

Captain Moroni's Title of Liberty. Another Book of Mormon custom on which the discovery of the Scrolls has thrown brilliant light is what might be called the cult of the banner. A text designated by the modern title of "The Rule of Battle for the Sons of Light" shows that the Jews shared with other people of antiquity "a mystical conception of war," according to which the carnage of the battlefield was "a sacred act" surrounded by definite ritual.[85]

The document in question contains special instructions for the Children of the Covenant on the marshaling of the hosts for war: "On the great ensign placed at the head of all the army shall be inscribed: 'Army of God' together with the name of the twelve tribes of Israel. On the ensign

NEW APPROACHES TO BOOK OF MORMON STUDY

of the thousand group shall be inscribed: 'Wrath of God, full of anger, against Belial and all the people of his party, without any survivors.' On the ensign of the hundred group shall be inscribed 'From God comes the energy to fight against all sinful flesh.' " Other inscriptions are given for the other military units, all of them more or less lengthy and proclaiming some inspiring principle or program to guide the hosts, and there are special inscriptions for entering battle, engaging in battle, and returning from battle.[86]

The flag is an Asiatic invention,[87] and there is a very ancient legend of how in the beginning when Iran was under the rule of the serpent, a blacksmith named Kawe put his leather apron upon a pole, and "that was the flag of Iranian independence, which, under the name of *dirafsh-i-kâwiyâni* [Flag of Kawe], remained the national standard down to the time of the Arab conquest." To lead the nation under its new flag of liberation, the hero Threataona was raised up in the mountains.[88] This Threataona is a doublet of King Cyrus, founder of the Persian nation, who holds such a high and holy place in Jewish tradition that he is next to Solomon alone the holiest of kings.[89]

Turning now to the Book of Mormon, we read how "it came to pass that he [Moroni] rent his coat; and he took a piece thereof, and wrote upon it — In memory of our God, our religion, and freedom, and our peace, our wives, and our children — and he fastened it upon the end of a pole. . . . And he took the pole, which had on the end thereof his rent coat, (and he called it the title of liberty)." All who followed Moroni on that occasion entered into a solemn covenant, and once Moroni gained the upper hand, "whomsoever . . . would not enter into a covenant to support the cause of freedom . . . he caused to be put to death" (Alma 46:12-13, 35). The surprising savagery and peculiarly Old-World concepts of "liberty" are matched perfectly in the special instructions to leaders in the "Rule

of Battle" scroll. These leaders are priests, whose duty
before the battle is to turn toward the enemy, denounce
them as a "congregation of wickedness," and formally
dedicate them to destruction. Their song of triumph,
"woven entirely of biblical texts," has a fierce and Asiatic
ring: "Bring the riches of the nations into Thy dwelling!
And may their kings serve Thee, and may all Thine op-
pressors prostrate themselves before Thee, and may they
lick [the dust] from Thy feet!"[90] However harsh and unsympathetic Moroni's character may appear to the modern
reader, he is a true child of ancient Israel.

The parallels between the Nephite and Old World practices deserve comment. The case of Kawe is not beside the
point here, for it has long been recognized by all scholars
in the field that there are numerous and clear affinities
between old Persian traditions and Jewish eschatological
lore—and Kawe is at the heart of the religion of the Magi,
his banner being the holiest symbol of their priesthood.[91]
The identity of Kawe with Cyrus, the darling of the Jewish
doctors, is enough in itself to justify referring to his story.
The fact that we are dealing with false priesthoods does
not obscure the significance of traditional institutions: (1)
the garment as a banner, (2) the long sermonizing inscription on it, (3) the idealistic program of liberation proclaimed
by the banner, (4) the ritual condemnation of all opponents
to death as children of darkness. These are now known to
be widespread concepts in the ancient world, but the discovery is recent.[92] What makes the Book of Mormon version
particularly significant is the fact that Moroni himself draws
the dramatic idea of the "title of liberty" directly from the
Old World pool when he attributes the the inspiration of
the banner not to his own invention but to the teachings
of the ancient Jacob, Lehi's son, who, as we have just
noted, was steeped in Old World lore and tradition, and
when he informs his followers that they are following in
the footsteps of their ancestor Joseph in rending their gar-

ments even as his garment was rent (see Alma 46:24). It is clear that the whole episode of the flag of liberty was consciously carried out in the spirit of the ancients, and that story, which might have been taken as pure fantasy up until about five years ago, is now substantiated by the discovery of the "Rule of Battle" scroll.

Relationships between Egypt and Israel. The position of 1 Nephi on things Egyptian receives confirmation from day to day. In 1949 Couroyer published a study in which he pointed out many notable parallels and a few points of contrast between Egyptian and Israelitish literature insofar as they deal with the subject of the Way of Life, a theme of great prominence in both literatures and a common bond between them.[93] Lehi, it will be recalled, was obsessed, dreaming and waking, by the concept of life as a way and a journey. Recently A. Mallon has declared that there is evidence for close and continual contact between Egyptian and Hebrew culture not only in Hebrew and Egyptian names (the proper names in the Book of Mormon seem to be split about half and half) but also in the peculiar role that dreams played among both peoples.[94] The long duration and remarkable constancy of relationships between Egypt and the Hebrews becomes plainer every day. Very recently Rowton has shown how the Exodus followed upon a period of Semitic domination in Egypt, and he argued that what prevented the occupation of Palestine by the children of Israel was an Egyptian occupation of that country.[95] So we find the people of these two cultures constantly trespassing on each other's lands. In his latest work, V. Gordon Childe describes the nature of the normal bond between Egypt and Palestine: "Native Giblite clerks were apparently trained in Egyptian hieroglyphic writing. In exchange for the cedars of Lebanon and perhaps olives and dyes, the Giblites received and adopted elements of Egyptian civilization, including writing and all that that implied, as well as manufactured articles and corn. They

remained a friendly but independent civilized community."[96] Long and intimate ties of commercial and cultural
rather than political and military nature are what is indicated by recent excavations, and that is precisely the background of Lehi's world as the Book of Mormon describes
it.

   The Language of the Book of Mormon. At present the problem of the original language of the Book of Mormon is one
which seems to be stirring considerable interest in some
quarters. It would be a very difficult and perhaps a useless
task to separate possible Egyptian elements in the Book of
Mormon from the Hebrew elements. For one thing, Egyptian influence is now known to have been far stronger in
Hebrew itself than we hitherto supposed,[97] so that when
we think we are dealing with a Hebraism, it might well
be an Egyptianism as well, and who is to say whether the
Egyptian flavor of the text is not actually stronger than the
Hebrew? Such speculations are a waste of time, however,
in view of Mormon's declaration that his people have altered the conventional ways of writing both Egyptian and
Hebrew to conform to their own peculiar manner of
speech, that is, both the writing and the language had
been changed, so that the prophet can state that "none
other people knoweth our language" (see Mormon 9:32-
34). Nephite was simply Nephite, as English is English,
whatever its original components may have been.

   Why all this concern, then, about the language or languages of the Book of Mormon? If we had the original
text, which we do not, and if we could read it, which we
cannot, any translation we might make of it would still be
inferior to that which was given, as we claim it was, by
the gift and power of God. If we had the original text,
scholars would be everlastingly squabbling about it and
getting out endless new and revised translations, as in the
case of the Bible. In fact, if our English text of the Book of
Mormon came to us in any other way than by revelation

it would be almost worthless! For members and investigators could ask of every verse: "But how do we know it is translated correctly?" A revealed text in English is infinitely to be preferred to an original in a language that no one on earth could claim as his own. It frees the members and leaders of the Church as it frees the investigating world from the necessity of becoming philologists, or, worse still, of having to rely on the judgment of philologists, as a prerequisite to understanding this great book. At the same time, it puts upon the modern world an obligation to study and learn, from which that world could easily plead immunity were the book in an ancient language or couched in the labored and pretentious idiom that learned men adopt when they try to decipher ancient texts.

To the question "What was the original language of the Book of Mormon?" the real answer is: It is English! For the English of the Book of Mormon comes by revelation, and no one can go beyond revelation in the search for ultimate sources. Let us, then, rejoice in the text we have and not attempt to reconstruct it in Hebrew or Egyptian so that we can then analyze and translate what we have written!

Proper Names. Yet, lest anyone charge the Book of Mormon with claiming to be beyond criticism, it supplies us with a goodly number of untranslated words that still await the attention of the philologist. There are the proper names, divided, as we have already noted, almost equally between Egyptian and Hebrew, which is what we would expect in view of Nephi's and Mormon's remarks about both languages being used and corrupted by the Nephites. In regard to Hebrew names, D. W. Thomas in 1950 confirmed our own observation in *Lehi in the Desert* that "the strong tendency [of Book of Mormon names] to end in *-iah* is very striking, since the vast majority of Hebrew names found at Lachish end in the same way, indicating that *-iah* names were very fashionable in Lehi's time."

Thomas notes that a "striking" peculiarity of Hebrew names in the age of Jeremiah is "the many personal names which end in -iah."[98] The same authority observes that the Lachish fragments prove the language of Zedekiah's time to have been classical Hebrew of a type which "aligns itself more especially with . . . the Book of Jeremiah," thereby vindicating the long-questioned accuracy and antiquity of the biblical records that purportedly come down to us from the time of Lehi.[99]

A well-known peculiarity of Book of Mormon names is that a very large percentage of them end in -m or -n. A glance at a name-list will show that mimation is overwhelmingly favored for Jaredite names, while nunation is the rule for Nephite and Lamanite ones. Jirku has declared that it is now known for certain that mimation was still current in the Semitic dialects of Palestine and Syria between 2100 and 1800 B.C., when the nominative (the subjective) case singular still ended in -m.[100] From Egyptian and Hittite records it is now clear that the dialects of Palestine and Syria dropped this mimation in the first half of the second millennium B.C. This old -m ending is preserved in the Bible only in a few pre-Hebrew words used in incantations and spells: Teraphim, Sanwerim, Urim, and Thummim.[101]

It is significant to Latter-day Saints that the last two words are not, as has always been supposed, Hebrew plural forms, but are archaic words in the singular. This means that the conventional attempts to determine the nature of Urim and Thummim from classical Hebrew are worthless and, as Jirku points out, that Urim and Thummim stands for two single implements or objects, and not for a multiplicity of things.

To judge by proper names in the Book of Mormon, the language of the Jaredites was related to a pre-Hebrew mimated language that has left its marks in a few very old and holy words in the Old Testament.

Jews. On no point have we been more often assailed since the appearance of the "Lehi" articles than our liberal use of the word *Jew* to describe Lehi and his contemporaries. A Jew is a member of the tribe of Judah, it is true, but that is not the whole story. The name is applied by experts today to any citizen of the ancient Jewish state or of Jerusalem, no matter what his tribe; to any inhabitant of Judaea, no matter what his tribe, religion, or citizenship; to anyone accepting the Jewish religion, no matter what his family background; to anyone descended from a family that had once practiced that religion, no matter what his present religion. The subject has recently received full treatment at the hands of Professor Solomon Zeitlin, whose conclusions may be helpful. The term *Hebrew*, according to Zeitlin, is never applied to the Israelites either in the Law or the Prophets.[102]

After the exile the people were called Judaeans, only rarely Israel, and "later the name Israel disappears, and that of Jews takes its place entirely." In the time of Josephus, all inhabitants of Judea, whether Jews or not, were called Judaeans, and in the Second Commonwealth all proselytes were also called Judaeans (Jews).[103] At that time the country itself was called *ha-aretz,* "the Land," as it is today, and the people were never called either Hebrews or Israelites. "The term *Jews* was applied in Egypt to the inhabitants who settled there and followed the same religion as the inhabitants of Judaea," regardless of ancestry or country of origin.[104] "When Paul was in Judaea," says Zeitlin, "he called himself a Judaean, . . . while when he was in the Diaspora he called himself a Hebrew, or Israeli, as the people [Jews] of the Diaspora did."[105] Since the Christians called themselves Israelites from the beginning, the Jews in order to combat their claims readopted the name of Israel, which they have employed freely to the present time.[106]

Throughout history, the determining factor of what

makes one a Jew has always been some association with the geographical area of Judaea, and since "Lehi . . . dwelt at Jerusalem in all his days" (1 Nephi 1:4), the best possible designation for him is *Jew*, regardless of his ancestry. Nephi's formula "the Jews who were at Jerusalem" (1 Nephi 2:13) makes it perfectly clear that he was acquainted with other settlements of Jews, and in his use of the term one may detect an undeniable feeling of detachment, if not of hostility, toward those city Jews. The Lachish Letters distinguish between the Jews of the country and the Jews of the city, and this distinction is also found in Nephi's account.

Babylon's Conquest of Jerusalem. In Omni 1:15, we read that "the people of Zarahemla came out from Jerusalem at the time that Zedekiah, king of Judah, was carried away captive into Babylon." Though this agrees with 2 Kings 25:7 and Jeremiah, scholars have doubted it. "Before the Chaldaean army laid siege to Jerusalem," according to Albright, "the Jewish King died or was assassinated, and his young son, Jehoiachin, went into exile in his place."[107]

It is with considerable surprise the experts now learn that in the Babylonian lists of prisoners brought to Babylon after the fall of Jerusalem "Jehoiachin is called 'the son of the king' of Judah,"[108] instead of king. While, according to Thomas, "it is possible that this is a mere scribal error,"[109] Weidner "suggests that the designation . . . may have been deliberately chosen, the Babylonians regarding Zedekiah as the legitimate king of Judah."[110] Along with that, it is notable that in the Book of Mormon Zedekiah plays absolutely no role at all, all government and dirty work being left, apparently, entirely to "the elders of the Jews" (1 Nephi 4:22, 27; cf. Jeremiah 26:17). This view is substantiated in a new book by Hölscher, who shows Zedekiah as a helpless puppet in the hands of "the potentates at the court, who now appear as sworn enemies of the Prophet whose predictions of disaster they regard as treason-able."[111] The prophet in question was Jeremiah, whom Lehi supported, thereby incurring the wrath of the same "elders" who attempted to liquidate him as well as Jeremiah.[112] Hölscher tells us that Jeremiah met with the weak king "in secret interviews," vainly attempting to persuade him to give up the fatal alliance with Egypt.[113] The decision of policy in "secret interviews" is exactly what we meet with in 1 Nephi, where the elders hold their councils in the deep of night. The "hysteria and gloom" that reigned in Lehi's Jerusalem are further reflected in an Aramaic letter discovered at Saqqarah in 1942 and dating from the time of Jeremiah: King Adon appeals to Pharaoh for aid in the very same terms that his ancestors used in calling upon Egypt in the Amarna age, centuries before: "[The armies] of the King of Babylon have come, they have reached Aphek; . . . do not forsake me."[114]

The Babylonian lists of prisoners to which we have just referred contain, along with the Jewish names, a respectable proportion of Egyptian names. This is what we find in the Book of Mormon name list as well, but the resemblance goes further, for the Egyptian names in the Old World list show, according to D. W. Thomas, that it was popular at the time to name children after famous Egyptian rulers of the past.[115] If the reader will consult our section on "Strange Names" in Lehi in the Desert, he will discover that a surprisingly large number of Egyptian names found among the Nephites were those of early Egyptian kings and heroes. The legendary first king of Egypt was Aha, whose name means "warrior," and, significantly enough, in the Book of Mormon this name is bestowed by a Nephite commander-in-chief on his son. Other royal and hero-names in the Book of Mormon are Himni, Korihor, Paanchi, Pacumeni, Sam, Zeezrom, Hem, Manti, Nephi, and Zenoch. Zeniff is certainly cognate with Arabic Zaynab, best known from the Latinized name of Zenobia, next to the Queen of Sheba the most famous woman in Egypt.[116]

The Babylonian captive-list also included Philistine, Phoenician, Elamite, Median, Persian, Greek, and Lydian names—all sweepings of a campaign into Lehi's country.[117] The variety of name-types in the Book of Mormon rosters is the much earlier Tell Ta'annek list, in which the element *bin* is prominent, for example, Bin-da-ni?-wa (cf. Book of Mormon Abinadi), as well as the *-zi-ra* and *-andi* combinations, the latter interpreted as East Canaanitish.[118]

Lehi in the Desert. Lehi's life in the desert receives new illustration steadily with new studies and explorations in the sand. In a recent study, Shalem has shown that the best evidence for the stability of climatic conditions in the East is the Bible itself; Shalem claims that man himself has been the main factor in changing the climate of Palestine from time to time, and he notes that there has been a "capital change" of climate in that country as a result of the return of the Jews to the land in our own time. Yet even while he pleads for the scriptures as the best guide to the understanding of the problem, this investigator passes by the words of the prophets in silence.[119]

As if they had not done enough already, our invaluable Scrolls supply the best explanations to date for Lehi's peculiar fondness for the desert. As a merchant and a Manassehite he cannot have escaped something of a desert background, but how do his exploits on the sand fit with his status as an orthodox Jew? From the Scrolls we learn that there existed among the Jews certain groups distinguished for their piety, prophetic zeal, and annoying insistence on a literal and not-too-distant coming of the Messiah. The Apocrypha teach us that such groups and such teaching were not confined to any one period of Jewish history but run like a scarlet cord through its whole texture. "Almost all our fathers," says Nephi, the son of Helaman, "testifed of the coming of Christ, and have looked forward, and have rejoiced in his day which is to come" (Helaman 8:22).

Now the Scrolls teach us that such holy men and their followers were wont to organize themselves in "encampments," actually living "outside the towns in the desert regions," where "they lived if not actually in tents at least in very simple dwellings. They thus avoided the corruption of the towns and once again realized the ideal of the nomad life handed down in the oldest of Israel's traditions."[120] As Israel of old, they were deliberately escaping from the wicked world to the air of the desert, carrying out in the life of the tent dwellers a symbolism which the Latter-day Saints preserve to this day when they speak of the "stakes" and the "center stake" of Zion. The earliest Arabic commentary on government is a poetic exposition in which, according to Nöldeke, we find not a brief for kingship but the "truly Arabic" concept of a free society in which the best rule by consent of all the governed:

No people are well off without proper leadership;
And there are no leaders when the more ignorant rule.
As the tent cannot be set up without poles,
And the poles cannot stand without the tent-stakes round about,
Even so, when both poles and stakes cooperate,
In that day has been achieved the goal which before
We only partly attained.[121]

The life of the tent-dwellers which Lehi and Ishmael followed was not the way of the Bedouin renegade, but the traditional choice of seekers after righteousness. Lehi's concern to keep his people from degenerating into Bedouins is thoroughly typical of an attitude illustrated in Jawad Ali's new two-volume *Arabs before Islam*, the first work of the kind to appear in Arabic. That author notes in his opening lines that the term *Jahiliyah*, "time of ignorance," is used to describe the pre-Islamic Arabs not because of their ignorance of Islam, but because of their low cultural level: They were nomadic tribesmen, living in ignorance and sloth, having no contacts with the outer

104 THE PROPHETIC BOOK OF MORMON

world, *and keeping no records*.[122] This state of things has
always been regarded as utterly abominable by the cultivated Arab (as it was by Lehi), proud though he is of his
desert heritage: the danger of degenerating into a desert
tramp is a real and constant one, and the only way of
combating it—by *adab*, a thorough training in the poetry
of the fathers, and by the keeping of records—has been
an obsession with the high-minded men of the desert
throughout their history.[123]

In the summer of 1953 a copy of the eighth book of
Hamdani's *Al-Iklīl* came into the author's possession from
the library of the late J. A. Montgomery, one of the great
Arabists of our time. Here is the key to one of Lehi's most
wonderful dreams, for this book of *Al-Iklīl* is devoted to
describing the early castles of Arabia, "great and spacious
buildings" which "stood as it were in the air, high above
the earth," filled with proud and finely dressed people
who held the wandering Bedouins in contempt. The imagery is Nephi's, but it might have taken right out of Hamdani: "And the castle of Ghumdan," he writes of one of
the most famous, "had twenty stories of upper chambers,
one above another." There is disagreement as to its height
and breadth, for some say each of its walls measured a
thousand by a thousand (a "great and spacious house"
indeed!), while others say it was greater, and that each of
its (20) stories was ten cubits (15 feet) high. And the poet
al-Aᶜsha says:

> And never was there a more splendid assemblage of
>   people
> Than the people of Ghumdan when they gathered.
> But dire calamity befell them,
> Even as a wailing woman who has been utterly bereft.[124]

Numerous other accounts of this and other castles are
cited but the moral is always the same: the magnificent
gathering in the great and spacious building high above

the earth is doomed to the destruction reserved for the haughty and the wicked. If no evidence for the provenience of the Book of Mormon existed except the eighth chapter of 1 Nephi, that alone would be quite adequate to establish its oriental origin beyond a doubt. Indeed, there is but one objection to its claims of authenticity, and that is a far-fetched story that a certain young man once told about an angel.

The reader may find in our above translations of Arabic poets ample proof of the claim that the greatest verses of those artists cannot be made into anything remotely resembling good literature in English and still preserve a trace of their original form or content. To judge the Book of Mormon as an exercise in English literary style, therefore, is the height of folly. Nicholson notes that the very best oriental poetry contains "much that to modern taste is absolutely incongruous with poetic style. Their finest pictures . . . often appear uncouth or grotesque, because without an intimate knowledge of the land and people it is impossible for us to see what the poet intended to convey, or to appreciate the truth and beauty of its expression."[125] One is constantly coming upon strange little expressions that recall the Book of Mormon. Thus the non-biblical use of *white* as the equivalent of *delightsome* in the Book of Mormon strongly suggests the Arabic *al-ḥasan wa'l-biyāḍ*—a very early expression,[126] while the designation of the sea by the earliest Arab poet as "the ocean spring" or "fountain" immediately recalls the term used by Lehi's wanderers, "the fountain of the Red Sea," and solves a knotty problem with a single cut.[127]

A recent study by Rosenblatt on oaths bears out well what we said about the episode of the swearing of Zoram (1 Nephi 4:35-37). Among both Arabs and Jews, says Rosenblatt, "an oath without God's name is no oath," while "both in Jewish and Mohammedan sources oaths by 'the life of God' are frequent."[128] So Nephi's "as the Lord liveth" is strictly correct.

Origins of Civilization. The whole picture of the racial and linguistic composition of the human race in the Jaredite era at the dawn of history has in our own day undergone such a complete alteration that those theories so stoutly defended in the 1920s and 1930s as the final verdict of scientific objectivity now appear almost pitifully biased. As Pittioni pointed out in 1952, a "sociologically oriented evolutionism" has so thoroughly preconditioned the thinking of the experts, who have "unconsciously and unquestioningly assumed a point of view sprung directly from the natural-science orientation of nineteenth-century cosmology," that they address themselves to the problem of origins with the implicit conviction that they already know exactly how everything happened![129] So ingrained is this childlike faith in the infallibility of the evolutionary rule of thumb, that it has enabled our colleges in the West to dispense almost entirely with libraries, and to offer large numbers of impressive courses in ancient life and culture without ever feeling the disquieting urge to consult original sources: why bother to read hard books when evolution gives you an easy answer to everything?

Every new discovery tends to substantiate the theory of a primary radiation of peoples from the "Jaredite country" in the northern reaches of the Tigris and the Euphrates. It is to that area that archaeologists have now turned for the solution to the problem of world civilization. Whether or not Jarmo, east of the Tigris in northern Iraq, is actually the oldest village in the world, as was announced in 1951 (and Braidwood estimates its age at only six thousand — *not* sixty million — years),[130] it certainly lies at the center of a series of radiating zones that embrace ruins of the same type that rival it in antiquity. The most ancient cities in the world are not strewn about the earth in haphazard fashion, but give every indication of spreading from a single center.[131]

The same tendency to converge toward a single point on the map has marked the study of linguistic origins during the past decades. The identification of exotic central and even eastern Asiatic languages as members of our own linguistic family was followed at the end of the 1920s by the surprising discovery that the mysterious Hittite was cousin to such homely western idioms as Latin and Welsh. Within the past year or two, archaeologists claim to have filled up the gap between the Indo-European and the Turanian languages; if that is so, almost all of Europe and Asia will turn out to be speaking variations of a single tongue.[132] In 1952, Carnoy announced that Etruscan, which has baffled researchers for centuries, belongs to a very early wave of Indo-European migration into the west, a wave which brought in with it such strange "Pelasgian" languages as Lydian and Lycian, and that Etruscan's closest relative is the thoroughly western Hittite.[133]

Along with this amazing predominance of "our own people" in times and places at which any suggestion of their presence a few years ago would have excited gales of contemptuous laughter goes the newly won conviction that the great civilizations of Egypt and Mesopotamia did not originate in those lands at all. At present the experts are meditating and arguing about the peculiar circumstance that writing was introduced into both areas suddenly and first appears in both places in an identical stage of development; this would indicate as plain as day that it must have come from the same source. But in that case, why are the earliest Egyptian and the earliest Babylonian writings so different from each other?[134] Whatever the answer, we must now give up the old illusion that the origin of civilization is to be sought in either Egypt or Babylonia. The once-popular theory that China saw the earliest beginnings must also be abandoned, though in view of the

impressive list of common cultural traits that bind ancient
Egypt, Babylonia, and China, one must assume that China,
too, drew from the common source.[135]

How far afield the authorities now range in their search
for Eden may be estimated from A. Herrmann's *Erdkarte
der Urbibel*. Herrmann believes that the oldest parts of Genesis are the geographical passages, and that these all have
one source, a lost "ur-Genesis" which was in fact originally
a History of Abraham, which he designates as the Ur-
Abraham, the ultimate source of Genesis.[136] The largest
surviving pieces of this lost Book of Abraham are to be
found in the Book of Jubilees, according to Herrmann,
which, interestingly enough, is of all questioned Apocrypha the one most thoroughly vindicated by the finding
of the Scrolls, which show Jubilees to be not a medieval
but a genuinely ancient document. According to this
source, the entire human race was living in the Land of
Eden (*not* the Garden of Eden, but the land where it had
been) when they were overwhelmed by water.[137] This cannot have taken place in Mesopotamia or Egypt, Herrmann
observes, since both those lands are described in the
sources as being uninhabited in Noah's day,[138] and Kraeling has noted that according to other sources the people
in the ark did not have the vaguest idea where they were
after the flood, but being in strange surroundings had to
learn of their location by revelation.[139] So Herrmann seeks
the Land of Eden in Abyssinia, South Arabia, and the
headwaters of the Nile — all dubious locales and all far from
the conventional Babylonian sites. It is a quest that would
have struck the dogmatic scholars of past years with amazement: they *knew* where the Garden of Eden was.

The Tower. No subject has been studied more diligently
of recent years than that of the ancient towers. In 1946 L.
H. Vincent showed that the ziggurat was designed from
the first as a means by which the *gigunu* could mount up
to heaven; it was "a scale model of the world," and a sort

of link between the heavenly and earthly temples and at the same time "a model of the universe" and a ladder to the upper world. The biblical explanation for the Tower of Babel is thus strictly correct.[140] G. Thausing in 1948 included the Egyptian pyramid among such structures, as "symbol of the outpouring of light, architectural manifestation of the idea of emanation and symbol of the uniting of Heaven and Earth. Its very name—*mr*, 'binding' [shows that] it is the Way to the world below, but also to the world above."[141] In the following year André Parrot published a large book on ziggurats, in which he sums up all the previous theories of the nature of these mysterious towers—for example, that they were meant to represent mountains, thrones, dwellings, the universe, altars, but especially that they are special structures "which the gods use in order to pass from their celestial habitation to their terrestrial residence, from invisibility to visibility. The ziggurat is thus nothing but the supporting structure for the edifice on its top, and a stairway between the upper and the lower world."[142] In a study on the Tower of Babel, Parrot in 1950 elaborated on this last conception as the true explanation for the towers: the god was thought to "land" with his escorting troupe at the "Hochtempel" at the top of the tower, and then to descend the stairs to the "Tieftempel" at the bottom, where everything was in readiness to receive him; the holy company was thought to return to heaven by the same route.[143] In the same year, Contenau in his book on the Babylonian Deluge concluded that the ziggurat of Babylon actually was the Tower of Babel, that such towers while serving as astronomical observatories were originally "temples of passage," reception places for divinity whenever it visited the earth; the holy mountain itself, according to this authority, was originally such a place of contact between heaven and earth.[144] There is no doubt at all, Contenau believes, that these Babylonian towers are the same as the Egyptian pyramids in their function of "pas-

sage for divinity from heaven to earth and back again,"
the two having a common but very ancient and unknown
origin.[145]

From a study of the archaic seals of Babylonia, the
oldest written documents in the world, Pierre Amiet in
1951 concluded that in the archaic period "the ziggurat
was at one and the same time an immense altar on which
were placed the gifts designed to attract the god, the platform where the priests raised themselves up to be nearer
to the divinity, as an aid of their prayers, and the support
for the stairway which the god, in response to those prayers, employed in order to descend to the earth."[146] The
same scholar in 1953 is more specific still: one idea is clear
above all others in these old tower-temples, "the idea of
ascension, of mounting up."[147] The steps of the tower, like
the steps of the altars in the most primitive seals, are stairways, "binding the heavens to the earth." The earliest of
all known temples is "the supra-terrestrial place, celestial
as it were, where the two aspects of divinity become fused
on the occasion of the performance of essential ordinances,
destined to assure fecundity upon the earth."[148] Thus a
hundred years of speculation have arrived at the point of
departure: there was a real tower that meant what the Bible
said it did.

A conspicuous aspect of the sacred tower is that it is
always thought of as standing at the exact center of the
earth; it is an observatory from which one takes one's
bearings on the universe. This being so, it is easy to see
how men would regard such a tower as the starting point
for the populating of the whole world. Thus in Jubilees
38:4, when the sons of Jacob went forth to claim their
heritage, "they divided themselves into companies on the
four sides of the tower." This is no mere mythological
concept: in every ancient land the seat of government was
an exalted structure thought to stand at the exact geographical center of the world.[149] The practical economy of

this is obvious; after all, most of our state capitals are placed as near the geographical center of the states as is practical. When the scriptures tell us that the people of the world had a great common center to which they repaired and from which, when it broke up, they scattered in all directions, it is not telling a fabulous or impossible tale but is rehearsing a well-known historic pattern.

Elephants, Glass, and Metal. By now many readers will be aware of an interesting study on "Men and Elephants in America" recently appearing in the *Scientific Monthly;* the writer concludes: "Archaeology has proved that the American Indian hunted and killed elephants; it has also strongly indicated that these elephants have been extinct for several thousand years. This means that the traditions of the Indians recalling these animals have retained their historical validity for great stretches of time. . . . Probably the minimum is three thousand years."[150] The author favors three thousand years ago as the terminal date for the existence of the elephant in America,[151] which would place its extinction about a thousand years B.C., when the Jaredite culture was already very old and Lehi's people were not to appear on the scene for some centuries. This suits very well with the Book of Mormon account, and in that case the Indian legends must go back to Jaredite times, and indeed the author of the study quoted insists that they must be at least three thousand years old. But since legends are word-of-mouth tradition, the presence of Jaredite legends among the Indians presumes a survival of the Jaredite strain among them, and at the very least such legends cannot have been transmitted from Jaredite to Lamanite hunters without long and intimate contact between the two groups. Here, then, is a strong argument for Jaredite survivors among the Indians, and if one refuses to interpret it as such one must certainly admit extensive intercourse between the two groups in order to transmit to the Lamanites knowledge which only the Jaredites possessed.

My own inclination is to see actual Jaredite heredity in the Indian strain. In the Doctrine and Covenants, it is promised that "the Lamanites shall blossom as the rose" (D&C 49:24). Yet many of the great nations of the eastern forests, the most formidable tribes of all, have entirely disappeared; whatever happens, they will never flourish. Can it be that those fierce and vanished tribes were predominantly of Jaredite stock and not true Lamanites at all?

Incidentally, the problem of the elephant in the Old World is no less puzzling than in the New, to judge by a philological study by Kretschmer, appearing in 1951.[152] According to that renowned philologian, the ancient Germans and Slavs actually confused the camel with the elephant, while the people of India, the classic land of the elephant, seem not to have been acquainted with the animal at first hand, since they had no word of their own for it! R. Walz, reviewing the whole problem of the domestication of the camel, has come to the conclusion that, at least up to 1951, the problem remains unsolved, in spite of all the work that has been done on it.[153]

As to glass and metal, it is now certain that their origin is to be sought neither in Egypt nor in Babylonia, but in the mountains to the north of the latter region, the area that we loosely describe as "Jaredite country."[154]

Weights and Measures. The names of weights and measures are among the most conservative properties of human society, as our own "foot," "yard," "mile," and "ounce" attest. But along with their conservatism, such terms give evidence at a glance of much borrowing and exchange between cultures. Thus common designations of weight and measure establish prehistoric ties between Egypt and Babylonia.[155] Now the fourteen odd names of measure given in the Book of Mormon are neither Semitic nor Egyptian; unlike the Nephite proper names, these terms have no parallels in the Old World. The explanation for this is obvious: they are Jaredite names. Clear evidence of borrowing by the Nephites can be seen in the words *shiblon, shiblum,* or *shublon,* for not only is the obvious confusion of mimation and nunation indicative of a transition, but the proper names of Shiblon and Shiblom, in both mimated and nunated form, are found among *both* Jaredites and Nephites. From this we may gain an idea of the really significant influence of the Jaredite upon the Nephite culture, for weights and measures are at the foundation of all material civilization. There is a remarkable and natural consistency in the picture which the most cunning calculations of a forger could not hope to achieve: the pains of the Nephite writer to explain the peculiar system; the names which, unlike other Book of Mormon names, have no known parallels in the Old World; the obvious overlapping of Nephite and Jaredite elements (seon, senine, senum); the well-known tendency of established systems of metrology to hold their own, no matter how quaint and antiquated, so that the older system would necessarily have priority over the newer; the equally well-known tendency to combine various foreign elements in a single system; the material superiority and materialistic orientation of Jaredite culture, betrayed by the incurable worldliness of men with Jaredite names. All this is found in the Nephite account, in which the sinister Jaredite influence constantly lurks in the background.

Conclusion. This brings us to a final reflection on the Book of Mormon as a fraudulent production.

There is wisdom in the rule laid down by Blass, that whoever presumes to doubt the purported source and authorship of a document cannot possibly escape the obligation of supplying a more plausible account in its stead.[156] The critic has made the accusation; therefore he must have his reasons—let us hear them. No intolerable burden is put upon him by the demand, for the more obviously fraudulent an account of origin is, the easier it should be to think up a better explanation. The critic is not required to tell exactly what the true origin of the text was, but merely to supply a more likely story than the one given. The world which rejects the official account of the Book of Mormon is not under obligation to tell us exactly when, where, and how the book was produced, but it is most emphatically under obligation to furnish a clear and convincing account of how it *could* have been created in view of all the positively known circumstances of its actual appearance. Clever people have not shirked from this duty, but until now not a single explanation has been offered that is not in glaring conflict with itself or with certain facts upon which all, Mormons and non-Mormons, are in agreement. Above all, it will not do to say that the book is a fraud because angels do not bring books to people, for that is the very point at issue. Joseph Smith may have been very shrewd and very lucky, but there are impassable bounds set to the reach of human wit and fortune. Consider the cases of Scaliger and Bentley, the two greatest scholars of modern, if not of all, times. The former, a mental marvel without compare, whose prodigious achievements in the field of scholarship make all others appear as novices,[157] could not, for all his immense perspicacity and learning, avoid the normal lapses of human knowledge or the pitfalls of vanity. With a record for accurate observation and penetrating discovery that no other can approach, he nonetheless "corrupts his own magnificent work by an anxious and morose over-diligence, and by his insane desire to display his erudition."[158] "In particular," says Housman, "he will often propound interpretations which have no bearing either on his own text . . . or on any other, but pertain to things which he has read elsewhere, and which hang like mists in his memory and veil from his eyes the verses which he thinks he is explaining. Furthermore it must be said that Scaliger's conjectures . . . are often uncouth and sometimes monstrous."[159] Housman then quotes Haupt: "Without doing injury to his fame, one may say that no great scholar ever set beside sure discoveries of the most brilliant penetration so much that is grammatically preposterous." "And," says Housman, "the worse the conjecture the louder does Scaliger applaud himself."[160]

Of Bentley, Housman writes: "The firm strength and piercing edge and arrowy swiftness of his intellect, his matchless facility and adroitness and resource, were never so triumphant as where defeat seemed sure; and yet it is other virtues that one most admires: . . . his lucidity, his sanity, his just and simple and straight-forward fashion of thought."[161] If anyone could produce a flawless reconstruction of a text, this paragon should, but what do we find? "The faults of this edition, which are abundant, are the faults of Bentley's other critical works. He was impatient, he was tyrannical, and he was too sure of himself. Hence he corrupts sound verses which he will not wait to understand, alters what offends his taste. . . . His buoyant mind, elated by the exercise of its powers, too often forgot the nature of its business, and turned from work to play; and many a time when he feigned and half fancied that he was correcting the scribe, he knew in his heart . . . that he was revising the author."[162]

Now "the nature of the business" of these two men was very close to that of the author of the Book of Mormon: it was to produce ancient texts "in their purity" by correcting the corrupt manuscripts that the world has inherited from early copyists. The correction was done on the basis of what the editor, using all the information at his disposal about the writer in question and the world in which he lived, conjectured that the author would have written in place of the badly copied text before him. Scaliger, Bentley, and the author of the Book of Mormon are all engaged in the proper business of scholarship, that of bringing out of obscurity and darkness ancient texts that present a true and faithful picture of the past. If the former two suffer serious reverses on almost every page, due to inevitable defects of knowledge and judgment, what should we expect of the last, even assuming him to be the most honest of men? To say that he may have made no *more* frightful mistakes per page than a Scaliger or a Bentley is to pay him the highest tribute. More cleverness and luck than that we simply cannot allow him. If any modern man, however great his genius, composed the Book of Mormon, it must of necessity swarm with the uncouth, monstrous, impossible, contradictory, and absurd.[163] But it does not.

The few odds and ends we have touched upon in this short study should be enough to show what teeming opportunities the writer of the Book of Mormon had to make a complete fool of himself, and the world will give a handsome reward to anyone who can show it but one clear and unmistakable instance in which he did so. We must grant, therefore, that the current explanation of the Book of Mormon — that the man who wrote it was both smart and unscrupulous — explains nothing.

Notes

1. Hugh W. Nibley, "Lehi in the Desert," *Improvement Era* 53 (January-October 1950); "The World of the Jaredites," *Improvement Era* 54 (September-December 1951), and 55 (January-July 1952); in book form, *Lehi in the Desert and the World of the Jaredites* (Salt Lake City: Bookcraft, 1952); reprinted in *CWHN* 5:1-282.

2. The best available treatment in English of the nature and rules of textual criticism is to be found in the introductions of the five volumes of A. E. Housman, *M. Manilii Astronomicon*, 5 vols. (London: Cambridge University Press, 1937); see esp. vols. 1 and 5.

3. Friedrich Blass, "Hermeneutik und Kritik," *Einleitende und Hilfs-Disziplinen*, vol. 1 of Iwan von Müller's *Handbuch der klassichen Altertumswissenschaft* (Munich: Beck, 1886), 127-272.

4. Ibid., 270-71.

5. Felix Jacoby, *Atthis: The Local Chronicles of Ancient Athens* (Oxford: Clarendon, 1949), 131.

6. Blass, "Hermeneutik und Kritik," 268.

7. Ibid., 271.

8. Ibid., 269.

9. Ibid., 268, 271.

10. Nibley, *Lehi in the Desert and the World of the Jaredites*, 128-39, 261-66; in *CWHN* 5:114-23, 259-63.

11. Blass, "Hermeneutik und Kritik," 271.

12. Nibley, *Lehi in the Desert and the World of the Jaredites*, 257; in *CWHN* 5:255.

13. Blass, "Hermeneutik und Kritik," 271.

14. Ibid.

15. Ibid.

16. Reynold A. Nicholson, *A Literary History of the Arabs* (London: Unwin, 1907; reprinted Cambridge: Cambridge University Press, 1953), 134.

17. Johannes Haller, *Nikolaus I und Pseudoisidor* (Stuttgart: Cotta, 1936), 158-59.

18. See ibid., 155-72, for Haller's discussion of the Pseudo-Isidor document.

19. Ibid., 181-82.

20. Ibid., 182-83.

21. Blass, "Hermeneutik und Kritik," 271.

22. Hugo Willrich, *Urkundenfälschung in der hellenistisch-jüdischen Literatur*, Heft 21 of *Forschungen zur Religion und Literatur des Alten und Neuen Testaments* (Göttingen: Vandenhoeck and Ruprecht, 1924), 3-4.

23. Ibid., 4.

24. Heinrich Böhmer, *Die Fälschungen Erzbischof Lanfrancs von Canterbury* (Leipzig: Dieterich 1902; reprinted Aalen: Scientia Verlag, 1972), being vol. 7, no. 1 of *Studien zur Geschichte der Theologie und Kirche*, 126-27.

25. This is the usual classification. Friedrich Leist, *Urkundenlehre* (Leipzig: Weber, 1893), divides his whole book into external, internal characteristics of documents; this differs slightly from external vs. internal evidence, the former being information coming from outside, the latter information contained entirely in the document itself.

26. Thus Housman, *M. Manilii Astronomicon*, 1:lxv: "Now where all MSS give nonsense and are therefore corrupt, those MSS are to be preferred which give the worst nonsense, because they are likely to be the least interpolated." Cf. ibid., 5:xxxiii-xxxv.

27. Blass, "Hermeneutik und Kritik," 270-71.

28. Ibid., 268.

29. This aspect of the Book of Mormon is the subject of a thesis

written by Robert K. Thomas, "A Literary Analysis of the Book of Mormon," at Reed College in 1947.

30. John Chrysostom, *De Sacerdotio (On the Priesthood)* I, 5, in *PG* 48:624.

31. Blass, "Hermeneutik und Kritik," 271.

32. Eduard Meyer, *Ursprung und Geschichte der Mormonen* (Halle: Niemeyer, 1912), 59-83, esp. 72, 80-83; published also as *The Origin and History of the Mormons*, tr. H. Rahde and E. Seaich (Salt Lake City: University of Utah Press, 1961), 37-56.

33. Franklin S. Harris, *The Book of Mormon Message and Evidences* (Salt Lake City: Deseret, 1953).

34. Paul E. Kahle, *The Cairo Geniza* (London: Oxford University Press, 1947).

35. An account and description of some of these texts, only a portion of which have been made available to students to date, may be found in Sidney B. Sperry, "The Sensational Discovery of Jerusalem Scrolls," *Improvement Era* 52 (1949): 636.

36. The best general studies of the scrolls to appear to date [1953] are André Dupont-Sommer, *The Dead Sea Scrolls, A Preliminary Survey* (New York: Macmillan, 1952), and Harold H. Rowley, *The Zadokite Fragments and the Dead Sea Scrolls* (Oxford: Blackwell, 1952). As new knowledge comes forth on these discoveries, it is made available to the public as soon as possible in the *Bulletin of the American Schools of Oriental Research* and in the *Biblical Archaeologist*. Most instructive are William H. Brownlee, "A Comparison of the Covenanters of the Dead Sea Scrolls with Pre-Christian Jewish Sects," *Biblical Archaeologist* 13 (1950): 49-72; William H. Brownlee, "Biblical Interpretation among the Sectaries of the Dead Sea Scrolls," *Biblical Archaeologist* 14 (1951): 54-76; William H. Brownlee, "The Dead Sea Manual of Discipline," *BASOR* Supplementary Studies, nos. 10-12 (1951).

37. E.g., Assumption of Moses 1:16-17, in Robert H. Charles, *The Assumption of Moses* (London: Black, 1897), 6-7; Carl Clemen, *Die Himmelfahrt des Mose*, in *Kleine Texte* no. 10 (1904), 2:3; James H. Charlesworth, *Old Testament Pseudepigrapha*, 2 vols. (Garden City: Doubleday, 1983), 1:927.

38. Eusebius, *Chronicon* I, 3, in *PG* 19:115-16. Nu'man, the fabulous King of Hira (around A.D. 400) when he built his marvelous palace ordered a "Songs of the Arabs" to be compiled and buried beneath it for future generations, Jawād ᶜAlī, *Tārīkh al-ᶜArab qabl al-Islām* (Baghdad: Matbacat, 1950), 1:14.

39. Dupont-Sommer, *The Dead Sea Scrolls*, 14-15.

40. See "Ancient Records on Metal Plates," ch. 10 in Harris, *The Book of Mormon Message and Evidences*, esp. 95.

41. Muhibble Anstock-Darga, "Semitische Inschriften auf Silbertäfelchen aus dem 'Beriz'-Tal (Umgebung von 'Maras')," *Jahrbuch für kleinasiatische Forschung* 1 (1950): 199-200.

42. André Dupont-Sommer, "Deux lamelles d'argent á inscription hébréo-araméenne trouvées á agabeyli (Turque)," *Jahrbuch für kleinasiastische Forschung* 1 (1950): 201-17. See also, Levi E. Young, "Goldsmiths of Ancient Times," *Improvement Era* 52 (1949): 206-8.

43. Bleddyn J. Roberts, "The Jerusalem Scrolls," *Zeitschrift für die alttestamentliche Wissenschaft* 62 (1950): 241.

44. Dupont-Sommer, *The Dead Sea Scrolls*, 95.

45. Ibid., 96.

46. Hermann Gunkel, *Zum religionsgeschichtlichen Verständnis des Neuen Testaments* (Göttingen: Vandenhoeck and Ruprecht, 1910). Though Gunkel became the founder of a "school," the consensus went against him, and in his latest book, *Christian Beginnings* (London: University of London Press, 1924), 27, F. C. Burkitt writes: "Christians have been too apt in the past to assume that there already existed among the Jews a fairly definite and uniform conception of the Messiah who was expected to come. That indeed is a notion presupposed in many Christian documents, . . . but it is not borne out by a study of Jewish literature." If anything, conventional Jewry has been opposed to the idea, but the Scrolls and sects among the Jews show it flourishing among the more pious element all along.

47. Dupont-Sommer, *The Dead Sea Scrolls*, 96.

48. A good collection of texts has been made by August von Gall, *Basileia tou Theou* (Heidelberg: Winter, 1926).

49. Hilel Ragaf, "The Origin of the Religious Sect of Mormons," *Vorwärts* (26 April 1953).

50. Solomon Zeitlin, "The Hebrew Pogrom and the Hebrew Scrolls," *Jewish Quarterly Review* 42 (1952-53): 146-47.

51. Paul E. Kahle, *The Cairo Geniza*, 130-31.

52. Tovia Wechsler, "Origin of the So-Called Dead Sea Scrolls," *Jewish Quarterly Review* 43 (1952-53): 121-39.

53. J. L. Teicher, "The Dead Sea Scrolls—Documents of the Jewish-Christian Sect of Ebionites," *Journal of Jewish Studies* 2 (1951): 69.

54. Ibid., 78 (emphasis added).

55. Ibid., 86.

56. Dupont-Sommer, *The Dead Sea Scrolls*, 100, 96.

57. Frederick A. M. Spencer, "The Second Advent According to the Gospels," *Church Quarterly Review* 126 (1938): 18.

58. William A. Irwin, "Ezekiel Research since 1943," *Vetus Testamentum* 3 (1953): 62 (emphasis added).

120   THE PROPHETIC BOOK OF MORMON

59. Ibid., 56.
60. Ibid., 59.
61. Ibid., 61.
62. Von Gall, *Basileia tou Theou*, 65-68, 164-74.
63. The process of "intellectualizing" the message of the prophets is well illustrated by the Talmud. See Moses Mielziner, *Introduction to the Talmud* (Chicago: Bloch, 1894), 103-14.
64. L. Guerrier, "Le Testament en Galilée de Notre-Seigneur Jésus-Christ," in *PO* 9:148-49.
65. Edward Chiera, *They Wrote on Clay* (Chicago: University of Chicago Press, 1938), 133.
66. See note 48 above, and the following note below.
67. For an extensive study of these groups, Robert Eisler, *Iesous Basileus ou Basileusas*, 2 vols. (Heidelberg: Winter, 1930), vol. 2, chapters 5-10.
68. Jeremiah seems to have been the leader of the opposition to the government party, to judge by the Lachish Letters; see sources cited in Nibley, *Lehi in the Desert and the World of the Jaredites*, 5-13; in *CWHN* 5:6-13.
69. Ethan Smith, *View of the Hebrews: Or the Tribes of Israel in America* (Poultney, Vt.: Smith and Shute, 1823 and 1825).
70. Sir Richard F. Burton, *The City of the Saints* (New York: Harper, 1862; reprinted New York: AMS, 1971), 258.
71. Dupont-Sommer, *The Dead Sea Scrolls*, 69.
72. D. Winton Thomas, "The Age of Jeremiah in the Light of Recent Archaeological Discovery," *PEFQ* (1950), 3-4. Both quotations are from Thomas.
73. Blass, "Hermeneutik und Kritik," 269.
74. A. E. Silverstone, "God as King," *Journal of the Manchester Egyptian and Oriental Society* 17 (1932): 47, on the Rabbinical interpretation of *amen*, with Messianic connotations.
75. The oldest Semitic version of Hebrews 11:1, the Syriac, employs the word *haimanutha*, from the conventional AMN root.
76. When Paul himself speaks of apocryphal matters, his writing "is nothing but a tissue of ancient prophetic formulas, borrowed ready-made," according to Denis Buzy, "L'Adversaire et l'Obstacle," *Recherches de science religieuse* 24 (1934): 409.
77. Friedrich Delitzsch, *Das Land ohne Heimkehr: Die Gedanken der Babylonier und Assyrer über Tod und Jenseits* (Stuttgart: Deutsche Verlags-Anstalt, 1911).
78. Peter C. A. Jensen, *Assyrisch-babylonische Mythen und Epen* (Berlin: Reuther and Reichard, 1900), 80-81.

79. Knut Tallquist, "Sumerisch-Akkadische Namen der Toten-welt," *Studia Orientalia* 4 (1934): 3, 15-17.

80. Nibley, *Lehi in the Desert and The World of the Jaredites*, 11, 97; in *CWHN* 5:11, 86.

81. Alfred Bloch, "Qasida," *Asiatische Studien* 3-4 (1948): 116-24.

82. Nibley, *Lehi in the Desert and The World of the Jaredites*, 102-4; in *CWHN* 5:89-90.

83. Nicholson, *A Literary History of the Arabs*, 74.

84. G. Adolf Deissmann, *Light from the Ancient East* (New York: Doran, 1927), 369-73. The idea is not of Hellenistic origin, for it is familiar in Egyptian literature where Pharaoh brings joy to the lands through which he takes his royal tours, letting his countenance shine (*wbn*) on each turn, just as his father Re makes the rounds (*shenen*) of the universe with his inspecting eye that gives both dread and joy to all beholders. The concept is even more conspicuous in Asia, where "the monarch moves like the beneficent sun in a tireless round among his people." The theme is treated by us in "The Hierocentric State," *Western Political Quarterly* 4 (1951): 241-42.

85. Dupont-Sommer, *The Dead Sea Scrolls*, 79-84.

86. Ibid., 82.

87. Hugh W. Nibley, "The Arrow, the Hunter, and the State," *Western Political Quarterly* 2 (1949): 340-41.

88. Clément Huart and Louis Delaporte, *L'Iran Antique* (Paris: Michel, 1943), 454-55.

89. Von Gall, *Basileia tou Theou*, 182-83, 186-88, 219, 456.

90. Dupont-Sommer, *The Dead Sea Scrolls*, 83.

91. Huart and Delaporte, *L'Iran Antique*, 329-30, 359, 379.

92. Nibley, "The Hierocentric State," 230-35, 244-47.

93. B. Couroyer, "Le Chemin de Vie en Egypte et en Israel," *Revue Biblique* 56 (1949): 412-32.

94. Alexis Mallon, "Les Hébreux en Egypte," *Orientalia* 3 (1921): 68-72.

95. M. B. Rowton, "The Problem of the Exodus," *PEFQ* (1953), 46-60.

96. V. Gordon Childe, *What Happened in History* (New York: Penguin, 1946), 133.

97. Thus Albright, following Gardiner, notes that the recently discovered Chester Beatty Papyri prove the Song of Songs to be of Egyptian origin; William F. Albright, *Archaeology and the Religion of Israel* (Baltimore: Johns Hopkins University Press, 1942), 21.

98. Nibley, *Lehi in the Desert and the World of the Jaredites*, 33; in *CWHN* 5:32. Thomas, "The Age of Jeremiah in the Light of Recent Archaeological Discovery," 2.

99. Ibid., 4.

100. Anton Jirku, "Die Mimation in den nordsemitischen Sprachen und einige Bezeichnungen der altisraelitischen Mantik," *Biblica* 34 (1953): 78-79.

101. Ibid., 80.

102. Solomon Zeitlin, "The Names Hebrew, Jew and Israel: A Historical Study," *Jewish Quarterly Review* 43 (1953): 367, the word "Hebrew" is used only in connection with slaves or with foreigners (non-Jews).

103. Ibid., 368 (emphasis added).

104. Ibid., 369-70 (emphasis added).

105. Ibid., 371.

106. Ibid., 374-75.

107. William F. Albright, "A Brief History of Judah from the Days of Josiah to Alexander the Great," *Biblical Archaeologist* 9 (1946): 2.

108. Thomas, "The Age of Jeremiah in the Light of Recent Archaeological Discovery," 6.

109. Ibid.

110. Ibid., citing E. F. Weidner," Jojachin, König von Juda, in babylonischen Keilschrifttexten," in *Mélanges syriens offerts a Monsieur R. Dussard* (1939), 923-35.

111. Gustav Hölscher, *Geschichtsschreibung in Israel* (Lund: Gleerup, 1952), 193.

112. See Nibley, *Lehi in the Desert and the World of the Jaredites*, 112-13; in *CWHN* 5:97-99.

113. Hölscher, *Geschichtsschreibung in Israel*, 193.

114. Thomas, "The Age of Jeremiah in the Light of Recent Archaeological Discovery," 8-9. The remarkable resemblance of this to the Amarna letters, upon which Thomas comments, justifies occasional use of Amarna material to illustrate the Book of Mormon, notably with regard to proper names.

115. Ibid., 7.

116. Nibley, *Lehi in the Desert and the World of the Jaredites*, 27-32; in *CWHN* 5:25-31.

117. Ibid.

118. A. Gustavs, "Die Personnennamen in den Tontafeln von Tell Ta'annek, I," *ZDPV* 50 (1927): 1-18; A. Gustavs, "Die Personnennamen in den Tontafeln von Tell Ta'annek, II," *ZDPV* 51 (1928): 191, 198, 207. There are nine Subaraean, five Asia Minor (Hittite), one Egyptian, one Sumerian, one Iranian, one Kossaean, one Indian, ten Akkadian (Babylonian), 21 Canaanitish, two Amorite, and five Arabic (Aramaic?) names, ibid., 209-10.

119. N. Shalem, "La Stabilité du Climat en Palestine," *Revue Biblique* 58 (1951): 54-74.

120. Dupont-Sommer, *The Dead Sea Scrolls*, 61.

121. Theodor Nöldeke, *Delectus Veterum Carminum Arabicorum* (Berlin: Ruether, 1890), 4, with note.

122. Jawād ʿAlī, *Tārīkh al-ʿArab qabl al-Islām* (Baghdad: Matbaʿat, 1950), 1:6.

123. At the beginning of their long wandering, the Sheikh of the *Banī Hilāl* ordered them to keep a record of each important event, "that its memory might remain for the members of the tribe, and that the people might read it and retain their civilized status [*ifada*]," *Kitāb Taghribat Banī Hilāl*, Damascus edition, 14. Accordingly, verses recited on notable occasions were written down on the spot, just as Nephi wrote down his father's utterances by the River of Laman.

124. Hamdani, *Al-Iklil* (Baghdad, 1931), Book 8, pp. 15-16. The work was translated in 1940 by Nahib Amin Faris (Princeton: Princeton University Press, 1940), but I have not seen the translation.

125. Nicholson, *A Literary History of the Arabs*, 103.

126. The expression is found in an Arabic rendering of a very early Christian Logion (saying attributed to Christ), no. 102 in the collection of Michaël Asin and Palacios, *Logia et Agrapha Domini Jesu*, in *PO* 13:426.

127. I have not been able to see the original text of the poem of Ḥassān ibn Thābit, which Nicholson, *A Literary History of the Arabs*, 18, renders: "Followed he [the hero Dhū 'l-Qarnayn] the Sun to view its setting, when it sank into the sombre ocean-spring."

128. Samuel Rosenblatt, "The Relations between Jewish and Muslim Laws Concerning Oaths and Vows," *American Academy of Jewish Research* (1936), 231, 238. For an account of the various things the Arabs swear by, Tadeusz Kowalski, "Zu dem Eid bei den Alten Arabern," *Archiv Orientalni* 6 (1934): 68-81.

129. Richard Pittioni, "Urzeitliche Kulturveränderungen als historisches Problem," *Anzeiger der Oesterreichische Akademie der Wissenschaft*, no. 11 (1952): 162-63.

130. Robert J. Braidwood, "Discovering the World's Earliest Village Community: The Claims of Jarmo as the Cradle of Civilization," *Illustrated London News* (15 December 1951), 992-95.

131. See the map in *Archaeologia* (Autumn 1952), 158.

132. V. Altman, "Ancient Khorezmian Civilization in the Light of the Latest Archaeological Discoveries (1932-45)," *JAOS* 67 (1947): 82-83. J. J. Gelb, "A Contribution to the Proto-Indo-European Question," *Jahrbuch für kleinasiatische Forschung* 2 (1951): 34, proclaims

"the common ancestry of the Semites, Hamites, and Indo- Europeans," a proposition that would have shocked and amused the experts of twenty years ago.

133. Albert J. Carnoy, "La Langue etrusque et ses origines," *L'antiquité classique* 21 (1952): 328.

134. R. Engelbach, "An Essay on the Advent of the Dynastic Race in Egypt and Its Consequences," *Annales du service des antiquités de l'égypte* 42 (1943): 193-221, esp. 208. M. Frankfort, *Birth of Civilization in the Near East* (London: William and Norgate, 1951), 106-7.

135. Arthur von Rosthorn, "Sind die Tschinesen ein autochthones Volk?" *Berichte des Forschungs-Instituts für Osten und Orient* 3 (1918): 28-33; Albert Wesselski, "Einstige Brücken zwischen Orient und Okzident," *Archiv Orientalni* 1 (1929): 88-84; Margaret A. Murray, "China and Egypt," *Ancient Egypt and the East* (1933), 39-42.

136. Albert Herrmann, *Die Erdkarte der Urbibel* (Braunschweig: Westermann, 1931), 124.

137. Ibid., 30.

138. Ibid., 106.

139. Emil G. Kraeling, "The Earliest Hebrew Flood Story," *JBL* 56 (1947): 285.

140. L. H. Vincent, "De la tour de babel au temple," *Revue Biblique* 53 (1946): 403-40, quotes from 439.

141. Gertrud Thausing, in *Oesterreichische Akademie Anzeiger*, no. 7 (1948): 130.

142. André Parrot, *Ziggurats et tour de babel* (Paris: Michel, 1949), 208.

143. André Parrot, "La tour de babel et les ziggurats," *Nouvelle Clio* 1-2 (1949-50): 153-61.

144. Georges Contenau, *Le déluge babylonien* (Paris: Payot, 1952), 244, 246.

145. Ibid., 245, 249-50, 260; quote is from 260.

146. Pierre Amiet, "La Ziggurat, d'aprés les cylindres de l'époque dynastique archaïque," *Revue d'Assyriologie et d'Archéologie* 45 (1951): 87.

147. Pierre Amiet, "Ziggurats et 'Culte en Hauteur' des origines à l'Époque d'Akkad," *Revue d'Assyriologie* 47 (1953): 23-33.

148. Ibid., 30-31.

149. Nibley, "The Hierocentric State," 235-38.

150. Ludwell H. Johnson, III, "Men and Elephants in America," *Scientific Monthly* 75 (1952): 220.

151. Ibid., 216, 220.

152. Paul Kretschmer, "Der Name des Elefanten," *Oesterreichische Akademie Anzeiger*, no. 21 (1951): 324-25.

153. Reinhard Walz, "Zum Problem des Zeitpunkts der Domestikation der altweltlichen Cameliden," *ZDMG* 101 (1951): 29-51.

154. For the latest philological evidence, Paul Kretschmer, "Zu den ältesten Metallnamen," *Glotta* 32 (1952): 1-16: the *oldest* of all names for metal is neither Egyptian nor Babylonian, but Indo-European — our own word "ore." For the classic treatment of the home of metallurgy, see Jacques de Morgan, *La Préhistoire Orientale*, 3 vols. (Paris: Guethner, 1925-27), 1:184-99. H. C. Beck, "Glass before 1500," *Ancient Egypt and the East*, part 1 (June 1934), 7-21, proposes Mesopotamia as the home of glass making.

155. De Morgan, *La Préhistoire Orientale*, 2:315-19.

156. Blass, "Hermeneutik und Kritik," 271.

157. "Scaliger," wrote the great Niebuhr, "stood on the summit of universal solid philological learning, in a degree that none have reached since; so high in every branch of knowledge, that from the resources of his own mind he could comprehend, apply, and decide on, whatever came in his way." Quoted by Mark Pattison, *Essays by the Late Mark Pattison*, 2 vols. (Oxford: Clarendon, 1889), 1:133. Pattison himself, ibid., 195, calls Scaliger's "the most richly-stored intellect which ever spent itself in acquiring knowledge." George W. Robinson writes: "Whether Joseph Scaliger should be reckoned the greatest scholar of all time, or should share that palm with Aristotle, is, perhaps, an open question; of his primacy beyond all rivalry among the scholars of modern times there can be no doubt." Joseph Scaliger, *Autobiography of Joseph Scaliger*, tr. George W. Robinson (Cambridge, Mass.: Harvard University Press, 1927), 8. "[His] only possible rival," writes H. W. Garrod in his *Manili Astronomicon Liber II* (Oxford: E. Typographeo Academico, 1911), lxxxii, "is Bentley — so much inferior in knowledge, in patience, in circumspection, and in the faculty of grasping a whole, that only a native levity of the caprice of reaction could place him on the same height as Scaliger." "He came nearer than any other man before or since his time to reaching the ideal of a universal grasp of antiquity," thus Jacob Bernays, *Joseph Justus Scaliger* (Berlin, 1855; reprinted New York: Franklin, n.d.), 1. For other references to Scaliger's achievements, Hugh W. Nibley, "New Light on Scaliger," *Classical Journal* 37 (1942): 291-95.

158. Huet, quoted in Housman, *M. Manilii Astronomicon*, 1:xiv.

159. Ibid.

160. Ibid.

161. Ibid., xvii.

162. Ibid., xvii-xviii, with much more to the same effect.

163. After immense labor and research, a movie of Lloyd Douglas's epic, *The Robe*, has been released. Almost the opening scene shows two lovers parting at a dock—Ostia. Their last embraces are curtailed by the voice of an importunate captain or mate of the ship, who keeps crying from the deck that unless our hero hastens they will surely miss the tide. "The tide, sir! The tide!" wails the voice. As any schoolboy knows who has read his Caesar, there are no tides in the Mediterranean. What if the Book of Mormon had made a slip like that? *The Robe* is full of them.

4

Kangaroo Court

It is the inalienable right of every questioned document, as of every accused person, to be represented by competent counsel, heard by an impartial jury, and sentenced by a qualified judge, being convicted or acquitted only on solid evidence and not on hearsay. To expect such extravagant justice for the Book of Mormon is to ask for the moon. Counsel for the defense often does the client more harm than good and is automatically branded as prejudiced merely by taking the job; and where will one find an impartial jury, a disinterested judge, or a willingness to test the Book of Mormon on its merits and not on the authority of wild and conflicting rumors about the manner of its origin? Still, however faint the chances of a fair trial may be, even that book has a right to its day in court, if only on the hazard that it may be genuine after all.

Has the Book of Mormon ever been given a fair hearing? From the statements of policy which we are about to quote it will be quite apparent that it most definitely has not. For such a procedure would require a perfectly straight-faced examination of its claims *as if* they were valid! Let us suppose, for the sake of argument and legal theory, that the accused is innocent, that the Book of Mormon is not a fraud but a genuine text as it purports to be. By what

This article first appeared in two parts, published in the Improvement Era (March 1959 to April 1959). The article was part of a series of five articles, published in nine parts under the title " 'Mixed Voices': A Study on Book of Mormon Criticism."

divination would its latest critics, Mrs. Brodie and Doctors
O'Dea and Cross (representatives of the English, sociology,
and history departments, respectively) be able to detect its
authenticity? What do they pretend to know about ancient
texts? The one man best qualified to make the tests indicated, though he was interested enough in the Mormons
to write a whole book about them, frankly confessed that
he had never read the Book of Mormon.[1] That was the
celebrated Eduard Meyer, who wrote with complete finality: "There can be no doubt at all that the golden plates,
though described by his mother and others as reposing in
a box in Smith's house, never existed in the real world."[2]
For him that settled the matter: He can speak with absolute assurance, *not* because he has examined the Book of
Mormon—he didn't need to!—but because he knows perfectly well that there are no such things as angels and gold
plates.

Justified or not, this has been the standard and accepted
position taken by Book of Mormon critics from the beginning, and it should be obvious to any reader that such an
attitude, however sincere, effectively closes the door on
any serious investigation of the book on its own merits.
The dice are always loaded before the game begins: It is
not the Book of Mormon, but the Angel Moroni who is on
trial. Let us glance at a few frank confessions by the leading
critics of the Book of Mormon in the past, to see whether
they ever intended to give it a fair trial.

The first non-Mormon to report on the book was David
Marks, who, after hearing the story of the angel and the
plates from the Whitmer family, approached his task with
a settled conviction that the thing was a fraud: "I wished
to read it, but could not, in good conscience, purchase a
copy, lest I should support a deception"[3]—a fine, open-
minded approach which ran small risk of disillusionment.
Before he was halfway through, Marks gave up the job,
finding "the style is so insipid, and the work so filled with

manifest imposture, that I could feel no interest in a further perusal." Yet generations of Book of Mormon critics were to quote Marks's final verdict on the book as the ultimate in scholarly objectivity.[4]

Within a year of the publication of the Book of Mormon, Alexander Campbell delivered a blast against it which was hailed at the time as demolishing once and for all its claims to divine revelation. By the author's confession, it was a superficial study, his intention being "not to honor him [Smith] by a too minute examination and exposition. . . . If this prophet and his three prophetic witnesses had aught of speciosity [that is, any attractive or challenging quality] about them or their book,"[5] Campbell explains, he *"would have* examined it and exposed it in a different manner."[6] As it is, he begs his readers' pardon for even looking at the thing: "For noticing of which I would have asked forgiveness from all my readers, had not several hundred persons of different denominations believed in it. On this account alone has it become necessary to notice it."[7]

Campbell's last remark is significant: an urgent sense of public duty has animated the Book of Mormon critics from the first, and rightly so. Unless the Book of Mormon is what it pretends to be, it is a regrettable imposture. If scholarship has any obligations to society to protect the layman from predatory quacks and impostors, no more urgent occasion or perfect opportunity for the exercise of true learning can be imagined than that offered by the bold, uncompromising challenge of the Book of Mormon. If it is weak, it should have been knocked over long ago; if it can't be knocked over, the public should be told as much. As long as it stands, it is a standing rebuke to scholarship.

The call to duty was heard from the first. Even a month before Campbell's attack, a newspaper editorial voiced dissatisfaction with the delinquency of the learned:

We have long been waiting, with considerable anxiety, to see some of our contemporaries attempt to explain the immediate causes, which produced that anomaly [sic] in religion and literature, . . . the Book of
Mormon, or the Gold Bible. The few notices heretofore
given in the public prints, are quite vague and uncertain,
and throw but a faint light on the subject.[8]

Thus from the very beginning the challenge was
thrown out to the world to explain the Book of Mormon
if it could, and a flood of conflicting stories and theories
soon followed — but no one ever put the Book of Mormon
to a real test.

The first full-time scholar to comment on the Book of
Mormon was Professor Rafinesque of Philadelphia. His
views were reported by Josiah Priest, who in 1832 observed, "This work is ridiculous enough, it is true; as the
whole Book of Mormon bears the stamp of folly, and is a
poor attempt at an imitation of the Old Testament Scriptures, and is without connection, object, or aim, . . . and
how can it be otherwise as it was written in *Ontario* County,
New York."[9] We are grateful to no end for this staunch
confession of faith, that a religious book produced in Ontario County could not possibly be anything but a fraud
("can there any good come out of Nazareth?"); for while
he has done the Book of Mormon no damage, he leaves
the world no doubt that he has firmly closed his mind
against any serious investigation of it.

What was intended to be a thorough and conclusive
examination of the whole Mormon position, *Mormonism
Exposed, Internally and Externally,* by Origen Bacheler in
1838, was prefaced by the enlightening admission that "to
make an earnest attack on Mormonism as if it had any
plausible pretentions to credibility, would argue great want
of discernment and good sense on the part of the one who
might thus assail it." Even to raise the hypothetical question "Could this be true?" is to brand oneself an idiot; yet

only by that approach can the Book of Mormon or any suspected text be examined. After promising to demolish the Book of Mormon once for all, Mr. Bacheler lamely decided to limit his examination to an absolute minimum, "briefly to expose some of the defects and absurdities of the book."[10] Thus, following a common practice of Book of Mormon critics, he attemps to disarm his jilted public by begging their pardon not for having delivered so little after promising so much, but for having written anything at all on such an offensive theme. Only a sense of obligation toward his "fellow citizens," he protests, can "justify the course I pursue, in stooping to notice an affair so intrinsically worthless and contemptible as the Mormon imposture."[11]

In the same year in which Bacheler's work appeared, the Scotchman, H. Stevenson, was fighting the fires of fanaticism in the Old World with a widely acclaimed lecture against the Book of Mormon, in which he stood foursquare on the proposition "that a Church which pretends to work miracles in these latter ages, proves itself to be an apostate Church."[12] How refreshingly direct! Even to propose testing the Book of Mormon as one does the Bible is for Stevenson a proposition outrageous "for its foolishness and its wickedness!" Nay, true or false, the Book of Mormon simply cannot be tested: "As the Book of Mormon has a suspicious aspect, on account of there being no history to contradict it, so, likewise, it has the disadvantage of no history to confirm it."[13] It is beyond examination.

E. D. Howe, in the 1840 edition of his anti-Mormon classic, which first appeared in 1834, recognizes in the usual terms both the necessity and the futility of attacking the Book of Mormon. "The task has been a laborious one, and we acknowledge but little has been effected," he confesses. "We should have abandoned the task, were it not that so many of our worthy fellow citizens have been seduced by the witcheries and mysterious necromances of

Smith and his colleagues, from the paths of wisdom and
truth, into folly and madness."[14] "The task," he announces
in his introduction, "however loathsome, shall be honestly
pursued." He admits he is helpless against those who are
foolish enough to read the Book of Mormon: "In our review, we are left without weapons to combat the credulous
Mormon believer," his only hope being to reach "any
man . . . who has not inhaled of the malaria of the impostor."[15] With all his talk of base passions, witcheries,
spells, and loathsome tasks, no one is going to accuse Mr.
Howe of a cool and unemotional approach to the Book of
Mormon, however much he may protest that his appeal
is all to the wisdom and sanity of an enlightened age.

In 1841 William Harris repeated the now familiar formula: Public duty requires an investigation of the Book of
Mormon, but no serious approach is required by the subject
itself. The only apology which he offers, this author says
of himself, "for having treated that which is in itself so
contemptibly ridiculous, with so much gravity, is, that well
meaning, though weak minded persons, are daily imposed
upon by the plausible statements of Mormon teachers."[16]

Three famous anti-Mormon books appeared in 1842,
each one containing plain statements of its author's conviction that study of the Book of Mormon is a sheer waste
of time. For the Reverend Clark, "deceit and imposture
are enstamped upon every feature of this monster, evoked
by a money digger and juggler from the shades of darkness."[17] "That its claims to divine origin are wholly un-
founded," he has his star witness say, "needs no proof to
a mind unperverted by the grossest delusions."[18] As for
himself, "This we consider one of the most pernicious
features of this *historical romance,* — that it claims for itself
an entire equality in point of divine authority with the
sacred canon."[19] This was Mr. Stevenson's objection, it
will be recalled: The question is not whether the claim is
true or not but simply whether the claim is made. *Any*

book that claims to be as holy as the Bible is proved by
that very claim to be a monstrous deception—there is no
need at all to search the book to see what it says.

Mr. Kidder is quite blunt: "Our own humble opinion
is, that just as much correct knowledge and real information may be drawn from the above nondescript and
heterogeneous medley of contents, as from a perusal of
the entire volume of 570 pages."[20] The "medley of contents" referred to is a very brief outline of the Book of
Mormon; the author admits freely that it isn't even a good
outline, a "nondescript and heterogeneous" thing, and yet
he solemnly assures the student that he can learn just as
much from that garbled table of contents about the Book
of Mormon as he can from reading the whole book. What
a program for the serious scholar! Of course Kidder assures
us that the only reason he would touch the thing at all is
that duty calls him: "American Christians have . . . been
criminally indifferent to their duty both of informing themselves and the world of its true character. . . . The leaven
of corruption has begun to work far and near."[21] If it is
criminal indifference to neglect the Book of Mormon under
such dire circumstances, what shall we say of this scholar
who, having taken up the challenge with a yell of defiance,
tells us that he can go no farther than to give us a little
outline of the Book of Mormon, and lets it go at that?

In a letter addressed to Joseph Smith, Professor Turner
minces no words in the matter of public duty. "It is my
right, it is the right of every American citizen, of every
Christian, of every honest man, to arraign and resent the
perfidy of your career," he writes, protesting that only that
sense of obligation can induce him to "submit to the un-
grateful task" of dealing with a book and an author which
"might well be left to putrefy, amid the moral pestilence
which you have produced." Under such circumstances,
impartiality in our scholar would be a positive vice: "To
treat you with even ordinary respect, is to treat them

['your . . . awfully deluded people'] with the most wanton and unfeeling cruelty."[22] Obviously these were the days when professors read their Cicero. What blows the top from this particular vessel of high-pressure academic righteousness is not the specific message of Joseph Smith and his book, but the idea of the thing: "It is not your peculiar *opinions*, as you well know, but your *impious pretentions*, which honest and Christian men reject, with loathing and abhorrence."[23] Again, it is not on the basis of its particular contents but solely on its claims to revelation that the Book of Mormon is to be judged.

This point is well illustrated in Mr. Kidder's review of Professor Turner's book. If Turner is all twisted up about the authorship of the Book of Mormon, as Kidder claims he is, who cares? The question at issue here is one of comparative unimportance. Turner's reasoning may be weak and his evidence shaky, but that is all one as long as we agree that the Book of Mormon is a vicious fraud: "We hail his work as one of . . . an eminently practical bearing."[24]

These three masterpieces usually keep company with the latter work of Thomas Gregg, which contains the usual declarations of contempt for the Book of Mormon and alarm at its effectiveness: "That such a book, . . . below the dignity of criticism, should find tens of thousands of persons of ordinary intelligence throughout Christendom, who have accepted it as a Revelation from God to man, is indeed a moral phenomenon unparalleled in the nineteenth century. . . . Many pages might be written, filled with instances of the senseless, ridiculous, incongruous, and blasphemous character of the work," to accept which "is to eschew holiness and goodness, and to dethrone the Almighty."[25] To save the world from such devastation, one might suppose that no number of pages would be too great to dedicate to the cause—as many as "might be written." Still our investigator limits himself to a few brief notices because after all, the book, he says, is "below the dignity of criticism."

J. H. Hunt, a relatively conscientious critic, was frank enough to entitle a chapter of his on the Book of Mormon (1844), "A Brief Notice of Several Books, Deemed Unworthy of Serious Attention."[26] So deemed by whom? The critic who deems a book unworthy of his attention should leave the criticizing of it to others who are willing to give it serious thought.

Here we have a paradox. Having announced that nothing is so urgently needed as a thorough study of the Book of Mormon, one crusader after another stops dead in his tracks with the lame excuse that the thing is not worth bothering about. And while we are told again and again that no human being in possession of his faculties would give a second thought to the book, we are also told that it is making terrible inroads among an enlightened citizenry. "No argument, or mode of reasoning, could induce anyone to believe that in the nineteenth century, in the United States, and in the blaze of science, literature, and civilization, a sect of religionists could arise on *delusion* and *imposition*." So one intellectual wrote in 1855, and adds the bemused confession: "But such are the facts, and we are forced to believe them."[27] This might be taken as an interesting commentary on the Book of Mormon: An intelligent man is confronted by a situation which, he tells us in the strongest language, nothing on earth could induce him to accept as possible—but there it is! Though they are contrary to everything we can or will believe, "such are the facts, and we are *forced* to believe them." Had he examined the Book of Mormon itself more closely, Mr. Reynolds might have been forced to believe many things which his training and vanity had told him were impossible.

"The reader will not be long," Mr. Taylder promises in the introduction to *The Mormon's Own Book*, "in judging whether his [Joseph Smith's] statements are the transcript of an enthusiast who unconsciously invested facts with the colouring of his imagination, or the cunningly-concocted after-thoughts of a knave."[28] Here the reader is given two damning alternatives in advance and told which one he is going to choose. With such helpful prompting he need not be long in reaching his conclusion, and the irksome obligations of serious research are gracefully sidestepped. With the same considerate forethought, Mr. Bays sent copies of the Anthon Transcript to a number of scholars, asking for their opinion of it—but *not* for their impartial opinion! With the transcript went a lurid covering letter, making it perfectly clear just what infamous claims were made for the document, and leaving the recipients in no doubt as to what effect a word in its favor might have on their reputations. The answer of the most eminent of the professors consulted gives the whole thing away. "The document which you enclose," the reply begins, "raises a *moral* rather than an *linguistic* problem." And as a moral problem the professor treats it.[29] Any chance of an impartial linguistic test was out of the question under such circumstances, yet this was one of the few attempts made to judge the Book of Mormon by severely objective standards.

The first volume of the eminent *American Anthropologist* includes a study of some length with the promising title, "The Origin of the Book of Mormon." Instead of displaying the deep scientific penetration and archaeological acumen we have a right to expect from such a source, the author confines his entire study to the grammatical mistakes in the book, resting his case principally on the antiquated use of "which" for "who," apparently unaware of the same usage in the Bible. He dismisses the book itself as "only grotesque." Yet for all that, it is a "portentous danger sign, . . . [a] monstrosity, born of deceit and bred in falsehood, . . . a monster of iniquity and deceit." And what is it in the book that makes this expert so forget his cool scientific detachment? It is not anything the Book of Mormon actually *says* that upsets him: its "teachings and precepts are not in themselves immoral. For, the Book of Mormon is not in itself immoral. There is no polygamy in it; . . . there is nothing immoral in the book." No, what alarms and enrages him is not what the Book of Mormon says, but what it pretends to be: "Its adherents have discovered a most dangerous weapon against the moral world in this doctrine of *'a continuing revelation.'* " That is the cloven hoof. As usual, it is not the Book of Mormon, but the Angel Moroni that is being put on trial: "To accept . . . any dispensation formulated in the terms of 'Thus saith the Lord,' is a portentous danger-sign to enlightened civilization."[30] Note that since this gentleman is not willing to accept *any* claim to revelation, the problem of *testing* such a claim never arises. In the same spirit, Professor Beardsley founds his Book of Mormon criticism on the unshakable rock that the modern mind rejects everything supernatural.[31] Granted that premise, *of course* the Book of Mormon is a fraud. But the challenge of the Prophet is to test the possibility of revelation by using the book as evidence, in which case we cannot start out by rejecting the book out of hand because we know that revelation is impossible. That is exactly what we do *not* know.

The work of Linn, often hailed as the first really scientific study of Mormonism, is a good example of the backward approach. "The Mormon Bible," he announces, "both in a literary and theological sense, is just such a production as would be expected to result from handing over to Smith and his fellow-'translators' a mass of Spaulding's material and new doctrinal matter for collation and copying."[32] Notice that he begins with definite expectations and finds in the Book of Mormon exactly what he expects. He advises the student to do the same: "An examination of its contents is useful, therefore, rather as a means of proving the fraudulent character of its pretention to divine revelation than as a means of ascertaining what the members of the Mormon church are taught."[33] Here the student is actually warned against reading the book to learn whether it is true or not, but is instructed to approach it with just one object in mind, "as a means of proving the fraudulent character of its pretention to divine revelation." And what rules does Mr. Linn have for telling when a writing is or is not the product of divine revelation? The usual rule, of course: There is no such thing!

Shortly after Linn's book appeared, the Fallows published their widely circulated *Mormon Menace*. "What sane person," they ask at the outset, "can believe that this man really believed that a glorious angel came from God and revealed to him the hiding place of these golden plates?"[34] The question is rhetorical; merely to state it is to have your answer. However effective polemically, it closes the door to any real investigation. If the whole thing is simply out of the question to any sane person, what sane person is even going to think about it?

One of the few critics ever to do a serious piece of work on the Book of Mormon was H. C. Sheldon. In coming to grips with the problem, he tells us exactly what his position is. "The primary question is: Are those claims credible, or do they bear unmistakably the stamp of falsehood and imposture?" A leading question, indeed, but at last we have someone who at least recognized the possibility of an alternative—Linn reads the book avowedly to prove it false, Taylder gives us our choice of whether Smith was one kind of liar or another, but Mr. Sheldon is actually willing to recognize an "either/or" situation. Only in the next sentence he takes it all back: "Many conditions, some of which are of compelling force, *shut up the critical investigator to the second alternative*."[35] What chicanery! Our guide tells us that the "primary question" for consideration is whether the Book of Mormon is true *or* false, and then calmly informs us that the first alternative is under no circumstances to be examined. The jury is instructed to choose between A and B, with the specification that A has been disqualified before the contest; with that understandable limitation the jury may favor whomever they will.

As early as 1835 one editor announced a policy that was to become standard procedure in dealing with the Book of Mormon, "an artifice so vile, shallow and contemptible, that it can never deceive one intelligent person; therefore we think it unworthy of so much as a contradiction!"[36] This is exactly the position taken in what has been hailed as recently as 1950 as the most thorough and devastating attack ever made on the Book of Mormon, a study by W. F. Prince, published in the *American Journal of Psychology* in 1917.[37] We shall deal with this study later, but first let Dr. Prince tell us how matters stand with science and the Book of Mormon: "Since the odd contents of the volume lamentably or ludicrously fall before every canon of historical criticism, scholars have not thought it worth while to discuss the notion of its ancient authorship, unless briefly for pragmatic reasons and missionary purposes."[38]

Here we have it again: the only reason any scholar consults the Book of Mormon is to debunk it for polemical purposes — pragmatic and missionary. The historical question raised by the book is purely and simply that of its ancient authorship — a problem that scholars have never discussed, according to Prince. Why not? we ask. Because it cannot stand up to critical investigation — it falls before every canon of historical criticism. Has it been tested by *any* of those canons? Of course not, it isn't worth the trouble!

This absurd position, that the Book of Mormon has failed to pass a test which has never been given it because of its failure to pass, etc., is neatly confirmed by the learned LaRue in 1919. "What of the book itself?" he asks, "*No serious consideration has ever been given it by men of science. It is considered fabrication.*"[39] Since it is a fabrication, why should any man of science waste his time with it? The answer is, that only by spending a lot of time with it can any man of science prove that it is a fabrication in the first place. But such reasoning does not count: "How could three rational men address 'all nations, kindreds, tongues, and people,' " LaRue asks, "and say that God had told them that these plates had been 'translated by the gift and power of God'?"[40] Another rhetorical question, and quite pointless besides, since the problem of how they *could* do so is overridden by the admitted fact that they *did*.

Writing in the following year, C. S. Jones, after an almost unbelievably confused and inaccurate account of the contents of the Book of Mormon, makes his point: "It would be easy, pitiably easy, if it were not supererogatory, to pulverize this claim, . . . but *cui bono?*"[41] *Cui bono* being Latin for "what's the use?" We now have the comforting assurance that if the scholars and scientists have neglected the Book of Mormon, it has not been because they were too busy with more important things — for anything "pitiably easy" as the debunking of the book, a crying need in our society, should not require more than a few easy hours of a good man's time. Why don't they get at it? "What's the use?" asks Mr. Jones, a strange question from one who feels that the world is in desperate need of a book by him entitled *The Truth about the Mormons.*

No anti-Mormon book has been pushed more diligently in high places than Arbaugh's University of Chicago thesis on *Revelation in Mormonism*. Arbaugh informs us that "apart from specialized treatises, there is only one scientific book on Mormonism," and that is Linn's work, "quite incomplete, out of date, and defective, presenting a maze of undigested facts."[42] In view of such a state of sorry neglect, one might expect Arbaugh himself to do some real digging on the Book of Mormon, especially since revelation is his story. But no: he disarmingly informs us that where the book is concerned, he is going to take his information from a single collection of third- and fourth-hand reports made by the Reverend Charles A. Shook in 1912.[43] For Mr. Arbaugh, "the fact that Mormonism is fantastic, interesting, and available for study as no other religion is, makes its study a pleasant task."[44] It presents no real problem because it is simply fantastic—you don't have to worry about proving or disproving fantastic things, do you?

As recently as 1957 the same Arbaugh has got out a pamphlet which he modestly describes as "an authoritative handbook on Mormonism—concise, . . . scholarly, . . . objective." "This is not an exposure of Mormonism," he cries with liberal magnanimity. "One complaint which can be urged against the exposures is that they sometimes confuse hearsay with fact."[45] But not Arbaugh; no prejudice for him! He will write no scandalized exposure, but give his little book the neutral and unemotional title of *Gods, Sex, and Saints: The Mormon Story,* and promises to tell us, without a spark of ill feeling, how "the integrative principle of sex" operates in this "polytheistic mystery cult." Thus with a preliminary barrage of loaded words, Mr. Arbaugh prepares us for his exercise in semantics— for he admits that he has shifted his ground from the historical to the semantic approach—no need to bother about facts here![46]

One of the "exposures" which Dr. Arbaugh condemns for confusing hearsay with fact is Mrs. Brodie's much-heralded novel, recently hailed by a reviewer as *the* work of "primary scholarship" on the Mormons.[47] "Scholars of American literary history have remained persistently uninterested in the Book of Mormon and other sacred books, like the Koran, and Science and Health, though all are . . . an obscure compound of folklore, moral platitude, mysticism, and millennialism."[48] That should be enough to show how deep Mrs. Brodie herself has gone in her "primary scholarship." She is quite unaware of Eduard Meyer's work, though she could not possibly have avoided him in any serious study of the Book of Mormon or the

Koran, and she apparently thinks that people who study and compare ancient and modern religious texts are known as sociologists.[49] But she is right about one thing—the Book of Mormon has been persistently neglected. A search in the latest encyclopedias, American and foreign, will disclose long articles on the Dead Sea Scrolls but never an article on the Book of Mormon.[50]

Mr. C. S. Braden, in a book devoted to the subject of modern scriptures, refuses to touch the Book of Mormon except to note: "Naturally it [the story of the Book of Mormon] has been doubted by those outside the faith and every effort has been made to find a more plausible explanation of the sources of this scripture. . . . In an age such as ours," he writes, "critical of all claims that run counter to what may be scientifically proven, the Mormon has a heavy burden of proof upon him."[51] Here, surely, is a convenient concept of the function of a textual critic. Mr. Braden it is who challenges the book, and then Mr. Braden denies any responsibility for proving his case. He dares the Mormons to convince him and refuses to study their book.

A Catholic priest prefaces a recent discussion of the Book of Mormon with a helpful statement of policy: "I, of course, hold that Mormon beliefs, differing as they do from the beliefs of Christians during two thousand years, are irreconcilable with the Christian faith."[52] In view of that "of course," one wonders why Father Rumble bothers even to pretend to be investigating the thing, but a reading of the pamphlet will readily show that he is innocent of any dangerous researches.

In an ambitious historical study of the Book of Mormon published in 1954, Professor Meinhold of Kiel wrote: "To presume to believe on the existence of the 'golden plates,' is in spite of the witnesses, *unerhört* [unheard of, unthinkable]."[53] *Unerhört* is no argument and no proof; it is the evasion of a task which the world has a right to expect of an honest scholar, and, like Eduard Meyer before him, Meinhold sidesteps the responsibility with a shrug. Speaking of such responsibility, A. E. Housman wrote, years ago, that no scholar, no matter how learned, may be "allowed to fling his opinions in the reader's face without being called to account and asked for his reasons."[54] One of the best commentaries on this text is one of the latest: Dr. O'Dea has observed, not without a touch of Irish wit, that "the Book of Mormon has not been universally considered by its critics as one of those books that must be read in order to have an opinion of it."[55] We have seen why.

From the brief survey of critical policy just presented, one fact stands out conspicuously—the fact that from first to last the foremost objection to the book, an objection that far outweighs all others both as to the frequency and feeling with which it is put forward, is that it is hopelessly out of place in our modern, scientific, enlightened society. What amazes the first commentator is that such a thing can exist "at this enlightened age of the world"; Campbell "sets the question . . . forever at rest, to every *rational* mind"; E.D. Howe is alarmed that "great numbers of people in our enlightened country" should fall for such a thing; the Reverend Clark is astonished that it should find followers "in enlightened New England"; Gregg finds it "simply astounding that any human being . . . can be found so credulous as to believe it"; and so on. This completely disqualifies the comfortable thesis that while the Book of Mormon may have impressed the rustic America of a century ago, "in an age such as ours" it simply won't hold up. Forty years ago a critic wrote that if Joseph Smith had "lived at a later date, he would have been laughed to scorn at once."[56] The fact is that he *was* laughed to scorn at once: in 1830 his book was if anything even more obnoxious to enlightened liberalism and modern education than it is today. "We must not forget," one investigator reminds us, that "Mormonism arose almost yesterday, amid universities and libraries," and not in a primitive world.[57] "The modern mind," writes Beardsley, "will reject the Mormon version of the golden plates and Urim and Thummim, as either delusions or fraud."[58] But in that respect the mind of 1830 was quite as "modern" as the mind of 1930. When Mrs. Brodie announces that twentieth-century science has finally "disembowelled" the Book of Mormon, we wait for the lurid details—but we wait in vain. Not a single twentieth-century argument does she produce: hardly a single new argument against the Book of Mormon has come forth since the first decade of its appearance!

Notes

1. Eduard Meyer, *Ursprung und Geschichte der Mormonen* (Halle: Niemeyer, 1912), p. 5, n. 1; published also as *Origin and History of the Mormons*, tr. H. Rahde and E. Séaich (Salt Lake City: University of Utah Press, 1961).

2. Ibid., 19.

3. *The Life of David Marks, To the 26th Year of His Age, Written by Himself* (Limerick, ME: Office of the *Morning Star*, 1831), 341. This happened on March 29, 1830. Marks' statement, p. 341, "From all the circumstances, I thought it probably had been written originally by an *infidel*, to see how much he could impose on the credulity of men" is quoted with slight alteration and no acknowledgment by E. D. Howe, and lifted from him by others in the same way.

4. Ibid.

5. Alexander Campbell's study first appeared in the *Millennial Harbinger* 2 (February 7, 1831): 85-96; it is most readily available in Francis W. Kirkham, *A New Witness for Christ in America*, 2 vols. (Independence, MO: Zion's, 1951), 2:101-9. Our quotations are from Kirkham, 106 (emphasis added).

6. Ibid., 107.

7. Ibid., 105.

8. Editorial, *Palmyra Reflector* (6 January 1831); quoted by Kirkham, *A New Witness for Christ in America*, 2:65.

9. Josiah Priest, *American Antiquities*, 5th ed. (Albany: Hoffman and White, 1835), 76. The first edition was in 1832. Constantine S. Rafinesque published his views in his *Atlantic Journal and Friend of Knowledge*, vol. 1, no. 3 (Autumn 1832; reprinted Cambridge: Murray, 1946): 98-99.

10. Origen Bacheler, *Mormonism Exposed, Internally and Externally* (New York: 162 Nassau Street, February 1838), 1, quoted by Kirkham, *A New Witness for Christ in America*, 2:159.

11. Ibid., 6.

12. H. Stevenson, *Lecture on Mormonism* (Newcastle, England: Blackwell, 1839; reprinted New Haven, Conn.: Research Publications, 1967), 24.

13. Ibid., 8-9.

14. E. D. Howe, *History of Mormonism: or a Faithful Account of that Singular Imposition and Delusion* (Painesville: Printed by the Author, 1840), 93-94.

15. Ibid., 74-75.

16. William Harris, *Mormonism Portrayed* (Warsaw, Ill.: Sharp and Gamble, 1841), Introduction, cited in Kirkham, *A New Witness for Christ in America*, 2:166-67.

17. John Alonzo Clark, *Gleanings by the Way* (Philadelphia: Simon, 1842), 259.

18. Ibid., 250.

19. Ibid., 282.

20. Daniel P. Kidder, *Mormonism and the Mormons* (New York: Carlton and Porter, 1842), 60.

21. Ibid., 8.

22. J. B. Turner, *Mormonism in All Ages* (New York: Platt and Peters, 1842), 300; Kirkham, *A New Witness for Christ in America*, 2:190.

23. Ibid., 302; Kirkham, *A New Witness for Christ in America*, 2:190-92.

24. Kidder, *Mormonism and the Mormons*, 336-37, esp. 337.

25. Thomas Gregg, *The Prophet of Palmyra* (New York: Alden, 1890), 35, 95, and 8, respectively. The first statement is quoted by Gregg from S. S. Harding.

26. James H. Hunt, *Mormonism* (St. Louis: Ustick and Davies, 1844), ch. 4, p. 39.

27. John Reynolds, *My Own Times* (Belleville, Ill.: Perryman and Davison, 1855), 563.

28. T. W. P. Taylder, *The Mormon's Own Book* (London: Partridge, Paternoster Row, 1857), xxiv.

29. Davis H. Bays, *The Doctrines and Dogmas of Mormonism* (St. Louis: Christian, 1897), 263.

30. Perry B. Pierce, "The Origin of the Book of Mormon," *American Anthropologist* new series, 1 (1899): 694 (emphasis added).

31. Harry M. Beardsley, *Joseph Smith and His Mormon Empire* (Bos-

ton: Houghton Mifflin, 1931), 79-80. Beardsley is ready to accept "The Mormon version" of the story of the Book of Mormon "if we relate it in modern terms . . . shorn of its supernatural aspect." As if the wise men of 1830 objected to anything else than its supernatural aspects!

32. William A. Linn, *The Story of the Mormons* (New York: Macmillan, 1923), 89.

33. Ibid., 90.

34. Samuel Fallows and Helen M. Fallows, *The Mormon Menace* (Chicago: Woman's Temperance Association, 1903), 16.

35. Henry C. Sheldon, *A Fourfold Test of Mormonism* (New York: Abingdon, 1914), 10 (emphasis added).

36. A. H. M., "Ancient and Modern Mormonism," *Western Examiner*, ed. J. Bobb (10 December 1835), col. 4.

37. Prince's study "proved beyond dispute thirty years ago" exactly when and where the Book of Mormon was conceived, according to Whitney R. Cross, *The Burned-over District* (Ithaca: Cornell University Press, 1950), 144.

38. Walter F. Prince, "Psychological Tests for the Authorship of the Book of Mormon," *American Journal of Psychology* 28 (1917): 373.

39. William Earl LaRue, *The Foundations of Mormonism* (New York: Revell, 1919), 77 (emphasis added). "A higher critical appraisal of the Book of Mormon, which was the result of this creative effort of Joseph Smith, *would be* extremely interesting," wrote Charles F. Potter, *The Story of Religion as Told in the Lives of its Leaders* (New York: Simon and Schuster, 1929), 531, but such has never been undertaken.

40. La Rue, *The Foundations of Mormonism*, 65.

41. C. Sheridan Jones, *The Truth about the Mormons* (London: Rider, 1920), 4-5.

42. George B. Arbaugh, *Revelation in Mormonism* (University of Chicago Thesis, 1932; reprinted 1950), v.

43. Ibid., vii.

44. Ibid., v.

45. George B. Arbaugh, *Gods, Sex, and Saints: The Mormon Story* (Rock Island, IL: Augustana, 1957), 5. "There is need for clarity at the point of semantics rather than for stories about the latest polygamists," ibid., 6.

46. Ibid., 5.

47. Dale L. Morgan, "The 'Peculiar People,' " *Saturday Review* (28 December 1957), 9.

48. Fawn M. Brodie, *No Man Knows My History* (New York: Knopf,

1946), 67. Meyer's work (see note 1 above) contains not only the classic comparison of Joseph Smith with Mohammed but also a detailed comparison of their revelations and their books. The work is not mentioned by Mrs. Brodie.

49. Ibid.

50. All that the *Encylopedia Americana* (1957), s.v. "Mormon," has to say about the Book of Mormon itself is that "many editions have been published, millions of copies have been distributed, and the work has been translated into many different languages." The *Britannica* (1957) has not a word to say about the contents of the Book of Mormon. [This situation is, fortunately, no longer the case – ed.]

51. Charles S. Braden, *The Scriptures of Mankind, An Introduction* (New York: Macmillan, 1952), 481-82.

52. L. Rumble, *Mormons or Latter-day Saints* (St. Paul, 1950), Introduction; reprinted in Kirkham, *A New Witness for Christ in America*, 2:304.

53. Peter Meinhold, "Die Anfänge des Amerikanischen Geschichtsbewusstseins," *Saeculum* 5 (1954): 85-86.

54. In Alfred E. Housman's edition of Manilius, *Astronomicon*, 5:xxxiii.

55. Thomas F. O'Dea, *The Mormons* (Chicago: University of Chicago Press, 1957), 26.

56. Stuart Martin, *The Mystery of Mormonism* (New York: Dutton, 1920), 16.

57. George Seibel, *The Mormon Saints* (Pittsburgh: Lessing, 1919), 7.

58. Beardsley, *Joseph Smith and His Mormon Empire*, 79-80.

5

Just Another Book?

Here We Are Again: The logical point of departure for a study of Book of Mormon criticism happens to be, at present, the present; for today's researches have just achieved the completion of a full circle in the mystic discipline. At the moment the critics are right back where they started from 130 years ago. Such is the progress of scholarship. Today we are being told that the Book of Mormon can be explained fully as a faithful reflection of the mind of Joseph Smith and the world he grew up in. Which is exactly what Alexander Campbell said in the beginning.[1] Indeed, the latest criticisms of the book can do no better than to quote Campbell's thesis word for word: "This prophet Smith, through his stone spectacles, wrote on the plates of Nephi, in his Book of Mormon, every error and almost every truth discussed in New York in the last ten years."[2]

Furthermore, Campbell observes, "there never was a book more evidently written by one set of fingers. . . . I cannot doubt for a single moment but that he is the sole author and proprietor of it."[3] That pretty well covers it: Smith was the author of the book, and its substance is a distorted image of his own times.

Now if all this was so perfectly obvious, then as now,

This article first appeared in two parts, published in the Improvement Era *(May 1959 to June 1959). The article was part of a series of five articles, published in nine parts under the title " 'Mixed Voices': A Study on Book of Mormon Criticism."*

why on earth did the critics forsake such a neat and comfortable explanation to wander for a hundred years in a
wilderness of speculation and contradiction? It was because the theory of the local origin collapsed at a touch.
No sooner had Mr. Campbell's explanation been received
with cries of joy and relief[4] than it was seen that the picture
had not been clarified by it at all, but made much messier.
An article in the *American Whig Review* explains the new
embarrassment: "Those who were acquainted with the
early life of the founder of Mormonism, with his ignorance
and character for stupidity, wondered much at the publication of so invention-displaying and elaborate a work,
of which he claimed to be sole author and proprietor; and
as the prophet daily lived down his own boasts of superior
value and wisdom, the wonder grew into a suspicion of
the genuineness of his claims of exclusive authorship. A
short time served to give this suspicion basis and confirmation, and a number of affidavits filed almost simultaneously in different parts of New York and Pennsylvania,
and by witnesses between whom there was no opportunity
of collusion, showed clearly the sources of the pretended
inspiration."[5]

The statement deserves close examination. Note first
of all that it was quickly realized, not only by the Mormons,
but by the anti-Mormons as well, that Joseph Smith by his
own wits could not possibly have written the Book of Mormon — and so farewell to Mr. Campbell's sublime certi-
tudes: "I cannot doubt for a single moment but that he is
the sole author and proprietor of it!" Note in the second
place the admission that this obvious fact left the critics in
a quandary — they "wondered much." And since quan-
daries are intolerable to critics, who are never at a loss to
invent explanations, it is not the least surprising that "the
wonder grew into a suspicion." From embarrassment to
wonder and from wonder to suspicion: is there any doubt
what the next step will be? Is suspicion ever at a loss to

discover villainy? All at once, and last of all, comes the evidence: "almost simultaneously" people everywhere start remembering a certain unpublished and unregretted novel, a dull, befuddled composition that no one had the patience to read but the names of whose characters were remembered with crystal clarity by people who had forgotten all about the book until then. Then another "double-take" made it necessary to explain how Smith could have got hold of the book, and, presto! another brain-wave hit the public, and here and there people suddenly remembered a "mysterious stranger" who used to visit the Smiths by night, some three to ten and more years before! There is your answer, and no funny business, either: "There was no opportunity of collusion" between the "witnesses."

Only in such a case one does not look for collusion but for control. We do not have to look far for the controlling and coordinating agencies in the case of the affidavits against Joseph Smith and the Book of Mormon, for they were all systematically sought out and collected by two or three individuals, going from door to door and from town to town, telling people what they wanted and finding certain parties only too glad to oblige. No collusion, indeed![6]

So Campbell's solution was short-lived, as the *Whig Review* has told us, and another had to be found. Accordingly we find a learned historian in 1835 voicing his and his fellows' relief at the new solution: "It has come out *at last*, that the Golden Bible was originally composed for a Novel, and being turned into a Bible by the ingenuity of two or three leading men among the Mormons, was printed and published as the basis of their religion. This developement we trust will speedily extinguish the new lights."[7] The "at last" is typical: through the years the experts have continued to attack from every angle, and periodically we hear the joyful cry that *at last* they have struck pay dirt.[8]

The alternative theory having collapsed, and since it is

much too late in the day to think up another one, the critics
have no choice today but to go back to the old original
theory of Campbell. But if that theory was so readily dis-
credited (please note: it was *not* supplanted by the Spaulding theory but broke down of its own accord, and the
Spaulding substitute was only found after a desperate in-
terval of frantic searching), if it could not stand up for a
year on its own merits, why should it work now? For the
good reason that lots of things are forgotten in 125 years!
The theory that Joseph Smith composed the Book of Mormon raises questions and involves corollaries which a
hundred years ago were readily seen to present an insu-
perable obstacle to its acceptance. But the modern world
can very easily overlook those questions and corollaries,
and present-day critics are trying hard to do so.

One of the latest and most conscientious critics of the
Book of Mormon, Dr. O'Dea, finds the answer to the whole
thing just as simple and obvious as it was to Alexander
Campbell: "There is a simple common-sense explanation
which states that Joseph Smith was a normal person living
in an atmosphere of religious excitement that . . . led him
from necromancy into revelation, from revelation to prophecy, and from prophecy to leadership. . . . To the non-
Mormon . . . such an explanation on the basis of the evidence at hand seems by far the most likely and safest."[9]

The trouble with this position is that all "the evidence
at hand" refutes it. To be consistent with his own position,
Dr. O'Dea must accept without question a number of perfectly untenable corollaries; for example, he accepts emphatically the proposition that as "a normal person" Smith
reacted to the common stimulus of his environment just
the way other people did, so that his Book of Mormon is
in fact a "primary source for the intellectual history of the
common man."[10] Even his claims to revelation were but a
"legitimate product of the intensified experience of the
region."[11] Dr. Cross goes even further; for him all of the

prophet's revelations, including the Book of Mormon, are "nothing more than [what] happens to any man who enjoys great responsibilities. . . . It might have happened to almost any one of Joseph's fellow Yankee migrants."[12] Even the alleged treasure-digging and the finding of the plates "was by no means peculiar and quite naturally seemed authentic to ordinary folks," according to this authority, who notes that such a composition as the Book of Mormon "would scarcely seem fanciful, possibly not even novel, to their contemporaries."[13]

The modern school has dug in so deeply on this ground that it will be necessary for us to labor the obvious by way of calling their reluctant attention to it. Two fundamental corollaries of the theorem that Joseph Smith wrote the Book of Mormon are (1) that it was not beyond his ability to write such a book, and (2) that the book itself, as the product of a normal mind under the influences of everyday stimuli supplied by a given environment, was necessarily quite at home in that environment. Our modern critics accept these corollaries, but the contemporaries of Joseph Smith *could not*, however eager they were to explain the Book of Mormon. For they knew too much and they saw too much. Dr. Francis Kirkham has devoted the better part of a large book to quotations in which contemporaries of Joseph Smith, hostile or friendly, all express complete conviction that he could not possibly have written the book. And even more clear and emphatic is the unanimous verdict that nothing could be more completely out of place in nineteenth-century America than Joseph Smith and his book.

We are apt to forget this unless we look at the record. Today, the experts find it not only convenient but also essential to their argument to forget how the world has reacted to Joseph Smith and the Book of Mormon. Let us refresh their memories by listing in chronological order some thoroughly representative remarks by leading critics.

1830s

A month after the appearance of the Book of Mormon, the liberal Palmyra *Reflector* warned Oliver Cowdery that he might end up being sent as a convict to the Simsbury Mines for daring to proclaim its message in "the principal cities of the Union."[14] Could this be the doctrine that "quite naturally seemed authentic to ordinary folks"? In July 1833 a widely heralded mass-meeting in Jackson County, Missouri, unanimously voted that all Mormons should leave "the country," that no more should be allowed to enter "the country," that the Mormon printing press should be destroyed (this was immediately done) and all publication by Mormons forthwith and forever cease. The reason for this perfectly illegal action was clearly stated and clearly understood: The community especially feared that their lives and property were in danger "in the hands of jurors and witnesses, who do not blush to declare, and would not hesitate upon occasion to swear, that they have . . . been the subjects of miracles and supernatural cures; have conversed with God and his Angels, and possess and exercise the gift of Divination, and of unknown tongues."[15]

In vain the newspapers around the country pointed out that you could not throw the Constitution out of the window simply because people had crazy religious ideas: "We regard the Mormons as a set of deluded and deceived fanatics, yet they have their rights and privileges."[16] In vain the governor of the state asked why the Mormons *alone* of all fanatics should be so treated: "It is not long," he wrote, "since an impostor assumed the character of Jesus Christ, and attempted to minister as such; but I never heard of any combination to deprive *him* of his rights."[17] At the same time a learned judge in the same state, acting in his official capacity, urged the Mormons to give up the cause of all their troubles, and warned them of what would happen, rights or no rights, if they did not: "The Honorable

Judge Ryland . . . addressed the Mormons warning them against the danger of suffering themselves to be led by pretenders to the high prerogatives of the Prophets of God."[18] Such is the specific crime with which he charges them. A year later a western editor compared the Mormons with the early Christians; he also called the Book of Mormon "an artifice so vile, shallow, and contemptible that it can never deceive one intelligent individual; therefore [we] think it unworthy of so much notice as a contradiction!" But the remarkable thing about this perfectly orthodox statement is that the author, who was a freethinker, speaks of Moses and Christ and of the Old and New Testaments in the very same terms, sagely observing that the world's opinion of the Book of Mormon was also "unquestionably the opinion of the learned ancients, concerning the former revelations."[19] It was a direct hit which went unnoticed in the general cry, voiced by the *Missouri Argus* in 1838, that though the Mormons may be Christians, still they were "a sect with a peculiar creed, distinct from that professed by the rest of Christians."[20] The general impression of the Mormons on American society at the time is eloquently expressed in the verse of Josiah Canning, the New England "poet":

> Now Mormon, with his golden plates,
> Says he has opened heaven's gates,
> And hangs out many tempting baits
> To prove the fact;
> And old Joe Smith, his agent, prates
> With school-boy tact.
>
> . . .
>
> Here in our own, our goodly land,
> Some zealot has enrolled a band,
> From heaven, I think!
> The last accounts they seem to stand
> Upon the brink.
>
> . . .

That heathenism should be done
Beneath New England's Christian sun,
'S a crying shame—a grievous one;
And into jail
The imps should tarred and feathered run,
Or ride a rail.[21]

Here it will be seen that the same objections are raised
to the Mormons in staid New England as in wild Missouri
(and they are purely religious objections), and the same
rough treatment is recommended for them. But today we
are being told that such doctrines "would scarcely seem
fanciful, possibly not even novel" in those early times.
Who is kidding whom?

1840s

It was the oddness of Mormonism that arrested the
attention of the Fabulous Forties, when the critics looked
for the peculiar and found it everywhere. Everything about
Mormonism was fantastic. Josiah Quincy said of the stately
Nauvoo Temple, "It certainly cannot be compared to any
ecclesiastical building which may be discerned by the natural eyesight."[22] To Mr. Kidder, Mormonism was "threatening to unsettle the grounds of all rational belief."[23] Wherever the Mormons went, "their fanatical religious zeal and
some of their tenets and practices . . . [were] inconsistent
or incompatible with the civilization surrounding them."[24]
"We are accustomed to boast of the intelligence of the
nineteenth century," wrote the scandalized editor of the
eminent Dublin *University Magazine* in 1843, "to laud ourselves on the march of mind in these modern days, and
to speak of the popular delusions by which past generations were misled, as of the spectral shadows of 'the long
night now gone down the sky.' Mormonism is a bitter
reply to our self-laudation."[25] "How, in the name of common sense," an English minister wrote to his nephew who
had become a Mormon elder, "could you be so simple, as

to let such a poor weak deluded creature, commit such *blasphemy,* as to put his hands on your head, and tell you that you should have the Holy Ghost descend upon you? — I would much rather have a pig's foot on my head, if it was well boiled."[26]

1850s

Everyone knows that the Mormons "are a queer, eccentric set; that they have got odd notions into their heads respecting religion and the Bible," a London editor observed in 1850.[27] Charles Dickens was bemused at the idea of people "seeing visions in an age of railways"; it was just too incongruous for words.[28] "It is most humiliating to our country and our age!" cries a devout American commenting on the same anomaly in 1853. "Who could opine that, in our happy land, in a nation of voters, freemen, newspapers, periodical literature, and general reading, such a gross and detestable imposture as Mormonism could find disciples and devotees?"[29] Speaking of the death of the Prophet, the most noted literary journal of the age says, "We cannot deny that in his punishment, the wrath of lawless men fulfilled the righteousness of God." Actually it was "a death too honourable for his deserts. . . . To call such a man a martyr is an abuse of language."[30] When one considers that this was written in Scotland, far from the political or economic troubles of the American frontier, and by a man who prided himself on his cool intellectual detachment, who had never had any contact with Joseph Smith, it is hard to argue that Mormonism was simply a normal product of the times. "It has been observed with some reason," an important American journal remarked in 1854, "that had a Rabelais or a Swift told the story of the Mormons under the vail of allegory, mankind would probably have entered a protest against the extravagance of the satirist."[31]

An editorial in the eminent *Putnam's Monthly* for March

1855 replies with a resounding "No!" to its own question: "Shall Utah be admitted to the Union?" It is the doctrines of the Church regarding God and man that decide the issue.[32] A later thesis on the same subject in the *Forum* reached the same conclusions: the Mormons are as different from the rest of society as the wild redskins, totally devoid of "the virtues upon which alone Christian people can build republican institutions."[33] In the same year, John Reynolds, a shrewd observer, wrote: "In all the great events and revolutions in the various nations of the earth nothing surpasses the extraordinary history of the Mormons. The facts in relation to this singular people are so strange, so opposite to common sense, and so great and important, that they would not obtain our belief if we did not see the events transpire before our eyes. No argument, or mode of reasoning, could induce any one to believe that in the nineteenth century, in the United States . . . a sect of religionists could arise on *delusion* and *imposition*."[34]

Yet our present-day critics do not even raise an eyebrow. They were born yesterday. A hundred years ago the critics agreed that "Mormonism is . . . the product of a bewildered brain, when it has evidence both to a *moral* and *metaphysical* nature, to prove that it cannot by *possibility* — I may almost say human or divine—be true! Before Mormonism can be true, the *nature of man*, the *nature of truth*, and the *nature of Deity* himself, must be *totally* subverted. . . . Nothing less than a total abcession in these parts can be tolerated."[35]

1860s

While American passions had full play in other directions in the 1860s, England carried on the great tradition of anti-Mormon raillery. "Although it is not in general a Christian duty to speak ill of any one, especially after he has gone to answer for himself before his Judge," wrote a venerable vicar in a long dissertation on Joseph Smith, "yet in the case of a deceiver, whose lying doctrines are perverting thousands from the right way, the ordinary course of duty is reversed."[36] For Smith alone the otherwise universal law of Christian charity is suspended. Another English divine describes Mormonism as "the great masterpiece of Satan in these last days, embracing every possible principle of antagonism to the word of God, whilst unblushingly parading itself as the purest form of Christianity extant."[37] Yet the same man "thoroughly endorses" the statement of an American clergyman: "I have never yet conversed with a lay Mormon whom I believed to be a hypocrite. Their whole soul seems launched upon their infatuation, and for it they readily leave home and property. . . . What churchmen and churchwomen such people would make—humble although they are—if they were correctly informed and judiciously controlled!"[38]

1870s

"Intercourse with Gentiles has already revealed to many of the Mormons the fact," C. H. Brigham reported in 1870, "that their system has no sympathy outside of their own community, that the civilized world is against them, and that they are classed with Pariahs and lepers. . . . The gracious doctor who praises them from their platform, holds them up to scorn and horror in the pages of his book."[39] As if the Mormons had not had reason before 1870 to know that! The "Mormon Problem," according to this authority, is the challenge of the question: "What is to become of this people? . . . Can this small body of insolent religionists defy much longer the will and force of the American nation? Can this blot on the civilization of the nineteenth century be longer tolerated?"[40]

An interesting editorial in *Scribner's*, 1877, noted that the treatment of the Mormons "is the *sole* apparent exception to the American rule of universal toleration. . . . The only church born in the country, with American prophets and apostles . . . has passed through what its own historians call 'ten general persecutions.'

"Here is a suggestive record: The Latter-day Saints have settled in twelve different places in the United States, and have invariably become embroiled with their neighbors unless the latter abandoned the vicinity *en masse*. In New York, while the church was yet confined to two families, they kept three townships in an uproar with quarrels and lawsuits, and sixty neighbors of the Prophet united in a deposition that they would not believe him or any of his party on oath."

Here there can be no question of the threat of growing political or economic power. Polygamy? our editor asks: "But the record excludes that idea; the Mormons had more trouble with the world before they adopted polygamy than since." At a loss for an explanation, he must seek it in "something peculiar to Mormonism [that] takes it out of the sphere of religion."[41] Here he entirely forgets that as the persecution was uniform, so the explanation for it is uniform in every decade. Economic, political, social, and geographical circumstances changed rapidly, but the attacks did not change—the two unchanging factors in the picture are the persecutions and the religious teaching of the Mormons, and the persecution is always explicitly leveled at the teaching.

1880s

The "gracious doctor" referred to above was T. deWitt Talmage, whose sermons, delivered from his huge Brooklyn Tabernacle, were the most widely syndicated in the country. When deWitt Talmage spoke, all America listened and approved. And he called for nothing less than an extermination of the Mormons: "O good people of the United States, . . . I have to tell you that unless we destroy Mormonism, Mormonism will destroy us. . . . Every day as a nation we consent to Mormonism we are defying the

hail and the lightning . . . and the earthquake of an in-
censed God."

It made no difference that the Mormons seemed to be
very nice people—"I never addressed a more genial audience in my life"—the whole thing had to go, if necessary
by "howitzer and bombshell, and bullets and cannon-ball.
If a gang of thieves should squat on a territory and make
thievery a religion how long would the United States government stand that?"[42]

All through the eighties eminent ministers echoed
these sentiments. Mormonism was "an evil, peculiar, enormous, and prophetic of untold disaster."[43] "It is acknowledged to be the Great Modern Abomination, the most
pernicious heresy of this century. . . . Throughout our
whole land it is universally despised and execrated; and
if popular odium could extinguish it, it would speedily be
sunk in the slimy depths of the Great Salt Lake."[44] In 1889
the Reverend J. P. Newman meditated and commented on
the impossibility of ever assimilating the Mormons into
civilized society.

"We prophesied that it would be short-lived; we esteemed it as a standing joke. . . . Then it was said that the
evil would succumb under the march of civilization. . . .
They said the locomotive would sound the death-knell of
Mormonism, that it would be the trump of its doom. They
said, 'Complete the railway from the Atlantic to the Pacific,
and this relic of barbarism will disappear.' Whereas the
neigh of the iron horse has been the bugle of advance for
Mormonism. . . . Then it was foretold that Mormonism
was an anomaly, out of accord with the spirit of the age;
that its perpetuity was an impossibility; that it would
wither under the genius of our institutions; that the very
spirit of the age would rise in its majesty and over-shadow
the evil; whereas, this evil genius has remained and hurled
defiance at the genius of our civilization. . . . They said,
'Let Congress legislate . . . and before the authority of the

law the evil would disappear. . . . The people said, 'Let
this Arch-Mormon die! . . . let that man, Brigham Young,
die, and Mormonism cease!' "[45]

Newman's own solution for the problem was simple,
direct, and unconstitutional: "Disfranchise the Mormon,
not merely the polygamist, but the Mormon."[46] The
thought of treating any other religious body in such a way
would have filled the good man with horror, but the rules
don't count where Mormons are concerned.

1890s

In 1898 the League for Social Service published a declaration with the title *Ten Reasons Why Christians Cannot
Fellowship the Mormon Church*. The list of officers of the
league, including such eminent names as those of Washington Choate, Jane Addams, Margaret Sangster, and the
Reverend Edward Everett Hale, reads like a roster of American liberalism. Those good people did originate the document but, generously and impulsively sponsoring any
cause put before them as liberal, had approved it on rec-
ommendation by the leading churches.[47] So here we are
as near as we can get to an official statement of why Mormons are not Christians: "Christians of every name most
earnestly desire to unite with the Mormon people in all
feasible plans that have as their end the social, political
and moral advancement of our commonwealth. There is,
however, a line of demarcation that Christians cannot overlook, that they cannot disregard. . . . The question is
purely a religious question. It goes to the very root of
Christian belief and duty."[48]

So the objection to the Mormons is not social, economic, political, or moral after all, but *purely religious*. The
"Mormon Problem" is simply, "Why cannot Christians
walk in fellowship with Mormons, in religion, as they do
with each other?" The first objection is that the Mormons
claim that they alone have the true gospel; the second that

"their so-called revelations of the present are put on the same level with the Bible"; the third that they regard "Joseph Smith as a prophet of God"; the fourth that they believe "that authority to officiate in the gospel is vested only in the said priesthood, . . . that it is invested with the very power of God himself"; the fifth that "the Mormon church teaches a doctrine of God that is antagonistic to the Scriptures, dishonoring to the Divine Being and debasing to man."[49] Note these objections to the Mormons are all about what they *believe*, not what they have done; and that these beliefs are accurately described as "purely religious" ones. These beliefs alone set them off completely from all the Christian world. After adding five more intolerable beliefs to the list—which, unlike the first five, are incorrectly presented and not very convincing—the indictment reaches its ringing conclusion: "Nothing in common. With such a so-called church and system of doctrine, Christians can have nothing in common but the need of the great salvation of the God-Man, Christ Jesus."[50]

"It is a very curious and remarkable fact," wrote British scientist Samuel Laing in 1898, "that while so many highly intellectual attempts have been made in vain in modern times to found new sects and religions, the only one which has had any real success is that which is based on the most gross and vulgar imposture—Mormonism."[51]

1900s

The verdict of a much-reprinted book appearing first in 1900 is that "for *climacteric comicality* Mormonism should be awarded the palm. Its romancing is refreshing in its very audaciousness. Jules Verne dreaming is here eclipsed; Baron Munchausen marvels seem commonplace. Of absurdities Pelions are piled upon Ossas, but the pile rises ever higher. Untruth was never more picturesque. From first to last the history of this cult is dramatic and spectacular. One feels that he has stumbled upon a scene in the Arabian Nights, rather than upon a sober chapter of a real religion."[52]

An investigator in 1906 found that all the peculiarities of the Mormons "center in and are the outgrowth of their strange religious beliefs," beliefs which he can only describe as "grotesque and monstrous," yet which "at the same time have won a following unsurpassed in devotion."[53] If the Mormons could only cure themselves of their bizarre taste for the grotesque and monstrous, and purge their religion "of its gross errors of doctrine," all would be well.[54] "It seems almost beyond belief," one scholar wrote in 1919, "that such a crude farrago of superstition, if not fraud, as Mormonism could be brought forth by the most enlightened age of the world; . . . a terrible canker has attacked the heart of Christianity at home."[55] Mormonism "may hope to survive," writes a typical representative of the new "liberal" school, "only if it is brave enough to jettison its out-of-date creed and face the future boldly, shorn of its absurdities and blasphemies. . . . That the Mormon Church will become the force predicted for it by its leaders, early and present-day, is impossible. That its doctrine could attract intellectual men is an insult to intellect. That it can continue to exist as a religious force is to expect too much."[56]

"We talk much about 'respecting' this or that person's religion," wrote G. K. Chesterton in an essay on the Mormons, "but the way to respect a religion is to treat it as a religion: to ask what are its tenets and what are their consequences."[57] For Chesterton, "the basic Mormon belief is one that comes out of the morning of the earth, from the most primitive and even infantile attitude," namely the idea regarding God, "not that He was materialized once, as all Christians believe, . . . but that He was materially embodied from all time; that He has a local habitation as well as a name."[58] This he calls a "barbaric but violently vivid conception," and bids us view the Mormons as "a number of dull, earnest, ignorant, black-coated men with chimney-pot hats, chin beards or mutton-chop whiskers [who] managed to reproduce in their own souls the richness and the peril of an ancient Oriental experience."[59]

It is a gaudy picture, and a phony one, but it leaves us in no doubt as to how a top-flight intellectual of the 1920s classified the Mormons: the only parallel Chesterton can think of is not that of the ancient Hebrews but of his own weird idea of them.[60] It was at least an improvement on the psychic deductions of Theodore Schroeder, who a few years before had found the whole key to Mormonism in the doctrine of a heaven "whose greatest and only advertised bliss will be intensified animalism, prolonged through eternity."[61]

In all this it would be hard to tell who rates the Mormons lower, the Liberals or the Fundamentalists. The cry of the latter is that "from first to last there is not one teaching peculiar to Mormonism which is not contrary to the Bible and to evangelical Christianity." Its "ghastly ideas" of a God who has a body, the necessity of good works for salvation, and so on, "cannot but be viewed with abhorrence by all true Christians. . . . We ought to care greatly that such evil beliefs are even held by Mormons themselves."[62] There should be a limit to freedom of religion, and Mormonism is it. A very recent "study" deplores the fact that "Mormons are generally considered by many to be 'Fundamentalists,' " since nothing could be greater than the gap between the two: "Mormons deny the Scriptural doctrine of the Trinity and the Deity of the Lord Jesus Christ. . . . Mormonism denies the authority of the Bible. . . . Mormon theology denies the virgin birth of our Lord Jesus Christ."[63] Such conclusions may be absurd, but they make it clear enough that the "Fundamentalists" are as determined as anyone else to have no part of the Mormons.

Anyone familiar enough with the febrile literature from

which we have been quoting to attempt writing his own book on the Mormons should recognize that nothing is more characteristic than the insistence of the critics on every side, that the Mormons are not like any other Christians or like any other people in the Western world. They may be compared with primitive Christians by freethinkers, or with primitive Hebrews or Moslems by people who have only the vaguest homemade conception of what these might have been like, but all are agreed that their presence in our Western civilization is completely and incredibly incongruous.

Critics may be permitted at this late date to try their hand at winning friends and influencing people by telling the Mormons of today that they are just ordinary folk with an ordinary church. But to say that such was also the case in the days of Joseph Smith and Brigham Young is neither honest nor sporting. The genial and forced camaraderie of some of the present-day critics of Mormonism is that of the man who finds it easier to pick your pocket by affectionately locking arms with you than by hitting you over the head. The new humane approach is simply an obvious maneuver to rob the Church of a glorious history and to play down every remarkable circumstance of its origin. When it reaches the point of being told that while the Book of Mormon may seem very strange to *us*, to the *contemporaries* of Joseph Smith it "would scarcely seem fanciful, possibly not even novel," it is high time to protest. For even the most superficial acquaintance with the literature will show that the Book of Mormon was as baffling, scandalizing, and hated a book in the first week of its appearance as it has ever been since. The idea that the Book of Mormon was simply a product of its time may be a necessary fiction to explain it, but it is fiction nonetheless. If they may be trusted in nothing else, the voluminous writings of the anti-Mormons stand as monumental evidence for one fact: that Mormonism and the Book of Mormon

were in no way a product of the society in which they
arose.

Notes

1. Alexander Campbell, "Delusions," *The Millennial Harbinger* 2
(Bethany Virginia, 1831; reprinted, Joplin, Mo.: College Press): 93.
The passage is cited at length by Whitney R. Cross, *The Burned-over
District* (Ithaca: Cornell University Press, 1950), as an authentic ex-
planation of the Book of Mormon.

2. Campbell, "Delusions," 93.

3. Ibid.

4. Campbell "unequivocally and triumphantly sets the question
of the divine authenticity of the 'Book' forever at rest, to every *rational*
mind." Thus, the Painesville *Telegraph*, 1 March 1831, cited by Francis W. Kirkham, *A New Witness for Christ in America*, 2 vols. (Independence, Mo.: Zion's, 1951), 2:96.

5. "The Yankee Mahomet," *American Whig Review* 7 (June 1851):
554.

6. The subject of the affidavits is treated in Hugh Nibley, *The
Myth Makers* (Salt Lake City: Bookcraft, 1961); see also Richard L.
Anderson, "The Reliability of the Early History of Lucy and Joseph
Smith," *Dialogue* 4 (Summer, 1969): 13-28, and "Joseph Smith's New
York Reputation Reappraised," *BYU Studies* 10 (1970): 283-314.

7. D. Griffiths, *Two Years' Residence in the New Settlements of Ohio*
(London: Westley and Davis, 1835), 140-41 (emphasis added).

8. The works of Linn, Arbaugh, Brodie, Morgan, Davis, to name
only a few, all promise to produce the true story of the Book of
Mormon—at last! In such pathetic hopefulness the Rev. James E.
Mahaffey published his *Found at Last! 'Positive Proof' that Mormonism
Is a Fraud and the Book of Mormon a Fable* (Augusta, Georgia: Chronicle
Job Office, 1902).

9. Thomas F. O'Dea, *The Mormons* (Chicago: University of Chicago Press, 1957), 24.

10. Ibid., 27.

11. Ibid., 13. O'Dea is speaking of the foundation of Mormonism
generally, which includes Joseph's claim to revelation.

12. Cross, *The Burned-over District*, 143.

13. Ibid., 81.

14. Palmyra *Reflector* (Palmyra, New York), 1 June 1830, in Francis
W. Kirkham, *A New Witness for Christ in America*, 2:50.

15. "Mormonism!" *Missouri Intelligencer and Boon's [sic] Lick Ad-*

vertiser (10 August 1833), col. 3. Also reported in the *Jeffersonian Republican* (Missouri, 17 August 1833).

16. "The Mormons," *Missouri Intelligencer and Boon's Lick Advertiser* (21 June 1834), col. 2.

17. Letter from Governor Daniel Dunklin, 6 June 1834, printed in *Missouri Intelligencer and Boon's Lick Advertiser* (5 July 1834), col. 4 (emphasis added).

18. "The Mormons," *Missouri Intelligencer and Boon's Lick Advertiser* (28 June 1834), col. 1.

19. A. H. M., "Ancient and Modern Mormonism," *Western Examiner*, ed. John Bobb (10 December 1835).

20. Letter to the editor, written from Jefferson City, *Missouri Argus* (20 December 1838), col. 3.

21. Josiah D. Canning, "The Review," in *Poems* (Greenfield, Mass.: Phelps and Ingersoll, 1838), 107-8. The poem is dedicated to Daniel Webster.

22. Josiah Quincy, *Figures of the Past* (Boston: Roberts, 1883), 389.

23. Daniel P. Kidder, *Mormonism and the Mormons* (New York: Carlton and Porter, 1842), 337.

24. J. Sterling Morton, *Illustrated History of Nebraska*, 3 vols. (Lincoln: Jacob North, 1907), 2:125, speaking of the 1840s. This is clearly illustrated in Francis Parkman's *Oregon Trail* (New York: Modern Library, 1949).

25. Editorial, "Mormonism; or, New Mohammedanism in England and America," *Dublin University Magazine* (March 1843): 283.

26. Rev. P. Alcock, *Latter-day Saints, A Letter to His Nephew, E. H. Webb, Elder in the Church of the Latter-day Saints* (Bristol: William Taylor, 39 Temple Street, 1842), 3.

27. Editorial, "What Is Mormonism?" *Sharpe's London Magazine* 5 (1850): 55.

28. Charles Dickens, "In the Name of the Prophet—Smith!" *Household Words* (19 July 1851): 385.

29. Samuel H. Cox, *Interviews: Memorable and Useful* (New York: Harper, 1853), 293.

30. William J. Conybeare, *Edinburgh Review* (London: Longman, Brown, 1854), 169-70; reprinted in the Traveller's Library (London: Jonathan Cape, 1854).

31. Editorial, *National Magazine* 4, no. 6 (June 1854): 481-82.

32. Editorial, "Shall Utah Be Admitted Into the Union?" *Putnam's Monthly* 5, no. 37 (March 1855): 225-36, esp. 226 and 236.

33. Henry L. Dawes, "The Admission of Utah," *Forum* (January 1888): 483; the comparison with savages and anarchists is on 482.

168 THE PROPHETIC BOOK OF MORMON

34. John Reynolds, *My Own Times* (Bellevue, Ill.: Perryman and Davison, 1855), 562-63.

35. [The source of this quotation has not been found—ed.] See also Jesse T. Peck, *The History of the Great Republic* (New York: Broughton and Wyman, 1868), 499-504.

36. H. Caswall, quoted in William S. Parrott, *The Veil Uplifted; or the Religious Conspirators of the Latter-Day Exposed* (Bristol: Taylor, 1865), 19.

37. Ibid., 33.

38. Ibid., 39, quoting Rev. O. C. Duke of Omaha.

39. Charles H. Brigham, "The Mormon Problem," *Old and New* (May 1870): 638.

40. Ibid., 628.

41. Editorial, "The Mormon Theocracy," *Scribner's* (July 1877): 391-92 (emphasis added).

42. Thomas deWitt Talmage, *The Brooklyn Tabernacle, A Collection of 104 Sermons* (New York: Funk and Wagnalls, 1884), 55-56. In an earlier sermon, pp. 36-37, Talmage labors to implicate the Mormons in the assassination of President Garfield.

43. F. A. Noble, *The Mormon Iniquity* (Chicago: Jameson and Morse, 1884), 3.

44. Robert W. Beers, *The Mormon Puzzle and How to Solve It* (New York: Funk and Wagnalls, 1887), 17, reluctantly adding: "But thus far it has successfully withstood even the fiercest opposition."

45. J. P. Newman, "The Mormon Question," in S. Fallows, *Hot Shot Fired at Fashion's Follies and Society's Abominations* (Chicago: Standard, 1890), 99-101.

46. Ibid., 108.

47. It was drawn up "by order of the Presbytery of Utah, April 8, 1897. Endorsed by the Congregational Association of Utah, October 14, 1897. Endorsed by the Baptist Association of Utah, September 7, 1898." *Ten Reasons Why Christians Cannot Fellowship the Mormon Church* (New York: League for Social Service, 1898), 12.

48. Ibid., 1 (emphasis added).

49. These objections are found in ibid., 2-6.

50. Ibid., 12. The expression "God-Man" would shock a Moslem or Jew quite as much as any Mormon teaching about God shocked these liberal Protestants!

51. Samuel Laing, *Modern Science and Modern Thought* (London: Chapman and Hall, 1898), 231.

52. Edgar E. Volk, *The Mormon Monster* (Chicago: Revell, 1900), 17, quoting George H. Combs, *Some Latter Day Religions* (Chicago: Revell, 1900). This is the "standard" Baptist work on Mormonism.

53. G. A. Irving, "The Ways of Mormons," *Outlook* (December 29, 1906): 1064.

54. Ibid., 1068.

55. George Seibel, *The Mormon Saints* (Pittsburgh: Lessing, 1919), 7-8, protesting that in this study "nought is set down in malice," 9.

56. Stuart Martin, *The Mystery of Mormonism* (New York: Dutton, 1920), 307-8.

57. G. K. Chesterton, *The Uses of Diversity* (New York: Dodd, Mead, 1921), 184.

58. Ibid., 185.

59. Ibid., 186.

60. Ibid., 189; "In other words, this strange sect, by soaking itself solely in the Hebrew Scriptures, had really managed to reproduce the atmosphere of those Scriptures as they are felt by Hebrews rather than by Christians." How does Chesterton know how an "atmosphere" feels to another person?

61. Theodore Schroeder, "The Sex-Determinant in Mormon Theology," *Alienist and Neurologist* (May 1908): 219.

62. John D. Nutting, *Why Care about Mormonism?* (tract) (Cleveland: Utah Gospel Mission, 1926), 1-2.

63. Walter R. Martin, *The Rise of the Cults* (Grand Rapids: Zondervan, 1955), 51-53.

6

The Grab Bag

How does the Book of Mormon critic of today go about his work? His point of departure is an article of faith: "Painstaking research can uncover the sources of all [Joseph Smith's] ideas."[1] Actually this statement of Mrs. Brodie's is nonsense, since no research can ever uncover the indisputable source of any man's ideas, let alone those of a man whose world, with all the myriad sights and sounds that *might* conceivably have given him those ideas, has passed away over a century ago. Armed with this naive credo and a determination to "uncover" something, the critic looks about him for something in the Book of Mormon, and as soon as he has found it announces to the world that he has at last discovered the indubitable source of the Book of Mormon.

Silly as it sounds, this is exactly how the critics operate.[2] They begin by declaring the book a typical product of its times; but if it is typical, it must be of a type—there must be other books like it. Where were they? Search as they would, the scholars could find nothing closer to the Book of Mormon than, of all things, the Koran, a writing about as far from Smith's time, place, and culture as it is possible to get.[3] The most casual reading will show, moreover, that it would be hard to name two writings less alike than those two. Many Moslems, for example, have rejected the pop-

This article first appeared in the Improvement Era (July 1959). The article was part of a series of five articles, published in nine parts under the title " 'Mixed Voices': A Study on Book of Mormon Criticism."

ular nineteenth *sura* (chapter) of the Koran because it contains in the story of Joseph and his brethren an episode of
human history: "It is entirely worldly history [they protest];
and it is unthinkable that this physical history should ever
be part of the holy Book revealed by God."[4] The reader
can soon convince himself that the Koran really is remarkably innocent of "physical history," while the Book
of Mormon purports to contain whole books of it. That
alone should indicate how much the two books have in
common.

But while some saw in Smith "another *Mohammed* preparing another *Koran*,"[5] others found in his work typical
"*Swedenborgian* illusions,"[6] a writer in Hastings *Encyclopedia*
even discovering in the Book of Mormon "references to
Swedenborgianism with its three heavens." The fact that
there is no such doctrine mentioned in the book does not
deter this investigator, who finds in the same source traces
of "the 'Washingtonian' movement for total abstinence."[7]
Though religious men in every age have abstained from
strong drink, yet the Mormons can only have got the Word
of Wisdom (*not* mentioned in the Book of Mormon!) from
the Washingtonians, because they happened to be active
at the time. These two instances illustrate how the critics
operate.

"The theological ideas of the Book of Mormon," according to J. H. Snowden, "are also easily traced to their
sources; . . . the [Nephites] were *Old School Presbyterians*."[8]
Since that is such an easy and obvious conclusion, it is
strange that Mr. John Hyde in a very thorough attack on
the Book of Mormon comes to the opposite conclusion,
that in the book "Calvinism repels him [Smith], and he
opposes it," while actually "Universalism affects his sym-
pathies."[9] Yet E. D. Howe insists that Universalism is not
the hero but the villain of the book,[10] which shows strong
influence of the seventeenth century *French Mystics*.[11] According to the same authority, in the Book of Mormon "the

Arian doctrine is denied";[12] yet the Rev. H. Mattison insists
that "the Mormons are strong advocates of Arianism."[13]
Others find that " 'free grace' abounds in the Book of Mormon" and can flatly declare: "The Mormons are Wesley-
ans."[14] But Charles Francis Adams, who visited Joseph
Smith in 1844, just as flatly declares, "His theological
system is very nearly Christian *Unitarianism*."[15] Today,
however, Mr. Davis tells us that "it opposed deism, evan-
gelism, and the Arminianism of Methodists and Unitarians."[16] Mr. Beers and others see in the Book of Mormon
a rehash of *Millerism*, ignoring the fact that
"Miller . . . began his lectures in 1831," after the book was
well on its way.[17] Dr. Biederwolf insists that the new
Church was nothing but a *Baptist* community,[18] while the
Baptists themselves insist that the Mormons were *Campbellites*, though Campbell for his part classed them with
the first *Quakers*.[19] At the other extreme scholars not only
charge Smith with toying with *Catholicism*,[20] but even insist
that "the Church of the Latter-Day Saints . . . is in connection with the Church of Rome, and is even daughter
to that great scarlet whore of Babylon."[21] With equal confidence others accuse the Book of Mormon of being an anti-
Catholic book.[22] "The doctrine of the book is wholeheartedly and completely *Arminian*,"[23] according to Dr.
O'Dea, while Davis counters by describing Mormonism as
the antithesis of Arminianism, especially in its rejection of
"the omnipresent, inscrutable, 'Buddhistic' God of modern
Arminian religions."[24] A German encyclopedia, the *Grosse
Brockhaus*, sees predominant *Gnostic* elements in both Mormonism and the Book of Mormon,[25] while a learned journal
of fifty years ago found their doctrine "formed on *Buddhistic*
principles."[26] The astute Gunnison thought Mormonism
was strongly influenced by the teachings of the *Transcen-
dentalists* and that Joseph Smith "and his followers have
fallen in with the spiritual philosophy of the day, and
added the doctrine of affinities of minds and the sympathy

of souls."[27] Others argued that the Book of Mormon "must have been written by an *atheist*," as a sort of practical joke, the work of "a fearless infidel" undertaken as "a ridicule upon the Holy Bible."[28] With the charges of atheism went those of "*Deism, Owenism, Socialism.*"[29] Chesterton sees the Mormon Church "soaking itself solely in the Hebrew Scriptures."[30]

"Mormonism borrowed most of its ideas from the 'Campbellite,' or *Disciples of Christ Church,*" according to the new Arbaugh, who proceeds to describe the basic Campbellite doctrines in a way that makes it clear that nothing could be less like Mormonism.[31] Certainly none was better qualified to speak for Campbellism than the elder Campbell, who in denouncing "the infernal Book of Mormon" stated as the basic proposition of his own faith "the all-sufficiency and alone-sufficiency of the . . . Bible," which makes the Book of Mormon the embodied antithesis of Campbellism.[32] The Campbellites accused the Baptists of trying to fob off Mormonism on them and the latter returned the charge.[33] This is an amusing game of hot potato that the sects played among themselves, tossing the Book of Mormon at each other as a deadly missile. It is still going on, for in 1956 a Jesuit writer described Mormonism as "derived from the Reformation principle of religious freedom carried to the extreme."[34] Mr. Davis, on the contrary, informs us that the Mormons were actually "opposed to individualism of any kind."[35] And while one school of thought sees in the new religion "a reaction against stern New England Calvinism," the same Mr. Davis assures us that the very opposite was the case: it was rather a reaction against the "rising tide of liberalism and individualism."[36]

This business of capitalizing on chance resemblances of detail to explain the Book of Mormon reaches the consummation of absurdity in the recent revival of the theory that the book was simply a steal from the writings of a

thirteenth-century monk, the Abbot Joachim of Flora, because Joachim uses the expression "the everlasting Gospel" which is found in the Bible but *not* in the Book of
Mormon![37] It seems that the Book of Mormon incorporates
"many of the almost forgotten tales of the monk Cyril and
the Abbot Joachim,"[38] though Smith could only have found
out about them from Mosheim, whose work did not appear
in English until 1839, who quotes none of the "forgotten
tales" in his unflattering paragraph on Joachim, who never
mentions Cyril.[39]

One expert confidently assures us that it was the great
French satirist Rabelais who inspired the Book of Mormon,
for in his *Gargantua* Rabelais tells of "a man digging in the
earth, and suddenly alighting upon a brazen tomb, in
which were deposited nine gold flagons, upon which were
engraved innumerable Egyptian hieroglyphics, and with
them a large pair of golden spectacles, by the employ of
which the said man was enabled to decipher the said mysterious characters. With this fancy of the Frenchman Smith
had become acquainted; and being full of craft and cunning, at once appropriated it to his deceptive purposes,
and out of it concocted the story of his golden bible and
spectacles."[40]

Others have pointed to suspicious doctrinal parallels
between the Book of Mormon and the writings of St. Anselm — though they are unwilling to read the one and unable to read the other. Even so, these scholars have missed
the really striking resemblance between Joseph Smith and
Anselm, for the latter "as a simple, innocent boy" firmly
believed and "publicly asserted before others" that he had
climbed the mountains near his home one day and seen
God face to face.[41] Isn't that Joseph Smith all over?

If you want parallels we can give you dozens of them.
In the book *An Approach to the Book of Mormon*, we quoted
a long passage from Solon of Athens that might have come
right out of the Book of Mormon — why not take that as

proof positive that the book is simply a steal from the Greeks? The evidence is just as good as any other.[42] The old cycle, prosperity, pride, sin, and destruction, is found again and again in Greek and other literature, ancient and modern; there is no need for Dr. O'Dea to brand it Arminianism when it occurs in the Book of Mormon—it would be just as accurate to label it by any of a dozen other names.

The Book of Mormon critics have made an art of explaining a very big whole by a very small part. The game is to look for some mysterious person or document from which Joseph Smith might have got the few simple and obvious ideas and then cry triumphantly, "At last we have it! Now we know where the Book of Mormon came from!"

"If someone will only show me how to draw a circle," cries the youthful Joseph Smith, "I will make you a fine Swiss watch!" So Joachim or Anslem or Ethan Smith or Rabelais or somebody takes a stick and draws a circle in the sand, and forthwith the adroit and wily Joseph turns out a beautifully running mechanism that tells perfect time!

This is not an exaggeration. The Book of Mormon in structure and design is every bit as complicated, involved, and ingenious as the works of a Swiss watch, and withal just as smoothly running. With no model to follow and no instruction of any kind (Where was the model? Who could instruct?), the writer of that book brought together thousands of ideas and events and knit them together in a most marvelous unity. Yet the critics like to think they have explained the Book of Mormon completely if they can just discover where Joseph Smith *might* have got *one* of his ideas or expressions!

It does not relieve the absurdity of the situation very much to point to more than one possible source for the Book of Mormon. "The ecclesiastical student will not fail to remark that Mormonism is an eclectic religious philosophy, drawn from *Brahmin mysticism* in the dependence of

God, the *Platonic* and *Gnostic* notion of Eons, . . .
Mohammedan sensualism, and the fanaticism of the sects
of the *early church;* and there is the good and evil of Ah-
rimaism, with the convenient idea of the transmigration
of souls, from the *Persian.*"[43] It is all as easy as that—the
student "will not fail to remark" these parallels. Why a
feeling of dependence on God must come from the Brah-
mins instead of Schleiermacher, or what resemblance there
is between Gnostic aeons and Mormon dispensations, or
why anthropomorphism is identical with sensualism, or
when and where any Mormon has ever preached transmigration of souls, our authority does not explain. An
eminent encyclopedia of religion can tell us that in the
Book of Mormon "Calvinism, Universalism, Methodism,
chiliasm, Catholicism, deism, and freemasonry are discussed, . . . not by name," of course, but "in a manner
that strikingly corresponds to Smith's relations to these
systems,"[44] thereby proving the Book of Mormon a fraud.
But just where will one find out exactly what Smith's
"relations to these systems" were, in order to make the
"striking" comparison? Why, in the Book of Mormon, naturally, since there is no other source!

The Schaff-Herzog Encyclopedia informs us that in the
Book of Mormon "there are passages also which betray a
dependence upon other books, such as the Westminster
Confession of Faith and the Methodist *Discipline.*"[45] Since
the passages in question are quite short, one wonders why
our authority does not produce them; the reason for the
omission is quite plain: the passages actually "betray a
dependence" no greater than any two texts chosen at random on the same subject would betray.[46] Yet another religious encyclopedia, taking up where the Schaff-Herzog
leaves off, informs an unsuspecting world that "the speech
of Nephi [which speech?] contains *quotations* from the
Westminster Confession of Faith."[47] With such a fine start,
a contemporary treatise takes up the cry: "Nephi, who

purports to be a pre-Christian prophet, uses *verbatim quotations* from the seventeenth-century Westminster *Confession of Faith.*"[48]

Finally, Father Rumble assures us that "Mormon managed . . . to engrave on his golden plates *quotations word for word* from the Westminster Confessions."[49] What started out as passages that "betray a dependence" of one text on another—a purely subjective judgment—finally emerge after passing from hand to hand, with no checking of original sources, as nothing less than word-for-word quotations. This is a highly characteristic procedure in Book of Mormon criticism, converting cautious speculation to damning certitude by the simple process of whispering from ear to ear.

To prove that Campbellite teaching "pervades the Mormon Bible," one critic has only to point out that to both "great emphasis on the efficacy of baptism . . . [and] expectation of the coming and millennial reign of Christ, are unequivocally reproduced."[50] Of course these things have been basic in Jewish and Christian eschatology from the beginning—but Joseph Smith could only have got them from the Campbellites, because this particular writer wants it that way. One seminarist has sought to demonstrate that "in its theological positions and coloring the Book of Mormon is a volume of Disciple theology." Only to support his thesis he must argue that the book underwent "two several [sic] redactions" which cleverly conceal the fact.[51] Mormons have no right to resent such tricks, however, since the Bible is treated with the same perfect liberty by the same critics: "Every scholar goes his own way, and according to his private predilection chooses what is genuine and what is secondary in the book."[52] "Private predilection" is the key to the grab-bag method.

Notes

1. See Fawn M. Brodie, *No Man Knows My History* (New York: Knopf, 1946), 67.

2. The method is discussed by Solomon Zeitlin, "The Hebrew Scrolls and the Status of Biblical Scholarship," *Jewish Quarterly Review* 42 (1952): 150-52, 189-90, who notes generally that one can always find for one's purpose ideas parallel with those in ancient writings, or modern.

3. "The parallel between Joseph Smith and Mohammed was frequently noted even by contemporaries of the Mormon prophet," writes Eduard Meyer, *Ursprung und Geschichte der Mormonen* (Halle: Niemeyer, 1912), 67. A recent reflection on this is worth quoting: it is George B. Arbaugh's remark, in *Gods, Sex and Saints: The Mormon Story* (Rock Island, Ill.: Augustana, 1957), 10, that Mormonism "in fundamental respects is more alien to Christianity than is Islam," i.e., modern Christianity is closer to Islam than Mormonism is. How true!

4. Ignaz Goldziher, *Vorlesungen über den Islam* (Heidelberg: Winter, 1925), 194.

5. T. W. Young, *Mormonism: Its Origin, Doctrines and Dangers* (Ann Arbor: George Wahr, 1900), 7-8.

6. Charles W. Ferguson, *The Confusion of Tongues, A Review of Modern Isms* (Garden City, New York: Doubleday, 1929), 369.

7. James Hastings, ed., *Encyclopedia of Religion and Ethics*, 13 vols. (New York: Scribner's, 1951), 11:85.

8. James H. Snowden, *The Truth about Mormonism* (New York: Doran, 1926), 112-13. Snowden quotes I. W. Riley concerning "Old School Presbyterians."

9. John Hyde, *Mormonism, Its Leaders and Designs* (New York: Fetridge, 1857), 281.

10. E. D. Howe, *History of Mormonism* (Painesville: Printed by the Author, 1840), 70.

11. E. D. Howe, *Painesville Telegraph* (15 February 1831), in Francis W. Kirkham, *A New Witness for Christ in America*, 2 vols. (Independence, Mo.: Zion's, 1951), 2:57-58.

12. Howe, *History of Mormonism*, 40.

13. Hiram Mattison, *A Scriptural Defence of the Doctrine of the Trinity, or a Check to Modern Arianism*, 4th ed. (New York: Colby, 1850), v.

14. Hyde, *Mormonism, Its Leaders and Designs*, 281. Editor of *Galaxy Magazine* 2 (New York, 1866): 356. The *Encyclopedia Illustrada* in its article on Mormons, p. 1126, describes the Book of Mormon as a mixture of the Spaulding manuscripts "and Joseph Smith's fanatical Wesleyan ideas."

15. Henry Adams, "Charles Francis Adams Visits the Mormons in 1844," *Proceedings of the Massachussetts Historical Society* 68 (October

1944–May 1947; reprinted Boston, 1952), 286. Quotation is found on p. 22 of reprint.

16. David B. Davis, "The New England Origins of Mormonism," *New England Quarterly* 26 (1953): 158.

17. Robert W. Beers, *The Mormon Puzzle and How to Solve It* (New York: Funk and Wagnalls, 1887), 34: "Millerism in particular was attracting great attention at that time, and so they incorporated into the 'Book of Mormon' its leading tenets." The remark as to the date of Miller's teaching, which began when "the Mormon church was only a year old," is from John D. Kingsbury, *Mormonism* (New York: Congregational Home Missionary Society, n.d.), 7.

18. William E. Biederwolf, *Mormonism under the Searchlight* (Grand Rapids: Eerdmans, 1956), 3: "The first 2,000 converts came, nearly every one of them, out of the Baptist churches of western Pennsylvania and eastern Ohio." This is strictly untrue. The article in *Galaxy Magazine* 2:356 calls the Mormons "Wesleyan Baptists."

19. Thomas Campbell, quoted in *Painesville Telegraph* (15 February 1831); Kirkham, *A New Witness for Christ in America*, 2:93.

20. Jules Remy, *A Journey to Great Salt Lake City*, 2 vols. (London: Jeffs, 1861), 1:231-32.

21. J. Theobald, *Mormonism Harpooned* (London: Horsell, 1855), 24.

22. Thus Brodie, *No Man Knows My History*, 59-60.

23. Thomas F. O'Dea, *The Mormons* (Chicago: University of Chicago Press, 1957), 28.

24. Davis, "The New England Origins of Mormonism," 155.

25. *Der Grosse Brockhaus*, 14 vols. (Wiesbaden: Brockhaus, 1952-63), s.v. "Mormonen."

26. Editor in *Knowledge, A Weekly Magazine* (New York), 1, no. 9 (2 August 1890): 186.

27. John W. Gunnison, *The Mormons or Latter-day Saints* (Philadelphia: Lippincot, 1856), 61.

28. Howe, *History of Mormonism*, 54, 19 (emphasis added); this is actually a quotation from David Marks. Cf. J. B. Turner, *Mormonism in All Ages* (New York: Platt and Peters, 1842), 8: "Atheism and Romanism [are] its natural allies."

29. John Theobald, *The Overthrow of Infidel Mormonism* (London: Horsell, 1850), 18. The charge was a common one.

30. G. K. Chesteron, *The Uses of Diversity* (New York: Dodd, Mead, 1921), 189.

31. Arbaugh, *Gods, Sex, and Saints*, 9-10 (emphasis added).

32. See Kirkham, *A New Witness for Christ in America*, 2:89, 92,

quoting the *Painesville Telegraph* (15 February 1831). A Campbellite preacher refused to occupy a pulpit in which a Mormon had been invited to speak, protesting that "the man proclaimed *another gospel* written in another book." Ibid., 2:113. Campbellites do not believe there ever was a great apostasy, that the Holy Ghost was ever had among any but the original apostles, that rebaptism is necessary, that a definite organization is required for the church, etc., to name only a few of the fundamental differences listed by Campbell, *Painesville Telegraph* (15 February 1831).

33. David I. Burnett, a Campbellite leader, discusses this (7 April 1831), in Kirkham, *A New Witness for Christ in America*, 2:113.

34. John A. Hardon, *The Protestant Churches of America* (Westminster, Md.: Newman, 1956), 179.

35. Davis, "The New England Origins of Mormonism," 163.

36. Ibid., 148, 154.

37. Daniel H. C. Bartlett, *The Mormons or, Latter-Day Saints, Whence Came They?* (Liverpool: Thompson, 1911), 9.

38. A. M. Redwood, "Mormonism," in William C. Irvine, ed., *Heresies Exposed*, 28th printing (New York: Loizeaux, 1955), 129.

39. Redwood suggests, "Mormonism," 128, 130, that Rigdon's copy (hypothetical) of Mosheim was used. John Mosheim, in his *Ecclesiastical History*, (1839), 2:312-14; (1842), 1:356, describes the teaching of Joachim as Franciscan mysticism, maintaining that after two imperfect ages "the true and eternal Gospel" was finally taught by St. Francis, who was the angel mentioned in Revelation 14:6, and "that the Gospel of Christ would be abrogated in the year 1260," etc. And this is supposed to be the source of the Book of Mormon!

40. William S. Parrott, *The Veil Uplifted; or the Religious Conspirators of the Latter-Day Exposed* (Bristol: Taylor, 1865), 13.

41. Eadmer, *Vita Anselmi*, 2, in *PL* 158:50-51. The scholars in question refer to the doctrine of atonement in Anselm's *Cur Deus homo?*, oblivious of its remarkably feudalistic and chivalric quality.

42. Hugh Nibley, *An Approach to the Book of Mormon* (Salt Lake City: Deseret, 1957), 42; reprinted in *CWHN* 6:50-51.

43. Gunnison, *The Mormons or Latter-Day Saints*, 61.

44. *Schaff-Herzog Encylopedia of Religious Knowledge*, 15 vols. (Grand Rapids: Baker, 1950), 8:13.

45. Ibid., 8:12.

46. The passage in the *Confession of Faith*, ch. 32-33, reads: "After death the souls of the wicked are cast into hell, where they remain in torments, reserved to the judgment of the great day. In which day all persons shall appear before the tribunal of Christ, to give

an account of their thoughts, words and deeds, and to receive according to that which they have done in the body, whether good or evil. The end of God's appointing this day is for the manifestation of His justice. For then shall the righteous go into everlasting life, but the wicked shall be cast into eternal torments." Quoted in I. Woodbridge Riley, *Founder of Mormonism* (New York: Dodd, Mead, 1902), 132-33. It would be hard to find a more thoroughly standardized statement of biblical teachings regarding the last judgment. The official Catholic teaching is the same, Bernhard Bartmann, *Manuale de Teologia Dogmatica* 3 (Alba: Edizioni Paoline, 1949): 430-33. Indeed, this is one of the few Christian doctrines on which nearly all churches, as well as the Jewish doctors, agree, and it could hardly be otherwise, since it is all set forth so clearly in the scriptures. The last judgment is a favorite theme of churchmen, ancient, medieval, and modern, who never tire of repeating over and over again almost word for word the story quoted above. "If the speech of Nephi, to his brethren, be compared with the Westminster Standards," writes Riley, *Founder of Mormonism*, 132, "a close parallelism will be disclosed." But no closer than with a hundred other sources.

47. Hastings, *Encyclopedia of Religion and Ethics*, 11:86.

48. Horton Davies, *Christian Deviations* (London: SCM, 1954), 80 (emphasis added).

49. L. Rumble, *Mormons or Latter-Day Saints* (tract) (St. Paul, 1950), reprinted in Kirkham, *A New Witness for Christ in America*, 2:304 (emphasis added).

50. Henry C. Sheldon, *A Fourfold Test of Mormonism* (New York: Abingdon, 1914), 43-44. Cf. Daniel P. Kidder, *Mormonism and the Mormons* (New York: Carlton and Porter, 1842), 337; Hyde, *Mormonism, Its Leaders and Designs*, 281.

51. William H. Whitsitt, *Concise Dictionary of Religious Knowledge*, ed. Samuel M. Jackson (New York: Christian Literature, 1891), 616.

52. William A. Irwin, "Ezekiel Research Since 1943," *Vetus Testamentum* 3 (1953): 61, speaking of research on Ezekiel.

7

What Frontier,
What Camp Meeting?

Nearly all present-day critics insist on an atmosphere of extreme religious hysteria, "a time of strange, wild religious excitement," as essential to the production of the Book of Mormon.[1] The heat and passion of the backwoods revival meeting provide the fiery crucible in which the book was forged.[2] The frontier and the camp meeting between them set the stage for the Book of Mormon.

"In spite of its respectable distant New England background," a recent and typical study reports, "Mormonism was unquestionably a product of the frontier, the strangest, most ambiguous, adventurous, and colorful of all the movements emanating from that turbulent region."[3] The latest investigators, however, have been seriously questioning this proposition. Mrs. Brodie has an easy time showing that western New York in Joseph Smith's time was not primitive frontier at all, but thoroughly settled and civilized. Yet after all that she remains true to the party line: the matter of the Book of Mormon "is drawn directly from the American frontier."[4] But others have now taken the magic out of that magic word and demythologized the myth of the frontier.

"Mormonism has usually been described as a frontier

This article first appeared in the Improvement Era (August 1959). The article was part of a series of five articles, published in nine parts under the title " 'Mixed Voices': A Study on Book of Mormon Criticism."

religion," writes Cross, and hastens to correct the error: "The church did not rise during the pioneering era of western New York. Its early recruits came from many sects, but invariably from the longest settled neighborhoods of the region. Joseph's peregrinations [in the early days] . . . were always eastward, not westward. . . . The Church of the Saints was not a frontier phenomenon in origin."[5] Even if you call Western New York the frontier, "its impact upon the region and period from which it sprang was extremely limited," Mormonism receiving its greatest strength from abroad.[6] Mr. Davis confirms this verdict: "But Upstate New York in the 1820's," he writes, "was not a frontier. . . . Actually, the frontier was the place where Mormonism was nearly extinguished, while the final settlement came a thousand miles beyond the frontier."[7] The theory that Mormonism was a product of the frontier will not stand up to any examination.

Equally groundless is the common claim that the element of supernatural intervention in the Book of Mormon was a response to the stimulus of the camp meeting. "There are no detailed descriptions of the revivals in Palmyra and Manchester between 1822 and 1827, when they were at their wildest," writes Mrs. Brodie.[8] If she had really wanted to find out what the revivals were like at the time and place indicated, Mrs. Brodie could have had a quite adequate description from the autobiography of Nancy Towle, the traveling revivalist who operated in upper New York State between the years 1818 and 1831. From her we learn that the pathological camp meetings that Smith is supposed to have attended are a myth of the critics.[9] The preaching routine of the time was standardized and stereotyped: if Smith ever got his religion "from the mouth of the wilderness preacher," it is passing strange that his own sermons and writings do not remotely resemble theirs. Particularly repugnant to Miss Towle and her fellow evangelists is Smith's claim that "the gift has returned back again, as in former times, to illiterate fishermen." To which Miss Towle's reaction was: "Are you not ashamed, of such pretentions? You who are no more ashamed, than any ignorant, ploughboy of our land! Oh! blush, at such abominations!"[10] So far were the revivalists from admitting any kind of inspiration. The idea of supernatural manifestations, which Joseph Smith is also supposed to have picked up from the revivals, was completely foreign to them. When she speaks of healing, Miss Nancy makes it perfectly clear that she means only the healing of the soul; when she rushes to the side of the sick and the dying, it is to exhort them to prepare to meet Jesus; when she speaks of death it is with genuine terror and despair.[11] She is constantly on guard against accepting for a moment as supernatural any of the many experiences and manifestations that she so often meets with in the course of her neurotic career.[12] The revivalists had a definite technique and enthusiasm of their own, but it was of a totally different nature from that found among the Mormons, concerning which one observer noted ninety years ago: "This enthusiasm is different in style and expression from the religious enthusiasm of many of the Christian sects. The excesses of revivals are not favored by the leaders for this practical Church. There is no frenzy in their prayers, and the worship in their Tabernacle is as decent as that of a Puritan Church. But under this quiet exterior, there is a spirit of fanatical devotion, deep and earnest."[13]

Could one ask for plainer evidence that the Mormon tradition is not that of the camp meeting and the frontier? From Miss Towle we learn that the revival meetings of Joseph Smith's day were not held in fields, woods, and tents, but in regular churches and in good order.[14] It was only in the British Isles that Miss Towle herself preached in the open air: her message there was the same as in America, and met with the same response — there was nothing "frontier" about it.[15]

Miss Towle has a good deal to say about the bitter rivalries among the ministers ("rotten-hearted professors. . . . Oh! these men-appointed leaders, how despicable they often, to me, appear!"), and so makes it clear that Joseph Smith was not exaggerating (as is often claimed) when he told of how meanly they treated him.[16] From Nancy Towle we can learn what the atmosphere of the revivals really was: Religious feeling ran high; rivalry was intense and sometimes bitter;[17] but the wild, orgiastic rites of the camp meeting, of which we have heard so much, were totally foreign to her experience and to the world of the youthful Joseph Smith. Only twice in all her long experience did Miss Towle see anyone faint at a meeting—once in Cumberland and once in Nova Scotia—and the sight surprised and disturbed her: such a thing, she says, never happens in the New England revivals.[18]

As early as 1843 the *Methodist Quarterly Review* severely criticized an English writer for describing Mormonism as a frontier religion. The Mormon converts, the reviewer pointed out, came not from the frontier or even from America, but from that very "sound, enlightened, Protestant England" that the British writer boasts about![19] As to the Book of Mormon resembling American preaching, at revivals or anywhere else, nothing could be more absurd to the American reviewer: "Now we fear that the reviewer [in England] knows just as little about what is said 'at meeting' as he does about the contents of the Book of Mormon, and this is almost nothing at all."[20]

Dr. O'Dea Bloweth Where He Listeth

Dr. O'Dea should have considered some of these things before propounding his favorite thesis on the Book of Mormon: "The book is obviously an American work." How, "obviously"? Well, "American sentiments permeate the work." For example? "Taxation is oppressive, and lawyers are not to be trusted."[21] In what nations is that not true?

Has Dr. O'Dea never heard of Molière or Aristophanes or Rabelais? Again the "obligation of the clergymen to work" in Alma's church is right out of New England: but why not right out of Cluny, or the Qumran Community, or the *Didache?* Alma's going "from one body to another, preaching unto the people repentance and faith on the Lord" (Mosiah 25:15) is for O'Dea "a scene strongly reminiscent of the camp meeting," though he admits elsewhere that camp meetings belong to the *post* Book of Mormon period.[22] But Dr. O'Dea's job as a critic is not simply to report what Book of Mormon scenes and incidents suggest to his mind, but to prove, when he suggests a source, that the matter concerned *could not possibly have come* from any other source. After all, the man who by some mysterious process can borrow the ideas of thirteenth-century monks, Brahmin sages, French satirists, and Washingtonian reformers may at any given moment be stealing from *any* conceivable source, so that no critic can ever be sure of his ground. But Dr. O'Dea is: he finds that in the Book of Mormon "the closeness to violence was thoroughly American."[23] But what could be more thoroughly Italian or Greek or Irish or Roman or Arabic or Hebrew, and so on, than "closeness to violence"? Nancy Towle actually left England to get away from a "closeness to violence," in comparison of which America was a haven of calm.[24]

In his too-ready analysis Dr. O'Dea goes far enough to contradict himself soundly, for though the Book of Mormon according to him draws its "fundamental theme" from Calvinism and revivalism, it does so "without either the stress on human depravity of the former or the excessive emotionalism of the latter."[25] That is to say, what we find in the book is Calvinism and revivalism—but with their essential elements left out: "In contrast to the extremes of religious enthusiasm that were soon to follow upon the revivals . . . later in the decade, the intellectuality of the Book of Mormon and its appeal as a reasonable answer to

the problems of existence and salvation are quite obvious."[26] So what the Book of Mormon offers is not a resemblance but a "quite obvious" *contrast* to the ways and
teachings of those religious enthusiasts who are supposed
to have inspired it! O'Dea even labors the indiscretion: "In
fact, in catching and committing to print the hopes and
exaltations of the revival meeting and in doing so without
the distractions and emotional excesses, . . . the Book of
Mormon was admirably suited to become . . . the scriptures of an American Church."[27] Passing by the fact that
the book was never meant to become *the* scriptures of any
church, and that the great appeal of Mormonism and the
Book of Mormon has in the past not been to Americans
but to people of other lands, we must hasten to point out
that "emotional excesses" are no extraneous fixture of the
revival meeting but the very substance of those "hopes
and exaltations" without which it would not be a revival
meeting. To say that the young fanatic Joseph Smith succeeded in separating revivalism from emotionalism makes
about as much sense as to talk of separating Romanism
from Rome or separating the front of a piece of paper from
the back. Calvinism and revivalism "without either the
stress on human depravity of the former or the excessive
emotionalism of the latter" are simply *Hamlet* with Hamlet
left out.

   Though Riley assures us that "Joseph Smith knew as
little about Arminius as Arminius did about Joseph
Smith,"[28] and Davis insists that Mormonism is a revolt
against Arminianism,[29] Dr. O'Dea finds "the doctrine of
the book is wholeheartedly and completely Arminian."
The proof? "Men," says the Book of Mormon, "[will] be
judged [by God] according to their works" (Alma 41:3),
which Arminius also taught.[30] But so did a thousand other
Christian teachers, ancient, medieval, and modern, to say
nothing of the scripture itself (e.g., Ecclesiastes 12:13-14).

   And, we learn that the democratic creed of the Book

of Mormon is purely American — except that it is not: "Yet
this confession of democratic faith, so characteristic of the
milieu, did not pass without qualification. . . . Whether it
was the problems of developing his 92 B.C. plot or his
reflection upon his experience with his contemporaries that
gave him pause, Joseph appended a profound warning."[31]
That is, it *should* have been "characteristic of the milieu,"
according to Dr. O'Dea's calculations, yet it was not, because that rascal Joseph Smith insisted on forcing it into
another milieu — that of 92 B.C. We challenge Dr. O'Dea to
name a century between the first and the twentieth A.D.
in which the "content" of which he speaks was not only
present but also conspicuous in the Christian world: the
Reformation was only one of many expressions it has taken
through the centuries. Again, it is impossible to take any
position regarding baptism that has not been taken by one
religious group or another in the past: so while the Book
of Mormon concept of baptism conforms to none of the
familiar Christian patterns, it may be broken down arbi-
trarily into fragments that may be held to suggest aspects
of baptism as practiced by somebody or other, and so claim
to have discovered the source of the Book of Mormon ideas
on the subject, as Dr. O'Dea does.[32]

Parallels to Taste

The grab-bag method exemplified by Dr. O'Dea makes
it possible for the experts, each feeling his own part of the
elephant, to propound with perfect confidence diametri-
cally conflicting explanations of the Book of Mormon. Thus
some scholars tell us that the Book of Mormon could only
have been written by "a man of learning," that "the real
author . . . was well acquainted with the classics,"[33] while
others insist that "only an ignorant man could have produced it."[34]

Today certain professors find that "the intellectuality
of the Book of Mormon and its appeal to its adherents as

a reasonable answer to problems of existence and salvation are quite obvious,"[35] and assure us that the book "satisfied the inbred desire of Yorkers to achieve an orderly, intellectual formulation of their beliefs."[36] Can this be the same book which Dr. Davis is calling "the gibberish of a crazy boy?"[37]

For Professor Meinhold the Book of Mormon contains no history, but a wonderful *philosophy* of history.[38] For Professor Arbaugh it is the other way around: "Mormon scriptures contain items of purported history, but, significantly, *no* philosophy of history."[39]

Investigators as different as Gibbs, Brodie, and Eduard Meyer have commented on the remarkable consistency of the Book of Mormon, which for Mr. Bernard De Voto was nothing but a "yeasty fermentation, formless, aimless, and inconceivably absurd."[40] Years later, to be sure, De Voto admitted he had been "ignorant, brash, prejudiced, malicious, . . . irresponsible, . . . in the . . . mood of illegitimate and dishonest attack."[41]

Critics have detected fraud in the Book of Mormon on the one hand in their discovery that it "determines none of the great questions pending in the world at large, but only the minor difficulties that would have been likely to have reached a western village,"[42] and on the other hand in the equally astute discovery that it simply reflects the great issues about which "men in various parts of the country were thinking."[43] Again, which is it to be, great issues or small, that damn the Book of Mormon?

While one school of investigators sees in the Book of Mormon an "altogether remarkable production of an overimaginative mind," the work of "an audacious and original mind, . . . fecund imagination," and so on,[44] others can detect only a "perfect . . . destitution of inventive power in its writer, . . . [a] complete inability to perceive, and to conceal, its inconsistencies."[45]

A learned English divine in 1886 felt to reject the Book

of Mormon *in spite of* "all its air of sincerity and truth: for all the striking and often beautiful passages that it contains."[46] Yet how many critics detect those qualities in the work? The usual reaction is: "In nothing does the line, style, invention, conception, content and purpose reveal the hand of a master, let alone of Divine inspiration."[47]

Notes

1. The quotation is from John D. Kingsbury, *Mormonism* (New York: Congregational Home Missionary Society, n.d.), 6-7.

2. The Book of Mormon itself is "interspersed with the catchwords of the Methodist camp-meeting exhorter," according to James Hastings, ed., *Encyclopedia of Religion and Ethics*, 13 vols. (New York: Scribner's, 1951), 11:86. For a particularly gaudy description, see Leon Leomonnier, *Les Mormons* (Paris: Gallimard, 1948), 17; and George Townshend, *The Conversion of Mormonism* (Hartford: Church Missions, 1911), 13-14.

3. Ernest S. Bates, *American Faith* (New York: Norton, 1940), 341. Cf. I. Woodbridge Riley, *Founder of Mormonism* (New York: Dodd, Mead, 1902), 85.

4. Fawn M. Brodie, *No Man Knows My History* (New York: Knopf, 1946), 9-10. The quotation is from page 69.

5. Whitney R. Cross, *The Burned-over District* (Ithaca: Cornell University Press, 1950), 146.

6. Ibid., 138.

7. David B. Davis, "The New England Origins of Mormonism," *New England Quarterly* 26 (1953): 151, 154.

8. Brodie, *No Man Knows My History*, 14.

9. Nancy Towle, *Vicissitudes Illustrated* (Charleston: Burges, 1832). It is plain that Mrs. Brodie read only the part dealing with Towle's visit to Kirtland in 1831, which she distorts in her usual fashion, reporting, for example, that Miss Towle "blundered" into Kirtland, Brodie, *No Man Knows My History*, 103, while Miss Towle's own account is that she had long planned and carefully arranged her visit to that place.

10. Towle, *Vicissitudes Illustrated*, 145.

11. Ibid., 198-200.

12. For example, ibid., 124-25. The worst thing she can call people is "superstitious," ibid., 54.

13. Jules Remy, *A Journey to Great Salt Lake City*, 2 vols. (London: W. Jeffs, 1861), 1:103.

14. She commiserates a fellow-evangelist for being forced by un-usual circumstances to preach in the open air at the risk of her health; Towle, *Vicissitudes Illustrated*, 33, cf. 82.

15. Ibid., 53, 60.

16. Ibid., 185, 170-71, 22, 16.

17. She tells how "the very bigoted Methodists" of Geneva, New York, near Palmyra, refused her their chapel, p. 152. Though she would have welcomed imprisonment or physical persecution, "that honor," she reports, "was denied me." Ibid., 62-63, cf. 17, 23, 28, 41, 54, 94. Only the Mormons had that honor, ibid., 146.

18. Ibid., 165, n. 1; 164-65.

19. "Mormonism and the Mormons," *Methodist Quarterly Review*, ed. George Peck, 25, series 3 (1843): 126.

20. Ibid., 125.

21. Thomas F. O'Dea, *The Mormons* (Chicago: University of Chicago Press, 1957), 32.

22. Ibid., 28. Page 31 notes that "the extremes of religious en-thusiasm . . . follow upon the revivals . . . later in the decade." Yet these extremes are supposed to have produced the Book of Mormon.

23. Ibid., 33.

24. Only in the British Isles did Miss Towle have fears for her life, Towle, *Vicissitudes Illustrated*, 57-59; she vividly describes the poverty, violence, and insecurity of English lower society. Chief Justice Jackson has observed that the American public differs most sharply from the European in its abhorrence of violence: mob action is the rule in European political history, the exception in America.

25. O'Dea, *The Mormons*, 27.

26. Ibid., 31.

27. Ibid., 40.

28. Riley, *Founder of Mormonism*, 135.

29. Davis, "The New England Origins of Mormonism," 154-55, 158.

30. O'Dea, *The Mormons*, 28, cf. 27: "[The Book of Mormon's] fundamental theme combines the concomitance of righteousness and prosperity of the later Calvinism with the call to repentance and humility of revivalistic Christianity." If Dr. O'Dea troubled to read such odd items as the Bible, the Greek Poets, or the Fathers of the Church, he would discover that these teachings are by no means a monopoly of Calvinists and revivalists.

31. Ibid., 34.

32. Ibid., 35-36, accusing the Book of Mormon of "ambiguity on the question of baptism" because it does not conform to one pattern, but suggests Baptist, Arminian, Catholic, and Episcopalian ideas.

33. E. D. Howe, *History of Mormonism: or a Faithful Account of that Singular Imposition and Delusion* (Painesville: Printed by the Author, 1840), 19, 21.

34. *Schaff-Herzog Encyclopedia of Religious Knowledge*, 15 vols. (Grand Rapids: Baker, 1950), 8:13.

35. O'Dea, *The Mormons*, 31.

36. Cross, *The Burned-over District*, 145.

37. Davis, "The New England Origins of Mormonism," 148.

38. Peter Meinhold, "Die Anfänge des amerikanischen Geschichtsbewusstseins," *Saeculum* 5 (1954): 86.

39. George B. Arbaugh, *Revelation in Mormonism* (Chicago: University of Chicago Press, 1932; reprinted 1950), 5.

40. Eduard Meyer, *Ursprung und Geschichte der Mormonen* (Halle: Niemeyer, 1912), 78; Meinhold, "Die Anfänge des amerikanischen Geschichtsbewusstseins," 66-67; Bernard De Voto, "The Centennial of Mormonism," *American Mercury* (January 1930), 5.

41. Bernard De Voto, "A Revaluation," *Improvement Era* 49 (March 1946): 154. De Voto's letter, reprinted in the *Improvement Era* with his permission, is a reflective and honest self-evaluation of his earlier writing, as well as a fine statement on the interchange of ideas, from an older writer. But the majority of scholars still remember only his earlier position. See also Francis W. Kirkham, *A New Witness for Christ in America*, 2 vols. (Independence, Mo.: Zion's, 1951), 2:351-53. David B. Davis's article of 1953, "The New England Origins of Mormonism," is a faithful echo of the earlier De Voto.

42. John Hyde, *Mormonism, Its Leaders and Designs* (New York: Fetridge, 1857), 281; cf. J. B. Turner, *Mormonism in All Ages* (New York: Platt and Peters, 1842), 203.

43. Harry M. Beardsley, *Joseph Smith and His Mormon Empire* (Boston: Houghton Mifflin, 1931), 87.

44. M. A. Sbresny, *Mormonism: As It Is Today* (London: Stockwell, n.d.), 25; cf. Beardsley, *Joseph Smith and His Mormon Empire*, 4; Josiah F. Gibbs, *Lights and Shadows of Mormonism* (Salt Lake Tribune, 1909), 57; Brodie, *No Man Knows My History*, 48, 69.

45. Daniel P. Kidder, *Mormonism and the Mormons* (New York: Carlton and Porter, 1842), 255.

46. George Wotherspoon, *Mormonism* (London: Sunday Lecture Society, 1886), 16.

47. M. H. A. Van Der Valk, *De Profeet der Mormonen Joseph Smith, Jr.* (Kampen: Kok, 1921), 107.

8

The Comparative Method

The comparative method as such is neither good nor bad. It can be abused (what tool can not?), and to condemn it outright because of its imperfections would put an end to all scholarship.

The fundamental rule of the comparative method is that if things resemble each other there must be some connection between them, and the closer the resemblance the closer the connection. For example, if anyone were to argue that the Book of Mormon was obviously stolen from Solomon Spaulding's *Manuscript Story* (the document now at Oberlin College) because the word "and" is found to occur frequently in both texts, we would simply laugh at him. If he brought forth as evidence the fact that kings are mentioned in both books, he might not appear quite so ridiculous. But if the *Manuscript Story* actually referred by name to "cureloms and cumoms" we would be quite sure of a possible borrowing (though even then we would not have proven a direct borrowing). The hypothetical case illustrates the fact that there are degrees of significance in parallels. Recently a Protestant minister pointed to seventy-five resemblances between the Book of Mormon and the *Manuscript Story*: None of them alone is worth anything, but his position is that there are so many that

This article first appeared in two parts, published in the Improvement Era *(October and November 1959). The article was part of a series of five articles, published in nine parts under the title " 'Mixed Voices': A Study on Book of Mormon Criticism."*

taken altogether they must be significant.¹ The trouble is that it would be very easy to find seventy-five equally good parallels between the Book of Mormon and any other book you can name. As an actual example, to prove that the Book of Mormon and the *Manuscript Story* are related, this investigator shrewdly notes that in both books "men arise and make addresses," "both [books] pronounce woe unto the wicked mortals," "both mention milk," in both "adultery was a crime," "both had counsellors," and so on. What kind of "parallels" are these? Seventy-five or seven hundred fifty, it is all the same—such stuff adds up to nothing.²

But the most publicized list of parallels of the Book of Mormon and another work is B. H. Roberts's comparison of that book with Ethan Smith's *View of the Hebrews*.³ Commenting on this, Mrs. Brodie wrote: "The scholarly Mormon historian B. H. Roberts once made a careful and impressive list of parallels between the *View of the Hebrews* and the Book of Mormon, but for obvious reasons it was never published."⁴ The most obvious reason for not publishing it would be, to any textual critic as it was to Elder Roberts, that the "careful and impressive list of parallels" is quite worthless either to prove or disprove the Book of Mormon.

In the first place, only eighteen parallels are listed, and neither Mrs. Brodie nor Mr. Hogan adds anything to the list. This, then, is the best we can do for Ethan Smith's parallels. If there were only eighteen ideas in all the Book of Mormon and about the same number in Ethan Smith's book, then the eighteen parallels would be indeed suspicious. But there are not only eighteen ideas in the Book of Mormon—there are hundreds! So if we are going to use such a tiny handful as evidence, they had better be good. But when we consider the Roberts parallels, we find that they are not only very few but without exception all perfectly ordinary. In fact, Mr. Hogan in his recent treatment of the subject has unwittingly robbed the eighteen parallels of any significance by going to considerable pains to point out in his introduction that the ideas shared by Ethan and Joseph Smith were not original to either of them but were as common in the world they lived in as the name Smith itself. He would agree with Mr. Cross that "neither Solomon Spaulding, for whom some have claimed authorship of a manuscript which became the basis of the Book of Mormon, nor Joseph Smith required any originality to speculate in this direction."[5] No originality was required in these matters because these things were public property. This being the case, why would Joseph Smith need to steal them from Ethan Smith?

Take Parallels Numbers 2 and 4 in Roberts's list for example: *Both claim a Hebraic origin for the Indian.* But so did everybody else. In 1833 Josiah Priest wrote, "The opinion that the American Indians are the descendants of the lost Ten Tribes, is now a popular one, and generally believed."[6] In that case Joseph Smith must have known as much about it as Ethan Smith—no need for pilfering.

No. 5, *the idea of a lost or buried book,* is found in both documents. Again, what could be commoner? This is Mr. Hogan's prize exhibit and parting shot: Ethan Smith had suggested that the best evidence for a connection between the Indians and the ancient Hebrews would be the finding of an actual inscription "on some durable substance in evident Hebrew language and character."[7] Of course it would: inscriptions in ancient languages on durable material (they could hardly be in modern languages on perishable materials) have been throughout history the best-known link between ancient and living civilizations. Yet Ethan Smith's idea that a Hebrew inscription would be the best tie-up between the Jews and the Indians is presented here as a brilliant and novel idea, the provocation that set Joseph Smith on the high road to forgery, according to Mr. Hogan, who concludes his study with the weighty words:

"If an enterprising and imaginative writer needed any final provocation, this would seem to be it."[8] As if "an energetic and imaginative writer," of all people, needed to be told that it is ancient writings that tell about ancient people.

No. 14. In Ethan Smith's book is reported that an Indian chief once said that "he knew it to be wrong, if a poor man came to his door hungry and naked, to turn him away empty. For he believed God loved the poorest of men better than he did proud rich men."[9] Again, would Joseph Smith or any Christian have to go to Ethan Smith's book to learn this? If the Indian's words were quoted in the Book of Mormon, it would be a different thing: but what compassionate human being, Christian or not, has not held this philosophy? Here is another version of the same thing:

No. 16. An early trader quoted by Ethan Smith tells of some Indians who were "loving and affectionate to their wives and relations."[10] The Book of Mormon reports indirectly that the Nephites also loved *their* children. And this, believe it or not, is taken as strong proof that the Book of Mormon was stolen from the *View of the Hebrews*.

No. 15. It is the same with polygamy: in Ethan Smith's book a Delaware chief deplores the recently adopted practice in his tribe of picking up a number of wives and casting them off as soon as one grew tired of them. The fact that the Indian recognizes such a practice as immoral can only indicate, according to Ethan Smith, the influence of "Israelitish tradition . . . as taught by the Old Testament,"[11] as if mankind had no other source of morality. Yet here his naive reasoning is sounder than the proposition that the prohibition of more than one wife to the Nephites must have come from this particular source. Actually, this is no parallel at all since there is no resemblance between the practices described.

A number of parallels in the list are attributed to Joseph Smith's stealing from the *View of the Hebrews*, when he could more easily have found the same material in the

Bible. This reaches the point of absurdity in parallel No. 12, where Joseph Smith gets the idea of quoting Isaiah from Ethan since the latter "quotes copiously and chiefly from Isaiah in relation to the scattering and gathering of Israel."[12] This is the equivalent of accusing one scholar of stealing from another because they both quote "copiously and chiefly" from Homer in their studies of Troy. Since ancient times, Isaiah has been *the* source for information on the scattering and gathering of Israel. Any student writing a term paper on that subject would deserve to be flunked if he failed to quote from that prophet without ever having heard of Ethan Smith!

Parallel No. 11 is a related case: "The view of the Hebrews has many references to both the scattering and the gathering of Israel 'in the last days.' The second chapter . . . is entitled 'The Certain Restoration of Judah and Israel' and in this section is quoted nearly all the references to Isaiah that are referred to, but quoted *more fully*, in the Book of Mormon."[13] Which would Joseph Smith be more likely to go to in treating this subject, Mr. Ethan Smith or the Bible? Obviously the Bible is the more likely source. But would Joseph need Ethan to tell him to consult the Bible in the first place?

Again, No. 10, the first chapter of the *Views of the Hebrews* is devoted to the destruction of Jerusalem. Since the book claims to be searching out the lost ten tribes, it is hard to conceive how it could begin otherwise. There have been many dispersions from Jerusalem, as the Book of Mormon tells us, and many destructions: the one told of in the Book of Mormon is a *totally different* one from that described by Ethan Smith, which took place hundreds of years before it. It is hardly likely that the Bible-reading Smiths first discovered that Jerusalem was destroyed by perusing the pages of Ethan's book. Neither did Joseph need Ethan Smith to tell him that God's people anciently had inspired prophets and heavenly gifts (No. 6). This has always been a conspicuous part of Indian tradition, but given the popular belief that the ancient Americans were of Israel, Joseph Smith would have no choice but to attribute to them the divine gifts possessed by God's people. Among these divine gifts was the Urim and Thummim (No. 7) *described* in the Bible, and only dimly and indirectly hinted at by Ethan Smith in describing an article of clothing worn by medicine men—quite a different article from the Urim and Thummim of either the Book of Mormon or the Bible.

The trouble with this last parallel is that it is not a parallel at all, but only something that is made into one by egregiously taking the part for the whole. The same faulty reasoning characterizes the first of the parallels in the list. No. 1: the *place of origin of the two works*. Ethan Smith's book was written in Vermont, and Joseph Smith was born in Vermont. That would be a very suspicious coincidence were it not that Joseph Smith left Vermont as a child at least eight years before the *View of the Hebrews* was published. The time scale which invalidates the argument of place of origin is actually given as another parallel between the two books. No. 3: *the time of production*— it is held to be most significant that the publication of Ethan Smith's first edition and the appearance of the Angel Moroni occurred in the same year. We must confess our failure to detect anything in Ethan Smith's book that might have suggested the Angel Moroni. All that is proved by the dates is that the *View of the Hebrews* came out first, so that Joseph Smith *could* have used it. Of course, if *View of the Hebrews* had appeared *after* the Book of Mormon there would be no case—though Mrs. Brodie tries very hard to hint that Joseph Smith covered his tracks by later referring to Josiah Priest, whose book did not appear until 1833![14] Even Mrs. Brodie concedes that "it may never be proven that Joseph saw *View of the Hebrews*,"[15] but even if he had seen it, that would prove nothing unless we could discover something in the Book of Mormon that could not possibly come from any other source.

What the critics seem to consider the most devastating of all the parallels in the list, the one most often mentioned and on which B. H. Roberts concentrates most of his attention, is No. 9, which deals with the general relations of the ancient Americans to each other. The most obvious and immediate objection to the popular theory that the Indians were the ten tribes was that the ten tribes were civilized and the Indians were not. Since colonial times there were two things that everybody knew about aboriginal America: (1) that it was full of savages, and (2) that it was full of ruins left by people who were *not* savages. If the Indians were from the ten tribes, then they must have fallen from a higher estate, and that estate was mutely witnessed by the ruins. Using these general speculations as his starting point, Ethan Smith, like any intelligent man, goes on with his own surmises: When the civilized ten tribes arrived in the New World, they found themselves in a wilderness teeming with game, (1) *"inviting them to the chase;* most of them (2) *fell into a wandering* idle hunt-life,"* while the "more sensible parts of this people"[16] continued in their civilized ways and left behind them the ruins that fill the land. "It is highly probable," Ethan Smith continues to speculate, "that the more civilized part of the tribes of Israel, after they settled in America, became (3) *wholly separated* from the hunting and savage tribes of their brethren; that the latter (4) *lost the knowledge* of their having descended from the same family with themselves; that the more civilized part continued for many centuries; that (5) *tremendous wars were frequent* between them and their savage brethren."[17] Then gradually (6) *"in process of time* their savage jealousies and rage annihilated their more civilized brethren."[18] No other explanation is possible, he thinks: "What account can be given of this, but that the savages extirpated them, after (7) *long and dismal wars.*"[19] As to the state of the savages, "We cannot so well account for their evident degeneracy in any way" except the Bible way: "as that it took place under a vindictive Providence, as has been noted, to accomplish (8) *divine judgments denounced against the idolatrous ten tribes of Israel*"[20] (emphasis added).

Now consider the eight points from the viewpoint of the Book of Mormon. (1) It was *not* the joy of the chase that led the Lamanites into the wilderness—the greatest hunters in the Book of Mormon are Nephites. (2) The less civilized group did *not* upon arriving in America "fall into a wandering . . . life." They were wanderers when they got here, and so were their brethren. (3) In the Book of Mormon "the more civilized part" of the people *never* becomes "wholly separated . . . from their brethren," the two remaining always in contact. (4) The more savage element never "lost the knowledge" of their descent: The Lamanites always claimed, in fact, that the Nephites had stolen their birthright. (5) The wars were neither tremendous nor frequent—they are almost all in the nature of sudden raids; they involved small numbers of people, and, except for the last great war, they are relatively brief. (6) It was *not* the savage jealousy and rage of an inferior civilization that destroyed the higher civilization—that higher civilization had broken up completely before the last war by its own corruption, and at the time of their destruction the Nephites were as debased as their rivals. (7) It was *not* a process of gradual extermination but of a quick and violent end. (8) Finally, the downgrading of the Lamanites is *not* the fulfillment of prophecies about the ten tribes after the pattern of the destruction of God's people (that would be the *Nephites*); their degeneracy is given a unique explanation that cannot be found in either Ethan Smith or the Bible.

To establish any connection at all between the books of the two Smiths, it is absolutely imperative to find something perfectly unique and peculiar in both of them. Yet there is not *one single thing* in common between *View of the Hebrews* and the Book of Mormon that is not also found in the Bible. Parallel No. 9, discussed above, promises to be the exception to this, containing as it does significant details that are not found in the Bible; yet it is in these very details that the two books are in complete disagreement! Another false parallel is No. 10, the destruction of Jerusalem: Ethan Smith speaks of one destruction, the Book of Mormon of another, but the Bible speaks of both. Here the parallel is not between the two Smiths at all—they are talking of wholly different events—but between them and the Bible only. Again there is no indirect reference to American hieroglyphics in Ethan Smith, which leads to parallel No. 8 with the query: "Was this sufficient to suggest the strange manner of writing in the Book of Mormon in the 'learning of the Jews and language of the Egyptians' but in altered Egyptian?"[21] In other words, the two sources have the mention of *Egyptian hieroglyphics* in common—only the word *Egyptian* does *not* appear in Ethan Smith; and the word *hieroglyphics* does *not* appear in the Book of Mormon; but if you put the two together, what do you get? Egyptian hieroglyphics! In the same way, Ethan Smith contains a brief mention of Quetzalcoatl, though nothing could be farther from his mind than to suggest that Quetzalcoatl might be Christ, while the Book of Mormon contains mention of Christ without the slightest hint that he might be Quetzalcoatl: put *them* together, and you have parallel No. 18: The common teaching of both books that Christ was Quetzalcoatl! Again, because Joseph Smith (*not* the Book of Mormon) and Ethan Smith both mention Ezekiel 37, our critics are convinced that the former is stealing from the latter, though their interpretations of the celebrated passage are *entirely different*: it is suspicious for Joseph Smith even to mention a universally discussed chapter of the Bible if Ethan Smith has already mentioned it.

Finally parallel No. 13: Granted that the Indians are

the descendants of the lost ten tribes, as everyone believed
in 1830, what Christian would not feel an obligation toward
them? Ethan Smith's view that "the American Gentile nation [the United States]" should "become the Savior of
Israel in America" is a perfectly natural one, and is assumed
to offer another parallel to the teaching of the Book of
Mormon. Nothing could be further from the mark: the
Book of Mormon never looks to the United States government, the American people, or Christian civilization to save
the Indians—it tells a very different story of what is to
happen.

So after all Ethan Smith turns in a perfect score; not a
single blemish mars the target. In every case where the
Book of Mormon *might* have borrowed from him, it might
much more easily have borrowed from the Bible or prevailing popular beliefs. In the few cases where he deals in
common with the Book of Mormon with matters not treated
in those other sources, the two books are completely at
variance.

Grab-bag Research

Any conscientious student likes to find support for his
own theories and ideas in the writings of others, and when
he comes upon a particularly helpful or enlightening passage joyfully quotes it. Yet if Joseph Smith says there was
once a great civilization in Central America, and quotes
Josiah Stout to back him up, it is plain that Smith is stealing
from Stout—even though Stout's book came out three
years later than his! Plagiarists conceal the sources of their
information; they do not shout them from the housetops;
but if a Mormon leader is so careless as to quote a non-
Mormon writer by way of illustrating or supporting a Mormon teaching, he has given everything away; he has
openly declared the true source of Mormon revelation.
"Sidney Rigdon quoted openly from [a book by Thomas]
Dick" on one occasion. This proves to Mrs. Brodie that he

had read the book[22] — therefore Joseph Smith had read it or heard of it — therefore Smith got his cosmology from it — therefore Mr. Davis now tells us that Mormon leaders "drew in ideas at random from local preachers, pseudo-scientific books, and 'philosophers' like Thomas Dick."[23] And this statement is bred of nothing more than an airy word from Mrs. Brodie.[24]

If we were to ask an IBM machine, a super-electronic memorizer, associator, and classifier of data, to tell us which cultural, historical, and intellectual influences are most prominent in the Book of Mormon, we would consider the machine's response utterly worthless unless we had first stocked it with ten thousand times more facts than any human mind contains. Yet every Book of Mormon critic thinks he can answer the question by referring to whatever tiny patch of knowledge he happens to sit on. What do we trust in the critics? Certainly it cannot be their knowledge — it must be instinct. Today we are asked to accept mystic explanations of the Book of Mormon which, lacking any solid foundation, rest their case on Joseph Smith's reactions to "latent facets" of Puritanism (O'Dea) or to "historic responses" of the Reformation (Davis). All the prevailing environmental theories of Mormonism and the Book of Mormon insist that both were the product of an intensely local setting, suited to the extremely limited intellectual horizon of Smith and his followers. Yet Mr. Cross and Dr. O'Dea tell us that it was not Mr. Davis's old New Englanders to whose thoughts Joseph Smith gave such welcome expression but a very different stock, the "Yorkers." Mr. Armytage, however, shows us that Mormonism was exactly and peculiarly what the sturdy north-country farmers and artisans of England wanted to hear,[25] while the same holds true for Welsh miners, Scandinavian fishermen, prosperous Swiss burghers, and South Pacific Islanders. Davis's "fourteen-year-old ragamuffin" certainly had a knack: "Why should the gibberish of a crazy

boy," he asks, "send thousands of people trekking off to
establish a theocracy beyond the Rocky Mountains?"²⁶ The
question is admirably put, and he can find but one possible
answer for it: It was because the crazy boy told all those
people exactly what they wanted to hear, giving them
doctrine so perfectly suited to their taste that they would
undergo any toil or danger for it. One hundred years ago
Monsieur Remy accounted for the success of Joseph Smith
by observing that he had simply combined all that was
most enticing in all religions into one religion. Look what
our crazy boy Joseph is doing! What we want to know is
how he does it. After all, what the latest explanations of
Smith and his book amount to is the profound discovery
that he succeeded where others failed because he always
happened to do just the right thing.

The vast depth and breadth of the grab-bag guarantee
that our Book of Mormon investigators will never run out
of parallels and analogies which they may hail as significant
or not as they choose. But it also guarantees that none of
them will ever have the last word. To the end, their ideas
about the Book of Mormon remain strictly their own, and
they are welcome to them. But any pretense to scientific
or scholarly finality under the circumstances is but an illusion. Our poorly trained scholars, satisfied that modern
science has emancipated them from old methods and
chores, are quite unaware that the critics of an earlier day
were just as well-educated and emancipated as they, and
that they are only repeating in their shallow researches
what has already been done by men of greater diligence
and authority—and duly marked off as wasted effort.

Notes

1. James D. Bales, *The Book of Mormon?* (Rosemead, CA: Old
Paths, 1958), 142-46. Even to work out the small number of seventy-
five parallels, Bales had to pad heavily. Thus, both the Book of
Mormon and the Spaulding Manuscript talk about great civilizations, as what history does not? This parallel is broken down into

such inevitable points of resemblance as "both [books] refer to great cities," "both . . . represented as having some scientific knowledge," "both knew something of mechanical arts," "both used iron," "both used coins" (the words "coin" and "coins," however, are not mentioned in the Book of Mormon), "both constructed fortifications," "both exceeded the present Indians in works of art and ingenuity," etc. Now all these things are inevitable accompaniments of any civilization; they are not separate and distinct points of resemblance at all. One might as well argue that since both books mention people, both imply that people have hands, hands have fingers, etc., and thus accumulate "parallels" by the score.

2. Ibid.

3. Mervin B. Hogan, " 'A Parallel': A Matter of Chance Versus Coincidence," *Rocky Mountain Mason* (January 1956): 17-31. Elder Roberts's manuscript is still in manuscript form. [It has recently been published in Brigham D. Madsen, ed., *B. H. Roberts: Studies of the Book of Mormon* (Urbana: University of Illinois, 1985), 323-44— ed.]

4. Fawn M. Brodie, *No Man Knows My History* (New York: Knopf, 1946), 47, n. 2.

5. Whitney R. Cross, *The Burned-over District* (Ithaca: Cornell University Press, 1950), 81.

6. Josiah Priest, *American Antiquities*, 5th ed. (Albany: Hoffman and White, 1835), 75-76.

7. Hogan, " 'A Parallel,' " 30; citing Ethan Smith, *View of the Hebrews: Or the Tribes of Israel in America* (Poultney, VT: Smith and Shute, 1823), 167.

8. Hogan, " 'A Parallel,' " 30.

9. Hogan, " 'A Parallel,' " 28; citing Smith, *View of the Hebrews*, 2nd ed., 104.

10. Ibid., 29; citing Smith, *View of the Hebrews*, 2nd ed., 175.

11. Smith, *View of the Hebrews*, 2nd ed., 104.

12. Hogan, " 'A Parallel,' " 25.

13. Ibid. (emphasis added).

14. Brodie, *No Man Knows My History*, 47.

15. Ibid., 47.

16. Hogan, " 'A Parallel,' " 23; citing Smith, *View of the Hebrews*, 2nd ed., 172-73.

17. Ibid.

18. Ibid.

19. Ibid.

20. Smith, *View of the Hebrews*, 2nd ed., 172.

21. Hogan, " 'A Parallel,' " 22.

22. Brodie, *No Man Knows My History*, 171.

23. David B. Davis, "The New England Origins of Mormonism," *New England Quarterly* 26 (1953): 167.

24. Brodie, *No Man Knows My History*, 69, asserts that "the book can best be explained . . . by his responsiveness to the provincial opinions of his time."

25. W. H. G. Armytage, "Liverpool, Gateway to Zion," *Pacific Northwest Quarterly* 48 (1957): 39-40. For sheer misinformation, Mr. Armytage's article sets a record even among anti-Mormon writers.

26. Davis, "The New England Origins of Mormonism," 167.

9

The Boy Nephi in Jerusalem

Editor's Note [from the *Instructor*]: This story is the author's concept of what might have been in the Jerusalem of about 600 B.C. While not scriptural, the details of trade and politics, and the general background indicated herein are supported by the author's extensive research and by artifacts of the period.

We can best imagine what life was like in Lehi's Jerusalem if we visit the city, not during the frightening days just before it fell, but in happier times a few years earlier, when Nephi was a boy of, say, eleven or twelve.

The elegant Syrian sundial in the courtyard showed just "half-past four" in the afternoon (for in those days at Jerusalem they counted twenty-four hours to a day and sixty minutes to an hour—exactly as we do!), and Nephi had just finished his lessons. His teacher, a clever old Hebrew who had joined his father's employ at the big (mostly ruined) market town of Zoan in Egypt, had given him a bad time. He was now making Nephi put all the books and pens and tablets back in their proper places among the scrolls, inkpots, and writing plates (the ones used for important contracts) in the big book closet. Nephi deserved the extra disciplining, for his mind had wandered during the lesson. He had been quick enough in arithmetic and had had no trouble with Hebrew, which even the poor country people read and wrote in those days; but that

---

This article first appeared in the Instructor *96 (March 1961): 84-85.*

cramped and squiggly Egyptian stuff was awful. Nephi's father, like every educated man of his day, knew all about the great centers of learning that stretched from Egypt to India, where even Jews had to go to study if they wanted to become important men—priests, physicians, scholars, statesmen—and he was determined that his sons should not lack learning.

But today Nephi had other things to think about, for that morning in the kitchen he had learned that Uncle Ishmael was coming down from Sidon with a load of goods. Last year his uncle had promised to bring Jonadab with him next time—and now it was next time. Of the same age, Jonadab and Nephi had had wonderful times together the summer they manned the watchtower in Father Lehi's vineyards. The caravan should arrive, as usual, about sundown; and poor Nephi was in agony during the last hour of the lesson. Once released, he raced down the winding, narrow streets like a skillful quarterback carrying the ball, barely missing dirty children playing tag or King-of-the-Mountain, servant girls with huge jugs of water, poor peasants peddling loads of firewood, donkeys burdened with dried fish from Galilee or cheese from Bethlehem.

Nephi always liked to visit the big square at the West Gate where most of the caravans unloaded. The little shops under the wooden arcades around the sides of the square were always interesting. Sharp-eyed, sharp-tongued storekeepers skillfully, but not too honestly, manipulated their little hand scales amid piles of textiles or sandals or dried figs or pots and pans or skins or herbs or watermelons. But even they could not compete with the wonderful bales and crates of stuff that the camels brought in from goodness knows where—much of it so valuable that it was opened only in the presence of great merchants such as Nephi's father. Sometimes a drove of splendid horses, pampered like princes by their drovers, would spend the night in a corner of the great square. One could even see huge, gray brahma bulls for sale. Originally from India, these great beasts were very popular in Egypt and Babylonia. Every visit to the big *suq* held some surprise.

But this time, the surprise was Jonadab. For just as Nephi burst panting into the square, there was Jonadab tugging away at the halter of a stately yellow camel to get the beast into position for unloading. With a glad cry of greeting, Nephi jumped over a huge pile of Cappadocian rugs and rushed to join his friend. But before he could reach him, he had to stop short, for there right in front of him was Uncle Ishmael, an impressive figure in his big, floppy traveling cap and his long, red robe with its lordly array of dusty fringes and tassels. Nephi went down on his knees and bowed so low that he almost touched the ground with his head—for that was the proper way to salute a respected person. His uncle asked him how things were at home and why he happened to be in town when tomorrow was a holiday.

"I came to take Jonadab with me," said Nephi; and, reminding Ishmael of his promise, "We'll stay here tonight and go out to the country the first thing in the morning."

Ishmael released the happy boy after promising Nephi that he would follow along later for dinner. It was an exciting place where the boys were going tomorrow: Father Lehi's "inheritance," or big family estate, was right on the edge of the desert. Here a boy could become really handy with a bow and arrow and learn to track things almost as well as the desert people themselves.

As the two boys toiled upward through the streets carrying Jonadab's things, Nephi remembered that if they were going to leave in the morning, he would have to show his cousin the wonders of the new wall right now. So he veered off toward the northwest corner of town. Soon the boys were looking up with interest and admiration at the huge, idle derricks and soaring scaffoldings. Nephi set his bundle down amid a great litter of stone chips and started up a ladder; Jonadab hesitated only a second and then followed.

"They're always building these walls," Jonadab panted as they climbed, "and now they are working even harder than they were the last time!"

"I know," said Nephi. "Laman says it's silly, because Necho is our friend, and Egypt is stronger than anybody in the world. Next year or perhaps the next they are going to beat the daylights out of the Babylonians, so we have nothing to worry about. Father's not so sure, though. He says the prosperity of Jerusalem can pass away just as quickly as it came."

"Well, anyway, the temple is the same as ever," Jonadab observed as he reached the top of the wall and looked around.

"Yes," Nephi rejoined, "they say it hasn't changed much since King Solomon built it over 300 years ago. But there was a man who visited us last week who said that even the temple can be destroyed if the people aren't more righteous."

"Oh, I know; one of those crazy prophets. They're always saying things like that." Jonadab shrugged his shoulders.

"This one's different. He isn't one of the poor ones who live in little rooms in the temple. His name's Jeremiah, and he is an important man. He even knows the King of Babylon—they say he's related to him, or something like that. So Laman says it's all just politics, because Laman's for Egypt. But father talked with the prophet all night long. Look out there. There's going to be a storm."

Against a darkening, stormy sky to the south and east, the temple stood out in the rays of the setting sun like dazzling gold.

"Let's go up to the end of the wall. The guard won't care. It's the highest point in the city except for the temple. Do you know that you can see the great sea from the top of the temple? And that's the way to the south desert, over those hills. My father has been there lots of times, clear down to Elath on the Red Sea! I wonder if I'll ever get that far."

Nephi chattered on until they reached their goal and the city lay beneath them: Jerusalem, one of the very oldest cities in the world, was an intricate jumble of square stone houses, broken here and there by the dark little canyon of some street. The bright plaster of the buildings was quiet and subdued in the dusk under the thin pall of blue smoke. The broad litter of flat roofs (the rugs, couches, and screens were gone, for the warm season was over) gave way here and there to a cluster of little cupolas or the looming mass of some public building. In the background, the lines of the battlements and gate towers of the city wall stood out in sharp silhouette against the evening sky. To the east, the Mount of Olives caught the full benefit of the sunset; but it was the temple that made both boys cry out in wonder as it changed from gold to deep coppery red. From the southeast came a rumble of thunder; and with the nightfall, a desert wind began to blow.

"It's kind of scary, isn't it?" said Jonadab as they started back to the ladder. "I wonder if the prophet was right— about the temple, I mean."

"There's lightning out there in the desert. I wonder what it is like there. They say there are places there where nobody has ever been. Maybe mother will let us go camping."

Back on the ground, the boys picked up Jonadab's luggage and trudged across town to dinner.

10

Literary Style Used in
Book of Mormon
Insured Accurate Translation

Editor's Note [from the *Church News*]: The *Church News* recently received a letter from an interested non-member of the Church making the inquiry about why the Prophet Joseph Smith, in translating the Book of Mormon, did not use contemporary English instead of using the "King James English" as found in the Bible. We forwarded this letter on to Dr. Hugh Nibley of the Brigham Young University Department of Religion, asking him to prepare the answer. Dr. Nibley's reply, published herewith, is worth the reading of every Latter-day Saint.

The editor of the *Church News* has forwarded to me your question about the Book of Mormon and the King James Bible. I welcome this opportunity to try to clear up that and a number of related points.

Readers of that valuable periodical *Christianity Today* have been treated to a number of lively discussions of the Book of Mormon in recent issues.[1] To me the most significant aspect of the various attacks on that book has been their concentration on the philological aspects of the problem.

This response to a letter to the editor was printed in the Church News *section of the* Deseret News *(29 July 1961): 10, 15. It was reprinted in* Saints' Herald *108 (9 October 1961): 968-69, 975.*

All the old "scientific" objections seem to have fallen by the way, so that today we are back where we started, with heavy emphasis on the relationship of the Book of Mormon to the Bible, specifically to the King James Version. The main arguments, past and present, are these:

1. For many years the most crushing argument against the Book of Mormon was that it proclaimed itself to be the Word of God, right beside the Bible. Since the fourth century the doctors of the church had argued that since the Bible is the word of God, and God is perfect, the Bible itself must be perfect, and therefore complete. This no longer holds today; the discovery of other ancient and holy texts leads such devout scholars as F. M. Cross to exclaim: "It is as though God had added to his 'once for all' revelation."[2] But where does the Bible itself ever claim "once for all" revelation? Nowhere. As Professor C. M. Torrey points out, our Bible as we have it is the result of picking and choosing by men who claimed no inspiration for themselves, yet on their own authority decided what should be considered "revelation" and what should be labeled apocryphal or "outside" books.[3]

"Outside books?" writes Torrey. "By what authority? The authority was duly declared, but it continued to be disputed . . . down even to the nineteenth century. . . . A new terminology is needed; . . . the current classification . . . as Apocrypha and Pseudepigrapha is outworn and misleading, supported neither by history nor by present fact."[4]

The idea that any book not found in the Bible must be denied the status of revelation has thus been rejected today, yet for many years it was the principal argument against the Book of Mormon.

2. The next most crushing argument—a dead giveaway in the eyes of the critics—was the admission on the title page of the Book of Mormon that it contained "the mistakes of men." How, it was asked, could an inspired book have

THE PROPHETIC BOOK OF MORMON

any mistake at all? Today the answer is only too well-known, and you will find in the very pages of *Christianity Today* long articles by ministers discussing frankly the imperfections of all our Bible manuscripts and translations.

"A first point is the obvious one," writes G. W. Bromiley, "that a human authorship is also assumed for all books of the Bible. . . . These men used ordinary media. They adopted or adapted known literary genres. . . . As the Lord Jesus Christ Himself took flesh, so the written word was clothed in the form of human writings."[5]

And E. M. Good writes: "And if we must await the time when biblical scholars happen to come with all the right guesses in them, what will we do meantime on Sunday morning? Every translation is provisional; . . . a translation is always also an interpretation. . . . No translation of the Bible into English will ever be more than a provisional translation."[6] The title of Good's article is "With All Its Faults" — and these men are talking about the Bible! It was because the Book of Mormon recognized these now well-known facts of scripture that it was assailed for a century as the most outrageous blasphemy.

3. The next most devastating argument against the Book of Mormon was that it actually quoted the Bible. The early critics were simply staggered by the incredible stupidity of including large sections of the Bible in a book which they insisted was specifically designed to fool the Bible-reading public. They screamed blasphemy and plagiarism at the top of their lungs, but today any biblical scholar knows that it would be extremely suspicious if a book purporting to be the product of a society of pious emigrants from Jerusalem in ancient times did not quote the Bible. No lengthy religious writing of the Hebrews could conceivably be genuine if it was not full of scriptural quotations.

These were once the three commonest arguments against the Book of Mormon. Since they have been silenced by the progress of discovery, the emphasis has now shifted to two other points, (1) that the Book of Mormon contains, to quote another writer of *Christianity Today,* "passages lifted bodily from the King James Version,"[7] and (2) that it quotes, not only from the Old Testament, but also the New Testament as well. Your own question, I leave to the last.

4. As to the "passages lifted bodily from the King James Version," we first ask, "How else does one quote scripture if not bodily?" And why should anyone quoting the Bible to American readers of 1830 not follow the only version of the Bible known to them?

Actually the Bible passages quoted in the Book of Mormon often differ from the King James Version, but where the latter is correct there is every reason why it should be followed. When Jesus and the Apostles and, for that matter, the Angel Gabriel quote the scriptures in the New Testament, do they recite from some mysterious Urtext? Do they quote the prophets of old in the ultimate original? Do they give their own inspired translations? No, they do not. They quote the Septuagint, a Greek version of the Old Testament prepared in the third century B.C. Why so? Because that happened to be the received standard version of the Bible accepted by the readers of the Greek New Testament. When "holy men of God" quote the scriptures it is always in the received standard version of the people they are addressing.

We do not claim the King James Version of the Septuagint to be the original scriptures—in fact, nobody on earth today knows where the original scriptures are or what they say. Inspired men have in every age been content to accept the received version of the people among whom they labored, with the Spirit giving correction where correction was necessary.

Since the Book of Mormon is a translation, "with all its faults," into English for English-speaking people whose fathers for generations had known no other scriptures but the standard English Bible, it would be both pointless and confusing to present the scriptures to them in any other form, so far as their teachings were correct.

5. What is thought to be a very serious charge against the Book of Mormon today is that it, a book written down long before New Testament times and on the other side of the world, actually quotes the New Testament! True, it is the same Savior speaking in both, and the same Holy Ghost, and so we can expect the same doctrines in the same language.

But what about the "Faith, Hope and Charity" passage in Moroni 7:45? Its resemblance to 1 Corinthians 13 is undeniable. This particular passage, recently singled out for attack in *Christianity Today*, is actually one of those things that turn out to be a striking vindication of the Book of Mormon. For the whole passage, which scholars have labeled "the Hymn to Charity," was shown early in this century by a number of first-rate investigators working independently (A. Harnack, J. Weiss, R. Reizenstein) to have originated not with Paul at all, but to go back to some older but unknown source: Paul is merely quoting from the record.[8]

Now it so happens that other Book of Mormon writers were also peculiarly fond of quoting from the record. Captain Moroni, for example, reminds his people of an old tradition about the two garments of Joseph, telling them a detailed story which I have found only in a thousand-year-old commentary on the Old Testament, a work still untranslated and quite unknown to the world of Joseph Smith.[9] So I find it not a refutation but a confirmation of the authenticity of the Book of Mormon when Paul and Moroni both quote from a once well-known but now lost Hebrew writing.

6. Now as to your question, "Why did Joseph Smith, a nineteenth century American farm boy, translate the

Book of Mormon into seventeenth century King James English instead of into contemporary language?"

The first thing to note is that the "contemporary language" of the country-people of New England 130 years ago was not so far from King James English. Even the New England writers of later generations, like Webster, Melville, and Emerson, lapse into its stately periods and "thees and thous" in their loftier passages.

For that matter, we still pray in that language and teach our small children to do the same; that is, we still recognize the validity of a special speech set apart for special occasions. My old Hebrew and Arabic teacher, Professor Popper, would throw a student out of the class who did not use "thee" and "thou" in constructing. "This is the word of God!" he would cry indignantly. "This is the Bible! Let us show a little respect; let us have a little formal English here!"

Furthermore, the Book of Mormon is full of scripture, and for the world of Joseph Smith's day, the King James Version was the Scripture, as we have noted; large sections of the Book of Mormon, therefore, had to be in the language of the King James Version—and what of the rest of it? That is scripture, too.

One can think of lots of arguments for using King James English in the Book of Mormon, but the clearest comes out of very recent experience. In the past decade, as you know, certain ancient nonbiblical texts, discovered near the Dead Sea, have been translated by modern, up-to-date American readers. I open at random a contemporary Protestant scholar's modern translation of the Dead Sea Scrolls, and what do I read? "For thine is the battle, and by the strength of thy hand their corpses were scattered without burial. Goliath the Hittite, a mighty man of valor, thou didst deliver into the hand of thy servant David."[10]

Obviously the man who wrote this knew the Bible, and we must not forget that ancient scribes were consciously

archaic in their writing, so that most of the scriptures were
probably in old-fashioned language the day they were written down. To efface that solemn antique style by the latest
up-to-date usage is to translate falsely.

At any rate, Professor Burrows, in 1955 (not 1835!), falls
naturally and without apology into the language of the
King James Bible. Or take a modern Jewish scholar who
purposely avoids archaisms in his translation of the Scrolls
for modern American readers: "All things are inscribed
before Thee in a recording script, for every moment of
time, for the infinite cycles of years, in their several appointed times. No single thing is hidden, naught missing
from Thy presence."[11] Professor Gaster, too, falls under
the spell of our religious idiom.

By frankly using that idiom, the Book of Mormon
avoids the necessity of having to be redone into "modern
English" every thirty or forty years. If the plates were being
translated for the first time today, it would still be King
James English!

Notes

1. Wesley P. Walters, "Mormonism," *Christianity Today* 5/6 (19
December 1960): 8-10 [228-30]; editorial, "The Challenge of the
Cults," *Christianity Today* 5/6 (19 December 1960): 20 [240].
2. Frank M. Cross, "The Scrolls from the Judean Wilderness,"
Christian Century 72 (1955): 890.
3. Charles C. Torrey, *The Apocryphal Literature* (New Haven: Yale
University Press, 1945), 4.
4. Ibid., 10-11.
5. Geoffrey W. Bromiley, "The Bible Doctrine of Inspiration,"
Christianity Today 4/4 (1959): 10.
6. Edwin M. Good, "With All Its Faults," *Christianity Today* 5/8
(1961): 6-7.
7. Walters, "Mormonism," 8.
8. See references in *CWHN* 7:455, n. 4.
9. See references in *CWHN* 6:487-88, notes 12-17.
10. Millar Burrows, *The Dead Sea Scrolls* (Michigan: Baker, 1955;
reprinted 1978), 1:397.
11. Theodore H. Gaster, *The Dead Sea Scriptures* (New York: Doubleday, 1964), 136.

11

The Book of Mormon:
True or False?

It is impossible to read the Book of Mormon with an "open mind." Confronted on every page with the steady assurance that what he is reading is both holy scripture and true history, the reader is soon forced to acknowledge a prevailing mood of assent or resentment.

It was the same uncompromising "yea or nay" in the teaching of Jesus that infuriated the scribes and Pharisees against him; the claims of the Christ allowed no one the comfortable neutrality of a middle ground. Critics of the Book of Mormon have from the beginning attempted to escape the responsibility of reading it by simple appeal to the story of its miraculous origin; that is enough to discredit it without further investigation.

Thanks to its title page, the Book of Mormon "has not been universally considered by its critics," as one of them recently wrote, "as one of those books that must be read in order to have an opinion of it."[1] Even Eduard Meyer, who wrote an ambitious study of Mormon origins, confessed that he had never read the Book of Mormon through.[2]

So it was something of an event when, not long since, an eminent German historian read enough of the strange volume to be thoroughly disturbed by it. He found in it

This article appeared in the Millennial Star 124 (November 1962): 274-77.

"the expression of a mighty awakening historical consciousness"[3] and declared that "the problem of America and Europe has in fact never again been so clearly perceived and pregnantly treated as here."[4]

Clear perception? Skillful treatment? In *that* book? Of course the whole thing is a monstrous hoax; Professor Meinhold will not even deign to consider any alternative: in spite of the witnesses and all that, the story of its origin needs and deserves no examination; it is simply *unerhört* ("unheard of"), and we don't discuss things that are *unerhört*.[5]

Worst of all, the Book of Mormon bears such alarming resemblance to scripture that, for Meinhold, it not only undermines but threatens in a spirit of "nihilistic skepticism" to discredit the Bible altogether.[6] Since one can reject the Book of Mormon without in any way jeopardizing one's faith in the Bible, and since no one ever can accept or ever has accepted the Book of Mormon without complete and unreserved belief in the Bible, the theory that the Book of Mormon is a fiendish attempt to undermine faith in the Bible is an argument of sheer desperation. Recently Professor Albright has noted that the Bible is first and last a historical document, and that of all the religions of the world, only Judaeo-Christianity can be said to have a completely "historical orientation."[7]

Modern scholarship has, up to recent years, steadily undermined that historical orientation and with it the authority of the Bible; but today the process is being reversed and the glory of our Judaeo-Christian tradition vindicated. "Characteristic of the compelling force of this orientation," according to Albright, are the "marked historical tendencies" of Islam and Mormonism, the most complete expression of which is Mormonism's "alleged historical authentication in the form of the Book of Mormon."[8]

What shocks Professor Meinhold in the Book of Mormon is the very thing that shocked the past generations

of German professors in the Bible: its claims to be a genuine
history. When the whole Christian world had forgotten
that "historical orientation," which was one unique distinction, the Book of Mormon alone preserved it completely
intact.

It is said that John Stuart Mill, the man with the fabulous I.Q. (and little else), read the New Testament with
relish until he got to the Gospel of John, when he tossed
the book aside before reaching the sixth chapter with the
crushing and final verdict, "This is poor stuff!" Any book
is a fraud if we choose to regard it as such, but Professor Meinhold cannot be nearly so experienced or well-
educated as John Stuart Mill that he can simply serve notice
that this book is a laughing matter.

But why would anybody be upset by what a Harvard
pedant of our own day calls "the gibberish of a crazy boy"?
Because the Book of Mormon is anything but gibberish to
one who takes the trouble to read it. Here is an assignment
which we like to give to classes of Oriental (mostly Moslem)
students studying the Book of Mormon (it is required) at
the Brigham Young University:

> Since Joseph Smith was younger than most of you
> and not nearly so experienced or well-educated as any
> of you at the time he copyrighted the Book of Mormon,
> it should not be too much to ask you to hand in by the
> end of the semester (which will give you more time than
> he had) a paper of, say, five to six hundred pages in
> length. Call it a sacred book if you will, and give it the
> form of a history. Tell of a community of wandering Jews
> in ancient times; have all sorts of characters in your story,
> and involve them in all sorts of public and private vi-
> cissitudes; give them names—hundreds of them—pre-
> tending that they are real Hebrew and Egyptian names
> of circa 600 B.C.; be lavish with cultural and technical
> details—manners and customs, arts and industries, po-
> litical and religious institutions, rites, and traditions, in-

clude long and complicated military and economic histories; have your narrative cover a thousand years
without any large gaps; keep a number of interrelated
local histories going at once; feel free to introduce religious controversy and philosophical discussion, but always in a plausible setting; observe the appropriate literary conventions and explain the derivation and
transmission of your varied historical materials. Above
all, do not ever contradict yourself! For now we come
to the really hard part of this little assignment. You and
I know that you are making this all up—we have our
little joke—but just the same you are going to be required
to have your paper published when you finish it, not as
fiction or romance, but as a true history! After you have
handed it in you may make no changes in it (in this class
we always use the first edition of the Book of Mormon);
what is more, you are to invite any and all scholars to
read and criticize your work freely, explaining to them
that it is a sacred book on a par with the Bible. If they
seem over-skeptical, you might tell them that you translated the book from original records by the aid of the
Urim and Thummim—they will love that! Further to allay
their misgivings, you might tell them that the original
manuscript was on golden plates, and that you got the
plates from an angel. Now go to work and good luck!

To date no student has carried out this assignment,
which, of course, was not meant seriously. But why not?
If anybody could write the Book of Mormon, as we have
been so often assured, it is high time that somebody, some
devoted and learned minister of the gospel, let us say,
performed the invaluable public service of showing the
world that it can be done.

Assuming that it was not Joseph Smith but somebody
else who wrote it gets us nowhere. If he did not write it,
Joseph Smith ran an even greater risk in claiming authorship than if he had. For the first important man among
his followers to turn against him would infallibly give him

away. Sidney Rigdon, full of ambition and jealous of the Prophet, never claimed authorship of the Book of Mormon (which has often been claimed for him) or any part in it, nor in all the years during which he fought Smith from outside the Church did he ever hint the possibility of any other explanation for the Book of Mormon than Joseph Smith's own story.

Martin Harris, Oliver Cowdery, David Whitmer all turned against the Prophet at one time or another, but neither they nor any other of the early associates of Smith, no matter how embittered, ever gave the slightest indication that they knew of anybody besides Smith himself who had any part whatever in the composition of the Book of Mormon.[9] For years men searched desperately to discover some other possible candidate for authorship, making every effort to find a more plausible explanation of the sources of these scriptures.

From the first, all admitted that Joseph Smith was much too ignorant for the job. We grant that willingly, but who on earth in 1829 was not too ignorant for it? Who is up to it today? If the disproportion between the learning of Smith and the stature of the Book of Mormon is simply comical, that between the qualifications of an Anthon or a Lepsius and the production of such a book is hardly less so. We can't get rid of Joseph Smith, but then it would do us no good if we could. Just consider the scope and variety of the work as briefly as possible.

First Nephi gives us first a clear and vivid look at the world of Lehi, a citizen of Jerusalem but much at home in the general world of the New East of 600 B.C. Then it takes us to the desert, where Lehi and his family wander for eight years, doing all the things that wandering families in the desert should do.[10] The manner of their crossing the ocean is described, as is the first settlement and hard pioneer life in the New World dealt with in the book of Jacob and a number of short and gloomy other books. The eth-

nological picture becomes very complicated as we learn
that the real foundations of New World civilization were
not laid by Lehi's people at all, but that there were far
larger groups coming from the Middle East at about the
same time (this was the greatest era of exploration and
colonization in the history of the ancient world), as well
as numerous survivors of archaic hunting cultures of
Asiatic origin that had thousands of years before crossed
the North Pacific and roamed all over the north country.[11]

The book of Mosiah describes a coronation rite in all
its details and presents extensive religious and political
histories mixed in with a complicated background of exploration and colonization.[12] The book of Alma is marked
by long eschatological discourses and a remarkably full
and circumstantial military history.[13] The main theme of
the book of Helaman is the undermining of society by moral
decay and criminal conspiracy; the powerful essay on crime
is carried into the next book, where the ultimate dissolution
of the Nephite government is described.[14]

Then comes the account of the great storm and earthquakes, in which the writer, ignoring a splendid opportunity for exaggeration, has as accurately depicted the typical behavior of the elements on such occasions as if he
were copying out of a modern textbook on seismology.[15]
The damage was not by any means total, and soon after
the catastrophe, Jesus Christ appeared to the most pious
sectaries who had gathered at the temple.

The account of Christ's visits to the earth after his
resurrection are exceedingly fragmentary in the New Testament, and zealous efforts are made in early Christian
apocryphal writing to eke them out;[16] his mission to the
Nephites is the most remarkable part of the Book of Mormon. Can anyone now imagine the terrifying prospect of
confronting the Christian world of 1830 with the very
words of Christ? Professor Meinhold still shudders with
horror at the presumption of it,[17] and well he might, as

the work of an impudent impostor who knew a year ahead of time just what mortal peril he was risking. The project is indeed *unerhört;* as the work of an honest, well-meaning Christian it is equally unthinkable.

But the boldness of the thing is matched by the directness and nobility with which the preaching of the Savior and the organization of the church are described. After this comes a happy history and then the usual signs of decline and demoralization. The death-struggle of the Nephite civilization is described with due attention to all the complex factors that make up an exceedingly complicated but perfectly consistent picture of decline and fall.[18] Only one who attempts to make a full outline of Book of Mormon history can begin to appreciate its immense complexity; and never once does the author get lost (as the student repeatedly does, picking his way out of one maze after another only with the greatest effort), and never once does he contradict himself. We should be glad to learn of any other like performance in the history of literature.

The book of Ether takes us back thousands of years before Lehi's time to the dawn of history and the first of the great world migrations. A vivid description of *Völkerwanderungszeit* concentrates on the migration of a particular party—a large one, moving through the years with their vast flocks and herds across central Asia (described at that time as a land of swollen inland seas), and then undertaking a terrifying crossing of the North Pacific. Totally unlike the rest of the Book of Mormon, this archaic tale conjures up the "heroic" ages, the "epic milieu" of the great migrations and the "saga time" that follows, describing in detail the customs and usages of a cultural complex that Chadwick was first to describe in our own day.[19]

Here in this early epic, far beyond the reach of any checks and controls, our foolish farm-boy had unlimited opportunity to let his imagination run wild. What an invitation to the most gorgeously funny extravaganza! And instead we get a sober, factual, but completely strange and unfamiliar tale.

Even this brief and sketchy indication of thematic material should be enough to show that we are not dealing here with a typical product of American or any other modern literature. Lord Raglan has recently observed that the evolution of religions has been not from the simple to the complex, but the other way around: "The modern tendency in religion, as in language, is towards simplicity. The youngest world religion, Islam, is simpler both in ritual and dogma than its predecessors, and such modern cults as Quakerism, Baabism, Theosophy, and Christian Science are simpler still."[20]

The work of Joseph Smith completely ignores this basic tendency; whatever he is, he is not a product of the times. The mere mass, charge, and variety of Mormonism has perplexed and offended many; but it is never too much to digest. The big, ponderous, detailed plot of the Book of Mormon, for example, is no more impressive than the ease, confidence, and precision with which the material is handled. The prose is terse, condensed, and fast-moving; the writer never wanders or speculates; beginning, middle, and ending are equally powerful, with no signs of fatigue or boredom; there is no rhetoric, no purple patches, nothing lurid or melodramatic—everything is kept sober and factual.

The Book of Mormon betrays none of the marks of "fine writing" of its day; it does not view the Gorgeous East with the eyes of any American of 1830, nor does it share in the prevailing ideas of what makes great or moving literature. The grandiose, awesome, terrible, and magnificent may be indicated in these pages, but they are never described; there is no attempt to be clever or display learning; the Book of Mormon vocabulary is less than 3,000 words! There are no favorite characters, no milking of particularly colorful or romantic episodes or situations, no reveling in terror and gore.

The book starts out with a colophon telling us whose hand wrote it, what his sources were, and what it is about; the author boasts of his pious parents and good education, explaining that his background was an equal mixture of Egyptian and Jewish, and then moves into this history establishing time, place, and background; the situation at Jerusalem and the reaction of Nephi's father to it, his misgivings, his prayers, a manifestation that came to him in the desert as he traveled on business and sent him back post-haste "to his own house at Jerusalem," where he has a great apocalyptic vision.[21]

All this and more in the first seven verses of the Book of Mormon. The writer knows exactly what he is going to say and wastes no time in saying it. Throughout the book we get the impression that it really is what its authors claim it to be, a highly condensed account from much fuller records. We can imagine our young rustic getting off to this flying start, but can we imagine him keeping up the pace for ten pages? For 588 pages the story never drags, the author never hesitates or wanders, he is never at a loss. What is really amazing is that he never contradicts himself.

Long ago Friedrich Blass laid down rules for testing any document for forgery.[22] Let us paraphrase these as rules to be followed by a successful forger and consider whether Joseph paid any attention to any of them.

1. Keep out of the range of unsympathetic critics. There is, Blass insists, no such thing as a clever forgery. No forger can escape detection if somebody really wants to expose him; all the great forgeries discovered to date have been crudely executed (for example, the Piltdown skull), depending for their success on the enthusiastic support of the public or the experts. The Book of Mormon has enjoyed no such support. From the day it appeared, important

persons at the urgent demand of an impatient public did
everything they could to show it a forgery. And Joseph
Smith, far from keeping it out of the hands of unsympathetic critics, did everything he could to put it into those
hands. Surely this is not the way of a deceiver.

2. Keep your document as short as possible.[23] The
longer a forgery is the more easily it may be exposed, the
danger increasing geometrically with the length of the writing. By the time he had gone ten pages, the author of the
Book of Mormon knew only too well what a dangerous
game he was playing *if* it was a hoax; yet he carries on
undismayed for six hundred pages.

3. Above all, *don't* write a *historical* document! They are
by far the easiest of all to expose, being full of "things too
trifling, too inconspicuous, and too troublesome" for the
forger to check up on.[24]

4. After you have perpetrated your forgery, go into
retirement or disappear completely. For vanity, according
to Blass, is the Achilles' heel of *every* forger.[25] A forger is
not only a cheat but also a show-off, attempting to put one
over on society; he cannot resist the temptation to enjoy
his triumph, and if he remains in circulation, inevitably he
gives himself away. Joseph Smith ignored any opportunity
of taking credit for the Book of Mormon—he took only the
responsibility for it.

5. Always leave an escape door open.[26] Be vague and
general, philosophize and moralize. Religious immunity
has been the refuge of most eminent forgers in the past,
beautiful thoughts and pious allegories, deep interpretations of scriptures, mystic communication to the initiated
few, these are safe grounds for the *pia fraus* ("pious fraud").
But the Book of Mormon never uses them. It does not even
exploit the convenient philological loophole of being a
translation: as an inspired translation it claims all the authority and responsibility of the original.

Granted that any explanation is preferable to Joseph

Smith's, where is any explanation? The chances against such a book ever coming into existence are astronomical: Who would write it? Why? Trouble, danger, and unpopularity are promised its defenders in the book itself. Did someone else write it so that Joseph Smith could take all the credit? Did Smith, knowing it was somebody else's fraud, claim authorship so that he could take all the blame?

The work involved in producing the thing was staggering, the danger terrifying; long before publication time the newspapers and clergy were howling for blood. Who would want to go on with such a suicidal project? All that trouble and danger just to fool people? But the author of this book is not trying to fool anybody: he claims no religious immunity, makes no effort to mystify, employs no rhetorical or allegorical license.

There are other things to consider too, such as the youth and inexperience of Smith when (regardless of who the author might be) he took sole responsibility for the Book of Mormon. Faced with a point-blank challenge by the learned world, any impostor would have collapsed in an instant, but Joseph Smith never weakened though the opposition quickly mounted to a roar of national indignation. Then there were the witnesses, real men who, though leaving the Church for various real or imagined offenses, never altered or retracted their testimonies of what they had seen and heard.

The fact that only one version of the Book of Mormon was ever published and that Joseph Smith's attitude toward it never changed is also significant. After copyrighting it in the spring of 1829, he had a year to think it over before publication and yield sensibly to social pressure; after that he had the rest of his life to correct his youthful indiscretion; years later, an important public figure and a skillful writer, knowing that his book was a fraud, knowing the horrible risk he ran on every page of it, and knowing how hopelessly naive he had been when he wrote it, he

230 THE PROPHETIC BOOK OF MORMON

should at least have soft-pedaled the Book of Mormon theme. Instead he insisted to the end of his life that it was the truest book on earth, and that a man could get nearer to God by observing its precepts than in any other way.[27]

Parallelomania has recently been defined as the double process which "first overdoes the supposed similarity in passages and then proceeds to describe source and derivation as if implying literary connections flowing in an inevitable or predetermined direction."[28] It isn't merely that one sees parallels everywhere, but especially that one instantly concludes that there can be only one possible explanation for such. From the beginning the Book of Mormon has enjoyed the full treatment from Parallelomaniacs. Its origin has been found in the Koran, in Swedenborg, in the teachings of Old School Presbyterians, French Mystics, Methodists, Unitarians, Millerites, Baptists, Campbellites, and Quakers; in Roman Catholicism, Arminianism, Gnosticism, Transcendentalism, Atheism, Deism, Owenism, Socialism, and Platonism; in the writing of Rabelais, Milton, Anselm, Joachim of Flores, Ethan Smith, and the Early Church; in Old Iranian doctrines, Brahmin mysticism, Free Masonry, and so on.

Now a person who has read only Milton, or Defoe, or Rabelais would have an easy time discovering parallels all through the Book of Mormon, or any other book he might read thereafter. It is not surprising that people who have studied only English literature are the most eager to condemn the Book of Mormon.[29]

Notes

1. Thomas F. O'Dea, The Mormons (Chicago: University of Chicago Press, 1957), 26.
2. Eduard Meyer, Ursprung and Geschichte der Mormonen (Halle: Niemeyer, 1912); published also as The Origin and History of the Mormons, tr. H. Rahde and E. Seaich (Salt Lake City: University of Utah, 1961), iii.
3. Peter Meinhold, "Die Anfänge des amerikanischen Geschichtsbewusstseins," Saeculum 5 (1954): 67.

4. Ibid., 86.
5. Ibid., 85-86.
6. Ibid., 86.
7. William F. Albright, "Archaeology and Religion," Cross Currents 9 (1959): 112.
8. Ibid., 111.
9. More recently, see Richard Lloyd Anderson, Investigating the Book of Mormon Witnesses (Salt Lake City: Deseret, 1981).
10. Hugh W. Nibley, An Approach to the Book of Mormon (Salt Lake City: Deseret, 1957), 47-57, 79-91; reprinted in CWHN 6:59-70, 95-108.
11. Hugh W. Nibley, Lehi in the Desert and the World of the Jaredites (Salt Lake City: Bookcraft, 1952); reprinted in CWHN 5.
12. Nibley, An Approach to the Book of Mormon, 256-70; CWHN 6:295-310.
13. Ibid., 164-89; CWHN 6:194-221.
14. Ibid., 336-50; CWHN 6:378-99.
15. Hugh W. Nibley, Since Cumorah (Salt Lake City: Deseret, 1970), 261-96; reprinted in CWHN 7:231-63.
16. Hugh W. Nibley, "Evangelium Quadraginta Dierum," Vigiliae Christianae 20 (1966): 1-24; reprinted in CWHN 4:10-44.
17. Meinhold, "Die Anfänge des amerikanischen Geschichtsbewusstseins," 76-78.
18. Nibley, An Approach to the Book of Mormon, 351-65; CWHN 6:416-30.
19. Hugh W. Nibley, "There Were Jaredites," Improvement Era 59 (January 1956): 30-32, 58-61; reprinted in CWHN 5:285-307, 380-94; H. Munro Chadwick, The Growth of Literature, 3 vols. (Cambridge: Cambridge University, 1932-40), vol. 1.
20. Lord Raglan, The Origins of Religion (London: Watts, 1949), 44.
21. Nibley, Lehi in the Desert and The World of the Jaredites, 1-26; in CWHN 5:3-24.
22. Friedrich W. Blass, "Hermeneutik and Kritik," Einleitende und Hilfsdisziplinen, vol. 1 of Handbuch der klassischen Altertumswissenschaft (Nördlingen: Beck, 1886), 269, 271.
23. Ibid., 270.
24. Ibid., 271.
25. Ibid., 270.
26. Ibid., 269.
27. Joseph Fielding Smith, ed., Teachings of the Prophet Joseph Smith (Salt Lake City: Deseret, 1976), 194.

28. Hugh W. Nibley, "Mixed Voices: The Comparative Method," *Improvement Era* (October-November 1959): 744-47, 759, 848, 854, 856; see above 193-206.

29. At a Portland Institute Symposium, Nibley subsequently gave a talk that developed several of these same themes further, along with discussing the negative reviews of Fawn Brodie's biography of Thomas Jefferson. The main body of the talk is included in the following transcript:

There are two rigorous tests to which we can subject the Book of Mormon: There is the internal test and the external test. This is true for every document. At the time of the Renaissance, which they usually say began with the fall of Constantinople (actually that is not true—the Turks treasured those documents from ancient times), all of a sudden they discovered them, not so much in the East as in the monasteries. They discovered thousands of manuscripts from ancient times. They didn't know what to do with them, or how to arrange them in order, or whether they were genuine or not. It became the stock assignment of scholarship to go through a great big pile of nondescript documents in quite a number of languages and decide what can they tell us about the human race—what here is authentic, what isn't, what have they been doing. It was just a mess, and some of the great scholars devised a very efficient method for processing these documents, and also for testing them for authenticity. Their test became foolproof, not only just intuitive; they could do marvelous things. They could take documents damaged almost beyond recognition and restore them. And later, years later, they would discover a complete document, and, sure enough, the restoration was correct. They were often going on mere intuition.

The first question that you have when you get an ancient document is—is it real? That is the first question they wanted to know. They could very well be not just copies of copies, but they could be fakes. That is very common too and, well, what part of it is real? Because there is no such thing as a perfect document. There *is* no such thing as a flawless document—never has been, never will be. The Book of Mormon recognized this—remember in the title page: "If there are mistakes therein they are the mistakes of men." And men do make mistakes. Well, if parts are real, what parts? What has been going on? How have they been treating the document? An interesting thing—you read the document itself without any reference to anything outside. If it is a historical document, you say, "Oh, sure, this claims to be at a certain time and place"—you can go back and check to see if this was going on. You do not have to do that. The classic work on the criticism of ancient documents is by Frederick Blass. It was written almost a hundred years ago. It is a massive work by a German. I think he is most memorable because of his equally classical work on classical rhetoric. He begins by saying (which is so typical of German scholarship), "I have never been able to get interested in classical rhetoric." Then the great man begins to exhaust the field and the reader too. I don't think anybody ever read it through except me, once. Well, as Blass says, you never have to go outside of a document, you never have to check from outside sources; just read the thing itself and it easily becomes clear whether it is authentic or not. Regardless of the period, regardless of how much else is known about it, regardless of what other documents go along with it, simply read it and see if it is convincing in itself.

Now today interesting things are happening on many fronts. They are dealing with things differently than they ever have before. If it looks like an elephant, call it an elephant; no matter how queer it may sound, you have to pay attention to it now. Things must be explained. You just can't fit everything into the well-known, established patterns. Before, if anything seemed odd, strange, or weird, you just discounted it; but you can't do that anymore. It is these things that are odd that are most significant. For example, speaking of documents, the best kind of document is the one that has fantastic mistakes in it—when you get a weird anomaly or contradiction or something impossible. That is the time to start looking; that is not the kind of thing that copyists put in. Copyists have a weakness for correcting texts they don't understand, so they write it so they can understand. So if you have a flawless text, look out; it has been faked, doctored; the copyists have taken care of it, they have brought it up to date. But if you have one that is full of the weirdest stuff, there you have a real gem, because that stuff came from somewhere. Someone picked it up from somewhere, and you just need to look at the document itself. It is not necessary to go beyond the internal evidence, because it is impossible to fake an ancient document on two conditions, first the internal—especially if it is of any length at all (and the Book of Mormon is long) you multiply the danger, you compound it with every word you add (mathematical progression). Every time you add a word you get yourself in deeper and deeper. So keep your documents short if you want to fake one. Never write a long document—that will hang you just as sure as anything. Nobody has ever faked one successfully.

The second condition, of course, is external. Does it purport to be historical? If you are going to write a document, write one of beautiful thoughts, and no one can object. If you say it is history, then you are in trouble because it has to be checked at various points. So this first thought is going to be about internal evidence of the Book of Mormon, just the internal evidence. I'm not going to use anything outside at all. The internal evidence for the super-human origins of the Book of Mormon is so overwhelming today that the story of the angel, as far as I am concerned, has become the least baffling explanation. If you think of other explanations, good—but they rejected the story of the angel out of hand because it was absurd. Well, Blass says (this is a very important principle) you should always begin by assuming that a document is authentic. Why not give it the benefit of the doubt? It will quickly become apparent if it isn't. If you proceed on the grounds of authenticity, and if it isn't, the first thing you will know you will be caught up short. So, the first thing, you begin by assuming that your document is authentic, and you say, "Well, that isn't playing fair." All right then, you think of a better explanation. If it isn't a fourteenth-century document, were did it come from? If the famous Turk map of North America of pre-Columbian times isn't authentic, then who did pro-duce it? The more fantastic it is, the easier it is to select a substitute and alternative. Well, I can't think of a more fantastic explanation of the Book of Mormon than the story of the angel. Think of another way to explain it. By George, it turns out that the story of the angel is the least fantastic story that you can think of—everything else is even more weird.

You are welcome to try to explain how the Book of Mormon came to exist. What would be your plausible explanation of the existence of the Book of Mormon? How would you explain its mere existence? "Well," you say "let me give some parallel examples." Okay, tell us of another book, anything like that at all. The only way you can do it is to reconstruct the crime yourself. How did Joseph Smith get or how did he produce this book? You ask yourself how you would go about it. Try to imagine how you would go about reproducing the book.

I tried this out at family home evening last week on some very, very literary students, some foreign students, some investigators— a very skeptical group. And since they were literature people, I asked them, "How would you do it?" Consider the problems facing you if you are undertaking to do what Joseph Smith did. Mere physical problems: he must produce a big book. All right, sit down and produce a big book. That means a lot of work, just putting it together. It means you have to find the time, you have to find the resources, you have to find the continued motivation to keep going. Just try to keep any student or anybody going on a project like that! What is the motivation, what is going to keep you going right up until the end? Again you see, immediately the internal evidence comes. Does it have an even flow, does he run out, does he peter out, does he start repeating himself, does he weaken? These are all internal evidences. The Book of Mormon starts out with a bang, a rush — it is a marvelous beginning and it never drags, things happen very rapidly. You will find that it is when people don't know exactly what they are going to write about that they can string things out endlessly. All your big books do that. But the pace of the Book of Mormon is quite breathtaking — the number of episodes that occur, the rapidity of things that occur. You would be surprised to compare any ten pages with the next ten pages and see what happens — you are in a different world entirely. Things really keep moving, and they keep moving, so it not only starts out with a rush like a rocket, but it ends up like a rocket. It ends up with a magnificent display of fireworks. It never loses from beginning to end, and in the middle it is the most exciting of all.

So this is the test we put to our book. Remember, you are a young man struggling to make a living, tied up in such projects. Of all the things to get tied up in when you are trying to make a living! Remember, Jesse Knight's father tells in his journal how he first met Joseph Smith and Oliver Cowdery, and they were living in a shack translating the Book of Mormon. He said they were hungry and they didn't have a penny, and he brought them a sack of potatoes; and it was that sack of potatoes that enabled them to survive the winter. They were that hungry doing it — he should have better things to think of than a long, long book and a very complicated book that no one was going to believe in. So you have to have the motivation just to create a big book.

You ask the people, "Can you think of any other such performance for comparison?" Who else wrote a long book like the Book of Mormon? What young fellow ever produced anything like that? We think of the great, massive, impressive works in English literature. There is Macaulay and the *History of England*, Carlyle's *Frederick the Great*, Gibbons' *Decline and Fall*; but you see how different these all are. There are plenty of big historical works, but these men were paraphrasing. They had all the records in front of them. They rearranged the chronological order and told the story. They just retold the story, and sometimes very interestingly, but they had all their materials provided them. They could do what they wanted with the materials as far as that was concerned. Joseph Smith had no such handbook. The most terrifying assignment that you can ever give students is to say, "Write on anything you want," because that is where you give yourself away. Joseph Smith could write anything at all; no one knew about Central America in those times long ago. That is just the challenge; that is the hardest thing of all to do. Just try doing it. If you can follow a text, if you have historical records or something to follow, you are on safe ground; you can move securely, you can go step by step, you have handles. He had no such thing to go by.

Joseph Smith had to start from scratch and produce a brand new epic. Instead of making things easier for himself, he made something never seen before. Now we have epics being produced in our generation, and some of them become very popular, strangely popular. Begin with Walter Scott at the beginning of the nineteenth century producing his ponderous works, or, in our time, C. S. Lewis, Tolkien, who have invented cultures and worlds all of their own. They are free to do this, but notice here they are not held to historical accuracy at all, though they still have material supplied. Walter Scott is nothing else but a story, and he read and read and read for years. He was thoroughly saturated in the literature, and so was Tolkien, a professor of Anglo-Saxon at Oxford. He just retold old English stories. Shakespeare was the greatest creative genius of them all, but not a single plot, not a single sentiment in all of Shakespeare, is original. They are all lifted from somewhere else but fit in a real and marvelous new structure. It is like saying, "Oh, yes, he used all those words you will find in the dictionary, so there is nothing original about that." You can say, "Bach just used the eight notes of the scale and composed this; anybody could do that if he had a piano." No, you can't compose like Bach. Joseph Smith does not write like that. These men have this license; they can be creative as they wish, but they are all completely saturated from material from a time and place and are just rewriting it in their imagination. The same thing with C. S. Lewis; he mixed his religion in with the theme, a sort of science fiction, and he goes off into the blue. These people were not held to historic accuracy, and their material is already provided. And then they are given a special license by the reading public and they write, and even so they are all monotonous. Nobody reads Walter Scott today. Tolkien had a big run with young people a while ago, but what do Tolkien's characters do? They are always eating and traveling and having wars and having things in court.

They just go through the regular thing of the Medieval court—hunting and feeding and traveling and fighting. That is it, the same routine. Joseph Smith isn't going to be able to get away with anything as easy as that. C. S. Lewis always has boy meets girl on Jupiter, or boy meets girl on Mars. It is the same story, you just put it in a different setting. That is what all your science fiction people do anyway.

Well, back to Brother Joseph—you can do the same with your piece you are writing. Remember, you are writing a big book—nothing has to be trimmed—just a big book. Right there you have a terrific challenge. What am I going to do? I'll go crazy. I can't go on writing day after day, year after year. What is this? Won't you give me some help, won't you tell me what to say? Oh sure, you can go to the Bible. They tell us again and again that anyone looking at the Bible can write a Book of Mormon. It is all there after all—just try that again. You can do the same thing with our piece; you can put in anything you want to. But as soon as you start borrowing, you will give yourself away. As the scripture tells us, "My words shall be of the uprightness of my heart" (Job 33:3).

Brigham Young used to have a black leather couch in his office. A window faced the couch; when people came to see him, they would sit on the couch with Brigham Young's back to the window, the desk between them. Brigham Young would just look at the person for three minutes, that was all. He was never fooled; he could figure them out every time. After all, they had come to see him; he didn't ask for them. If they had anything to say, they could talk and he would say nothing. He would just let them talk, and lots of rascals came, people plotting against his life, people wanting to get money from him, all sorts of things. The man never had to talk more than three minutes. Here is your nondirect interview which is so effective to the psychologist—Brigham had it worked out completely. My grandfather said he was never wrong. After three minutes he knew his man. Well, the same way, if you sit down and write a book 600 pages long, you are going to give yourself away all over the place—what a revelation of your character. Your background will come to the fore all over the place. Enemies tried to catch Joseph Smith in this trap. There are things common to all human affairs. For example, in the Book of Mormon, people eat; well, they eat in the Bible—aha! See, he stole it from the Bible. Somebody actually used that as an argument. The problem here is to make a big book.

Secondly, the book has to have some sort of quality. You didn't have to make your book good, but Joseph Smith had to make his book good. So it would be nice, if you are going to write a book, to write a decent one while you are at it. The book can't be complete nonsense. You can't waste your time and everyone else's. You've got to make a book that is something. Well, now you are in real trouble, because 99 percent of the books published today are not worth the paper they are printed on. Here you are, twenty-three years old, and you must live with this book over your head the rest of your life. No matter who writes it, you are going to be wholly and completely responsible for it—Joseph Smith, author and proprietor. He had to do that for the sake of the copyright. Before the book even came out, all the scandalous stories were circulating, and in the *Painesville Telegraph* they made a parody of what it must be. In order to protect it against complete manipulation, the author had to copyright it under the copyright law. Joseph Smith authored the Book of Mormon just as James was the author of the Epistle of James. Although he could write, the author was the Lord. It was given by revelation. That would never do—we assign the authorship of the Bible to the men who wrote it, by revelation or not. Joseph Smith takes complete responsibility—no matter who wrote it; that isn't the question. He is going to be responsible for it, and be responsible for it the rest of his life. How often he must think back, "Oh, what I did when I was a fool kid. If I could only amend that book!" It would be easy—get more inspiration and have a revised edition. The first edition was reprinted by Wilford C. Wood. It is very useful; it hasn't been divided up into chapters and verses—Orson Pratt and Brother Talmage did that later. It is an interesting book to use. There are some mistakes, but the text is actually a better one than the 1920 edition. The point is, it was never changed, and Joseph Smith was never haunted by it. Right to the end, he kept insisting, "This is the most correct book on the earth today." Imagine that—even more correct than a book on mathematics. Sure, I have books of mathematics that are hopelessly out of date today. They are not used today. They were when I was in school. They are not used anymore because they are hopelessly wrong. You are going to be stuck with the correctness of the book.

It should have some literary quality, don't you think? If you are going to have to live with it the rest of your days, it should be consistent; it should hang together. You are feeling bad when you write one part, you are feeling good when you write another. The thing must drag out for years. What are the different parts going to read like? What are they going to be like? In talking or writing for 600 pages, you can't choose but to lay bare your own soul. That is going to be exposing your mental quality and your mental bankruptcy. It will show if you have nothing but gibberish, if you are devious and scheming, if you are honest, and also the degree of education. You can see what Blass means when he says you don't need anything but internal evidence.

You can tell whether a man is faking a book or not if it is long enough, if he gives himself enough room — and it doesn't take much. The only successful forgeries have been very short ones, just brief inscriptions, two or three words or a half-dozen words. As soon as forgeries get long, and there have been some famous ones, it becomes easy to discover. Why do you think Blass states this as a categorical principle: "There never has been a clever forgery." People say the Book of Mormon was a clever forgery. There never has been a clever forgery. "Well, how do you know? A really clever one would have never been discovered," you say. "You won't have even known he was a forger." Such a statement can be justified on the grounds that every forgery discovered so far has not been clever but crude and very obvious. The only reason it ever got by at all is that people wanted to accept it, wanted to very badly. The Royalist boy Chatterly is an example. He was just a child when he faked a lot of Middle English poetry, and everyone was so thrilled about the discovery of old documents that they never bothered to read them with particular care. The first person who read them with any critical eye discovered they were done by a kid, and very crudely. See, when you discover a forgery, it is very obvious; the author gives himself away.

This brings up an interesting thing: When I taught at Claremont, I had a next-door neighbor who was the wife of the most famous of all American scholars. Her husband had just died the year she came to live in Claremont, and since we both rode bicycles, we got to be pretty good friends. She told me that her husband, a very conscientious, public-minded man, decided he would do the world a good deed and save a lot of people the trouble of mixing themselves up and being confused in their ignorance and hopelessness by taking a few hours off and going through the Book of Mormon (and that was all it would take, a few hours) and showing them it was a fraud. He would thereby perform a valuable service to the Mormons, too, because it was of no value to them to be led astray. If they were being fooled, they should be grateful to him to know that. So he began to do it. He thought it would take twenty minutes or so. Twenty hours, twenty days, and his work never came out. I asked

her what happened to that public service—well he just dropped it,
that was all.

It should be very easy under these circumstances, the Book of
Mormon being produced under such conditions, to make a monkey
out of Joseph Smith, because, as I say, there is no such thing as a
clever forgery. You just can't get away with it. It was many years
later when he had developed a fine style of his own, yet he still
proclaimed, "This is the most correct book around."

All right, you have just the work of producing the book, and you
can smell the quality all over. Then the disposal of it after you write
it: What are you going to do with it? Do you really expect this to
be popular? Are you crazy? In competition with the Bible? People
don't read the Bible anyway, but when they do, you now tell them
there is more Bible to read! They won't thank you for that, I'm sure.
As a holy book, it is going to be kept perpetually before the public.
They are going to be dogged with it, they are going to be bothered
with it, you are going to wear them down with it. I was on a short-
term mission here many years ago, and by that time everyone in
Portland had been visited so much by the Mormons they were sick
and tired of them, but they are still hearing of the Book of Mormon.
This is an important thing. This book has to be kept perpetually
before the public. Also, through the years literary tastes are going
to change, and styles in reading are going to change. Sometimes
they go for things, sometimes not. You notice the Book of Mormon
is being peddled back East now. You see it in the Chicago airport,
for example.

This takes us into external evidence. This is a very great risk you
are taking now: you are going far beyond a book of opinion, sage
remarks, the wisdom of the ages, which are always very repetitious.
There is nothing original in any of those books. The expressions
are sometimes very catching, the forms in which they are conveyed
to us. As I said, Shakespeare was not original, but how he says it
was excellent. The Jewish rabbis will tell you that there is nothing
in the philosophy in the Sermon on the Mount that you won't find
in the Old Testament or in the rabbinical writings, and that is true,
too. You are not going to issue this just as a book of your ideas and
thoughts. It is not a book of essays, but a story of things that really
happened. It has got to be reality. It has to have substance in this
book. And you can expect unlimited criticism, unsparing criticism
without a supporting voice, because no critic in his right mind is
going to accept this book just on your say-so. And what lies at the
end—what can you look forward to in this dangerous product? It

is dangerous: terror not only knocks at the door, but every time you leave the house someone is waiting for you. Shots are fired in the night, and mobs come. The worst rioting and mobbing occurred before the Book of Mormon ever came out. Some of the most harrowing experiences that the Prophet Joseph ever had were caused simply by the Book of Mormon. The advance publicity brought down such a storm of denunciation that it put his life in the most imminent danger. Here is another motive. Are you going to write that kind of book? Yes, you are not in any doubt about that. You get a horrifying foretaste of what merely the process of getting it into print is going to get you into while you are dictating the book. This is no way to win friends; you are asking for trouble. Every day while writing the book, the sheer audacity of the theme is brought to you with great force.

Read the literature about Joseph Smith's undertaking. Who were his critics from the first? They say he was writing for some gullible bumpkins, a lot of yokels that would swallow anything. No, it was the ministers and teachers. It was the establishment back East that immediately had this book in their hands and were criticizing it. It was the ministers that wanted to defend their ignorant flocks against Joseph Smith. You might be able to fool the gullible people, but they weren't the ones who read it and they weren't the ones Joseph Smith was concerned about, as far as that goes. What did these men protest? They protested, "Blasphemy, alias the Golden Bible." The main protest was that in this enlightened age, in the advanced nineteenth century, in this age of science and understanding, that such a fraud should appear, such a scandal. This was the thing they couldn't stand. It was an offense to the intellect. It was an offense to the mind of men. It wasn't on spiritual or religious grounds that they protested. Those were the reasons they gave their flocks, the religious mobs, that it was a blasphemous work. But always the writings against the Book of Mormon were that it was an offense to intelligent people. So these were the people that criticized it.

Speaking of only internal contradictions here, historical and literary epics fairly shriek their folly to anyone who reads them. Here we have a long history. It is full of proper names and of people and places; it recounts their comings and goings and even their thoughts and prayers and their dealings with each other; their wars and their contentions and rumors of wars; their economic, social, dynastic, military, religious, and intellectual history. Now the main problem here, from an internal point of view, is how in all this human comedy can you as the author establish a ring of similitude from readers who have read a lot of stuff, who know how things are supposed to happen or how they do happen, who spent their lives immersing themselves in the doings of dynasties or families or nations? A thousand clues spring to the ear immediately of any educated practitioner: "This reads all right. This sounds pretty good. Oh, this is bad here." And you are not educated. Do you have any idea what you are up against?

12
Howlers in the Book of Mormon

It is the "howlers" with which the Book of Mormon abounds that furnish the best index to its authenticity. They show, first of all, that the book was definitely not a typical product of its time, and secondly, when they are examined more closely in the light of present-day evidence, they appear very different indeed than they did a hundred years ago. Consider some of the queer gadgets mentioned in the Book of Mormon:

1. According to the book of Ether, the first migrants to America were Asiatics who crossed the violently stormy waters of the North Pacific in eight ships constructed "like unto the ark of Noah" (Ether 6:7). To wit, they had covered decks, "and the top thereof was tight like unto a dish; . . . and the door thereof, when it was shut, was tight like unto a dish," and "the ends thereof were peaked" (Ether 2:17). It was driven before the wind without sails and was often covered by the heavy seas, "for the mountain waves shall dash upon you" (Ether 2:24).

Within the strange ships, men and animals were safe, as "they were tossed upon the waves of the sea before the wind" (Ether 6:5).[1] The oldest accounts of the ark of Noah, the Sumerian ones, describe it as a "magur boat," peaked at the ends, completely covered but for a door, without sails, and completely covered by the waters from time to time, as men and animals rode safe within.[2] But the re-

This article appeared in the Millennial Star, 125 (February 1963): 28-34.

markable thing about Jared's boats was their illumination by stones which shone in the dark because they had been touched by the finger of the Lord (Ether 3:6, 6:3).

The Rabbis tell of a mysterious Zohar that illuminated the ark, but for further instruction we must go to much older sources: the Pyrophilus is traced back to the *Jalakanta* stone of India, which shines in the dark and enables its owner to pass unharmed beneath the waters; this in turn has been traced back through classical and Oriental sources to the Gilgamesh Epic, where Alexander's wonderful Pyrophilus stone turns up as the Plant of Life in the possession of the Babylonian Noah.[3]

A large number of ancient traditions, first brought together in the present century, justify one in assuming some sort of legendary shining stones in the ark of Noah. Whether or not there is any historical reality behind it, the fact is that we now know, from sources completely inaccessible to the world of Joseph Smith, that such a tradition actually did exist in very ancient times. It is nothing to laugh at after all.

2. As a laugh-getter, the shining stones of the Jaredites have always had a close competitor in the Liahona. The Liahona was a hollow bronze sphere in which were mounted two pointers, headless arrows that bore mysterious inscriptions and pointed the way that Lehi's party should travel in the desert. Besides pointing the direction, the arrows and the inscriptions also provided special instructions for the journey. They only worked during the expedition to the New World, after which they ceased to function and were preserved among the national treasures as a curiosity.

A recent study by an Arabic scholar has called attention to the long-forgotten custom of the ancient Arabs and Hebrews of consulting two headless arrows whenever they were about to undertake a journey; the usual thing was to consult the things at a special shrine, though it was common also to take such divination arrows along on the trip in a special container. The message of the arrows, which were mere sticks without heads or feathers, was conveyed by their pointing and especially by the inscriptions that were on them, giving detailed directions as to the journey. Mr. Fahd deserves our thanks for having called attention to this interesting and forgotten gadget in 1958; but how would Joseph Smith know about it in 1829?[4]

3. Nothing in the Book of Mormon itself has excited greater hilarity and derision than Joseph Smith's report that the original record was engraved on gold plates, the account being condensed from much fuller records on bronze plates. Today scores of examples of ancient historical and religious writings on sacred and profane plates of gold, silver, and bronze make this part of Joseph Smith's story seem rather commonplace.[5] But it was anything but commonplace a hundred years ago, when the idea of sacred records being written on metal plates was thought just too funny for words.

4. For years the most frequent and what was thought to be the most unanswerably devastating charge against the Book of Mormon was that it mentioned steel. Steel as early as 600 B.C. was considered a whopping anachronism: If Laban had a ceremonial sword with a pure gold handle and a blade of "precious steel," so did generations of potentates before him.[6]

5. The earliest immigrants to America domesticated elephants, the Book of Mormon tells us, hundreds of years before Lehi's time; there is no mention of elephants in the later Nephite period. This is another absurdity that has recently become a possibility.[7]

6. Critics have been scathing in denouncing what they consider an obvious fraud in the Book of Mormon's mention of Nephite money—not coins, but money. Today we know that the ancients, notably the Egyptians, had real money a thousand years before the purported invention

of coinage by the Lydians. The really remarkable thing about the Nephite monetary system, however, was that it was practical rather than traditional: "They altered their reckoning and their measure, according to the minds and the circumstances of the people, in every generation" (Alma 11:4). Their sole interest was to get the *best* monetary system possible, and they did so: for the system of monetary weights given in Alma (units of 1, 2, 4, and 7) has been shown by mathematicians to be the most efficient system possible; that is, for carrying out business transactions, it requires fewer "coins," or whatever weights or measures or monetary units were used, than any other system devisable, including our own.[8]

Whatever Joseph Smith was, he was no mathematician: wasn't it sly of him to devise the perfect monetary system for his mythical Nephites? Or maybe he wasn't so sly after all; since nobody noticed the fact until the present decade, maybe he was simply wasting his talents.

7. No less impressive than the gadgets in the Book of Mormon are the proper names. The Hebrew names often have peculiar nonbiblical forms; highly characteristic is the ending in *-iah*. The discovery of lists of prisoners from Lehi's own Jerusalem now makes it possible to check on these name types, and the *-iah* ending is found to be highly characteristic of them too.[9] Lehi as a traveling merchant had frequent contacts with the Arabs, and his elder sons have good Arab names; indeed, it was not until 1940 that the name of Lehi itself started turning up as a personal name, first in the old Hebrew settlement at Elath.[10]

The great emphasis in the Book of Mormon on the name of Ammon (and to a lesser degree Manti), both alone and in components, faithfully reflects conditions in the Old World in Lehi's day, and there is not much room for quibbling about the "Egypticity" of such Book of Mormon names as Korihor, Paanchi, Pacumeni, or Giddianhi.[11] There is one name that always gave this writer a jolt: Hermounts. What a name! Like nothing you ever heard before. So until about a month ago, we completely ignored it. Then the question was raised, What is Hermounts? It is not a person; it is the name used to designate wilderness country, "which was infested by wild and ravenous beasts" (Alma 2:37). Right away we thought of Min (good old Book of Mormon Ammoron) of Hermonthis, the Egyptian Pan, the God of wild places and wild animals. Some explain the name Hermonthis as meaning "House of Month" (good old Book of Mormon Manti!), referring to the shrine of the southern frontier. "Month" is the patron of war and colonization, and next to Ammon, Manti is the most common name of the persons and places in the Book of Mormon.[12] Whatever the real explanation, Hermounts does not offend the ear anymore. If the Egyptians want to designate their wild country as Hermonthis and the Nephites as Hermounts, that is their business.

8. Passing from the particular to the more general, the cultural patterns of the Book of Mormon are not to be ignored. The close cultural ties between Jerusalem and Egypt insisted on by the Book of Mormon have been thoroughly vindicated. There is a great deal about desert life in 1 Nephi: Lehi's dreams of the perils of the way, yawning gulfs, mists of darkness, flash-floods, and proud and contemptuous dwellers in lofty, desert skyscraper palaces are matched by everyday manners and customs: passionate debate in the tent of the sheikh, an authentic qaṣida, ceaseless scouting and prowling, covered fires and breathless escapes, fierce family feuds and deadly rivalries, starvation, hunting, avoiding raiders, and losing the way.[13]

9. More impressive still are the fullness and detail with which the rites of a royal coronation are described: here we have that ritual complex known as "patternism" set forth with great clarity. The theory and practice of kingship, which of recent years has become almost an independent discipline, are explained in the book of Mosiah

with due attention to its Old World background and its inevitable corruptions. It is only since 1930 that the common ritual pattern of coronation in the ancient Near East, with its complicated political, economic, priestly, and eschatological connections, has become the object of intensive and extensive comparative study.[14]

At the coronation of King Benjamin, all the elements are met within their proper setting and relationships, the coronation rite itself being the subject of a long moral and didactic discourse by the king. The great annual assembly is often referred to in the Book of Mormon; the case of Benjamin is far from being an isolated instance.[15]

10. A rather gaudy and sensational aspect of the royal cult, which has been the subject of some recent historical novels, was that sinister mode of succession that prevailed in the earliest days, when the old king would be beheaded by the new king, who would then proceed to marry the queen.[16] The Jaredites had hardly arrived in the Western Hemisphere, ages before Lehi's people, when a certain princess inaugurated this system, which was unknown in later times. She did not invent it, we are told, but brought it to her father's attention from ancient sources: "Hath he not read the record which our fathers brought across the great deep? Behold, is there not an account concerning them of old?" (Ether 8:9). She goes on to explain the beheading to the old king, who unwittingly becomes the first victim (Ether 8:10, 9:6).

Here on the borderline between the historical and the legendary, the thing to note is not the historical accuracy of the Book of Mormon, but its perfect legendary consistency. The various people who came to the New World from the Old are supposed to have brought certain traditions and legends with them, as the last instance demonstrates. The rustic youth in upper New York shrewdly included a good deal of this old apocryphal stuff in the

Book of Mormon, stuff quite inaccessible to him or the world he lived in. Take a few examples.

11. The Nephite prophet Moroni tells a story, which he says was common property of his people, concerning the death of the patriarch Jacob (Alma 46:24-25). I have never come across this story except in Tha'labi—who in Joseph Smith's America had access to Tha'labi? Tha'labi, a Persian in the tenth century A.D., went about collecting old stories of the prophets from his Jewish neighbors. The story in barest outline is that when the garment of Joseph was brought to Jacob on his deathbed, he rejoiced because part of it was sound and whole, signifying that some of his descendants would always remain true; but he wept because another part of the garment was befouled and rotted away, signifying that part of his descendants that would fall away. The same story is told with the same interpretation in Tha'labi and in the book of Alma, in the latter significantly as a popular folk-tale. The presence of such a story among the Hebrews has been indicated in a recent study by a Jewish scholar, but could Joseph Smith wait until 1953 to read about it?[17]

12. Moroni tells the story of Joseph's garment as a commentary on his own garment. He had written a high-sounding motto on his cloak, put it on a pole, and gone through the land raising recruits to fight the battles of the Lord. His improvised banner he calls the Title of Liberty (Alma 46:12-15). One is reminded of the founding of the order of the Magi by an ancient hero who did much the same thing, but even more of the war standards of the Dead Sea Scrolls.[18] The point is that the Book of Mormon tells us that it was a typical and familiar thing that Moroni was doing. The people who came to join his holy host knew just how to go about it, "rending their garments in token, or as a covenant, that they would not forsake the Lord their God; or, in other words, if they should trans-gress, . . . the Lord should rend them even as they had

rent their garments" (Alma 46:21). There is much more of this "enacting of a mystery" in the Book of Mormon, one of the most interesting examples being:

13. The peculiar rite of hanging. When the celebrated liberal-preacher Nehor killed an opponent in his rage, he was condemned to death: "And they carried him upon the top of the hill Manti, and there he was caused, or rather did acknowledge, between the heavens and the earth, that what he had taught to the people was contrary to the word of God; and there he suffered an ignominious death" (Alma 1:15). Centuries later the traitor Zemnarihah suffered a like hanging "upon a tree, yea, even upon the top thereof, until he was dead" (3 Nephi 4:28). This acknowledging of one's crime between heaven and earth takes us back to the first sinners, Harut and Marut (another tradition of the Magi), and in the Jewish tradition the angel Shamhozi who "repented, and by way of penance, hung himself up between heaven and earth."[19]

14. What religious group has not sought aid and comfort from the Dead Sea Scrolls since their discovery? The most crushing argument against the authenticity of the Book of Mormon has ever been its attributing of Christian expressions and ideas to people whose ancestors are supposed to have left Jerusalem 600 years *before* Christ: how could such people ever have brought New Testament ideas with them? The Dead Sea Scrolls, to the surprise and alarm of the learned, have now broken down the late and artificial barrier which the Jewish and Christian doctors erected between the world of the Old Testament and the New. Except where the learned themselves hold sway, they were not two separate worlds at all.

Recently Professor E. R. Goodenough has pointed out with great fullness and clarity that what has long been accepted in the schools as the Jewish tradition is only one Jewish tradition, the Rabbinical or "horizontal" tradition, as he designates it. After long years of dedicated effort, the Rabbis succeeded in so discrediting and effacing the ancient and genuine rival Jewish tradition that few today, even among scholars of Judaism, are aware of its existence.[20] This older tradition Goodenough calls the "mystic" or "vertical" tradition, the term being suggested by the basic belief that the leaders of Israel should have prophetic inspiration — direct "vertical" ties with the other-world revelation, instead of the mere "horizontal" transmission of knowledge from human teacher to student. To judge by Goodenough's presentation, the Book of Mormon is a mine of authentic "vertical" Judaism. To give some examples:

15. A very common motif in the oldest surviving examples of Jewish and Christian art is the figure of a prophet clothed in a white robe or of three men likewise attired. The white robe is a symbolic garment showing that the wearer has reached a state of celestial purity and enlightenment, and, according to Professor Goodenough, is of immense importance for the understanding of "vertical Judaism." Alma in the Book of Mormon is an authority on vertical Judaism and knows all about the white-robed figures, individually and in threes: "There were many who were ordained and became high priests of God . . . and were sanctified, and their garments were washed white, . . . having their garments made white, being pure and spotless before God" (Alma 13:10-12). He appeals to the people: "Keep your garments spotless, that ye may at last be brought to sit down with Abraham, Isaac, and Jacob, and the holy prophets who have been ever since the world began, having your garments spotless, even as their garments are spotless, in the kingdom of heaven" (Alma 7:25; cf. Alma 13:11-12).

He discourses at length on the things which Goodenough designates as peculiar to vertical Judaism: life beyond the grave, the virgin mother of the Messiah, baptism, the importance of a Savior, and the peculiar status of Melchizedek, an unpopular figure in "Rabbinic Juda-

ism" but a great favorite in the "vertical" tradition. All this
is typical of the book of Alma. And who was Alma?

16. Alma was the son of another Alma, who was a
priest in the employ of a small-time despot called King
Noah. Alma the Elder listened to the preaching of a prophet
Abinadi, who knew the old vertical prophetic tradition
right back to the beginning; in his teaching, Abinadi cited
extensively from the books and records. When Abinadi
was put to death, Alma went into hiding and thought
things over; he promptly wrote down all he could remember of Abinadi's teachings and then went out in the desert
and secretly founded his own religious community at a
place where there were springs and a grove of trees. The
organization and teachings of his "church in the wilderness" present almost a perfect duplicate of the Qumran
community. The surprising thing is that the Book of Mormon traces the institution right back to the old desert sectaries, explaining that Lehi himself was one of many pious
Jews who incurred the wrath of the authorities at Jerusalem
and deliberately went out into the desert where he could
live the Law of Moses in its purity and look forward to the
coming of the Messiah.[21] If the least be said, the scrolls
from the Dead Sea make a lot of the Book of Mormon
sound very familiar.

17. Speaking of vertical Judaism, one should not overlook Zenos, an ancient Hebrew prophet who lived before
the days of Lehi but who is often cited in the Book of
Mormon as one of the prophets who spoke most clearly
and explicitly of the coming of the Messiah. He represents
strikingly the suppression of "vertical" Judaism by the
doctors at Jerusalem; for we learn (quite between the lines)
that he prayed in a strictly private capacity in his home
and was a commoner and a farmer who called upon God
in his field and in his house, that God heard his prayer,
that he spent some time in the desert, that he succeeded
in converting some of the opposition, that he was cast out

and despised, but that the tables were turned and his enemies suffered a severe setback (Alma 33:4-10), that he prophesied things about the Nephites and much about the coming of the Messiah and the gathering of Israel (1 Nephi 19:11-16), and that "Zenos did testify boldly; for the which he was slain" (Helaman 8:19). A typical representative of the *ma'asim* ("deeds"), one might say.

We have chosen the above examples out of hundreds because they have been cited in the past as the strongest possible arguments against the Book of Mormon. They are the last sort of thing any forger would introduce into a book designed to fool people; they are the sort of thing nobody would dream of in Joseph Smith's day; and they are the sort of thing that one would tend to look for today in a genuine record of the sort indicated.

18. The first and foremost objection to the Book of Mormon was summed up in the first word of Alexander Campbell's opening blast against it: "Blasphemy!" The first thing that would hit any Christian on opening to the title page was the claim of this book to be nothing less than the Word of God—right beside the Bible! " 'Ye have heard the blasphemy: What think ye?' (Mark 14:64). Is further testimony necessary?"[22] Again the Book of Mormon has the last word: rare indeed is the Christian scholar today who would maintain that every word declared canonical in the past, by committees claiming no inspiration whatever, is the absolute Word of God; or that all the writings given noncanonical status by the same learned conclaves are, when they claim the status of scripture, to be condemned out of hand as fraudulent. That won't do anymore; today religious journals are full of perplexed and controversial articles on "What is Scripture?"

19. Again, the statement on the front page of the Book of Mormon, explaining that if it contains mistakes they are the mistakes of men, has always been exploited as a dead giveaway: How, it was asked, could an inspired book have

any mistakes at all? Today it would be hard to find a scholar who does not recognize that all the scriptures in our possession bear all over them the marks of having passed through the hands of ordinary, fallible human beings.

20. For over a century critics have loudly voiced their shock and amazement that the Book of Mormon should stoop to the transparent and suicidal device of actually quoting the Bible. Today any biblical scholar would be extremely suspicious of a book claiming the background and origin of the Book of Mormon that did not quote the Bible a great deal. But what about "passages lifted bodily from the King James Version" about which the critics are clamoring? They are simply following the accepted ancient procedure, in which "holy men of God," when they quote earlier scriptures, favor not the original language or their own translation, but whatever version of the scriptures is most familiar *to the people they are addressing*. The Book of Mormon was addressed to a society which knew only the King James Version.

21. As all the classic arguments against the Book of Mormon fall by the wayside one by one, we are left with one which is being put forward at the moment as unanswerable refutation, namely the quoting of the New Testament by people whose ancestors left the Old World 600 years before Christ. Here again the argument backfires against the critics, for if one examines the critical quotation that has been questioned, it is found to belong to a class of scriptures which is not original to the New Testament at all. The main exhibit is Moroni's "faith, hope, and charity," lifted, we are told, right out of 1 Corinthians 13:13. Only now we know that Paul got the expression from a much older and unknown source, and that he was much fonder of quoting from old Jewish and Greek sources than has been heretofore suspected.[23] While bits of apocryphal writing common to Paul and the Book of Mormon may

conceivably confirm the authenticity of the latter, they can no longer be taken as positive evidence against it.

22. But of all the arguments thrown at the Book of Mormon in the past, one completely overshadows all the rest. It is simply this: the book is a fraud because its existence is attributed to divine revelation. A writer in the first volume of the *American Anthropologist*, while dismissing the Book of Mormon as "only grotesque," warned against it as "a portentous danger sign. A monstrosity, born of deceit and bred in falsehood, . . . a monster of iniquity and deceit."[24] He thus shares the verdict of Professor Meinhold but, like him, finds nothing bad in the book itself: "Its teachings and precepts . . . are not in themselves immoral," he explains; "the Book of Mormon is not in itself immoral. . . . There is nothing immoral in the book." Then what is all the fuss about? It all comes down to one thing: "Its adherents have discovered a most dangerous weapon against the moral world in this doctrine of 'a continuing revelation.' . . . 'Thus saith the Lord,' is a portentous danger sign to enlightened civilization."[25]

In 1899, the leading American intellectuals and liberals signed a statement that had first been drawn up and approved by the leading churches of the land: *Ten Reasons Why Christians Cannot Fellowship the Mormon Church*. Polygamy had nothing to do with it; the writers were at considerable pains to point out that the question is a purely religious question. They summarized their ten religious objections in one neat rule-of-thumb: "Their so-called revelations."[26]

But what do we see today? We turn to the current Protestant journals and come upon articles entitled "Revelation and Religion," "The Need for Revelation," "Why not Prophetic-Apocalyptic?" and "The Church and its Prophets." The opening words of the last-named, from an eminently authoritative and respectable journal, are as follows: "If Christianity is, as it were, congenitally prophetic, the prophetic charisma [gift] must always have existed in some authentic form among Christians. What is that form today?"[27]

The same study tells us that speaking in tongues "has appeared in the Episcopal Church, of all bodies," very recently, and hails it with approval.[28] Slightly dizzy, we turn to the Catholic publications and find such titles as "Problems in the Field of Inspiration," "Reason without Revelation," "On Inspiration," and an article asking whether St. Augustine really received revelation. Of recent years, the religious seem unable to leave revelation alone. The one thing that once made them recoil with horror and loathing from Joseph Smith and the Book of Mormon is the very thing they are now seeking.

Notes

1. Hugh W. Nibley, "Strange Ships and Shining Stones," *A Book of Mormon Treasury* (Salt Lake City: Bookcraft, 1959), 133-51; reprinted in *CWHN* 6:340-58.

2. For a complete description of the "magur boat," see H. V. Hilprecht, *The Earliest Version of the Babylonian Deluge Story and the Temple Library of Nippur; The Babylonian Expedition of the University of Pennsylvania*, vol. 5, fasc. i (Philadelphia: University of Philadelphia, 1910): 52-56; and other sources in Nibley, "Strange Ships and Shining Stones," 150; in *CWHN* 6:343-48.

3. Discussed in Nibley, "Strange Ships and Shining Stones," 140-51; in *CWHN* 6:348-58.

4. Hugh W. Nibley, "The Liahona's Cousins," *Improvement Era* 64 (1961): 87-89, 104-6, 108-11; in *CWHN* 7:251-63.

5. For some examples, see Franklin S. Harris, *The Book of Mormon: Message and Evidences* (Salt Lake City: Deseret, 1953), 95-105; and Hugh W. Nibley, "New Approaches to Book of Mormon Study," *Improvement Era* 57 (February 1954): 125-26, see above, 54-126.

6. The Egyptians had been making steel since 1200 B.C.; see J. R. Forbes, "The Coming of Iron," *Ex Oriente Lux* 9 (1944): 210-11; cf. Gerald A. Wainwright, "The Coming of Iron," *Antiquity* 10 (1936): 16; Max Ebert, *Reallexikon der Vorgeschichte*, 14 vols. (Berlin: De Gruyter, 1924-29), 3:63; and the frontispiece of the *Journal of Egyptian Archeology* 28 (1942).

7. Ludwell H. Johnson, "Man and Elephants in America," *Scientific Monthly* 75 (1952): 215-21.

8. Richard P. Smith, "The Nephite Monetary System," *Improvement Era* 57 (1954): 316-17.

9. D. Winton Thomas, "The Age of Jeremiah in the Light of Recent Archaeological Discovery," *PEFQ* (1950), 2.

10. Nelson Glueck, "Ostraca from Elath," *Bulletin of the American Schools of Oriental Research,* 80 (1940): 3-10, esp. 4-6.

11. Names are discussed in Hugh W. Nibley, *Lehi in the Desert and the World of the Jaredites* (Salt Lake City: Bookcraft, 1952), 20-36; reprinted in *CWHN* 5:19-34; Hugh W. Nibley, *An Approach to the Book of Mormon* (Salt Lake City: Deseret, 1957), 242-55; in *CWHN* 6:75-77, 281-94.

12. See M. Grapow, "Hermonthis," *RE* 8:901-2.

13. *Lehi in the Desert and the World of the Jaredites,* 1-139; in *CWHN* 5:3-149.

14. S. H. Hooke, ed., *Myth, Ritual and Kingship* (Oxford: Clarendon, 1958).

15. Nibley, *An Approach to the Book of Mormon,* 256-70; in *CWHN* 6:295-310.

16. Examples given in Robert Graves, *The Greek Myths,* 2 vols. (New York: Penguin, 1960); Marie Renault, *The King Must Die* (New York: Pantheon, 1958); cf. Ether 8:7-18 and Ether 9.

17. Tha'labi, *Qisas al-Anbiyyā* (Cairo: Mustāfā al Bābi al-Halabi wa-Awlāduhu, A. H. 1345), 80-81, 97; Eberhard Baumann, "Der Linnene Schurz, Jer. 13:1-11," *Zeitschrift für die alttestamentliche Wissenschaft* 65 (1953): 77-81.

18. Alma 46, discussed in Nibley, *An Approach to the Book of Mormon,* 178-89; in *CWHN* 6:209-21.

19. See George Sale's commentary in his translation of *Koran,* 5th ed. (Philadelphia: Lippincott, 1870), ch. 2, pp. 13-14, note v.

20. Erwin R. Goodenough, *Jewish Symbolism in the Greco-Roman World,* 13 vols. (New York: Pantheon, 1953-68), 1:8-11, 18-21, 24-29.

21. Nibley, *An Approach to the Book of Mormon,* 133-42; in *CWHN* 6:157-67.

22. Alexander Campbell, "Delusions," *Millennial Harbinger* 2 (February 7, 1831), 85-96.

23. Richard Reitzenstein, "Die Entstehung der Formel 'Glaube, Liebe, Hoffnung,' " *Historische Zeitschrift* 116 (1916): 189-208. Isidore Levy, "Sur I Corinth. II.9 et l'apocalypse d'Elie," *Revue des Etudes Juives* 82 (1926): 161-63.

24. Perry B. Pierce, "The Origin of the Book of Mormon," *American Anthropologist* 1 (1899): 694 (emphasis added).

25. Ibid.

26. League for Social Service, *Ten Reasons Why Christians Cannot Fellowship the Mormon Church* (New York: 105 E. 22 St., 1898), 3-8. Endorsed by Presbyterian, Congregational, and Baptist Churches of America.

27. Walter C. Klein, "The Church and Its Prophets," *Anglican Theological Review* 44 (1962): 1.

28. Ibid., 17.

13

The Mormon View
of the Book of Mormon

The first step in what the Mormons consider the Restoration of the Gospel in the Dispensation of the Fulness
of Times was the coming forth of the Book of Mormon.
More than anything else this fixed the unique status of the
new religion, of which Eduard Meyer wrote: "Mormonism . . . is not just another of those innumerable new sects,
but a new religion of revelation (*Offenbarungsreligion*)."[1]
The Latter-day Saints "believe the Book of Mormon to be
the word of God" in exactly the same sense as the Bible
(Article of Faith No. 8) — a proposition which has caused
great offense to many Christians and led to long and severe
persecutions, the Book of Mormon being the principal object of attack.

The book does not, however, take the place of the Bible
in Mormonism. But just as the New Testament clarified
the long-misunderstood message of the Old, so the Book
of Mormon is held to reiterate the messages of both Tes-

This article was published in the multilingual journal Concilium: Theology in the Age of Renewal, 30 (New York: Paulist Press, 1968), 170-
73; also printed in England under the same title in Concilium: An International Review of Theology, 10 (December 1967), 82-83, and in
other foreign-language editions of this journal in French, pages 151-53;
Portuguese, pages 144-47; and German, pages 855-56. It was reprinted in
Nibley on the Timely and the Timeless (Salt Lake City: Bookcraft,
1978), 149-53, under the title "The Book of Mormon: A Minimal Statement" with the note that appears here as a postscript.

taments in a way that restores their full meaning. Its professed mission, as announced on its title page, is "to show unto the remnant of the House of Israel what great things the Lord hath done for their fathers; and that they may know the covenants of the Lord, that they are not cast off forever — And also to the convincing of the Jew and Gentile that Jesus is the Christ, the Eternal God, manifesting himself unto all nations." Until recently, most Mormons have not been zealous in the study of the book, considering it on the whole a strange and alien document with little relationship to modern life. Its peculiar effectiveness has indeed been as a messenger (it was brought by an angel) to the world at large.

The Book of Mormon professes to present in highly abridged form the history of a peculiar civilization, transplanted from the Old World to the New around 600 B.C. Of complex cultural background and mixed racial stock, the society endured only a thousand years, of which period the Book of Mormon contains an unbroken account, taken supposedly from records kept almost entirely by the leaders of a minority religious group. The first of the line was Lehi, who with his family and some others fled from Jerusalem to the desert to live the Law in its purity and prepare for the coming Messiah. Commanded by God after much wandering to cross the seas, the community reached the New World and there broke up, only a minority choosing to continue the ways of the pious sectaries of the desert. Lehi's descendants in time met and mingled with yet other migrants from the Old World, and indeed for almost five hundred years they had, unawares, as their northern neighbors, warlike hunting tribes which, according to the Book of Mormon, had come from Asia thousands of years before. The racial and cultural picture of the Book of Mormon is anything but the oversimplified thing its critics have made it out to be. For the Mormons, the Book of Mormon contains "the fulness of the gospel." Six hundred years of its history transpire before the coming of Christ, and four hundred after that. In the earlier period the faithful minority formed a church of anticipation, their charismatic leaders "teaching the law of Moses, and the intent for which it was given; persuading them to look forward unto the Messiah, and believe in him to come as though he already was" (Jarom 1:11). There are extensive quotations from the Old Testament prophets, especially Isaiah, with remarkable variant readings, and much that is reminiscent in language and imagery of early Jewish apocryphal writings. The boldest part of the Book of Mormon is the detailed account of the visit of Jesus Christ to his "other sheep" in the New World after the Resurrection, including his instructions and commandments to the new church. This episode closely parallels certain of early Christian apocrypha dealing with post-resurrectional teachings of the Lord to his disciples in Galilee and on the Mount of Olives, although none of these sources was available in Joseph Smith's day.

The historical parts of the Book of Mormon bear witness to its good faith, which never claims for it any sort of immunity, religious or otherwise, from the most searching scientific and scholarly criticism. Lack of comparative historical documents is offset by an abundance of cultural data: over two hundred nonbiblical Hebrew and Egyptian names offer ample material to the philologist, and a wealth of technical detail invites critical examination, thanks to precise descriptions of such things as the life of a family wandering in the Arabian desert, a great earthquake, the ancient craft of olive-culture, a major war in all its phases, the ways of the early desert sectaries, and the state of the world during a protohistoric *Völkerwanderung*, and so on.

Along with cultural-historical particulars the religious message of the book is richly interspersed with peculiar expressions, legends, traditions, and customs supposedly derived from the Old World, which may today be checked against ancient sources. Thus it describes certain practices of arrow-divination, an odd custom of treading on garments, a coronation ceremony (in great detail), the evils of the archaic matriarchy, peculiar ways of keeping and transmitting sacred records, the intricacies of an ingenious monetary system, and the like.

Of particular interest to Latter-day Saints are the prophetic parts of the Book of Mormon, which seem to depict the present state of the world most convincingly. The past 140 years have borne out exactly what the book foretold would be its own reception and influence in the world; and its predictions for the Mormons, the Jews, and the other remnants of scattered Israel (among which are included the American Indians) seem to be on the way to fulfillment. The Book of Mormon allows an ample timescale for the realization of its prophecies, according to which the deepening perplexities of the nations, when "the Lord God shall cause a great division among the people" (2 Nephi 30:10), shall lead to worldwide destructions by fire, for "blood, and fire, and vapor of smoke must come; and it must needs be upon the face of this earth." After this, the survivors (for this is not to be the end of the world) shall have learned enough to coexist peaceably "for the space of many years," when "all nations, kindreds, tongues and people shall dwell safely in the Holy One of Israel if it so be that they will repent" (1 Nephi 22:26, 28).

The Book of Mormon is the history of a polarized world in which two irreconcilable ideologies confronted each other, and is addressed explicitly to our own age, faced by the same predicament and the same impending threat of destruction. It is a call to faith and repentance couched in the language of history and prophecy, but above all it is a witness of God's concern for all his children, and to the intimate proximity of Jesus Christ to all who will receive him.

Postscript: The preceding statement was written on request for a journal which is published in eight languages and therefore insists on conciseness and brevity. Teaching a Book of Mormon Sunday School class ten years later, I am impressed more than anything by something I completely overlooked until now, namely, the immense skill with which the editors of that book put the thing together. The long Book of Alma, for example, is followed through with a smooth and logical sequence in which an incredible amount of detailed and widely varying material is handled in the most lucid and apparently effortless manner. Whether Alma is addressing a king and his court, a throng of ragged paupers sitting on the ground, or his own three sons, each a distinctly different character, his eloquence is always suited to his audience, and he goes unfailingly to the peculiar problems of each hearer.

Throughout this big and complex volume, we are aware of much shuffling and winnowing of documents, and informed from time to time of the method used by an editor distilling the contents of a large library into edifying lessons for the dedicated and pious minority among the people. The overall picture reflects before all a limited geographical and cultural point of view — small localized operations, with only occasional flights and expeditions into the wilderness; one might almost be moving in the cultural circuit of the Hopi villages. The focusing of the whole account on religious themes as well as the limited cultural scope leaves all the rest of the stage clear for any other activities that might have been going on in the vast reaches of the New World, including the hypothetical Norsemen, Celts, Phoenicians, Libyans, or prehistoric infiltrations via the Bering Straits. Indeed, the more varied the ancient American scene becomes, as newly discovered artifacts and even inscriptions hint at local populations of Near Eastern, Far Eastern, and European origin, the more hospitable it is to the activities of one tragically short-lived religious civilization that once flourished in Mesoamerica and then vanished toward the northeast in the course of a series of confused tribal wars that was one long, drawn-out retreat into oblivion. Such considerations would now have to be included in any "minimal statement" this reader would make about the Book of Mormon.

Notes

1. Eduard Meyer, *Ursprung und Geschichte der Mormonen* (Halle: 1912), 1; published also as *The Origin and History of the Mormons*, tr. H. Rahde and E. Seaich (Salt Lake City: University of Utah Press, 1961), 1.

14

Ancient Temples: What Do They Signify?

What most impressed me last summer on my first and only expedition to Central America was the complete lack of definite information about anything. We knew ahead of time that of the knowledge of the ancient cultures there wasn't much to be expected, but we were quite unprepared for the poverty of information that confronted us in the guided tours of ruins, museums, and lecture halls. It was not that our gracious guides knew less than they should. It is just a fact of life that no one knows much at all about these oft-photographed and much-talked-about ruins.

In the almost complete absence of written records, one must be permitted to guess, because there is nothing else to do; and when guessing is the only method of determination, one man's skill is almost as good as another's. An informed guess is a contradiction of terms, so our initial shock of nondiscovery was tempered by a warm glow of complacency, on finding that the rankest amateur in our party was able to pontificate on the identity and nature of most objects as well as anybody else.

One would suppose it to be a relatively easy thing to decide whether a given structure had served as a hospital, a monastery, a palace, a storeroom, a barracks, a temple, a tomb, or an office. But it is not easy at all, with everything looking just alike. Usually, we do not even know who the

This article appeared in the Ensign *(September 1972), 46-49.*

builders were or what their names were or where they came from.

Stock phrases, such as "We know as little about the history of the Mixtecs as we do about the Zapotecs," may confirm a scientist's integrity, but they hardly establish him as an authority. Admission of ignorance, though a constant refrain in guidebooks and articles, is really no substitute for knowledge. This writer is as ill-equipped as any ten-year-old to write about the people of ancient America, because he has never seen their records — but then who has?

The vast archives of the Old World civilizations that bring their identities and their histories to life simply do not exist for the New World, and so all we can do as we sit drinking lemonade in the shade is to gaze and emote and speculate and rest our weary feet.

There are two things, however, about ancient American ruins upon which everyone seems to agree: (1) the reliefs that adorn the walls of some of these structures with ritual games, sacrifices, processions, audiences, and well-known religious symbols leave little doubt that they were designed to be the scenes of religious activities, and (2) some of these religious structures were laid out to harmonize with the structure and motion of the cosmos itself, as witness the perfectly straight axial ways that point directly to the place of the rising and setting sun at solstices and equinoxes or the total of 364 steps and 52 slabs to a side that adorn the great pyramid of Chichen Itza.

It is an eloquent commentary on the bankruptcy of the modern mind, as Giorio de Santillana points out, that we can find so little purpose or meaning in the magnificent and peculiar structures erected by the ancients with such immense skill and obvious zeal and dedication.[1] These great edifices are found throughout the entire world and seem to represent a common tradition; and if they do, then we have surely lost our way.

Counterparts to the great ritual complexes of Central America once dotted the entire eastern United States, the most notable being the Hopewell culture centering in Ohio and spreading out for hundreds of miles along the entire length of the Mississippi River. These are now believed to be definitely related to corresponding centers in Mesoamerica.[2]

Ranging further abroad, we see a convincing resemblance when we visit the famous ritual complex sites of the Old World and find the same combination of oddities on the same awesome scale. Pyramids and towers first catch our eye whether in Asia or America, and closer inspection reveals the familiar processional ways, stone alignments and colonnades, ceremonial gates, labyrinthine subterranean passages and chambers with their massive sarcophagi for priests and kings, reliefs depicting processions and combats, images of kings, gods, priests, and dangerous carnivores and serpents in stone.

While those who dig in the ruins of both hemispheres discover many similarities in the use of gold, turquoise, seashells, feathers, cotton textiles, and abstract designs, such as key patterns, spirals, and swastikas, the Western experts doggedly defend their domain as New World specialists. They are unencumbered by extensive knowledge of the Old World and still insist that there was absolutely no similarity in the details of development in America and the Mediterranean countries. Then they mention similarity after similarity with, of course, the understanding that such likenesses are the result of mere coincidence.

As for the idea of possible contact between the hemispheres, a magisterial gesture toward the map has always been thought sufficient to explain everything, obviating the necessity of reading the rich and wonderful libraries of the ancients who could tell us a great deal about the real and possible intercourse over the waters if we would only give them our attention.

Whole rooms full of ancient writings have been found in the Old World at actual ruin sites with which they were contemporary, and from such we may learn the nature and purpose of the great buildings. Strangely enough, it is only in the present generation that really extensive comparative studies among these documents and ruins have been undertaken. Serious study of the Egyptian temples, with the aid of inscriptions found in and near them, is only now being systematically pursued for the first time.

Because of this neglect, it is not surprising that comparison of Old World ritual complexes with their counterparts in the New World has hardly even begun, though resemblances between the two have never failed to impress even the most casual observer of the past 150 years. However, such studies as have been undertaken invariably suggest emerging patterns common to both worlds. Without committing ourselves to any dogmatic position (it is still too early for that), we can still indulge like stout Cortez in a few wild surmises from a peak in Darien.

In his recent study of a primitive Egyptian temple complex, Egyptologist Philippe Derchain declares that "one can almost compare the ancient Egyptian temple to a powerhouse where diverse energies are converted into electric current or to a control room where, by the application of very little effort, . . . one can safely produce and distribute energy as needed along the proper power lines."[3] Such powerhouses were not confined to Egypt; we find them everywhere, in the Old World and the New.

The ruins of such centers of power and control still comprise by far the most impressive remnants of the human past. Today the great plants are broken down and deserted; the power has been shut off. They mean nothing to us anymore, because we don't understand how they worked.

The most sophisticated electronic gadget in perfect working order is nothing in the hands of one who has never heard of electricity, and it would only frustrate even an expert if he found no power outlet to plug into. Perhaps the old powerhouses were something like that. And did they ever really work?

A great many people went to a lot of trouble for an unusually long time to set up these mysterious dynamos all over the world. What could they possibly have derived from all this effort? They must have gotten something, to have kept at it so long and so enthusiastically. For that matter, some of the holy places still carry on: pilgrims still travel in vast numbers to Mecca, Jerusalem, Rome, and Benares, hoping to experience manifestations of supernatural power.

Countless reports are on record at those famous sites of ingenious attempts to duplicate by fraud certain miraculous displays during the pilgrimages, attesting the fading or fictive nature of the vaunted powers from on high.

It is remarkable that some principal centers of world power are still located at the ancient sites where the corporate life of the race was thought to be renewed in the great New Year rites presided over by the king as god on earth. These sacred centers flourished in the heart of Rome, at the Altar of the Sun in Peking, in the Kremlin, in Jerusalem, in Cairo (the ancient Memphis), in Mexico City, and elsewhere. Such pouring of new forces into fossil molds is what the philosopher Oswald Spengler calls "pseudomorphs," endowing a new power structure with a specious authority in which no one any longer believes.[4]

The idea that divine power can be conveyed to men and used by them through the implementation of tangible earthly contrivances and that these become mere antique oddities once the power is shut off is surprisingly confirmed and illustrated by the Book of Mormon. Thus the Liahona and the Urim and Thummim were kept among the national treasures of the Nephites long after they had ceased their miraculous functions.

Before the finger of the Lord touched the sixteen stones of the brother of Jared, they were mere pieces of glass, and they probably became so after they had fulfilled their purpose. And the gold plates had no message to deliver until a special line of communication was opened by supernatural power.

In themselves these objects were nothing; they did not work by magic, a power that resided *in the objects themselves* so that a person has only to get hold of the magical staff, seal, ring, robe, book of Moses or Solomon or Peter in order to become master of the world. The aids and implements that God gives to men work on no magic or automatic or mechanical principle, but only "according to the faith and diligence and heed which we . . . give unto them" (1 Nephi 16:28) and cease to work because of wickedness (1 Nephi 18:12).

Some have thought it strange that God should use any earthly implements and agents at all, when he could do all things himself just as easily. But even the Moslems, who protest that Christianity places needless intermediaries, notably Jesus and the Holy Ghost, between God and man, declare in their creed that they believe "in God and his Angels and his Prophets and his Books."[5] Does God need all these to do his work with men? However we may rationalize, the fact is that he does make use of them.

But what about all these ancient powerhouses – what would happen if they were restored? Nothing, in my opinion. They might be repaired and put in working order, but that would no more make them work than setting up a Liahona or Urim and Thummim, with all of the working parts in order, would enable us to use them. Without power from above, nothing will happen, for this is not magic.

It is doubtful if any of the known powerhouses ever really worked, except for the temple at Jerusalem (of which duplicates were made all over the Christian world as centers of pilgrimage in the Middle Ages), where the key manifestations in the life of the Savior took place. But what of the others? If they enjoyed no real dispensations of heavenly power, they really did not need to justify their existence, with all the trouble and expense of building them or keeping them in operation as the focal centers of the world's religious life.

The gesture of faith was not without its reward, however, and the by-products of the ancient temple were easily worth the time and effort that went into constructing and operating it, since the result was nothing less than civilization itself.

Ancient civilization was hierocentric, so that everything came from the temple. The Egyptians carried on for centuries like "a people searching in the dark for a key to truth," as I.E.S. Edwards put it.[6]

Abraham, while he pitied the futility of Pharaoh's zeal, respected his sincerity: though "cursed . . . as pertaining to the Priesthood," Pharaoh was nonetheless "a righteous man, . . . seeking earnestly to imitate the order . . . of the first patriarchal reign." In return he was blessed "with the blessings of the earth, and with the blessings of wisdom" (Abraham 1:26), and with the most stable, humane, and enlightened of civilizations.

If the Egyptian religion fed on its hopes, so do all the others; the Jews ever hoping for Jerusalem, the temple, and the Messiah; the Latter-day Saints still hoping for the fulfillment of the promises of the tenth Article of Faith.

One thing that leads us to suspect that most of the great powerhouses whose traces still remain were never anything more than pompous imitations or replicas is their sheer magnificence. The archaeologist finds virtually nothing of the remains of the primitive Christian church until the fourth century, because the true church was not interested in buildings and deliberately avoided the acquisition of lands and edifices that might bind it and its interests to this world.

The Book of Mormon is a history of a related primitive church, and one may well ask what kind of remains the Nephites would leave us from their more virtuous days. A closer approximation to the Book of Mormon picture of Nephite culture is seen in the earth and palisade structures of the Hopewell and Adena culture areas than in the later stately piles of stone in Mesoamerica.

C. Northcote Parkinson has demonstrated with withering insight how throughout history really ornate, tasteless, and pompous building programs have tended to come as the aftermath of civilization.[7] After the vital powers are spent, then is the time for the super-buildings, the piling of stone upon stone for monuments of staggering mass and proportion. It was after the disciples of the early church decided to give up waiting for the Messiah and to go out for satisfaction here and now that the Christians of the fourth century took to staging festivals and erecting monuments in the grand manner, covering the whole Near East with structures of theatrical magnificence and questionable taste.

How unlike the building program of the Church today, which can barely erect enough of our very functional, almost plain chapels to keep abreast of the growing needs of the Latter-day Saints.

Though such piles as the great pyramid-temple of Chichen Itza are surpassed by few buildings in the world in beauty of proportion and grandeur of conception, there is something disturbing about most of these overpowering ruins. Writers describing them through the years have ever confessed to feelings of sadness and oppression as they contemplate the moldy magnificence — the futility of it all: "They have all gone away from the house on the hill," and today we don't even know who they were.

Amid the ruins of the New World, as in Rome, we feel

something of both the greatness and the misery, the genuine aspiration and the dull oppression, the idealism and the arrogance imposed by the heavy hand of priestcraft and kingcraft, and we wonder how the ruins of our own super buildings will look someday.

The great monuments do not represent what the Nephites stood for; rather, they stand for what their descendants, mixed with the blood of their brethren, descended to. But seen in the newer and wider perspective of comparative religious studies, they suggest to us not only the vanity of mankind and the futility of man's unaided efforts, but also something nobler: the constant search of men to recapture a time when the powers of heaven were truly at the disposal of a righteous people.

Notes

1. Giorgio de Santillana, *Hamlet's Mill* (Boston: Gambit, 1969), 3-5.

2. James B. Griffin, "Mesoamerica and the Eastern United States in Prehistoric Times," in *Handbook of Middle American Indians*, ed. Robert Wauchope (Austin: University of Texas, 1966), 4:111-31; D. S. Brose and N. Greber, *Hopewell Archaeology* (Kent: Kent State University, 1979).

3. Philippe Derchain, *Le Papyrus Salt 5825*, in *Memoirs of the Royal Academy* 58 (Brussels, 1965): 14.

4. Oswald Spengler, *The Decline of the West*, 2 vols. (New York: Knopf, 1928), 2:189, speaks of "historic pseudomorphosis."

5. George Sale, *The Koran* (London: Warne, n.d.), 55, 105, 109.

6. Iorwerth E. S. Edwards, *The Pyramids of Egypt* (Maryland: Penguin, 1964), 29.

7. Cyril Northcote Parkinson, *Parkinson's Law or the Pursuit of Progress* (Boston: Houghton Mifflin, 1957), 59-69.

15

Bar-Kochba and Book of Mormon Backgrounds

Almost a quarter of a century ago this investigator wrote a study of life in the Arabian desert in ancient times. It first appeared in the pages of the *Improvement Era* under the title of "Lehi in the Desert," and drew almost exclusively on the writings of European visitors to those arid regions during the past 200 years and the works of medieval and modern Arabic writers.[1] Some years later in a study called "Qumran and the Companions of the Cave," he again explored the subject, this time with extensive flights into the early Arabic writers.[2] Since the ways of Bedouins are notoriously unchanging, the idea was that the Arabic report of how things were out there would apply in ancient as well as in medieval and modern times, and thereby supply us with a "control" over Nephi's history of his family's travels and tribulations in those same deserts early in the sixth century B.C. The main reason for using Arabic sources was, of course, that there were no other specialized studies in the field. But just as the articles began to appear, the first copies of the Dead Sea Scrolls began to be available—and that changed everything. We no longer had to ask the Arabs how the Jews may have behaved in the desert in ancient times, since we now had first-hand reports of how they actually did. Those reports

---

This book review appeared in BYU Studies 14 *(Autumn 1973): 115-26.*

have steadily increased in volume, and Professor Yadin's book now carries the Book of Mormon student far beyond the former speculations.

The reaction to these marvelous discoveries by their finders is convincing confirmation of the Book of Mormon thesis that these new findings were meant to be. The Israeli scholars are understandably moved by the one thing that makes these documents of supreme importance for them: the fact that they belong to their own ancestors. "We found that our emotions were a mixture of tension and awe," writes Yadin, "yet astonishment and pride at being part of the reborn State of Israel after a Diaspora of 1,800 years."[3] Compare this with Nephi's moving lines: "And it shall be as if the fruit of thy loins had cried unto them from the dust; for I know their faith. And they shall cry from the dust, . . . even after many generations have gone by them" (2 Nephi 3:19-20). Their own people after all those years! How often has it happened that ancient docu-ments—2,000 years old—have been dug up in their own homeland by the very descendants of the men who wrote those documents and, what is still more marvelous, who could still read them on the spot? We know of no other such instance in the history of scholarship.

Nephi continues: "For those who shall be destroyed shall speak unto them out of the ground, and their speech shall be low out of the dust and their voice shall be as one that hath a familiar spirit; for the Lord God will give unto him power, that he may whisper concerning them, even as it were out of the ground; and their speech shall whisper out of the dust" (2 Nephi 26:16). All this talk about dust. Well, anyone who visits the sites or reads Yadin's books soon finds himself deep in dust. Every text discussed in Dr. Yadin's new book was found by the searchers delib-erately buried under the floor of a very dusty cave. They have not survived accidentally, as most other ancient writ-ings have, but were hidden away on purpose; nor were they simply left behind or misplaced or forgotten by people who moved on and lived out their lives elsewhere — the people who left these records died soon after they buried them and died on the spot, the victims of a savage religious war. "For those who shall be destroyed shall speak unto them out of the ground" (2 Nephi 26:16). What do these records contain? Accounts of contemporary affairs in private letters, legal documents, military and civil correspondence, or, in the words of the Book of Mormon, "For thus saith the Lord God: They shall write the *things which shall be done among them.* . . . Wherefore, as those who have been destroyed have been destroyed speedily" (2 Nephi 26:17-18). Not only all their letters and legal papers, but their household effects and their bones were left behind in the caves, for the simple reason that they did not have time to escape. As to their destroyers, "Nothing remains here today of the Romans save a heap of stones on the face of the desert," writes Yadin, "but here the descendants of the besieged were returning to salvage their ancestors' precious belongings."[4] Again the Book of Mormon: "And the multitude of their terrible ones shall be as chaff that passeth away" (2 Nephi 26:18).

The future of the Book of Mormon is fittingly made the subject of prophecy by the first man and the last one to write in it. Moroni ends and seals up the book with the prophecy that when its words shall be "like as one crying from the dead, yea, even as one speaking out of the dust" (Moroni 10:27), then shall the invitation go forth to the Jews: "Awake, and arise from the dust, O Jerusalem; . . . enlarge thy borders forever, that thou mayest no more be confounded" (Moroni 10:31), which is exactly what they are doing today.

In reading Professor Yadin's account of the findings of the ancient artifacts and documents in a cave in the Nahal Hever cliffs, we seem to shift back and forth between the refugees and the fighters under Bar Kochba, or, in Book of Mormon terms, between Lehi, the refugee in the desert, and Moroni, the hero, fighting against fearful odds to save his people.

First consider Lehi, warned by dreams and portents of the imminent fall of Jerusalem to the Babylonians, fleeing by night with his family to the south desert with the intention of founding some sort of community there. His sons, sent back to the city to obtain valuable family documents, hid in nearby caves as they sized up the situation and laid their plans. The caves in which the Bar Kochba documents were found were places of hiding, and the people who wrote and owned them had brought them from home, for they too were refugees from the approaching armies of a mighty world-conquering power determined to hold Palestine and to subdue the Jews for that purpose.

In Lehi's day we find many well-to-do Jews putting their trust in Egypt and finally fleeing thither when things got too hot in Jerusalem. The same sort of thing meets us in the letters of a rich lady named Babata, found in the Cave of Letters. She had real-estate dealings in 130 A.D. with a Roman lady, Julia Crispina, who turns up in mid-133 A.D. in the Fayyum in Egypt, where she owned property. Babata might have joined her associate and gotten out of the country before it was too late, but apparently she was too attached to her lands and goods (like Lot's wife in nearby Sodom) to make the break. It is interesting to find rich and autocratic women busy in Palestine, even as they flourished there in the succeeding centuries, when it was the safest refuge in the Empire for investments (especially in real-estate) and for refugees fleeing before the barbarian invaders.[5] Lehi burned his bridges behind him, and he did not expect to return to Jerusalem, but to find a "promised land" in the desert. Nothing was further from his mind than crossing the ocean—Nephi was simply staggered when he was commanded to build a ship, and his brothers laughed their heads off at his presumption. On the other hand, it was never hinted that there was anything strange about Lehi's taking to the wastelands, or even proposing that he should found a colony with his son Nephi as its ruler, because that sort of thing was being done all the time. Lehi's story takes place 700 years before Bar Kochba's day, and yet the two tales present astonishing points of resemblance which, we believe, are more than purely coincidental, for the same cave that yielded the Bar Kochba materials also brought forth evidence of much earlier occupations. The diggers working under Bar-Adon in a neighboring cave in the Nahal Mishmar discovered a treasure of 429 metal objects, some of them quite beautiful, and as the things were brought to light the workers spontaneously burst into "a very well-known Hebrew song of the Temple," for the beautiful bronze objects strongly suggested temple vessels to their minds.[6] Yet those objects were found by carbon-14 dating to be no less than 5,000 years old! The most plausible explanation of how they got to the cave is that people fleeing from the advances of the first kings of Egypt into Palestine brought and hid them there.[7] In all probability they were sacred vessels, but what, and whose? Even without an inkling of the answer, it is clear that the practice of people fleeing to these caves with their sacred and profane treasure is far older than Lehi's day. The same caves also yielded objects from the Iron Age of the eighth and seventh centuries B.C.; that is, from Lehi's own time, making it "quite clear," according to Yadin, "that these remote caves . . . served as places of refuge . . . for people who were forced by circumstances to flee the rulers of the land."[8] We are also reminded of how Lehi's sons were impressed by the "precious steel" of a sword (1 Nephi 4:9; cf. 1 Nephi 16:18), that being a time when the stuff was available (iron could not be smelted without a carbon mixture which made it steel), but was still very costly.

The most welcome aspect of the new findings is that the families who fled from the town to the desert took along collections of writings with them—legal documents, correspondence, family records, scriptures—quite in the manner of Lehi. Unfortunately the modern Bedouins of the region, knowing the monetary value of the ancient scrolls, had thoroughly sacked nearly all the caves before the scholars could get to them; but the scraps of writing dropped by them in their hasty departure happen to be passages of scripture which peculiarly fitted the situation of the people in their desert hiding places. Though this may be a coincidence, it does remind us that Nephi in the desert made it a point to read to his people just those scriptures which applied to their present situation: "And I did read many things unto them which were written in the books of Moses; but that I might more fully persuade them to believe. . . . I did liken all scriptures unto us, that it might be for our profit and learning" (1 Nephi 19:23). This practice of applying ancient stories and prophecies to their own peculiar condition was found to be a special practice of the religious community at Qumran, who compared themselves to Israel driven into the wilderness and sorely afflicted by Gentile armies in ages past. This is exactly what Nephi did to hearten his people wandering in the sands, and it was the Book of Mormon that first pointed up the practice.

As might be expected, the most interesting and important documents of all to their discoverers were the personal letters, including an autograph of Bar Kochba himself. These take us not into the world of Lehi so much as into that of the great Book of Mormon general, Moroni. Thus we find that Bar Kochba's people reissued Roman coins with a new stamp upon them bearing slogans of liberty resembling those on the trumpets of the armies in the Battle Scroll. Such devices are, "Year 1, Redemption of Israel," "Year 2, Freedom of Israel," or simply "Freedom of Jerusalem." These slogans were to inspire the people to resistance, inscription money having long been used in the ancient world, especially by the Romans, as a convenient means of spreading government propaganda. Compare this with Moroni's standards: "In memory of our God, our religion, and freedom, and our peace, our wives, and our children. . . . And he took the pole, which had on the end thereof his rent coat, (and he called it the title of liberty)" (Alma 46:12-13). It has been objected that such talk of liberty smacks suspiciously of nineteenth-century America rather than ancient Israel, but the constant recurrence of the word liberty (*kherut*) in the Dead Sea Scrolls, to say nothing of the Bar Kochba coins, shows that it is entirely in order in Moroni's world. But what has that world of around 70 B.C. in the Western Hemisphere to do with Bar Kochba's world of 131-32 A.D. in Palestine? Surprisingly, a great deal. Not only have the new discoveries shown the Jews to be phenomenally conservative in their ways, but the Book of Mormon itself accounts for Moroni's familiarity with old-world customs. The title of liberty which he inscribed on his own cloak was suggested to him, according to his own report, by an ancient tradition which the people had brought with them to the New World: "Let us preserve our liberty as a remnant of Joseph: yea, let us remember the words of Jacob [when] . . . he saw that a part of the remnant of the coat of Joseph was preserved" (Alma 46:24). He then goes on to tell a story of how the garment of Joseph was preserved in two parts, which the aged Jacob recognized on his deathbed, weeping for the one part which was defiled, and rejoicing over the other which was miraculously preserved. This was a story that went back to the Old Country which the people were enjoined to remember — it is not in the Bible, and I have not found reference to it in any Jewish source; and though my resources are far from unlimited, still they go immeasurably beyond what Joseph Smith possessed, and yet he knew this story, which I have found preserved in the pages of Tha'labi, who got it from an old Jewish informant somewhere in Persia in the tenth century. The point is that Moroni bases his military practices on the customs of the Jews in the homeland.[9]

The story of Moroni's war of liberation with its liberty slogans is taken from the book of Alma in the Book of Mormon, and this provides us with another tangible link to the Old World, namely, the name of Alma, which deserves a momentary digression. The more exotic proper names of the Book of Mormon have been matched up extensively and sometimes quite convincingly with real Egyptian and Semitic names (which is what they claim to be). Such an odd monicker as Paanchi (who ever heard of a double "a" in English?) not only turned up in the Egyptian records a generation after the Book of Mormon came out, but it turns out to be a rather prominent and important name in the bargain.[10] And such a very un-Egyptian, un-Oriental, indeed un-anything name as "Hermounts" was applied by the Book of Mormon Nephites to a region on the extremity of the land where wild animals abounded, a territory whose description perfectly matches that part of the world to which the Egyptians gave the name of Hermonthis.[11] But strangely enough, the name in the Book of Mormon that has brought the most derision on that book, and caused the greatest embarrassment to the Latter-day Saints, especially among those holders of the priesthood who have borne it among the children of men, is the simple and unpretentious Alma. Roman priests have found in this obviously Latin and obviously feminine name — (who does not know that Alma Mater means "fostering mother"?) — gratifying evidence of the ignorance and naiveté of the youthful Joseph Smith — how could he have been simple enough to let such a thing get by? At least his more sophisticated followers should have known better! It is therefore gratifying to announce that at the extreme

end of the Cave of Letters, on the north side of the Nahal
Hever, between three and four o'clock of the afternoon of
15 March 1961, Professor Yadin put his hand into a crevice
in the floor of the cave and lifted out a goat-skin bag containing a woman's materials for mending her family's
clothes on their sad and enforced vacation; and hidden
away under the stuff, at the very bottom of the bag, was
a bundle of papyrus rolls wrapped in a cloth. And among
them was a deed to some land near En-Gedi (the nearest
town to the cave) owned by four men, one of whom signed
himself, or rather dictated his name since he was illiterate,
as "Alma the son of Judah." The deed is reproduced in
color on page 177 of the book, and there at the end of the
fourth line from the top, as large as life, is *A-l-m-a ben
Yehudah,* which Professor Yadin sensibly renders "Alma"
with no reservations. And speaking of names, it is interesting that the Jews who reissued Roman coins as Bar
Kochba coins with their pious patriotic inscriptions gave
the coins new names and denominations,[12] with the same
freedom with which Alma says his people invented new
names and denominations for their weights and measures
(Alma 11).

Bar Kochba's war, like Moroni's, was a holy war, a
"Messianic war," with fanatical concern for the temple.[13]
In the struggle for liberation, the hero found his hands full
dealing with all kinds of people and problems. For one
thing, he found that "some of the wealthier citizens" of a
city were "evaders of national duties" in his day, as their
ancestors had been in the days of Nehemiah.[14] Specifically,
they were "disregarding the mobilization orders of Bar
Kochba," who became exceedingly angry and issued dire
threats against them, including even the death penalty.
Compare this with Moroni in a like situation: "And it came
to pass that whomsoever of the Amalickiahites that would
not enter into a covenant to support the cause of freedom, . . . he caused to be put to death; and there were

but few who denied the covenant of freedom" (Alma
46:35). And who were the Amalickiahites? A coalition of
those who "because of their exceedingly great riches" opposed government controls (Alma 45:24); those who considered themselves the aristocracy "who professed the
blood of nobility" (Alma 51:21); the "king-men" led by
"the lower judges of the land, . . . seeking for power"
(Alma 46:4); local judges, officials, and other upper crust
bound together by family ties as "kindreds," whose boast
was that they had "acquired much riches by the hand of
[their] industry" (Alma 10:4, 3 Nephi 6:27); these were not
pacifists or draft-evaders but were armed to the teeth,
"those men of Pachus and those king-men, whosoever
would not take up arms in the defence of their country,
but would fight against it" (Alma 62:9-11). These Moroni
put to death. Bar Kochba had to deal with just such characters, and he did it in the same way. To the "brothers"
(for so he calls them, as Moroni does all to whom he writes)
in the city of En-Gedi, he personally wrote a letter in Hebrew that survives to this day: "To Masabala and to Yehonathan bar Be'ayan, peace. In comfort you sit, eat and
drink from the property of the House of Israel, and *care
nothing for your brothers.*" Thus Yadin.[15] We have italicized
certain words to point up the parallels to Moroni's letter
from the field: "To Pahoran, in the city of Zarahemla . . . and also to all those who have been chosen by
this people to govern and manage the affairs of this war"
(Alma 60:1). "Can you think to sit upon your thrones in
a state of *thoughtless stupor,* while your enemies are spreading the work of death around you? Yea, while they are
murdering thousands of *your brethren?*" (Alma 60:7). To
such people Moroni issues a dire threat: "And I will come
unto you, and . . . behold I will stir up insurrections
among you, even until those who have desires to usurp
power and authority shall become extinct" (Alma 60:27).
If this sounds shockingly severe, the provocation was as

terrible: Moroni, like Bar Kochba, was holding on by the skin of his teeth: "Whatever we may think of Bar Kochba's harsh tone," writes Yadin, "it is quite clear that Yehonathan [an important leader] was not the most loyal of subordinates," and there were others like him in high office, especially as things grew worse.[16] But if the secret of Moroni's success was his essential gentleness—he always called a halt to the fighting the instant the enemy, whom he called his "brethren," showed the least inclination to parley—it has often been said that Bar Kochba's undoing was the lack of such a redeeming quality. "His brutality, according to some sources, was manifested in the way he killed the revered Rabbi Eleazar of Modi'in, . . . who Bar Kochba suspected of betraying the secrets of Bethar [a city under attack] to the Romans. This cruel act, according to the same sources, caused Bar Kochba's death, and the fall of Bethar."[17]

When another leader, Galgoula, was called to task for holding out supplies, including a cow, he wrote to his superiors to explain: "Were it not for the Gentiles [that is, the Romans] who are near us, I would have given up and satisfied you concerning this, lest you will say that it is out of contempt that I did not go up to you."[18] Moroni ran into just such a misunderstanding, when he accused Pahoran of withholding supplies, to which Pahoran replied just as Galgoula did: "It is those who have sought to take away the judgment-seat from me that have been the cause of this great iniquity; . . . they have withheld our provisions, and have daunted our freemen *that they have not come unto you*. . . . In your epistle you have censured me, but it mattereth not; I am not angry, but do rejoice in the greatness of your heart" (Alma 61:4, 9).

If the Book of Mormon were a product of our own day, such striking parallels (and there are many others) would be not only a suspicious but a damning circumstance. As it is, one is still forced to ask for an explanation for a phenomenon which can hardly be mere coincidence. The explanation is to be found in the nature and genius of the Jewish people, whose internal and external history has a way of falling into almost rigid patterns. The kind of squabbles that go on among themselves are typically and thoroughly Jewish, and you will find them everywhere; the same temperament or culture places them at odds with the "outside world" in a particular way so that the atrocities committed against them seem to fall into the same mold whether in the first or fifteenth or twentieth centuries and whether in Spain, Germany, or Russia. This is the familiar theme of the prophets—rebellion, punishment, repentance, the same old cycle round and round. Just as the Six Week War of 1948 broke out, the Battle Scroll of the Dead Sea Scrolls came to light—it read like a series of editorials to inspire twentieth-century Jews to deeds of heroism, and as such it was joyfully received. The Battle Scroll, now edited by Professor Yadin, shows to what an amazing degree, even in such a technical and dating operation as warfare, the ancient image fits the modern situation.

Since the discovery of the Dead Sea Scrolls, it has become plain that one of the constants of Jewish history in ancient times was the small band of pious souls who would leave Jerusalem, which they deemed doomed and corrupted, to go into the desert to form their own community there and to attempt to carry on in a manner of Israel in the wilderness under Moses. Lehi is a classic example of such an operation, and the tradition was carried over right into the New World, Lehi's descendants forming such groups of pious sectaries from time to time. The most notable of these was Alma's colony, and we are told how it came about. Alma, as a young priest serving under a corrupt king, became a secret disciple of the prophet Abinadi, who was a master of the old Jewish lore, and a caustic wit. Abinadi was a walking Bible, and after he was put to death, Alma hid out in a cave and wrote from mem-

ory, and probably from notes, all he could recall of
Abinadi's teachings. Then he went out into a desert place
to a spot called the Waters of Mormon, and there set up
his community, organized in companies of fifty with visiting inspectors, engaging in pious activities, self-sup-
porting and industrious. He initiated members by baptism
in the waters of Mormon. Even down to details his organization resembles very closely the sectaries of the Dead
Sea.[19] Yadin points out in his book the presence at Qumran
of "numerous cisterns and ritual baths,"[20] whose ritual
nature was stoutly denied by Jewish and Christian scholars
alike as being an altogether unlikely circumstance.

Of the thirty-five private letters of the wealthy woman
Babata, mentioned above, twenty-three "belonged to the
type commonly known as 'double deeds' " or "tied
deeds," whose use "is a very old and known practice in
the ancient world," though until this, no actual examples
had ever been found from ancient times.[21] It was an arrangement by which a legal agreement was written twice
on the same piece of papyrus or parchment, the first time
very small at one end of the paper, which was then rolled
into a tight cylinder, sewn closed, and signed over with
the participants' signatures. The rest of the sheet, the
greater part of it, then received the same writing in bolder
letters; it was not sealed, so that it could be freely consulted
while the other copy of the text, though on the same sheet,
remained tightly sealed until the time came to settle the
contract; then it was unrolled and compared with the other
writing, and if the two were exactly the same, all would
be in order. The purpose, of course, was "to safeguard the
original deed from falsification, while at the same time to
enable its holder to use the lower exterior half for daily
reference as required."[22] This is simply an elaboration of
the old tally-stick technique which we have discussed at
length elsewhere.[23] Very early, strips of parchment or cloth
were attached to the sticks and wrapped around them,

since there was not room enough on a stick for writing a lengthy contract. This was the origin of the Jewish scroll wrapped around a staff resembling a scepter. The original tally-stick was a staff on which the contract and names of the contracting parties were written; the staff was then split down the middle; and one half, the "stock," was kept by one of the parties, while the other, "the bill," was held by the other. When the time came to settle the contract, the two parties would bring their sticks together in the presence of the king, and if they matched perfectly, it was plain that neither party had attempted to tinker with the document, and the two would then be bound with a string in the king's hand and laid away in the archives. The Bar Kochba cave has now produced twenty-three examples of this technique, and this is another score for the Book of Mormon, which claims to be that very "stick of Joseph" which in the last days would be joined to the "stick of Judah," so that the two would come together "and they shall be one in mine hand" (Ezekiel 37:19). The word of the Lord assures us that it is "Moroni, whom I have sent unto you to reveal the Book of Mormon, containing the fulness of my everlasting gospel, to whom I have com- mitted the keys of the record of the stick of Ephraim" (D&C 27:5). There are many "sticks," but no more significant joining of sticks than that now taking place between the Jewish and the Nephite records:

> And it shall come to pass that the Jews shall have the words of the Nephites, and the Nephites shall have the words of the Jews; and the Nephites and the Jews shall have the words of the lost tribes of Israel. . . . And it shall come to pass that my people, which are of the house of Israel, shall be gathered home unto the lands of their possessions; and my word also shall be gathered in one. And I will show unto them that fight against my word and against . . . the house of Israel, that I am God, and that I covenanted with Abraham that I would re- member his seed forever (2 Nephi 29:13-14).

Notes

1. Hugh W. Nibley, *Lehi in the Desert* (Salt Lake City: Bookcraft, 1952), 1-139; reprinted in *CWHN* 5:3-146.

2. Hugh W. Nibley, "Qumran and the Companions of the Cave," *Revue de Qumran* 5 (1965), 177-98; reprinted in *CWHN* 1:253-84.

3. Yigael Yadin, *Bar-Kochba* (New York: Random House, 1971), 253.

4. Ibid., 253.

5. Ibid., 247-48.

6. Ibid., 218.

7. Ibid., 221.

8. Ibid., 30.

9. Discussed in detail in Hugh W. Nibley, *An Approach to the Book of Mormon* (Salt Lake City: Deseret Book, 1957), 178-89; reprinted in *CWHN* 6:209-21.

10. Nibley, *Lehi in the Desert*, 24-32; in *CWHN* 5:22-30.

11. See above, page 247.

12. Ibid., 176.

13. Ibid., 27.

14. Ibid., 125; cf. Nehemiah 3:5.

15. Ibid., 133 (emphasis added).

16. Ibid., 134.

17. Ibid., 26.

18. Ibid., 136.

19. Nibley, *An Approach to the Book of Mormon*, 154-63; in *CWHN* 6:183-93.

20. Ibid., 189.

21. Ibid., 229.

22. Ibid., 230.

23. See above, pages 16-21.

16

Churches in the Wilderness

If all the Dead Sea Scrolls which are *now known* to scholars but have not yet been published were to go through the press at the same rate that the others have, we might well be talking about *new* Dead Sea Scrolls for at least two centuries to come. This is about some scrolls and some readings hitherto quite unknown to the public.[1]

The first is the Enoch Scroll, which became accessible not long ago. I want to call attention to just one item which caught my attention. In the Joseph Smith book of Enoch is an episode that stands out conspicuously for the strangely intimate twist it gives to the story. That is when out of the blue comes "a man . . . whose name was Mahijah," who asks Enoch point-blank, "Tell us plainly who thou art, and from whence thou comest?" (Moses 6:40). This triggers Enoch's great sermon in response, in which he reads to the people from the book of Adam and puts them to shame for their sins. As far as I know, the episode is not found in the Ethiopian, Old Slavonic, Hebrew, or Greek Enoch text, so I was brought up with a start when, upon reading the final fragments of the newly published Aramaic Enoch from the Dead Sea Scrolls, the name *MHWY* started popping up repeatedly. Before telling the story of *MHWY* from Qumran, a word about the name is in order.

It is, of course, the *MHWY-EL* of Genesis 4:18, where

This article first appeared as a chapter in Nibley on the Timely and the Timeless *(Provo: Religious Studies Center, 1978), 155-86.*

the other Enoch's grandfather is given the name appearing in our King James Bible as Mehujael. This is not our hero, whose name lacks the -el ending; on the contrary, he belongs to the Cainite branch of the family, which would make the Sethite missionary Enoch an alien to his people. In the Joseph Smith Enoch both forms of the name appear, Mahijah and Mahujah (Moses 6:40; 7:2), which should not be surprising; for in Semitic languages the consonants abide, as everyone knows, while the vowels undergo all manner of vicissitudes; and of all the vowels the w and the y are the most active. (One need mention only such obvious examples as the Hebrew *yeled* and Arabic *walad*, "boy," or the way the w and y constantly supplant each other in Egyptian participles, depending on time and place of writing.) The name *MHWY* is written exactly the same in the Qumran texts as in the Hebrew Bible. In the Greek Septuagint it is Mai-el (the Greeks, having letters for neither h nor w, could end up with Ma[hu]y[ah] as Mai); the trace of the *waw* is preserved in the Latin Vulgate: Mavia-el; but in both cases the semi-vowel *waw* is weakened, and the y sound dominates. Mahujah and Mahijah obviously have the same root. The Ma- prefix may denote the place of an action or in derived forms of the verb the person acting, reminding us that it was "upon the place Mahujah" that Enoch inquired of the Lord and received his missionary assignment in a glorious theophany (Moses 7:2), while the man who boldly put the questions to Enoch himself was Mahijah, the asker. And, since we are playing games, what the Ma- most strongly suggests is certainly the all-but-universal ancient interrogative, *Ma*, what? so that the names Mahujah and Mahijah both sound to the student of Semitics like questions. In the newly discovered texts from Ebla (Tel-Mardikh), the same names are written with Ma- (Amorite) and Mi- (Phoenician-Hebrew.)

But the important thing about *MHWY* in the Aramaic Enoch — by far the oldest Enoch text so far known — is what

CHURCHES IN THE WILDERNESS   291

the man does. Let me read you some parallel passages,
following the translation of Professors Milik and Black, so
that you won't think I have been loading the dice to come
out this way.

The presence of Enoch was a disturbing one, "a strange
thing in the land," and in the Joseph Smith version, "a
wild man hath come among us." And so this is what we
get:

Moses 6:39. When they heard him, . . . *fear came* on all them that heard him.	4QEnGiants[b] 1.20. [Thereupon] all the giants [and the *nephilim*] *took fright,*
Moses 6:40. And there came a man unto him, whose name was *Mahijah,* and said unto him: *Tell us plainly* who thou art, and from whence thou comest?	and they summoned *Mahawai* [*Mahujah*] and he came to them. And the giants asked him and sent him to Enoch . . . saying to him: Go then . . . and under pain of death you must . . . listen to his voice; and tell him that *he is to explain* to you and to interpret the dreams.

So here comes Mahujah-Mahijah to Enoch, represent-
ing a disturbed constituency, to ask the holy man just what
the situation is. That *MHWY* was sent "under pain of
death" shows that not only the dreams but the presence
of Enoch was a cause of dread. In reply the messenger
learns that Enoch comes from a special and holy place:

Moses 6:41. And he said unto them: I came out from . . . the land of my father, a *land of righteousness* unto this day.	4QEnGiants[c] (Ohyah, following MHWY's report): My accusers . . . dwell in [heaven]s, and they live in *holy abodes,* . . . they are more powerful than I.

Enoch tells the man about a revelation and call he received as he traveled in the mountains on a missionary

journey. The journey here seems to be transferred to *MHWY* himself, who crosses the deserts on high to behold Enoch and receive an oracle from him, while in the Joseph Smith version Enoch himself makes such a journey to receive instructions from God:

Moses 6:42. And . . . as I journeyed . . . by the sea east, I beheld a vision; and lo, the heavens I saw.

Moses 7:2-3. As I was journeying, . . . I . . . went up on the mount; . . . I beheld the heavens open.

4QEnGiants[b]. [MHWY . . . rose up into the air] like the whirlwinds, and he flew . . . and crossed Solitude, the great desert. . . . And he caught sight of Enoch, and he called to him and said to him: An oracle.

It is in reply to Mahijah-*MHWY* that Enoch refers the people to an ancient book which he bears with him, having according to some sources (Jubilees, XII Patriarchs) copied it with his own hand from heavenly tablets:

Moses 6:45-46. [Enoch]: We . . . cannot deny, . . . for a book of remembrance we have *written* among us,

according to the pattern given *by the finger* of God, . . . in our own language.

4QEnGiants[a] 7-8. To you, Mah[awai . . .] the two tablets . . . and the second has not been read up till now. The boo[k of . . .]

the copy of the second tablet of the E[pistle . . . *written*] *by* Enoch, the distinguished *scribe's own hand* . . . and the Holy One, to Shemîhazah and to all [his] com[panions].

The teachings of the book (from Adam's time in the Joseph Smith version) strike home, and the hearers are overcome:

Moses 6:47. And as

6Q8a. Ohya and he said

Enoch spake forth the words of God, the people *trembled, and could not stand* in his presence.

to Mahawai: And [I(?)] do not *tremble.* Who showed you all (that) tell [us(?)]. . . . And Mahawai said: . . . Baraq'el, my father, was with me.

4QEnGiants*a* Frg. 4. Ohyah said to Ha]hyah, his brother. . . . They *prostrated themselves* and began to weep before [Enoch (?)].

The name Baraq'el is interesting in this context since Joseph Smith was designated in the Doctrine and Covenants both as Enoch and as Baurak Ale (e.g., D&C 78:9; 103:21-22). Next comes a resounding declaration of general depravity, which in two verses of the Joseph Smith text powerfully sums up the same message in the longest of the Aramaic Enoch fragments:

Moses 6:48-49. And he said unto them, . . . we are made partakers of misery and woe, . . . carnal, sensual, and devilish, and are *shut out from the presence of God.*

4QEnGiants*a* Frg. 8 (The longest fragment): The depravity and misery of the people is described. Their petition is rejected: *God has cast them out.* All is for the worst.

But then, interestingly enough, both the Qumran and the Joseph Smith sermons end on a note of hope—which is *not* found in the other versions of the Book of Enoch:

Moses 6:52. If thou wilt *turn unto me,* . . . and repent, . . . *asking* all things in his name, . . . it shall be given you.

4QEnGiants*a* Frg. 8 (Closing line): And now, *loosen your bonds* [of sin?] which tie [you] up . . . and begin to *pray.*

Now comes what I consider an important theological note. Enoch tells how the Lord told Adam of the natural inclination to sin that came with the Fall. This is converted in the Aramaic version to a denunciation of the wicked people of Enoch's day, who did indeed conceive their children in sin, since they were illegitimate offspring of a totally amoral society:

Moses 6:55-57. Inasmuch as thy *children* are *conceived in sin,* even so . . . sin conceiveth in their hearts. . . . Wherefore teach it unto your children, that all men, everywhere, must repent.

4QEnGiants 8. Let it be known to you that, . . . and your works and those of your wives [. . .] themselves [and their] *children* and the wives of [their children] *by your prostitution* on the earth. And it befell you.

Next the wicked move against Enoch and his people in force but are themselves forced to acknowledge the superior power supporting the patriarch:

Moses 7:13. And . . . he [Enoch] led the people of God, and their enemies *came to battle against them;* and he spake the word of the Lord, and the earth trembled.

4QEnGiants^c (Ohyah the enemy of Enoch): By the strength of my power, [I had attacked] all flesh and I have *made war with them;* . . . they live in holy abodes, and . . . they are more powerful than I.

And then comes that striking passage, so surprisingly vindicated in other Enoch texts, of the roaring lions amidst scenes of general terror:

Moses 7:13. And the *roar of the lions* was heard out of the wilderness;

[Thereupon . . .] the *roaring of the wild beasts* came and the multitude of the wild animals began to cry out.

and all nations *feared greatly.*

And Ohyah spoke . . . : My dream has *overwhelmed* [me . . . and the s]leep of my eyes [has fled].

Finally comes the prediction of utter destruction and

the confining in prison that is to follow:

Moses 7:37-38. These shall suffer. . . . These . . . *shall perish* in the floods; and behold, I will *shut* them up; a *prison* have I prepared for them.	4QEnGiants^a Frg. 7. Then Ohyah [said] to Hehya[h, his brother. . .]. Then he (i.e., God?) punished . . . [the sons] of the Watchers, the giants, and all [their] beloved ones *will not be spared;* . . . he has *imprisoned* us and you, he has subdued [*tqaf,* "seized, *confined"*].

Among new Dead Sea Scrolls we may number those found in 1966 not at Qumran but in the all but inaccessible caves that line the precipitous walls of the Naḥal Ḥever, or, as we would say, "Heber Valley." Instead of a valley it is a deep gorge, like Rock Canyon; it is the next canyon just south of En Gedi where the people bathe in the Dead Sea today. In those caves Jews fleeing from the Romans in the time of Bar Kochba holed up with their families and their most precious portable possessions. A cave in the side of a cliff that can be approached only by one man at a time is easy to defend; and the Romans did not bother to attack them there, but simply set up camps on the flat mesas on either side of the canyon, from which they could look right down into the caves and make sure that no one escaped. Thus trapped, the poor Jews perished miserably in their hideouts; refusing to surrender, they left behind not only all matter of artifacts, kitchenware, clothing, baskets in excellent condition, shoes, and so on, but a priceless harvest of their personal papers and books. These throw a great deal of light on practices described in the Book of Mormon.

For what these people were doing in fleeing from the farms and cities of Judea, as digging in these very caves has shown, was exactly what had been done at other times when the land was overrun by foreign armies. The evi-

dence goes clear back to mysterious bronze vessels hidden
there about 3000 B.C., supposedly by people fleeing from
the armies of the first king of Egypt! I will be quoting from
the review of Professor Yigael Yadin's book *Bar Kochba* on
the subject.

First of all, there is something almost alarmingly literal
about these "voices from the dust." For these documents
were deliberately buried in the deep dust of the cave floors
and came forth in choking clouds of dust—the finders had
to wear masks: "For those who shall be destroyed shall
speak unto them out of the ground, and their speech shall
be low out of the dust, and their voice shall be as one that
hath a familiar spirit; for the Lord God will give unto him
power, that he may whisper concerning them, even as it
were out of the ground; and their speech shall whisper
out of the dust" (2 Nephi 26:16). They have not survived
accidentally, as most other ancient writings have, but were
hidden away on purpose; nor were they simply left behind
or misplaced or forgotten by people who moved on and
lived out their lives elsewhere—the people who left these
records died soon after they buried them and died on the
spot, the victims of a savage religious war. "For those who
shall be destroyed shall speak unto them out of the
ground" (2 Nephi 26:16). What do these records contain?
Accounts of contemporary affairs in private letters, legal
documents, military and civil correspondence, or, in the
words of the Book of Mormon: "For thus saith the Lord
God: They shall write the things which shall be done
among them. . . . Wherefore, as those who have been destroyed have been destroyed speedily" (2 Nephi 26:17-18).

Not only all their letters and legal papers, but their
household effects and their bones were left behind in the
caves, for the simple reason that they did not have time
to escape. As to their destroyers, "Nothing remains here
today of the Romans save a heap of stones on the face of
the desert," writes Yadin, "but here the descendants of

the besieged were returning to salvage their ancestors' precious belongings." Again the Book of Mormon: "And the multitude of their terrible ones shall be as chaff that passeth away" (2 Nephi 26:18).

With the Dead Sea Scrolls we have something new under the sun; even if they simply repeated what we already know, their principal contribution would be the same — a new dimension of reality to our religion. It has been a long time since scholars asked, "Are there really such things as this? Did this really happen?" They have learned to be content with the easy assumption that it really makes no difference in dealing with spiritual, allegorical, moral emblems whether or not there is a physical reality to our stories. The most shocking thing that Joseph Smith brought before the world was the announcement that things men had been talking about for centuries were literally true and would have to be viewed as such. The restoration of the gospel brought a new reality but found few believers — it was more comfortable the old way, when you could take things just as you wanted them.

But with the scrolls from the caves, the reality of things hits us in the face with a shock. How often does it happen that documents thousands of years old have been dug up by the very descendants of the people who wrote those documents, who could actually read them on the spot, not referring them to pedantic decipherment in distant studies and laboratories, but reading them right off as messages from their own grandparents? "We found that our emotions were a mixture of tension and awe," writes Professor Yadin, "yet astonishment and pride at being a part of the reborn State of Israel after a Diaspora of 1,800 years."[2] Compare this with Nephi's moving lines: "And it shall be as if the fruit of thy loins had cried unto them from the dust, . . . even after many generations have gone by them" (2 Nephi 3:19-20).

Nothing illustrates this better than Ezekiel's dry bones.

The question in Ezekiel 37:3 is, "Can these bones live?" And the answer is, Yes, *when* "the stick of Ephraim, [for Joseph] and for all the house of Israel," is joined "with the stick of Judah," "one to another into one stick; and they shall become one in thine hand" (Ezekiel 37:16-19). I once wrote a series of articles on the ancient tally-sticks. The true tally-stick was a staff (originally an arrow-shaft) on which the contract and names of the contracting parties were written. The staff was then split down the middle; and one half, called "the stock," was kept by one of the parties, while the other, "the bill," was held by the other. When the time came to settle the contract, the two parties would present their halves of the stick to the king. If they matched perfectly it was plain that neither party had attempted to tinker with the document; and all conditions having been met, the two halves, joined together again to make one, would be bound with string in the king's hand and laid away in the archives. The oldest known tallies are written in Latin and, surprisingly, in Hebrew. Are such the "sticks" to which Ezekiel refers? They are. The Bar Kochba cave has now produced no fewer than twenty-three examples of this technique in those letters of "the type commonly known as 'double deeds' or 'tied deeds,' " whose use "is a very old and known practice in the ancient world."[3] The idea was to write the same contract twice, once very small; roll it into a tight cylinder; sew it closed; and sign it over with the participants' signatures, not to be opened until the final settlement — plainly the technique of the tally-stick.

So here the Dead Sea Scrolls confirm our own interpretation of what the sticks of Ephraim and Judah were: matching documents to be brought together and placed side by side to make one book at that particular moment when God would set his hand to resurrecting the dry bones of dead Israel. The word of the Lord assures us now that it is indeed "Moroni, whom I have sent unto you to reveal

the Book of Mormon, containing the fulness of my everlasting gospel, to whom I have committed the keys of the
record of the stick of Ephraim" (D&C 27:5). It is specifically
with the bringing forth of these documents that the work
of the last days is to start moving. Moroni, who brought
the book again, sealed it up anciently with the prophecy
that when its word shall be "like as one crying from the
dead, yea, even as one speaking out of the dust" (Moroni
10:27); *then* shall the invitation go forth to the Jews:
"Awake, and arise from the dust, O Jerusalem, . . . enlarge thy borders forever, that thou mayest no more be
confounded" (Moroni 10:31). Which is exactly what they
are doing today: the only way they can keep from being
"confounded" is to have defensible borders.

In 1948 the world turned a corner. Overnight modern
Israel became a reality, *and so did ancient Israel.* The Battle
Scroll appeared just at the moment that Israel was called
to arms, and according to Yadin had not only a moral but
even a practical value in that great crisis. Suddenly scriptures became "relevant." In the same year the oldest Jewish
library and the oldest Christian library were discovered:
both were threatened with destruction; both were challenged as hoaxes; both were viewed as the work of irresponsible and fanatic sectaries. Yet through the years there
has been a growing respect for both the Nag Hammadi
and the Qumran writings, both because of their impressive
spiritual content and also the number of other pseudepigrapha that are being discovered or rediscovered to confirm
their proximity to the authentic Judaism and Christianity
that flourished in the days before the Jewish and Christian doctors of Alexandria changed everything.

To me this seems to be an obvious sequel to what
happened in 1830, when another book appeared from the
dust, and another Israel was established. There are three
main parts to the Restoration, as was made clear in a revelation given a year later: "But before the great day of the

Lord shall come, Jacob shall flourish in the wilderness, and the Lamanites shall blossom as the rose. Zion shall flourish upon the hills and rejoice upon the mountains, and shall be assembled together unto the place which I have appointed" (D&C 49:24-25). And the three shall combine their records, for "it shall come to pass that the Jews shall have the words of the Nephites, and the Nephites shall have the words of the Jews; and the Nephites and the Jews shall have the words of the lost tribes of Israel; and the lost tribes of Israel shall have the words of the Nephites and the Jews. And it shall come to pass that my people, which are of the house of Israel, shall be gathered home unto the lands of their possessions; and my word also shall be gathered in one. And I will show unto them that fight against my word and against my people, who are of the house of Israel, that I am God, and that I covenanted with Abraham that I would remember his seed forever" (2 Nephi 29:13-14). The Dead Sea Scrolls bind the Old Testament and the New Testament together as nothing else, and almost all the Scrolls so far published show affinity to the Book of Mormon, as well as the restored church. Why should this be? Or am I just imagining things? The proper cure for "parallelomania" is not to avoid parallels but to explain them: every parallel has a proper explanation, even if it is only mere coincidence or illusion. There are marks on rocks that sometimes look like writing or like fossilized plants; these are not to be ignored even though they often turn out to be misleading, because once in a while they really are true writing and true fossils. Resemblances between the Bible and the Book of Mormon are not hard to explain; far from being evidence of fraud, they are rather confirmation of authenticity. If the Book of Mormon is what it purports to be, we should expect to find a strong biblical influence in it. Its prophets sound like those of the Old Testament because they studied and consciously quoted the words of those prophets, and all prophets moreover are programmed to sound alike, being called for the same purpose under much the same conditions.

But the Book of Mormon goes far beyond such generalities when it takes us into worlds hitherto undreamed of, namely those societies of desert sectaries, Jewish and Christian, which since the discovery of the Dead Sea Scrolls and Nag Hammadi documents have come to life in our histories and commentaries. The Book of Mormon deals with both types of religious community, for 3 Nephi gives us the Christian version, as other books do the Jewish. The presence of Jewish colonies that look strangely Christian has been disturbing to both conventional "normative" Judaism and conventional Christianity, and has already called for drastic revisions of doctrine and liturgy.

In the Dead Sea Scrolls we learn of the peculiar way of life of the sectaries of the desert, whose Rekhabite tradition goes back to Lehi's day and long before, and survives long after, as is very apparent from the 2nd Sura of the Koran. The people of Lehi were rooted in this tradition. When John Welch was studying at Duke University a few years ago, he was struck by the close resemblance between the story of Lehi and the writing of Zosimus, a Greek of the third century A.D.[4] What would a Greek know about Lehi almost a thousand years after? Zosimus was looking for the model society of the saints, and he attempted to find it in the desert among the Rekhabites—that is the common tradition; I pointed out long ago that Lehi was in the proper sense a Rekhabite and certainly acquainted with the pious sectaries of Jeremiah 30. The writing of Zosimus shows that we are dealing with a pervasive and persistent pattern. Since the rise of "patternism" in the 1930s, scholars have come to recognize all manner of common religious forms and stereotypes throughout the world. But it is important to remember that Joseph Smith in his day was running in an open field, a boundless plain where there was nothing to check or restrain him. Mrs. Brodie saw in the Book of Mormon only the product of a completely untrained, unbridled, undisciplined imagination that ran over like a spring freshet, as she put it. A hundred and forty years ago, Joseph Smith might have gotten away with it, but now surely comes the day of reckoning! And it is not he but the critics who are confounded.

The Book of Mormon is, as it often reminds us, a selective history. It deals with small groups of pious believers, intensely conservative by nature and tradition; consciously identifying themselves with their ancestors, Israel in the wilderness of long ago (see 1 Nephi 19:23). It was this characteristic tendency of the sectaries to identify themselves with earlier trials and tribulations of Israel that at first made the Dead Sea Scrolls so hard to date: the same situations seem to obtain again and again through history, so that the Kittim of the scrolls might be the Eyptians, Assyrians, Babylonians, Greeks, or Romans. Though carrying on in the New World, the Book of Mormon people preserve their ancient culture for centuries: which should not surprise us — do not the present inhabitants of America speak the English, Spanish, and Portuguese and preserve the customs of the Old World after four hundred years? With this strong cultural carry-over, the Nephites are aware of being special and apart — as the sectaries always are — "a lonesome and a solemn people" (Jacob 7:26) is the moving expression of Nephi's brother. And strangely enough, they are peculiarly bound to the written word, as are the people of Qumran. One of the most important discoveries of the Book of Mormon was the process and techniques of recording, transmitting, concealing, editing, translating, and duplicating ancient writings. Here is something the world refused to see in the Bible, the most sealed of books, but it has been thoroughly vindicated in the Dead Sea Scrolls.

Of many striking parallels, I would like to speak of one here that goes to the root of things. It is an episode that opens in the Book of Mormon in the middle of the second century B.C. with "a man whose name was Abinadi," in deep trouble with the establishment. In the Old World we find about the same time a certain "Teacher of Righteousness" in much the same fix: his story is told in the Manual of Discipline, the Damascus or Zadokite Fragment, the commentary on Habakkuk, and the Thanksgiving Hymns from Qumran. He is being given a bad time by certain corrupt priests who are in the saddle. In the Book of Mormon we find them cross-examining the righteous man as they sit at a special tribunal with comfortable seats:

1QH 4:9-10. The common formula is *lying* speakers and vain seers [*m*ᵉ*litsey kazav w-khozey rᵉmiyah*].

Mosiah 11:11. That they [the priests] might rest their bodies . . . while they should speak *lying* and *vain words* to his people.

1QH 4:7. But they lead thy people astray by speaking smooth things to them, practitioners of *vain rhetoric* [*m*ᵉ*l-itse remiyah*, preachers of deceit].

1QH 4:20. They are men of deceit [*mirmah*] and seers who lead astray [*khozey ṭaᶜut*].

1QH 4:15-16. In their insolence they would sit in judgment on thee [investigate, persecute: *yidreshu ka*] . . . from the mouths of lying prophets led astray by error.

Mosiah 11:19. They . . . did delight in . . . shedding . . . the blood of their brethren, and this because of the wickedness of their king and priests.

CD 1:20. And they took the offensive [*yagudu*] against the life of the Righteous One and all who walked uprightly [perfectly]; they hated in their hearts, and pursued them

with the sword and rejoiced
in controversy.

CD 19:3-7. The princes of
Judah . . . have transgressed
in a bond of conspiracy [*tshu-
vah*]. . . . In vengeance and
wrath, every man against his
brother, and everyone hating
his neighbor, . . . greedy for
gain.

Mosiah 11:26. They were
wroth with him and *sought to
take away his life;* but the Lord
delivered him out of their
hands.

1QH 2:21-23, 32-35. The
ruthless ones *sought my
life,* . . . a gang of no-goods
[*sodh shawe'*], a conspiracy of
Belial. But they knew not that
my security [*ma'amadhi*]
rested on Thee, and that
through thy mercy is my soul
delivered. . . . They *sought to
take away my life* . . . and shed
my blood, . . . but Thou God
hast helped the weak and
suffering out of the hand of
the one who was stronger
than he.

Mosiah 11:28. Abinadi
. . . has said these things that
he might stir up my people
to anger one with another,
and to raise contentions
among my people; therefore I
will slay him.

1QH 2:14. I became a
man of controversy [*'ish riv,*
"a troublemaker"] to the
preachers of error.

(Cf. Joseph Smith–History
1:20. I was destined to prove
a disturber and annoyer of
his [Satan's] kingdom.)

Mosiah 12:1. After the
space of two years . . .
Abinadi came among them in
disguise, that they knew him

IQH 4:8-9. For they drove
me out of my land, like a
bird from its nest, and all my
friends and relatives, they

not, and began to prophesy.   turned against me [cf. Odes
of Solomon 42].

Next Abinadi uses an interesting figure, combining two elements of fire and weaving, as the Damascus text also does, but in a quite different combination:

Mosiah 12:3. The life of King Noah shall be valued even as a *garment* in a *hot furnace.*

CD 2:5. For those who stubbornly oppose [God] there shall be violence and overpowering of great terror by the flame of *fire.*

CD 5:13-14. They are playing with *fire* and throwing sparks around [or setting fires]. . . . Their *weaving* is a flimsy thing, the weaving of spiders.

Here both prophets are borrowing from Isaiah 50:9, 11: "Who is he that shall condemn me? lo, they all shall wax old as a garment; the moth shall eat them up. Behold, all ye that kindle a fire, that compass yourselves about with sparks; walk in the light of your fire, and in the sparks that ye have kindled." The idea is that those who have foolishly started such fires will themselves perish by them. In the Zadokite Fragment the precarious position of the persecutors is compared with playing with fire and a flimsy weaving of spiders. Abinadi combines the images with characteristic wit: Noah himself is the flimsy garment in the hot fire, to suffer the very death he is inflicting on Abinadi. In the next verses he employs figures also found in the scrolls:

Mosiah 12:10. He [Abinadi] . . . saith that thy life shall be as a *garment* in a *furnace of fire.*

Mosiah 12:12. And again,   1QH 7:20-21. Thou . . .

he saith thou shall be blossoms of a thistle, which . . .
the *wind* bloweth.

Mosiah 12:19. [The
priests] began to question
him, that they might cross
him, . . . to accuse him; . . .
but . . . to their astonishment, . . . he did withstand
them in all their questions,
and did confound them in all
their words.

Mosiah 12:25-26. [You]
pretend to teach this
people. . . . If ye understand
these things ye have not
taught them; therefore, ye
have perverted the ways of
the Lord.

Mosiah 12:27-29. Ye have
not applied your hearts to
understanding, . . . and they
said: We teach the law of
Moses. . . . If ye teach the
law of Moses why do ye not
keep it? Why do ye *set your
hearts upon riches?* Why do ye

scatterest the remnant of the
men who fight against me
like chaff before the *wind* [cf.
Psalm 1].

1QH 2:29-33. They spread
a net to catch me, but it
caught their own foot. . . .
Thou deliverest me from the
spite of the manipulators
[rhetoricians] of lies, from the
council of those who seek
smooth things; . . . thou has
rescued the soul of the Poor
One whom they desired to
destroy because of his service
to thee.

1QH 14:14. I was zealous
against . . . the deceitful
men, for all who are near
to Thee resist not thy
mouth . . . nor change thy
words.

1QH 2:15-16. I became an
accusing spirit [of *qinah*]
against all who taught
smooth things; and all the
men of false teaching [*rᵉmiyah*, "deception, illusion"]
stormed against me.

commit *whoredoms* and spend your strength with harlots?

Mosiah 12:33. I know if ye keep the commandments of God ye shall be saved, yea, if ye keep the commandments which the Lord delivered unto Moses in the mount of Sinai.

CD 8:4-8; 19:15-20. They professed to be in the covenant of repentance. But they have not departed from the way of the apostates, but have wallowed in the ways of *whoredoms,* and godlessness. . . . Everyone has deserted his family for immoral practices, *zealous in the acquisition of wealth* and property, every man doing what is right in his own eyes, confirming the people in their sins [cf. Alma 30:17].

Mosiah 12:37. Have ye done all this? . . . And have ye taught this people that they should do all these things? I say unto you, Nay, ye have not.

1QH 4:9-12. The preachers of lies and seers of illusions contrive devil's tricks against me to make me exchange the Law which thou has engraved in my heart for the smooth things they teach to the people. They who shut up the drink of knowledge from the thirsting ones to give them vinegar, to turn them to false teachings that they fall into your nets!

Then comes a long sermon to the wicked priests in which Abinadi chides them with their indifference to the scriptures and lays it on with a caustic tongue, showing himself well-versed in the ancient writings: "And now I read unto you the remainder of the commandments of God, for I perceive that they are not written in your hearts; I perceive that ye have studied and taught iniquity the most part of your lives" (Mosiah 13:11). Like the Teacher of Righteousness, Abinadi sees in the law a preparation for the Messiah to come. Professor Frank Cross called the Qumran community "the church of anticipation."

Mosiah 13:27. I say unto you that it is expedient that ye should keep the law of Moses *as yet*; but I say unto you, that the time shall come when it shall no more be expedient to keep the law of Moses.

1QS 9:9-11. And from no precept of the Law [*torah*] shall they depart, . . . *until* there shall come the Prophet and the Messiah of Aaron and Israel.

Mosiah 13:30-32. Therefore there was a law given, . . . a law of performances and of ordinances, . . . which they were to observe strictly from day to day. . . . But behold . . . all these things were types of things to come. . . . And now . . . they did not all understand the law; and this because of the hardness of their hearts.

CD 12:21-23. And according to this rule shall they walk even the seed of Israel ;. . . and this is the way [*serekh*] of living for the camp, by which they walk in the time of the wicked, *until* the Anointed One [Messiah] of Aaron arises.

Mosiah 13:33. Did not *Moses* prophesy . . . concerning the coming of the Messiah, and that God should redeem his people? Yea, and even all the prophets who have prophesied ever since the world began— have they not spoken more or less concerning these things?

1QS 1:3. . . . as was commanded by the hand of *Moses* and by the hand of his servants the prophets.

1QS 9:4-5. . . . to atone for the sins . . . to please God in the land *more* than the flesh of burnt offerings and the fat of sacrifices: the heave-offering of the lips for a *mishpaṭ*, like the sacrificial odor [*kᵉ-nikhoakh*], the offering acceptable to him.

Being perfect in the way means keeping the covenants one has made; the expression is found at the opening of the book of Luke, where we find the parents of John the Baptist following precepts like these:

Mosiah 15:10-11. And who shall be his seed? . . . Whosoever has heard the words of the prophets . . . and believed that the Lord would redeem his people, and have looked forward to that day, . . . these are his *seed*, or they are the heirs of the kingdom of God.

1QSb 3:2-5. May he lift up his face upon all thy assembly and place upon thy head the crown. . . . In eternal glory and sanctify thy *seed* with eternal glory . . . and give thee peace and the kingdom [*malkuth*, kingship].

1QS 5:21-22. A covenant of the Church to establish forever the kingship of his people.

Mosiah 15:26. Behold, and fear, and tremble, . . . ye . . . that have known the commandments of God, and would not keep them.

1QS 2:26-3:1. For his soul has turned away and departed from the knowledge [counsel] of the ordinances [*mishpaṭim*] of truth; he did not remain firm in his dedication [changing of his life].

Mosiah 16:1-3. The time shall come when all shall see the salvation of the Lord. . . . And then shall the wicked be cast out, . . . and the devil has power over them.

CD 20:26. When the glory of God is openly revealed to Israel, then shall all the evildoers of Judah be cast out from the midst of the camp and the people.

During the trial of Abinadi, Alma, one of the priests of Noah who had been converted by the teaching of the holy man, pleaded on his behalf, and being in danger of his own life (Mosiah 17:2), withdrew from circulation while he could put everything down in writing. The name of Alma, incidentally, has turned up in one of the newly discovered scrolls. In 1966, Professor Yadin found deeply buried in the floor of the Cave of Manuscripts the deed to a farm. Today the visitor entering the Shrine of the Book of Jerusalem will find the very first display on his left hand to be this deed, a strip of papyrus mounted on glass with a light shining through; and there, written in a neat and legible hand, is the name "Alma, son of Judah" — one of the owners of the farm. This deserves mention because the critics have always made great fun of the name of Alma (both Latin and feminine), comically out of place among the ancient Jews.

Mosiah 17:3-4. The king . . . caused that Alma should be cast out . . . and sent his servants after him that they might slay him. But he fled from before them and hid himself that they found him not. And he being concealed for many days did write all the words which Abinadi had spoken.

1QH 5:5-13. I praise thee Lord for thou didst not desert me when I was among the people . . . and didst not leave me in my secret affairs, but saved my life out of the pit . . . in the midst of lions. . . . Thou didst take me to a place removed among the fisherfolk and hunters. . . . Thou didst hide me, O God, from the children of men, and hid thy law in me, until the time that thy help should be revealed to me. . . . Thou didst preserve the life of the Poor One in the place of lions.

This is something of a standard situation — preparation for a holy mission by a retreat into the wilderness; we see the same thing in the cases of Ether, Moroni, Lehi and his sons, of Moses, John the Baptist, and the Lord himself. The wilderness motif is preparation for the more ambitious

Rekhabite motif, about which Robert Eisler wrote so learnedly many years ago. Alma came out of hiding, to do his work among the people; and in the Hodiyot we see the leader building up just such a following in the towns:

Mosiah 18:1-3. Alma . . . went about privately among the people . . . to *teach* the words of Abinadi. . . . And he taught them privately.	1QH 4:23-25. Thou hast not kept hiding for shame all those who permitted me to visit [or *instruct*] them, who came together in a church [*yahad*] of thy covenant to listen to me, and to follow the ways of thy heart. They rallied to my defense as a group of Saints.

And now comes the New World Qumran:

Mosiah 18:4. And . . . as many as did believe him did go forth to a place which was called Mormon, . . . being in the borders of the land . . . infested by times or at seasons by wild beasts. (Note: This is not the howling wilderness, but the *midhbar*, the places where desert and cultivation or grazing infringe upon each other; the next verse shows that it was a desert terrain.)	CD 6:4-8. The volunteers from the people are those who bear the staff [cf. of wandering Moses] and the Fountain [or spring] is the Law, . . . and they are the inhabitants of Israel who depart from the land of Judah and dwell in the land of Damascus as strangers. . . . The staff is the one who teaches them the Law, as Isaiah says.
Mosiah 18:5. Now, there was in Mormon a fountain of pure water, . . . there being near the water a thicket of small trees [like Ain Feshka?], where [Alma] did hide himself in the daytime from the	1QS 8:13-16. At the fulfillment of these signs they shall separate themselves from dwelling in the midst of a perverse people, and go forth into the desert to prepare a way for Him. . . . Even by

searches of the king.

the study of the Law as it was given to Moses according to what has been revealed from time to time as it was shown to the prophet through the Holy Ghost.

Mosiah 18:6-8. As many as believed him went thither to hear his words. And . . . after many days there were a goodly number gathered together at the place of Mormon, to hear the words of Alma. . . . And he did teach them, and did preach unto them. . . . And . . . he said unto them: . . . as ye are . . . willing to bear one another's burdens.

1QS 9:18-20. . . . to lead and instruct [le*hinkhotam*] in knowledge and so give them understanding in the hidden wonders and truth[s] in the midst of the men of the Church; to walk each one blamelessly [perfect] with his neighbor in all that has been revealed to them in this time of preparing the way in the wilderness, and to instruct them in all that must be done at this time.

Such communities were not without precedent in Israel. There were fraudulent prophets and quacks who led such groups into the wilderness.[5] The Dead Sea Scrolls have a good deal to say about such ambitious would-be Moseses. There is one instance in the early Christian literature which is interesting because it tells of one impostor who led his people to a place of filthy water—reminding us of Ignatius's charge that the apostate leaders of his day are giving the thirsting people poison to drink.[6] So too we read in CD 1:14: "The man of deception [*latson*—the phony] arose who preached lying waters to Israel and led them astray in the pathless desert, away from the paths of righteousness." In 1QH 2:16 the Righteous Teacher tells how "all the men of falsehood [*remiyah*] stormed against me like a mass of mighty waters." In 1QH 2:12, "The assembly of the wicked rushed upon me like a stormy sea, whose waves cast up all manner of mud," and in 1QH 2:13, "filth." This is the "filthy water" of Nephi's vision, an image found also in the desert Arab poets. What could be worse to one dying of thirst in the desert than to be led to waters that could not be drunk!

Mosiah 18:8-10. [Alma says], here are the waters of Mormon. . . . What have you against being *baptized* in the name of the Lord, as a witness . . . that ye have entered into a covenant, . . . that ye will serve him and keep *his commandments?*

1QS 3:8-10. [In *baptism*] he submits his soul in all humility to every *commandment of God,* . . . [after which] he applies himself to walking carefully [perfectly] in all the ways of God as he commanded for the specified time and conditions in turning aside to the right or to the left.

Mosiah 18:13. . . . as a testimony that ye have entered into a *covenant* to serve him.

1QS 3:11-12. Then he will truly be a *covenant* member of God's eternal church.

Mosiah 18:8-9. . . . willing to bear one another's burdens, that they may be light; . . . and willing to mourn with those that mourn; yea, and comfort those that stand in need of comfort.

1QS 2:24-25. For all shall be united in one true church [oneness of truth], and in becoming humility, and love of mercy and fair dealing [dealings of righteousness] each man with his neighbor.

1QS 5:24-25. . . . to be perfect each in supporting his fellow in truth and humility and love of mercy towards all.

Mosiah 18:8-9. As ye are desirous to come into the fold of God, and to be called his people,

CD 4:2-4. The sons of Zadok are following the patterns: The priests are penitent Israel who have left the Land of Judah [and they are the Levites], . . . they are the elect of Israel who will be called up by name in the last days.

and to stand as witnesses of God at all times and in all things, and in all places . . . even until death,

1QS 1:17-18. And not to turn away from him out of any fear or terror or any burning that may threaten in the government of Belial.

that ye may be redeemed . . . and be numbered with those of the first resurrection, that ye may have eternal life.

1QH 6:7-9. I was comforted amidst all the raging of the people gathering together. For I know that after a time thou wilt raise up the Living One in the midst of thy people, and a remnant in thine inheritance, and purify them with the purification of forgiveness, for all their deeds. They trust on thee.

2 Nephi 9:41-43. The keeper of the gate is the Holy One of Israel; and he employeth no servant there. . . . And whoso knocketh, to him will he open; . . . [to give them] . . . that happiness which is prepared for the saints.

1QH 6:13-14. And there is no go-between [melitz benayim, "servant, representative"] for thy Saints, . . . for they answer in the presence of thy glory and become thy princes in an eternal inheritance.

The 1QH 6:25-28 here uses the same language as the Shepherd of Hermas: "O God thou layest a foundation upon a Rock, . . . according to the true rule and plummet [made] of thy chosen stones, . . . and none stumbles, who walketh hence. For no stranger will enter into its gates, protective gates, . . . whose strong bolts cannot be forced." These verses plainly refer to the mysteries of godliness both in the Book of Mormon and the Qumran texts (cf. 2 Nephi 9:42-43). When I first visited Qumran, in 1966 (Dr. Joseph Saad, Vontella Kimball, Moses Kader, and I were the only persons on the site, for it was during a time of troubles), Christian and Jewish scholars vigorously denied that the tanks, basins, and water conduits connecting them had anything to do with baptism or ritual ablutions; but last year our group visiting the place noted with interest that the Israeli authorities had put up signs designating such places as meant for ritual ablutions. The baptism of Alma is the old Jewish baptism, strictly an ordinance of purification and initiation with no mention of death and resurrection.

Mosiah 18:10. . . . baptized . . . as a witness . . . that ye have entered into a covenant, . . . that ye will serve him and keep his commandments, that he may pour out his Spirit more abundantly upon you.	1QH 14:17-18. Thine abundant goodness have I recognized by an oath, not to sin against thee or to do anything that is evil in thine eyes. And so I have joined in the fellowship of all who share my faith [*sodh*].
Mosiah 18:11. [Alma put the proposition before all the people gathered]; when the people had heard these words, they clapped their hands for joy, and exclaimed: This is the desire of our hearts.	1QS 1:19-20. And all those desiring to enter into the covenant shall say after them [the Levite who preaches repentance and the Priest who proposes the new covenant] Amen! Amen!

Reference to baptism has naturally caused a good deal of discussion among Christians and Jews alike. It is plain from the scrolls that there was both an initiatory baptism and frequent ritual washings:

Mosiah 18:10-13. . . . being baptized . . .	1QS 3:4-5 (Introductory admonition): The backsliders

that he may pour out his
Spirit. . . . O Lord, pour out
thy Spirit upon thy ser-
vant. . . . May the Spirit of
the Lord be poured out upon
you; and . . . grant unto you
eternal life, through the redemption of Christ, . . .
prepared from the foundation
of the world.

from the covenant "shall not
be purified and cleansed by
the waters of *niddah* [removal
of ritual impurity] nor sanctified by the water of the running streams, nor cleansed
by the waters of washing,
[bathing; *rakhāts*].

Now we come to the organization of Alma's church —
Jewish in some respects, early Christian in others. The
writers of the scrolls call their organization a *yaḥad*, the
word meaning simply "oneness." Some would translate
it as "unity," others as "community," others as "oneness."
Georg Molin, the eminent Roman Catholic student of the
scrolls, insists that the usage and context of the word requires it to be translated simply as "church," while the
name the people gave to themselves, according to him,
was "Latter-day Saints."[7] The emphasis on oneness is a
reminder that these churches in the wilderness thought of
themselves as little scale models of Enoch, City of Zion,
so-called "because they were of one heart and one mind"
(Moses 7:18):

Mosiah 18:21. He [Alma]
commanded . . . that there
should be no contention one
with another, but that they
should look forward with *one*
eye, having *one* faith and *one*
baptism, having their hearts
knit together in *unity* and in
love one towards another.

1QS 5:25-26. No one shall
speak to his brother in anger
or peevishness, or haughtily
[with stiff neck] or with any
unkind feeling [*qinah*], but
everyone shall admonish his
fellow in truth, humility and
loving-kindness.

1QS 1:3-9. And to love all
the Chosen . . . and to love
all the Sons of Light in the
quorum [council, brother-

hood; *etsath*] of God .

As to organization:

| Mosiah 18:17. And they were called the church of God, or the church of Christ [Messiah]. . . . And . . . whosoever was baptized by the power and authority of God was added to his church. | 1QSa 2:11-12, 17-23. This is the assembly of the men of the name, the meeting of the council of the church [*yahad*] whenever God causes the Messiah [Anointed One, Christ] to be born among them. . . . And whenever they come together for the table of the church [*yahad*, "unity"] or to drink the new wine, and the table of the *yahad* is set, and the new wine is mixed for drinking, no one shall put forth his hand toward the bread and wine at first before the Priest, for he must bless the first-fruits of the bread and wine; and he takes the bread before them, and after that the Messiah of Israel puts forth his hand on the bread; and after that, all the assembly of the church shall bless [or be blessed, served], each in order of his office [dignity], . . . and this is how they shall do it on every formal occasion [*ma'rakhah*], when as many as ten come together. |

If this sounds disturbingly Christian, it is no more so than

1QS 8:1: In the council of the church there shall be

twelve men, and three priests, perfectly instructed in all that has been revealed.

Mosiah 23:14. Trust no one to be your teacher nor your minister, except he be a man of God, walking in his ways and keeping his commandments.

1QS 8:1-2. . . . in the entire Torah, to act in truth and justice and judgment and love of mercy, walking in humility with their brethren.

Mosiah 23:16. Alma was their high priest . . . [and] founder of their church.

Mosiah 23:17. None received authority to preach or to teach except it were by him from God. . . . He consecrated all their priests and all their teachers.

1QS 6:3-4; 7:1-2. Ten men shall not meet without a priest to preside. . . . There must never be a priest failing to teach the word of God.

1QS 6:6. And there shall not be missing in any place where there are as many as ten men a *doresh* [reader, expounder] in the Torah, whether by day or night.

1QS 2:19-23. The priests shall enter [or move on] first of all, . . . the Levites come next, and all the people in third place, . . . for thousands and hundreds and fifties, and then tens, so that every man may know his place in the church of God for the doctrine of the eternities.

1QS 6:8-10. The priests sit in the first place, the elders in the second and then all the

other people each according
to his dignity. And they shall
be consulted concerning the
law and all the decisions
whatsoever that come before
the congregation, so that
every member . . . may place
his knowledge at the disposal
of all.

1QSa 1:24. All things are
directed by the Sons of Zadok the priests.

CD 13:2-3. In a place of
ten people there must be a
priest learned in the Book of
Haggai, and all must follow
his instructions. If he does
not know enough, a Levite.

Mosiah 18:19. [The
priests] should teach nothing
save it were . . . [what Alma]
had taught, and which had
been spoken by the mouth of
the holy prophets.

1QS 9:7. Only the Sons of
Aaron shall decide matters of
law and property and administer the affairs of the society.

1QS 2:1. The priests shall
bless all the active members
[men who share the lot] who
are in good standing [who
are walking perfectly].

Mosiah 18:23. They
should observe the sabbath
day, . . . and *also* every day
they should give thanks.

CD 10:14-12:6. Anyone
who desecrates the Sabbath
or the special day (*mo^cadhoth*)
is put on probation for seven
years, before he is permitted
again to attend all the meetings.

Mosiah 18:25. And there
was one day in every week

1QS 6:7-8. The entire congregation shall watch to-

that was set apart that they should gather themselves together to teach the people, and to worship the Lord their God, and also, as often as it was in their power, to assemble themselves together.

gether for a third of every night, to read in the book, discuss the Law, and sing hymns together.

Mosiah 18:24, 26. The priests . . . should labor with their own hands for their support. . . . And the priests were not to depend upon the people for their support; . . . for their labor they were to receive the grace of God, that they might . . . teach with power.

1QS 6:2. And the small shall heed the superior regarding work and property [*mammon,* "business"] and they shall eat together.

CD 13:11. And everyone who joins the community shall be examined for his past activities, his knowledge and skills, his physical capacity, his energy, and his possession. [All contribute these.]

Mosiah 18:27-28. The people of the church should impart of their substance, every one according to that which he had. . . . They should impart of their substance of their own free will . . . to those priests that stood in need, . . . and to every needy, naked soul.

1QS 6:19-20. Anyone accepted into the community shall turn over his property agreeable to the priests and the congregation, and receive a receipt from the official in charge.

1QS 7:6-7. Anyone careless with the common property must replace it.

Mosiah 18:29. And they did walk uprightly before God, imparting to one another both temporally and spiritually according to their needs and their wants.

CD 13:7-10. The overseer of the Camp shall direct the generality in the works of God, and teach them about the wonderful things he has done, . . . and have compassion like a father with his

children, saving them from
their erring ways as a Shepherd his sheep . . . that there
be no oppressor or smiter in
his group [*adhatho*].

CD 14:12-14. The grain
[*shkar*] from at least two days
a month shall be placed in
the hands of the Overseer
and the judges, . . . for the
support of the widows, the
ailing and the poor and aged.
[In the Pastor of Hermas the
rule is one day's income a
month.]

As he sums up the achievements of this holy band,
struggling to be real saints, and to a degree succeeding,
the author of our account breaks out into an ecstatic little
hymn of joy. The author of which account? Of both! The
author of Mosiah 18:30 precedes the hymn with a satisfying
summary to his story: "And they did walk uprightly before
God, imparting to one another both temporally and spiritually" (Mosiah 18:29). The writer of the Thanksgiving
Hymns prefaces this particular one with an account of the
wicked world in which he lived, but then he sees the
community in the desert as a light shining all the more
brightly by contrast:

1QH 6:11-13. The people
of thy counsel in the midst of
those of the world [the *bne
adam*], telling for endless generations thy marvellous
things and meditating upon
thy greatness without ceasing, . . . for thou sendest thy
glory to all the men of thy

counsel, sharing a common lot with the angels of thy presence.

1QH 6:5-8. From the world of *shaw* [vanity] and *khamas* [violence], . . . God will establish a new life for his people, the remnant who will be heirs.

1QH 6:13-18. Everyone who accepts his counsel receiving a common share with the angels of the presence [cf. the Zion of Enoch motif]. There is no "go between" between the Holy One and the Saints [cf. 2 Nephi 9:41]. . . . They are like a congregation of princes sharing in the eternal glory of the presence. . . . Blossoming fruit forever, putting forth shoots to bear foliage in endless planting [renewal], to cast their shade over the earth, . . . until . . . their roots reach to the foundations of the earth [*tehom*]: they strike the cosmic waters, and all the streams of Eden water them. . . . And [it] has become the place of springs of light for an unfailing fountain that knows no ceasing. [Then the account goes back to the wicked.]

After this brief, happy vision of the community as a well-watered garden, an oasis in the desert, the poet plunges back into the dreary and wicked world. But the most remarkable parallel to Alma's hymn is No. 8 of the Thanksgiving Hymns from Qumran: The Book of Mormon hymn is divided into two stanzas, the first about the waters of Mormon, the second about the trees of Mormon. IQH8 emphasizes the same dependence of the water and the trees on each other:

Mosiah 18:30. And . . . all this was done in Mormon, yea, by the waters of Mormon, in the forest that was near the waters of Mormon; yea, the place of Mormon, the waters of Mormon, the forest of Mormon, how beautiful are they to the eyes of them who there came to the knowledge of their Redeemer; yea and how blessed are they, for they shall sing to his praise forever.	1QH 8:4-6. I praise the Lord, for Thou didst bring me to a place of water in a dry land, to a fountain of water in a parched land, and to a water of a garden, . . . a growth [planting] of junipers, poplars and cedars; along with thy glory, trees of life are hidden amidst secret springs in the midst of all the trees, by the water, and they shall bring forth shoots for an eternal planting to salvation.

Even without the last line and the formal word of conclusion—"forever"—it would be plain that the Book of Mormon verses are a hymn with a melody hovering about the word *Mormon*. In both songs the imagery is that of the wanderer in the desert saved by the water of life and the tree of life, saved from spiritual death to find redemption and salvation. As might be expected, the trees and the water give knowledge—life-giving knowledge as sustenance.

1 Nephi 2:9 (Lehi's song *qasida*, in the desert): O that thou mightest be like unto this river, continually running into the *fountain of all righteousness!* [cf. Ether 8:26].	1QS 10:9-14. I will sing and play . . . to . . . the Most High, the *fountain of my good,* the source of my well-being, a fountain of knowledge, a flowing spring of holiness. . . . I will praise him

at my going out and coming
in.

Even the end of the colony is much the same in the
two stories. Neither Qumran nor the waters of Mormon
were unknown to the king's men (Noah's in one case,
Herod's in the other); after all, the places were not too far
out in the wilderness—numbers of people streamed out
to them, and only one spy could find out or suspect all
that was necessary. What happened in the Book of Mormon suggests quite sensibly what could have happened
at Qumran, with a jealous monarch keeping the place under surveillance until he decided it would have to go.

> Mosiah 18:32-33. The
> king . . . sent his servants to
> watch them . . . and . . . said
> that Alma was stirring up the
> people to rebellion against
> him; therefore he sent his
> army to destroy them.

So they had to move on—but they were used to that,
for that is the Rekhabite tradition: Israel is ever "das wan-
dernde Gottesvolk," God's Wandering People—indeed the
present pope of Rome is partial to the title "Wayfaring
Church" to describe his own flock.

> Mosiah 18:34-35. And
> . . . Alma and the people of
> the Lord . . . took their tents
> and their families and de-
> parted into the wilderness.
> And they were in number
> about four hundred and fifty
> souls.
>
> (Then they repeat Opera-
> tion Flight into the Wilder-
> ness.)

> CD 6:3-8. They went into
> the desert [Numbers 21:8] to
> dig a well, that is, to study
> the Law, namely the noble
> ones with the staff, that of Is-
> rael who had repented
> ["been converted," *shuv*]; and
> they departed from the land
> of Judah and sojourned in
> the Land of Damascus [a land
> that was strange]. God has

Mosiah 23:1-5. Now
Alma . . . made it known to
his people, therefore they
gathered together their
flocks, and took of their
grain, and departed into the
wilderness. . . . And they
fled eight days' journey into
the wilderness. And they
came to . . . a very beautiful
and pleasant land, a land of
pure water. And they pitched
their tents, and began to till
the ground, and began to
build buildings; yea, they
were industrious, and did labor exceedingly.

called them princes because
they sought after him, . . .
and the Staff [their leader] is
he who studies the Law [cf.
Isaiah 54:16], . . . an imple-
ment in the hands of God to
bring about his purposes.

It would be easy to supply many times more such
parallels between the Book of Mormon and the other ancient records. If the latter are authentic (and both the Qumran and the Enoch writings were once challenged as late
forgeries), it is hard to see how we can brush aside the
Joseph Smith production as nonsense. Even if every parallel were the purest coincidence, we would still have to
explain how the prophet contrived to pack such a dense
succession of happy accidents into the scriptures he gave
us. Where the world has a perfect right to expect a great
potpourri of the most outrageous nonsense, and in anticipation has indeed rushed to judgment with all manner of
premature accusations, we discover whenever ancient
texts turn up to offer the necessary checks and controls,
that the man was astonishingly on target in his depiction
of general situations, in the almost casual mention of peculiar oddities, in the strange proper names, and countless
other unaccountable details. What have Joseph Smith's
critics really known about the true nature of those ancient

societies into which his apocalyptic writings propose to take us? As the evidence accumulates, it is not the Prophet but his critics who find themselves with a lot of explaining to do.

Notes

1. This chapter in *Nibley on the Timely and the Timeless* (Provo: Religious Studies Center, 1978), 155-86, began with the following introductory statement written by Nibley:

Long before the Dead Sea Scrolls were found, Robert Eisler called attention to the existence of societies of ancient sectaries, including the early Christians, who fled to the desert and formed pious communities there, after the manner of the order of Rekhabites (Jeremiah 35:4). More recently, E. Käsemann and U. W. Mauser have taken up the theme, and now the Pope himself refers to his followers as "the Wayfaring Church," of all things. No aspect of the gospel is more fundamental than that which calls the Saints out of the world; it has recently been recognized as fundamental to the universal apocalyptic pattern, and is now recognized as a basic teaching of the prophets of Israel, including the Lord himself. It is the central theme of the Book of Mormon, and Lehi's people faithfully follow the correct routine of flights to the desert as their stories now merge with new manuscript finds from the Dead Sea and elsewhere. And while many Christian communities have consciously sought to imitate the dramatic flight into the wilderness, from monastic orders to Pilgrim Fathers, only the followers of Joseph Smith can claim the distinction of a wholesale, involuntary and total expulsion into a most authentic wilderness. Now, the Book of Mormon is not only a typical product of a religious people driven to the wilds—surprisingly we have learned since 1950 that such people had a veritable passion for writing books and keeping records—but it actually contains passages that match some of the Dead Sea Scrolls almost word for word. Isn't that going too far? How, one may ask, would Alma be able to quote from a book written on the other side of the world among people with whom his own had lost all contact for five hundred years? Joseph Smith must have possessed supernatural cunning to have foreseen such an impasse, yet his Book of Mormon explains it easily: Alma informs us that the passages in question are not his, but he is quoting them directly from an ancient source, the work of an early prophet of Israel named Zenos. Alma and the author of the Thanksgiving Scroll are drawing from the same ancient source. No wonder they sound alike.

2. Yigael Yadin, *Bar-Kochba* (New York: Random House, 1971), 253.

3. Ibid., 229-30. For the earlier articles by Nibley, see chapter 1 in the present volume.

4. John W. Welch, "The Narrative of Zosimus and the Book of Mormon," *BYU Studies* 22 (1982): 311-32.

5. Robert Eisler, *Iesous Basileus ou Basileusas*, 2 vols. (Heidelberg: Winter, 1929), 2:171.

6. Ignatius, *Epistle to the Ephesians* 7, *Epistle to Polycarp* 3.

7. Georg Molin, *Die Söhne des Lichtes* (Vienna: Herold, 1954), 146.

17

Freemen and King-men in the Book of Mormon

In recent years Mesoamerican archaeologists have directed their attention with increasing concern to evidence that might explain the strange and sudden demise of the great ancient American centers of civilization that left behind those imposing ruins "abandoned by unknown builders at an unknown time for unknown reasons."[1] In attempting to get at the root of the matter the experts have, it would seem at present, come to some sort of consensus or convergence of ideas favoring one explanation over all the others. While not excluding the roles played by the upheavals of nature, disease, change of climate, depletion of resources, and so on, the specialists now conclude that the primary reason for the rapid decline and fall of those civilizations, far outweighing the rest, was the pressure brought to bear by one segment of the population, which they designate as "the elite," on another, which they call "the commoners." This matches the tales told in the pre-Columbian literary accounts transmitted and translated by the European Conquistadors of the sixteenth century, with their repeated reference to the tragic confrontations between "los señores" and "la gente comun." The theme is not confined to one area of Middle America nor to any one period of time; it is, in fact, one of the constants of history.

This is an edited and annotated transcript of a talk given in 1981 at the J. Reuben Clark Law School of Brigham Young University.

And so it is not going out of bounds to recall the long and exciting account in the Book of Mormon of the rivalry between the "king-men" and the "freemen" and what it led to.

As a completely self-consistent and convincing story, the epic tale of the "freemen" stands on its own feet; but the new double-check of ancient evidence plus modern relevance now invites us to examine it more closely and take it to heart more seriously than ever before. We cannot do better than to let the Book of Mormon tell the story in its own powerful and moving prose, leading off with the basic question:

Q. Who were the freemen?

A. The term is first used in the Book of Mormon to designate the people who supported the government of the Nephites, around 67 B.C., during a political crisis: "And those who were desirous that [the newly elected] Pahoran should remain chief judge over the land took upon them the name of freemen" (Alma 51:6).

Q. Shouldn't the name be capitalized?

A. It does not designate a political party, organization, or society, but simply denotes the body of common citizens supporting Moroni in his opposition to a group known as the "king-men." When the king-men's candidate lost and "the voice of the people came in favor of the freemen" (Alma 51:7), the king-men refused to accept defeat; it was their continued hostility which gave rise to the popular countermovement led by Moroni and designated by the name of freemen.

Q. Did Moroni organize them into a party?

A. No, he did not need to. He was acting in his official capacity, having been appointed to be "chief captain over the Nephites" (Alma 43:16), with emergency powers granted "by the chief judges and the voice of the people" (Alma 46:34). He was simply fulfilling the duties of his office in alerting the public to the dangerous nature of the opposition.

Q. What was the nature of that danger?

A. The king-men at the time represented the resurgence of an element which had plagued the Nephites from the beginning. Just six years before the affair in question Moroni had overcome a coalition formed to overthrow the government and establish a monarchy. The name of freemen was not mentioned at that time, but the king-men ye have always with you: "Now those who were in favor of kings were those of high birth and they sought to be kings; and they were supported by those who sought power and authority over the people" (Alma 51:8).

Q. Wouldn't it have been within their rights to change the form of government if they got enough votes?

A. That is what they were aiming at, but it was their methods that brought Moroni into action against them. They were secretly preparing a coup to take over the government by force, and were in communication with the king of the Lamanites, with whom Moroni had just concluded a dangerous war brought on by Nephite dissenters (Alma 43:44). With peace barely achieved, the new threat made the affairs of the people of Nephi "exceedingly precarious and dangerous" (Alma 46:7).

Q. Who comprised the powerful coalition?

A. The original nucleus was composed of people who were making a lot of money in the postwar boom. When Helaman and other leaders of the church reprimanded their practices, calling upon them to walk uprightly before God, "there arose a dissension among them, and they would not give heed to the words of Helaman and his brethren; but they grew proud, being lifted up in their hearts, because of their exceedingly great riches; therefore they grew rich in their own eyes, and would not give heed to their words" (Alma 45:23-24).

Q. Were they organized from the first?

A. No. The new trouble began with "many little dissensions and disturbances . . . among the people" (Alma 45:21). But as was usual in these periodic slips back into the old materialism, the discontent crystallized around the person of a dynamic leader who was able to bring jarring and dissident elements together.

Q. Why did he oppose the government?

A. The old story—he wanted to run things himself. "Desirous to be king" (Alma 46:4), he took skillful advantage of the ground-swell favoring a monarchy in an atmosphere of sudden prosperity in which many "grew proud, being lifted up in their hearts" (Alma 45:24). The man who led them was Amalickiah, who is, in Moroni's opinion, another example of the "great wickedness one very wicked man can cause to take place among the children of men" (Alma 46:9).

Q. Ambition is hardly a rare human quality—what made him so very wicked?

A. It depends on how you define wickedness. This man was really quite a charmer, "a man of many flattering words," who won a great personal following and "led away the hearts of many people" (Alma 46:10). "A large and a strong man" of imposing presence (Alma 46:3); to a powerful and persuasive rhetoric he added the fierce resolve of one who "had sworn to drink the blood of Moroni," his chief opponent (Alma 51:9). Shrewd and calculating, "a man of cunning device" (Alma 46:10), he knew how to preserve himself: "He did not come down himself to battle" (Alma 49:11). Amalickiah was willing to pay any price in blood to gain his objective, for "he did care not for the blood of his people" (Alma 49:10). His plan was skillfully conceived and executed.

Q. What did he do?

A. He not only brought together the conflicting factions of selfish and greedy Nephites but united them for war. At the same time, he arranged a coordination of activities with an invasion by the Lamanites as he "stirred up the hearts of the people of the Lamanites against the people of the Nephites," among whom "he was gathering together soldiers from all parts of his land, and arming them, and preparing for war" (Alma 51:9). For Amalickiah the answer to his problems and the realization of his ambitions lay in military action. That was his last campaign, and it was brilliantly successful until he was assassinated in his tent. Unpopular with most of the Nephites, he had to use Lamanite manpower in his various operations.

Q. How was he able to do that?

A. Once by poisoning he gained complete control of a renegade Lamanite army of war-protesters (Alma 47:5-19); then he got command of the main Lamanite force by assassinating the king. Putting himself forward as the champion of law and order, he then married the mourning queen and mounted the Lamanite throne (Alma 47:32-35). Then he stirred up the war-weary Lamanites to a pitch of warfever entirely contrary to all their interests and inclinations but beneficial to his own. He accomplished that feat by masterful use of the media. As in later Mesoamerica, it seems that towers were a conspicuous part of public architecture, used among other things for public presentations and announcements. When Amalickiah became king, "he began to inspire the hearts of the Lamanites against the people of Nephi; yea, he did appoint men to speak unto the Lamanites from their towers, against the Nephites" (Alma 48:1). He saturated the airwaves, so to speak, and his propaganda worked. Finally this consummate dissembler and master liar was able to march at the head of a mighty army which he thought would make him king in Zarahemla.

Q. Did he think the Nephites would support him after Moroni had thrown him out the first time?

A. He could always count on strong backing by the king-men. Let us go back to his first enterprise when he found a field ripe for his talents among those who were made fighting mad—"exceeding wroth"—by "the words of Helaman and his brethren." They had decided to take action and "were gathered together against their brethren," not merely to oppose them at the polls, but "determined to slay them" (Alma 46:1-2). Playing upon the king-men's disaffection and anger, Amalickiah became the man of the hour: "And those people who were wroth were also desirous that he should be their king" (Alma 46:4). By working on a common hostility to the government, Amalickiah was able to weld half a dozen divergent interests into a single military force of king-men.

Q. I believe we started out asking what those divergent elements were.

A. First, as we have noted, the original core of those who refused all instruction, "because of their exceedingly great riches" (Alma 45:24), "gathered together" as a hate-group—"exceeding wroth"—to plan the extremist measures against those who stood in their way (Alma 46:1-2). Then there were passionate monarchists, who not only were "in favor of kings" but, being of "high birth, . . . sought to be kings" (Alma 51:8)—every one in line for the throne. After them were those who may not have claimed royal blood but nevertheless "professed the blood of no-

bility" — whether they could prove it or not (Alma 51:21).
Then, as in the Late Roman Empire, intermarriage put
aspiring judges and high clergy into the picture as aristocratic families intermarried and intrigued together.
"Those judges had many friends and kindreds;
and . . . almost all the lawyers and high priests, did gather
themselves together, and unite with the kindreds of those
judges" (3 Nephi 6:27). All those who aspire to be in the
upper crust, "the elite," "los señores," gravitate toward
the king-men in every period of Book of Mormon history.
Though they were lower in the scale, "the lower judges
of the land" were Amalickiah's strongest supporters, and
he knew how to make use of them: "And they were seeking
for power. And they had been led by the flatteries of Amalickiah, that if [the local magistrates] would support him
and establish him to be their king, that he would make
them rulers over the people" (Alma 46:4-5). Finally he used
his cunning arguments and gratifying rhetoric on the
people of the church with considerable success, as "there
were many in the church who believed in the flattering
words of Amalickiah" (Alma 46:7). This was six years before the name of freemen marked the opposition. It was
by the tried and true method of hard, persistent work,
constantly stirring up and playing upon the discontent,
aspirations, and fears of various groups, with a ceaseless
flow of clever and impassioned rhetoric, that Amalickiah
was able to lay the solid foundation for his armed takeover
of the country. It seems to have been kept very secret, or
else nobody took it very seriously, for Moroni exploded
when he heard about it.

Q. Do you think Moroni was surprised?
A. His behavior was that of a man caught off guard by
acts of such vicious and deceitful nature that his own guile-
less spirit was slow to anticipate what it was loathe to
attribute to any fellow creature: "When Moroni, who was

the chief commander of the armies, . . . had heard of these dissensions, he was angry with Amalickiah" (Alma 46:11), and he reacted in a quick and spectacular manner; the drastic measures he took to alert the people show that they needed waking up in a great hurry. "He rent his coat, . . . took a piece thereof, and wrote upon it — In memory of our God, our religion, and freedom, and our peace, our wives, and our children" (Alma 46:12). This vividly recalls the inscriptions that the ancient Jews would put on their banners and trumpets before going out to war, as reported in the Battle Scroll of the Dead Sea Scrolls. During times of war, the priests would go forth before the ranks of warriors immediately before the battle, stirring their spirits with just such words as Moroni used when, having put the cloak on a pole and calling it the "title of liberty" (Alma 46:13), he went forth among the people, calling upon them "with a loud voice." Hearing Moroni, and seeing the banner, "the people came running together" (Alma 46:19-21). It was all according to ancient custom, as is clear from the sermons Moroni gave on the occasion, recalling their traditions to mind and giving us the official statement of just what it was freemen stood for.

The people who answered Moroni's summons came girding on their armor and "rending their garments in token, or as a covenant, that they would not forsake the Lord their God; or, in other words, if they should transgress the commandments of God, . . . the Lord should rend them even as they had rent their garments" (Alma 46:21). "And they cast their garments at the feet of Moroni, saying: . . . We shall be destroyed, even as our brethren in the land northward [the Jaredites], if we shall fall into transgression; yea, [God] may cast us at the feet of our enemies, . . . to be trodden underfoot, if we shall fall into transgression" (Alma 46:22). Recent studies have called attention to the forgotten but peculiar old Jewish rite of treading on one's garments while making a covenant.

Moroni, in addressing the people on the occasion, sheds more light on the subject: "Surely God shall not suffer that we, who are despised . . . shall be trodden down and destroyed, until we bring it upon us by our own transgressions" (Alma 46:18). Then he reminds them of a tradition that takes the origin of the rent garment symbolism back to their ancestor Joseph, the suffering outcast, with whom they are to identify themselves: "Yea, let us preserve our liberty as a remnant of Joseph; yea, let us remember the words of Jacob, before his death." For Jacob, noting that part of the torn garment of Joseph was bloody and decayed and part of it perfectly preserved, saw in that a token of the future of his descendants (Alma 46:24-26). The story, exactly as Moroni recalls it, was also preserved among Jews living in Persia in the Middle Ages—a powerful confirmation of the reality of all this. Moroni asks the people: Which is the remnant of the garment that shall perish— could it perhaps be the people who have dissented from us, the king-men? Don't be smug about it! "Yea, and even it shall be ourselves if we do not stand fast in the faith of Christ" (Alma 46:27). In this episode we see just how the freemen think of themselves: two ideas are of primary importance.

Q. What two ideas?

A. First, as the descendants of Joseph they march under his banner—not the banner of the Grand Vizier of Egypt, but the torn and tattered garment of Joseph the outcast child, who was beaten, stripped, and sold into bondage. His cloak was taken from him, then torn and bloodied to prove that he was finished forever, while he went on to be a suffering servant and a prisoner in Egypt. Moroni calls upon his people to recognize their position as the meek and humble of the world, "we, who are despised" (Alma 46:18); it is the perennial call of the prophets of Israel, with Isaiah at the head. This is in vivid contrast to the rich and well-born, whose "pride and nobility" Moroni denounces as loudly as he proclaims the humility of the freemen (Alma 51:17, 18, 21). The second point is more important. You will notice that every time the dedication of the people to the cause of God is mentioned, it is followed immediately by a qualifying clause, proclaiming that the people who enter the covenant are not to be considered righteous simply by virtue of party affiliation. They do not represent the Good People as opposed to the Bad People: their own transgression can spoil everything at any time; they are quite as capable of sinning and incurring destruction as their enemies; they can bring down upon themselves the same calamities as the dissenters; their garments can be rent along with the most wicked; and they can be as completely destroyed as the Jaredites of old, for there is no guarantee that they are the Good People. This is an extremely important lesson driven home repeatedly in the Book of Mormon, that righteousness does not consist in being identified with this or that nation, party, church, or group. When you find a particularly wicked society in the story (as in Helaman 5:2), look back a few pages and you will probably find that not many years before, those same people were counted righteous. Or, when you find a particularly godless and ferocious lot of Lamanites, if you look a few pages ahead you may find them among the most blessed and favored of God's people (Helaman 6:36; Alma 26:23-33).

Q. But at any given time, surely, or in any particular conflict, you have right against wrong.

A. On the contrary, whenever the Nephites and Lamanites come to blows there is little to choose between them. If the "bad people" more often provoke war, the "good people" have equal responsibility, since they have the greater light. Take what must be the most clear-cut case of a good guy fighting a bad guy in the Book of

Mormon: "And it came to pass that Alma fought with Amlici with the sword, face to face; and they did contend mightily, one with another" (Alma 2:29) — the righteous leader Alma versus the wicked arch–king-man Amlici.

Q. Right out of *Star Wars*.

A. That is exactly how the average reader would see it, knowing that "Alma, being a man of God, . . . was strengthened, insomuch that he slew Amlici with the sword" (Alma 2:30-31). And yet how did the Nephites, under Alma's instruction, view this particular showdown? "They believed that it was the judgments of God sent upon them because of their wickedness and their abominations; therefore they were awakened to a remembrance of their duty" (Alma 4:3). It was not a case of right against wrong at all, but of two wrongs teaching a grim lesson of mutual destruction; for what kind of a victory was it for the Nephites? "The people were . . . greatly afflicted for the loss of their brethren; . . . their flocks and herds [and] . . . their fields of grain . . . were trodden under foot and destroyed by the Lamanites. And so great were their afflictions that every soul had cause to mourn" (Alma 4:2-3).

Q. Admittedly war is hell. But they *had* to repel those Lamanite attacks!

A. Yes, Lamanite attacks which they knew perfectly well would never have taken place if they had not brought it on themselves. While Lehi's fleeing family was still within range of Jerusalem, the Lord told Nephi that it was his intention henceforward to keep the descendants of Laman and Lemuel (who were already making trouble as the original king-men!) in a position to threaten Nephi's people with destruction at all times, as "a scourge unto [his] seed, to stir them up in the ways of remembrance" (1 Nephi 2:24).

Q. In that case, can you blame the Nephites for being trigger-happy?

A. Yes, because the Lord also made it perfectly clear to Nephi that the Lamanites, no matter how formidable and threatening, "shall have no power over thy seed except they shall rebel against me also" (1 Nephi 2:23). Accordingly, if there was any war at all the Nephites shared the guilt for it.

Q. But can't we distinguish the Nephites and Lamanites as the right and wrong in a general sense?

A. Hardly. Moroni opposed and denounced his own head-of-state when he thought, quite wrongly as it turned out (and let that too be a lesson to us!), that he was guilty of the "great wickedness of those who are seeking for power and authority, yea, even those king-men" (Alma 60:17). It is the individual, not the society, that sins. At the time, the king-men were actually the official Nephite nation, in control of the city and the government. Yet not long after, we find some of the most brutal and bloodthirsty of these king-men enjoying pentecostal manifestations (Helaman 5:26-51). Repeatedly the Book of Mormon admonishes us not to judge people by labels. Lehi's family was still in Arabia when Nephi gave his brothers a lesson in that important principle. Laman and Lemuel had insisted that they were doing right because they were identified with the dominant traditionalist party in Jerusalem (who happened to be Zedekiah's king-men), who were righteous because they were the Chosen People and because they went to church. Nonsense! said Nephi: "Do ye suppose that the children of this land, . . . who were driven out by our fathers, do ye suppose that they were righteous? . . . Do ye suppose that our fathers would have been more choice than they if they had been righteous? I say unto you, Nay. Behold, the Lord esteemeth all flesh in one; he that is righteous is favored of God" (1 Nephi 17:33-35).

Q. But if the Law is a moral code, to observe the Law implies upright behavior.

A. That was the position of the Pharisees; but when the Lord was asked how one could be sure one was ful-filling the Law, he replied by holding up to his apostles as the perfect example of a righteous person ("Go ye there-fore and do likewise!"), a Samaritan. This man was a mem-ber of the wrong nation, the wrong party, and the wrong church. He did a very unpleasant, messy, and inconve-nient thing in helping a total stranger who for all he knew and to all appearances was a dirty, drunken, no-good tramp. At least two members of the right party, and the right nation, and the right religion, who were respected authorities and priests in Israel, discreetly and quietly de-clined the awkward involvement (which could certainly lead to complications) by passing down on the other side of the road (Luke 10:27-37). Now the "title of liberty," like the Good Samaritan, proclaimed the cause of the outcast and downtrodden against "the great wickedness of those who are seeking for power and authority, yea, even those king-men" (Alma 60:17).

Q. How do you distinguish the righteous from the wicked, then?

A. You don't; that is not your prerogative: "As you cannot always tell the wicked from the righteous," the Lord told the Prophet Joseph, "therefore I say unto you, hold your peace until I shall see fit to make all things known" (D&C 10:37). In this connection another parable of Jesus bids us consider a very important principle, namely that we are never to take people's own estimate of their virtue at face value. When "two men went up into the temple to pray," one of them proclaimed his righteousness and the other his sinful condition; as it turned out, the true labels were reversed (Luke 18:10-14). This is important, because throughout the Book of Mormon the king-men routinely described themselves as the champions of freedom. Right at the outset, Laman falsely accused Nephi of being a king-man: "He has thought to make himself a king and a ruler over us, that he may do with us according to his will and pleasure. And after this manner did my brother Laman stir up their hearts to anger" (1 Nephi 16:38). Of course it was Laman himself who was aspiring to be top dog (1 Nephi 17:44), while he put himself forward as the champion of freedom. Giddianhi was one of the most rabid of king-men, "the leader and the governor of this band of robbers" aspiring to take over the government (3 Nephi 3:1). He wrote a most high-flown and idealistic letter to Lachoneus, the real governor, praising his dedication to "that which ye suppose to be your right and liberty," and insisting that his own followers were the real freedom-fighters with "their unconquerable spirit" and determination to right "the many wrongs which ye have done unto them" (3 Nephi 3:2-4). But magnanimously "feeling for your welfare" (3 Nephi 3:5), he urges them to "become our brethren . . . not our slaves, but our brethren and partners of all our substance" (3 Nephi 3:7) — a blow for freedom. He invites them to join his dignified and venerable society — "The works thereof I know to be good; and they are of ancient date, . . . handed down unto us" (3 Nephi 3:9). He pleads for avoidance of bloodshed by returning to his people "their rights and government" which they had lost through the Nephites' "wickedness in retaining from them their rights of government" (3 Nephi 3:10). Lachoneus the governor was astonished at the sheer effrontery of the thing (3 Nephi 3:11), in which the modern reader cannot help but detect familiar echoes of "liberationist" terror groups throughout the world: the king-men

have always made a big thing of sounding like freemen.
One of the cleverest such twisters was Korihor.

Q. Who was he?

A. Korihor was another ambitious man who rallied
people of property to free themselves from the oppressive
restraints of sacral government and the "foolish ordinances
and performances" by which "this people bind themselves . . . that they may not lift up their heads" (Alma
30:23). He said that thanks to the government, people
"durst not enjoy their rights and privileges"; in particular,
"they durst not make use of that which is their own, lest
they should offend their priests" (Alma 30:27-28). His appeal was for freedom from restraints laid down by ancient
priests (Alma 30:23), freedom to do business without interference from church or state, freedom to follow the natural order in which every man prospered according to his
genius, and "every man conquered according to his
strength." Korihor also preached that "whatsoever a man
did was no crime" (Alma 30:17).

Q. What was Alma's answer to that?

A. He showed that Korihor was deliberately misinter-
preting everything, being "possessed with a lying spirit"
(Alma 30:42). He answered him patiently, point by point,
but it was his exemplary restraint that gave Korihor the
lie.

Q. How so?

A. Alma showed Korihor what real freedom was, putting him under no restraint whatsoever, though he openly
defied the highest authorities. Korihor was perfectly free
to teach the people anything he chose, for "there was no
law against a man's belief; for it was strictly contrary to
the commands of God that there should be a law which
should bring men on to unequal grounds" (Alma 30:7).

"Now if a man desired to serve God, it was his privilege, . . . but if he did not believe in him there was no law
to punish him" (Alma 30:9) or to put him at a disadvantage,
for the idea was that "all men were on equal grounds"
(Alma 30:11).

Q. Do you mean that Alma, the high priest and chief
judge of the land, actually permitted people to preach atheism?

A. When Alma's own son went around the country
with King Mosiah's sons preaching publicly against everything their fathers stood for, those two powerful men took
no action against them (Mosiah 27:8-10). It took an angel
to stop the young smart-alecks, and even he made it perfectly clear that God would not revoke the agency of those
who opposed his purposes: "This is my church, . . . and
nothing shall overthrow it, save it is the transgression of
my people" (Mosiah 27:13). God guarantees the integrity
of his church against all external enemies, but he will not
deny the members the right to transgress and destroy it.
So with Korihor: Alma the chief judge, whose determination equaled that of Moroni to pull down the pride and
the nobility of the king-men (Alma 4:19), passed no sentence against him (Alma 30:30-55).

Q. What happened to Korihor?

A. Poetic justice caught up with him. Uncomfortable
among the Nephites, he sought out a community of certain
dissenters who were as proud and independent as himself,
people who had separated themselves from the Nephites
and called themselves Zoramites after their leader. There,
Korihor was killed by a mob (Alma 30:59). These Zoramites
are a perfect example of a phenomenon to which American
archaeologists are calling attention, since they seem to represent one of those "incursions by small expansionist 'elite'
groups" into areas where they imposed "political control

and their own religious cults" on the less militant inhabitants; the conquered peoples thereafter "maintained the elite and constructed the great ceremonial centers under their direction."[2] So we find the common people complaining to Alma the missionary: "They have cast us out of our synagogues which we have labored abundantly to build with our own hands" (Alma 32:5). Although we cannot pursue this striking piece of evidence here, we should not ignore the principal message of the Zoramites to us.

Q. What is that?

A. The deceitfulness of the self-image. This is perfectly understandable, since people have to live with themselves, but also quite dangerous, since it easily covers a multitude of sins. Thus the people of Zarahemla angrily rebuffed calls to repentance by Samuel the Lamanite. They insist on being told not what is *wrong* with Zarahemla—for that "ye . . . cast him out and seek all manner of ways to destroy him; . . . ye say that he is a false prophet . . . of the devil," and so on (Helaman 13:26). They only want to hear what is *right* with Zarahemla, for which "ye will lift him up, . . . give unto him of your substance, . . . of your gold and of your silver, and ye will clothe him with costly apparel" (Helaman 13:28). This is, incidentally, exactly how prophets were treated in Ancient America, where the Chilans (prophets) "were held in such high esteem that they were carried on men's shoulders when they went abroad"—lifted up.[3] Another bull's-eye for the Book of Mormon.

Now these Zoramites had their virtues as well as their vices, as every society does if it is to survive for a month or more. They were strong-minded, independent people who went off to found their own nation and in so doing showed themselves exceedingly enterprising and industrious. A disciplined people, they turned out the ablest military officers that Moroni ever had to contend with

(Alma 43:6, 44; 48:5). Enjoying great prosperity, they were strict in their religious observances, giving fulsome thanks to God for his goodness in fervid personal testimonies every week, and preserving an atmosphere of high respectability with unswerving adherence to proper dress standards (Alma 32:2).

Q. They seem the right kind of people to me.

A. They certainly thought they were, giving themselves a five-star rating in everything. And yet to Alma, who had seen as much as any man of the depravity of which men are capable, these were beyond a doubt the most wicked people he had ever come up against: "Oh Lord," he cried, "wilt thou suffer that thy servants shall dwell here below in the flesh, to behold such gross wickedness among the children of men?" (Alma 31:26).

Q. What was so wicked about them?

A. The peculiarly deadly combination of total selfishness with the assiduous cultivation of an air of saintliness was what stunned Alma, who was "astonished beyond all measure" at their performance (Alma 31:19). "Behold, O God, they cry unto thee" (Alma 31:27).

Q. What is wrong with that?

A. "And yet" is what is wrong with it, as Alma continues, "and yet their hearts are swallowed up in their pride. . . . They cry unto thee with their mouths, while they are puffed up, even to greatness, with the vain things of the world. Behold, O my God, their costly apparel . . . and all their precious things; . . . and behold, their hearts are set upon them, and yet they cry unto thee and say— We thank thee, O God, for we are a chosen people" (Alma 31:27-28). It was that combination of covetousness and self-righteousness, to which the Prophet Joseph found the people of his day also highly susceptible, that condemned the Zoramites. Who can doubt that Mormon, who saw our day in detail, had a very good reason for including the strange case of the Zoramites in his message to us? The story is equally impressive for its manifestly authentic ancient setting and its prophetic relevance to the modern situation. The Zoramites were the very type and model of the king-men.

Q. It seems to me that a little more discipline would not have harmed the sons of King Mosiah and Alma. Why didn't the King simply forbid his sons from making all that mischief?

A. Because he was Mosiah, who had given the Nephites their ideal constitution based on the old Israelite rule of judges. "Behold, it is not expedient that we should have a king; for thus saith the Lord: Ye shall not esteem one flesh above another, or one man shall not think himself above another; therefore I say unto you it is not expedient that ye should have a king" (Mosiah 23:7). Here you have in a nutshell the difference between the king-men and the freemen, and the issue is purely that of equality. Where persuasion would not work with the young men, an angel had to take over.

Q. Exactly what did Moroni want in dealing with the king-men?

A. Before all else, peace: Moroni was thus "breaking down the wars and contentions among his own people" (Alma 51:22). The nation desperately needed peace — that is why he fairly exploded when he learned that Amalickiah was stirring up war-fever at home and abroad (Alma 46:11-35). Personally his grand passion was for equality — a positive mania with him — without which, according to the Book of Mormon, there can be no freedom.

Q. But if ever there was an *un-average* man, it was Moroni!

A. Yes, Mormon comments on that—for him Moroni was a sort of superman (Alma 48:16-17). But Moroni was wholly dedicated to defending that constitution which Mosiah had given the nation when he laid down the kingship, in which the sum of wisdom was equality, as set forth in the great speech of his father King Benjamin at a former abdication: "And I . . . am no better than ye yourselves are; for I am also of the dust" (Mosiah 2:26). Mosiah reiterated the theme in his own farewell address: "For thus saith the Lord: Ye shall not esteem one flesh above another, or one man shall not think himself above another" (Mosiah 23:7). "I desire that this inequality should be no more in this land; . . . but I desire that this land be a land of liberty, and every man may enjoy his rights and privileges alike" (Mosiah 29:32). He tells us what kind of equality is indispensable if a people are to enjoy liberty, namely "that every man should have an equal chance throughout all the land . . . to answer for his own sins" (Mosiah 29:38).

Q. What's to prevent any man from answering for his own sins?

A. Being in bondage to another, so that he is not free to arrange his own actions. We might get into all sorts of fine distinctions here, but fortunately the Book of Mormon is full and explicit on the subject, allowing a generous sampling of relevant and enlightening passages. Right at the beginning, Nephi, following Isaiah, singles out the greatest enemy of equality: "For because they are rich they despise the poor; . . . their hearts are upon their treasures; wherefore, their treasure is their god" (2 Nephi 9:30). The "economy" is the culprit, "and they that are rich, . . . puffed up because of their learning, and their wisdom, and their riches—yea, they are they whom he [God] despiseth" (2 Nephi 9:42). This is the only time we ever read of God despising anything—not his creatures but their base, self-imposed condition. Next Jacob, the brother of Nephi, puts his finger on the spot: "You have obtained many riches; and because some of you have obtained more abundantly than that of your brethren, . . . ye suppose that ye are better than they. . . . God . . . condemneth you, and if ye persist in these things his judgments must speedily come unto you. . . . O that he would rid you from this iniquity and abomination" (Jacob 2:13-16). The danger does not lie in riches as such, which Jacob points out. Nothing would please him better than to have everybody rich: "Think of your brethren like unto yourselves, and be familiar with all and free with your substance, that they may be rich like unto you" (Jacob 2:17). But in the unequal distribution, which is an abomination to God, Jacob says, "Do ye not suppose that such things are abominable to him who created all flesh? And the one being is as precious in his sight as the other" (Jacob 2:21). King Benjamin recognizes the same perennial threat to freedom in the processes of acquisition: "I . . . have not sought gold nor silver nor any manner of riches of you; neither have I suffered . . . that ye should make slaves one of another, . . . and . . . I, myself have labored with mine own hands that I might serve you" (Mosiah 2:12-14). "For, behold, are we not all beggars? Do we not all depend upon the same Being . . . for all the riches which we have of every kind?" (Mosiah 4:19). When Alma organized his model church, the members "were all equal, and they did all labor, . . . and they did impart of their substance, every man according to that which he had" (Alma 1:26-27). As a result, because of "the steadiness of the church they began to be exceedingly rich, having abundance of all things" (Alma 1:29).

Q. That sounds good to me.

A. So mark well what happened soon. These same good people "because of their exceeding riches . . . which they had obtained by their industry [Note that—they worked for it!] . . . were . . . lifted up in the pride of their eyes" (Alma 4:6). "The people of the church began . . . to set their hearts upon riches, . . . that they began to be scornful, one towards another" (Alma 4:8). The result was great inequality among the people (Alma 4:15). "Will ye still persist," Alma said to the people, "in the wearing of costly apparel and in setting your hearts upon . . . your riches? Yea, will ye persist in supposing that ye are better one than another?" (Alma 5:53-54). This state of things inevitably led to social and economic collapse.

Q. How?

A. Through the operation of what we may call Samuel's Law. The Prophet Samuel the Lamanite sets forth the interesting rule that when "the Economy" becomes the main and engrossing concern of a society — or in the routine Book of Mormon phrase, when "they begin to set their hearts upon their riches" — the economy will self-destruct. This is how he puts it: "Ye do always remember your riches; . . . your hearts are not drawn out unto the Lord, but they do swell with great pride, . . . envyings, strifes, malice, persecutions and murders, and all manner of iniquities" (Helaman 13:22). Note well the sequence of folly: first we are well pleased with ourselves because of our wealth, then comes the game of status and prestige, leading to competitive maneuvers, hatred, and dirty tricks, and finally the ultimate solution. Where wealth guarantees respectability, principles melt away as the criminal element rises to the top: "For this cause hath the Lord God caused that a curse should come upon the land, and also upon your riches" (Helaman 13:23). "And behold, the time cometh that he curseth your riches, that they become slippery, that ye cannot hold them; and in the days of your poverty ye cannot retain them" (Helaman 13:31). "And then shall ye lament and say, . . . our riches . . . have become slippery that we should lose them; for behold, our riches are gone from us. Behold, we lay a tool here and on the morrow it is gone" (Helaman 13:32-34). "Yea, we have hid up our treasures and they have slipped away from us, because of the curse of the land, . . . for behold the land is cursed, and all things are become slippery and we cannot hold them. Behold, we are surrounded by demons" (Helaman 13:35-37). It ends in utter frustration and total insecurity as morals and the market collapse together and the baffled experts surrender. It happened also in Alma's day, when he attributed the "wars and contentions among the Nephites" (Alma 28:9) to the same human weakness: "And thus we see how great the inequality of man is because of sin and transgression" (Alma 28:13). This was at the very time that Korihor emerged with a fervid dialectic giving philosophical sanction to that inequality, as "every man fared in this life according to the management of the creature," and so on (Alma 30:17).

Q. How long does the problem persist in the Book of Mormon?

A. Right to the end. Many years after Alma, a righteous people were again "lifted up unto pride and boastings because of their exceedingly great riches" (3 Nephi 6:10). Careerism became the order of the day in a business-society of "many merchants . . . and also many lawyers, and many officers. And the people began to be distinguished by ranks, according to their riches and their chances for learning" (3 Nephi 6:11-12). "And thus there became a great inequality in all the land, insomuch that the church began to be broken up" (3 Nephi 6:14). Then came great natural calamities, after which the church was established again by the Lord himself, and the "people were all converted unto the Lord, . . . and they had all things common among them; therefore there were not rich and poor, bond and free, but they were all made free" (4 Nephi 1:2-3). And there we see what it means to be true freemen, but as long as Satan is permitted to try men and to tempt them by the gold and silver and treasures of the earth, we can expect a counterattack. In time the ideal society established by the Lord was broken up, as "there began to be among them those who were lifted up in pride, such as the wearing of costly apparel. . . . And from that time forth they did have their goods and their substance no more common among them" (4 Nephi 1:24-25).

Q. Shouldn't we change the subject and get back to Moroni?

A. Moroni is still the subject—he was the greatest champion of equality of them all. He had been elected to defend his people, "and thus he was preparing to support their liberty . . . and their peace. . . . Moroni . . . did not delight in bloodshed; [he was] a man whose soul did joy in the liberty and the freedom of his country" (Alma 48:10-11). For him peace and freedom were as inseparable from each other as both were from equality. So "Moroni commanded that his army should go against those king-men, to pull down their pride and their nobility and level them with the earth. . . . And . . . the armies did march forth against them; and they did pull down their pride and their nobility" (Alma 51:17-18). "And thus Moroni put an end to those king-men, that there were not any known by the appellation of king-men; and thus he put an end to the stubbornness and the pride of those people who professed the blood of nobility; but they were brought down to humble themselves like unto their brethren" (Alma 51:21).

Q. There seems to be a note of gloating there.

A. There is no doubt that the king-men had made a horrible nuisance of themselves. But the final settlement left them no worse off than anybody else—no hint of punishment or reprisal. Moroni is quite impartial; when he suspects his own superiors of arrogance in government he writes to them: "I will stir up insurrections among you, even until those who have desires to usurp power and authority shall become extinct. Yea, behold I do not fear your power nor your authority, but it is my God whom I fear" (Alma 60:27-28). "Behold, I am Moroni, your chief captain. I seek not for power, but to pull it down. I seek not for honor of the world but for the glory of my God" (Alma 60:36).

Q. Doesn't all that pulling down sound rather drastic?
A. Moroni explains: "Had it not been for . . . these king-men, who caused so much bloodshed among ourselves, . . . yea, had it not been for the desire of power and authority which those king-men had over us, . . . we should have dispersed our enemies" (Alma 60:16). He notes that ambitious Nephites are more guilty than Lamanite invaders, for "it is the tradition of [the Lamanites'] fathers that has caused their hatred; . . . while your iniquity is for the cause of your love of glory and the vain things of the world" (Alma 60:32).

Q. Moroni was a great warrior, a great general, and you say all that he wanted was peace?
A. His first move against Amalickiah was to gather all the people together and make a "covenant to keep the peace" (Alma 46:31), and the immediate result of the lightning campaign that followed was that the Nephites "began to have peace again in the land; and thus they did maintain peace" —for four years. "They did have much peace," thanks to Moroni (Alma 46:37-38). And as soon as the long war was over, what did he do? As the savior of his country and a national hero, he could have been elected to any position he chose, including that of king or dictator—he had achieved the very thing for which Amalickiah had plotted and struggled so long. But instead of going on to a brilliant career, Moroni, though still a young man (Alma 43:17), "yielded up the command of his armies, . . . and

he retired to his own house that he might spend the remainder of his days in peace" — all his words about peace
and equality had not been just talk (Alma 62:43).

Q. But he was a fierce fighter.

A. High-spirited and short-tempered he certainly was,
as his ill-advised letters to Pahoran (Alma 60:1-36) and
Ammoron (Alma 54:11-13) amply attest. But his magnan-
imous nature as a lover of peace and fair play always prevailed. He always calls the enemy his brothers, with whom
he is loathe to contend. You cannot ask for a less warlike
spirit than that of an army who "were compelled reluctantly to contend with their brethren, the Lamanites," who
waged war "for the space of many years, . . . notwithstanding their much reluctance"; who were "sorry to take
up arms against the Lamanites, because they did not delight in the shedding of blood; yea . . . they were sorry to
be the means of sending so many of their brethren out of
this world" (Alma 48:21-23). In battle Moroni always calls
an end to the fighting and proposes a settlement the moment the enemy shows signs of weakening (Alma 43:54;
44:1, 20); and though surprise and deception are the essence of strategy, he refused to take advantage of an enemy
who was too drunk to fight — that would be an "injustice"
(Alma 55:19). He even made special excuses for sending
spies behind enemy lines (Alma 43:27-30). With never a
thought of punishing a beaten foe, Moroni sought no re-
prisals even after the gravest provocations. He was satisfied to take his defeated adversaries at their word and trust
them to return to their homes or settle among the Nephites
as they chose (Alma 44:6, 11, 19-20), even granting them
Nephite lands for their rehabilitation (Alma 62:16-17). His
attitude is well expressed in an exchange of letters with
his friend Pahoran, who writes: "We would not shed the
blood of the Lamanites if they would stay in their own
land. We would not shed the blood of our [Nephite] breth-

ren if they would not rise up in rebellion and take the sword against us. We would subject ourselves to the yoke of bondage if it were requisite with the justice of God" — which, indeed, in the Book of Mormon story it sometimes was (Alma 61:10-13). "We do not desire to be men of blood," says Moroni on the battlefield; "ye are in our hands, yet we do not desire to slay you. . . . We have not come . . . that we might shed your blood for power" (Alma 44:1-2).

Moroni's wars were all defensive: "Now the Nephites were taught to defend themselves" but "never to raise the sword except it were against an enemy . . . to preserve their lives" (Alma 48:14). While Moroni prepared fortifications for defense "to support their liberty . . . and their peace, . . . he . . . did not delight in bloodshed; [for he was] a man whose soul did joy in the liberty and the freedom of his country" (Alma 48:8-10). Above all, this great general renounced the standard military solution to problems of defense.

Q. What is that?
A. The strategic approach. Strategy is by definition deception — its purpose is to fool the opposition. Moroni's "unrealistic" approach to the problem of power is vividly contrasted with the methods of Amalickiah: "While Amalickiah had thus been obtaining power by fraud and deceit, Moroni, on the other hand, had been preparing the minds of the people to be faithful unto the Lord their God" (Alma 48:7). For him, in the end, faithfulness was the only guarantee of true security. Mormon tells us that Moroni "was a man like unto Ammon . . . and also Alma" (Alma 48:18). Alma, it will be recalled, after ably functioning as commander of the armies, high priest of the church, and chief judge of the land, laid down all his high offices to go out and try to save things by "bearing down in pure testimony" among a stiffnecked people (Alma 4:19). They gave him a

bad time when he came before them without any official clout, but he knew that the gospel was the only solution. Ammon, the mightiest fighting man in the Book of Mormon, laid aside his invincible sword to go tracting from door to door among a bloody-minded enemy nation. His friends and fellow church members laughed at the deed: "Do [you] suppose that [you] can bring the Lamanites to the knowledge of the truth, . . . as stiffnecked a people as they are; whose hearts delight in the shedding of bloodshed; whose days have been spent in the grossest iniquity; whose ways have been the ways of a transgressor from the beginning?" (Alma 26:24). That is how they made fun of Ammon's insane proposal. There is only one way to deal with these people, they said — only one language they understand: "Let us take up arms against them, that we destroy them and their iniquity out of the land, lest *they* overrun us and destroy *us*" (Alma 26:25). Kill or be killed — the basic creed of the military to this day. "Now my brethren, ye remember that this was their language," says Ammon, recalling it (Alma 26:24). But what did Ammon do, the most terrible fighter of them all? With his companions, "patient in our sufferings, . . . we have traveled from house to house," teaching anyone who would listen, "and we have been cast out, and mocked, and spit upon, and smote upon our cheeks" (Alma 26:28-29).

Q. You say this man was the greatest of all Book of Mormon warriors?
A. In single combat no one could hold a candle to him.

Q. And he let people laugh at him, and slap his face, and spit on him?
A. He tells us why: "And we have suffered . . . all this, that perhaps we might be the means of saving some soul; and we supposed that our joy would be full if perhaps we could be the means of saving some" (Alma 26:30). He knew

that the harder way of winning over an enemy was the better way, and all his converts underwent a most marvelous change of heart: "Now there was not one soul among all the people who had been converted unto the Lord that would take up arms against their brethren; nay, they would not even make any preparations for war; yea, and also their king commanded them that they should not" (Alma 24:6). No less than eight times do they refer to their former deeds of arms as acts of murder for which they are deeply contrite (Alma 24:9-25). They were complete pacifists, and Moroni gave them his unqualified support along with Helaman, another great commander, who labored successfully to dissuade the Ammonites from taking up arms even to come to the aid of his own sorely pressed troops in a desperate military crisis (Alma 53:14). As a result of that, many Lamanites surrendered and were sent by Moroni and Helaman to "dwell with the people of Ammon" (Alma 62:17). These repentant Lamanites were "desirous to join the people of Ammon and become a free people" (Alma 62:27).

Q. Strange that those pacifists should be singled out as a free people.

A. Who is free to do as he will in a state of war? Once the shooting starts the options vanish. That is why people rush into war—because they think it will put an end to their problems.

Q. But hold on! What about all those men who were put to death for not joining Moroni's army?

A. They have been represented as conscientious objectors and pacifists, but they were the exact opposite. Note that Moroni specifies that he sheds the blood of his Nephite brethren only when they take the sword against him (Alma 61:11). He explains the situation: "Were it not for these king-men, who caused so much bloodshed among ourselves; . . . had they been true to the cause of our freedom, and united with us, and gone forth against our enemies, instead of *taking up their swords against us,* which was the cause of so much bloodshed among ourselves; . . . we should have dispersed our enemies" (Alma 60:16). These were no pacifists or foot-dragging Nephites, but a para-military combine out to use force to gain political ends. They were Amalickiahites, both stirring up war with the Lamanites and planning to shed the blood of the opposition at home: "And . . . whomsoever of the Amalickiahites that would not enter into a covenant to support the cause of freedom, . . . [Moroni] caused to be put to death, . . . and there were but few" (Alma 46:35). The Amalickiahites had welcomed the approaching Lamanites, glad in their hearts that the government was in trouble, and though Moroni reasoned with them and appealed to their sense of grati-tude and fair play, they would not budge from their hostile position: "When Moroni saw . . . that the Lamanites were coming into the borders of the land, he was exceedingly wroth because of the stubbornness of those people whom he had labored with so much diligence to preserve" (Alma 51:14). Even so, the Amalickiahites were not taken from their homes or cut down in the streets, but all met their fate on the battlefield in the very act of laying about them with their swords — they were fairly beaten in an open fight which they invited. "The armies did march forth against them; and they did pull down their pride and their nobility, insomuch that *as they did lift their weapons of war to fight against the men of Moroni,* they were hewn down and leveled to the earth" (Alma 51:18). The victims were not helpless prisoners but armed warriors on the field of battle.

Q. But were not those cut down who refused to take up arms in defense of their country?

A. Cut down, but only on the battlefield during the battle: "Those of their leaders who were not *slain in battle* were taken and cast into prison, for there was no time for their trials at this period" (Alma 51:19). Those not slain in battle had also refused to take up arms in defense of their country, yet they were not put to death even when taken with arms in their hands, but were remanded for trial.

Q. How did the trial go?
A. They were all released when they surrendered rather than be smitten down by the sword. They were not even executed for treason, but were only required henceforth to "fight valiantly for their freedom from bondage" (Alma 51:21), which I think they willingly did in the face of what followed.

Q. What was that?
A. The sight of Amalickiah, the king-men's idea of a Nephite patriot, leading a Lamanite army against the Nephites. When they saw him in his true colors after having won them over "by fraud and deceit" they were willing enough to switch to the faithful Moroni. Four years later, under a new leader of the king-men, the problem of disaffected Nephites came up again, with this solution: "Those men of Pachus [the new leader] and those king-men whosoever would not take up arms in defense of their country, *but would fight against it,* were put to death," this time after being captured and tried (Alma 62:9). They had actually joined the Lamanites in the attack, which indeed they had arranged; yet even so they were given a chance to change their minds, and only those were put to death who stubbornly insisted on "denying their freedom" (Alma 62:10). They are all warriors – anything but pacifists or conscientious objectors. There are indeed some very conspicuous pacifists and war-objectors in the Book of Mormon besides Ammon and his people, and interestingly enough they include some of the most valiant warriors and

seasoned fighters, but we cannot go into their stories here. We are concerned only with king-men and freemen.

Q. Did the Pachus episode put an end to the king-men?
A. Far from it. Though we never hear of the freemen by that name again, the king-men persevere right to the end. They were able to become so numerous in Zarahemla during the war that the governor Pahoran had to flee for his life (Alma 61:3-5); but the people flocked to him in exile as they had flocked to Moroni's banner, and the two leaders were able to join forces and bring the war to a successful conclusion (Alma 62:7-8). Then Moroni went into permanent retirement—free of ambition to the end (Alma 62:43-44). But the king-men were not finished.

Q. What next?
A. They went underground—standard procedure when they are beaten—and made themselves indistinguishable from the general public as they bided their time and carried the secret plans and programs that such people love (Helaman 1:12). Their leader, Kishkumen, sought out the services of a professional hit man by the name of Gadianton, a talented killer, "exceedingly expert . . . in his craft" (Helaman 2:3-4), who could be trusted to carry out the secret work of murder and robbing in a business-like and professional manner. He worked out a plan which he guaranteed would put Kishkumen and his gang in complete control of the government. All they had to do was murder the chief judge Helaman, as they had already murdered his predecessor Pahoran II, and make Gadianton himself judge—he would take care of the rest (Helaman 2:4-5). The plan miscarried and the villains had to skip town, and yet before many years "this Gadianton did prove the overthrow, yea, almost the entire destruction of the people of Nephi" (Helaman 2:13).

Q. How was that possible?

A. By broadening his operation. The cloak-and-dagger stuff was all very well, but big money has to be respectable money from a visible source. Gadianton's new plan was to bring the public into his operation in a big way, allowing anyone to buy in, so that they "seduced the more part of the righteous," who, seeing how the business prospered, "had come down to believe in their works and partake of their spoils" (Helaman 6:38). Public opinion was so much on their side that "the Nephites did build them up and support them, beginning at the more wicked part of them." Gadianton's band grew ever more respectable "until they had overspread all the land" (Helaman 6:38).

Q. But how could the Nephites be so crude or so naive as to invest in a corporation whose business was robbery?

A. That was the clever part of the plan. As the Nephites "did turn unto their own ways, and did build up unto themselves idols of their gold and their silver" (Helaman 6:31), it was easy for the society to swing elections in its favor and to put its people in complete control of the law-courts: from then on they could make whatever they chose to do perfectly legal. Speaking of the days of Moroni, Mormon observes that it was the lawyers and judges who started laying the foundation of the "destruction of this people" (Alma 10:27). So with the public in a state of awful wickedness and the combine in control of the nation's wealth, in the "space of not many years" (Helaman 6:32) there was little opposition when those Gadianton robbers filling the judgment seats established their kind of justice. They did whatever they pleased under color of legality, "condemning the righteous because of their righteousness; letting the guilty and the wicked go unpunished because of their money. . . . [They were] held in office at the head of government, to rule and do according to their wills" — after all, they *were* the government — "that they might get gain and glory of the world" (Helaman 7:5). This was no undercover operation, but government heavy with the symbols of power and majesty. Ironically, at this very time the Gadianton robbers were hunted down and "utterly destroyed from among the Lamanites" (Helaman 6:37).

Q. Good police work?

A. Of the right kind. They borrowed a page from Ammon and sent out missionaries everywhere to "preach the word of God among the more wicked part of them," and that did it—they gave up the whole evil business (Helaman 6:37).

Q. That sounds unrealistic.

A. As indeed it is, to those who do not know the power of the gospel. But Alma had used the same method to pull down "the pride and craftiness . . . which were among his people" years before (Alma 4:19). That is, instead of marching forth with an army or a posse, though he was at that time the commander-in-chief (Alma 4:16), Alma armed himself with no other weapon than the word of God, "seeing no way that he might reclaim them save it were in bearing down in pure testimony against them" (Alma 4:19). But it worked—we make a tragic mistake in underestimating the power of the gospel to change men's lives if only it is brought to them. Also we are prone to look to force for solutions, though the final word and summing-up of the last great commander in the Book of Mormon is: "Therefore, he that smiteth shall be smitten again, of the Lord. Behold what the scripture says—man shall not smite, neither shall he judge" (Mormon 8:19-20). The Lamanites got rid of the Gadiantons, but not the Nephites.

Q. Who was left for them to loot if everybody belonged?

A. There were levels of control and profit-taking, as in a modern franchise set-up; at the heart of everything was the original band of charter members, a sort of central committee, whose meetings and manipulations were top-secret (Helaman 6:22-24). But there is no love lost among criminals, "the devil will not support his children at the last day," says Mormon, "but doth speedily drag them down to hell" (Alma 30:60). Inevitably interests and ambitions conflict, and so with criminal interests fighting each other "there were wars throughout all the land among the people of Nephi. And it was this secret band of robbers who did carry on this work of destruction and wickedness" (Helaman 11:1-2).

Q. Why weren't the Nephites destroyed at that time?

A. The intervention of the prophet Nephi saved them when he deliberately asked God to wipe out the economy completely. Nephi prayed for a super-depression: "O Lord, do not suffer that this people shall be destroyed by the sword; but O Lord, rather let there be a famine . . . to stir them up in remembrance" (Helaman 11:4). The famine was horrendous and put a stop to everything, so finally the people were willing to give up their stocks and bonds and settle for just their lives. When "the people saw that they were about to perish by famine" (Helaman 11:7), they appealed to Nephi, who prayed: "O Lord, wilt thou turn away thine anger, and try again if they will serve thee?" (Helaman 11:16). So they were given another chance and the robbers went, literally, underground: "The band of Gadianton . . . have become extinct, and they [the repentant people] have concealed their secret plans in the earth" (Helaman 11:10). That concealing in the earth is a very important part of the story. The mischief is not finished off—it only sleeps. Since it is Satan's prerogative to try men and to tempt them with the treasures of the earth, the means of doing so will always be within his reach. Accordingly, only four years after the great famine we find a "certain number of dissenters from the people of Nephi" who had permanently joined the Lamanites some years before, bent on stirring up another war (Helaman 11:24). Their motive was robbery.

Q. Hadn't they learned their lesson?
A. They thought they had, for this time they were resorting to a wholly new strategy—terrorism: "They did commit murder and plunder; and then they would retreat back into the mountains, and into . . . secret places, hiding themselves that they could not be discovered, receiving daily an addition to their numbers" (Helaman 11:25). Their appeal was mostly to the young, who found it exciting (3 Nephi 1:29-30). Their unrelenting campaign of terrorism "did make great havoc . . . among the people of Nephi" (Helaman 11:27). Armies were sent against them, but to no avail—it was not that kind of war; the terrorists were winning (Helaman 11:28-33). But this had one good re-sult—it kept the rest of the people from slipping back into their old ways: "Now this great evil, which came unto the people because of their iniquity, did stir them up again in remembrance of the Lord their God" (Helaman 11:34). But here we have another demonstration of the folly of labelling good guys and bad guys, for only three years later "they [the Nephites] began to wax strong in iniquity" (Helaman 11:36), and this time "they did not mend their ways" (Helaman 11:36). So for another two years "they did wax stronger and stronger in their pride, and in their wicked-ness; and thus they were ripening again for destruction" (Helaman 11:37). Nephi the prophet did his best, but got little support. As usual, it was the king-men who ended up in the saddle, led by a man called Jacob. Under this renewed pressure the central government finally collapsed and the people followed their local tribal leaders and tra-ditions, "and thus they did destroy the government of the land" (3 Nephi 7:2). The "secret combination" had engi-neered the whole thing (3 Nephi 7:9) by stirring up con-

tention everywhere (3 Nephi 7:7), and taking advantage
of a climate in which the people "did yield themselves
unto the power of Satan" (3 Nephi 7:5), since even "the
more righteous part of the people had nearly all become
wicked" (3 Nephi 7:7). The secret organization put their
man Jacob on the throne (3 Nephi 7:9), but then the rest
of the populace, "notwithstanding they were not a righteous people, yet they were united in the hatred of those
who had entered into a covenant to destroy the government" (3 Nephi 7:11). Having finally gotten rid of their
favorite target, the central government, the people immediately regretted its loss and turned with fury on those
whom they held responsible for terminating it.

Q. By now the story is getting a bit monotonous.
A. Yes, and it is the same monotonous scenario that
tells us of decline and fall in other times and places, including the days that lie ahead of us—for the story has
been preserved and published for our benefit.

Q. But don't the recurrent transitions from Good
People to Bad People and back again take place awfully
fast?
A. The Book of Mormon writers themselves often marvel at the speed with which the picture changes. In the
instance last cited, the writer notes, "And thus six years
had not passed away since the more part of the people
had turned from their righteousness" (3 Nephi 7:8). And
yet if we examine our own experience and history, people
do post with such dexterity from one extreme to the other—
where wealth is concerned, that is; and in the Book of
Mormon, money is the key to the situation. "Now the
cause of this iniquity . . . was this," Mormon observes;
"Satan had great power, unto the stirring up of the people
to do all manner of iniquity, and to the puffing them up
with pride, tempting them to seek for power, and au-

thority, and riches, and the vain things of the world" (3 Nephi 6:15). Need we remind you that "power, authority, and riches" are what the king-men are always after, and what Moroni and his freemen were determined to "pull down"? Mormon's remark was by way of explaining why the nation had declined so quickly, why they "had enjoyed peace but a few years" (3 Nephi 6:16). Money gets quick results, and the effects of newly acquired riches are almost instantaneous. At once the happy recipient of a big promotion is expected to change his lifestyle, move to a better part of town, join different clubs, send his children to different schools, even change his church affiliation for a more fashionable one, or drop an intended bride for one more acceptable to the president's wife and her exalted circle. The instant pride of the foolish milkmaid in the prospects of a new affluence was the same ambition that made a monster of the noble and generous Macbeth overnight. History, literature, and folklore are full of the Fatal Gold—the deadly Rings, the Dragon's Treasure, the Golden Fleece, etc.—that brings quick and inevitable destruction on those that seek and find it. No, my friends, the Book of Mormon does not exaggerate either the relentless efficiency or the speed with which wealth corrupts all those who "set their hearts upon riches and the things of the world."

Q. But just how far can we go in applying the story to ourselves?

A. Why do you think the book was given to us? Angels do not come on trivial errands, to deliver books for occasional light reading to people whom they do not really concern. The matter in the Book of Mormon was selected, as we are often reminded, with scrupulous care and with particular readers in mind. For some reason there has been chosen for our attention a story of how and why two previous civilizations on this continent were utterly destroyed.

Lest the modern reader of this sad and disturbing tale from the dust choose to pass lightly over those fearful passages that come too close to home, the main theme is repeated again and again, so that almost any Latter-day Saint child can tell you what it is: The people were good so God made them prosperous, and when they were bad, they got wiped out. What few people can tell you are the steps by which the fatal declension took place, without which the story is juvenile and naive.

Q. Can you sum up the steps? I take it they are more or less what you have been talking about.

A. In their prosperity the people "begin to set their hearts on riches," an oft-repeated formula which rings like the stroke of doom. It reminds one of the four steps in Greek tragedy, each leading inexorably to the next—*olbia*, *koros*, *hybris*, and *ate*—there, too, power and gain is the theme. With wealth the measure of all things, a class-conscious and covetous society ends up under the domination of powerful combinations, leading to internal rivalries and international intrigue that inevitably lead to armed conflict. A war of extermination results from the willful polarization between equally guilty nations, each justifiably feeling threatened by the other, and each determined to see the sole source of its troubles in the wickedness of the other. The wars solve nothing, even for the winners.

Q. I can see endless debate growing out of those propositions.

A. Fortunately we are not obliged to speculate on the purpose of the Book of Mormon in telling us all this, for its authors and editors have addressed themselves specifically to our generation on the point. Hear the moving appeal of Mormon: "And then, O ye Gentiles, how can ye stand before the power of God, except ye shall repent and turn from your evil ways?" (Mormon 5:22). "[God] hath made manifest unto you *our* imperfections, that *ye* may learn to be more wise than *we* have been" (Mormon 9:31). "There shall be great pollutions upon the face of the earth [the expression definitely implies ecology]; there shall be murders, and robbing, and lying, and deceivings, and whoredoms. . . . Many . . . will say, Do this, or do that, and it mattereth not, . . . but wo unto such[!]" (Mormon 8:31). "Behold, I speak unto you as if ye were present, and yet ye are not. . . . But . . . Jesus Christ hath shown you unto me, and I know your doing. And I know that ye do walk in the pride of your hearts . . . unto the wearing of very fine apparel, unto envying, and strifes, and malice, and persecutions. . . . For behold, ye do love money, and your substance, and your fine apparel, and the adorning of your churches, more than ye love the poor and the needy, the sick and the afflicted. O ye pollutions, ye hyp- ocrites, ye teachers, who sell yourselves for that which will canker, why have ye polluted the holy church of God? . . . Why do ye adorn yourselves with that which hath no life, and yet suffer the hungry, and the needy, and the naked, and the sick and the afflicted to pass by you, and notice them not? Yea, why do ye build up your secret abominations to get gain, and cause that widows should mourn before the Lord, and also orphans, . . . and also the blood of their fathers and their husbands to cry unto the Lord from the ground, for vengeance upon your heads? Behold, the sword of vengeance hangeth over you; and the time soon cometh" (Mormon 8:35-41). I used to think that those words about blood crying from the ground were possibly a bit overdrawn—but not after seeing what is going on throughout the world today!

Q. How do you know that these things apply to our particular generation?

A. Mormon's son, Moroni, tells us that the teachings

of the book will apply to that generation that recognizes the symptoms: the shoe will belong to the one it fits. Up until now the Book of Mormon has been for the Mormons themselves a romantic tale of the far-away and long-ago, as strange as the Arabian Nights—such things just do not happen in the real world! But now: "O ye Gentiles, it is wisdom in God that these things should be shown unto you, that thereby ye may repent of your sins, and suffer not that these murderous combinations shall get above you, which are built up to get power and gain—and the work, yea, even the work of destruction come upon you, yea, even the sword of the justice of the Eternal God shall fall upon you, to your overthrow and destruction if ye shall suffer these things to be. Wherefore, the Lord commandeth you, when ye shall see these things come among you that ye shall awake to a sense of your awful situation, because of this secret combination which shall be among you; or wo be unto it, because of the blood of them who have been slain" (Ether 8:23-24).

Q. But what can anyone do about combinations as secret and as powerful as those mentioned? Who can oppose them?

A. First of all, we are told, we can cease to build them up, for "whoso buildeth it up seeketh to overthrow the freedom of all lands, . . . and it bringeth to pass the destruction of all people" (Ether 8:25).

Q. How can you build up a combination if you don't know where it is or even what it is?

A. You can do that by playing the game its way. Once you have been warned, as we have been here, that things are being run by such elements, then you know very well that if you aspire to power and gain, influence, status, and prestige; in other words, if you aspire to success by present-day standards, you can only achieve it by doing everything their way. One ceases to uphold those elements only by rejecting a whole way of life, regardless of the risk or inconvenience involved.

Q. So you don't uphold them; but they are still there. How can you get at them?

A. As Alma and Ammon did in their day. They went forth "bearing down in pure testimony" to whoever would hear them, suffering the worst the opposition had to offer, "not with the intent to destroy our brethren [who were very wicked and depraved, you will recall], but with the intent that *perhaps* we *might* save *some few* of their souls" (Alma 26:26). Admittedly it was a risky and dangerous business, but it was all they could do. We are not called upon to seize and occupy enemy territory, for the evil we are combatting is everywhere (D&C 1), and the only place we can confront it and overcome it is in our own hearts. I cannot make a bad person good by pulling a trigger, yet conversion of sinners to saints is exactly what the Lord requires: to persuade the children of men to do good continually, so that Satan may have no more power over their hearts (Ether 8:26). If men are to overcome Satan in this world, they must be alive to do it—shooting them solves nothing.

Q. But we must overcome the hosts of evil.

A. Where are they? "This is my doctrine, . . . that the Father commandeth all men, everywhere, to repent" (3 Nephi 11:32). Will you ask God which people you are to love and which you are to hate? Which to deal fairly with and which to cheat? Which to speak the truth to and which to lie to? Which to be kind to and which to be cruel to? The word of God answers all such questions with the greatest clarity; we have only one game-plan, and that is the call to faith, repentance, and charity with which Moroni sums up the Book of Mormon.

Q. You mean we should treat freemen and king-men alike?

A. Of course. In our society, who is going to call himself a king-man or not call himself a freeman? To lay official claim to the title is as fatuous as forming a club called "The Great Men" in the expectation of being accepted as such. It is the title in its Book of Mormon context that has concerned us here, and though the definition has taken us on a longer journey than we expected, we have not been wandering, for the ways of the king-men must also be understood if we are to understand the freemen.

Q. How, then, would you define the freemen in the Book of Mormon?

A. The freemen are the Nephites who supported Moroni in his opposition to a dangerous coalition led by Amalickiah. The king-men's combination consisted of rich Nephites who were outraged by what they considered interference by "Helaman and his brethren" in their private affairs. Other king-men included monarchists, influential and intriguing families, a self-styled aristocracy, social climbers "lifted up in their hearts" by their new wealth (Alma 45:24), haughty and aspiring judges, power-hungry local officials—including "almost all the lawyers and the high priests"—men taking advantage of church positions (3 Nephi 6:27), and many ordinary church members beguiled by the powerful and impressive rhetoric of Amalickiah. Only one comprehensive label fits that combination.

Q. And you would call the freemen Left Wing?

A. Not at all. For them there were no wings—equality was their watchword, and their torn, trampled garments and tattered "title of liberty" announced to all that they considered themselves nothing more than God's typically weak and fallible children, whom he loves all alike.

Q. Would you say that the freemen as such had no distinctive characteristics?

A. On the contrary, from our point of view they would be a great oddity. For the Book of Mormon they are just ordinary people, but their character stands out in bold relief as they are pointedly contrasted to the king-men. To wit, they were not militant; it took a great deal to stir them to action, and they made war with heavy reluctance and without rancor, always keeping the fighting to a minimum. They were peace-loving, noncompetitive, and friendly, appealing to the power of the word above that of the sword. "Taught never to give offense," and never aggressive, they were terrible indeed when the king-men pushed them too far, but quick to spare and forgive. They were not class-conscious, but prized equality among the greatest of blessings. In their personal lives they placed no great value on the accumulation of wealth and abhorred displays of status and prestige, e.g., the wearing of fashionable and expensive clothes. Eschewing ambition, they were not desirous or envious of power and authority; they recognized that they were "despised" by the more success-oriented king-men, and thought of themselves as outcasts from the ways of the world. They shunned the climate of secrecy and conspiracy in which the king-men delighted, and avoided aristocratic pretenses and aspirations as well. They sought the solution to all their problems in fervid prayer and repentance.

Q. It sounds rather boring to me—too idealistic and unrealistic.

A. Yes, that is the way it seems to us. We have disqualified ourselves for that kind of life; nothing short of a fix moves our jaded and over-stimulated appetites anymore. But may I point out to you that there are still a few societies left on earth, or there were until recently, in which the freemen's way of life survived. I am thinking of certain societies of American Indians and Pacific Islanders.

Q. Come now! They are nature-people, savages.

A. By us they are "despised," to use Moroni's expression. But what stable societies from the New England village to the ancient dwellers on the Nile have not been "nature people," gladly accepting the world that God has given them? It is only in our own day that the bulldozers, freeways, high-rises, parking prairies, shopping palaces and industrial "parks" have claimed the land in the name of great combinations dedicated to power and gain. And in that denatured and dehumanized setting, modern man finds satisfaction in watching, reading, and living out those stories of contention, violence, intrigue, duels for power, grand theft, murder, high fashion and high sex which have become the daily fare of the millions as they once were for the king-men of old. And ever and always, *money* is the name of the game.

But there is a ray of hope in the circumstance that the freemen and king-men belong to the same race and culture; it is quite possible for people to move from one category to the other, as they often do in the Book of Mormon, where "one very wicked man" can get a huge following in short order, and just as quickly lose it. We are all both king-men and freemen at heart, just as we are all potential devils or gods.

Comparative Notes on Ancient Mesoamerica

At the center of ancient American studies today lies the sovereign question: Why did everything collapse so suddenly, so completely, and so mysteriously? To this question "no solution acceptable to the majority of students has yet appeared."[4] J. Eric Thompson's theory is that people "in an increasingly complex society had largely lost the ability to act for themselves." But the valuable collection of studies edited by T. P. Culbert reaches an overall consensus that is worth setting forth in the words of the various contributors. It may help to put the Book of Mormon statement in a roughly parallel column.

Culbert, p. 91: "Oversuccessful, overstrained, and probably overbearing, Tikal would have been at the mercy of . . . ecological, social or political catastrophes."

Jacob 2:13-14: "You have obtained many riches, . . . ye are lifted up in the pride of your hearts. . . . God . . . condemneth you, and if ye persist, . . . his judgments must speedily come unto you."

E. W. Andrews, p. 263: "As civilization becomes more complex, it becomes more vulnerable—as we are discovering to our increasing horror in recent years. . . . The problems of maintenance and unity increase geometrically."

3 Nephi 6:11-14: "Many merchants . . . and also many lawyers, and many officers . . . and . . . people began to be distinguished by ranks. . . . And thus there became a great inequality, . . . insomuch that the church began to be broken up."

W. T. Sanders, p. 359: There was "rise of population density, decline of per capita income, increasing local specialization in crops, heavier reliance . . . on the periphery for basic materials and more highly organized trade . . . closely correlated with militarism [and] . . . a shift from egalitarian to ranked to stratified society."

Sanders, p. 363: Recent studies favor "political and

Mormon 1:7-8, 12: "The whole face of the land had become covered with buildings, and the people were as numerous almost, as it were the sand of the sea. . . . And . . . there began to be a war between the Nephites . . . and the Lamanites and the Lemuelites and the Ishmaelites, . . . [until] the Lamanites withdrew their design [of conquest]."

Alma 28:10-13: "The de-

economic" causes. "Military incursions" disrupted the "trade network." Farmland gobbled up the forests.

Sanders, p. 364: There was "an increasing distance between peasant and noble, an economic deterioration in the average peasant's lifestyle, and an increase of nutritionally-based diseases." "The only reasonable explanation [for sudden and catastrophic population decline] . . . is migration, stimulated by peasant dissatisfaction and permitted by the breakdown of the political system."

M. C. Webb, pp. 402-3: "Rivalry over trade was a major cause of war. . . . Probably in many cases allegiance was simply transferred to the intruders." "The proximate cause [of the great collapse] was the resultant spread of the Postclassic pattern of secular trade and commercial war into the Maya area."

struction of many thousand lives, . . . an awful scene of bloodshed. . . . And thus we see how great the *inequality* of man is because of sin and transgression."

Alma 5:54: "Will ye persist in supposing that ye are better one than another . . . in the persecution of your brethren, who humble themselves?"

Alma 46:18, 24: "We, who are despised . . . shall [not] be trodden down. . . . Let us preserve our liberty."

Alma 60:27-28: "I will stir up insurrections. . . . I do not fear your power nor your authority."

Helaman 6:8, 9, 17: "Whether it were among the Lamanites or . . . the Nephites, . . . they did have free intercourse one with another, to buy and to sell, and to get gain, according to their desire. . . . And . . . they became exceedingly rich. . . . [Within a few years in order] to get gain, . . . they began to commit secret murders, and to rob and to plunder [leading to a series of wars]" (see Helaman 6:20).

General summary (G. R. Willey and D. B. Shimkin), p. 459: "Late Classic society was more sharply differentiated into elite and commoner strata than . . . Early Classic times. As this process of an elite consolidation went on, [there was] . . . a related development of a class of bureaucrats and craft specialists."

General summary, p. 461: In the seventh and eighth centuries, "Maya civilization . . . was integrated at the elite level in a more impressive fashion than ever before," as "signs of regionalism" appear.

General summary, p. 470: "Intensified . . . fighting, crop loss and destruction, malnutrition, and disease . . . reduced population greatly." (e.g., 90% at Tikal— Culbert).

General summary, p. 484: "The most vital . . . aspects" [of the collapse are] 1) the role of the elite class, 2) the widening social gulf between the elite and the commoner, 3) the competition between centers, 4) the agricultural problems, 5) the demographic pressures and disease bur-

3 Nephi 6:12: "And the people began to be distinguished by ranks, according to their riches and their chances for learning; yea, some were ignorant because of their poverty, and others did receive great learning because of their riches."

Helaman 13:22, 31: "Ye do always remember your riches . . . unto great swelling, envyings, strifes, malice, persecutions and murders. . . . The time cometh that he curseth your riches, that they become slippery, that ye cannot hold them."

Helaman 11:1: "Contentions did increase, insomuch that there were wars throughout all the land among all the people of Nephi."

Alma 45:21, 24: "[There were] many little dissensions and disturbances . . . among the people. . . . They grew proud . . . because of their exceedingly great riches."

Alma 32:4-5: "Upon the [Zoramite] hill Onidah, . . . they are despised . . . because of their

dens, and 6) the changing effects on . . . external trade." "The expansion of the hereditary elite population was clearly a major force in the geographical expansion of the Late Classic Maya Civilization."

General summary, p. 485: "The role of the elite must have become increasingly exploitative as resource margins declined; . . . widening social distance [was] an inevitable accompaniment of the evolution of ranked, and probably kin-based, society to a class structured one. . . . In some areas . . . the numbers of commoners were being maintained only by recruitment and capture from other centers. Yet the upper class continued to grow, to expand its demands for luxury . . . and to strive to compete with rival centers and aristocracies." "The priestly leaders of these great centers, in their efforts to outdo each other, to draw more wealth and prestige to themselves, . . . must have diverted all possible labor and capital to their aggrandizement."

General summary, p. 486: "Add to this the competition for trade, . . . and we can see

poverty, yea, and more especially by our priests; for they have cast us out of our synagogues which we have labored abundantly to build with our own hands; and they have cast us out because of our exceeding poverty; and we have no place to worship. . . . What shall we do?"

3 Nephi 6:27-28: "Those judges had many friends and kindreds; and . . . almost all the lawyers and the high priests, did gather . . . together, and unite with the kindreds of those judges. . . . And they did enter into a covenant one with another."

3 Nephi 30:2: "Turn . . . from . . . your idolatries, and . . . your murders, and your priestcrafts, and your envyings, and your strifes."

Helaman 6:31: "The Nephites . . . turned out of the way of righteousness . . . and did build up unto themselves idols of their gold and their silver."

3 Nephi 6:15: "Satan had great power, unto . . . stirring up . . . the people, . . . tempting them to seek for power, and authority, and riches, and the vain things of

the situation brought to a fighting pitch." All leading to a "rapid down-spiraling to extinction."

General summary, p. 488: "1) Population growth increased the demand on resources; 2) the growth of manpower [allowed] . . . economic expansion; 3) the differential growth and longevity . . . [divided] social classes [the poor were short-lived] . . . ; 4) efforts to compensate for manpower shortage . . . were increasingly important causes of warfare." The economy forced everything in the direction of war.

General summary, p. 490: "The Maya elite . . . shared like training, . . . prestige, beliefs, and interregional co-operation which acted to control warfare and promote . . . geographical expansion," while it "increasingly separated them from common-ers."

General summary, p. 491: The elite "made no technological or social adaptive innovations which might have mitigated these difficulties. In fact, the Maya managerial elite persisted in traditional directions up to the point of

the world."

3 Nephi 6:17: "And thus . . . they were in a state of awful wickedness."

Alma 26:25: "Let us take up arms against them, that we destroy them . . . out of the land, lest they overrun and destroy us."

Helaman 11:1-2: "There were wars throughout all the land among all the people of Nephi. And it was this secret band of robbers who did carry on this work of destruction."

3 Nephi 2:17-19: "[It was economic warfare] between the robbers and the people of Nephi. . . . The Gadianton robbers did gain many advantages over them . . . insomuch that they were about to be smitten down, . . . and this because of their iniquity."

Helaman 6:38: "The Nephites [instead of reform] did build them up and support them [the robber societies], . . . until they had come down to believe in their works and partake of their spoils."

collapse." With religion and law on their side, the elite needed to make no concessions.

Sejourne, p. 183: "The spiritual anemia was followed by a state of permanent struggles for power; . . . the whole country [Central Mexico] broke up into little communities, each claiming its own history and origin." The battle scenes show the fulfillment of the message of the American Prophet: "Mesoamerica fell little by little into a ruinous materialism. . . . It is as if the message of Quetzalcoatl, the American Prophet, had been consumed by the organic inertia which it was his mission to denounce."

Alma 10:27: "The foundation of the destruction of this people is beginning to be laid by . . . your lawyers and your judges."

3 Nephi 7:2-3: "The people . . . did separate one from another into tribes, every man according to his family and his kindred and his friends; and thus they did destroy the government of the land. And every tribe did appoint a chief."

3 Nephi 7:6-7: "And the regulations of the government were destroyed [by the king-men]. . . . The more righteous part of the people had nearly all become wicked."

3 Nephi 7:11: "The tribes of the people . . . were united [only] in the hatred of those who had entered into a covenant to destroy the government."

Notes

1. P. Tompkins, *Mysteries of the Mexican Pyramids* (New York: Harper and Row, 1976), xv.

2. J. A. Graham, G. R. Willey, and D. B. Shimkin, "The Maya Collapse: A Summary in View," in *The Classic Maya Collapse*, T. P. Culbert, ed. (Albuquerque: University of New Mexico, 1973), 477.

3. Ralph L. Roys, *The Book of Balam of Chumayel* (Washington: Carnegie Institute of Washington, 1933), 182.

4. E. W. Andrews, "The Development of Maya Civilization after Abandonment of the Southern Cities," in Culbert, ed., *The Classic*

Maya Collapse, 258. [Also, in the last part of an unpublished typescript entitled "The Book of Mormon and the Ruins—The Main Issues" (July 13, 1980), 10 pages, Nibley similarly organizes quotations from leading Mesoamerican archaeologists regarding their helplessness before the mystery of the collapse of Mesoamerican civilizations, the futility of arguments about Indian origins, the fact that people other than Nephites were present in Mesoamerica (as implied by Helaman 3:4-12), the racial complexity of Mesoamerican peoples, the limited types of migrations described in the Book of Mormon, the great mobility and uniformity amidst the complexity of these cultures, the feasibility of the great migrations of Book of Mormon peoples, and the existence of a dark, iniquitous side of all these civilizations—ed.]

18

The Lachish Letters

About twenty-five miles southwest of Jerusalem in Lehi's day lay the powerfully fortified city of Lachish, the strongest place in Judah outside of Jerusalem itself. Founded more than three thousand years before Christ, it was under Egyptian rule in the fourteenth century B.C. when the Khabiri (Hebrews) had just arrived. At that time, its king was charged with conspiring with the newcomers against his Egyptian master. A later king of Lachish fought against Joshua when the Israelites took the city about 1220 B.C. In a third phase, either David or Solomon fortified it strongly.

The city's strategic importance down through the years is reflected in the Babylonian, Assyrian, Egyptian, and biblical records. These describe a succession of intrigues, betrayals, sieges, and disasters that make the city's story a woefully typical Palestinian "idyll." Its fall in the days of Jeremiah is dramatically recounted in a number of letters found there in 1935 and 1938. These original letters, actually written at Jeremiah's time, turned up in the ruins of a guardhouse that stood at the main gate of the city—

This chapter combines two substantially similar publications, "The Lachish Letters: Documents from Lehi's Day," Ensign 10 (December 1981): 48-54, and "Dark Days in Jerusalem: The Lachish Letters and the Book of Mormon (1 Nephi)," in Book of Mormon Authorship, Noel B. Reynolds, ed. (Provo: Religious Studies Center, 1982), 103-21. Transcripts of two talks by Dr. Nibley covering the same topics have also circulated under the titles "The Jerusalem Scene" and "Souvenirs from Lehi's Jerusalem."

two letters a foot beneath the street paving in front of the guardhouse, and the other sixteen piled together below a stone bench set against the east wall. The wall had collapsed when a great bonfire was set against it from the outside.

The bonfire was probably set by the soldiers of Nebuchadnezzar because they wanted to bring down the wall, which enclosed the gate to the city. Nebuchadnezzar had to take the city because it was the strongest fortress in Israel and lay astride the road to Egypt, controlling all of western Judah. Jeremiah tells us that it and another fortified place, Azekah, were the last to fall to the invaders (see Jeremiah 34:7). An ominous passage from Lachish Letter 4:12-13 reports that the writer could no longer see the signalfires of Azekah—that means that Lachish itself was the last to go, beginning with the guardhouse in flames.

The letters survived the heat because they were written on potsherds.

They were written on potsherds because the usual papyrus was unobtainable.

It was unobtainable because the supply from Egypt was cut off.

The supply was cut off because of the war.

The letters were in the guardhouse because they were being kept as evidence in the pending trial of a military commander whose name was Hoshaᶜyahu.

He was being court-martialled because he was suspected of treason.

He was suspected of treason because someone had been reading top-secret dispatches sent from the court at Jerusalem to the commander at Lachish, whose name was Ya'ush.

Hoshaᶜyahu was a likely suspect because all the mail had to pass through his hands.

It had to pass through his hands because he was in

command of a fortified town on the road between Jerusalem and Lachish, probably Qiryat Ye'arim. His duty,
among other things, was to forward the king's mail—not
to read it.

That the confidential letters had been read was apparent because somebody had tipped off a certain prophet
that he was in danger.

He was in danger because the king's soldiers had been
put on his trail.

They were on his trail because he was fleeing to Egypt.

He was fleeing because he was wanted by the police
in Jerusalem.

He was wanted by the police because he and other
prophets were considered by the king's supporters to be
subversives.

They were considered subversives because they were
opposing the official policy and undermining morale by
their preaching. As Jeremiah puts it: "The princes [the
important people] said unto the king: We beseech thee,
let this man be put to death: for thus he weakeneth the
hands of the men of war that remain in this city, and the
hands of all the people, in speaking such words unto them"
(Jeremiah 38:4). As Lachish Letter 6:5-6 puts it: "The words
of the [prophet] are not good [and are liable] to loosen the
hands." The Book of Mormon adds another reinforcement:
"In that same year there came many prophets, prophesying unto the people they they must repent, or the great
city Jerusalem must be destroyed" (1 Nephi 1:4)—distress-
ing news indeed. The prophet who was tipped off to escape
"was surely Uriah of Qiryat Ye'arim."[1]

The Lachish Letters are the best evidence so far discovered for the authenticity of Bible history. In Lachish
Letter 3:13-21, for example, Hoshacyahu says that it was
reported to him that "the commander of the army
[Yi]khbaryahu the son of Elnathan [went down] to Egypt"
to fetch (lᵉqaḥat) something, and that other men were also

sent, and that there was a letter of warning to the prophet. The same story is told in Jeremiah 26:22 (cf. 36:12, 25), where "the king sent . . . Elnathan the son of Achbor, and certain men with him into Egypt." One or the other scribes has transposed the names, not an uncommon occurrence. For what is the likelihood of two such pairs with identical names being involved in the idential mission to Egypt? Torczyner concludes that the scribe indeed "wrote one for the other." The Bible story and the Lachish Letters are full of such striking coincidences; for example, when Letter 4:6-7 tells of a man having the same peculiar name as Uriah's father, Shemaᶜyahu, going up from Uriah's village to Jerusalem on urgent business, accompanied by the chief inspector of military outposts. On what business? Perhaps, Torczyner suggests, "to use his influence with the king" in behalf of his son.[2] "In these letters," wrote Harry Torczyner, whose edition and commentary is a standard work on the subject, "we have the most valuable discovery yet made in the biblical archaeology of Palestine and the most intimate corroboration of the Bible to this day."[3] They are also star witnesses for the correctness of the Book of Mormon, whose opening scenes take place in exactly the same setting and time as the Letters. Both records paint pictures which are far removed from those supplied in any other known sources, and yet the two pictures are as alike as postcards of the Eiffel Tower.

The first contribution of the Lachish Letters to ancient studies was the revelation that such documents existed. Until their discovery in 1935, it was thought that the Hebrew alphabet of that time (shortly after 600 B.C.) was used only for the writing of inscriptions; indeed, all known inscriptions of comparable antiquity to the Letters are so scarce and scanty that it has been impossible even to put together a complete exemplar of the Hebrew alphabet from their contents. But with the finding of the Lachish Letters, it suddenly became clear the "the ancient Jews could write quickly and boldly, in an artistic flowing hand."⁴ The same arresting discovery was repeated at Qumran, where again the revelation of writing in common use among the Jews of another Jerusalem six hundred years later came as a distinct surprise. While the Lachish Letters were written on potsherds, the scrolls were kept in the pots, both practices reminding us that since prehistoric times symbolic marks on pottery had been used to convey messages.

Potsherds, however, do not lend themselves to convenient filing, and the contents of important Lachish Letters were duly abridged for transfer to the official archives,⁵ in the form of *delathoth*, as would appear from Letter 4:2-4, in which the writer reports that he is writing *'al ha-DLT*. What is a *deleth?* Torczyner puzzled that such a word should be used to indicate "a sheet or page of papyrus," since the word originally meant "doorboard, then board in general," being applied according to the dictionary to a "board, plaque, plate, or tablet."⁶ Torczyner finds the root meaning of the Akkadian word *edeln,* from *wdl, ydl,* "to lock or shut," the collective noun indicating things locked, hinged, or joined together—a reminder that the very ancient codex form of the book was joined pages of wood, ivory, or metal. The scanty evidence, confined to the time of Jeremiah, is enough to justify speculation of the possibility of the *delathoth* being such "plates" or metal tablets as turn up in the Book of Mormon study.⁷

More specific resemblances in the records are evident, beginning with the same obsessive concern with writing and recording and the same association with the name of Jeremiah. Nephi informs us that Jeremiah's words had been put into writing from time to time (rather than appearing as a single completed book), and that the process was still going on at the time his family left Jerusalem (1 Nephi 5:13). From the Lachish Letters we learn that Jeremiah himself made use of other writings circulating at that time, including the Lachish Letters themselves, which may be "some of the actual documents" upon which the prophet based his account of his fellow prophet Uriah; Jeremiah 38:4, in fact, is a direct quotation from Letter 6.[8] (Jeremiah could hardly have visited the enemy stronghold of Lachish to consult the original potsherd text.)

Nephi's father, Lehi, kept a written account of things as they happened, including even his dreams and visions (1 Nephi 1:16), which things Nephi faithfully transfers to his record, but only after he has abridged and added his own account. This process of transmitting, abridging, compiling, and commenting as we find it at Lachish goes on throughout the Book of Mormon. Preservation on *delathoth* was no invention of Lehi's, since the story begins with the fetching of records written on bronze plates from the archives of Laban, the military governor of Jerusalem. Is metal plates carrying *delathoth* too far? The Copper Scroll of the Dead Sea Scrolls assures us that it is not. That scroll was made of separate plates riveted together, admittedly an unusual and inconvenient arrangement but nonetheless one necessary to insure the survival of particularly precious records. Joseph Smith's insistence on books made of metal plates was a favorite target of his detractors; metal plates were strange enough to seem ludicrous, and impractical enough to cause difficulties. This was not the normal way of writing; John Allegro comments that "the scribe [of the Copper Scroll], not without reason, appears to have tired toward the end, and the last lines of writing are badly formed and rather small. One can almost hear his sigh of relief as he punched out the last two words in the middle of the final line."[9] Compare this with the sighs of Nephi's younger brother: "I cannot write but a little of my words, because of the difficulty of engraving our words upon plates. . . . But whatsoever things we write upon anything save it be upon plates must perish and vanish away; but we can write a few words upon plates, . . . and we labor diligently to engraven these words upon plates, hoping that our beloved brethren and our children will receive them" (Jacob 4:1-3).

Equally significant for the Book of Mormon study is Torczyner's emphasis on the *Egyptian* manner of keeping records in the days of Zedekiah. The Lachish Letters were written on potsherds, he notes, only because of a severe shortage of papyrus, the normal writing material. With the use of Egyptian paper went the Egyptian scribal practices in general: "The new writing material first appears under Tiglath Pileser III," that is, its general use throughout the Near East begins a century before Lehi's day, "and thereafter [writes A. T. Olmstead] every expedition has its two scribes, the chief with stylus and tablet, his assistant with papyrus roll or parchment and Egyptian pen."[10] More than sixty years before Lehi left Jerusalem, the kings of Assyria were also pharaohs of Egypt, their Egyptian scribes glorifying them in Egyptian records. At the same time the Assyrian court "found it necessary to possess an Aramaic scribe" as well, to record in that language.[11] Thus the idea of Lehi's bilingual record keeping, which caused considerable trouble to the recorders, is not entirely out of place. The reason given for it is economy of space. In Lehi's day a new type of Egyptian writing, demotic, was coming to its own, as much quicker and briefer than hieratic, as hieratic was than hieroglyphic. This is perhaps what Lehi would have used. Only a thousand years later do we learn of "characters which are *called among us* the reformed Egyptian," something not recognizable to any Egyptologist today, altered beyond recognition even as "Hebrew hath been altered by us also" (Mormon 9:32-33). It should be noted however, that the only known example of supposed Nephite writing, the so-called Anthon Transcript, compares with Meroitic writing—another type of "reformed Egyptian" developed at the same time as the Nephite script by people also fleeing from destroyers of Jerusalem, who in a short time transformed demotic or hieratic into their own new and mysterious writing.

The dates *post* and *ante quem* of the Lachish Letters are not disputed. The majority date to 589-88 B.C., shortly before the city's destruction in 587 B.C.,[12] weeks before the fall of Lachish, "while others possibly cover a period of a few years."[13] There is definitely a conflict in the record as to who was the king at the time. The scribe of Jeremiah 27:1-3 says that Zedekiah was not yet king, but scholars now insist that he was wrong and that Zedekiah was ruling earlier than the Masoretic text says he was, so 1 Nephi 1:4 may not be an anachronism. While Lehi's story begins in the first year of Zedekiah, the background of the ostraca actually happened in the last year of the reign of Zedekiah.[14] After his vision in the desert Lehi spent some time at Jerusalem entering into the activity of the other prophets and getting himself into the same trouble: "In that same year there came many prophets, prophesying unto the people that they must repent, or the great city Jerusalem must be destroyed" (1 Nephi 1:4). This was the very message ("not good!") that caused "the hands to sink," even the hands of those in "the country and the city," according to the Lachish Letters.[15]

The *proper names* in the Lachish Letters and the Book of Mormon belong to one particular period in Jewish history — the same period. Seven of the nine proper names in Letter 1 end in -*yahu*, which later became -*iah*, and during the Babylonian period lost the "h" entirely. In all the letters there are no Baal names and no El names — whose lack was once thought to be a serious defect in the Book of Mormon. Torczyner finds "the spelling of the names compounded with -iah" to be most important. The -*yahu* ending is also found as -*yah* about a century later among the Jews in Elephantine, who were "perhaps the descendants of those Jews who, after the fall of the Judaean kingdom, went down to Egypt, taking with them the prophet Jeremiah."[16]

Here we have another control over the Lehi story. The discovery of the Elephantine documents in 1925 showed that colonies of Jews actually did flee into the desert in the manner of Lehi, during his lifetime, and for the same reasons; arriving in their new home far up the Nile, they proceeded to build a replica of Solomon's Temple, exactly as Lehi did upon landing in the New World. Both of these oddities, especially the latter, were once considered damning refutations of the Book of Mormon. The -*yahu* ending of personal names abounds at Elephantine, but in a more abbreviated form (-*iah*) than at Lachish (-*yahu*) a hundred years earlier. The same variety of *endings* is found in the Book of Mormon, for example, the Lachish name *Mattanyahu* appears at Elephantine as *Mtn,* and in the Book of Mormon both as Mathonihah and Mathoni. The Book of Mormon has both long and short forms in the names Amalickiah, Amaleki and Amlici (cf. Elephantine MLKih).[17] The Assyrian inscriptions show that the final "h" was dropped in the Hebrew spelling after Lehi left, when the Jews "lost their pronunciation of the consonant 'll' under the influence of the Babylonian language."[18] Of the two names in Letter 1 *not* ending in -*yahu,* the one, Tb-Shlm (which Torczyner renders Tobshillem), suggests Book of Mormon Shilom and Shelem, while the other, Hgb, resembles Book of Mormon Hagoth.

More significant are the indications that the -*yahu* names are "certainly a token of a changed inner Judaean relationship to Yhwh. . . . This practice," Torczyner suggests, "is in some way *parallel* to . . . the first reformation by Moses"; what we have in the predominance of -*yahu* names reflects "the act of general reformation inaugurated by King Josiah (Yoshiyahu) [the father of Zedekiah]" (2 Kings 22-23).[19] Another interesting coincidence is: A Book of Mormon king 450 years after Lehi undertook a general reformation of the national constitution and revival of the religious life of the people. He and his brothers had been rigorously trained by their father, King Benjamin, "in all the language of his fathers, that thereby they might become men of understanding," familiar with the writings of the ancient prophets and also "concerning the records which were engraven on the plates of brass," without which records, he tells them, "even our fathers would have dwindled in unbelief. . . . And now my sons, I would that ye should remember to search them diligently, that ye may profit thereby" (Mosiah 1:2-3, 5, 7). Fittingly, this king named his eldest son, the great reforming king, Mosiah, suggesting both the early reform of Moses and its later imitation by Josiah. This would be altogether too much of a coincidence were it not that the book of Mosiah supplies the information that fully accounts for the resemblances when it explains just how Nephite names and customs were preserved intact in the transplanting of cultures from the Old World to the New. Lehi's ties to the Yahwist tradition are reflected in the only female name given in his history, that of his wife, Sari*ah*; such feminine names turn up at Elephantine—Mibtahyah, though in female names the -*yahu* element usually comes first.[20]

The action of the Lachish Letters centers around the activities of the prophets in the land, who are causing grave concern to the government. The Book of Mormon opens on a similar note: "And in that same year there came many prophets, prophesying unto the people that they must repent, or the great city Jerusalem must be destroyed" (1 Nephi 1:4). The identity of all but two of these prophets has now been lost, but it is clear from both the Lachish Letters and the Book of Mormon that there were more of them. "It must certainly be admitted," writes Torczyner, "that there was more than one prophet at this time."[21] The central figure is of course Jeremiah, but it is only by chance that we even know about him, for he is not mentioned in the book of Kings—it is the prophetess Huldah, "an otherwise quite unknown figure," whom Josiah consults.[22]

Jeremiah in turn mentions the prophet Uriah, "in only a few passages," and his name turns up nowhere else, though Uriah's "religious" influence must have been of great extent and long standing![23] Uriah "prophesied against this city and against this land according to all the words of Jeremiah" (Jeremiah 26:20). The words of such prophets were dangerously undermining morale both of the military and the people. "Behold the words of the [prophet] are not good, [liable] to weaken the hands of the country and the city."[24]

As the Book of Mormon opens, we see Lehi as one of those citizens distressed and discouraged by the preaching of the "many prophets. . . . As he went forth," apparently on a business journey, for he was a rich merchant, he "prayed unto the Lord, yea, even with all his heart, in behalf of his people" (1 Nephi 1:4-5). In reply to his prayer he received a vision which sent him out to join the prophets: "My father . . . went forth among the people, and began to prophesy and to declare unto them" (1 Nephi 1:18). He indeed was teaching "in the spirit of Jeremiah," for Nephi explicitly links him to the prophet's vicissitudes: "For behold, they have rejected the prophets, and Jeremiah have they cast into prison. And they have sought to take away the life of my father, insomuch that they have driven him out of the land" (1 Nephi 7:14). Torczyner suggests that Uriah "may have *hidden in the hills* of Western Judah . . . for a long time,"[25] and we find Lehi doing the same thing. Indeed, as Torczyner points out, what we are dealing with here is a type of thing, Uriah's story being told only "as a parallel to Jeremiah's not less dangerous position."[26] To their number we may add Lehi, whose story has every mark of authenticity.

As the Book of Mormon leads us into a world of Rekhabites and sectaries of the desert, so the Lachish Letters give us "for the first time . . . authentic and intimate contemporary reports from Jews, faithfully following their

God, about their inner political and religious struggles."[27] Torczyner sees in the -*yahu* names a sure indication of a loyal reformist faction which included even the highest military officers. Ya'ush and his men are the prophet's followers,[28] even though they are necessarily the king's defenders. We see Uriah hiding out in the wilderness "where he had friends and followers, for a long time."[29] The Dead Sea Scrolls have put flesh on these sectarian bones, showing how from the earliest times communities of the faithful would withdraw from Jerusalem to bide their time in the wilderness. Lehi's activities were not confined to the city, he was in the desert when he received the manifestation that sent him hurrying back to his house in Jerusalem, from which later he "went forth among the people" as a prophet (1 Nephi 1:18). Badly received, he was warned in a dream that his life was in danger (1 Nephi 2:1), and was ordered to go into the wilderness and leave all his worldly things behind (1 Nephi 2:2). It was the idea behind the Rekhabites (Jeremiah 35) and the people of Qumran; Nephi, inviting a new recruit, Zoram, to come and "have place with us," points out to him that only so could he "be a free man like unto us," and that to "go down into the wilderness" was the only way to "be diligent in keeping the commandments of the Lord" (1 Nephi 4:33-34).[30] This is the firm conviction of the sectaries of the desert, later expressed in the writings of St. Anthony. So Zoram duly takes an oath and joins the pious company (1 Nephi 4:35).

One important aspect of Lehi's account has surfaced very recently in the light of what Klaus Koch calls the rediscovery of apocalyptic.[31] It seems that almost every ancient patriarch, prophet, and apostle is credited with having left behind a testament or apocalypse bearing his name. A key figure is Jeremiah, whose two assistants, Ezra and Baruch, are responsible for two of the six basic Jewish apocalypses. Some of these stories are very old, and a consistent pattern emerges from the telling of them, though they are widely scattered in space and time. Briefly summed up, the general plot is this: A righteous man, sorely distressed by the depravity of the world or of Israel, prays fervidly for light and knowledge, and in due time receives a divine manifestation, when a heavenly messenger comes to teach him and takes him on a celestial journey, climaxing in a theophany, after which he returns to earth and reports his experience to family and friends; often this is just before he dies, and he bestows a patriarchal blessing—his testament—upon his sons. Often he also goes forth to preach to the people, who reject his message with scorn, whereupon he departs into the wilderness with his faithful followers to establish a more righteous if tentative order of things in the desert, a sort of "church of anticipation." All of which things Lehi also does in due and proper order; the first part of Nephi's writing, he says, is but an abridgment of his father's record, which may properly be called the Testament or Apocalypse of Lehi. It also relates to the Lachish Letters, for Jeremiah was the champion of the Rekhabites (Jeremiah 35) and his assistants (cf. 4 Ezra and 2 Baruch) both headed such communities of refugees. Lehi is definitely doing the accepted thing for men of God in his time.

That the Rekhabite ideal of the desert sectaries was in full flower in Lehi's day, as many other sources now indicate, is clear from the accusation that Nephi's elder brothers brought against him, that he was planning to set up such a society with himself as "our ruler and our teacher," leading them by his false claims of prophetic inspiration to believe "that the Lord has talked with him, . . . thinking, perhaps, that he may lead us away into some strange wilderness [some unoccupied tract]; and after he has led us away, he has thought to make himself a king and a ruler over us" (1 Nephi 16:37-38). Plainly they know about that sort of thing. When after eight years of wandering, the party was commanded to build a ship and sail on the waters, they were all at their wit's end, because they had never dreamed of such a thing as a promised land beyond the sea; theirs was strictly the tradition of the desert sectaries, "a lonesome and a solemn people," as Nephi's younger brother put it (Jacob 7:26).

Against the larger background of national calamity, which is never lost from view, both the Lachish Letters and the Lehi story are concerned with relatively narrow circles of friends and relations.[32] Clandestine flights from the city in both stories involve friends and families; Nephi and his brethren go back to town to persuade Ishmael and his family to join them in flight (1 Nephi 7:2-5). But soon the group begins to split up as Laman, Lemuel, and the two daughters of Ishmael whom they later married, as well as two of Ishmael's sons, vote to return to Jerusalem (1 Nephi 7:6-7). They find the whole idea of giving up their opulent life-style and renouncing their fashionable friends quite unacceptable: "Behold, these many years we have suffered in the wilderness, which time we might have enjoyed our possessions and . . . been happy. And we know that the people . . . of Jerusalem were a righteous people; for they kept the statutes and judgments of the Lord; . . . they are a righteous people; and our father hath judged them" (1 Nephi 17:21-22).

They are especially disgruntled at having to defer to a quality in their father for which the Lachish Letters have a particular expression characterizing the man of prophetic calling as *ha-piqqeah*, which Torczyner finds to mean "the open-eyed"[33] or *visionary man*, "the seer," the man whose eyes God had "opened to see,"[34] that is, to see things that other people do not see. So in the Book of Mormon the brothers use it in a critical sense against their father, arguing that he is being unrealistic and impractical: "They did murmur in many things against their father, because he was a *visionary man*, and had led them out of the land of Jerusalem, to leave the land of their inheritance, and their gold, and their silver, and their precious things, to perish in the wilderness. And this they said he had done because of the *foolish imaginations of his heart*" (1 Nephi 2:11).

They make fun of their father for being *piqqeah*, a "visionary man." Torczyner explains the word by referring to the instance in 2 Kings 6:17, where Elisha asks the Lord to open the eyes of his servant so he could see realities, horses and chariots, which otherwise only Elisha could see. In the same way the uncooperative brothers of Nephi hiding out with him in a cave in the Judaean wilderness had their eyes opened so they could see "an angel of the Lord" while he was reprimanding them (1 Nephi 3:29; 7:10).

When feelings run high the Lachish Letters resort to an unpleasant expression which Torczyner notes because of its peculiarity: "Another interesting phrase may be 'to curse the seed of somebody,' used apparently in the form *ya-or zera ha-melek*, 'he curses [the] seed to the King,'[35] reminding us of . . . the Arabic curse: 'May Allah destroy thy house.' "[36] The exact Lachish practice, however, is not found in the Bible,[37] but the closest thing to it is found in Alma 3:9, "And it came to pass that whosoever did mingle his seed with that of the Lamanites did bring the same curse upon his seed."

If the Lachish Letters reflect "the mind, the struggles, sorrows and feelings of ancient Judah in the last days of the kingdom,"[38] so to an even greater extent does the book of Nephi, where families split along political lines in a tragic conflict of loyalties. And if the situation of Uriah parallels that of Jeremiah, as Torczyner points out, even more closely does it parallel that of Lehi when we learn from the Letters of "*a warning from the prophet* to one of *his* friends [Slm], who is apparently in the same danger as he himself [cf. Ishmael]. It is, therefore, a prophet fleeing from his home and his friends, a prophet wanted by the military authorities."[39]

The leading character of the Lachish Letters is a high military officer, Hoshacyahu at Qiryat Ye'arim, suspected by one party, as reported to his superior Ya'ush, of treachery to the king in aiding the prophet, and by the other of betraying the prophet by revealing the contents of his warning letter to the king: this letter revealed to the king that the prophet was fleeing to Egypt. Likewise his superior officer, Ya'ush, who had been ordered to investigate him, "appears to be on the best of terms with the king. But still both men respect the prophet and believe in him, in spite of the king's attitude to him, and their hearts ache that they should be responsible for his destruction."[40] The same tragic confusion exists in the Lehi story. This is borne out in the relationship of the actors to the Egyptians in both dramas. Though Lehi supports the anti-Egyptian party, his sons have Egyptian names and Egyptian educations and they keep their records after the Egyptian manner. Moreover, the party flees toward Egyptian territory. The same anomaly confronts us in the Lachish Letters, which tell of a certain general sent down to Egypt to fetch a prophet back to Jerusalem for execution.[41] But why on earth, asks Torczyner, would the good man flee to Egypt, of all places, when his crime was supporting Jeremiah in calling "for peace with Babylonia"? Our informant finds "this astonishing fact," that he fled towards Egypt instead of Babylonia, quite inexplicable.[42]

As the main actors in the Lachish drama are high military officers, so also in the Book of Mormon the key figure in the Jerusalem episode is another high military officer. This was Laban, whose official position resembles that of Ya'ush in Lachish very closely. "Thus Ya'ush must be the military governor of Lachish, . . . this greatest fortress of Judah";[43] along with that, " 'lord Ya'ush' may have been Governor of the city, whose *archives* would probably have been housed in the region of the palace-fort or keep, or perhaps he was only the senior military officer."[44] All of which applies with equal force to Laban, the military governor of Jerusalem, "a mighty man" who can command fifty in his garrison (1 Nephi 3:31) and "his tens of thousands" in the field (1 Nephi 4:1). Among the nonbiblical names in the Book of Mormon which excited amusement and derision among its critics, we remember one Josh, identified in Reynolds's *Concordance* as "a Nephite general, who commanded a corps of ten thousand men" at Cumorah—an interesting comment on the conservatism of Nephite tradition (Mormon 6:14).[45] Where is the king in all this? In both stories he appears as a rather shadowy character in the background. As for Ya'ush, "the king appeals to him in everything concerning this part of the country,"[46] that is, the whole western part of the kingdom[47]— he left things pretty much up to his general, as according to the Book of Mormon he also did in Jerusalem. Laban was of noble descent, of the same ancestry as Lehi himself and of a more direct line to the patriarch Joseph, for the genealogy was kept in Laban's family (1 Nephi 5:16), and the archives were housed at his official residence, as the archives of Lachish "would probably be housed" at the headquarters and residence of Ya'ush. When Lehi's sons went to get the records from Laban, they talked with him intimately as he sat in his house, and proposed buying the plates. He refused to give up the brass plates and so they decided to bribe him with what was left of their own family treasures. They knew their man, but not quite well enough, for he kept the treasure but chased them out of the house and sent his servants after them to get rid of them (1 Nephi 3:24-25). The young men escaped and hid out in a cave, but the cat was out of the bag—Lehi's flight was now known to Laban as Uriah's was to Ya'ush, and Laban's troops would soon be on the trail of the refugees as Ya'ush's were already in pursuit of Uriah. Lehi was spared, however, because Laban never got into action on the case. That very night Nephi found him dead drunk in a street near his house and dispatched him with his own sword (1 Nephi 4:5-18). Going toward the house, Nephi met Laban's servant and got the keys to the treasury and archives from him by a ruse. In the dark the man thought that Nephi was Laban, for he was expecting his boss to be returning very late (and drunk) from an emergency council of "the elders of the Jews; . . . Laban had been *out by night* among them" (1 Nephi 4:22). There is a world of inference in this — secret emergency sessions, tension, danger, and intrigue — as there is in Lachish Letter 18, which must be forwarded from Ya'ush to the king through the village of Qiryat Ye'arim *by night*.[48] Lehi's boys took Laban's servant along with them "that the Jews might not know concerning our flight . . . lest they should pursue us and destroy us" (1 Nephi 4:36). Even so we see in the Lachish Letters "a prophet fleeing from his home and friends, and a prophet wanted by the military authorities."[49] Zoram was carried along by force but was persuaded that it was in his own interest to join a pious escape-group in the desert, and he duly exchanged oaths with his captors, his conscience not overly bothered by the change of sides; he displays the same hesitant and divided loyalties as everyone else in the Book of Mormon and the Lachish Letters. The military correspondence of the Lachish Letters, with its grim suspicions of disloyalty and double-dealing, fervid denials, charges, investigations, and reports, reminds one of the much later Bar Kochba letters (discovered in 1966) which in turn present truly astonishing parallels to some of the military correspondence in the Book of Mormon.[50]

One peculiar situation in the Lachish Letters casts a good deal of light on an equally peculiar and highly significant episode in the Book of Mormon. Hosha'yahu protests to his boss in Lachish, "and the letter [which] Nedabyahu, the NKD of the King, had brought . . . has thy slave sent to my lord."[51] The title NKD suggests that "the prophet's warning letter . . . could have been sent while the prophet was still near his hometown, through a little boy, most suited as an unsuspected messenger," in view of the fact that little boys performed such offices in the time of David (2 Samuel 15:36; 17:17-21), and that "such small boys are used also today in Palestine, often for quite responsible missions."[52] What suggests the idea to Torczyner is the mention of "Nedabyahu, the NKD of the king," as the one who delivered a letter from the prophet to SHLM warning him of the danger he was in.[53] The word NKD suggests first of all grandson. There is a Nedabiah, grandson of King Jehoiakim, in 1 Chronicles 3:18, and Torczyner finds it "possible and even probable" that he is the very one named here. What, the king's own grandson bearing letters for his opponent the prophet? The exact meaning of NKD is "unfortunately . . . not definitely established" so that the king referred to may be "either Jehoiakim . . . or less likely, Jeconiah, . . . or Zedekiah."[54] It is not a direct line of descent, Jeconiah being not the father but the nephew of Zedekiah; but since most scholars maintain, along with the Septuagint, that NKD simply means offspring or descendant, "it would be quite possible . . . to call somebody the 'grandson' [NKD] of his grandfather's brother," in this case of Zedekiah. "The Hebrew *nekedh* may certainly have been used at least for *grandson-nephew* as well as for grandson."[55] This Nedabiah, whose title "may equally well mean the grandson of Jehoiakim as the grand-nephew of Zedekiah," was quite young; "one would prefer the age of 10-13 to that of 5 years,"[56] carrying dangerous letters between the towns and camps for the prophet's people. Since he was running errands for the opposition party, the boy was, of course, away from home most of the time; and since he was specifically carrying letters of warning telling people to decamp and save their lives, he could surely count on escaping with them. When news reached them that the royal family was wiped out, only one course of action was open to the child [as survivor] and his friends. Where would they go? Torczyner suggests the date of 590-588 for this episode, that is, the year 589, just eleven years after 600 B.C. According to the Book of Mormon, eleven years after Lehi left Jerusalem — 589 — a company escaped from the land of Jerusalem bearing with them a son of Zedekiah, the only member of the family not put to death when Jerusalem was taken. From the descendants of these people in the New World, the Nephites learned that Jerusalem actually did fall as prophesied: "Will you dispute that Jerusalem was destroyed? Will ye say that the sons of Zedekiah were not slain, all except it were *Mulek?* Yea, and do ye not behold that the seed of Zedekiah are with us, and *they* were driven out of the land of Jerusalem?" (Helaman 8:21). By an interesting coincidence, the Septuagint translates the word NKD, by which Nedabyahu is designated in Hebrew, simply as "seed,"[57] as apparently does the Book of Mormon — "the seed of Zedekiah." The land north where they settled in the New World "was called Mulek, which was after the son of Zedekiah; for the Lord did bring Mulek into the land north" (Helaman 6:10). Nowhere are we told that Mulek was the leader of the company, and indeed at his age that would be unthinkable — his father Zedekiah was only about thirty-one when he was taken prisoner and blinded. But as the sole survivor of the royal family and heir presumptive to the throne, he was certainly the most important person in the company, a source of legitimate pride to the group. The name tells everything — "Mulek" is not found anywhere in the Bible, but any student of Semitic languages will instantly recognize it as the best-known form of diminutive or caritative, a term of affection and endearment meaning "little king." What could they call the uncrowned child, last of his line, but their little king? And what could they call themselves but Mulekiyah or Mulekites?

And so the coincidences go on accumulating. It is time to turn to the computer, as we do today whenever questions and problems arise. What are the chances of the many parallels between the Lachish Letters and the opening chapter of the Book of Mormon being the product of mere coincidence?

1. First consider the fact that only one piece of evidence could possibly bring us into the Lehi picture, and that one piece of evidence happens to be the *only* firsthand writing surviving from the entire scope of Old Testament history. Lehi's story covers less than ten years in the thousand-year history of the Book of Mormon, and the Lachish Letters cover the same tiny band of a vast spectrum — and they both happen to be the *same* years!

2. Not only in time but in place do they fit neatly into the same narrow slot, and the people with which they deal also belong to the same classes of society and are confronted by the same peculiar problems.

3. With the Book of Mormon account being as detailed and specific as it is, it is quite a piece of luck that there is nothing in the Lachish Letters that in any way contradicts its story — that in itself should be given serious consideration. Is it just luck?

4. Both documents account for their existence by indicating specifically the techniques and usages of writing and recording in their day, telling of the same means of transmitting, editing, and storing records.

5. The proximity of Egypt and its influence on writing has a paramount place in both stories.

6. Both stories confront us with dynastic confusion during a transition of kingship.

7. Both abound in proper names in which the *-yahu* ending is prominent in a number of forms.

8. In both, the religious significance of those names

gives indication of a pious reformist movement among the people.

9. The peculiar name of Jaush (Josh), since it is not found in the Bible, is remarkable as the name borne by a high-ranking field officer in both the Lachish Letters and the Book of Mormon.

10. In both reports, prophets of gloom operating in and around Jerusalem are sought by the government as criminals for spreading defeatism.

11. The Rekhabite background is strongly suggested in both accounts, with inspired leaders and their followers fleeing to the hills and caves.

12. Political partisanship and international connections cause division, recriminations, and heartbreak in the best of families.

13. The conflicting ideologies—practical vs. religious, materialist vs. spiritual—emerge in two views of the religious leader or prophet as a *piqqeah*, "a visionary man," a term either of praise or of contempt—an impractical dreamer.

14. For some unexplained reason, the anti-king parties both flee not towards Babylon but towards Egypt, "the broken reed."

15. The offices and doings of Laban and Jaush present a complex parallel, indicative of a special military type and calling not found in the Bible.

16. Almost casual references to certain doings by night create the same atmosphere of tension and danger in both stories.

17. Little Nedabyahu fits almost too well into the slot occupied by the Book of Mormon Mulek, "the little king," who never came to rule but escaped with a party of refugees to the New World.

18. The whole business of keeping, transmitting, and storing records follows the same procedures in both books.

Other parallels may be added to taste, but this should

be enough to show that Joseph Smith was either extravagantly lucky in the opening episodes of his Book of Mormon — that should be demonstrated by computer — or else he had help from someone who knew a great deal.

Notes

1. These introductory paragraphs appeared in Hugh W. Nibley, "The Lachish Letters: Documents from Lehi's Day," *Ensign* (December 1981): 48-50.

2. Harry Torczyner, *Lachish I (Tell ed-Duweir): The Lachish Letters* (London: Oxford, 1938), 86. On the transposition of the names, see ibid., 67. If Achbor's name was written backwards by the scribe of Jeremiah, it would not be his only or even most serious slip in the matter; the scribe assigns the Uriah episode to the time of Jehoiakim (608-597), but scholars are now agreed on the evidence of Jeremiah 27:1-3 that the scribe has mistakenly put things in the reign of Jehoiakim which rightfully belong to the reign of Zedekiah; ibid., 69.

3. Ibid., 18. Fifteen years after Torczyner's work, another translation of the Lachish Letters appeared in David Diringer, "Early Hebrew Inscriptions," in Olga Tufnell, *Lachish III (Tell ed-Duweir): The Iron Age Text* (London: Oxford, 1953), 331-359, esp. 331-339. The Letters were discovered in Stratum II at Tell ed-Duweir; Tufnell, *Lachish III*, 48, which was destroyed by Nebuchadnezzar in 587 B.C., and the majority of the letters date to 589-88 B.C. See John Bright, *A History of Israel*, 3rd ed. (Philadelphia: Westminster, 1981), 330, n. 58, 60. In recent years, much discussion about the dating of Stratum III's destruction has occurred. The consensus now is that Stratum III was destroyed in 701 B.C. by Sennacherib. See David Ussishkin, "Answers at Lachish," *Biblical Archaeology Review* 5 (1979): 16-39. Earlier scholars believed that Stratum III reflected an attack by Nebuchadnezzar in 597 B.C., but that claim no longer seems tenable. See David Ussishkin, "The Renewed Archaeological Excavations at Lachish," *Buried History* 13 (1977): 2-16; Yohanan Aharoni, *The Archaeology of the Land of Israel*, ed. Miriam Aharoni, tr. Anson F. Rainey (Philadelphia: Westminster, 1982), 272-73. The earlier date for Stratum III does not change the dating for the Letters. Regardless of other uncertainties, all seem to agree that the Letters come from Stratum II and the destruction by Nebuchadnezzar in 587-86 B.C. See Torczyner, *Lachish I*, 18; Tufnell, *Lachish III*, 57; John Bright, "A New Letter in Aramaic, Written to a Pharaoh in Egypt," ed. G. Earnest Wright and David Noel Freeman, *The Biblical Ar-*

chaeology Reader, 3 vols. (Garden City, New York: Doubleday, 1961), 1:98; Yohanan Aharoni, *The Land of the Bible: A Historical Geography*, ed. and tr. Anson F. Rainey (Philadelphia: Westminster, 1978), 340-46; Aharoni, *The Archaeology of the Land of Israel*, 272, 279. In the *Ensign* 10 (December, 1981): 50, Nibley added, "Even without the archaeological sites, the setting and situation in which the letters were written could be determined by their style as well as their content. They contain '90 . . . lines of clear writing, beautiful language, and highly important contents.' Torczyner, *Lachish I*, 15. The language is pure Hebrew, most closely resembling that of the books of Jeremiah and of Kings. Ibid., 17. They show, to everyone's surprise that in 600 B.C. 'writing was almost common knowledge, and not a secret art known only to a very few.' Ibid., 19."

4. Torczyner, *Lachish I*, 15.

5. Ibid., 80.

6. The one passage in the Old Testament that would justify calling a *deleth* a roll of papyrus is Jeremiah 36:23: "When Jehudi had read three or four leaves [*delathoth* = *pagellas*], he cut it with a knife and cast it into the fire, until all the roll [*megillah, volumen*] was consumed with fire." Papyrus tears easily, yet instead of ripping the roll to shreds in his wrath, the king had to go after it with a knife — surely it was more solid than paper. David Diringer, "Early Hebrew Inscriptions," 333, renders *deleth* as "door," but he places a question mark after the word to indicate that he is not certain about the translation. The question is open.

7. In the *Ensign* 10 (December, 1981): 50, Nibley similarly wrote: "In Letter No. 4:2-4, Hoshaᶜyahu assures his superior in Lachish that he has carried out his written orders to the letter: 'According to whatever my lord has sent, so has thy servant done.' Furthermore, 'I have written down in the *deleth* whatever my lord has sent [written] me.' Plainly he copied it down for the official record. Though 'the Bible throughout speaks of rolls of writing,' meaning papyrus or, more rarely, parchment rolls, Letter 4 specifically uses the rare word *deleth* for the form in which Hoshaᶜyahu copied down or registered his official correspondence. Torczyner assumed that *deleth* must refer to a 'papyrus sheet,' or 'page,' since a *deleth* is not a roll and is certainly not a potsherd. Torczyner, *Lachish I*, 80. An alternative is a tablet or plate of solid material."

8. Torczyner, *Lachish I*, 18.

9. John M. Allegro, *The Treasure of the Copper Scroll* (New York: Doubleday, 1960), 27.

10. A. T. Olmstead, *History of Assyria* (Chicago: University of Chicago, 1960), 583. In the *Ensign* 10 (December, 1981): 51, Nibley explained further that "the assistant was needed not so much for his skill with Egyptian writing materials, which had been introduced quite recently in the time of Tiglath-Pileser III and which anyone could learn to handle, but for the same reason 'the court found it necessary to possess an Aramaic scribe'—namely to deal with the language, ibid., 581-82, so widespread was the Egyptian tradition of record keeping at that time. Would the Egyptian scribes of a Babylonian or Assyrian king employ their skill to write in cuneiform or any other language but Egyptian? There were plenty of native scribes for that. Though a wealth of cuneiform writings on clay have been found in Egypt, cuneiform writings on papyrus are not known in the East."

11. Ibid., 581-82.

12. Bright, *A History of Israel*, 106, n. 58, 60. An earlier version of this paper asserted that the two layers of ashes represented destructions of Jerusalem in 597 and 588 B.C. between which the Letters were found. "Two Shots in the Dark," 107. Present scholarship favors the date of 701 B.C. for the earlier layer of ashes, but this does not change the dating of the Lachish Letters. See above, note 3—ed.

13. Torczyner, *Lachish I*, 18.

14. Ibid., 69.

15. Ibid., Letter 6:6-7.

16. Ibid., 27.

17. Ibid., 24.

18. Ibid., 25.

19. Ibid., 29.

20. Ibid., 27-28.

21. Ibid., 65.

22. Ibid., 70.

23. Ibid.

24. Ibid., Letter 6:5-6; cf. Jeremiah 38:4.

25. Ibid., 70 (emphasis added).

26. Ibid., 69 (emphasis added).

27. Ibid., 18.

28. Ibid., 66.

29. Ibid., 70.

30. Compare similar expressions of piety in 1QS 1.

31. Klaus Koch, *Ratlos vor der Apokalyptik* (Gütersloh: Mohr, 1970).

32. "The Lachish Letters are the first personal documents found,

reflecting the mind, the struggles, sorrows and feelings of ancient Judah in the last days of the kingdom, within the typical form of ancient letter writing. . . . Here for the first time we have authentic and intimate contemporary reports from Jews, faithfully following their God, about their inner political and religious struggles, as told in the book of Jeremiah." Torczyner, *Lachish I*, 18. The Lehi history, as shown in *Lehi in the Desert and the World of the Jaredites* (Salt Lake City: Bookcraft, 1952), in *CWHN* 5, is nothing if not intimate.

33. Torczyner, *Lachish I*, 53. Diringer, "Early Hebrew Inscriptions," 332, also translates this term as "open-eyed," but places a question mark after the translation to indicate uncertainty. Diringer finds the characters preceding and following "open-eyed" to be illegible.

34. Torczyner, *Lachish I*, 65.

35. Ibid., Letter 5:10. This type of cursing is widely attested in the ancient world, although its presence in Lachish Letter 5 is debatable. See Diringer, "Early Hebrew Inscriptions," 333.

36. Torczyner, *Lachish I*, 17.

37. Ibid., 17, points out that the closest biblical example of cursing seed is in Malachi 2:2-3, "I will corrupt your seed."

38. Torczyner, *Lachish I*, 18.

39. Ibid., 64 (emphasis added).

40. Ibid., 113.

41. Ibid., 63.

42. Ibid., 67.

43. Ibid., 87.

44. Ibid., 12 (emphasis added).

45. George Reynolds, *A Complete Concordance of the Book of Mormon* (Salt Lake City: Deseret, 1900).

46. Torczyner, *Lachish I*, 118.

47. Ibid., 87.

48. Ibid., 183.

49. Ibid., 64.

50. Discussed in Hugh W. Nibley, "Review Essay on Yigael Yadin's Bar-Kochba: The Rediscovery of the Legendary Hero of the Second Jewish Revolt Against Rome," *BYU Studies* 14 (Autumn 1973): 120-24; above, pages 279-86.

51. Torczyner, *Lachish I*, 64, n. 1; Letter 3:19-21. Diringer, "Early Hebrew Inscriptions," 333, does not see NKD, but rather YBD, a common name for "servant." Therefore, Diringer's translation describes the servant of the king rather than the NKD (grandson or grand-nephew) of the king. Both readings are possible.

52. Torczyner, *Lachish I*, 68.

53. Ibid., Letter 3:19-21. Diringer, "Early Hebrew Inscriptions," 333, alternatively reads "Tobyahu" rather than "Nedabyahu."

54. Torczyner, *Lachish I*, 61.

55. Ibid., 61.

56. Ibid., 69.

57. Ibid., 61.

19

Christ among the Ruins

The great boldness and originality of writings attributed to Joseph Smith are displayed in their full scope and
splendor in the account, contained in what is called 3 Nephi
in the Book of Mormon, of how the Lord Jesus Christ after
his resurrection visited some of his "other sheep" in the
New World and set up his church among them. It would
be hard to imagine a project more dangerous to life and
limb or perilous to the soul than that of authoring, and
recommending to the Christian world as holy scripture,
writings purporting to contain an accurate account of the
deeds of the Lord among men after his resurrection, including lengthy transcripts of the very words he spoke.
Nothing short of absolute integrity could stand up to the
consequences of such daring in nineteenth-century America. We know exactly how his neighbors reacted to the
claims of Joseph Smith, and it was not (as it has become
customary to insist) with the complacent or sympathetic
tolerance of backwoods "Yorkers," to whom such things
were supposedly everyday experience: nothing could
equal the indignation and rage excited among them by the
name and message of Joseph Smith.

And yet the particular part of the Book of Mormon to
which we refer, the postresurrectional mission of Christ

This article was first published in Book of Mormon Authorship, *ed.
Noel B. Reynolds (Provo: Religious Studies Center, Brigham Young University, 1982), 121-41. A popular version of the same material subsequently
appeared in* Ensign 13 (1983): 14-19.

in the New World, has not been singled out for condemnation; it has, in fact, met with surprisingly little criticism. Why is that? Experience has shown, for one thing, that the tone and content of this particular history are so elevated and profoundly sincere as to silence and abash the would-be critic. When the austere dean of the Harvard Divinity School can take 3 Nephi seriously as a religious outpouring, who can laugh at it?[1] More to the point, the story of Christ's ministry among men during the forty days following his return from the tomb is one to which the churchmen have always given a wide berth, frankly disapproving of the crass literalism of Luke's almost clinical account. What can one say about events for which, as one scholar puts it, "no metaphysical or psychological explanation can be given?" What controls does one have for testing matters that lie totally beyond our experience?

Of recent years the discovery and rediscovery of a wealth of very early Christian writings suggest at least one type of control over the elusive history of the forty days. For with surprising frequency the oldest of these texts purport to contain "The Secret Teachings of Our Lord to His Disciples" after his return from the dead, or titles to that effect. Since this is the theme of the history in 3 Nephi, ordinary curiosity prompts us to ask how that document compares with the ancient ones in form and content. That question in turn waits on the prior necessity of comparing the older writings with each other to see whether, taken all together, they tell anything like a consistent story. When this writer brought a number of the "forty-day" texts together some years ago (the amount of available material has grown considerably since then), it became at once apparent that they do have certain themes and episodes in common.[2] At that time nothing could have been farther from this person's mind than the Book of Mormon, and yet if we set those findings over against the long account of Nephi, the latter takes its place in the bona fide apocalyptic library so easily and naturally that with the title removed, any scholar would be hard put to it to detect its irregular origin. That is only our opinion, but fortunately copies of the Book of Mormon are not hard to come by in our society, and the reader is free to control the whole thing for himself. Permit me to run down the list of common features in the forty-day writings in the order in which we presented them in the article referred to.

First, we noted that the large literature of the forty-day mission of the Lord was early lost from sight by the Christian world because it was never very popular, and that for a number of reasons. In almost all the accounts, for example, the apostles, who are about to go forth on their missions and establish the church throughout the world, anxiously ask the Lord what the future of that church is to be, and are given a surprisingly pessimistic answer: the church will fall prey to the machinations of evil and after two generations will pass away. "The apostles protest, as we do today: Is this a time for speaking of death and disaster? Can all that has transpired be but for the salvation of a few and the condemnation of many? But Jesus remains unyielding: that is not for us to decide or to question."[3] A strangely negative message for the church, understandably unacceptable to the conventional Christianity of later times. One would hardly expect such a thing in the Book of Mormon, but there it is, the same paradox: the glad message of the resurrection and the glorious unifying of the Saints is saddened, dampened by the forthright declaration that the church is only to survive for a limited time. To speak of the world in negative terms is permissible—but the church?

> And now, behold, my joy is great even unto fulness, because of you, and also this generation; . . . for none of them are lost. Behold, I would that ye should understand; for I mean them who are now alive of this generation. But behold, it sorroweth me because of the

fourth generation [in the Old World it was the second generation] from this generation, for they are led away captive by him even as was the son of perdition; for they will sell me for silver and for gold. . . . And in that day will I visit them, even in turning their works upon their own heads (3 Nephi 27:30-32; cf. 17:14, 21-23).

On both hemispheres the people of the church were only too willing to forget such disturbing prophecies and insist that God would never desert his church.

The loss of the "forty-day literature" was clearly hastened by the secrecy with which the various writings were guarded. The usual title or instruction to the texts specifies that "these are the secret teachings" of the risen Lord, and as such they were treasured and guarded by the communities possessing them. This secrecy made possible all sorts of sectarian misrepresentations, forgeries, and Gnostic aberrations, which flourished throughout the Christian world of the second century and served to bring the final discredit and oblivion on the writings and the sects that exploited them. The apocryphal literature contains no better explanation of the original observance of secrecy than the book of 3 Nephi itself:

And now there cannot be written in this book even a hundredth part of the things which Jesus did truly teach unto the people (3 Nephi 26:6).

And if . . . they will not believe these things, then shall the greater things be withheld from them, unto their condemnation. Behold, I was about to write them, all which were engraven upon the plates of Nephi, but the Lord forbade it, saying: I will try the faith of my people (3 Nephi 26:10-11).

Write the things which ye have seen and heard, save it be those which are forbidden (3 Nephi 27:23).

Besides things which *should* not be recorded were those which by their nature *could* not be:

And no tongue *can* speak, neither *can* there be written by any man . . . so great and marvelous things as
we both saw and heard Jesus speak (3 Nephi 17:17).

And tongue *cannot* speak the words which he
prayed, neither *can* be written by man the words which
he prayed. (3 Nephi 19:32).

So great and marvelous were the words which he
prayed that they *cannot* be written, neither *can* they be
uttered by man. (3 Nephi 26:34).

Peculiar to the "forty-day literature" is the emphasis
on certain teachings neglected or vigorously opposed by
the intellectual churchmen of later Christianity. Whether
or not one chooses to accept them as authentic, it is their
presence in the preachings of the risen Lord in 3 Nephi
which interests us here. One aspect of his activity which
does not receive particular attention in Luke's accounts is
the worldwide circulation of the Savior among his servants
in the apocalyptic versions. Luke has the Lord come and
go with great freedom and frequency among his people in
Judaea, but in the "forty-day literature" he appears to them
in all parts of the world.[4] So also in the Book of Mormon:

I have other sheep which are not of this land, neither
of the land of Jerusalem, neither in any parts of that land
round about whither I have been to minister. They . . .
have not as yet heard my voice. But . . . I shall go unto
them, and . . . they shall hear my voice, and shall be
numbered among my sheep (3 Nephi 16:1-3; cf. 3 Nephi
15:14-24; 17:4).

In the early Christian texts, the teaching of the risen
Lord is prophetic and apocalyptic, reviewing the history
of God's dealing with men on earth from the beginning
and carrying it down to its glorious culmination at the
Parousia; the story is usually presented in a series of "dispensations," alternating periods of light and darkness
through which the world and the saints must pass. The
3 Nephi version faithfully follows the pattern in a long

exposition which goes back to the beginning of the law, its presence among peoples scattered in divers places, not in just one place (3 Nephi 15); its future among them and its spread throughout the world among the Gentiles, with the vicissitudes through which both Israel and the Gentiles must pass (3 Nephi 16). Chapter 20 carries the coming history of Israel and especially of the Nephites themselves right through to the end, including the climactic events of our own day, as chapter 21 sets forth God's dealings to come with the people on this hemisphere until the establishing of the New Jerusalem.

The most natural questions to ask anyone returning to earth after being away would be, Where did you go and what did you see? These questions, put by the disciples in the Old World accounts, lead to discussions of the *Descensus* and the *Kerygma*, that is, the Savior's descent to the prison-house to preach to those spirits who were disobedient in the days of Noah (1 Peter 3:19-20). This theme became the subject of the "Harrowing of Hell" drama of the Gospel of Nicodemus and the medieval mystery plays. Does the Book of Mormon version have anything about that? Yes, and the *Descensus* and the *Kerygma* described there are uniquely glorious. Let us recall that the *Descensus* closely parallels the earthly mission of John the Baptist "to give light to them that sit in darkness and in the shadow of death" (Luke 1:79). In the Book of Mormon, the hosts that sit in darkness are the Nephites themselves, exhausted and in utter despair and desolation after three days of destruction followed by total darkness, and awful lamentations followed by even more awful silence. The Lord three days after his crucifixion leaves the spirits in prison and now descends to them as a figure of light, "descending out of heaven . . . clothed in a white robe" (3 Nephi 11:8), exactly as he does to the spirits in hell in the Old World writings; announcing to them "I am the light and the life of the world" (3 Nephi 1:11) who has come directly from the agony of the "bitter cup" to bring light and deliverance to them. And they accepted him as such, as "the whole multitude fell to the earth" (3 Nephi 11:12); then he identified himself to them and announced his mission, and "they did cry out with one accord, saying: Hosanna! Blessed be the name of the Most High God! And they did fall down at the feet of Jesus, and did worship him" (3 Nephi 11:16-17). For they knew that he had come to lead them out of their prison. The first thing he did was to address them as disobedient spirits, as he promised, "And this is my doctrine . . . that the Father commandeth all men, everywhere, to repent and believe in me" (3 Nephi 11:32)—we are all disobedient spirits in prison! The next thing was to insist that they all be baptized—exactly as in the *Descensus* accounts; he must give the "seal" of baptism to all to whom he preaches in the underworld before they can follow him out of darkness up into his kingdom. Jesus puts it to them as an act of deliverance. Then the Lord says a striking thing to the Nephites: "Verily, verily . . . this is my doctrine, and whoso buildeth upon this buildeth upon my rock, and the gates of hell shall not prevail against them. And whoso shall declare more or less than this, . . . the gates of hell stand open to receive such when the floods come and the winds beat upon them" (3 Nephi 39:40). He has come to deliver them from the Gates of Hell that hold them in bondage; this is the "smashing of the Gates theme," the "Harrowing of Hell" motif all the way through. As he is about to leave, there is a great sorrowing among them as if they were being left behind in darkness. This vividly recalls like situations in the royal Parousias of Egyptian rulers, a concept going back at least as far as the text of the Am Duat.[5]

To show his people that he is really a resurrected being and not a spirit, both in the New Testament account and in the apocryphal version, Jesus calls for food—real food— and insists that they share it with him in a sacred meal.

The meal usually follows the baptism, putting its seal upon
the initiation and the union of those who follow the Lord.
In 3 Nephi the sacral meal with the risen Lord, repeated
more than once, is an event of transcendent importance,
to which we shall refer below.

Most scholars and theologians have seen the purpose
of the forty days to be the laying of a firm foundation for
the sending out of the disciples into all the world to lay a
foundation for the church. At the time of the crucifixion
they were utterly demoralized and scattered, in no condition to go forth as powerful ambassadors of the Lord
into all the world. The forty-day teaching has the object
of preparing them for their missions. This is exactly the
case in the Book of Mormon. After the founding of the
church among the people come two chapters (3 Nephi 27-
28) dealing exclusively with the preparation of the chosen
disciples for their special missions into the world, upon
which after his departure they immediately set forth.

As might be expected, the appearances of the Lord to
the astonished multitude, as well as his departures from
them, are events of celestial splendor, nowhere more mov-
ingly described than in chapter 11 of 3 Nephi. The utter
glory of his presence among the people or with the disciples
is a constant theme in both the Book of Mormon and the
other sources. And yet it is combined with a feeling of the
closest and most loving intimacy, especially moving in the
Book of Mormon accounts of his dealings with the children.

The comings and goings of God himself, moving between heaven and earth, must needs be surrounded by
an aura of mystery and excitement. Can such things really
be? Luke, in his meticulous, almost clinically exact and
factual reports, wants us to know once and for all that they
really can be. The wonder of it, something akin to the
excitement of Christmas, quickens the reader's pulse, but
how could we describe the state of mind of those who
actually experienced it? The apocryphal writings go all out

to make us feel with them, but it is 3 Nephi who really catches the spirit:

> When Jesus had ascended into heaven, the multitude did disperse, and every man did take his wife and his children and did return to his own home. And it was noised abroad among the people immediately, before it was yet dark, that the multitude had seen Jesus, . . . and that he would also show himself on the morrow unto the multitude. Yea, and even all the night it was noised abroad concerning Jesus; and insomuch did they send forth unto the people that . . . an exceedingly great number, did labor exceedingly all that night, that they might be on the morrow in the place where Jesus should show himself unto the multitude (3 Nephi 19:1-3).

Nothing could convey the atmosphere of the electrifying "forty-day" message better than that. In 3 Nephi we see the celestial splendor of his comings and goings. We see the utter glory of his presence. And we see the Savior's closest and most loving intimacy, which is especially tender in the accounts of his dealings with children.

But now it is time to turn to a particular text. When E. Revillout announced the discovery of a Coptic manuscript of the Gospel of the Twelve Apostles in 1904, he declared it to be the text which Origen and Jerome "considered . . . to be perhaps earlier than Saint Luke and referred to by him in his prologue," a work esteemed by the church fathers as of "capital importance," uniquely free of any hint of heresy, carrying the tradition of Christ's visits to the earth beyond the scope of Luke—even to an event fifteen years later.[6] German scholarship promptly and routinely minimized the claims of Revillout, and went too far in the process. If the fragments of the Coptic Gospel of the Twelve Apostles do not necessarily occur in the order in which Revillout arranged them (the order which we will follow), subsequent discoveries make it clear that they

really are connected parts of a single—and typical—forty-
day manuscript, and that they belong to the earliest stratum of early Christian writing. Revillout's arrangement
does not follow quite the same order as 3 Nephi, either,
but a comparison of the two may be instructive.

The Lord's condescension: He came and ate with them:

Evangile des douze apôtres, Fragment 2, in *PO* 2:132.

Friends: Have you ever seen, Brethren, such a loving Lord, promising his apostles his own kingdom? Where they would eat and drink with him upon a heavenly table even as he had eaten with them on earth at an earthly table.

Thereby he put them in mind of the heavenly table, considering the things of this world [*kosmos*] as nothing.

3 Nephi 10:18-19. And it came to pass that in the ending of the thirty and fourth year, behold, I will show unto you that the people of Nephi who were spared, and also those who had been called Lamanites, who had been spared, did have great *favors* shown unto them, and great *blessings* poured out upon their heads, insomuch that soon after the ascension of Christ into heaven he did truly manifest himself unto them—Showing his body unto them, and ministering unto them; and an account of his ministry shall be given hereafter.

3 Nephi 26:13. Therefore I would that ye should behold that the Lord truly did teach the people, for the space of three days; and after that he did show himself unto them oft, and did break bread oft, and bless it, and give it unto them.

To make them one with him and with each other:

PO 2:132-33. If you really want to know, listen and I will tell you. Did not God feel an equal love for all his apostles? Listen to John the Evangelist, testifying how the Christ used to plead with [*sops*] his Father on their behalf, even that "they become one even as we are one."

PO 2:133. Do you want to know the truth about that? It is that he chose the Twelve.

PO 2:132. Listen to John the Evangelist testifying. [On this matter he refers them back to the testimony of John.]

3 Nephi 19:23. That they may believe in me, that I may be in them as thou, Father, art in me, that we may be one.

3 Nephi 19:29. Father, I pray . . . for those whom thou hast given me out of the world, . . . that they may be purified in me, that I may be in them as thou, Father, art in me, that we may be one, that I may be glorified in them.

3 Nephi 28:6 [In another matter he also refers the disciples back to John]: I know your thoughts, and ye have desired the thing which John, my beloved . . . desired of me.

The loaves and the fishes:

PO 2:133. . . . upon them, saying, I feel concerned [pity] for this multitude; for behold they have been with me for three days, and [now] they have nothing to eat. I don't want to let them leave here hungry, lest they faint by the wayside.

Andrew said to him, My Lord, where will we find bread in this wilderness?

Jesus said to Thomas: Go to a certain [*pei*] man who

3 Nephi 17:6. And he said unto them: Behold my bowels are filled with compassion towards you.

3 Nephi 8:23. For the space of three days [preceding, all had been deprived. The place was now desolate.]

3 Nephi 20:6. Now there had been no bread, neither wine brought by the disciples, neither by the multitude.

has with him fives loaves of barley bread and two fishes, and bring them to me here.

Andrew said to him Lord, how far would five loaves go with such a huge crowd?

Jesus saith to him: Bring them to me and there will be enough.

(While they go for the food Jesus talks with a little child.)

And so they went [for the food]. A small child was brought to Jesus, and straightway, he began to worship him. The small child said to Jesus, Lord I have suffered much because of these [i.e., at the hands of people. The puzzled scribe connects this with the loaves: the child must have suffered because of *them*, as if the child had been sent to fetch them]. Jesus saith to the child, Give me the five loaves which have been entrusted to you.

PO 2:134. Thou has not saved [rescued] this multitude in time of need, but it is the *toikonomia* [arrangement, ordinance, divine intent] that

3 Nephi 18:2. And while they were gone for bread and wine, he commanded the multitude that they should sit themselves down upon the earth.

3 Nephi 17:11-12. And it came to pass that he commanded that their little children should be brought. So they brought their little children and set them down upon the ground round about him, and Jesus stood in the midst; and the multitude gave way till they had all been brought unto him.

3 Nephi 26:14. And it came to pass that he did teach and minister unto the children of the multitude of whom hath been spoken, and

[they] behold a marvelous thing, the *remembrance* of which shall never pass away, nor the food with which they are filled.

he did loose their tongues, and they did speak unto their fathers great and marvelous things, even greater than he had revealed unto the people; and he loosed their tongues that they could utter.

Note here the strange precocity of the child and the sacramental (memorial) nature of the meal.

3 Nephi 18:5, 7, 11. And when the multitude had eaten and were filled, he said unto the disciples: . . . This shall ye do in *remembrance* of my body, which I have shown unto you . . . that ye do always *remember* me. And if ye do always *remember* me ye shall have my spirit to be with you. . . . And this shall ye always do to those who repent and are baptized in my name; and ye shall do it in *remembrance* of my blood, which I have shed for you, that ye may witness unto the Father that ye do always *remember* me. And if ye do always *remember* me ye shall have my Spirit to be with you.

The sacrament administered:

PO 2:134. And Jesus (1) took the loaves

3 Nephi 18:3-4. And when the disciples had come with bread and wine, he (1) took of the bread

and (2) blessed them [gave thanks over them]

and (2) brake

and (3) divided them

and (4) gave them to the apostles

(5) that they might bear them to the multitude.

and (3) blessed it;

and (4) he gave unto the disciples and commanded that they should eat.

And when they were filled, he commanded that (5) they should give unto the multitude.

The sacrament withheld:

PO 2:134. For Judas [had been] the last to partake of the loaves [this refers back to the Last Supper, to illustrate a principle].

3 Nephi 18:28-29. And now behold, this is the commandment which I give unto you, that ye shall not suffer any one knowingly to partake of my flesh and blood unworthily, when ye shall minister it;

Andrew said to Jesus, O Master [*sah*], Judas did not receive a *kleronomia* [of] loaves . . . to bear to the multitude . . . [such as] . . . we were to give to them.

That is because he to whom I did *not* give a share of the loaves from my hands was *not worthy* of a part [share] of my flesh.

Neither did he care to share with the poor, but thought only of the *glosogomon* [finance].

3 Nephi 18:29. For whoso eateth and drinketh my flesh and blood unworthily eateth and drinketh damnation to his soul; therefore if ye know that a man is unworthy to eat and drink of my flesh and blood ye shall forbid him.

The sacramental prayer:

PO 2:134. It is a mystery of my Father . . . which con[cern]s . . . the partaking [dividing] of my flesh.

And forthwith he blessed them, saying, O my *Father,* root [source] of all good, *I ask thee to bless these* five barley *loaves* that *all these* [multitude] may be filled, that thy son may be glorified in thee; and that those whom thou hast drawn to thee out of the world might *hearken to* [after, obey] *him.*

The actual words of the prayer (Moroni 4:1-2) are given by Moroni (compare 3 Nephi 18:6-11):

Moroni 4:3. O God, the Eternal *Father, we ask thee* in the name of thy Son, Jesus Christ, *to bless* and sanctify *this bread* to the souls of *all those* who partake of it; that they may eat in *remembrance* of the body of thy Son and . . . always remember him, and *keep his commandments,* which he hath given them, that they may always have his Spirit to be with them. Amen.

PO 2:134-35. And straightway his word came to pass in *exousia* [authority, as requested]. His blessing fell upon [*shope*] the bread in the apostles' hands.

And all the people ate and were filled. They *gave praise* to God.

Moroni 5:2. . . . wine . . . that they do always *remember* him, that they may have his *Spirit* to be with them. Amen.

3 Nephi 20:9. Now when the multitude had all eaten and drunk, behold, they were filled with the Spirit; and they did cry out with one voice, and gave *glory* to Jesus, whom they both saw and heard.

Jesus prays three times:

PO 2:134-35. You have seen, O my beloved one,

3 Nephi 28:13-14. And behold, the heavens were

what love Jesus had toward his apostles, insomuch that he kept [hid] nothing from them of any of the things touching upon his godhead [relationship to God].

opened, and they were caught up into heaven, and saw and heard unspeakable things. And it was forbidden them that they should utter; neither was it given unto them power that they could utter the things which they saw.

The first time while blessing the five loaves of barley bread.

3 Nephi 19:19-20. And it came to pass that Jesus departed out of the midst of them, and went a little way off from them and bowed himself to the earth, and he said: Father, I thank thee that thou hast given the Holy Ghost unto these whom I have chosen . . . out of the world.

3 Nephi 19:24-25. When Jesus had thus prayed . . . he came unto his disciples and . . . blessed them as they did pray unto him; . . . and behold they were as white as the countenance and also the garments of Jesus.

The second time in his giving thanks to his Father [the prayer is not quoted].

3 Nephi 19:28-30. Father, I thank thee that thou hast purified those whom I have chosen, . . . and I pray for them, and also for them who shall believe on their words. . . . Father, I pray not for the world, but for those whom thou hast given

me out of the world. . . .
And [Jesus] . . . came again
unto his disciples; . . . and
behold they were white, even
as Jesus.

The third time in giving
thanks for the seven loaves
[the prayer is not quoted].

3 Nephi 19:31-33. And
. . . he went again a little
way off and prayed unto the
Father; and tongue cannot
speak, . . . neither can be
written by man the words
which he prayed. And the
multitude did hear and do
bear record; and their hearts
were open and they did understand in their hearts the
words which he prayed.

The Lord invites the disciples to ask for higher things:

PO 2:135. Have you seen
[considered], O my beloved
ones, the love of Jesus towards his apostles; insomuch
that he did not conceal anything from them, even all the
things concerning his godhead?

3 Nephi 27:2. And Jesus
again showed himself unto
them, for they were praying
unto the Father in his name;
and Jesus came and stood in
the midst of them, and said
unto them: What will ye that
I shall give unto you?

They are abashed and have to be encouraged:

PO 2:135-36. Jesus saith
unto Thomas: Thomas my
friend, you and your brethren are free to ask me whatsoever you please and I will
keep nothing back from you.
Insomuch that you may see,
and feel [palpitate] and be
convinced in your heart. If

3 Nephi 28:1. And it
came to pass when Jesus had
said these words, he spake
unto his disciples, one by
one, saying unto them: What
is it that ye desire of me,
after that I am gone to the
Father?

3 Nephi 28:6. And he

you want to see those in their tombs revived, you do well to ask for a sign of the resurrection. For it was I myself who said to you, "I am the resurrection and the life" [John 11:25]. And also, if the ear of wheat does not die, there will be no yield [*karpos*]. And if you yourselves do not see with your eyes [1 John 1:1], your heart will not be confirmed in this.

PO 2:138-39. *Thomas wept* and said to Jesus: Thou hast taken all this trouble to come to the tomb . . . *because of my incredulity*. Let thy will be done and this tomb receive me until the day of the resurrection.

PO 2:136. Jesus said: *Thomas, be not afflicted;* that which I do, you know not; . . . I told you to move the stone so that a witness of the resurrection might appear in the tomb of death.

PO 2:136. You likewise, if you do not see with your eyes, you will not be strengthened in your hearts.

Have I not told you: More blessed are ye who have not seen and have believed than *ye who have seen* and not believed.

said unto them: Behold, I know your thoughts, and ye have desired the thing which John, my beloved, who was with me in my ministry, before that I was lifted up by the Jews, desired of me.

3 Nephi 28:3-6. And he said unto them: Blessed are ye because ye desired this thing of me; therefore, after that ye are seventy and two years old ye shall come unto me in my kingdom; and with me ye shall find rest. . . . He turned himself unto the three, and said unto them: What will ye that I should do unto you, when I am gone unto the Father? And *they sorrowed in their hearts, for they durst not speak* unto him the thing which they desired. And he said unto them: Behold, I know your thoughts, and ye desire the thing which John . . . desired of me.

3 Nephi 19:35-36. And it came to pass that when Jesus had made an end of praying he came again to the disciples, and said unto them: So great faith have I never seen *among all the Jews;* wherefore I could not show unto them so great miracles, because of their unbelief.

Ye had seen how many wonders and miracles I did in the presence of *the Jews*, and they *believed not* on me.

Verily I say unto you, there are *none of them* that have seen so *great things as ye have seen;* neither have they heard so great things as ye have heard.

The disciples are understandably embarrassed at having to ask questions which argue a lack of faith in the very presence of the resurrection. Here was the living Jesus before them, risen from the dead; and yet he knows that they are still unsettled in their minds. For how could they be guaranteed their own resurrection? After all, Jesus was a special case, the Son of God; but the men, women, and children he raised from the dead all had to die again. What about this? Are there levels and degrees of immortality? Is there a transition zone between the living and the dead? On these questions both of our sources at this point launch into earnest discussions. For the type of the human who is dead but not dead, raised from the dead but still not resurrected, the Gospel of the Twelve Apostles gives us Lazarus, while the Book of Mormon discusses the same matters as represented by the strange case of the Three Nephites.

PO 2:135. Thomas said to Jesus: My Lord, behold thou has granted us every favor in thy goodness. *There is just one thing* which we would like you to bestow on us. We want to see, O Lord, those people who were dead and buried, whom you revived [raised up], as a sign of thy *resurrection* which is to take place for us.

We know, Lord, that

thou didst raise up the son of the widow of Nain. But we are thinking of *another kind* of miracle, for you met with that multitude going along the road. What we want to see is the bones that have fallen apart in the tombs and are able to join together so that they can speak on the spot.

PO 2:137. Didymus boldly [took heart] said to him: My Lord, how shall we go to him since the Jews are seeking to stone thee? [He said this because he was worried by the things which Jesus had said about Lazarus and did not want to go.]

PO 2:136. Didymus [Thomas], come with me, let us go to Bethany, so that *I can show you the type of the resurrection* at the last day in the grave, that your heart may be strengthened that I am the resurrection and the life.

Come with me O Didymus, and I will show you the bones that have come apart in the tomb uniting themselves together again. . . . I will show the body hollow, putrefied eye-sockets

3 Nephi 28:7-8. Therefore, more blessed are ye, for ye shall never taste of death; . . . ye shall never endure the pains of death; but . . . ye shall be changed in the twinkling of an eye from mortality to immortality; and then shall ye be blessed in the kingdom of my Father.

3 Nephi 28:13. And they [all the disciples] were caught up into heaven.

3 Nephi 28:15. And whether they were in the body, they could not tell, for it did seem unto them *like a*

. . . devoid . . . the tongue of Lazarus, rotted away, which *will speak again* with thee.

transfiguration, . . . changed from this body of flesh into an immortal state.

3 Nephi 28:17. Now, whether they were mortal or immortal, from the day of their transfiguration, I know not.

PO 2:136-37. See that which the worm have eaten coming forth at my voice when I call. . . . *Thou seekest a sign of the resurrection, Thomas,* come and I will show it to you at the tomb of Lazarus.

3 Nephi 28:37. There must needs be a change wrought upon their bodies.

3 Nephi 28:39. Now this change was not equal to that which shall take place at the last day; but there was a change wrought upon them.

PO 2:137. You have asked about the stretched out hands; come and I will show you the hands of Lazarus wrapped in their bandages, tight in their shroud, which will be raised up as they come out of the tomb.

Didymus my friend, come with me to the tomb of Lazarus, for *my mouth desires what thou thought.*

3 Nephi 28:6. *I know your thoughts.*

3 Nephi 28:3. Blessed are ye because *ye desired* this thing of me.

PO 2:138. Jesus said to him: Didymus, *he who walks in the light trembleth not* [nor, is not offended]. Jesus said this to Thomas to console him when he saw that he

3 Nephi 18:16. And as I have prayed among you even so shall ye pray in my church, among my people who do repent and are baptized in my name. Behold *I*

was afflicted because of the
death of Lazarus.

am the light; I have set an example for you.

PO 2:137. And these are
the things which Jesus said to
his apostles.

PO 2:140. Jesus cried out,
saying: *My Father,* My Father,
root of all goodness, *I pray
unto thee,* for the moment has
come to *give glory to thy Son,*
that all may know that it is
Thou who hast sent *me* for
this. Glory unto thee unto
the eternity of the eternities.
Amen.

3 Nephi 19:29. *Father, I
pray* . . . for those whom
thou hast given me, . . . that
I may be in them as thou, Father, art in me, that we may
be one, *that I may be glorified
in them.*

No passage of scripture has puzzled theologians more
since the days of the primitive church than 1 Peter 3:18-
19; 4:6, the brief notice of the descent of Christ to preach
to the dead, "regarded by some," as MacCulloch observes,
"as wholly enigmatic," because "the plain meaning of the
passages conflicted with the interpreters' views of the nature of life beyond the grave."[7] Descent to *what?* was the
question. Not to the Underworld, certainly, was St. Augustine's conclusion—too primitive and naive for words.[8]
To what, then? There are three missions of Christ, three
descents in the Gospels: (1) As a mortal condescending to
mortals, (2) as a spirit, ministering to spirits in their deep
prison, (3) as a glorified, resurrected being who frequently
descends during the forty days to minister to certain mortals who share in his glory in special manifestations,
as described in the Gospel of the Twelve Apostles and
3 Nephi. Since the second mission is rejected by the doctors
of the church, in the allegorizing spirit of the times they
had no trouble in making the Petrine passage refer to the
first: The Lord descended to those in this life only who sat
in the dark prison of ignorance, who were disobedient *like*

those of Noah's day, and so on. Thus they confine the Petrine doctrine to the Lord's mortal mission, as does the modern Catholic explanation, that "the effect of Christ's preaching extended to the lost [in Limbo, not in Hell], without His having actually descended to them."⁹

But that third mission was hard to shake. "Whether the Petrine passages referred to the descent or not, the doctrine itself, wherever derived, soon became a most vital one in early Christian thought."¹⁰ And the farther back we go in the record the more conspicuous it becomes. The famous "Harrowing of Hell" mystery play is only its final expression, taken from the earlier Gospel of Nicodemus and other still earlier sources well attested at least in the second century.¹¹ Indeed, MacCulloch suggests that "Jewish belief in the possibility of good news being announced to the dead" goes clear back to the ancient prophets, including Isaiah (Isaiah 51:1; 52:7; 49:9).¹²

In this third realm we run into a strangely ambiguous state of things, confronted by an impressive cast of characters who have died, are raised from the dead as an earnest of the resurrection, and then have to die again! There was the host of those risen from the dead of Galilee; the pair Lenthius and Charinus who went to Jerusalem to deposit their written affidavits to the resurrection and then returned to their tombs;¹³ or the two in Arimathaea who, "having given up their writings . . . were transfigured, exceeding white, and were no more seen." On the way to enlist the testimonies of Charinus and Lenthius, Nicodemus, Joseph, and three rabbis "meet twelve thousand who have risen."¹⁴ All of these were raised from the dead only to return to the grave.

Since none of these risen ones are mentioned in the scriptures, however, the test case would have to be Lazarus, who appears at all three levels in the Gospels. We find *a* Lazarus speaking from "Abraham's bosom" on high to one in the depths of hell—communicating between the worlds (Luke 16:20-25). On earth we find a very human Lazarus, the friend of Jesus, who goes the way of mortality only to be recalled from the tomb (John 11:1-43). He is the obvious candidate to witness what went on in both worlds; the perfect living example of those ambivalent beings who in their persons prove the resurrection and yet are still subject to death, like the three Nephites and the host of witnesses mentioned above. Lazarus's experience is put to good use in the early Christian dramatizations. In the dialogue between Death and Hades that is the opening scene of the "Harrowing of Hell," Hades is distressed at the prospect of one who has but recently snatched Lazarus from his power; "Have mercy on me," cries Hades; "do not bring Him here, for He is great!"[15] Lazarus is the test case, the proof of the reality of the whole thing. As such he appears frequently in the accounts of the *Kerygma*.[16]

Viewing the three types of descent, we must admit that one is not more miraculous than the other; actually, Christ's visits during the forty-day mission are no more incredible than the other two, and all are attested by an interesting interweaving of documents which deserve much closer study in which the Book of Mormon scores many points.

In early Christian ordinances, ties are clearly established between the three levels. Thus, the designation of baptism as *photismos* or "light-bringing" was by the early saints "sometimes symbolized as an actual light, the result of Christ's presence, shining in the gloom of hades," which is mentioned as early as the Odes of Solomon. Does that mean baptism was connected with the Lord's visits to the world below as well as to the world above? MacCulloch thinks so, for the preaching must be followed by baptism: "All this is in keeping with the custom of vicarious baptism" (1 Corinthians 15:29). [17] So the overpoweringly dramatic appearance of the Lord to the Nephites sitting in darkness, identifying himself to them as "the light and the life," has its counterpart in the world below. Baptism was an initiation into the church, and an important part of the Lord's Descent to the Underworld is the way in which he galvanizes the spirits there (*excitavit et erexit*), and organizes them, as they form up in special marshaling areas[18] or form into a procession behind Adam and the Patriarchs, the grand parade that is the climax and conclusion of the "Harrowing of Hell."[19] In a word, the Lord organizes the church, as he does in the Book of Mormon, of those who are about to be saved and led out of darkness.

And so, we may well ask, "What imposter with no text or precedent to guide him could hope to venture into the unexplored morass of the Old World forty-day accounts where to this day the student finds no solid foothold, without quickly coming to grief?" The calm, unhesitating deliberation with which the author of 3 Nephi proceeds where religious scholars and poets have feared to tread has been explained as an example of Joseph Smith's impudence—a desperate argument. The other explanation—that he was translating an authentic document—deserves a fair hearing.

Notes

1. See Krister Stendahl, "The Sermon on the Mount and Third Nephi," in *Reflections on Mormonism*, ed. Truman G. Madsen (Provo: BYU Religious Studies Center, 1978), 139-54.

2. Hugh W. Nibley, "Evangelium Quadraginta Dierum," *Vigiliae Christianae* 20 (1966): 1-24; reprinted in *CWHN* 4:10-44.

3. Ibid., 7; in *CWHN* 4:13.

4. Ibid., 18-21; in *CWHN* 4:18-19.

5. E.g., Erik Hornung, "Des Amduat: Die Schrift des verborgenen Raumes, Teil 3," in *Aegyptische Abhandlungen* (Wiesbaden: Harrassowitz, 1967).

6. E. Revillout, *Les Apocryphes Coptes, Première Partie, Les évangiles des douze apôtres et de Saint Barthélemy*, in *PO* 2:123-30.

7. John A. MacCulloch, *The Harrowing of Hell* (Edinburgh: Clark, 1930), 50.

8. Ibid., 50-51.

9. Ibid., 50-56, discusses six different interpretations. Quote is

THE PROPHETIC BOOK OF MORMON

from 53.

10. Ibid., 65.

11. In such early Christian classics as Ignatius, Clement, the Odes of Solomon, etc., ibid., 241. In the Shepherd of Hermas, and the Epistle of the Apostles, which are all very early, ibid., 246.

12. MacCulloch, *The Harrowing of Hell*, 252.

13. Ibid., 158-60.

14. Ibid., 158-60, 170-71.

15. Ibid., 177-78.

16. Ibid., 177; cf. 290, n. 2; 333.

17. Ibid., cf. 15, 240-52; quote is from 248.

18. Ibid., 260-65; cf. 15.

19. The most available text of the "Harrowing of Hell" is found in The Gospel of Nicodemus in the popular reprint volume entitled *The Lost Books of the Bible and the Forgotten Book of Eden*, ed. Rutherford H. Pratt (Cleveland: World Publishing, 1926), 63-91. The magazine version of this material, *Ensign* 13 (July 1983):17-18, added the following synopsis of the "Harrowing of Hell" in the Gospel of Nicodemus:

"When the Lord returned from his Easter absence in another world, 'the question was bound to arise,' writes MacCulloch, 'What did Christ's soul do there?' And the answer: 'As Christ was active for good on earth, so also would He be in Hades [world of spirits]. . . . As he preached the good news on earth, so also would he preach it in Hades' (p. 315). For the early Christians, 'Hades, Paradise, Heaven, were regarded as *local* places,' the spirit world not being utterly removed from anything earthly (p. 318). In the Old World Descent literature, the same type of work by the Lord and the Apostles—preaching, baptizing, teaching—goes on whether on earth or in the spirit world (pp. 55, 169).

"It is such parallels as these that could well cause religious scholars to ask if the writer of 3 Nephi drew upon the Descent Literature and the Old World forty-day stories as source material. The problem is that the forty-day literature was unknown in the 1820s, and the Descent literature had no credit with the clergy. MacCulloch himself is left in a quandary: 'The old doctrine of the Descent . . . need not be taken literally. Yet we cannot regard it as mere "dead wood" as the clergy do today' (p. 232). The many hints in the scriptures only sowed confusion among the theologians—due, they said, to (1) 'our Lord's constant reticence both with regard to the Other World and with regard to Himself, and (2) the whole nature of the Descent doctrine with its notions of a *local* underworld' (p. 317).

"These concepts the doctors of the church simply could not accept. Exactly like the Old World forty-day teachings, the Descent was a carefully guarded doctrine. Its most famous expression was in the apocryphal Gospel of Nicodemus. The Gospel was written by 'an early writer, using traditional materials,' which was later 'transformed into one of the most popular of mystery Plays—the Harrowing of Hell.' A brief look at Nicodemus with 3 Nephi in mind is in order. Keep in mind that the Gospel of Nicodemus is apocryphal and as such contains some details that will not jibe with the true accounts found in scripture. Still, the similarities are numerous.

"The *Descensus* story begins 'with our fathers in the depth of hell, the blackness of darkness' (Nic. 13:3). Suddenly a great light appears, and Adam announces, 'That light is the author of everlasting light' (13:3–4). Chapter 16 is devoted to the Gates of Hell, which no longer prevail against those who accept the King of Glory. Then Jesus 'stretched forth his hand, and said, Come unto me, all ye my saints' (19:1), and proceeded to organize the Church among them (19:1–3). Adam and all the rest cast themselves at the Savior's feet and with one voice acknowledge him as their Redeemer (19:4–8). Stretching forth his hand again, he introduces Adam and then 'all his saints' to the mark of the crucifixion (19:11). Then, 'taking hold of Adam by his right hand, he ascended from hell' into a higher realm, 'and all the saints of God followed him' (19:12).

"A strange episode concludes the story in this aprocryphal tale. We are faced with the condition of Enoch and Elijah, 'who have not tasted death' but must still go on a three-day mission to Jerusalem, be put to death, and 'be taken up again into the clouds' (20:1–4). Similarly, the final chapter reports that the whole account has been written by two special witnesses. These were 'Charinus and Lenthius,' who were 'not allowed to declare the other mysteries of God,' or to communicate with men except on special occasions (21:3). 'We have only three days allowed' in Jerusalem, they note, after which 'now they are not seen by anyone' (21:5). The reason is that they have been 'commanded to go beyond Jordan, to an excellent far country' to continue their labors (21:4). These two men, according to the story, were the pair also known as the sons of Simeon, who supposedly after being raised from the dead were sent on this special mission by the Lord to testify of his resurrection. After finishing their work in the Old World, they 'were changed into exceeding white forms and were seen no more' (21:8).

"The account of the Savior's visit to the New World ends on a similar note. Just before his departure, three of his disciples ask to remain on the earth to minister among men. Their request is granted, and a 'change' is 'wrought upon their bodies' that 'they might not taste of death' (3 Nephi 28:38). Thereafter they ministered to the Nephites and Lamanites, eventually to go 'unto all nations, kindreds, tongues and people. . . . They are as angels of God,' although unrecognized and unknown. (See 3 Nephi 28:25–32.)"

20

The Prophetic Book of Mormon

There are many prophecies in the Book of Mormon, far more than the casual reader would suspect. Some have been fulfilled; some have yet to be. I want to talk about one dominant prophetic theme, which is for us here and now the most important of them all. The editors of the Book of Mormon, Mormon and Moroni, give this theme top priority and bring it to our attention as a matter of life and death. The whole Book of Mormon from beginning to end gives it maximum emphasis. As we all know, that strange and powerful book is a voice from the dust, a message from a departed people, a step-by-step account of how all their deeds and accomplishments came to be expunged from the memory of man while other far older civilizations in the Old World have survived to this day.

At the center of ancient American studies today lies the overriding question, "Why did the major civilizations collapse so suddenly, so completely, and so mysteriously?" The answer now given by the overwhelming majority of those scholars as contained, for example, in T. P. Culbert's valuable collection of studies on the subject, is that society as a whole suffered a process of *polarization* into two separate and opposing ways of life, an increased distance between peasant and noble, as W. T. Sanders puts it, that went along with growing hostility between cities and na-

This speech was delivered at the BYU Alumni House, September 23, 1981, and was printed under the same title in Seventh East Press, 1 (27 March 1982): 6-8, 16-17.

tions as resource margins declined.[1] The polarizing syndrome is a habit of thought and action that operates at all levels, from family feuds like Lehi's to the battle of galaxies. It is the pervasive polarization described in the Book of Mormon and sources from other cultures which I wish now to discuss briefly, ever bearing in mind that the Book of Mormon account is addressed to future generations, not to "harrow up their souls," but to tell them how to get out of the type of dire impasse which it describes. Moroni is explicit: "And this cometh unto you, O ye Gentiles, . . . that ye may repent, . . . that ye may not bring down the fulness of the wrath of God upon you as the inhabitants of the land have hitherto done" (Ether 2:11). And again Moroni says: "Give thanks unto God that he hath made manifest unto you our imperfections, that ye may learn to be more wise than we have been" (Mormon 9:31).

What we are to avoid in particular is that polarizing process that begins on the first page of the Book of Mormon and continues to the last. In the opening scene it is Egypt versus Babylon, West versus East, with Lehi's people caught in the middle; and the book ends with the climactic confrontation at Cumorah, with Moroni caught between two wicked and warring peoples in a battle of annihilation. The Book of Mormon is the story of the fearful passage that led from the one situation to the other. Every Latter-day Saint knows that it is a tale of Nephites versus Lamanites, conveniently classified as the Good Guys versus the Bad Guys. In a book called *Since Cumorah,* I pointed out that a line drawn between the two peoples does not automatically separate the righteous from the wicked at all.[2] Far from it—the Lamanites were often the good guys and the Nephites the bad guys; and they had a way of shifting back and forth from one category to the other with disturbing frequency. In the end, as Mormon sadly observes in letters to his son, it is a toss-up as to which of the two is the worse. Cumorah was no showdown between good and evil; it was not even a contest to pick the winner, for while the Nephites did get wiped out, the Lamanites went right on wiping each other out, "and no one knoweth the end of the war" (Mormon 8:8). Speaking of another final showdown, which ended in the extermination of *both* nations, Moroni turns to address us directly: "And thus *we* see that the Lord did visit them" when "*their* wickedness and abominations [not their enemies!] had prepared a way for *their* everlasting destruction" (Ether 14:25). He wants to make sure we do not miss the point.

The often dangerous polarization between Nephites and Lamanites was no imaginary thing. It was very real, from beginning to end. Right at the outset God explained to Nephi that it was going to be both real and permanent. He wanted it that way for a definite purpose: "Inasmuch as thy brethren shall rebel against thee, they shall be cut off from the presence of the Lord. . . . I will curse them even with a sore curse, and they shall have no power over thy seed except they shall rebel against me also"; *then* "they shall be a scourge unto thy seed, to stir them up in the ways of remembrance" (1 Nephi 2:21-24). The Nephites would never be able to remove the Lamanite threat by knocking them out. Every time the Nephites tried that solution they suffered severe losses, and in the end, when after a series of brilliant victories they determined to "cut them off from the face of the land" (Mormon 3:10) and end the Lamanite menace once and for all, the Nephites got themselves exterminated.

The process of polarization works like the elimination in a tennis tournament that begins with a large number of contestants for the prize, and by pairing them off two by two ends up with a final pair and winds up with a single Numero Uno. Thus Amalickiah, the most competent of a long line of ambitious and unscrupulous men in the Book of Mormon, removes all competitors one by one, uniting ever growing numbers of his opponents' followers into a political party and then into a mighty conglomerate army. All this he does in preparation for a showdown with his archenemy, Moroni, whose blood he swore to drink. Moroni was the intolerable obstacle between Amalickiah and his goal, which was to be Number One. It is the age-old story of the three rivals for the kingdom, the treasure, and the inheritance, in which two combine in secret to surprise and kill the third, after which they must fight it out between themselves, each of them having prepared a trap ahead of time that destroys the other.

How it works in history may be viewed in a terrible account of conditions in the Christian churches of the fourth century as given by St. Basil. In the confused political situation at the beginning of the century, he says, everyone wanted to give orders and nobody would take them; men were willing to cooperate on anything only as the most effective means of crippling the common enemy, after which they would turn against each other. The final survivor and undisputed Number One was Constantine the Great. But, to quote our own study on the subject: "No sooner had Constantine removed his last civil and *military* opponents than the issue between his Christian and pagan subjects became acute." No sooner had he put the pagans in their place, than "the churchmen started accusing each other of heresy with a wild abandon that surpassed—as the Emperor himself observed—any performance of the heathen. No sooner had his successors removed the last heretic and received the undying thanks of the church, than the *true* believers were at each others' throats."[3] The problem was never solved, for in this life we can expect opposition in all things.

The Jaredite Experience

Nowhere is the process brought into sharper analytical focus than in a history that Moroni inserted between his father's book and his own as the supreme example of the polarizing mania that destroyed his own people. That history is the story of the Jaredites, "who were destroyed by the hand of the Lord upon the face of this north country" (Ether 1:1). While the Nephite epic is told with all the depth and power of a Thucydides, the case of the Jaredites, whom Moroni never knew, is set forth as a clinical study. In reading it we seem to be watching some organism through a microscope, first undergoing a process of fission, after which one part attacks and convulsively consumes part or all of the other, and then after a pause begins to show signs of splitting to start the process all over again.

It will be necessary to run through this dismal tale at some length to bring out the full flavor of its insanity. A grand cycle running from unity of the nation to division, conflict, and hence to paralysis or extinction is repeated at least a dozen times, with significant variations over which we cannot linger here.

The sorry round begins when one Corihor, the great-grandson of the original Jared, rebelled against his father the king, moved out of the land, and "drew away many people after him" (Ether 7:4), until he had an army that was able to beat the king and take him captive. Corihor was now what he wanted to be — Number One — until his brother Shule beat him and restored the kingdom to their father, again Number One. Then Corihor does a surprising thing — he repents — and Shule gives him a share of the kingdoms; that is the first time around. Each cycle ends with repentance; it is repentance alone that saves the people from total extinction as they move from one period to the next.

Later Corihor's son rebelled "and drew away . . . all his brethren and many of the people" (Ether 7:15), whereupon he captured Shule and became Number One, until the sons of Shule conspired and murdered him, and Shule became Number One for the third time. Under his rule there came prophets telling the people to repent or be destroyed. The people did repent — and prospered: Second cycle.

Years later one Jared "did flatter many people . . . until he had gained the half of the kingdom" (Ether 8:2) from his father Omer, whose other sons beat Jared and reinstated Omer as Number One. To get back the kingdom, Jared formed secret combinations bound by oaths: "The oaths . . . were given by them of old who also sought power . . . to help such as sought power to gain power" (Ether 8:15-16). The secret of the operation was "to keep [the people] in darkness" (Ether 8:16). We shall have something to say of *power* hereafter — the word occurs some 386 times in the Book of Mormon. Jared was killed by his son-in-law Akish; then Akish, wary of his own son, starved him to death, whereupon another son left the country and joined the deposed king Omer with his followers. Akish was a hard man to beat because he had "won the hearts of the people" by knowing just what they wanted: "The people of Akish were desirous for gain, even as Akish was desirous for power" (Ether 9:11); but his sons could also play the game, and with money "they drew away the more part of the people after them" (Ether 9:11). The war that ensued encompassed "the destruction of nearly all the people of the kingdom" (Ether 9:12), only thirty having the good sense to leave the scene instead of standing up to be counted.

With things thus sadly set to rights, the Lord took the curse off the land, until one Heth "began to embrace the secret plans again of old, to destroy his father" (Ether 9:26), and (need we add?) to become Number One: he "slew him with his own sword; and he did reign in his stead" (Ether 9:27). Enter the prophets again, announcing that the people "should be destroyed if they did not repent" (Ether 9:28). It was a terrible drought and famine that brought repentance and better conditions until one "Morianton . . . gathered together an army of outcasts," and after a long war "he did gain power over all the land, and did establish himself king over all the land" (Ether 10:9). And Morianton was a very good king; his son and successor Kim was captured by his brother, who became Number One, but Kim's son Levi made war against him and thus became Number One. Levi was also a good king. One Com, whose father had lost the kingdom and had been imprisoned for twenty-four years, "drew away the half of the kingdom," and after forty years challenged the king of the other half, Amgid. Following a long war, Com "obtained power over the remainder of the kingdom" (Ether 10:32). His son Shiblom slew the prophets, who had again stated the proposition that the people must repent or be utterly destroyed (Ether 11:5). Yet later the people began to repent and were blessed.

After yet another killer came "many prophets" with the usual message: "The Lord would utterly destroy them . . . except they repented of their iniquities" (Ether 11:12). This time there was no repentance, for the people "hardened their hearts, . . . and the prophets mourned and withdrew from among the people" (Ether 11:13). From that time on it was all downhill. A mighty man led a revolt against the king and kept half the kingdom for many years until the king overcame him and became Number One again. Then another mighty man took *him* captive. Again many prophets came with the usual warning and the assurance that "God would send or bring forth another people to possess the land" (Ether 11:21), while Ether himself preached from sunrise to sunset, exhorting the people "unto repentance lest they should be destroyed" (Ether 12:3). Then the thing became a free-for-all, with "many who rose up, who were mighty men" (Ether 13:15), all zeroing in on King Coriantumr. But he was a great survivor—he knew all the tricks, and he kept afloat while people around him died like flies. Bad as the king was, Ether told him that "the Lord would give unto him his kingdom and spare the people" (Ether 13:20) if they would repent. But the polarizing process had gone too far—nobody could afford to repent (in war, one has only one thought in mind), "and the wars ceased not" (Ether 13:22). Shared put Coriantumr in captivity and became Number One, until Coriantumr's son freed and restored Coriantumr to that glorious position. By then there was a complete breakdown of all government, with "every man with his band fighting for that which he desired" (Ether 13:25). Coriantumr and Shared became obsessed with the necessity of ridding the world of each other and chased each other back and forth as the land went to pot—nothing was secure anywhere, everything would get ripped off—it was as bad as a modern city. This insecurity led to a gun-and-shelter mania, as "every man did cleave unto that which was his own, . . . and every man kept the hilt of his sword in his right hand [to get it you would have to pry it from his cold, dead fingers], in the defense of his property and his own life and of his wives and children" (Ether 14:2). When Shared defeated one of Coriantumr's armies, he raced to the capital and put himself on the man's throne— Number One at any price.

Then the process of polarization began in earnest: Coriantumr gathered "great strength to his army" (Ether 14:7) for the space of two years, while Gilead, the brother and successor of Shared, was doing the same, assisted by secret combinations. They were dangerous associates, however, for they soon murdered Gilead and then liquidated his murderer, while a giant by the name of Lib became king. He was killed fighting Coriantumr, but his brother continued the feud—he was Shiz. As he "[swept] the earth before him," the "people began to flock together in armies, throughout all the face of the land. And they were divided; and a part of them fled to the army of Shiz, and a part of them fled to the army of Coriantumr" (Ether 14:18-20). Now polarization had reached the critical stage: "And thus we see that the Lord . . . had prepared a way for their everlasting destruction" (Ether 14:25), says Moroni, looking straight at us. As the people of Shiz retreated, they "swept off the inhabitants before them, all them that would not join them" (Ether 14:27). Meanwhile, "Coriantumr did gather his armies together upon the hill Comner, and did sound a trumpet unto the armies of Shiz to invite them forth to battle" (Ether 14:28), suggesting the formal set battles of epic literature and the Middle Ages, as "polarized" as a chess game.

After losing millions of people in battles, Coriantumr "began to repent" and wrote to Shiz, "desiring him that he would spare the people, and he would give up the kingdom for the sake of the lives of the people" (Ether 15:3-4). It was of course a personal feud—the world polarizes around over-rated individuals—and Shiz agreed, "if [Coriantumr] would give himself up, that [Shiz] might slay him with his own sword" (Ether 15:5). That was going too far—nobody repented, and both sides "were stirred up to anger" (Ether 15:6) and would have nothing but total victory. Now comes the last act: "They did gather together all the people upon all the face of the land, . . . the people who were for Coriantumr were gathered together to the army of Coriantumr; and the people who were for Shiz were gathered together to the army of Shiz. . . . For the space of four years [they were] gathering together the people," total mobilization including women and children, "every one to the army which he would" (Ether 15:12-15). Everybody had to stand up and be counted. Coriantumr, sizing up the situation, repeated his offer of coexistence to Shiz, but nobody would have it, "for they were given up unto the hardness of their hearts, and the blindness of their minds that they might be destroyed; wherefore they went again to battle" (Ether 15:19). But the insanity could have been halted even then if they would have thought of repenting. Not a chance: "They were drunken with anger, even as a man who is drunken with wine; and they slept again upon their swords" (Ether 15:22). Then "Shiz arose, and also his men, and he swore in his wrath that he would slay Coriantumr or he would perish by the sword" (Ether 15:28), which he did. Coriantumr enjoyed the advantage of being a little less bad (he had suggested peace talks) and was allowed to live a little longer, alone in utter misery. Thus the polar tension was dissolved, the wicked destroyed the wicked, and Coriantumr remained all alone, the undisputed Number One. In *The World of the Jaredites*, we showed that the Jaredite scenario is not at all as fantastic as it sounds to us: it was the normal perennial Asiatic madness of the great Khans and War-Lords of the Steppes.[4] But now, thirty years after, it does not sound fantastic at all, this picture of two halves of humanity destroying each other—it is alarmingly prophetic.

The Roman Experience

Thirty years ago I wrote another study of polarization in the ancient world—the situation in the time of Constantine. It is such an opposite illustration of what we are talking about that I may be forgiven for quoting from it at some length. Here the Romans and the new Super-States of the East were facing each other in a fatal showdown that exhausted both civilizations. At that time, I wrote, "the concept of Romanitas [was] . . . very close indeed to that 'Western Civilization' by which one conjures in our own day." "Rome [citing Aelius Aristides and Prudentius, for this was a well-documented article] . . . is civilization itself, the free world of free men, a new race sprung from the mixed blood of all the nations."[5] Its way of life was the only one for civilized men and was bound to become that of all mankind, and so on. The Romans were the Good Guys: "*Hic est Ausonia*, the Western World of clean, fresh, simple, unspoiled pioneers. . . . Rome was great because Rome was good. The emperors who . . . took the names of Pius and Felix were giving expression to the old Roman belief in the close association between piety and success. . . . Teachers and orators drilled the essentials of Western goodness into their pupils and auditors until, by the fourth century, when hardly a speck of ancient virtue remained, men could talk of nothing else but that virtue."[6] Again I cannot resist quoting what I wrote thirty years ago because it seems so prophetic, too. The principal exponents of the doctrine from the beginning had been the Roman Patres, "aristocratic, senatorial, traditionalist, anti-oriental." "No word was dearer to them than *libertas* [freedom], . . . but 'the *nobiles* conceived of this popular catchword as meaning freedom for them to exercise their *dignitas*,' and not for people without money. In the fourth century they 'had plenty to say about their *humanitas, philanthropia*, . . . their mercy, their pious serenity. . . . But such self-praise carries no weight; the choice words are mere empty form.' In the Senate they called loudly for arms to defend civilization—when no personal sacrifice was involved; and when the barbarians were at the gates they spent their time not in meeting the foe but in hysterical attacks on possible subversives."[7]

Scholars have marveled that the magnificent military equipment and huge armies of professional soldiers " 'were not more effective than they were, and that the closely knit network of skillfully deployed fortresses let the invaders pass through it many times.' This grim defect is attributed first to the economies of the government, which, while giving away enormous wealth to individuals, so reduced and neglected the personnel of the border forces that 'the strong places, badly manned, were simply forgotten, often without garrisons,' and second to the low morale and frequent desertions of the underpaid soldiers who remained [especially in Germany]. Nobody who could pay for defense was willing to do it."[8] "The great landowners, who were also the industrialists of the times, 'ap-

preciated civilization and culture very highly,' says Rostovtzeff, 'their political outlook was narrow, their servility
was unbounded. But their external appearance was majes-
tic, and their grand air impressed even the barbarians.' "⁹
" 'The earth is the mother of all of us,' said the starving
field-hands and factory workers, 'for she gives equally; but
you pretend that she is your mother only.' "¹⁰ "Skimming
the cream of the world's natural resources on their vast,
tax-free estates, these men thought of themselves as
natural-born leaders of men. . . . Under the early emperors 'the state's sphere of activity had been curtailed to an
astonishing degree; the state simply secured peace and law
in the world and then turned it over to private exploita-
tion.' "¹¹

"But when in the fourth century the Imperial government went after a larger share of the income in order to
support costly wars of defense," of which they approved
so loudly, the great landowners were not among the contributors. "They quickly became experts in evading taxation and shifting the expenses of war and government to
others." Their speculations in grain drove the Emperor
Julian to threaten publicly " 'to have all gentlemen arrested' for sabotaging his attempts at price control. They
in reply accused . . . [him] of low demagoguery in trying
to fix minimum grain prices in the face of drought and an
artificial boom market created by the army; and they not
only refused to sell at government prices, but bought up
what grain they could at those prices to resell on the black
market or outside the price-control zone. Small wonder
that bishops, government officials, and the common
people blamed 'the rich' for deliberately engineering famines that were profitable to themselves."¹²

We have much more to say in the article on the same
subject. What had kept a society, split down the middle
from the earliest times between *Patres* and *Plebs*, from falling apart was practiced application of the maxim *Externus*

timor, maximum concordiae vinculum, or, the secret of unity is to find an external foe. "Since Republican times Parthia had been 'the type and representative of the untamed Orient,' the Eastern peril, the symbol of Asiatic barbarism; but when the Parthians were absorbed by the revived and highly centralized Persian Empire, . . . or under a superman such as Attila, conditions were present for a true world-polarization, with the East replying in kind to Western charges of barbarism and aggression."[13] Each side described itself as the "free world and its rival as a slave-state" in one of those ideological debates in which neither side is ever beaten. "On both sides the ancient propaganda of freedom has a singularly hollow ring," because each was being torn and tattered by fits of internal polarization, that *factio,* the restless, narrow, angry and violent defense of special interests which, according to the ancient observers, was what really destroyed the Empire. Each half of the world "was in itself a world of factions and parties, of rival ideologies and rival cultures pitted against each other in deadly conflict, yet so exactly alike in everything but label [and usually the rivals were contending for the possession of some world-commanding label – the same label] as to give the impression that one antagonist is simply a mirror-image of the other."[14]

This is a very important principle. As the two poles conceive an ever-greater antipathy to each other, they become more and more *alike.* Everyone knows that it is like poles that repel each other. As each recognizes itself in the other, it resents the incriminating resemblance. "It was the custom of the emperors of Rome and Asia to describe themselves in identical terms, while each accused his rival of being nothing but a base forgery and depraved imitation of himself."[15] "We have not here a real clash of ideologies at all, but only the rivalry of parties animated by identical principles and racing for the same objectives."[16] What they were both after was, to use the Book of Mormon formula, "power and gain." And the secret of commanding loyalty on both sides was, of course, to play up the wickedness of the other. In the fourth century, this was done systematically in church and school.

"Just as all obedient subjects are embraced in a single shining community, so all outsiders are necessarily members of a single conspiracy of evil. . . . It can be shown by a most convenient syllogism that since God is on our side, we cannot show any degree of toleration for any opposition without incurring infinite guilt. . . . One does not need to quibble; there is no such thing as being partly wrong or mistaken; the painful virtue of forbearance and the labor of investigation no longer embarrass the champions of one-package loyalty. No matter how nobly and austerely the heretics may live, for St. Augustine they are still Anti-Christ — all of them, equally and indiscriminately; their virtues are really vices, their virginity carnality, their reason unreason, their patience in persecutions mere insolence; any cruelty shown to them is not really cruelty but kindness. . . . [For] heresy in any degree is a crime against God, and is not any crime against God an infinite sin?" As Alföldi points out, the logic of polarization is irrefutable — and utterly without conscience, but it is also inevitable.[17]

The empire of the fourth century was a world of displaced persons, inevitably drawn toward the big city. To take the place of the old, lost loyalty to hearth and home-land — the *prisca fides* — strong measures had to be taken; a new super-loyalty was needed to guarantee the permanence of the social order: men were taught to declare allegiance to a super-thing, a noble abstraction loosely designated as *Romania* or *Romanitas,* whose binding cement was a carefully cultivated hostility to *Barabria,* the threatening world of the Steppes of Asia. The idea of the two worlds was moreover no mere fiction of government propaganda; it was an intimate reality. It was "the age-long struggle to repel, check, or annihilate the perennial enemy," described by J. B. Bury as "the eternal question, . . . the strife between Europe and Asia, between East and West, between Aryan and non-Aryan."[18] All around the civilized periphery of Asia, "the hordes of the heartland" had for centuries been dealt with in the same ways: "By subtle and disruptive diplomacy, by the long and costly *limes,* by punitive and deterrent expeditions, and, when all else has failed, by the reluctant absorption of their barbarian conquerors."[19]

To command loyalty and secure their own power, the rulers of Rome made the most of this confrontation. "To the lessons of the schools, carefully supervised by the government, was added a more aggressive policy of deliberately widening the gulf between the Two Worlds" — Planned Polarization. "For centuries barbarian and Roman, East and West, had been mingling on terms of greatest intimacy, producing a borderline culture in which it was quite impossible to draw the line between one culture and another. Priscus mentions quite casually the presence of people from the West, visiting relatives in the camps of the Asiatics; he notes the busy coming and going of merchants between the Two Worlds, and he describes the kind hospitality shown him, a complete stranger, in the homes of the Easterners. But with this he gives us the other side of the picture — the official side: the ubiquitous activity of spies and agents in Roman pay, the infusion into the very court of Attila of large sums of Roman money to corrupt and divide, the insane and mounting conviction of the rulers of the two halves of the world (both barbarians!), each [believing] that his way was the divine calling to liberate the human race from the intolerable ambition of the other."[20]

Two Contemporary Cases of Dangerous Polarization

With the Jaredite and Roman examples before us, let us turn to the two most notable exponents of world-

polarization in the land today. Both accept the drastic splitting of the globe into mutually antithetical halves; but their
own interpretations are poles apart.

The position of the first, Richard Nixon, is supremely
simple and straightforward: It is the Good Guys on one
side and the Bad Guys on the other, and that explains
everything: "It may seem melodramatic," he writes in the
conclusion of his book, "to treat the twin poles of human
experience represented by the United States and the Soviet
Union as the equivalent of Good and Evil, Light and Darkness, God and the Devil; yet if we allow ourselves to think
of them that way, even hypothetically, it can help clarify
our perspective of the world struggle."[21] If it hardly clarifies
the picture, it certainly simplifies it, as the writer continues,
"The U.S. represents hope, freedom, security, and peace.
The Soviet Union stands for fear, tyranny, aggression, and
war. If these are not poles of good and evil in human affairs,
then the concepts of good and evil have no meaning. Those
who cannot see the distinction have little claim to lecture
on conscience."[22]

So there you have it: There are just two poles, and we
are all at one pole and they are all at the other. Their evil
deeds repel us, yet, strange to say, we do everything they
do—because *they* force us to! "Soviet strategy is not defensive; it is designed to secure victory. The only answer
to a strategy of victory on the Soviet side is [a] strategy of
victory for the West."[23] If they play dirty, "we too can fight
the twilight war . . . in the hazardous mufti of the CIA."
In another shrewd move, "the Russians have been giving
their clients guns, while we have been giving ours lectures
on human rights."[24] No more of that—we now do everything they do. We must fight them because they do all
those bad things—and to fight them, we too must do all
those same bad things. Thus, just like them, we must give
up desirable social goals to attain military aims.[25]

"We have no choice but to . . . counterpose our military strength to that of the Soviet Union," which, of course, leaves them no choice but to counter ours. "This is the way to avoid defeat,"[26] he tells us. Finding ourselves constantly threatened, in reply we should be as much a threat to them as they are to us. We should "knock down the 'no trespassing signs' " and "declare ourselves as free to forage on the Soviet's side as they have been to forage on ours."[27] "The Soviet leaders can be utterly ruthless in their use of power," which we can counter "only if the West develops a sense of purpose equal to theirs — though different from theirs."[28] How different? To the Soviets anyone who stands in the way of their supremacy — of their hegemony — is an adversary — and what else is anyone who stands in Mr. Nixon's way but an adversary on his enemy list? We can never have peace with them because "the Soviet leadership has no concept of 'peace' as we understand it, or of coexistence as we would define it. They do not believe in the concept of equals. An equal is, by their definition, a rival, to be eliminated before he eliminates you."[29] Mr. Nixon's sentiments exactly: No reconciliation, no coexistence, no avoidance of war is to be thought of — because they will not allow it. The thesis of Mr. Nixon's book, if not of his life, is that we are constantly being threatened; and there is only one way to meet the threat, coming as it does from a source of irredeemable evil, and that is by *power* — the enemy understands no other argument: "To meet the challenge of our own survival . . . we must drastically increase our military *power*, shore up our economic *power*, reinvigorate our will *power*, strengthen the *power* of our Presidents, and develop a strategy aimed not just at avoiding defeat [that would leave us still feeling threatened] but at attaining victory."[30] "Victory requires knowing when to use *power*." He quotes James M. Burns: "Presidents must have a will to *power*; . . . they must constantly search for *power*, building it, if necessary, out of every scrap of formal authority and personal influence they can locate. They must constantly guard whatever *power* they have achieved. They must hoard *power* so that it will be available in the future."[31] One man alone has "the specific responsibility" to ensure "the nation's survival and the free world's future," through the "effective use of power" that "only experience can teach," and so on.[32]

At this point we cannot but call to mind the situation in the days of Enoch: "In those days Satan had great dominion among men, and raged in their hearts; and from thenceforth came wars and bloodshed . . . because of secret works, seeking for *power*" (Moses 6:15). This also brings up Moroni's statement referred to above about "oaths . . . given by them of old who also sought *power*. . . . And they were kept up by the *power* of the devil to administer . . . unto the people, to keep them in darkness, to help such as sought *power* to gain *power*" (Ether 8:15-16). Granted that such power-seeking is bad on their side, what else can it be in those who imitate them? Secret works? To be sure, "secrecy is the *sine qua non* in the conduct of international relations, whether dealing with allies or adversaries."[33]

The Enoch situation recalls another quotation, far more recent, from President Spencer W. Kimball in his great bicentennial address: "We commit vast resources to the fabrication of . . . ships, planes, missiles, fortifications— and depend on them for deliverance. When threatened, we become anti-enemy instead of pro-kingdom of God. . . . What are we to fear when the Lord is with us? Can we not take the Lord at his word and exercise a particle of *faith* in him? . . . We must leave off the worship of modern-day idols and a reliance on the 'arm of flesh.' "[34] Mr. Nixon has an answer to that one: Faith without strength is futile.[35] What a revealing statement! Faith is the source of strength, the very power by which the worlds were created. To say it is helpless without military backing recalls an ancient saw: "I trust God but I feel better with money in the bank." In the spirit of the times we preach that to expect security without a four-man bodyguard is futile, when security is *not* to need a bodyguard; that charity without a guaranteed profit is futile, when charity means asking *no* profit; that free agency without strict supervision is futile, and so on. Mr. Nixon rejects Napoleon's dictum that in the end it is the spirit that always wins — Napoleon should know, but Nixon will have none of that: that goes only for the long run, he says, but "in that short run in which we all live, the sword is the essential shield for the spirit,"[36] and "in the final analysis victory will go to the side . . . [with the] *power*." "*Power* is the ability to make things happen, . . . to set the course of history."[37] "The uses of power cannot be divorced from the purposes of power."[38] In Mr. Nixon's book, God *is* indeed on the side of the big battalions.

Mr. Nixon insists that there can be no thought of avoiding World War III (because it is already begun) and that we can win it. "If we win World War III, all peoples can survive . . . with the chance to advance toward freedom and prosperity. If the Soviets win, all will become slaves and satellites."[39] He cannot resist an ethnic racial slur — anything to widen the breach — when he remarks, quite incorrectly, that "the word 'Slav' is itself related to the word 'slave.' "

All peoples can survive? Never once does he mention the suicidal — Jaredite — nature of the war he heralds. "The American people want to win [who doesn't?]. . . . The first necessity is to recognize that we can win, and that we should win. The next is to insist that we must win, and . . . that we will do whatever is necessary to ensure victory."[40] Does that mean that the end justifies the means? That immoral doctrine Mr. Nixon finds to be "meaningless in the abstract," but a particular end does justify a particular means: "Some ends . . . do justify some means that would not be justified in other circumstances." "Failure to [act on this principle] . . . would be an act of moral abdication."[41] In such circumstances the Ten Commandments apply to only half the human race, and it is not the voice of God from Sinai that lays down the rules but our own interest and convenience, as we choose to interpret them. Thus, thou shalt not lie—to your friends, that is. After all, the dictionary definition of strategy is "Deception," in particular, with the intention of "killing others, practiced on an enemy," an enemy being anyone who stands in your way, and whether in business or war, strategy is the name of the game. Thou shalt not kill—people on your side only, of course; for killing others you get medals. Thou shalt not steal—from your friends, naturally. I seem to recall that the Lord said that if you love only your friends you have no reward, because sinners and publicans do that much (Matthew 5:46-47).

To end his book with a resounding peroration in the best manner of the high-school debater, Mr. Nixon coins some new scripture to take the place of all those unpleasant things about "who takes up the sword," "cursed is he who puts his trust in the arm of flesh," "man shall not smite, neither shall he judge," and so on. "If we determine to win," he cries, "then the spirit gives edge to the sword, the sword preserves the spirit, and freedom will prevail."[42] He identifies "the spirit" with that determination to win and to be Number One at all cost, which was the spirit that annihilated the Jaredites and, according to Milton and the Bible, which motivated the indomitable Lucifer and got him thrown out of heaven.

Such a cleanly polarized world gives us supremely simple solutions and supremely confident leaders, whose decisions are as quick and spontaneous as a knee-jerk and as irrevocable as the Ten Commandments—men like Hitler, Stalin, Arafat, Khadafi, Khomeni, Somoza, and others—who reduce all troubles to one cause and all problems to just one enemy. What could be more unhealthy than to have all one's thoughts and actions dictated and conditioned by the policy of another, waiting for him to act so that we can react, noting what he does so that we can do the same, watching his career to know how to plan and direct our own? Well is Satan called the Adversary, the Destroyer, the Accuser, the Contender. All of his titles describe one who must wait for another to act before he can move. Nothing is more crippling to creative thinking than obsession with an enemy. The person who can think of only one solution to a given problem is mentally bankrupt; the person who can think of only one solution to *every* problem is doomed.

Our second preacher of world dichotomy is Aleksandr Solzhenitsyn. No one hates the Soviet regime and what it stands for more intensely than he, or with better reason. In an address delivered at Harvard, entitled *A World Split Apart,* he asks us to view "two world powers, each of them already capable of destroying the other." The West as he describes it is in exactly the position and mood of the Roman Empire in the fourth century, everyone being convinced that those without the Empire "are only being temporarily prevented by wicked governments, or by . . . their own barbarity, . . . from taking the way of Western pluralistic democracy and adopting the Western way of life."[43] Like the Romans, the West also displays, according to Solzhenitsyn, "a decline in courage among the ruling groups and the intellectual elite," revealed in "anger and inflexibility . . . when dealing with weak governments and weak countries," in other words, the tendency to bully characteristic of spoiled children, motivated by "the constant desire to have still more things and a still better life," which "imprints many Western faces with worry and anxiety," indicative of "active and intense competition." Though they have "almost unlimited enjoyment of freedom," they insist on preserving it not by teaching self-control, but by making laws to take care of everything:

"The limits of human rights and righteousness are determined by a system of laws" — everything must be settled
in court, "any conflict is solved according to the letter of
the law." "One almost never sees voluntary self-restraint.
Everybody operates at the extreme limit of the legal
frames."[44]

On the one hand "a Communist regime . . . *without*
any objective legal scale is a terrible one indeed. But a
society with no *other* scale but the legal one is not quite
worthy of man either." Thus "an oil company is legally
blameless when it purchases an invention for a new type
of energy in order to prevent its use. A food-product man-
ufacturer is legally blameless when he poisons his product
to make it last longer: after all, people are free not to buy
it."[45] Within the past ten days we have seen even more
shocking examples in the cases of the eight major oil companies and the three dominant cereal processors. Which
is good and which is bad in these two extremes? Solzhenitsyn will relegate neither society to either pole: "But
should someone ask me whether I would indicate the West
such as it is today as a model to my country, frankly I
would have to answer negatively; No, I could not rec-
ommend your society in its present state as an ideal for
the transformation of ours." In other words, we need repentance — and who would deny it? Over against "an abyss
of lawlessness," in the Soviet Union, "it is also demeaning
to elect such mechanical legalistic smoothness as you
have," which is far more dehumanizing. There is a "weakening of human beings in the West, while in the East they
are becoming firmer and stronger."[46]

This enervating "mechanical legalistic smoothness" is
nowhere more in evidence than here in our midst, where
for years short skirts were modest and long slacks im-
modest — because the rules said so; mustaches and beards,
mandatory among our grandfathers, became by decree carnal, sensual, and devilish. Last week students enrolling in

my classes had just one question to ask: How do we get grades? Grades are acquisitive, competitive, and phony; but they are the official legal certificates that everyone must have, issued in fixed denominations on a mathematically graduated scale, to be converted it is hoped hereafter into legal tender of the land—and that is the only thing that interests these young people in the study of *religion,* of all things! This is no trifling thing; the seeds of such corruption are all-pervasive.

Poles apart in some things, it is where they are *weakest* that the two societies described by Solzhenitsyn are most alike. Like poles repel each other, and it is when as in Roman times the two halves of the world are playing for the same stakes and using exactly the same methods that they most resent each other. They are rivals; for many years each has announced that it intends and expects to convert the world. The two great principles of action that dominate both communities are the same. First, the belief that the *economy* is the most important thing in the world— they are by profession "dialectical materialists," while we rest our case in all human affairs on the bottom line. Both sides fancy themselves before everything as realists. The second principle is that man is "the center of everything that exists," having no "higher task than the attainment of happiness on earth." Success is what we are both after, and success means *here* and *now;* no "pie in the sky" for either party. "Everything beyond physical well-being and the accumulation of material goods is . . . left outside the range of attention of the state and the social system." As *both* "state systems were becoming increasingly materialistic," it was all "endless materialism; freedom from religion, . . . concentration on social structures." Solzhenitsyn insists that in describing the West he has also been describing the East: "At first glance it seems an ugly parallel," he writes, "common traits in the thinking and way of life of today's West and today's East? But such is the logic of materialistic development." Nevertheless, "in our Eastern countries, Communism has suffered a complete ideological defeat; it is zero and less than zero." What is the danger, then? It is not miserable Marxism. On both sides "we have lost the concept of a Supreme Complete Entity which used to restrain our passions and our irresponsibility," lacking which we are "deprived of our most precious possession: our spiritual life. In the East it is destroyed by the dealings and machinations of the ruling party. In the West, commercial interests tend to suffocate it. *This is the real crisis.* The split world is less terrible than the fact that the same disease is plaguing the two main sections."[47] In *Since Cumorah* we called it "The Nephite disease."[48] But note well, Mr. Nixon names his book "The *Real* War," and he explains it by the total and irreconcilable *differences* between two societies; Mr. Solzhenitsyn on the other hand sees the exact opposite, that what he calls "the *real crisis*" is not caused by the two being so different, but by their being so very alike in the things they believe most strongly. Marx and Manchester both take their moral and rational standard four-square on the foundation that Darwin laid for them. "On the whole," said President Kimball, "*we* are an idolatrous people, a condition most repugnant to the Lord."[49]

The Real Polarity

The polarized condition of the world today, however silly, is not to be denied. But is it consistent with the real polarity of good and evil? If God and Satan stand each surrounded by his host, they are not human hosts. The human race is placed not at either pole but squarely *between* the two. In that position each individual is free to gravitate in either direction; that is the testing to which all are subjected during this time of probation, every day of their lives. As long as they are living here they are subject to being tried and tested. This is how Mormon puts it. First, the polar situation: "A man being a servant of the devil cannot follow Christ; and if he follow Christ he cannot be a servant of the devil. Wherefore, all things which are good cometh of God; and that which is evil cometh of the devil; for the devil is an enemy unto God, and fighteth against him continually, and inviteth and enticeth to sin, and to do that which is evil continually. But behold, that which is of God inviteth and enticeth to do good continually; wherefore every thing which inviteth and enticeth to do good, and to love God, and to serve him, is inspired of God" (Moroni 7:11-13).

Note the "broken symmetry." There is no mention of God's being an enemy to the devil, or of fighting against him. He could crush him in an instant if he chose. There is no mention of his followers fighting; their only invitation is to love God and to serve him by doing good continually. There are two powers, "inviting and enticing" us in op-posite directions — but not forcing anyone — the devil can-not do that, said the Prophet Joseph, and God will not. No one is forced in either direction, and everyone makes his own choice as an individual. This is carefully explained by Moroni in the verses that immediately follow. No one in this life reaches either pole or can consider himself safely home in either camp — for the whole purpose of this life, designed at the creation to be "a time of pro-bation," is to subject each individual to the test by allowing him to choose for himself, as long as he lives, which way he shall go.

But if evil is by definition that of which one does not approve, you ask, then what danger is there of anyone's deliberately choosing it? One does not; one follows "the desires of his heart" — the ultimate choice, as Alma ex-plains, and all the time insists that he is choosing what is good and in so doing puts the stamp of righteousness on his life (cf. Alma 41:3-5). Thus Satan enticeth and inviteth men to go his way by "puffing them up with pride, tempt-

ing them to seek for power, and authority, and riches, and
the vain things of the world" (3 Nephi 6:15), having taken
which course men invariably justify it by depicting it as
the very path of virtue. "Wherefore," says Mormon, "take
heed, my beloved brethren, that ye do not judge that which
is evil to be of God, or that which is good and of God to
be of the devil" (Moroni 7:14), from which it is apparent
that such neat perversions of value are not only possible
but common — something to be earnestly warned against.
And then comes the important principle: "For behold, my
brethren, it is given unto you to judge, that ye may know
good from evil; and the way to judge is as plain, that ye
may know with a perfect knowledge, as the daylight is
from the dark night" (Moroni 7:15). We cannot plead ignorance in yielding to temptation. "For behold, the Spirit
of Christ is given to *every man*, that he may know good
from evil." Mormon repeats then that everything which
"inviteth to do good, and to persuade to believe in Christ,
is sent forth by the power and gift of Christ; wherefore ye
may know with a *perfect* knowledge it is of God," while
"whatsoever thing persuadeth men to do evil, . . . then
ye may know with a *perfect* knowledge it is of the devil"
(Moroni 7:16-17). Again, there is no mention of force or
compulsion on either side. Again the admonition: "See
that ye do not judge wrongfully, . . . search diligently
in the light of Christ that ye may know good from evil"
(Moroni 7:18-19). The only deception here is self-deception,
since every individual can know perfectly which is right
and which is wrong. It is against self-deception that Moroni
passionately warns us.

The point is that all men find themselves between the
two poles. In this life no one has as yet arrived at a point
of complete perfection or of complete depravity. Ezekiel
devotes a whole chapter to this theme: "Have I any pleasure at all that the wicked should die? saith the Lord God:
and not that he should return from his ways, and live? But

when the righteous turneth away from his righteousness, and committeth iniquity, . . . shall he live? All his righteousness that he hath done shall not be mentioned: . . . and in his sin . . . shall he die" (Ezekiel 18:23-24). While we remain alive, it is never too late for the wicked to choose righteousness and vice versa; the pressure is always on— "the devil . . . inviteth and enticeth to sin . . . continually. But . . . God inviteth and enticeth to do good continually" (Moroni 7:12-13). To imagine the wicked as *already* gathered at one pole, and all the righteous at another is to reject the whole plan of probation; it renders the gospel of repentance null and void, the wicked being beyond repentance, the righteous not needing it; whereas God keeps the door open to both as long as they are in this time of testing. This life is "a probationary time, a time to repent and serve God" (Alma 42:4). Nay, the life of man is lengthened long beyond his prime to give him the full benefit of the doubt: "And we see that death comes upon mankind; . . . nevertheless there was a space granted unto man in which he might repent; therefore this life became a probationary state" (Alma 12:24). The door is left open, says Nephi, "until the end of the day of probation" (2 Nephi 33:9).

"The devil is an enemy unto God, and fighteth against him continually" (Moroni 7:12), and God *permits* it! He has expressly allowed Satan, the common enemy, to try men and to tempt them—that is the whole point of the thing; men must be exposed to both influences so each can make his own choice. None has gone so far in one direction that he may not still repent and turn back; and none has gone so far in the other that he does not need to repent and improve his ways. What, then, could be more retrograde to God's purpose than to see all mankind as the churchmen did in the fourth century, as solidly compacted and congealed at two opposite poles, with nothing between them; each animated and absorbed by one thought—implacable hatred of the other? The gospel of repentance is a constant reminder that the most righteous are still being tested and may yet fall, and that the most wicked are not yet beyond redemption and may still be saved. And that is what God wants: "Have I any pleasure at all that the wicked should die?" (Ezekiel 18:23). There are poles for all to see, but in this life no one has reached and few have ever approached either pole, and no one has any idea at what point between his neighbor stands. Only God knows that.

When the early church began to grow in power and influence and worldliness, the ancient doctrine of the *Two Ways* was quickly replaced by that of the *Two Parties*. The former specified that there lies before every mortal, at every moment of his life, a *choice* between the Way of Light and the Way of Darkness; but the latter doctrine taught that righteousness consisted in belonging to *one* party (ours), and wickedness in belonging to the *other* (theirs).

The doctrine of probation is the inescapable choice between Two Ways, everyone having a perfect knowledge of the way he should go. None may commit his decision to the judgment of a faction, a party, a leader, or a nation; none can delegate his free agency to another. "Thou shalt not follow a multitude to do evil" (Exodus 23:2). We cannot protest innocence on the grounds of having been given bad advice, doing what we did for the best interests of the country, doing only what others were doing, or being forced to do it by the need to check and frustrate a nefarious enemy. Those who make those pleas, which have become popular in our day, dismiss any thought of repentance for themselves. Has even one of the many convicted of great crimes in high places of recent years ever admitted moral wrongdoing? Has any ever even hinted at a need for repentance?

It is easy to imagine absolutes, and to think and argue in terms of absolutes, as the theologians have always done: Good and evil, light and darkness, hot and cold, black and white—we know exactly what they are; but in the real world we have rarely experienced the pure thing—our own experience lies between. Yet standing on that middle ground, we *are* faced with absolute decisions. It is not where we stand, says Ezekiel, that makes us good or evil in God's eyes—no one has reached the top or bottom in this short life—but the direction in which we are facing. There we have only two choices. The road up and the road down are the same, says Heracleitus.[50] It all depends on the way *you* are facing. You are taking either the up-road or the down-road; there is no third way, for if you try to compromise and go off at an angle, you will never reach either goal. You are either repenting or not repenting, and that is, according to the scriptures, the whole difference between being righteous or being wicked.

So it is indeed the Way of Light or the Way of Darkness, but when two ways were identified with the two parties by the churchmen—ours and yours—the doctrine was exploited with inexorable logic: Since there are only two sides, one totally evil and the other absolutely good, and I am not totally evil, I must be on God's side, and that puts you on the other side. This doctrine has been worked for many years in Utah as a political ploy. With withering contempt, Isaiah denounces the comfortable logic: It is not for you to say who is on the Lord's side, says the Lord; that is for me to say, and those who most loudly offer me their support and cry "Lord! Lord!" are those of whom I most disapprove (Matthew 7:21). "See the foe in countless numbers, marshalled in the ranks of sin," we sing, as if we have already chosen sides and know who the bad people are, because *we* are on the Lord's side. "Fight for Zion, down with error, flash the sword above the foe, every stroke disarms a foeman," and so on. No error on our side? The point of all such hymns is that it is sin and error that we are fighting, not people guilty of sin and error—for we are all such people, and each one can only confront and overcome sin and error in himself. You cannot tell the righteous from the wicked, the Lord told Joseph Smith, you cannot tell your friends from your enemies. Be still and let me decide the issue! (D&C 10:37).

In his last letter to his son, Mormon considers the battle already lost (Moroni 9:20); sometime before, he had decided that his people had passed the point of no return: "I saw that the day of grace was passed with them, both temporally and spiritually" (Mormon 2:15). Yet he insists that he must go right on struggling as long as he is alive: "For if we should cease to labor, we should be brought under condemnation; for we have a labor to perform whilst in this tabernacle of clay, that we may conquer the enemy of all righteousness, and rest our souls in the kingdom of God" (Moroni 9:6). Only after this life are we safe in home. And what was the "labor" he had to perform? Who was this "enemy of all righteousness"? Not the Lamanites! "Notwithstanding this great abomination of the Lamanites, it doth not exceed that of our people" (Moroni 9:9). No, the call was to "labor diligently" with his own people, "notwithstanding their hardness" (Moroni 9:6), even though "[he] fear[s] lest the Spirit of the Lord hath ceased striving with them. For . . . they have lost their love, one towards another; and they thirst after blood and revenge continually" (Moroni 9:4-5). Earlier, though, the leader of the army, Mormon, had laid down his arms and "utterly refused" to march against the Lamanites, because his own people were going to battle seeking revenge for the blood of their brethren. And what was wrong with the "Green Beret" scenario? The Lord had strictly forbidden it. And now, in the letter, he tells Moroni that he is actually praying for the "utter destruction" of the *Nephites* "except they repent" (Moroni 9:22). And they had not repented, and he had given up hope. And yet Mormon died fighting the *Lamanites*, who were not as wicked as his own people!

Is there no solution to the cruel dilemma? There is, and the Book of Mormon gives it to us in a number of powerful examples. Perhaps the foremost is Ammon, the mightiest man in battle of all the Nephites. He became wholly convinced that there was a better way of handling even the most vicious and determined enemy than by killing them. The Nephites laughed at him, but he went right ahead: he would go on a mission and preach to the Lamanites. You are crazy, they said, there is only one sermon those wretches understand: "Now do ye remember, my brethren, that we said unto our brethren in the land of Zarahemla, we go up to the land of Nephi, to preach unto our brethren, the Lamanites, and they laughed us to scorn? For they said unto us: Do ye suppose that ye can bring the Lamanites to the knowledge of the truth, . . . as stiffnecked a people as they are; whose hearts delight in the shedding of blood; whose days have been spent in the grossest iniquity; whose ways have been the ways of a transgressor from the beginning? Now my brethren, ye remember that this was their language" (Alma 26:23-24). And what could be more sensible? There is only one possible solution. "And moreover they did say: Let us take up arms against them, that we destroy them and their iniquity out of the land, lest *they* overrun us and destroy *us*" (Alma 26:25). But not for Ammon: "We came . . . not with the intent to destroy our brethren, but with the intent that perhaps we might save some few of their souls" (Alma 26:26). Nothing guaranteed, you understand, but anything was better than the other solution. So Ammon recalls how he and his friends went "forth amongst [the people], . . . patient in our sufferings," going "from house to house. . . . We have entered into their houses and taught them . . . in their streets, . . . and we have been cast out, and mocked, and spit upon, and smote upon our cheeks, . . . stoned, . . . bound, . . . and cast into prison" (Alma 26:28-29). What could have been worth paying such a price in inconvenience and humiliation? "We have suffered . . . all this, that perhaps we might be the means of saving some soul" (Alma 26:30). This alone could break the vicious circle of provocation and revenge that was destroying both people.

And Ammon brought thousands to his way of thinking. A whole nation of great warriors laid down their arms and refused to take them up again even at the cost of their lives. When they were moved by great compassion to come to the aid of Helaman and Alma, who had given them protection and who were being desperately sore-pressed by their enemies, those two heroes intervened with powerful preaching that persuaded them not to change their wise decision. The Ammonites became the most righteous, the most saintly people in the Book of Mormon, after a period of agonizing repentance, in which they repeatedly refer to their former deeds of valor on the battlefield as pure murder, and wonder whether God will ever forgive them. They utterly rejected taking up arms under any circumstances and turned the tide in the affairs of both Nephites and Lamanites.

Alma learned the same lesson. After holding the highest and most influential positions in the land, which enabled him to bring pressure to bear on decisive issues — commander of the armies, chief judge, head of the church — he laid aside all his high offices and did "go forth among his people, . . . that he might preach the word of God unto them, to stir them up in remembrance of their duty, and that he might pull down, by the word of God, all the pride and craftiness and all the contentions which were among his people, *seeing no way,*" after all his experience, "that he might reclaim them *save it were in bearing down in pure testimony*" (Alma 4:19). With all his vast experience Alma was convinced that he could do more good and actually have more influence as a simple missionary than as head of the state, head of the army, or head of the church! And so he takes his leave, disappearing all alone over the horizon into the midst of hostile and unbelieving people, never to be heard of again. Once the people saw that the great man had lost his official clout, they treated him almost as badly as they did Ammon.

We freely grant that this is an unlikely solution in the present world, as the Book of Mormon more than hints in God's reply to Moroni when, being shown by Jesus Christ the dangers in which the present inhabitants of the land and the church now find themselves, he "prayed unto the Lord that he would give unto the Gentiles grace, that they might have charity" (Ether 12:36). For the Lord had told him that the *only* hope of the Gentiles was to have *charity* (Ether 12:34-35), the one thing toward which the present world is least inclined. In reply to his request, the Lord gave Moroni no firm promise. His only answer was: "If they have not charity it mattereth not unto thee, thou hast been faithful" (Ether 12:37). God will not force any man to have charity—that would not be charity, which must be spontaneous and unsolicited, as Paul says, seeking nothing for itself (1 Corinthians 13:5). Charity is the one thing a person must have in himself and of himself. And so there Moroni leaves it: will we have charity, or will we not?

We can end on a cheery note in spite of everything. The mere fact that we have the Book of Mormon is reassuring. On this night of the Autumnal Equinox, the angel Moroni took the trouble to appear to Joseph Smith—four times on the first night, and on the same night in four successive years. Moroni has told us of the pains he took to compile, edit, preserve, and conceal the record, and he has made it clear that he did it all with the express understanding that someone in the future, reading it, might decide to repent; that some people might just be wiser than the Nephites, Lamanites, and Jaredites. As to the rest, those who will not listen and repent, "as it was in the days of Noah," they have been given fair warning "so that they are without excuse" (Romans 1:20). Either way, Moroni's efforts were not to be in vain.

After reading this over, I thought, So what else is new? Can't I say something a bit more original? Must we always deal in truisms and platitudes? What is new is this: that only a few years ago this little spiel would have sounded like the most extravagant science-fiction or futuristic horror-fantasy; it would have been quite unthinkable. In my youth I thought the Book of Mormon was much too preoccupied with extreme situations, situations that had little bearing on the real world of everyday life and ordinary human affairs. What on earth could the total extermination of nations have to do with life in the enlightened modern world? Today no comment on that is necessary. Moroni gives it to us straight: This is the way it was before, and this is the way it is going to be again, unless there is a great repentance.

Notes

1. W. T. Sanders, in T. P. Culbert, ed., *The Classic Maya Collapse* (Albuquerque: University of New Mexico Press, 1973), 345-46.

2. Hugh W. Nibley, *Since Cumorah* (Salt Lake City: Deseret Book, 1967), 373-409; reprinted in *CWHN* 7:337-72.

3. Hugh W. Nibley, "The Unsolved Loyalty Problem: Our Western Heritage," *Western Political Quarterly* 6 (1953): 648.

4. Hugh W. Nibley, *Lehi in the Desert and the World of the Jaredites* (Salt Lake City: Bookcraft, 1952), 231-38; reprinted in *CWHN* 5:231-37.

5. Nibley, "The Unsolved Loyalty Problem," 633.

6. Ibid., 638.

7. Ibid., 649.

8. C. Diehl, as quoted in ibid., 649.

9. M. Rostovtzeff, as quoted in ibid., 649.

10. Philostratus, as quoted in ibid., 649.

11. J. Vogt, as quoted in ibid., 650.

12. Ibid., 650-51.

13. Ibid., 633-34.

14. Ibid., 635.

15. Ibid., 636.

16. Ibid., 637.
17. Ibid., 645-46.
18. J. B. Bury, as quoted in ibid., 637.
19. Ibid., 637.
20. Ibid., 638-39.
21. Richard Nixon, *The Real War* (New York: Warner, 1980), 314.
22. Ibid.
23. Ibid., 297.
24. Ibid., 298.
25. Ibid., 199-201.
26. Ibid., 300.
27. Ibid., 299.
28. Ibid., 309.
29. Ibid., 20-21.
30. Ibid., 15-16.
31. James M. Burns, as quoted in ibid., 248.
32. Ibid., 249.
33. Ibid., 257.
34. Spencer W. Kimball, "The False Gods We Worship," *Ensign* 6 (1976): 6.
35. Nixon, *The Real War*, 310.
36. Ibid.
37. Ibid., 312.
38. Ibid., 313.
39. Ibid., 299.
40. Ibid., 280, 296.
41. Ibid., 313.
42. Ibid., 315.
43. Aleksandr Solzhenitsyn, "A World Split Apart," *National Review* 30 (1978): 836.
44. Ibid., 837.
45. Ibid.
46. Ibid., 839.
47. Ibid., 840-41.
48. Nibley, *Since Cumorah*, 390-405; in *CWHN* 7:354-68.
49. Kimball, "The False Gods We Worship," 6.
50. Fragment 60, in Hermann Diels and Walther Kranz, *Die Fragmente der Vorsokratiker*, 3 vols. (Berlin: Weidmann, 1951), 1:164.

21

Scriptural Perspectives on How to Survive the Calamities of the Last Days

"And this gospel of the kingdom shall be preached in all the world for a witness unto all nations; and then shall the end come" (Matthew 24:14). That is an established pattern: hard upon the preaching of the gospel comes its rejection, followed by destruction and darkness. Each time, it is called the end of the *aeon*, the age or dispensation. This description appears most plainly in Joseph Smith's inspired rendering of the so-called Little Apocalypse, the twenty-fourth chapter of Matthew, in which the end of the world is described three times.

First the Lord prophesies "great tribulation on the Jews, and upon Israel, . . . no, nor ever shall be sent again upon Israel" (JS–M 1:18; cf. Matthew 24:21). It was true prophecy; never were the Jews so completely obliterated as in the days of the Apostles (A.D. 70 and A.D. 130). And yet this was "only the beginning of the sorrows which shall come upon them" (JS–M 1:19) — the beginning of two thousand years of persecution. Time and again they were on the verge of extinction and only one thing saved them: "And except those days should be shortened, there should none of their flesh be saved"(JS–M 1:20). There is no point to foretelling woes from which there is no deliverance, and

---

This article appeared in BYU Studies 25 *(Winter 1985): 7-27.*

the Lord does not leave the people helpless but tells them specifically what they are to do.

In the first place, those who lived in the Judean area were to do what they had always done in such an emergency: they were to flee to the mountains containing hundreds of caves and gorges a few short miles from the city (see JS–M 1:13). But, unlike the other times, they were under no conditions to go back to the city again; no one was to "return to take anything out of his house; neither let him who is in the field return back to take his clothes" (JS–M 1:14-15); it was not to be the usual return to the city after the trouble had passed; there were no arrangements whatsoever for returning. The Lord gave fair warning that pregnant women should be got out of the city before it was too late. They were not to wait for winter, which would be a bad time to flee; and of course things should be arranged so as not to flee on the Sabbath (see JS–M 1:16-17).

So it was foretold and so it happened. The Lord then describes the next End, the end of the Church, which is to take place "after the tribulation of those days which shall come upon Jerusalem" (JS–M 1:21). At that time people will come claiming to have the gospel, but they are not to be believed. The Saints, "who are the elect according to the covenant," will be led astray by "false Christs, and false prophets" (JS–M 1:22; see also 1:21). To prepare them for this cruel blow which must come to pass, the Lord is giving them an explanation ahead of time: "See that ye be not troubled. . . . Behold, I have told you before" (JS–M 1:23-24). The next verse anticipates the sectaries of the desert and the secret conventicles which flourished in the second century; the Saints were to join none of them: "Wherefore, if they shall say unto you: Behold, he is in the desert; go not forth: Behold, he is in the secret chambers; believe it not" (JS–M 1:25).

Next comes the restoration of the gospel; some vivid imagery is used. First, "the morning breaks, the shadows flee"; "for as the light of the morning cometh out of the east, and shineth even unto the west, and covereth the whole earth," so should it be in the time of "the coming of the Son of Man" (JS–M 1:26). Now comes one of the most disturbing parables in the Bible, which in the true context as given here is perfectly clear. The manner of the gathering, we are told, will be in the same miraculous and mysterious way as the gathering of eagles to a carcass lying in the desert—they appear suddenly and inexplicably in the four quarters of the sky and come together from vast distances to that single spot (see JS–M 1:27). Just as the breaking of the light from the east describes the manner of the Restoration with no reference to geography, so this passage describes the manner of the gathering—no other comparison is implied in introducing such an unsavory object as a carcass.

It will be a terrible time, with "wars, and rumors of wars" (JS–M 1:28), with world unrest; "nation shall rise against nation, and kingdom against kingdom; there shall be famines, and pestilences, and earthquakes" (JS–M 1:29). "And again, because iniquity shall abound, the love of men shall wax cold" (JS–M 1:30). Yet at that very time "this Gospel of the Kingdom shall be preached in all the world, for a witness unto all nations, and then shall the end come" (JS–M 1:31). A thick pall of dust and smoke shall cover the earth, "the sun shall be darkened, and the moon shall not give her light" (JS–M 1:33). The generation in which these things happen will see the final end (see JS–M 1:34): unlike all the other great destructions, this one involves the entire globe, when "all the tribes of the earth mourn" (JS–M 1:36). Then the Son of Man shall come, but first "he shall send his angels before him with the great sound of a trumpet" for a last gathering—"and they shall gather together the remainder of his elect from the four winds" (JS–M 1:37). "As it was in the days which were before the flood," it will be business as usual right up until the end, which shall come suddenly and unexpectedly: "They were eating and drinking, marrying and giving in marriage; and knew not until the flood came, and took them all away; so shall also the coming of the Son of Man be" (JS–M 1:42-43). Again an interesting comparison occurs when the Lord likens himself to a thief in the night. There are no criminal connotations; the metaphor is used purely to describe the *manner* of his coming—it will be a complete surprise. How does one prepare for it, then? One does not. Jesus makes it very clear that the only preparation is to live every day as if the Lord were coming on that day. In striking contrast to the Jerusalem situation, he gives no specific instructions but explains that "then shall be fulfilled that which is written, that in the last days, two shall be in the field, the one shall be taken, and the other left; two shall be grinding at the mill, the one shall be taken, and the other left" (JS–M 1:44-45), which means that there is no point in devising ingenious schemes for survival. There is but one real course of escape. What you should do is to watch yourself at all times (see JS–M 1:46); to be found doing good all the time (see JS–M 1:49); to not act as if it were going to be business as usual indefinitely, as if the great event belonged to a vague and indefinite future (see JS–M 1:51). The one thing you can be sure of is that it will be "in such an hour as ye think not" (JS–M 1:48). So the only preparation is to do what? To abstain from taking advantage of others, oppressing the poor, and living in luxury (see JS–M 1:52).

Each of these ends is expressly called the end of the world, with the explicit statement of what is meant by the expression "the end of the world, or the destruction of the wicked, which is the end of the world" (JS–M 1:4; see also 1:31, 55). This is followed by the most important explanation of all, namely, that the end of these dispensations is not the destruction of the globe, for "the end of the earth is not yet, but by and by" (JS–M 1:55), that is, at some unspecified future date. Just as we do not believe that the creation of the world was the instantaneous beginning of everything, neither do we suppose a Star Wars ending. What we are plainly told is that the phrase *End of the World* refers expressly to the destruction of the wicked. So who are the "wicked," and how are they to be "destroyed"? The Book of Mormon is the complete handbook on the subject. Twenty times it tells us of the great overburn and each time assures us that while the wicked shall burn as stubble, the righteous need not fear. The question that concerns us, then, is not how such a miracle can be arranged—that is quite beyond our imagination at present—but who are the righteous and who are the wicked? We may think we have an easy answer to that one, but it is not the answer that the scriptures give us.

The righteous are whoever are *repenting,* and the wicked whoever are not repenting. "Two men went up into the temple to pray; the one a Pharisee" who gave thanks to God that he was not a crook or a lecher, that he fasted twice a week, paid a full tithe, and was very strict in his religious observances. All this was perfectly true. The other man was a tax collector and rather ashamed of some of the things he had done, and instead of thanking God by way of boasting, he only asked God to be merciful to him, a sinner (see Luke 18:10-13). The surprise is that the sinner was the righteous one—because he was repenting; the other one who "exalteth himself shall be abased"—because he was not repenting (Luke 18:14). None but the truly penitent are saved, and that is who the righteous are (see Alma 42:22-24).

What do you repent of and how do you repent? It is all a matter of *seeking*: when you repent you turn from seeking some things to seeking others. What you seek are the desires of your heart, as Alma says, and by them alone you will be judged (see Alma 41:3). "Now the cause of this iniquity of the people was this—Satan had great power, unto the stirring up of the people to do all manner of iniquity, and to the puffing them up with pride, tempting them to seek for power, and authority, and riches, and the vain things of the world" (3 Nephi 6:15). The condition is first laid out by Nephi and often repeated throughout the Book of Mormon: all who seek "to get gain, and all who are built up to get power over the flesh, and those who seek the lusts of the flesh and the things of the world, and to do all manner of iniquity; yea, in fine, all those who belong to the kingdom of the devil are they who need fear, and tremble, and quake; they are those who must be brought low in the dust; they are those who must be consumed as stubble; and this is according to the words of the prophet" (1 Nephi 22:23). The first commandment given to the restored Church was "seek not for riches but for wisdom" (D&C 6:7, 11:7), the Lord well knowing what most people are prone to seek. We need not expand on how those four things (gain, power, popularity, "lusts of the flesh") are inseparably joined "in one specious and glittering mass," as Gibbon says of the Romans; the appeal of the primitive TV show would be defective and our joy would not be full if any of the four were lacking in *Dallas, Dynasty,* or *Falconcrest.*

The Nephites of old had their own idea of who were righteous and who were wicked, as we do, which conveniently avoided the necessity of repentance until they were forced to it by violent events. And we are warned to "beware of pride lest ye become as the Nephites of old," who, the same verse tells us, sought the wrong kind of riches—that was their wickedness (D&C 38:39).

Very well, what do the righteous seek? Isn't "wisdom" rather vague? The righteous in the Book of Mormon sought to live "after the manner of happiness" (2 Nephi 5:27), and in at least five instances succeeded. It is their example we should follow, but I don't think we will until we get rid of our own definition of who are "the good guys" and who are "the bad guys."

All the writers in the Book of Mormon are worried men. Nephi ends his days disappointed, discouraged, and saddened. He had once led a society that lived "after the manner of happiness," but all that has changed.

> Wherefore, now after I have spoken these words, if ye cannot understand them it will be because ye ask not, neither do ye knock; wherefore, ye are not brought into the light, but must perish in the dark. . . . And now I, Nephi, cannot say more; the Spirit stoppeth mine utterance, and I am left to mourn because of the unbelief, and the wickedness, and the ignorance, and the stiffneckedness of men; for they will not search knowledge, nor understand great knowledge, when it is given unto them in plainness, even as plain as word can be. . . . It grieveth me that I must speak concerning this thing (2 Nephi 32:4, 7-8).

His last words show us the old Nephi, upright, passionate, obedient till the last: "These words shall condemn you at the last day. For what I seal on earth, shall be brought against you at the judgment bar; for thus hath the Lord commanded me, and I must obey" (2 Nephi 33:14-15).

If Nephi's last words are neither happy nor hopeful, the first words of Jacob, to whom he turns over the record, are positively alarming; he begins on a note of "great anxiety," because he has been shown what is going to happen (see Jacob 1:5). Jacob and his descendants are religious leaders, not kings, working to forestall a growing trend, trying to "persuade all men not to rebel against God" (Jacob 1:8). Already under Nephi the Second (see Jacob 1:11), they begin "to grow hard in their hearts," indulging "somewhat" in Solomon's luxurious vices and "lifted up somewhat in pride"—that "somewhat" still leaves the door open to repentance (Jacob 1:15-16). But they do all this under the guise of sanctity, justifying themselves by the scriptures (see Jacob 2:23). Jacob is very reluctant to speak about this sort of thing; he "shrink[s] with shame" at it

(Jacob 2:6). But things are definitely getting worse: "This day [I] am weighed down with much more desire and anxiety for the welfare of your souls than I have hitherto been. . . . I can tell you concerning your thoughts, how that ye are beginning to labor in sin" (Jacob 2:3, 5). At the launching of a new civilization which is to last for a thousand years, things must not get out of hand, and Jacob is desperate to control the situation. He is plainly embarrassed to bring up the sins, wickedness, crimes, and abominations under which the people are beginning to labor (see Jacob 2:5-6, 9-11).

Just what are these vices, we begin to wonder, and the answer is loud and clear: "This is the word which I declare unto you, that many of you have begun to search for gold"; they have not been opposed in this, he tells them, for God means the riches of the promised land to be enjoyed (Jacob 2:12). But what he does not like is the invidious comparison of a competitive economy: "*Because* some of you have obtained more abundantly than that of your brethren ye are lifted up in the pride of your hearts. . . . Ye suppose that ye are better than they" (Jacob 2:13). It is inequality that the prophets deplore throughout the Book of Mormon; pride stands at the head of every one of those many lists of crimes that beset the society. Above all, this reverence for wealth will not do, Jacob tells the people; do they have any idea how contemptible this thing is to God's sight? If they value his opinion, they will not set up their own artificial scale of values (see Jacob 2:16). There is nothing wrong with having plenty, but let's all be rich! "Be familiar with all and free with your substance, that they may be rich like unto you" (Jacob 2:17). Then comes a classic on equality: "Ye were proud in your hearts, of the things which God hath given you, what say ye of it? Do ye not suppose that such things are abominable unto him who created all flesh? And the one being is as precious in his sight as the other" (Jacob 2:20-21).

With seeking for wealth goes a "grosser" attendant vice
of licentious living (see Jacob 2:22-23). God does not bring
people to the promised land for a repeat of the Old World
follies; here he is determined to "raise up unto me a righteous branch from the fruit of the loins of Joseph. Wherefore, I the Lord God will not suffer that this people shall
do like unto them of old" (Jacob 2:25-26). God's people
may never enjoy the luxury of living after the manner of
the world (see D&C 105:3-5). The promised land is a testing
ground offering both great opportunity and corresponding
risk: "Wherefore, this people shall keep my commandments, saith the Lord of Hosts, or cursed be the land for
their sakes" (Jacob 2:29). In the Old World are civilizations
which were ancient at the time Lehi left Jerusalem, and
they still survive, but of those in the land of promise we
are told that when they are ripe in iniquity, when the cup
is full, they shall be swept off from the land. Compared
with other continents, this one has no history, no surviving
cultures, though far and wide civilizations whose identities
remain a mystery have left their ruins and their scattered
descendants.

The Nephites always fancied themselves to be good
people because the Lord had brought them to the land of
promise, and, accordingly, they styled their enemies as
the wicked. And indeed the enemy was a real and constant
element in all their operations. The dangerous illusion that
the populace may be classified simply as the good guys
(our side) and the bad guys (their side) becomes the main
theme of the book of Jacob, as of the Book of Mormon
itself. While Jacob spares no words in describing the
wickedness and depravity of the Lamanites, he can declare
of his own people at that early date: "Behold, ye have done
greater iniquities than the Lamanites" (Jacob 2:35). Where
does that leave us? With a polarized world that emerges
in Jacob 3:

Except ye repent the land is cursed for your sakes; and the Lamanites, which are not filthy like unto you, nevertheless they are cursed with a sore cursing, shall scourge you even unto destruction. And the time speedily cometh, that except ye repent they shall possess the land of your inheritance. . . . Behold, the Lamanites your brethren, whom ye hate because of their filthiness and the cursing which hath come upon their skins, are more righteous than you. . . . The Lord God will not destroy them, but will be merciful unto them (Jacob 3:3-6).

So later: "I will not utterly destroy them, but . . . concerning the people of the Nephites: If they will not repent, and observe to do my will, I will utterly destroy them" (Helaman 15:16-17). Bad guys? You "persecute your brethren because ye suppose that ye are better than they" (Jacob 2:13). As Isaiah told the Jews at Jerusalem, it is not for them to decide who are God's people—that is for God to decide (see Isaiah 1:12).

Throughout the Book of Mormon, the wicked have a perfectly beautiful self-image, to which Jacob now refers: "A commandment I give unto you, which is the word of God, that ye revile no more against them because of the darkness of their skins; neither shall ye revile against them because of their filthiness; but ye shall remember your own filthiness, and remember that their filthiness came because of their fathers," while "your filthiness, [may] bring your children unto destruction" (Jacob 3:9-10). Even Nephi in his youth recognizes and combats the natural tendency to put oneself on the right side: "Yea, why should I give way to temptations, that the evil one have place in my heart to destroy my peace and afflict my soul? Why am I angry because of mine enemy? Awake, my soul! No longer droop in sin. Rejoice, O my heart, and give place no more for the enemy of my soul. Do not anger again because of mine enemies" (2 Nephi 4:27-29). He recognizes that no matter how vicious his enemies are, they are not responsible for

his condition. We cannot repent for our enemies—what
do we know about their personal lives? *Repent* is a reflexive
verb—"I do repent me." I can sorrow for the wickedness
of another, but I cannot repent of it unless I have caused
it. For Nephi, the perennial tension is laid down as a condition of life for his people: "And inasmuch as ye shall
keep my commandments, ye shall prosper, and shall be
led to a land of promise; yea, even a land which I have
prepared for you; yea, a land which is choice above all
other lands. And inasmuch as thy brethren [the Lamanites]
shall rebel against thee, they shall be cut off from the
presence of the Lord. . . . For behold, in that day that they
shall rebel against me [fulfilled in Jacob 3:3], I will curse
them even with a sore curse, and they shall have no power
over thy seed except they shall rebel against me also. And
if it so be that they rebel against me, they shall be a scourge
unto thy seed, to stir them up in the ways of remembrance"
(1 Nephi 2:20-21, 23-24). Thus it is God's intention to keep
the "bad guys" in place permanently, and it is of no use
for the Nephites to try to get rid of them, since they can
be rendered harmless by the Nephites' righteousness.

The same message is given to Jacob's son Enos: "I will
visit thy brethren according to their diligence in keeping
my commandments. I have given unto them this land, and
it is a holy land; and I curse it not save it be for the cause
of iniquity" (Enos 1:10). With this goes a vivid description
of just how thoroughly bad the Lamanites are; every effort
of approach or conciliation by the Nephites is rebuffed:
"Our labors were vain; their hatred was fixed, and they
were led by their evil nature that they became wild, and
ferocious, and a blood-thirsty people; . . . and they were
continually seeking to destroy us" (Enos 1:20)—perfect
typecasting for the bad guys. And yet Enos declares that
this dangerous confrontation is exactly what the Nephites
need! They will not behave themselves without being thoroughly scared and admonished: "Nothing save it was

exceeding harshness, preaching and prophesying of wars, and contentions, and destructions, and continually reminding them of death" has the desired effect of "stirring them up continually to keep them in the fear of the Lord" (Enos 1:23). The prophecy of Nephi is being fulfilled: "They shall be a scourge unto thy seed, to stir them up in remembrance of me; and inasmuch as they will not remember me, and hearken unto my words, they shall scourge them even unto destruction" (2 Nephi 5:25). Isn't that all a bit severe? Not with "a stiffnecked people, hard to understand" (Enos 1:22). Jarom, the son of Enos, tells how "the prophets of the Lord did threaten the people of Nephi, according to the word of God, that if they did not keep the commandments, but should fall into transgression, they should be destroyed from off the face of the land"; and Jarom explains that "by so doing they kept them from being destroyed upon the face of the land; for they did prick their hearts with the word, continually stirring them up unto repentance" (Jarom 1:10, 12)—Nephi's formula again.

Strictly speaking, there are no good guys: "All men that are in a state of nature, or I would say, in a carnal state, are in the gall of bitterness and in the bonds of iniquity; they are without God in the world" (Alma 41:11). Hence, "this is my doctrine, . . . that the Father commandeth all men, everywhere, to repent and believe in me" (3 Nephi 11:32). It is as pointless, then, to ask who are the good guys and who are the bad guys as it is to ask who should repent. The answer is always the same: I am the sinner, and I must repent. How much? Until, like the Son of Man, I am "full of grace and truth" (2 Nephi 2:6). When will that be? Not in this life! Here, all one can hope for is a passing grade.

Jacob's warnings of destruction take on an ominous note when his son Enos prays to the Lord that "if it should so be, that my people, the Nephites, should fall into transgression, and by any means be destroyed," that their record be preserved for the Lamanites (Enos 1:13, 16). The most hopeful thing that Enos's son Jarom can say for his own people is that "God is exceedingly merciful unto them, and has not yet swept them off from the face of the land," in spite of "the hardness of their hearts, and the deafness of their ears, and the blindness of their minds, and the stiffness of their necks" (Jarom 1:3). Are the Lamanites, then, so deserving? At that time, Jarom tells us, they "loved murder and would drink the blood of beasts" (Jarom 1:6). The best Jarom can hope for is to postpone the tragic end, and many righteous people among the Nephites set themselves to the task: "The prophets of the Lord did threaten the people of Nephi, according to the word of God, that if they did not keep the commandments, but should fall into transgression, they should be destroyed from off the face of the land" (Jarom 1:10).

Why this constant insistence on destruction—can't the people simply be punished or corrected? The ceaseless labors of prophets, priests, and teachers are all that "kept them from being destroyed upon the face of the land; for they did prick their hearts with the word, continually stirring them up unto repentance" (Jarom 1:12). Apparently the severe penalty clause for those who fail to meet conditions of survival in the promised land comes with the territory.

And who are the righteous in this land of backsliding Nephites and depraved Lamanites? The answer is written all over the Book of Mormon—the righteous are whoever are *repenting*. "I say unto you that as many of the Gentiles as will repent are the covenant people of the Lord and as many of the Jews as will not repent shall be cast off; for the Lord covenanteth with none save it be with them that repent" (2 Nephi 30:2). Nephi is repeating a lesson given earlier to his brethren Laman and Lemuel, who assumed that they were the good guys and that the traditional enemies of Israel, the Amorites who formerly inhabited the land, were the bad guys. "Not at all!" says Nephi:

> Do ye suppose that the children of this land, who were in the land of promise, who were driven out by our fathers, do ye suppose that they were righteous? Behold, I say unto you, Nay. Do ye suppose that our fathers would have been more choice than they if they had been righteous? I say unto you, Nay. Behold, the Lord esteemeth all flesh in one; he that is righteous is favored of God. But behold, this people had rejected every word of God, and they were ripe in iniquity; and the fulness of the wrath of God was upon them; and the Lord did curse the land against them, and bless it unto our fathers; yea, he did curse it against them unto their destruction, and he did bless it unto our fathers (1 Nephi 17:33-35).

The same land is blessed and cursed depending entirely on how the people behave. "And he leadeth away the righteous into precious lands, and the wicked he destroyeth, and curseth the land unto them for their sakes" (1 Nephi 17:38). And now Nephi tells them it was the Jews' turn to come under the curse: "And now, after all these things, the time has come that they have become wicked, yea, nearly unto ripeness; and . . . the day must surely come that they must be destroyed" (1 Nephi 17:43).

Laman and Lemuel, being patriots, weren't having any of that; for them the Jews were ipso facto the good guys: "And we know that the people who were in the land of Jerusalem were a righteous people; for they kept the statutes and judgments of the Lord, and all his commandments, according to the law of Moses; wherefore, we know that they are a righteous people; and our father hath judged them" (1 Nephi 17:22). It is this very argument to which Isaiah gives such a stinging rebuke. Jarom's son Omni admits that he is a wicked man and has spent his time fighting Lamanites rather than keeping "the statutes and

the commandments of the Lord as I ought to have done"
(Omni 1:2). Omni's son, Amaron, announces the fulfillment of the prophecy in his own day, when

> the more wicked parts of the Nephites were destroyed.
> For the Lord would not suffer, after he had led them
> out of the land of Jerusalem and kept and preserved
> them from falling into the hands of their enemies, yea,
> he would not suffer that the words should not be ver-
> ified, which he spake unto our fathers, saying that: In-
> asmuch as ye will not keep my commandments ye shall
> not prosper in the land. Wherefore, the Lord did visit
> them in great judgment; nevertheless, he did spare the
> righteous that they should not perish (Omni 1:5-7).

How is it possible to be so selective in times of war and
confusion? It is done by the process of leading the righteous
away. When the lights go out and the grandson of Amaron
reports that there is "no revelation save that which has
been written, neither prophecy" in his day (Omni 1:11),
then the righteous man Mosiah is "warned of the Lord
that he should flee out of the land of Nephi" (Omni 1:12),
taking any who will go with him — it is Lehi all over again,
another society of saints in the wilderness.

Mosiah becomes a king in the land of Zarahemla, where
his son, the righteous King Benjamin, is able to establish
the semblance of a decent society by using "much sharp-
ness because of the stiffneckedness of the people," speaking "the word of God with power and with authority"
(Words of Mormon 1:17). At the time he hands over the
crown to his son King Mosiah at the conventional great
assembly of the nation, a *panegyric* is held after the manner
of the ancient everywhere: "I have not commanded you
to come up hither to trifle with the words which I shall
speak," he tells them (Mosiah 2:9). Benjamin is the idol of
his people to whom his courage and skill have brought
victory and prosperity. The meeting is in an ecstasy of
patriotic fervor. But what does the king do? He studiously

throws cold water over every spark of national pride. When he sees that in response to his words "they had fallen to the earth, for the fear of the Lord had come upon them" (Mosiah 4:1), he congratulates them on being awakened "to a sense of your nothingness, and your worthless and fallen state" (Mosiah 4:5). "Believe that ye must repent of your sins and forsake them, and humble yourselves before God. . . . I would that ye should remember, and always retain in remembrance, the greatness of God, and your own nothingness, and his goodness and long-suffering towards you, unworthy creatures, and humble yourselves even in the depths of humility" (Mosiah 4:10-11).

Why this relentless suppression of every impulse to self-congratulation? It is to prepare the people's minds to receive the doctrines of the Atonement and the Redemption, which otherwise appear strange and alien to prosperous people, and to prepare them to receive the Covenant. Only those who are aware of their lost and fallen state can take the mission of the Savior seriously, and before one can embrace it in terms of the eternities it must be grasped on the level of common, everyday reality— Benjamin's people know that they are in real danger a good deal of the time and, thanks to his teachings, know that there is only one way they can get through. And now he wishes to bring home to them the need for a Savior and Redeemer as something even more real and urgent than holding off the Lamanites. Their righteousness must be put to a very practical test: "Ye will administer of your substance unto him that standeth in need. . . . Perhaps thou shalt say: The man has brought upon himself his misery; therefore I will stay my hand, and will not give unto him of my food, nor impart unto him of my substance" (Mosiah 4:16-17). Justifying busy acquisition by equating it with righteousness is a great sin (cf. Alma 4:6), and unless one who commits it "repenteth of that which he hath done he perisheth forever," for he has denied our common dependence on God "and hath no interest in the kingdom of God. For behold, are we not all beggars?" (Mosiah 4:18-19). He wants them to realize that this dependence applies at every level: "If God . . . doth grant unto you whatsoever ye ask that is right, in faith, believing that ye shall receive, O then, how ye ought to impart of the substance that ye have one to another" (Mosiah 4:21). The essence of Benjamin's preaching is to purge the people, if possible, of their flattering self-image as good guys.

It is in the time of Benjamin's son Mosiah that Zeniff is sent on patrol to spy out the weak points of the Lamanite defenses, "that our army might come upon them and destroy them—but when I saw that which was good among them I was desirous that they should not be destroyed" (Mosiah 9:1). For this treason the leader of the patrol, "being an austere and a blood-thirsty man [a real commando] commanded that I should be slain" (Mosiah 9:2)—musn't be soft on the bad guys! After all, Zeniff tells us the Lamanites really "were a lazy and an idolatrous people; therefore they were desirous to bring us into bondage" (Mosiah 9:12). What is more, they "taught their children . . . an eternal hatred towards the children of Nephi" (Mosiah 10:17). How can you deal with such people? That problem is solved in the proper way at a later time by the mightiest warrior of the Nephites, the great Ammon.

One might expect Ammon, the super-swordsman of the Book of Mormon to whom no man or platoon of men can stand up, to wade in and teach the Lamanites a lesson; so when he proposes to go with a few companions among the Lamanites as a missionary, everybody "laughed us to scorn," as he reports it. "For they said unto us: Do ye suppose that ye can bring the Lamanites to the knowledge of the truth? Do ye suppose that ye can convince the Lamanites of the incorrectness of the traditions of their fathers, as stiffnecked a people as they are; whose hearts delight in the shedding of blood; whose days have been spent in the grossest iniquity; whose ways have been the ways of a transgressor from the beginning? Now my brethren, ye remember that this was their language" (Alma 26:23-24). Of course everybody is for the standard solution: "Let us take up arms against them, that we destroy them and their iniquity out of the land, lest they overrun us and destroy us" — the only realistic solution (Alma 26:25). But not for the mighty Ammon! "We came into the wilderness not with the intent to destroy our brethren, but with the intent that perhaps we might save some few of their souls" (Alma 26:26). And so the terrible warrior "traveled from house to house," patiently suffering every privation, "relying . . . upon the mercies of God," teaching the people in their houses and in their streets, being "cast out, and mocked, and spit upon, and smote upon our cheeks; and we have been stoned and bound with strong cords, and cast into prison. . . . And we have suffered all manner of afflictions, and all this, that perhaps we might be the means of saving some soul" (Alma 26:28-30). And that is the way you deal with the bad guys.

The result of that effort is a body of converts who accept Ammon's own philosophy, who "buried their weapons of war, and [who] fear to take them up lest by any means they should sin" (Helaman 15:9), the righteous people of Ammon, who spend their days repenting of the murders they had committed as acts of war and refusing to fight the bad guys under any circumstances (see Alma 24:5-30).

When Abinadi comes with the usual message — "except they repent I will utterly destroy them from off the face of the earth" (Mosiah 12:8) — the people of King Noah say Abinadi is crazy, because they are the good guys:

> And now, O king, what great evil hast thou done, or what great sins have thy people committed, that we should be condemned of God or judged of this man? And now, O king, behold, we are guiltless, and thou, O king, hast not sinned. . . . And behold, we are strong,

we shall not come into bondage, or be taken captive by
our enemies; yea, and thou hast prospered in the land,
and thou shalt also prosper [peace and prosperity, standing tall all the way]" (Mosiah 12:13-15).

In reply, Abinadi points out that while being actively
religious they are doing the two things so fervidly condemned by Jacob: "If ye teach the law of Moses why do
ye not keep it? Why do ye set your hearts upon riches?
Why do ye commit whoredoms and spend your strength
with harlots, yea, and cause this people to commit sin?"
(Mosiah 12:29).

We must not forget those Book of Mormon super-good
guys, the Zoramites—hard working, independent, fiercely
patriotic, brave, smart, prosperous Zoramites—strictly attending their meetings and observing proper dress
standards. What a perfectly wonderful self-image! "Holy
God, we believe that thou hast separated us from our
brethren. . . . We believe that thou hast elected us to be
thy holy children. . . . And thou hast elected us that we
shall be saved, whilst all around us are elected to be cast
by thy wrath down to hell; for the which holiness, O God,
we thank thee. . . . And again we thank thee, O God, that
we are a chosen and a holy people" (Alma 31:16-18). To
Alma, these quintessentially good guys are the wickedest
people he has ever known: "O Lord God, how long wilt
thou suffer that such wickedness and infidelity shall be
among this people? O Lord, wilt thou give me strength,
that I may bear with mine infirmities. For I am infirm, and
such wickedness among this people doth pain my soul"
(Alma 31:30). And yet instead of condemning them, he
prays God to give him strength to bear his afflictions among
them (see Alma 31:33), because "their souls are precious"
(Alma 31:35). And in what does the "gross wickedness"
of these people consist? In this, that "they cry unto thee,
and yet their hearts are swallowed up in their pride. Behold, O God, they cry unto thee with their mouths, while

they are puffed up, even to greatness, with the vain things of the world. Behold, O my God, their costly apparel . . . and all their precious things which they are ornamented with; and behold, their hearts are set upon them, and yet they cry unto thee and say—We thank thee, O God, for we are a chosen people unto thee, while others shall perish" (Alma 31:27-28).

The prophet Nephi makes the same charge against the people of Zarahemla: "Ye have set your hearts upon the riches and the vain things of this world, for the which ye do murder, and plunder, and steal, and bear false witness against your neighbor" (Helaman 7:21). But God is not going to put up with it; he is withdrawing his protection:

> The Lord will not grant unto you strength, as he has hitherto done, to withstand against your enemies. For behold, thus saith the Lord: I will not show unto the wicked of my strength, to one more than the other, save it be unto those who repent. . . . It shall be better for the Lamanites than for you except ye shall repent. For behold, they are more righteous than you, for they have not sinned against that great knowledge which ye have received; therefore the Lord will be merciful unto them; yea, he will lengthen out their days and increase their seed, even when thou shalt be utterly destroyed except thou shalt repent (Helaman 7:22-24).

How often does this have to be repeated? Why do you think such great pains and sufferings have been experienced to get the message of the Book of Mormon to us? Nephi goes on, "Yea, wo shall come unto you because of that pride which ye have suffered to enter your hearts, which has lifted you up beyond that which is good because of your exceedingly great riches" (Helaman 7:26).

In the twelfth chapter of Helaman the demoralizing effect of riches on society is stated as a general rule: "At the very time when he doth prosper his people, . . . then is the time that they do harden their hearts" (Helaman

12:2). Why do they do it? — "O how great is the nothingness of the children of men" — thus is their beautiful self-image rebuffed (Helaman 12:7).

Jesus Christ, visiting the Nephites, personally sees to it that the preaching of Samuel the Lamanite be included in the record, from which it had been omitted, perhaps because Samuel is an alien or speaks too frankly:

> For this cause hath the Lord God caused that a curse should come upon the land, and also upon your riches, and this because of your iniquities. . . . Ye do cast out the prophets, and do mock them. . . . And now when ye talk, ye say: If our days had been in the days of our fathers of old, we would not have slain the prophets; we would not have stoned them, and cast them out. Behold ye are worse than they; for as the Lord liveth, if a prophet come among you and declareth unto you the word of the Lord, which testifies of your sins and iniquities, ye are angry with him, and cast him out and seek all manner of ways to destroy him, yea, you will say that he is a false prophet, and that he is a sinner, and of the devil, because he testifieth that your deeds are evil (Helaman 13:23-26).

They want to be told that they are the good guys, and so when a man comes and tells them not what is wrong with Zarahemla but what is right with Zarahemla they will "say that he is a prophet" and reward him with large sums of money "because he speaketh flattering words unto you, and he saith that all is well, then ye will not find fault with him" (Helaman 13:27, 28).

Giddianhi, the robber leader, insists that his followers *are* the good guys who are only trying to protect their sacred rights and property against the bad guys, "because of the many wrongs which ye have done unto them" (3 Nephi 3:4). He is the chief of the large and powerful "secret society of Gadianton; which society and the works thereof I know to be good; and they are of ancient date and they have been handed down unto us" (3 Nephi 3:9). The chief is merely trying to "recover their rights and government," lost to them "because of your wickedness in retaining from them their rights" (3 Nephi 3:10). It is the rigid tribal morality of the Mafia.

The shining hero of the Book of Mormon is Moroni: "If all men had been, and were, and ever would be, like unto Moroni, behold, the very powers of hell would have been shaken forever; yea, the devil would never have power over the hearts of the children of men" (Alma 48:17). You do not expel evil from "the hearts of the children of men" by shooting them or blowing them up or torturing them—the Inquisition operated on that theory. Nor can "the powers of hell be shaken" by heavy artillery or nuclear warheads. The devil does not care who is fighting or why, as long as there is fighting; "[the devil] is the father of contention, and he stirreth up the hearts of men to contend with anger, one with another." "Behold, this is not my doctrine, to stir up the hearts of men with anger, one against another; but this is my doctrine, that such things should be done away. Behold, verily, verily, I say unto you, I will declare unto you my doctrine, . . . that the Father commandeth all men, everywhere, to repent and believe in me" (3 Nephi 11:29-32). There is no possibility of confrontation here between Good and Bad. This is best shown in Alma's duel with Amlici. The Amlicites are described as coming on in all the hideous and hellish trappings of one of our more colorful rock groups, glorying in the fiendish horror of their appearance (see Alma 3:4-6). Alma, on the other hand, is the "man of God" (Alma 2:30) who meets the monster Amlici "with the sword, face to face" (Alma 2:29), and of course wins. Yet the Nephites consider that debacle to be "the judgments of God sent upon them because of their wickedness and their abominations; therefore they are awakened to a remembrance of their duty" (Alma 4:3). The moral is that whenever there is a battle, both sides are guilty.

Nobody knows that better than Moroni, whose efforts to avoid conflict far exceed his labors in battle. When he sees trouble ahead, he gets ready for it by "preparing the minds of the people to be faithful unto the Lord their God" (Alma 48:7). His military preparations are strictly defensive, and he is careful to do nothing that will seem to threaten the Lamanites; all of his battles are fought on Nephite soil (see Alma 48:8-10). We are repeatedly reminded that Moroni is "a man that did not delight in bloodshed" (Alma 48:11). By him "the Nephites were taught to defend themselves against their enemies, even to the shedding of blood if it were necessary; yea, and they were also taught never to give an offense, yea, and never to raise the sword except it were against an enemy, except it were to preserve their lives" (Alma 48:14). Any thought of preemptive strike is out of the question; Moroni even apologizes for espionage, for if they only have sufficient faith God will "warn them to flee, or to prepare for war, according to their danger; and also, that God would make it known unto them whither they should go to defend themselves." This is a great load off their minds, "and [Moroni's] heart did glory in it; not in the shedding of blood but in doing good, in preserving his people, yea, in keeping the commandments of God, yea, and resisting iniquity" (Alma 48:15-16). Resisting iniquity where? In the only place it can be resisted—in their own hearts. Not only is a preemptive strike out of the question, but Moroni's people have to let the enemy attack at least twice before responding, to guarantee that their own action is purely defensive (see Alma 43:46). The highest compliment that Alma can pay Moroni is: "Behold, he was a man like unto Ammon" (Alma 48:18), who, as we have seen, renounced all military solutions to the Lamanite problem.

Later it is the decision of the Nephites, after a series

of brilliant victories, to take the initiative against the Lamanites and "cut them off from the face of the land" that
makes a conscientious objector of Mormon, their great
leader, who "did utterly refuse from this time forth to
be a commander and a leader of this people" (Mormon
3:10-11). "And when they had sworn by all that had been
forbidden them by our Lord and Savior Jesus Christ, that
they would go up unto their enemies to battle, and avenge
themselves of the blood of their brethren [a perfect John
Wayne situation], behold the voice of the Lord came [to
Mormon] saying: Vengeance is mine, and I will repay"
(Mormon 3:14-15). So Mormon, from being top brass, becomes a detached observer and reporter for our express
benefit: "I did stand as an idle witness. . . . Therefore I
write unto you, Gentiles, and unto you, house of Israel"
(Mormon 3:16-17). He explains that the fatal mistake of the
Nephites was to take the offensive: "And it was because
the armies of the Nephites went up unto the Lamanites
that they began to be smitten; for were it not for that, the
Lamanites could have had no power over them" (Mormon
4:4). Then comes the bottom line: "But, behold, the judgments of God will overtake the wicked; and it is by the
wicked that the wicked are punished; for it is the wicked
that stir up the hearts of the children of men unto bloodshed" (Mormon 4:5). The battle is not between Good and
Bad—the wicked shall destroy the wicked.

Mormon places the Nephites and the Lamanites side
by side for our benefit. As the war between them continues,
each sinks deeper and deeper into depravity. First, after
a Nephite victory, are four years of peace devoted not to
repentance but to warlike preparations as the Lord removes
his beloved disciples from among the Nephites because of
the wickedness and unbelief. The Lord even forbids Mormon to preach repentance, which preaching will now do
no good: "Because of the hardness of their hearts the land
was cursed for their sakes" (Mormon 1:17). They have

passed the point of no return. The people have begun to worry and seek safe investments, to "hide up their treasures in the earth." But the Dow Jones keeps going down as their riches "became slippery, because the Lord had cursed the land, that they could not hold them, nor retain them again" (Mormon 1:18). It is interesting that amid all this military fury, riches still hold the number-one position in their minds. Then, as at the end of the Antique World, total lack of security forces people to turn in desperation to "sorceries, and witchcrafts, and magics" (Mormon 1:19)—they feel haunted, helpless, surrounded by demons. "The land was filled with robbers"; insecurity is total, but "notwithstanding the great destruction which hung over my people, they did not repent, . . . and it was one complete revolution throughout all the face of the land" (Mormon 2:8). Then come those awful words: "And I saw that the day of grace was passed with them" (Mormon 2:15). Though Mormon relents under extreme pressure and leads the army to more victories (see Mormon 5:1), "nevertheless the strength of the Lord was not with us; yea, we were left to ourselves" (Mormon 2:26). After all the Lord has done for them, the poor fools "did not realize that it was the Lord that had spared them, and granted unto them a chance for repentance"—his arm is still stretched out (Mormon 3:3).

Meanwhile, what are the bad guys up to? The Lamanites have been sacrificing Nephite women and children (see Mormon 4:15), yet "notwithstanding this great abomination of the Lamanites, it doth not exceed that of our people," who practice cannibalism "for a token of bravery" (Moroni 9:9-10). When things reach this state, Mormon says: "I pray unto God that he will spare thy life, to witness the return of his people unto him, or their *utter destruction;* for I know that they must perish except they repent" (Moroni 9:22). "O the depravity of my people! They are without order and without mercy" (Moroni 9:18). Mormon prays for the people he had loved and led, though he knows his prayer cannot be answered (see Mormon 3:12). "And if they perish it will be like unto the Jaredites, because of the willfulness of their hearts, seeking for blood and revenge" (Moroni 9:23).

And all this is meant for us: "These things must surely be made known. . . . A knowledge of these things must come unto a remnant of these people, and also unto the Gentiles," by being "hid up unto the Lord that they may come forth in his own due time" (Mormon 5:8-9, 12). As to Mormon's own people, the Lord has reserved their blessings, which they might have received in the land, for the Gentiles who shall possess the land (see Mormon 5:19). But they will have another chance, for "after they have been driven and scattered by the Gentiles, behold, then will the Lord remember the covenant" (Mormon 5:20). Then it will be our turn to be concerned: "And then, O ye Gentiles, how can ye stand before the power of God, except ye shall repent and turn from your evil ways?" (Mormon 5:22). That hardly describes us as good guys; there is only one hope for us: "I prayed unto the Lord that he would give unto the Gentiles grace," says Moroni, "that they might have charity"—that is the only thing that can save us, unilateral generosity; if I expect anything in return for charity except the happiness of the recipient, then it is not charity. The Lord's answer to Moroni is chilling: "The Lord said unto me: If they have not charity it mattereth not unto thee" (Ether 12:36-37). Mormon was shown our generation, which he describes with photographic accuracy: "Behold, I speak unto you as if ye were present, and yet ye are not. But behold, Jesus Christ hath shown you unto me, and I know your doing" (Mormon 8:35). He then proceeds to describe a people immensely pleased with themselves: "There are none save a few only who do not lift themselves up in the pride of their hearts, unto the wearing of fine apparel, unto envying, and strifes, and

malice, and persecutions, and all manner of iniquities" —
the high-living, fiercely competitive, crime-ridden world
of the 1980s. And then to the heart of the matter: "For
behold, ye do love money, and your substance, and your
fine apparel, and the adorning of your churches [Com-
munists do not adorn churches], more than ye love the
poor and the needy, the sick and the afflicted." Why, he
asks, do we allow the underprivileged to "pass by you,
and notice them not," while placing high value on "that
which hath no life" (Mormon 8:36-37, 39). All the meanness
and smugness of our days speak in that phrase; and these
very self-satisfied, church-conscious, and wicked people
are about to be destroyed by war: "Behold, the sword of
vengeance hangeth over you; and the time soon cometh
that he avengeth the blood of the saints upon you, for he
will not suffer their cries any longer" (Mormon 8:41).

We have not mentioned the case of the Jaredites; it
should hardly be necessary to tell the story of Shiz and
Coriantumr, each obsessed with the necessity of ridding
the world of his evil adversary. Both sides were exterminated. Not many years ago all of this Book of Mormon
extravaganza belonged even for Latter-day Saints to the
world of pure fantasy, of things that could never happen
in the modern civilized world — total extermination of a
nation was utterly unthinkable in those days. But suddenly
even within the past few years a very ancient order of
things has emerged at the forefront of world affairs; who
would have thought it — the Holy War! the ultimate showdown of the Good Guys with God on their side versus the
Godless Enemy. It is the creed of the Ayatollah, the Jihad,
Dar-al-Islam versus Dar-al-Harb, the Roman *ager pacatus*
versus the *ager hosticus*. On the one side *Deus vult*, on the
other *Bi'smi-llah*; it is a replay of the twelfth century, the
only way the "good people" can be free — that is, safe — is
to exterminate the "bad people" or, as Mr. Lee counsels,

to lock them up before they do any mischief—that alone will preserve the freedom of "us good people."

And now there is even talk of Armageddon with Gog and Magog, the two giants of the North, ending in extermination. There are those who insist that we are the good guys fighting the bad guys at Armageddon, but there is no such affair in the scriptures, where the only actual fighting mentioned is when "every man's sword shall be against his brother"—the wicked against the wicked. Then God intervenes with pestilence, "hailstones, fire, and brimstone" (Ezekiel 38:21-22), with much slaughter, but no mortal army has a hand in it. In the New Testament version it all happens after the Millennium, when fire comes out of heaven and destroys the army besieging the Saints, but there is no mention of a battle anywhere (see Revelation 20:7-10). We have seen that for us there is only one way to prepare for the great events ahead, and that is to be found doing good when the Lord comes, with no one taking advantage of temporary prosperity "to smite his fellow-servants, and to eat and drink with the drunken" (JS–M 1:52).

Mormon's message to us is not without a word of hope and advice: "Behold, I speak unto you as though I spake from the dead; for I know that ye shall have my words. . . . Give thanks unto God that he hath made manifest unto you our imperfections that ye may learn to be more wise than we have been" (Mormon 9:30-31). His address is expressly to the inhabitants of "this land" into whose hands "this book" shall come—specifically, it is meant for us.

22

Last Call:
An Apocalyptic Warning
from the Book of Mormon

The message of the Book of Mormon is that Jesus is the Christ. On the truth of that proposition depends our only hope for eternal life, and without that we are going nowhere, as many a wise man now assures; life becomes absurd, much ado about nothing, "a tale told by an idiot," and so on. First and foremost, the Book of Mormon preaches the gospel, but it supports its presentation with strong evidence. It tells us frankly on the title page that its intent is to *show* and to *convince*. To convince is to overcome resistance—that is the object; and the method is to show, to demonstrate by evidence. The woman at the well hearkened to the Lord's message and urged the other villagers to do so because he told her all about herself, things that only she knew (John 4:6-30). So it is with the Book of Mormon; its message is the gospel, but as an inducement to consider the doctrine seriously an impressive historical superstructure has been erected.

Let us forego the discussion of the doctrinal and spiritual part and in the limited space given confine ourselves to the historical, though both parts deliver the same message.

This article is based on a transcript of a talk given at the 1986 Sunstone Theological Symposium in Salt Lake City. It was published in Sunstone 12 (January 1988): 14-25.

But is it history? Until specific sources are available one way or the other, can you tell me why it should not be treated as history? Here, a very young man (or somebody in the 1820s, perhaps the most barren and desolate decade in scholarship) has offered to present us with a complex history of a civilization covering a thousand years, and neglecting no major aspect of the human comedy from beginning to end. The author assures us that this is all history, and he has written it all out for us. This, by the rules of textual criticism, puts the ball in our court: The writer has done an awful lot of work, and it is now up to us to show that his work is not what he says it is.

Today, Egyptologists admit how very close to nothing at all is known about the ancient Egyptians, even though we have thousands of pages of their writings to read. But Egypt is our town, a crowded pageant of familiar faces, compared to the vast and total blank of the canvas which still awaits the portrait of the Americas of a mere thousand years ago. Do you think anyone is qualified at this time to tell the world just what went on and did not go on in that most lost of lost worlds?

For example, it is only since 1960, as Klaus Koch has shown, that we have seen "the rediscovery of apocalyptic."[1] The most significant form of that ancient literature is the *Himmelsreise der Seele [The Ascension of the Soul to Heaven]*, or as it is now somewhat pompously called, the *psychanodia*. The existence of the genre was first demonstrated by Martin Haug in 1872. The past twenty-five years have seen the emergence of two "psychanodic" heroes who quite overshadow all the others, namely Enoch and Abraham. Joseph Smith was only twenty-three years old when he produced the Book of Enoch and the Book of Mormon; the latter opens with the most perfect model of an ascension (*Himmelsreise*).[2] We find the righteous man in a doomed and wicked world supplicating God, carried aloft in an ascension in which "he thought he saw God

sitting upon his throne" (1 Nephi 1:8); he returns to earth
and begins to teach the people, who mock him and threaten
his life; he retires to the desert with a faithful following in
the expectation of founding a pious colony in the wilderness.

We have space to consider only certain specialized but
supremely important aspects of Book of Mormon history.
I have treated several others in some detail in the light of
more recent findings: the crisis in Jerusalem (illustrated by
the Lachish letters);[3] nomadic life in the deserts of Arabia
(as reported by mid–nineteenth-century and twentieth-
century travelers);[4] the communities of sectaries in desert
retreats (as described in the Dead Sea Scrolls);[5] ancient
religious rites, ordinances, and ceremonies (depicted in
documents found since the mid-nineteenth century);[6] ancient warfare (in the light of personal experience);[7] proper
names (from lists supplied by archaeology in Palestine and
Egypt);[8] and on and on. But if such a performance was
beyond the capacity of anyone living in the 1820s, what is
even more fantastic is the picture painted by the Book of
Mormon of another world entirely, even more removed
from the imagination of anyone living in 1830, namely our
own world of the 1980s. And this is the world with which
the Book of Mormon is primarily concerned.

For over a century, Mormons promoted the Book of
Mormon as the story of the Indians. "Wouldn't you like
to know where the American Indians came from?" my
missionary companions used to ask the factory workers
and peasants of Europe, who couldn't have cared less.
Why have we ignored the book's own insistent and repeated statements on why it was written and to whom it
is addressed? The first chapter is a prologue set in the Old
World which bluntly states the argument: "There came
many prophets, prophesying unto the people that they
must repent, or the great city Jerusalem must be destroyed"
(1 Nephi 1:4). In the last chapter of the Book of Mormon,

we find the identical proposition repeated for another and a distant people—a proud civilization which must repent or be destroyed (Moroni 10). In between the beginning and the end, the proposition is repeated more than a hundred times. "Destruction" is repeated some 513 times in the book, and "repentance" 385 times. "Destroy" is used in the proper sense as *de-struere*, to break down and scatter the elements, to smash the structure.[9]

A society on the brink of destruction is not a safe place to linger, and so we are immediately introduced into the *Rekhabite* motif: "Come out of her, oh my people! Partake not of her sins lest ye partake of her plagues" (cf. Jeremiah 35). After the ascension of Lehi, he does what other prophets did after such an experience and takes off into the wilderness. The Rekhabites were contemporaries of Lehi who did just that, and the discovery of the Dead Sea Scrolls shows us that such things actually did happen repeatedly.[10] The flight from Egypt, of course, had set the example, and to it the Book of Mormon preachers, like those in ancient Israel, often refer and compare themselves. The first psalm dramatizes the situation by comparing the righteous to a fruitful tree of life and the evil man to a barren plant; the one follows paths known to God, the other gets lost in the sand.

The Rekhabite move is repeated again and again in the Book of Mormon. Not long after the arrival of the family of Lehi in the New World, when the tension became unbearable between Nephi and his elder brothers, Nephi wrote, "The Lord did warn me, that I, Nephi, should depart from them and flee into the wilderness, and all those who would go with me" (2 Nephi 5:5). Even so, "Mosiah . . . being warned of the Lord that he should flee out of the land of Nephi, and as many as would hearken unto the voice of the Lord should also depart out of the land with him, into the wilderness . . . did according as the Lord had commanded him" (Omni 1:12-13). From his com-

munity in turn, others broke off and disappeared into the
wilderness (Omni 1:27-30). Likewise, Alma founded his
pious colony at the Waters of Mormon, a wild place (Mosiah 18:4); and when later his church had been absorbed
by a local kingdom, his people "gathered their flocks together" and while the guards slept, "Alma and his people
departed into the wilderness" (Mosiah 24:18, 20). After the
title of liberty was raised, many Lamanites gave up everything and went over to join the devout and peaceful society
of the Ammonites (Alma 62:27). Even so, the Latter-day
Saints, given the choice between Missouri and Illinois or
the desert, chose the wilderness.

So here we have two sharply divided societies to whose
irreconcilable views there is only one solution — separation.
But the trouble with idealistic communities fleeing from
the wicked world is that they take their tensions with them.
In the desert, trouble within the family, which began in
the city, only gets worse. Laman and Lemuel side with
the people at Jerusalem: "We perish if we leave Jerusalem,"
they said. "You perish if you stay," said Nephi, because
there isn't going to be any Jerusalem. How does he know?
"I have seen a vision" (2 Nephi 1:4). That is just what is
wrong, say Laman and Lemuel. Here they are being led
by the "foolish imaginations" of "a visionary man" — a
piqqeah, one who sees things that others do not — to give
up "the land of their inheritance, and their gold, and their
silver, and their precious things," and for what? "To perish
in the wilderness" (1 Nephi 2:11). Jerusalem offered Laman
and Lemuel wealth, social position, the security of a great
city with strong alliances (1 Nephi 2:13). What is more,
righteousness was on their side: "We know that the people
who were in the land of Jerusalem were a righteous people;
for they kept the statutes and judgments of the Lord, and
all his commandments, according to the law of Moses"
(1 Nephi 17:22). It was their father who was off base; what
did he and Nephi have to offer but "great desires to know

the mysteries of God" (1 Nephi 2:16)? Feelings ran so high that the brothers went so far as to conspire to remove Nephi and his father from the scene.

The hopeless impasse was an anguish of soul to the father and son, who received comfort and encouragement in inspired dreams, in which the high life and hunger in the sands become an allegory of the perennial choices before us. That is how Nephi explains it. Fashionably dressed beautiful people, partying in the top-priced upper apartments and penthouses of a splendid high-rise, have fun looking down and commenting on a bedraggled little band of transients eagerly eating fruit from a tree in a field (1 Nephi 8:10-27). "This great and spacious building," Nephi explains, "was the pride of the world" (1 Nephi 11:36), or rather is the "vain imaginations . . . of the children of men" (1 Nephi 12:18); the choice was narrowed when that "great and spacious building . . . fell, and the fall thereof was exceedingly great. . . . Thus shall be the destruction of all nations, kindreds, tongues and people, that shall fight against the twelve apostles of the Lamb" (1 Nephi 11:36).

This great dichotomy is the perennial order of the world, "opposition in all things," a symmetry as natural as that which pervades all matter, but it is a *broken* symmetry. Without the Rekhabite principle, the Book of Mormon would be nothing but a *vates malorum,* a wail of despair without hope. What breaks the symmetry is the indeterminate principle as stated by Heisenberg and also by Moroni in his final reflection on the fate of the Nephites: "The devil . . . inviteth and enticeth to sin, and to do that which is evil continually. But behold, that which is of God inviteth and enticeth to do good continually" (Moroni 7:12-13). Powerful forces exerting equal pull in opposite directions. What breaks the symmetry? The free will of the individual. The nation may go to hell, but the individual does not have to. Almost every leading character in the

Book of Mormon is one who breaks with the establishment and goes his way. So Moroni explains, "Wherefore, take heed . . . that ye do not judge that which is evil to be of God, or that which is good and of God to be of the devil. For . . . it is given unto you to judge, that ye may know good from evil . . . as the daylight is from the dark night" (Moroni 7:14-15). In the end this broken symmetry is the hope of salvation.

But God has more to offer those who break with the world than "wearying in a land of sands and thorns." The wilderness is only a transition, a difficult exercise of disengaging from the fashion of the world: "He did straiten them in the wilderness with his rod" (1 Nephi 17:41). Besides the "mysteries of God," there was more awaiting the faithful: "Ye shall prosper, and be led to a *land of promise* . . . which I have prepared for you; yea, even a land which is choice above all other lands" (1 Nephi 2:20). "He leadeth away the righteous into precious lands, and the wicked he destroyeth, and curseth the land unto them for their sakes" (1 Nephi 17:38). The idea is biblical — the promise to Abraham — and also classical, as we see in Tyrtaeus and the Aeneid.[11] It is the normal product of times of hardship and migration, when wandering tribes seek happy homelands, which finds its culmination in the hope of America.

This is the "choice land above all other lands" since the Flood, reserved for the New Jerusalem and the "remnant of the house of Joseph . . . like unto the Jerusalem of old" (Ether 13:2, 6-8). But God placed the promise upon it "in his *wrath*" (Jacob 1:7; Alma 12:35; Ether 1:33; 2:8; 15:28). Why that, of all things? Because his patience was at an end when men had defiled all the other lands in the glorious and beautiful world he had given them. He would set apart a place where he would stand for no nonsense; there men would be given such freedom as nowhere else, and could enjoy such prosperity as nowhere else.

But in return for this liberty, certain ground rules have to be observed. Perfect liberty means that you can go as far as you want, free of many of the age-old hampering restraints imposed by man; since this is a place of testing, that is the purpose of leaving everyone pretty much on his own. But when the inhabitants abuse that freedom until they "are ripened in iniquity," their presence will be no longer tolerated; "when the fulness of his wrath should come" they will be "swept off," suddenly and completely (Ether 2:8). As it was in the days of Noah, it shall be business as usual, right up until the last moment, for it is "not until the fulness of iniquity" is matched by "the fulness of his wrath," which "cometh upon them when they are ripened in iniquity," that they will be abruptly terminated (Ether 2:8-10). God was angry when he laid down these conditions: "These are my thoughts upon the land which I shall give you for your inheritance; for it shall be a land choice above all other lands." And these are the thoughts: "My Spirit will not always strive with man; wherefore, if ye will sin until ye are fully ripe ye shall be cut off from the presence of the Lord" (Ether 2:15). This promise is conveyed to us for our special benefit: "And this cometh to you, O ye Gentiles, that ye may know the decrees of God—that ye may repent, and not continue in your iniquities until the fulness come, that ye may not bring down the fulness of the wrath of God upon you as the inhabitants of the land have hitherto done" (Ether 2:11). It is Moroni's prophetic warning to stop doing what we are doing. Fullness and ripeness: when the cup is full, it can no longer be diluted; when the fruit is ripe, it can only rot—there is no point to continuing the game. But up to that point all is permitted.

"Promised land" has a nice upbeat sound that we like very much, but the great promise is worded as a curse: "Thus saith the Lord God—Cursed shall be the land, yea, this land, unto every nation, kindred, tongue, and people,

unto destruction, which do wickedly, when they are fully
ripe; . . . for this is the cursing and the blessing of God
upon this land" (Alma 45:16). When Lehi's party had barely
left Jerusalem, Nephi had a vision in which he "looked
and beheld the land of promise." And what did he see?
"A mist of darkness on the face of the land of promise,"
and horrible destruction and desolation (1 Nephi 12:4).
Obviously one is not home-free when he has set foot upon
the land of promise. Quite the opposite; from then on he
must watch his step and control the impulse to do whatever
he pleases and "have it all." For "God has sworn in his
wrath" that what went on in other lands should not go
on here. There are nations that were old when Nephi left
Jerusalem and whose cultures and languages, customs,
manners, and traditions still survive. They have all paid a
high price in human suffering as they go along from folly
to folly and disaster to disaster, but they are still there. It
is not so in the New World, where great civilizations vanish
without even leaving us their names, and where no high
civilization has survived. It is significant that with all the
warning and promising, only one penalty is ever mentioned, and only one means of avoiding it. "Prophets, and
the priests, and the teachers, did labor diligently; . . .
and . . . by so doing they kept them from being destroyed
upon the face of the land; for they did prick their hearts
with the word, continually stirring them up to repentance"
(Jarom 1:11-12). The penalty is destruction; the deliverance,
repentance.

To avoid the destruction of the righteous with the
wicked, God effects "a division of the people," the Rekhabite phenomenon, the awful gulf. It is the division between two ways of life, but *it* does not divide the good
guys from the bad guys into discrete societies. It is convenient to imagine all the righteous in one camp and the
wicked in another, and this has been the usual and comfortable interpretation of the Book of Mormon—it is the

good guys versus the bad guys. But this is exactly what the Book of Mormon tells us to avoid. God plays no favorites. Nephi rebukes his brothers for believing that because they are Jews they are righteous; God does not judge by party, he tells them; a good man is good and a bad one is bad, according to his own behavior: "Behold, the Lord esteemeth all flesh in one; he that is righteous is favored of God" (1 Nephi 17:35). Family and race and nationality account for nothing; "God is mindful of every people, whatsoever land they may be in; yea, he numbereth his people" (Alma 26:37). He numbers them as his own, not as being on one side or the other of a boundary; "the Lord doth grant unto all nations . . . to teach his word . . . all that he seeth fit that they should have" (Alma 29:8). Nephi finds the answer to the questions "Who are the bad guys? Where is the real enemy?" In himself. It is his own weakness that makes him frustrated and angry, he says. Why should he take it out on others? (2 Nephi 4:26-35). Though others may be seeking his life, his escape is to follow the path that God has shown him, "a way for mine escape before mine enemies!" It is not for him to settle the score with them: "I will not put my trust in the arm of flesh; for I know that cursed is he that putteth his trust in the arm of flesh. Yea, cursed is he that putteth his trust in man or maketh flesh his arm" (2 Nephi 4:33-34). He is to tell the people who their real enemy is. The Lamanites are not the problem: "And the Lord God said unto me: They shall be a scourge unto thy seed, to stir them up in the remembrance of me; and inasmuch as they will not remember me, and hearken unto my words, they shall scourge them even unto destruction" (2 Nephi 5:25). Did the wickedness of the Nephites make the Lamanites any less wicked or less dangerous? On the contrary, it made them more dangerous because God had planned it that way. As long as the Nephites behaved themselves, the Lamanites, "curse[d] . . . with a sore curse, . . . shall have no power

over thy seed except they shall rebel against me also." God
means to keep them in place right to the end as "a scourge
unto thy seed, to stir them up in the ways of remembrance"
(1 Nephi 2:23-24). The Lamanites "have not kept the commandments of God" and have "been cut off" (Alma 9:14).
Nevertheless, "the Lord will be merciful unto them and
prolong their existence in the land" (Alma 9:16),
"but . . . if ye [Nephites] persist in your wickedness . . . your days shall *not* be prolonged in the land, for
the Lamanites shall be sent upon you . . . and ye shall be
visited with utter destruction" (Alma 9:18-19).

The Book of Mormon goes to great lengths to describe
just what a wicked society looks like and how it operates,
with enough examples to type it beyond question; and
with clinical precision it describes the hysteria that leads
to its end.[12] It also tells us how to recognize a righteous
society, usually presenting the two types to us in close
proximity. With these two images firmly in mind we are
told why this presentation is being given, for whose benefit, and why it is so singularly important. The authors do
not ask us to make comparisons and see ourselves in the
picture, because that would be futile: the wickeder the
people are the more they balk at facing their real image
and the more skillful they become in evading, altering,
faking, and justifying. So the book does not tell us to make
the comparison — it does it for us, frankly and brutally. The
Book of Mormon does not need to tell us what the wickedness of Jerusalem consisted of, since we have that in the
Bible. The first display of evil is in the ambition of Laman,
who stirred everyone's hearts to anger by accusing Nephi
of thinking "to make himself a king and a ruler over us"
(1 Nephi 16:38), which is exactly what Laman was aspiring
to do (1 Nephi 17:44, 3:28-29). But the prime evil quickly
emerges and persists throughout the book. Nephi, following Isaiah, explains the situation with the Jews: "For because they are rich they despise the poor, . . . their hearts

are upon their treasures; wherefore, their treasure is their god" (2 Nephi 9:30). "And they that are rich, . . . puffed up because of their learning, and their wisdom, and their riches—yea, they are they whom he despiseth" (2 Nephi 9:42). That must be the all-time put-down.

Nephi's brother Jacob took over the leadership when the whole community was affected by the virus they had brought from Jerusalem: "You have obtained many riches; and because some of you have obtained more abundantly than that of your brethren, . . . ye suppose that ye are better than they. . . . [God] condemneth you, and if ye persist in these things his judgments must speedily come unto you. . . . O that you would rid you from this iniquity and abomination" (Jacob 2:13-16). In Alma's day, good, conscientious people, "because of their exceeding riches . . . which they had obtained by their industry [the work ethic, no less], . . . were lifted up in the pride of their eyes. . . . The people of the church began . . . to set their hearts upon riches . . . that they began to be scornful, one towards another" (Alma 4:6-8). The result was "great inequality among the people, . . . that Alma, seeing all their inequality, began to be very sorrowful" (Alma 4:12, 15). "Will ye persist, " he cried, "in the wearing of costly [not beautiful but always costly] apparel, and setting your hearts . . . upon your riches? Yea, will ye persist in supposing that ye are better one than another" (Alma 5:53-54). "And thus we see how great the inequality of man is because of sin and transgression" (Alma 28:13). The Book of Mormon describes the declension by which that mentality inevitably led to "wars and contentions among the Nephites, . . . an awful scene of bloodshed" (Alma 28:9-10).

Needless to say, advocates were not lacking to justify and even sanctify such behavior. Korihor, a contemporary of Alma, rallied the people of property to free themselves from the oppressive restraints of sacral government, "fool-

ish performances," he said, by which "this people bind
themselves . . . that they might not lift up their heads"
(Alma 30:23). Thanks to the government, said he, people
"durst not enjoy their rights and privileges." In particular,
"they durst not make use of that which was their own lest
they should offend their priests" (Alma 30:27-28); his appeal was for freedom from restraints "laid down by ancient
priests" (Alma 30:23), freedom to follow the natural order
in which "every man prospered according to his genius,
and that every man conquered according to his strength;
and whatsoever a man did was no crime" (Alma 30:17).
The bottom line was the common-sense creed, "when a
man was dead, that was the end thereof," all accounts
settled, all charges dropped, all moral objections canceled.
This was good news to the beautiful people, "causing them
to lift their heads in wickedness," enjoying unlimited criminal and sexual license, "leading away . . . women, and
also men, to commit whoredoms" (Alma 30:18)—a plain
but discreet way of hinting at rampant homosexuality.

When a long war was followed by a postwar boom,
there arose a dissension among them, and they would not
give heed to the words of Helaman and his brethren: "But
they grew proud, being lifted up in their hearts, because
of their exceedingly great riches; therefore, they grew rich
in their own eyes, and would not give heed to their words"
(Alma 45:24). Taking advantage of this backlash, one Amalickiah rode the wave to greatness. He is something of a
standard type in the Book of Mormon—quite a charmer,
"a man of many flattering words," who "led away the
hearts of many people" (Alma 46:10). Of large and imposing presence (Alma 46:3), he was shrewd and calculating, "a man of cunning device" (Alma 49:11), and
perfectly cynical—"he did not care for the blood of his
people" (Alma 49:10). He had solid support among "those
who were in favor of kings, . . . those of high birth, and
they sought to be kings; and they were supported by those

who sought power and authority over the people" (Alma 51:8). He wrought infinite mischief, as an example. Moroni reflects on "the great wickedness of those who are seeking for power and authority" (Alma 60:17). It was this "iniquity . . . for the cause of your love of glory and the vain things of the world" (Alma 60:32) that plunged the Nephites into that terrible war, and "caused so much bloodshed" among themselves; it was all due to "the desire [for] power and authority which those king-men had over [them]" (Alma 60:16).

The parallel path to power was that of organized crime. Kishkumen also aspired to head the government and began by employing the talents of one Gadianton, "exceedingly expert . . . in his craft," which was to "carry on the secret work of murder and of robbery" in a businesslike and professional manner (Helaman 2:4). Though their first plan failed, the campaign continued, and clever public relations "seduced the more part of the righteous" to invest in their numerous projects, "come down to believe in their works and partake of their spoils." Thus "the Nephites did build them up and support them, beginning at the more wicked part of them." But then growing ever more respectable "until they had overspread all the land" (Helaman 6:31), they found it an easy matter to swing elections in favor of the society, and to put their own people in office, especially filling the judgeships and getting complete control of the law courts: from then on they could make legal whatever they chose to do. Speaking of the days of Moroni, Mormon observes that it was the lawyers and judges who started laying "the foundation of the destruction of this people" (Alma 10:27). So with the public "in a state of . . . awful wickedness" (Helaman 4:25), the combination "did obtain the sole management of the government"; and the first thing they did was to "turn their backs upon the poor and the meek, and the humble followers of God" (Helaman 6:39). In control of the nation's wealth, "in the space of

not many years" (Helaman 6:32), the Gadianton society
had become perfectly respectable, "filling the judgment-
seats, . . . condemning the righteous; . . . letting the
guilty and the wicked go unpunished because of their
money, . . . held in office [perpetually] . . . to rule and do
according to their wills, that they might get gain and glory
of the world" (Helaman 7:4-5). It all goes back to one thing,
the line of ambitious men who beguile the public and aim
at absolute power, and always start out by "seeking for
gain, yea, for that lucre which doth corrupt the soul" (Mosiah 29:40). Among such men were religious promoters
like Nehor, who engaged in "the spreading of priestcraft
through the land . . . for the sake of riches and honor"
(Alma 1:16), or the wicked King Noah, who "placed his
heart upon riches" (Mosiah 11:14). There is one phrase
occurring some fifteen times in the Book of Mormon that
starts the alarm bell ringing and the red lights flashing;
the fatal words are: "They set their hearts on riches." If
you can have anything in this world for money, well,
money is what you want; how you get it, as the Roman
satirist says, is not too important as long as you keep things
respectable by keeping your murders secret — another main
theme of the Book of Mormon.

Nephi ended his days in deep discouragement: "I am
left to mourn because of the unbelief, and the wickedness,
and the ignorance, and the stiffneckedness of men; for
they will not search knowledge" (2 Nephi 32:7). His brother
Jacob takes up on an even more alarming note. In their
frontier condition his people had taken to the barbarian
custom of collecting wives, concubines, and the spectacular
loot that barbarians love. We should note here that the
savage Lamanites who lived by raiding and plunder sought
exactly the same things as the supposedly more civilized
Nephites did — the whole lot of them "set their hearts on
riches." Three hundred years after Christ, both the "people
of Nephi and the Lamanites had become exceedingly

wicked one like unto another" (4 Nephi 1:45). Who were the barbarians when "the people of Nephi began to be proud in their hearts, because of their exceeding riches, and become vain like unto their brethren, the Lamanites"? (4 Nephi 1:43). Love and display of wealth, as Plutarch tells us in his first Moral Essay, is the characteristic mark of the barbarians.[13] It is not surprising that "the robbers of Gadianton did spread over all the face of the land," with business booming everywhere—"gold and silver did they lay up in store in abundance, and did traffic in all manner of traffic" (4 Nephi 1:46). The work ethic paid off only too well when the "laborer in Zion" labored for money (2 Nephi 26:31), and "the hand of providence . . . smiled upon [them]" (Jacob 2:13).

The prosperity in the time of good king Mosiah produced a spoiled generation of smart-alecks, "many of the rising generation . . . did not believe"; actually, "they were a separate people to their faith, . . . even in their carnal and sinful state" (Mosiah 26:1-4). The sons of Alma and Mosiah were among the alienated generation; it took an angel to convert them, but the tradition never ceased out of the land (Mosiah 26:4). King Mosiah, to undertake reforms and make the country "a land of liberty," insisted that "this inequality should be no more in this land" and suggested a system of judges to equalize things (Mosiah 29:32). Under Alma the church was an ideal community (Alma 1:26-28), but the rest of the society indulged in the usual catalog of wrongdoing: "envyings and strife; wearing costly apparel; being lifted up in the pride of their own eyes; . . . lying, thieving, robbing, committing whoredoms, and murdering, and all manner of wickedness" (Alma 1:32). All the excitement of a highly competitive society, a night of prime-time TV. There are four things that can lead to certain destruction according to both Nephis: the desire for gain, for power, for popularity, and for "lusts of the flesh" — the lifestyles of the rich and famous (1 Nephi 22:23; 3 Nephi 6:15).

After the war with Amlici, the people repented and prosperity returned, whereupon "the people of the church began to wax proud, because of their exceeding riches, . . . which they had obtained by their industry" (Alma 4:6). "Many . . . were sorely grieved for the wickedness which they saw . . . [as] the people of the church began to be lifted up in the pride of their eyes, and to set their hearts upon riches" (Alma 4:7-8). The usual competitive escalation of unpleasantness followed: "Yea, there were envyings, and strife, and malice, and persecutions, and pride, even to exceed the pride of those who did not belong to the church" (Alma 4:9). When "Alma saw the wickedness of the church . . . thus bringing on the destruction of the people, [and when] he saw the great inequality among the people, . . . seeing all their inequality, [he] began to be very sorrowful" (Alma 4:11-12, 15). He laid down all his great offices of state, realizing that all the power and authority of the highest political and military (Mosiah 29:42; Alma 2:16) offices which he had held would not correct the evil, and spent the rest of his days preaching repentance (Alma 4:19-20): "Yea, will ye persist in supposing that ye are better one than another, . . . and will ye persist in turning your backs upon the poor, and the needy, and in withholding your substance from them?" (Alma 5:54-55). Things got worse, and there was a nasty war. Ammon was told by the Lord to save the people of Ammon, who wanted no part of the business. "Get this people out of this land that they perish not. . . . And they gathered together all their people . . . and . . . flocks and herds, and departed into the wilderness" (Alma 27:12-14). The Rekhabite solution was still the only way out. The Ammonites missed the tremendous battle that ensued and the great lamentation that followed: "And thus we see," says Mormon, "how great the inequality of man is because of sin and transgression, and the power of the devil, which comes by the cunning plans . . . to ensnare the hearts of men" (Alma 28:13). Need we go on?

What does a righteous society look like? Far less spectacular than the wicked, it keeps a low profile; a healthy body is not aware of the ailing organs that provide the interest, conversation, and titillation of a hypochondriac world. "Happy is the people whose annals is a blank!" says Voltaire. "What a drag!" says the overstimulated TV libertine. From the outside, the righteous society looks empty and boring to those who have not the remotest conception of what may go on inside. Alan Watts points this out in an essay in which he finds that the obscuring wall between the two worlds is simply money.[14] For those on either side of the veil it is the other side, naturally, that is not real—only our side is real. However, there are certain guidelines to what is a good society, though mostly given in negative terms—those who keep the ten commandments are praiseworthy for what they do *not* do. Jacob gives us some rules: "Think of your brethren like unto yourselves, and be familiar with all and free with your substance, that they may be rich like unto you" (Jacob 2:17)—it is not the wealth but the inequality that does the damage. Of unequal distribution he says, "Do ye not suppose that such things are abominable unto him who created all flesh? And the one being is as precious in his sight as the other" (Jacob 2:21). Benjamin recognizes the same danger of acquisitiveness: "I . . . have not sought gold nor silver nor any manner of riches of you; neither have I suffered . . . that ye should make slaves of one another. . . . And even I myself, have labored with mine own hands that I might serve you" (Mosiah 2:12-14). "For behold, are we not all beggars? Do we not all depend upon the same Being . . . for all riches which we have of every kind?" (Mosiah 4:19). And when Alma organized his church, "they were all equal, and they did all labor. . . .

And they did impart of their substance, every man according to that which he had" (Alma 1:26-27). The main theme is obvious: "For thus saith the Lord: Ye shall not esteem one flesh above another, or one man think himself above another" (Mosiah 23:7). "I desire that the inequality should be no more in this land . . . but I desire that this land be a land of liberty, and every man enjoy his rights and privileges alike" (Mosiah 29:32). For this reason, Mosiah laid down the kingship in favor of a system of judges, as a more equalitarian order (Mosiah 23:7). But the great obstacle to freedom was not government but money; to maintain their liberty, Alma's people "were all equal, and they did all labor, every man according to his strength" (Alma 1:26). (How could they be equal in wealth, we ask today, if no two of them were equal in strength?) Under the law of Mosiah and the judges, "there was no law against a man's belief; for it was strictly contrary to the commands of God that there should be a law which should bring men on to unequal grounds" (Alma 30:7). "Now if a man desired to serve God, it was his privilege; . . . but if he did not believe in him there was no law to punish him" (Alma 30:9) or to put him at a disadvantage, for the idea was that "all men were on equal grounds." So even Alma, the high priest and chief judge of the land, allowed people to go around preaching atheism. The righteous can preserve their liberty only by remembering the words of the patriarch Jacob, in all humility considering themselves despised and rejected in the manner of the youthful Joseph (Alma 46:24-27). Moroni calls upon his people to recognize their position as the meek and humble of the world, "we, who are despised" (Alma 46:18) by those whose "pride and nobility" he denounces (Alma 51:17, 18-21). The book of Alma begins with a happy picture. After a long war and great suffering, the people had learned their lesson, and here we have a picture of a righteous society: "And thus they were all equal, and they did all labor every man according to his strength. And they did impart of their substance, every man according to that which he had, to the poor, and the needy, and the sick, and the afflicted; and they did not wear costly apparel" (Alma 1:27). "Through the preaching of Ammon," many Lamanites "became a righteous people"—and here we have another important criterion of righteousness—"they did lay down the weapons of their rebellion" (Alma 23:7). And "there was not one soul among all the people who had been converted unto the Lord who would take up arms against their brethren; nay, they would not even make any preparations for war" (Alma 24:6). They repeatedly refer to all their former battles as murders (Alma 24:9-11; 27:8). When such groups got into trouble, Ammon recommended the Rekhabite solution—they "departed out of the land, and came into the wilderness" and carried on as "perfectly honest and upright in all things. . . . And they did look upon shedding the blood of their brethren with the greatest abhorrence" (Alma 27:14, 27-28).

When the Lord appeared among the people, he established his order of things, thereby demonstrating that it is not impossible for human beings on this earth to live after such an order without being bored by inactivity or lack of excitement. Fourth Nephi gives us the description of the model society:

> The people were all converted to the Lord, upon all the face of the land, both Nephites and Lamanites, and there were no contentions and disputations among them, and every man did deal justly one with another. And they had all things common among them; therefore there were not rich and poor, bond and free, but they were all made free, . . . continuing in fasting and prayer, and in meeting together oft both to pray and to hear the word of the Lord. . . . And . . . there was no contention in the land, because of the love of God which did dwell in the hearts of the people. And there were no envyings,

nor strifes, nor tumults, nor whoredoms, nor lyings, nor murders, nor any manner of lasciviousness; and surely there could not be a happier people. . . . There were no robbers, nor murders, neither . . . Lamanites nor any manner of -ites; but they were in one, the Children of Christ. . . . And how blessed they were!" (4 Nephi 1:2-3, 12, 15-18).

Does this sound tame? The wicked flaunt their riches and their learning in the highly visible manner; "they are they whom he [God] despises." To be righteous they must "consider themselves fools before God, and come down in the depths of humility" (2 Nephi 9:42), with no photo opportunities whatever. What counts is long suffering and patience—very low profile and nonspectacular; to call attention to one's patience is to be impatient, "the Lord . . . trieth their patience and their faith" (Mosiah 23:21). In fact, the whole program culminates in "a sense of your nothingness" (Mosiah 4:5). To discover that one is nothing is the first step in breaking loose; when you have done that, says Benjamin, "ye shall always rejoice, and be filled with the love of God." Yes, but what do you *do* to fill the time? "Ye shall grow in the knowledge of the glory of him that created you" (Mosiah 4:12). And what is that glory? Intelligence, the greatest fun of all, with no room for invidious comparison, rivalry, and jealousy that characterize the competitive business and professionalism, since truth alone is the object (Mosiah 4:13-16). In the end, we have no choice; Moroni prescribes the cure: "I give unto men weakness. . . . I will show unto the Gentiles their weakness, . . . that faith, hope, and charity bringeth unto me. . . . If the Gentiles have not charity . . . [I will] take away their talent" (Ether 12:27-28, 35). There is no other way than to be "meek and lowly in heart; . . . have charity; for if he have not charity he is nothing; . . . cleave unto charity, which is the greatest of all, . . . the pure love of Christ. . . . Pray unto the Father, that ye may be filled with this love, . . . that ye may become the sons of God" (Moroni 7:44-48). This is Moroni's summary of the situation.

We have ample material for an operational definition of righteousness and wickedness. One does not need to compose graduated lists of sins in the manner of the Jesuits. "I cannot tell you all the things whereby ye may commit sin," says King Benjamin, "for there are diverse ways and means, even so many that I cannot number them" (Mosiah 4:29). The same applies to deeds of righteousness: whether an act is a sin or a good deed depends on the state of mind of the person who does it. The Book of Mormon gives us the touchstone of righteousness, which is *repentance*. The test of righteousness or wickedness is not of location, a matter of being in one camp or the other, but of *direction*, as Ezekiel tells us (Ezekiel 18:26); one who has a low score in doing good, if he repents and does an about face, is counted as righteous, while one who has a long record of good deeds, if he turns around, has joined the wicked (Ezekiel 18:27). The person on the top step facing down is in worse condition than one on a bottom step facing up.

But isn't there a difference of degree? Not at all: is it not all the more reprehensible for the righteous person to backslide, and all the more commendable for the rascal to turn righteous? The Book of Mormon is full of examples on both sides: "Therefore, blessed are they who will repent, . . . for these are they that shall be saved" (Helaman 12:23). And Nephi assures us that "all nations, kindreds, tongues, and people shall dwell safely in the Holy One of Israel if it so be that they will repent" (1 Nephi 22:28). Indeed, "the days of the children of men were prolonged" for the express purpose "that they might repent while in the flesh; wherefore, their state became a state of probation, and their time was lengthened" (2 Nephi 2:21). This was done to give everyone the fullest opportunity, "for he gave commandment that all men must repent; for he showed unto all men that they were lost, because of the transgression of their parents" (2 Nephi 2:21). Christ's first pronouncement to the Nephites was, "I bear record that the Father commandeth all men, everywhere, to repent and believe in me" (3 Nephi 11:32). To carry on at all "we must call upon thee," "because we are unworthy before thee; because of the fall our natures have become evil continually" (Ether 3:2). Only little children are exempt from the command of constant repentance (Mosiah 3:21). Even the poor and despised must watch themselves and constantly correct their ways (Mosiah 4:24).

Does one person need repentance more than another? Until we have reached the shore, no one is home safe; a swimmer can drown fifty feet from the shore as easily as a mile from it; and in this life, none have reached the shore, for it is a probation right up until the last. Only one who is like the Son of Man, "full of grace and truth" (2 Nephi 2:6), may be exempt from repentance. While the great storm and earthquake were raging, the people were still given a chance to repent. "Wo unto the inhabitants of the whole earth, except they shall repent" (3 Nephi 9:2). "O ye house of Israel whom I have spared, how oft will I gather you as a hen gathereth her chickens under her wings, if ye will repent. . . . But if not, O house of Israel, the places of your dwellings shall become desolate" (3 Nephi 10:6-7).

This ongoing exercise that lasts all our lives is strictly a private affair. Repentance is an intransitive or rather a reflexive verb; you cannot repent another or for another or make another repent. In every single prophecy and promise of destruction in the Book of Mormon, there is a repent clause added. Repentance, and repentance alone, can save a land cursed with "workers of darkness and secret combinations." But if they accept repentance, that means "never [to] be weary of good works, but to be meek and lowly in heart; for such shall find rest to their souls"

(Alma 37:31-34). The long and puzzling story of the olive orchard in the fifth chapter of Jacob seems to present an endless combination of tactics to preserve the orchard. The point is that any combination is possible; God will try any scheme, general or local, to redeem the people. It is the plasticity of the thing that is impressive; sixteen times the trees are given a last chance to get growing again — there is no end to the Lord's patience. This is Nephi's message also to the Gentiles: "Therefore, cheer up your hearts and remember that ye are free to act for yourselves" (2 Nephi 10:23); this is still the time of probation, nothing is final. Christ "hath power given unto him from the Father to redeem them from their sins because of repentance" (Helaman 5:11). There were times when mass repentance turned history around, when the Nephites were completely converted (3 Nephi 5:1), and the robbers all rehabilitated (3 Nephi 6:3), but such times follow only upon great upsets, overthrows, and defeats, for without strong pressure what man is going to repent who thinks things are going his way? It usually amounts to being "awakened . . . out of a deep sleep" (Alma 5:7), and what is more annoying than being awakened out of a deep sleep?

In the need to rationalize their ways, it is not enough for the guilty to justify their position; it must be sanctified. There is a wonderful account in the Book of Mormon that shows how that is done. It is Alma's report on the Zoramites, which tells us how the vilest people he had ever known managed to project an image of extreme righteousness, loudly proclaiming themselves as "a holy people" (Alma 31:18), while their thoughts "were on their riches" (Alma 31:24-28). Independent, proud, enterprising, hard working, very prosperous, zealous in religious observances — including strict dress standards — brave and aggressive, the Zoramites in their time were the meddling catalyst that spread violence and war everywhere, even persuading the youth of the land to join up with the Gadianton robbers in order to embarrass the Nephites (3 Nephi 1:29).

Why does the Book of Mormon have so much to say about war, incidentally? Because it's the story of our own time. I have often heard generals deplore the awfulness of war, but the commander who really hates it is Captain Moroni. He is worthy of closer attention because he's the one who is held up as the model of military macho to LDS youth. Repeatedly, in the long account of Moroni, Alma reminds us that he did not "glory in . . . the shedding of blood" (Alma 48:16), as others do. His Nephites fought only when obliged to "contend with their brethren" (Alma 43:14) and only if they were "not guilty of the first offense, neither the second" offense (Alma 43:46), to say nothing of preemptive strikes. They celebrated their victories not by getting drunk but with fasting and prayer (Alma 45:1). "If all men had been like . . . Moroni . . . ," says Alma (Alma 48:17). Well, who was he like? and just what was he like? "He was a man like unto Ammon" (Alma 48:18). It was Ammon's people who refused to make war under any circumstances (Alma 26:32-34).

How did Moroni go about making war? First of all, the people humbled themselves: "They were free from wars and contentions among themselves." War was not a solution to internal unrest. They were reluctant "to contend with their brethren, . . . sorry to take up arms against the Lamanites, because they did not delight in the shedding of blood . . . and . . . they were sorry to be the means of sending so many of their brethren out of this world . . . unprepared to meet their God" (Alma 48:20-23). When Moroni had immobilized a guard house with a gift of wine, he refused to follow up the ruse, because he said it would be an "injustice" to perform a shameful act of taking advantage of a drunken enemy (Alma 55:19). Moroni was especially keen to watch for any slightest tendency of the enemy to give up; he was hypersensitive to that moment in the battle when the enemy falters, and the instant that came, when he sensed they were weakening, he would propose a stop to the fighting to talk things over (Alma 52:37-38). "We do not desire to be men of blood" (Alma 44:1), he tells them on the battlefield; "ye are in our hands, yet we do not desire to slay you. . . . We have not come . . . that we might shed your blood for power" (Alma 44:1-3). "We would not shed the blood of the Lamanites, if they would stay in their own land. We would not shed the blood of our [Nephite] brethren if they would not rise up in rebellion and take the sword against us. We would subject ourselves to the yoke of bondage if it were requisite with the justice of God" (Alma 61:10-12). He detested the power game that some men play; "I seek not for power," he says often, "but to pull it down. I seek not for the honor of the world" (Alma 60:36). He thinks more kindly of the Lamanite invaders than of the ambitious men on his own side. He says it is "the tradition of their fathers that has caused their hatred, . . . while your iniquity is for the cause of your love of glory and the vain things of the world" (Alma 60:32). He fought against people being "known by the appellation of kingmen, . . . and the pride of those people who professed the blood of nobility, . . . they were brought down to humble themselves like unto their brethren" (Alma 51:21). Inequality—that was the enemy in Moroni's eyes. When he raised the Title of Liberty, it was to teach his people to think of themselves as the poor and outcast of Israel (Alma 46:18, 23-24), not as a proud army with banners—reminding them that the rent garment could very well be their own condition (Alma 46:21) if they tried to match the enemy's own machismo.

Moroni's behavior gives point to the question "Who is the enemy?" The most clear-cut case of good guys fighting bad guys is Alma's duel with Amlici—right out of *Star Wars.* "Alma, being a man of God, . . . was strengthened, insomuch that he slew Amlici with the sword" (Alma

2:30-31). It came down to a single duel between the two leaders. Yet Alma taught the people right on the spot, and they believed him. He said it "was the judgments of God sent upon them because of *their* wickedness and *their* abominations" that brought the whole thing on (Alma 4:3). It wasn't the good guys fighting the bad guys at all. What kind of victory for the winners was it when "every soul had cause to mourn" (Alma 4:3)? Alma decided to preach to the enemy, as did Ammon, who rejected the stock argument for military interventionism: "Let us take up arms against them, . . . lest they overthrow and destroy us" (Alma 26:25). We have to sweep them from the land or they'll destroy us. In enemy territory, as you know, Ammon was "cast out and mocked and spit upon, and smote upon [his] cheeks" (Alma 26:29). He overruled the powerful reflexes to hit back, which you certainly would expect of the mightiest warrior of his time, which Ammon was. He would not do that; he said he just kept hoping that "perhaps we might be the means of saving some" (Alma 26:30). In that he was brilliantly successful.

Mormon also knew the futility of military operations, and he had lots of experience. When the army of Mormon, flush with new victory, started settling the Lamanite question once and for all under the noble call to "avenge . . . the blood of their brethren," he left his command and "utterly refused to go up against [his] enemies." Revenge, he said, was the one thing God absolutely would not tolerate (Mormon 3:9-16). For once that starts, there is no ending. Mormon shows us the military power completely out of control, practicing the usual atrocities, requisitioning everything for themselves while "many old women do faint by the way and die" (Moroni 9:16). Who were they defending? "My people!" he says. "They are without order and without mercy, . . . past feeling . . . [worse than] the Lamanites. . . . I pray . . . [for] their utter destruction" (Moroni 9:18-22). He's the one who has "loved" and "led them" (Mormon 3:12) for all those years; now, he prays for their destruction unless they repent (Moroni 9:22). But always repentance is open right unto the end. The fog and horror of battle pursue us right up to the end – the nation completely in arms at Cumorah with trained, experienced warriors, all a splendid sight marching forward. Alas, there's nothing heroic about it. How could they have been such fools? Pity was Mormon's only reflection on the splendid sight (Mormon 6:17-22). His last word to the survivors in the land is that they must lay down their arms and never take them up again, for they will never prevail by force. The only way they can prevail, he says (Mormon 7:3), is by repenting. Cumorah was no solution; the war went right on among the victors. Moroni's only comfort upon the earth is that "the hand of the Lord hath done it" (Mormon 8:8). And his word to us is, "Therefore, he that smiteth shall be smitten again, of the Lord. Behold what the scripture says – man shall not smite, neither shall he judge" (Mormon 8:19-20). That is the lesson of Cumorah: The calamities of the Nephites are due to their own wickedness. "It was their quarrelings, and . . . contentions, . . . murderings, . . . plunderings, . . . idolatry, whoredoms, . . . abominations . . . which brought upon them their wars and their destructions" (Alma 50:21).

Why does Moroni, vigorously pruning the record to make room for only what there is space for, insert his own long abridgment of the record of the Jaredites? He tells us why: What is going on in the world today, that's what the picture is. The Jaredites were plagued by that Asiatic tradition of kingship that required that a ruler should rule everything.[15] Where kingship or office itself is sacred, what is in the king's interest is moral and what is against the king's interest is immoral. As Cicero says, speaking of the ruling class in Rome, "everything becomes a pure power play." Any man who is strong enough can grab the power any way he can. The proof of his deserving it is that he has it. So we reach the final showdown in the story of the Jaredites. We find "war upon all the face of the land, every man with his band fighting for that which he desired" (Ether 13:25), every soldier of fortune out for himself. And "there were robbers, and in fine, all manner of wickedness upon all the face of the land" (Ether 13:26). And "every man did cleave unto that which was his own, with his hands, and would not borrow, neither would he lend" (Ether 14:2). Everyone for himself—this is free enterprise come to its conclusion. And "every man kept the hilt of his sword in his right hand, in the defense of his property and his own life and of his wives and children" (Ether 14:2). It all ends up in the family shelter. And the result: "All the people upon the face of the land were shedding blood, and there was none to restrain them" (Ether 13:31). It can actually come to that. War settles everything by a neat polarization: everything evil on one side and everything good on the other. No problem remains for anybody on either side but to kill people on the other side. So when Shiz set out with that noblest of intentions to "avenge himself" of the blood of his brother (Ether 14:24), his host forcibly recruited everyone who was not grabbed up by the other side. Shiz and Coriantumr are both obsessed with the paranoid conviction of an ever-threatening enemy whose rule of evil can only end with his extermination. The most significant thing about this polarization, of course, is that it puts an end once and for all to any thought of repentance, in which lies the only hope for survival and peace and leads in the end to the Book of Mormon phenomenon which until recently I thought was quite fantastically impossible—not just improbable—over-imaginative, and which some authorities in Washington still insist is unrealistic, namely, the "utter destruction" of *both* contestants in the war (Ether 11:20; Moroni 9:22). It nearly happened with the Nephites and Lamanites, and it did happen with the Jaredites.

To whom is all this addressed? To whom it may concern. And whom does it concern? To whom it may apply. In the midst of describing the plots and combinations of the Jaredites, Moroni pauses to explain, "I, Moroni, am commanded to write these things that evil may be done away, and that . . . Satan may have no power upon the hearts of the children of men, . . . that they may be persuaded to do good continually" (Ether 8:26). Notice that the program is entirely positive; it has to do with persuasion to do good, and it appeals to their hearts, not the mangling of their bodies. The book is addressed to a people very much in need of repentance: "And then, O ye gentiles, how can ye stand before the power of God, except ye shall repent and turn from your evil ways?" (Mormon 5:22). "He hath made manifest unto you our imperfections, that ye may learn to be more wise than we have been" (Mormon 9:31). The Lord in person spoke to the Nephites: "I command you that ye shall write these things after I am gone, . . . that these sayings which ye shall write shall be kept and shall be manifested unto the Gentiles" (3 Nephi 16:4). Nephi says, "I have spoken plainly to you, that ye cannot misunderstand. And the words which I have spoken shall stand as a testimony against you; for they are sufficient to teach any man the right way" (2 Nephi 25:28). "I, Mormon, do not desire to harrow the souls of men [by] casting before them such an awful scene of blood" (Mormon 5:8). Why, then, does he dwell on these pictures when he says he has no desire to do this? He says "but I . . . [know] that a knowledge of these things must come to the remnant of these people, and also unto the Gentiles, who the Lord hath said should scatter this people" (Mormon 5:8-9). "Wherefore, O ye Gentiles, it is wisdom in God that these things should be shown unto you, that thereby ye may repent . . . and suffer not that these murderous combinations shall get above you, which are built up to get power and gain [money, not ideology, is the motive] and the work, yea, even the work of destruction come upon you, . . . even the sword of . . . justice . . . shall fall upon you, to your overthrow and destruction if ye suffer these things to be" (Ether 8:23). Specifically, we are told to look out for one fatal symptom, the thing that has "caused the destruction of [the Jaredites] . . . and also the destruction of the people of Nephi," and will surely do the same for whatsoever nation in the future shall come under the control of the "secret combinations to get power and gain" (Ether 8:21-22).

The time came when the prophets did the only thing left for them to do: They "mourned and withdrew" (Ether 11:13). And Mormon was forbidden to write any more for them, but for us he directs his writings to another people living far in the future (Moroni 1:4): "I speak unto you as if ye were present, and yet ye are not. But . . . I know your doing, . . . [for] Jesus Christ has shown you unto me" (Mormon 8:35). Make no mistake about it, as the politicians say, it is our generation being described, when the manipulations of the combinations, far and wide, shed the blood of husbands and cause widows and "orphans to mourn, [be assured that] the sword of vengeance hangeth over you" (Mormon 8:40-41). "Wherefore, O ye Gentiles, it is wisdom in God that these things should be shown unto you, . . . that thereby ye may repent of your sins, and suffer not . . . these murderous combinations . . . which are built up to get power and gain—and the work, . . . even the work of destruction come upon you, . . . the sword of justice of the Eternal God shall fall" (Ether 8:23). Notice, first he says the sword of vengeance hangs over you because of the things you have done, and then the sword of justice [you deserve it] "shall fall upon you, to your overthrow and destruction if ye shall suffer these things to be" (Ether 8:23). So the great takeover is to be followed by the "great overburn." Now that phenomenon is mentioned more than thirty times in the Book of Mormon, when the wicked are burned as stubble and a vapor of smoke covers the earth (1 Nephi 22:15, 17-18, 23; 3 Nephi 10:13-14; 25:1; Mormon 8:29). "And thus commandeth the Father that I should say unto you: At that day when the Gentiles shall sin against my gospel, . . . and shall be lifted up in the pride of their hearts above all nations, and above all people of the whole earth, and shall be filled with all manner . . . of hypocrisy, and murders, and priestcrafts, and whoredoms, and of secret abominations; and . . . shall reject the fulness of my gospel, behold, saith the Father, I will bring the fulness of my gospel among them" (3 Nephi 16:10). Fortunately, that has not happened. "There shall be great pollutions upon the face of the earth; there shall be murders, and robbing, and lying, and deceivings, and whoredoms"; and as to the morality of it all, "there shall be many who . . . say, Do this, or do that, and it mattereth not, . . . but wo be unto such" (Mormon 8:31). "Wo be unto the Gentiles, . . . for notwithstanding . . . they *will* deny me; nevertheless, I will be merciful unto them, . . . if they will repent" (2 Nephi 28:32).

And so the timely reminder to the Church is this: Do not "suppose that ye are more righteous than the Gentiles. . . . For . . . ye shall . . . likewise perish; . . . ye need not suppose that the Gentiles are utterly destroyed" (2 Nephi 30:1). The Church is in the same danger as the Gentiles: "Wo be unto him that is at ease in Zion! Wo be unto him that crieth: All is well!" (2 Nephi 28:24-25). Here we see how the label of Zion has been processed in a smooth soft-sell by broadcasting: "All is well in Zion; yea, Zion prospereth, all is well . . . —the devil cheateth their souls, and leadeth them away carefully down to hell" (2 Nephi 28:21). That's the business of advertising, to cheat and to lead carefully.[16]

"When ye . . . receive this [word], repent all ye ends of the earth" (Ether 4:17-18). Whatever course they take, "all this shall stand as a testimony against the world at the last day" (Ether 5:4). The Gentiles will have their innings; they will be "lifted up by the power of God above all other nations, and prevail against the other inhabitants of the land" and so forth. But "the Lord God will not suffer . . . the Gentiles [to] utterly destroy" them (1 Nephi 13:30). But when that time is finished, "Wo be unto the Gentiles." Then it will be their turn, "if it so be in that day they harden their hearts" (1 Nephi 14:6). After the Gentiles take over completely and remove all rivals, then they become the endangered ones: "And then, O ye Gentiles, how can ye stand before the power of God, except ye . . . repent and turn from your evil ways?" (Mormon 5:22). For then, "the Lord God shall cause a great division among the people, and the wicked he will destroy . . . by fire" (2 Nephi 30:10).

About two hundred years after Christ visited the people, they became tired of intellectual integrity and self-control and opted to give up the law of consecration. From then on everything went in a fatal declension, each step of which has been duly marked and described in the Book of Mormon.

First they became *privatized*. They no longer had "their goods and their substance . . . [in] common" (4 Nephi 1:25). Then they became *ethnicized* as they "taught [their children] to hate" the Nephites and Lamanites they had been playing with (4 Nephi 1:39). Then they became *nationalized* by serving the careers of ambitious men. Then they became *militarized*, from the need for large-scale security when mutual trust gave way to self-interest. And they were *terrorized* as shrewd men saw the advantages of organized crime. Then they became *regionalized* as people began to form various combinations for protection and profit, entering through business relations with the criminal society and even sharing in their profits. Then they became *tribalized* as they finally succeeded at the urging of various powerful interests in abolishing the central government completely. Then they became *fragmentized* into paramilitary groups, wandering bands, family shelters, and so forth. Then they became *polarized*; to check the general disorder and insecurity, great armies were formed around competent leaders by forced recruitment or conquest. And they became *pulverized* as the great armies smashed each other and left the land utterly desolate. It is left for a future generation to take the final step and become *vaporized*. Viewing the state of the land at the American bicentennial, President Spencer W. Kimball declared himself "appalled and frightened" by what he saw, and in this and in his last published address he quoted many of the passages we have just cited from the Book of Mormon.[17] Now, President Ezra Taft Benson issues an inspired appeal to make the Book of Mormon an object of our most intense concern.[18] Suddenly, we find ourselves there: scenes and circumstances that not long ago seemed as distant as Nineveh and Tyre suddenly come to life about us. Could Joseph Smith have made all this up?

Notes

1. *Ratlos vor der Apokalyptik* (Gütersloh: Mohr, 1970), 11-12.

2. The Ascension Motif is discussed, for example, in Hugh W. Nibley, *Since Cumorah* (Salt Lake City: Deseret Book, 1967), 212-13; reprinted in *CWHN* 7:186-87; Blake T. Ostler, "The Throne-Theophany and Prophetic Commission in 1 Nephi: A Form-Critical Analysis," *BYU Studies* 26 (Fall 1986): 67-95; and John W. Welch, "The Calling of a Prophet," in *1 Nephi: The Doctrinal Foundation*, ed. Monte Nyman and Charles Tate (Salt Lake City: Bookcraft and BYU Religious Studies Center, 1988), 35-54.

3. The Lachish Letters are discussed, for example, in Hugh W. Nibley, "Dark Days in Jerusalem," in *Book of Mormon Authorship*, ed. Noel B. Reynolds (Salt Lake City: Bookcraft and BYU Religious Studies Center, 1982), 103-21; and Hugh W. Nibley, "The Lachish Letters: Documents from Lehi's Day," *Ensign* (December 1981): 48-54; see above, pages 380-406.

4. See Hugh W. Nibley, *Lehi in the Desert and the World of the*

Jaredites (Salt Lake City: Bookcraft, 1952), passim; reprinted in *CWHN* 5.

5. See Hugh W. Nibley, "Churches in the Wilderness," in *Nibley on the Timely and the Timeless* (Salt Lake City: Bookcraft and BYU Religious Studies Center, 1978), 155-86; see above, pages 289-327; Hugh W. Nibley, *An Approach to the Book of Mormon* (Salt Lake City: Deseret Book, 1957), 113-63; reprinted in *CWHN* 6:135-93.

6. See, for example, Nibley, *An Approach to the Book of Mormon*, 178-89; in *CWHN* 6:209-21; Nibley, *Since Cumorah*, 198-226; in *CWHN* 7:174-98.

7. Nibley, *Since Cumorah*, 328-70; in *CWHN* 7:291-333.

8. Nibley, *Lehi in the Desert*, 20-36; in *CWHN* 5:19-34.

9. Nibley, *Lehi in the Desert*, 240-42; in *CWHN* 5:239-41.

10. Jeremiah 35:1-10, 16, 18. The Rekhabites are discussed, for example, in Nibley, *An Approach to the Book of Mormon*, 123; in *CWHN* 6:146; Nibley, "Churches in the Wilderness," 165; see above, chapter 16.

11. Tyrtaeus, *Idylls of Theocritus with Bion and Moschus and the War Songs of Tyrtaeus*, tr. J. Banks (Bell, 1905); Vergil, *Aeneid*, IV, 259-78.

12. Nibley, *An Approach to the Book of Mormon*, 315-50; in *CWHN* 6:378-415; Nibley, *Since Cumorah*, 373-409; in *CWHN* 7:377-72; Nibley, "Freemen and Kingmen" (Provo: F.A.R.M.S. N-FRE, 1981); see above, chapter 17.

13. Plutarch, "On the Education of Children and On Love of Wealth," *Moralia* 1 and 7.

14. Alan Watts, *Does it Matter?* (New York: Pantheon, 1970), 6-24.

15. Nibley, *Lehi in the Desert*, 190-200; in *CWHN* 5:194-204.

16. Discussed in Hugh W. Nibley, "Victoriosa Loquacitas: The Rise of Rhetoric and the Decline of Everything Else," *Western Speech* 20 (1956): 57-82.

17. "The False Gods We Worship," *Ensign* (June 1976): 3.

18. "The Book of Mormon, Keystone of Our Religion," *Ensign* (November 1986): 7; "The Book of Mormon Is the Word of God," *Ensign* (May 1975): 65.

23

The Book of Mormon: Forty Years After

The talk I gave a year ago on this occasion was entitled, when it was published, "Last Call." That should have brought a sigh of relief to all who have suffered my apocalyptic fervor these many years. It was more than forty years ago that I started teaching the Book of Mormon in Provo. Last fall, after years away from it, I returned to the book. Was it weary, flat, stale, and unprofitable as any book would be after one hundred readings? On the contrary, it was a new book. But forget forty years. In the past year alone the world has stumbled, slipped, and slithered downward to a point where it has almost caught up with the later chapters of the Book of Mormon. The past year, as the culmination of forty years, bids me forward cast my eye and read, and fear!

When we were growing up, no one had any doubts at all about what the future would be like. It was simply a matter, as my old paleontology professor used to say, of "projecting the curve of experience into the curve of behavior," and that would tell you exactly where you were going. The two phrases constantly on our lips, the two factors which conditioned everything, were "unlimited opportunities" and "inexhaustible resources." We knew exactly where we were going. The mural in the public library

---

This talk was delivered on May 10, 1988, at the Sunstone Book of Mormon Lecture Series in Salt Lake City.

or high school showed you the hulking Neanderthal marching toward the Pyramids, the Parthenon, Notre Dame, the Washington Monument, and finally the triumphant culmination of the skyline of New York around 1930. Mr. Wells told us what the wonderful world of tomorrow would be, and he lived to see it become a nightmare. The one future that no one could have imagined was what we could read about in the Book of Mormon; but that we tolerantly consigned to a fantastic realm of the long-ago and far-away, a sort of overdone science fantasy. As it turned out, the Book of Mormon was not dashing off into Never-Never Land but bringing us down to reality if we had only believed it. But we did not and we still don't. But the past year has torn aside veils that we would prefer to have left in place, and we find ourselves enacting what our ancestors would have called a mad melodrama.

In the short time I have here, let me call your attention to some sixteen items among many which have not caught my attention until this year. They add to the impressive underpinning of evidence which is building up in support of the Book of Mormon, and I marvel that they should have escaped me for so long, and can only wonder how Joseph Smith or anyone else could have hit upon them by chance a hundred and sixty years ago.

First a few speculative points:

1. The documents discovered in the Cave of Letters in the Nahal Hever in 1966 show us a number of rich people fleeing from Jerusalem and taking important legal documents with them. These show how a well-heeled party living in Jerusalem could own estates and ranches off at the south end of the Dead Sea, and even have title to farms in Egypt. To one such estate a wealthy woman retreated when Jerusalem fell to the Romans.[1] Four centuries after the burying of the Scrolls, when the Barbarians invaded Europe, things were reversed, and rich Roman ladies bought up expensive places in Palestine to which they

could retire in what was then the safest place in the world. This is a picture of landholding and international ties which is truly surprising, quite modern, and wholly in keeping with the affairs of Father Lehi as they are set forth in 1 Nephi.

2. Clues to proper names keep turning up. Of course, they're all speculative, but some of them are pretty good. A new catalog of Bullae from the time of Jeremiah (and Lehi), has been published by Avigad.[2] Bullae were seals attached to formal documents. Among some hundred-odd familiar Old Testament names of important Jews living in Lehi's time, we find a scant dozen nonbiblical names. The chances of a Book of Mormon name turning up among them might appear astronomical, yet the theophoric name Mi-amon contains the Amon element which is dominant in the Book of Mormon and which one would hardly expect in this setting.

3. Then of course there is the work of the "Berkeley Group" under the guidance of John L. Hilton, which has demonstrated by word-prints that the statistical "confidence of Nephi and Alma having been written by different authors is greater than 99.5%."[3] But since this was none of my doing I need not pursue it here.

4. In the course of this year's teaching I have noticed literary qualities which have come as a complete surprise — language usages and cultural traits as distinctive as fingerprints. One example I like very much; it puts us into the mainstream of world literature.

The beginning of Enos's story in a hunting scene has always been treated as a picturesque detail and sometimes cited as justification for the philosophy of the National Rifle Association. It is the classic motif of the king's son engaged in an activity which should keep him out of mischief and trouble. However, royalty on the hunt is already at risk, and the next-in-line hunting alone is courting the fate of a Siegfried, or a William II, and no less than that of sixty-

seven Shahs of Persia or their heirs, all murdered on the
hunt. It is easy to see why princes should not hunt alone.
But it was not the risk to his life and crown that distressed
Enos. Prince Hal, kept safely in the sidelines until his time
would come, was indulged in all manner of wild and irresponsible horseplay. But intelligent princes, men worthy
to be kings, do not feel at ease wasting time and talents
in trivial pursuits. They become brooding and morose as
did Hamlet and the Buddha and also Enos. The discon-
tented prince is a stock figure in legend and literature but
no less in history. Enos, exactly like Gautama (Siddartha)
or Harūn al-Rashid, was not at all satisfied with the way
his life was going. He "wrestled" not with God but with
himself, struggling in the spirit before God "before [he]
received a remission of [his] sins" (Enos 1:2). He had to
come to peace with himself. It is an intensely personal
story. If he had nothing better to do than to hunt by himself, he was wasting his talents and he knew it: he knows
he is missing something, that this is not what he should
be doing—his father had told him about that. "And my
soul hungered; and I kneeled down before my Maker, and
I cried unto him in mighty prayer and supplication for
mine own soul" (Enos 1:4). He prayed all night long, determined to find release from an intolerable situation. He
felt implicitly as every intelligent person does, "Woe unto
him . . . that wasteth the day of his probation, for awful
is his state!" (2 Nephi 9:27). As a good prince, once his
frustration, or, as he says, "my guilt was swept away"
(Enos 1:6), his next thought was for his people; and when
he got what was clearly a highly conditioned promise for
them, the great-hearted young man then "prayed . . .
with many long strugglings for [his] brethren the Lamanites" (Enos 1:11). Here we have a situation which is recurrent in the history of royal houses and religions.

But the most significant parallel is certainly that between Enos and Gautama. The latter was born in 563 B.C.,

which makes him strictly contemporary with Enos, a grandson of Lehi. His father too bore the title of king, Rajan, but he was also like Jacob more of a counselor and tribal leader. Living in luxury, "the thoughtful young prince," according to his biographer, "must have become increasingly aware of the emptiness of such a life."[4] So he left his wife and child and, "as did many young people of his time, . . . sought higher knowledge in the silence and solitude of the forest."[5] Is the author of the Book of Mormon simply following the Buddhist story? Far from it. The two tales end up at opposite poles. Buddha found the answer to his quest in "the two fundamental principles of Buddhism," namely that there is no permanent existence, and that there is no enduring soul—no "I" nor "Self," since these depend on the five factors of body, feeling, awareness, the will, and consciousness. These things which Gautama renounced are the substance of Enos's salvation. And this parallel brings up a very important point which has never been sufficiently emphasized.

For many years critics of the Book of Mormon fondly believed that if they could find some striking parallel in the Bible or in U.S. history to a situation in the Book of Mormon, they had proven that Joseph Smith had plagiarized the whole thing. But when equally striking parallels are found to things of which the ancient Book of Mormon writers, had they existed, would surely have been aware, but of which no one in Joseph Smith's day could have had an inkling, they were ignored. Our lives consist of recurrent scenarios or syndromes, things that happen routinely, such as brushing one's teeth, having breakfast, going to work, and so on, all very minor scenarios. More pretentious scenarios are played out with crowds at church meetings, public games, banquets, plays, lectures, concerts, and the like. Such may cause great passing interest and have about them an element of ceremonial display but small historical importance. More significant are the ancient yearly practices of seasonal festivals, coronations, formal warfare, and the like. Eric Hornung (whom I consider the most enlightened Egyptologist of our time) has recently written of ancient Egypt: "For the people of that time history was no sociological or economic process, but a cultic activity and festive game."⁶ "Historical deeds repeat mythical events and are supposed to restore the perfect and primal condition of things."⁷ In the annals, everything the king does follows a prescribed sacred pattern; what an Egyptian pharaoh or Roman emperor or English monarch did was both ceremony and history, consisting of things that are done over and over again. That being the case, how can one hope to prove that an author is guilty of plagiarism when he recounts an event that strikingly resembles something that happened in another time or place?

But then how, on the other hand, can one confirm the bona fides of the Book of Mormon because it tells a story that has an authentic ancient ring? If these things happen all the time, how can we exploit apparent parallels as indicating either plagiarisms or sources? There is an answer to that; it is the oddities of each particular situation that make it different from all the others. The fall of ancient cities, for example, is a stock scenario rehearsed in the stereotyped lines of the poets and playwrights. But historically the fall of Troy, Jerusalem (which fall?), Rome, Constantinople, Paris, and so on, each had its peculiar attendant circumstances. The Lachish Letters tell of one of the many falls of Jerusalem, that in 587 B.C., and in many important aspects it was like no other taking of the city. And it is these aspects of the tragedy that receive full attention in Nephi's account of the event. Throughout history technology changes, but the issues remain the same; the styles of furniture, dress, and other properties of the play must alter, but the human comedy is always with us. It is that which makes the Book of Mormon highly relevant, now painfully relevant, to our own time. But in checking for historical accuracy, it is the oddities we must look for. I have time for only a few examples. First there is the affair at the waters of Sebus.

5. The whole affair at the waters of Sebus must strike anyone as very strange; I always thought that it was rather silly until the other day when I gave it a moment's thought. All the Lamanites would drive their flocks to a particular watering place (Alma 17:26). And when they got there, "a certain number of Lamanites, who had been with their flocks to water, stood and scattered the . . . [king's] flocks." After the flocks of the king "scattered . . . and fled many ways," the servants lamented that as a matter of course, "now the king will slay us, as he has our brethren" (Alma 17:28). And they began to weep. What insanity is this, the king kills his own servants for losing a contest that had been acted out before? In fact, "it was the *practice* of these Lamanites to stand by the waters of Sebus and scatter the flocks of the people," keeping what they could for themselves, "it being a *practice* of plunder among them" (Alma 18:7). So it was no secret to anyone; this was not an ambush but something to be expected. But the king's own flocks? Didn't he have enough men to protect them if this happened regularly? Well, for one thing the Lamanites played the game for sport; it was more than meat that they were after, for "they delighted in the destruction of their brethren; and for this cause they stood to scatter the flocks of the king" (Alma 17:35). The fun of it was their main interest, but Ammon spoiled the fun when he "stood forth and began to cast stones at them with his sling." They were outraged: "They began to be astonished . . . [and] angry" (Alma 17:36) — he wasn't playing fair. So they came after him with clubs; why only clubs? He had a sword. There is only one way you can wield a club; you cannot cut or thrust with it but have to raise it up over your head and thus expose your arms. Ammon took full advantage of the situation, slicing away at the arms raised against

him. And yet, with his overwhelming advantage, Ammon "slew none save it were their leader with his sword" (Alma 17:38). He knocked six of them out with his sling and cut off the arms of others as they raised their clubs, but he only contended with the leader to death. After that, the winning party or team brought back the trophies to the king, "bearing the arms which had been smitten off by the sword of Ammon" (Alma 17:39). By now it should be clear that we are dealing with a sort of game; a regular practice, following certain rules. This becomes apparent when a few days later, the very men "who had stood at the waters of Sebus and scattered the flocks" (Alma 19:21) mingled freely and openly with the crowd of people gathered at the palace at the report of strange things going on there. Some in the crowd said these things were happening because the king "slew his servants who had had their flocks scattered at the waters of Sebus" (Alma 19:20); and the very men who had scattered the king's flocks loudly announced their presence by shouting abuses at Ammon for what he had done "to their brethren at the waters of Sebus" (Alma 19:21). The brother of the head man (whom Ammon had killed with his sword) drew his own sword on the spot and made at Ammon (Alma 19:22). So the men had swords but only used clubs. Isn't that odd, and isn't it odd that those same wicked Lamanites walked around right in front of the king's palace where everybody recognized them, and nobody did anything about it? And no one held it against the winning team that they had stolen their flocks back, but the losers were only angry with Ammon because he had thrown rocks and used his sword against men bearing only ceremonial clubs.

All this reminds us of those many ceremonial games in which the loser also lost his life, beginning with an Aztec duel in which one of the contestants was tethered by the ankle and bore only a wooden mace while his heavily armored opponent wielded a weapon with sharp obsidian edges. Then there were the age-old chariot races of the princes in which one was to be killed by the *Taraxippus,* and the equally ancient game of Nemi made famous by Frazer's *Golden Bough.*[8] Add to these such vicious doings as the Platanista, the Kyrpteia, the old Norse brain-ball, the hanging games of the Celts, and so on. But the closest are those known to many of us here, namely the bloody fun of the famous basketball games played in the great ballcourts of the ceremonial complexes of Mesoamerica. In these games either the captain of the losing team or the whole team lost their heads. Surviving into the present century among the Pueblos was the race between the Coyote and the Swallow, in which the winner killed the loser as he crossed the finish line. Equally horrendous and popular was the Wa-Wa rite in which the participants swung head downward from around a great pole mounted at the edge of a mesa from which individuals were expected to fall to their death. The purpose of such games was to make a human sacrifice, but as at Olympia or in the Roman arena, the religious nature of the thing could be lost in the fun and excitement of the brutal contests. Granted that the Lamanites at Sebus were depraved barbarians and real Yahoos, what is the logical or ritual explanation, the aesthetic appeal, or sporting spirit of the tag-team wrestling, demolition- or roller-derbies, or laser-tag of our own enlightened age? Nothing could be closer psychologically and historically to the ancient version of this insanity than the doings by the waters of Sebus.

The games of chivalry were just as rough and deadly as the Sebus sport, and far more ancient. Sinuhe is a thousand years older than Achilles or David, and monuments from prehistoric Egypt show the first "pharaohs" bashing the heads of rival rulers with the ceremonial mace. The famous scenes of the battles of Megiddo and Carchemish display the piles of severed hands and arms brought as trophies to the king. Incidentally, the Egyptians commonly use one word — ᶜ3 — for both hand and arm. From the days of the Jaredites to the final battle at Cumorah, we find our Book of Mormon warriors observing the correct chivalric rules of battle — enemies agreeing to the time and place of the slaughter, chiefs challenging each other to single combat for the kingdom, and so on. I have written elsewhere of the martial formalities of the Battle Scroll observed in the Book of Mormon.[9]

6. One of the aspects of ancient American religion that archaeology is bringing increasingly to the fore is the dominance of the familiar Great Mother in religion: Where is she in the Book of Mormon? The Book of Mormon brands all non-Nephite cults as idolatry and does not go on to describe them — Nephi says he does not want to run the risk of conveying the details of such enticing abominations to posterity. But there is one broad hint. When Alma's youngest son wanted to misbehave with the harlot Isabel, he had to go into another country to do it (Alma 39:3). Parenthetically, Isabel was the name of the Patroness of Harlots in the religion of the Phoenicians.[10] Remembering that this took place in a Mulekite setting, we have more than immoral behavior here — Corianton could have misbehaved anywhere. But we are also told that the lady Isabel had a large following. Others went over to join in the rites which Alma declared to be "most abominable above all sins" (Alma 39:5). In such a guarded manner Alma also refers to other hierodules (Alma 30:18).

7. I think we have also in the Zoramites a clear example of the contamination of Nephite religion by older cults that may have been found in the land or transplanted from the Old World. The Zoramites were *dissenters* from the Nephites (Alma 31:8). Under a charismatic leader they went off by themselves and started "perverting the ways of the Lord" (Alma 31:1). These were no minor changes but "great errors," which effectively nullified "the commandments of God and his statutes according to the Law

of Moses" (Alma 31:9). Under the new system they would not "observe or keep them" (Alma 31:9). What amazes Alma is not the denial of Christ—everywhere Nephite intellectuals were teaching that—but the strange actions these people were up to, having departed from the "*performances* of the church" (Alma 31:10). The change had been abrupt and spectacular—Alma and his brethren were astonished by it "beyond measure" (Alma 31:12, 19). The brethren were horribly depressed by what they found; they could hardly stand it (Alma 31:30-33). The Zoramites had only been off by themselves for a short time, yet what they were doing was all new to Alma. At first sight it looked like pure idolatry (Alma 31:1). The Zoramites had meeting places like the Jews (synagogues) but worshipped "after a manner which Alma and his brethren *had never beheld*" (Alma 31:12). Where did they get all this stuff all of a sudden? The most prominent fixture of their ceremonial center was a praying-stand at the top of a stairway—suggesting, of course, the standard appointment of the ancient American ceremonial centers: the tall towers with their steep stairways (Alma 31:13). The stair-tower went by the very alien name of Rameumptom (Alma 31:21). Alma, who never accuses these people of immorality, is shocked that their prayers are accompanied with a great showing off of costly and ornate vestments. Heavily adorned—in striking contrast to the garments of the Mosiac priesthood, they paraded around in gorgeous attire while they prayed (Alma 31:27-28). This in turn reminds us of the indescribably heavy, lavish, ornate, awkward adornments of the priestly grandees who parade before us in the pre-Columbian murals and jar paintings. The rites were celebrated once a week (Alma 31:12), like the Hopi dances—were they on a lunar calendar exclusively? In drastic departure from the law of Moses, masses of people were forced by the priesthood to work on ceremonial buildings or meeting places, which were, however, taboo to the common people, who were not properly dressed (Alma 32:1-3). The Zoramites, a well-organized and enterprising body, had simply moved in and taken over among less sophisticated inhabitants — a procedure now believed by Americanists to be almost routine in Mesoamerica. Everybody, Alma tells us, was convinced that only at these holy centers was proper worship possible (Alma 32:5, 9-12).

So here we have a competition between two religions as well as a fusion. "Their souls are precious," says Alma, "and *many* of them are our brethren; . . . give unto us . . . power and wisdom that we may bring these, our brethren, again unto thee" (Alma 31:35). "Many" means not all; who were those who were not their brethren? They boasted a superior religion, and the Zoramite priesthood claimed to be eminently rational and spiritual, accusing the Nephites of "childish" beliefs and practices — Alma lays great stress upon their boasting, in the manner of all barbarians. In short, "they did pervert the ways of the Lord in very many instances" (Alma 31:11), but not in all. Did they still think of themselves as Israelites? They certainly thought of the Nephites as apostates. In particular, they rejected the redemption by the Messiah as naive and unnecessary (Alma 31:16-18, 29), for they considered themselves very advanced, very superior as they strutted amidst the almost comically exaggerated splendor of their Mesoamerican dress and architecture (Alma 31:25-27). The moral of this is that the bemused LDS tourist, when he walks through a Mayan or Aztec ruin of a museum, need not see either Nephites or wild Lamanites all around him; there were other things going on too, though the Book of Mormon is strictly edited to exclude them as demoralizing or irrelevant.

8. One point that every passing year makes clearer is the complete ethnic mix, not only of the people of the Americas, but no less of those in the Book of Mormon. With Lehi we already have a rich mixture of Near Eastern

blood. He was of the tribe of Half-Manasseh, which may mean that he was half Aramaic or Arabic to begin with.[11] The family of Ishmael belonging in that same tradition, with a name like that, should almost certainly have been of the desert strain. The Manasseh part was in turn half Egyptian, and the Egyptians from the beginning were a blend of "nomads, cattle raisers, farmers, Africans, Asiatics, Semites, and Hamites."[12] The infiltration of these people began in the earliest times and mounted steadily through the centuries, families of every class enjoying strong infusions of "foreign" blood. In Lehi's day both Egypt and Palestine were swarming with Greek mercenaries and sailors (the Egyptian fleet was Corinthian), which may explain the few Greek names that pop up in the Book of Mormon. Zoram was a servant or slave and hence probably not an Israelite. To the very end his descendants form a distinct ethnic group in the New World. So Lehi's company and the Mulekites, and especially the Jaredites from the primal mixing and mustering center of the Tower, were already about as mongrel a people as you could find when they arrived in the New World.

But it is in the New World itself that the mixing really goes on. Nephites and Lamanites from time to time freely mingle. Lamanite warriors favored stolen Nephite brides, and Nephites, like the priests of Noah and the people of Amulon, gladly took Lamanite wives. Throughout the Book of Mormon, there are from time to time massive migrations toward the north and east, the equivalent of the American frontier and the Western movement. These found extensive evidence of previous inhabitants in the land — not all of them Jaredites, though the Jaredites were swarming by the millions while Zarahemla flourished as a great city to the south. Though Zarahemla is the center of the action in the Book of Mormon, it was not a Nephite city at all, but one of the Mulekites'; and the Mulekites brought no records with them from Jerusalem — they were apparently more numerous and heterogenous than Lehi's company.

What everyone has overlooked, however, is that the Mestizos of both North and South America, whether from the Spanish or Portuguese side, are as qualified to be called Israelites as the Nephites themselves were. For, as is well known, for seven centuries the people of Spain and Portugal mingled and intermarried with their large and important Jewish populations. We have underestimated or rather completely ignored the European strain of Jacob in the New World. Ethnically, what we find in Mesoamerica is what the Book of Mormon should expect us to find if we read it with any care:

> These Pacific basin people whom the Spanish invaders found in Mexico showed a cross-bred physiognomy embracing every physical feature and skin color known anywhere around the Earth. They were so cross-bred that they could no longer be spontaneously differentiated into separate "color" races. This crossbreeding is most advanced in Mexico and India today, but now embraces all the European features as well. Every variety of angular pattern variation in physiognomy is found in both countries in every skin color and every shade from intensely dark to intensely light. Hair ranges through every known variety between straight to tight curly, in every hue from black to platinum blond, and all varieties of hair adorn all varieties of skin color in all degrees of shading from dark to light, which in turn adorn all varieties of facial features and head shapes, wherefore few Mexican individuals can be identified as being of any hybrid race. They are simply worldians.[13]

The worldian theme is very prominent in the Book of Mormon.

9. This is not the time to go into doctrinal matters, except to say that the Book of Mormon contains by far the clearest exposition "in words of exceeding plainness" of

the mysteries, beginning with the meaning of that elusive word itself. The mysteries are not magic or occultism, but any knowledge that men cannot obtain by their own efforts, knowledge to be had only by revelation. The whole Book of Mormon is such a mystery. There you will find clear, concrete definitions of such daunting words as faith, heaven, hell, creation, atonement, resurrection, redemption, preexistence, hereafter.

One point that stands out today deals with the all-important issues of authority. Every hero in the Book of Mormon is a dissenter, bucking the system, usually a Rekhabite type who goes off into the wilderness with whoever is willing to follow him. These men are at odds not with the godless, depraved, barbaric society, but with a community and nation that considers itself the heirs of true religion, the elect, pious, and proper people. The prophets usually appear in numbers, and often, like Samuel the Lamanite, hold no office; and indeed, Alma and others divested themselves of all official titles to be more effective in their prophetic mission.

All of man's dealings with God in the Book of Mormon are on an individual basis. All covenants and agreements made at the great national assembly convened by King Benjamin are made between the individual and Jehovah, beginning with the king, who protests that he is only a man, answerable to God alone for his management of the kingdom: "I myself have labored with my own hands" (Mosiah 2:14). "I can answer [with] a clear conscience before God this day" (Mosiah 2:15). "If that man repenteth not, . . . the demands of divine justice do awaken his immortal soul to a lively sense of his own guilt" (Mosiah 2:38). Eternal punishment and reward are entirely personal and individual: "They shall be judged, every man according to his works, . . . consigned to an awful view of their own guilt" (Mosiah 3:24-25). At the end the king "thought it was expedient [to] . . . take the names of all those who had entered into a covenant with God" (Mosiah 6:1). And to emphasize this individualism, the new king "also, himself, did till the earth" (Mosiah 6:7).

When the Lord comes in person to establish the true order of things, all his dealings are with individuals as such. Just before his arrival a voice from on high introduces the Lord as the one responsible for all the great natural upheavals that have occurred. Thirty times in 3 Nephi 9, the Lord says that he alone has done this because people have turned their backs on him. But by a natural screening the more righteous save themselves by moving toward the temple. Upon arriving in person simply as "a man . . . [dressed] in a white robe," the Lord introduced himself personally to everyone, the people "going forth *one by one*" (3 Nephi 11:14-15), giving to each the signs and tokens. The angels also appeared to individuals, "for they all of them did see and hear, every man for himself, . . . men, women, and children" (3 Nephi 17:25). Especially the children. When the Lord blessed them "he took their children, one by one, and blessed them, and prayed unto the Father for them" (3 Nephi 17:21). When he gave them the Ten Commandments, they were all in the singular. In short, we make all our covenants with him as individuals, person to person: "The keeper of the gate is the Holy One of Israel, and he employs no servant there" (2 Nephi 9:41). We can see why in his great sermon on faith, Alma speaks much of faith in the Father and the Son and the Holy Ghost and the Word of God but never mentions the church. In the Book of Mormon, the worst sinners of all are members of the traditional church, which was often under condemnation as the church has been in this dispensation. It is quite unthinkable, of course, that the gospel should ever be under condemnation, for that is the Word in which we can put our entire faith.

10. After centuries of buildup looking toward that greatest of events, the coming to earth of the Creator him-

self, when the day finally arrives, we ask, "Where are the special effects of Steven Spielberg or George Lucas?" All the people see is "a man dressed in a white robe" who has to introduce himself. Also, he brings a lot of angels along with him.

And what do they do? They "minister" to the people. What does that mean?

An angel is a messenger; when he visits he not only talks with people, he converses with them—that is the word used both in the Book of Mormon and in the Bible. The angels circulated among men, women, and especially the children and chatted with them. That is how they carry out their mission or ministry.

Why don't we see angels?

The people raise that question in the Book of Mormon, and the answer there is very clear. Angels do not pose as ornamental fixtures; they come only to deliver important messages and at moments of crisis. Throughout the Book of Mormon, when things reach a hopeless condition, it is the visit of an angel which moves things off dead center and invariably inaugurates a new turn of things. They appear only to specially qualified persons—men, women, and children—not high officials. But if angels do not come, we are left on our own resources in a perilous condition. How fortunate that the whole Book of Mormon story begins with Moroni, the clinically specific and detailed account of an angel's visit to Joseph!

We are clearly told by Moroni how things operate. First of all he says, "Neither have angels ceased to minister unto the children of men," but they minister only as messengers "subject unto *him* [God], to minister according to the word of *his* command," and they show themselves only "unto them of strong faith and a firm mind in every form of godliness" (Moroni 7:29-30), not to hysterical, overimaginative, or ambitious people, but only to sane, sober, and intelligent ones. And these highly qualified people, "not only men, but women also" (Alma 32:23), have, as "the office of *their* ministry, . . . to fulfill and to do the work of the covenants," and by teaching these covenants, have "to prepare the way . . . by declaring the word of Christ unto chosen vessels of the Lord" (Moroni 7:31). These in turn bear testimony of him, "that the residue of men may have faith in Christ" (Moroni 7:32).

Isn't that a sort of trickle-down theory, like the thirty Aeons of the Gnostics, with the low man on the totem pole miles removed from the sublime source? Nothing of the sort. The last person to receive the message has as much right to revelation as the first. For it is given to "the residue of men . . . that the Holy Ghost may have a place in *their hearts,* according to the power thereof; and after this manner bringeth to pass the Father, the covenants which he hath made unto the children of men" (Moroni 7:32). So here we go clear back to the Father of all sharing the power with all. How this is done is most perfectly shown in 3 Nephi.

11. This is one side of the picture. A fundamental teaching of the Book of Mormon is that of the "awful gulf" that separates the two ways of life from each other. The Book of Mormon is edited to give equal attention to each, because our business here is to make a choice between them: "The devil . . . inviteth and enticeth to sin, and to do that which is evil continually. . . . But behold that which is of God inviteth and enticeth to do good continually" (Moroni 7:12-13). Drawn with equal attractive force toward either orbit, it is the individual who makes the final choice. Let us look at the dark side.

The Book of Mormon ends as it begins amidst scenes of destruction. The fearful process of this deathmarked tale is the syndrome familiar to all Latter-day Saints. God causes a righteous people to prosper, and the prosperous inevitably become corrupted by their prosperity. Inevitably? So it would seem: "And thus we can behold how false and also the unsteadiness of the hearts of the children of men. . . . At the very time when he doth prosper his people, . . . then is the time that they do harden their hearts, and do forget the Lord their God, and do trample under their feet the Holy One—yea, and this because of their ease, and their exceedingly great prosperity" (Helaman 12:1-2). Must it be that way? Helaman, completely fed up with the exasperating routine, has composed a neat example of the mingled genres of ancient wisdom literature and lamentation literature, which is now recognized as shared by Egypt and Israel. Helaman has given us a little gem: "O how foolish, and how vain, and how evil, and devilish, and how quick to do iniquity, and how slow to do good, are the children of men; yea, how quick to hearken unto the words of the evil one, and to set their hearts upon the vain things of the world! . . . Yea, how slow to walk in *wisdom's* paths! . . . O how great is the nothingness of the children of men; yea, even they are less than the dust of the earth," and so on. (Helaman 12:4-7). This is precisely the conclusion of Sophocles: "O human race, after careful calculation I conclude that you are equal to exactly nothing!"[14]

In keeping with the genre, this particular piece is the only part of the Book of Mormon which considers *cosmology*, an indispensable element of ancient wisdom literature, and one which abounds in the book of Moses (published at the same time as the Book of Mormon) and the book of Abraham. It takes the form of the well-known apostrophe on the obedience of all nature to the eternal laws and even includes a sensational discovery that had been made back in Lehi's day, "for surely it is the earth that moveth and not the sun" (Helaman 12:15).

12. In turning again to economic matters I am, alas, not beating a dead horse.[15] Teaching a Book of Mormon class last semester, I was brought to my senses with a shock—the Book of Mormon has become alarmingly, ter-

rifyingly, relevant. If a superabundance of riches virtually guarantees destruction, why doesn't God put an end to the comedy by simply withholding the dangerous wealth, as he withheld the rain when Nephi asked him to? (Helaman 11:4). That is a question with which the Book of Mormon is especially concerned, laboring the point that this life is "a state of probation" in which all must be put to the test (2 Nephi 2:21); and for that "it must needs be that there was an opposition" (2 Nephi 2:15), and that men might be given a good chance to make their decisions: "And the days of the children of men were prolonged . . . that they might repent while in the flesh" (2 Nephi 2:21). And to be effective the test must be, as Karl Popper assures us,[16] the hardest possible test: Would you be willing to turn down a certificate which is good for "anything in this world"? As drugs are not the real problem in the world today, nor armaments, nor sex, nor pollution, nor corruption in business and government, and on and on, so likewise in the Book of Mormon a multitude of sins is invariably traced back to one source: it is, of course, money which is the spoiler: "Now the cause of this iniquity of the people was this: . . . pride, tempting them to seek for power, and authority, and riches, and the vain things of the world" (3 Nephi 6:15). It is the rich mix of our prime-time TV. This "common whore of mankind that put'st odds among the rout of nations"[17] leads in the Book of Mormon from great wars to the more assured way of acquiring power and gain—organized crime. Kishkumen wants to run things by occupying the chief judgment seat, from which he could reward his supporters and have his friends "placed in power and authority among the people" (Helaman 2:5). He hired a fast-talking professional hit man, Gadianton, who was "exceedingly expert in many words and also in his craft," to organize his mafia for a highly efficient brand of "secret work of murder and of robbery." He took over Kishkumen's operation (Helaman 2:4). But when a servant of Helaman the Chief Judge was able to penetrate the organization as a "plant," Gadianton had to get out of the country (Helaman 2:11). At this point we are assured that, in time, Gadianton's gang would prove "almost the entire destruction of the people of Nephi" (Helaman 2:13). If ever a story was worth heeding after that announcement, this is one to which we should pay the closest attention—a nation helpless to resist the march of crime!

In Helaman 3, after a thumbnail picture of a civilization—a skillfully condensed vignette like one of those astonishing ivory panoramas carved on a single elephant's tusk (Helaman 3:14), we are introduced into the underworld and are told how skillfully the crime families gradually infiltrate the whole society during a time of peace and prosperity, getting themselves "established in the more settled parts of the land" so quietly that their activities "were not known unto those who were at the head of the government" (Helaman 3:23). The prosperity of the time is actually called "astonishing beyond measure," a time of "peace and exceedingly great joy" (Helaman 3:25, 32). Yet scarcely two years later "pride . . . began to enter into the church" (Helaman 3:33), and soon "the more humble part of the people," suffering great persecutions, "did wax stronger and stronger in their humility" (Helaman 3:34-35), while the great majority had their vices "grow upon them from day to day, . . . because of their exceedingly great riches and their prosperity" (Helaman 3:36-37). Such was the way of the church. The general public (not the church members) were able to drive out the worst criminals, who went to stir things up among the Lamanites (Helaman 4:1-2) and finally persuaded them to make war against the Nephites who had thrown them out. The worst offenders in those days were "those who professed to belong to the church of God. And it was because of the pride of their hearts, because of their exceeding riches, yea, of their oppression of the poor, withholding their substance from the hungry," and so on (Helaman 4:11-12), that "in the space of not many years" (Helaman 4:26) the Nephites were reduced to a sorry, materialistic people, hopelessly outnumbered by their enemies but with no inclination whatsoever to call upon God. "The voice of the people . . . chose evil, . . . therefore they were ripening for destruction, for the laws had become corrupted" (Helaman 5:2). Nephi gave up the judgment seat in disgust (Helaman 5:4).

At this time, thanks to free and open intercourse with all trade barriers removed between the Lamanites and the Nephites, both enjoyed unparalleled prosperity. With the usual result: "For behold, the Lord had blessed them so long with the riches of the world that . . . they began to set their hearts upon their riches; yea, they began to seek to get gain that they might be lifted up one above another." In short, they became more competitive, "therefore they began to commit secret murders, and to rob and plunder, that they might get gain" (Helaman 6:17). It was time for the syndicate "formed by Kishkumen and Gadianton" to come out into the open (Helaman 6:18). Their system of protection worked so well that "the more part of the Nephites . . . did unite themselves with those bands of robbers, and did enter into their covenants and their oaths, that they would protect and preserve one another, . . . that they should not suffer for their murders . . . and their stealings" (Helaman 6:21). And this is ominous. They operated by the rules of their organization and "not according to the laws of their country," which they felt were too confining (Helaman 6:24). Money was the name of the game (Helaman 6:31); the prospect of huge profits "seduced the more part of the righteous until they had come down to believe in their works and partake of their spoils" (Helaman 6:38). With this solid public support, the crime syndicate was able to "obtain sole management of the government," and, as their first act, "turn their backs upon the poor and the meek and the humble followers of God" (Helaman 6:39).

The Gadiantons knew where the real power lay, and they were careful to fill the judgment seats with their own people who could make and interpret the laws to their own advantage, "letting the guilty and the wicked go unpunished because of their money." And what could anybody do about it, now they were the law, "held in office at the head of the government, to rule and do according to their wills" (Helaman 7:5), deciding for themselves what was right and wrong and enjoying unlimited power? Nephi was helpless in his high office and looked on "in the agony of his soul" (Helaman 7:6). I have told about these things before, but in the light of recent events, they begin to take on a new meaning. The Nephite society had achieved a rich mix of prime-time TV, which has become the domestic fare of our own time; with everybody out "to get gain, to be praised of men, . . . [setting] your hearts upon the riches and the vain things of this world, for the which ye do murder, and plunder, and steal, and bear false witness" (Helaman 7:21). And yet in all this they considered themselves very righteous—it was all perfectly legal (Helaman 7:5; 8:1-7). It was time for something to happen—a terrible drought at Nephi's request brought the people to their senses and broke the Gadianton power (Helaman 11:4-10).

But a new threat arose. The criminal element took to the hills and there established retreats where they built up strength from dissenters joining them until they were able to reestablish the Gadianton organization. Terrorism was the name of the game. From their secure places they would strike and withdraw, making a special effort to kidnap "especially women and children," to assure the permanence of their society (Helaman 11:33). At the same time, Zoramite recruiters brought a host of young Nephites into the organization by the prospect of such things as romantic adventure, gaudy makeup, danger, loot, and license to kill

(3 Nephi 1:28-30). Soldiers of fortune also flocked to the camps. The fact that at this time the victims too were becoming cynical and corrupt leads Helaman to his outburst of wisdom literature (Helaman 12).

13. At this point the Book of Mormon scores another hit. These bands of robbers it describes are not some exotic invention of romantic fancy, but a major factor in world history. We think of the age-old traditions of Seth and his robber bands in the Egyptian literature (al-ᶜArish, *Sieg über Seth*), of the Pompey's Pirates or the Algerians, the Vikings, the Free Companies of the fourteenth century, the Kazaks, the Robber Barons, the Assassins, the Bagaudi, the Druze, the militant orders that imitated them (Templars, Knights of Rhodes, and so on), the Vitalian Brothers, the Riffs, and finally the Medellin drug lords of the south, whose long arm can constrain the leaders of nations. All of these operators were terrorists, and they held whole armies at bay and overthrew kingdoms. The best and perhaps the earliest description of such bands in action is from the Amarna Letters, where we find Lehi's own ancestors, the wandering, plundering Khabiru of the fourteenth century B.C., actually overthrowing city after city in Palestine and disrupting the lives of nations.

In the manner of such hosts, the Gadiantons were able to defy the police and the military and put punitory forces to flight (3 Nephi 2:11-12). It took a general strike to starve them out because, like all military, "there was no way that they could subsist save it were to plunder and rob and murder" (3 Nephi 4:5). Then there came another time of peace, and many of the robbers were reformed and rehabilitated—they were human beings after all; "and now there was nothing in all the land to hinder the people from prospering continually, except they should fall into transgression" (3 Nephi 6:5). It was clear sailing ahead, a happy ending to a storm-tossed journey, a splendid economic boom and the flowering of a business civilization.

And how long did it stay on course? For about two years —
when "there became a great inequality in all the land,
insomuch that the church began to be broken up" (3 Nephi
6:14). Broken up into what? Why, to be sure, into "ranks,
according to their riches and chances for learning," a yup-
pie civilization (3 Nephi 6:12). And what caused it all? The
same rich TV mix: "Now the *cause* of this iniquity was
this: . . . Satan . . . [was] stirring up the people . . . with
pride, tempting them to seek for power, and authority,
and riches, and the vain things of the world" (3 Nephi
6:15).

14. And now comes another episode which in the past
few years has taken on painfully familiar aspects. There
was a law that every warrant of execution had to be signed
by the governor of the land, so that "no lawyer nor judge
nor high priest" could get rid of inconvenient witnesses
or critics (3 Nephi 6:22), as they had tried to get rid of
Nephi when only the force of public opinion stopped them
(Helaman 8:7-10). "Many . . . who testified of the things
pertaining to Christ . . . were taken and put to death secretly by the judges, so that the knowledge of their death
came not unto the governor . . . until after their death"
(3 Nephi 6:23). In other words, they sometimes found it
necessary to go beyond the law. Since that was grossly
unconstitutional "a complaint came . . . to the governor
of the land against these judges" (3 Nephi 6:25). There
was an investigation and indictment. When the time came
for the judges to be brought to trial, their supporters closed
ranks, determined to get them off: "Now . . . those judges
had many friends and kindreds; and . . . almost all the
lawyers and the high priests did gather themselves together and unite with the kindreds of those judges who
were to be tried according to the law" (3 Nephi 6:27). This
inbred and influential establishment was determined to
block any conviction of those upright judges. They agreed
on a coup to get the release of the guilty parties "from the

grasp of justice which was about to be administered according to the law [their Constitution]. And they did set at defiance the law and the rights of their country; and they did covenant one with another to destroy the governor, and to establish a king over the land" (3 Nephi 7:29-30). They wanted a leader who would not be hampered by legislative checks and restraints of any kind. The standard solution lay ready at hand: They murdered the chief executive. In the confusion that followed, the people broke up into tribes, "every man according to his family and his kindred and friends; and thus they did destroy the government of the land" (3 Nephi 7:2). At last they were free of annoying government regulations of which Korihor and others had complained long before: "And the regulations of the government were destroyed because of the secret combination of the friends and kindreds" (3 Nephi 7:6). Needless to say, everything was thrown into confusion and was a free-for-all game of grabbing, since "the more righteous part of the people had nearly all become wicked" (3 Nephi 7:7). And this, Nephi marvels, had all taken place in six short years. If we think these switches are too sudden, we have only to consider the changes that take place in our own society with a change of administrations, or compare the state of the world in one decade with that of the next. The people immediately missed the advantages of the central government and were united only in their hatred of the people who had led in its destruction (3 Nephi 7:11).

15. Less than a month ago I gave students in a Book of Mormon class the choice of writing a term paper on either a religious or economic theme. Ninety-four percent of the class chose the theme "Discuss the problem of riches in the Book of Mormon." Almost every scholar began by evoking the sacred cliche: there is nothing wrong with wealth itself; wealth as such is good. It is only how you use it that may be bad. They insisted that a free market

was the perfect and flawless order of things, the ordained sanction of free agency. It is only when the system is abused that things go wrong, and that in itself proves that it is good in itself.

How do we escape abuses? How do we avoid breathing polluted air on a busy street? Simply stop breathing. In the Book of Mormon, the destructive power of wealth is pervasive and inescapable, since, as Helaman discovered, we can always count on humanity to do foolish things. The question is, what economic system *would* suit such people? The Book of Mormon answer is clear: None that *they* could devise. The Nephites willfully and repeatedly rejected the way that is shown them "with exceedingly great plainness" (Enos 1:23); have we any assurance that we, whom the book is designed to warn against that very folly, are doing any better? Christ gave them the economic system by which they lived happily for a far longer period than any of the brief boom-cycles enjoyed by the Nephites. And we know what he taught; should that not suffice? Should not 4 Nephi put an end to all argument and sophistry? If we want answers, here they are. Yet, strangely, for Mormons this is off limits and out-of-bounds — so long ago and far away! But the purpose of the Book of Mormon is to make all things present to us; it has been edited to delete anything not relevant to our condition. It makes no difference where or in which dispensation we live (Mosiah 3:13), all are tested equally. And now the Book of Mormon is holding the mirror up to our ugliness — no wonder we look the other way as it pleads with us, "[O], be more wise than we have been!" (Mormon 9:31).

The two passages which the students choose to score their point are anything but a brief for riches if we read them with care. They were highly favored by the class because out of more than sixty statements on the seeking of wealth in the Book of Mormon, these are virtually the only ones that can be interpreted as giving countenance to the profit motive. The first of these passages is Jacob 2:18-19: "But before ye seek for riches, seek ye for the kingdom of God. And after ye have obtained a hope in Christ, ye shall obtain riches if ye seek them." That is the great favorite.

It is standard practice to stop there and leave it at that. But even if we go no further, the plain lesson of the injunction is to seek the kingdom of God first of all. And how do we build up the kingdom of God and establish Zion? By observing and keeping the law of consecration. What does that mean? The preceding verse, routinely overlooked, explains: "Think of your brethren like unto yourselves, and be familiar with all and free with your substance." How free? "That they may be rich like unto you" (Jacob 2:17). That looks suspiciously like equalizing the wealth—this is with reference to "substance"; you cannot get out of it by saying you will make them "spiritually rich." We give to the poor enough to make us feel virtuous and keep them on the leash, but the order here is for a basic redistribution of wealth. And when do you stop seeking the kingdom of God on the earth and turn to seeking riches? Certainly not as long as the Lord's Prayer is effective. If God's kingdom is to come (a place on earth where his will is done), then we must remove the great obstacle to it—the burden of debt which binds all mankind and robs them of freedom of choice and action. That removal is "the Lord's release" (like Solon's *seisachtheia*), the cancellation of all debts, required by what we think of as the primitive, savage, tribal law of Moses (Leviticus 25)—far more humane than our own. The Lord's Prayer given in the Book of Mormon preserves the correct business terminology of Matthew 6:12: "Forgive our debts as we forgive our debtors" (routinely softened to read "trespasses"). It is a literal cancellation of debt which is required by the Mosiac Law before we can have the kingdom of God on earth. "It is not given that one man should possess that

which is above another, wherefore the world lieth in sin"
(D&C 49:20). But when do you start seeking riches for
yourself? Never, according to Jacob, since your intent in
seeking them is to give to others. That is no way to max-
imize profits! But we are still ignoring that big "if," which
admonishes us to consider the context of the speech. Jacob
has gathered the people together because he has been
commanded to give them two messages which he is very
reluctant to deliver, the first being an impassioned rebuke
to people possessed with gold fever. He must hold their
attention and not lose them completely. The best he can
do is to tell them that *if* they must seek riches, they should
get them under only two conditions, (1) seeking for the
kingdom of God, which means not giving up until you
have found it, and (2) seeking with the intent to give to
others, to the point of achieving the kingdom.

Did anyone heed Jacob's advice? At the end of his life
he was still pleading desperately with his people (Jacob
6:5-13). And under his son Enos, we find that "the people
were a stiffnecked people, hard to understand. And there
was nothing save it was exceeding harshness, preaching
and prophesying of wars, . . . and continually reminding
them of death, . . . continually to keep them in the fear of
the Lord . . . [to] keep them from going down speedily to
destruction" (Enos 1:22-23). So much for the Jacob formula
as a franchise for big money.

The other passage they all love is Alma 1:29: "Because
of the steadiness of the church they began to be exceedingly
rich, . . . and thus in their prosperous circumstances, they
did not send away any who were naked or that were hungry, . . . and they did not set their hearts upon riches;
therefore they were liberal to all, . . . whether out of the
church or in the church, having no respect to persons as
to [not 'among'] those who stood in need." So much for
those convenient weasel-words "the deserving poor."
How long did the people thus described resist the eroding

effects of riches? Within five years "Alma saw the wickedness of the church. . . . Yea, he saw the great inequality
among the people, . . . some turning their backs upon the
needy; . . . and seeing all their inequality, [Alma] began
to be very sorrowful" (Alma 4:8-15).

Nothing has surprised me more this past year than to
discover how aware our young people are of the extent of
injustice, arrogance, and greed where it should not be. In
particular they have wide experience of the singular disregard by LDS employers of the Lord's command given
personally in the Book of Mormon not to "oppress the
hireling in his wages" (3 Nephi 24:5).

There is one remarkably lucid and direct fable on the
possibility of being both rich and righteous which should
pretty well settle the issue. Amulek was an eminently successful man, a direct descendent of Nephi (Alma 10:2-3)
and proud of his genealogy and important family connections—a true aristocrat: "I have many kindreds and friends,
and I have acquired also much riches by the hand of my
industry" (Alma 10:4). A model citizen, hardworking, rich,
well-born, immensely respectable: "And behold, I am also
a man of no small reputation among all those who know
me" (Alma 10:4). But to get rich this man could not neglect
his business; he was contracted to Mammon instead of
God: "Nevertheless, after all this, I never have known
much of the ways of the Lord," even though he had the
best opportunity to know them, "for I have seen much of
his mysteries and his marvelous power. . . . Nevertheless,
I did harden my heart, for I was called many times and I
would not hear. . . . I knew concerning these things, yet
I would not know; therefore I went on rebelling against
God, in the wickedness of my heart" (Alma 10:5-6). That
went on until an angel stopped him (Alma 10:7). Being
thus admonished, Amulek forsook "all his gold, and silver,
and his precious things which were in the land of Am-
monihah, for the word of God" (Alma 15:16). It had to be

one or the other. But all was not lost, you might say, he still had his old friends and admirers and loved ones. Please let us not underestimate the power of money. Having lost his fortune, he was promptly "rejected by those who were once his friends and also by his father and his kindred" (Alma 15:16). Had Joseph Smith studied Timon of Athens?

Now this Amulek, during the years of his prosperity, would have merited the praise of one student who told in his term paper how he lived in the richest ward in the stake which was full of very many, very rich and successful businessmen, who were none the less Christlike because they gave to the poor. So do the Mafiosi, thus purchasing public respect and even sanction for their gains. Students are fond of evoking the names of highly successful Latter-day Saint businessmen, who have endowed monuments to themselves with their left hand while none of their admirers knew what their right hand was doing. Wherever giving or money is the issue, "How much?" is the only question. The widow's mite? Were the donors still rich after they had given? Was it enough to bring everyone up to an equal level, as the Book of Mormon commands? (Jacob 2:17).

16. Let us recall how the Nephites had to be constantly brought into line by "exceeding harshness, preaching and prophesying of wars, and contentions, and destructions, and continually reminding them of death, . . . stirring them up continually to keep them in fear of the Lord. . . . Nothing short of these things . . . would keep them from going down speedily to destruction" (Enos 1:23). This is an important phenomenon in the history of the church. We always seem to be right on the brink—because we are. If world history is a succession of recurrent scenarios, then we must look forward to certain set situations, good and bad. We are told, for example, that Jerusalem was destroyed again and again: "And as one generation has been destroyed among the Jews because of iniquity, even so

have they been destroyed from generation to generation according to their iniquities; and never hath any of them been destroyed save it were foretold them by the prophets of the Lord" (2 Nephi 25:9). So here is our standard Book of Mormon scenario. For a hundred and sixty years we have been calling these the *last* days. The forlorn figure with the sign reading "The World Will End Tomorrow" is much nearer to reality than the smart readers of the *New Yorker* who laugh at him; merely change that "tomorrow" to "the near future," and the bell tolls for every one of them. Throughout the Book of Mormon, people are looking forward to the coming of the Lord, and the Master of the House does not want anyone to know the exact time — not even the angels (Matthew 25:13, D&C 49:7). He plans to catch us doing our normal thing. So the lesson is that we must keep plugging away at the business of repentance as if the Lord were to come and inspect us today.

Until that time, we must withhold judgment of others. Another teaching that is coming into full force just now is the Book of Mormon admonition to be more patient with the imperfections of the church and less patient with our own. The church is a training school in which everyone is there for the training. So don't waste time criticizing the authorities. In that regard the Book of Mormon gives us another neat example. Moroni had very good reason to complain about the top men of the nation "sitting upon [their] . . . thrones in a state of thoughtless stupor" while the work of death was going on all around them (Alma 60:7). Many today are complaining of a like situation. Anyone can see the horrendous abuses, incompetence, dishonesty, cruelty, and immorality thriving on all sides; but from the control centers comes only a dignified silence. Many are very disturbed by this. "Brutus, thou sleepest!" is the cry. But the moral of the story, as it turns out, is that Moroni in his criticism was wrong, completely out of order; he simply did not understand the situation. He was quite right about the crime, but it was not for him to apportion the guilt. So let us, when distressed by the inadequacies of others, remember the number-one instruction of the Book of Mormon: "This is my doctrine . . . that the Father commandeth all men everywhere to repent and believe in me" (3 Nephi 11:32). This life is "a state of probation" (2 Nephi 2:21). "Be wise in the days of your probation" (Mormon 9:28). "Wo unto him . . . that wasteth the days of his probation, for awful is his state!" (2 Nephi 9:27).

Repentance is the main message of the Book of Mormon, which also tells us what repentance is. *Metanoia,* the New Testament word, contains no hint as to how we go about it, but the Greeks had a better instruction in the two great maxims from the temple at Delphi: "Know thyself" and "Nothing in excess." Both are lamely translated as advice for making friends and influencing people. Actually they are the rules by which the universe is governed; the one sets us on the right track, and the other keeps us there. The Book of Mormon tells us that the essence of repentance is knowing exactly what we are. King Benjamin really rubs it in: "Therefore, of what have ye to boast? And now I ask, can ye say ought of yourselves? . . . Ye cannot say that ye are even as much as the dust of the earth" (Mosiah 2:24-25). "Retain in remembrance the greatness of God, and your own nothingness, and his goodness and longsuffering towards you, unworthy creatures, and humble yourselves even in the depths of humility. . . . If ye do this ye shall always rejoice" (Mosiah 4:11-12). And this was on the occasion of a great national assembly celebrating years of victory and prosperity — the king is careful to throw cold water on the slightest indication of self-congratulation. The very purpose of our being here is repentance, and repentance is an unsettling exercise in self-knowledge: "O how great is the nothingness of . . . men" (Helaman 12:7). This is the time of probation and preparation; though we are born innocent, there are flaws in our nature, and it is the purpose of our earthlife to bring them out in the open through repentance and eradicate them through baptism, to clear the way for further progression. If there is any weakness in our characters, this is the setting in which it is bound to show up, this life is the day of our probation; whether we find ourselves in an unstable and dangerous or a safe and prosperous environment, it makes no difference — the bad stuff in us will come to the surface. We all feel the unreality of this life, and it makes us afraid of everything, "living lives of quiet desperation." Young and old people today are beset by hidden anxieties and will go for anything that promises security. Latter-day Saints even know what it means when the Lord says, "My Father worked out his kingdom in fear and trembling, and I must do the same."[18] That is exactly what we are doing. Until the reality of existence is found not in the great and spacious high-rise, but in that wholly different ambience on the other side of the Yawning Gulf, there will be no peace on this distracted globe. Apart from the way the Book of Mormon puts it, nothing else makes sense of a world that works like a badly assembled, badly repaired, badly operated, but beautifully designed machine.

But in seeking to know ourselves, we must not forget that other injunction — "Nothing in excess." Once we are on the path, we must stay with it. "Because strait is the gate and narrow is the way" (3 Nephi 14:14, 27:33). This not only refers to the control of appetites, desires, and passions, but it is what keeps the universe itself viable — without it life would be impossible. It is that fine-tuning that guarantees that the earth is not too near or too far from the sun, not too wet or too dry, not too hot or too cold, does not move too fast or too slowly, is not too large or too small, and so on. It is that constant fine-tuning which correlates the fifteen constants and makes this life possible. The Book of Mormon teaches us that we must observe it in all that we do. It is interesting how the wicked in the Book of Mormon, like the Zoramites and the people of Zarahemla and even the Gadianton society, go overboard in *both* directions at once, balancing their excess of worldly vanity by an equally obnoxious excess of ceremonial piety.

Recently a scientist has written that we can philosophize and theologize all we want to, but still there is no saving ourselves from the ultimate tragedy of a life that suddenly stops. John G. Taylor has written,

> We have come to the end of our story about the universe. It is full of violent actions and grim forebodings. . . . The natural reaction to such a tale is [for] . . . each of us to live our lives untouched by these immensities, and by the catastrophes to come. The satisfaction gained from the simple round of life need be unaltered. . . . We may live and die without raising up our eyes to the heavens, secure in the safety of our cotton-wool globe. Yet that is false. We cannot divorce our lives from our understanding of the world around us, and especially the basic problems of existence, the impossible questions of the universe. It is our answers, or lack of them, which determine our actions, even from day to day. For whatever we do, we must somehow come to terms with the infinite before we can act.[19]

And we ask ourselves in view of our untouched potentialities, "Is that all there is?" That is the question of the day, the terrible question. We are in the position of the Nephites in their final stages who were frantic with grief—not for their sins, as Mormon laments, but because they could not go on enjoying them indefinitely; the whole society, so to speak, had the AIDS mentality: "But behold this my joy was vain, for their sorrowing was not unto repentance, . . . but it was rather the sorrowing of the damned, because the Lord would not always suffer them to take happiness in sin" (Mormon 2:13). Suddenly it becomes clear how the ultimate lessons of the Book of Mormon converge on the present scene. The futility of military solutions: "It is by the wicked that the wicked are punished" (Mormon 4:5). "Ye must lay down your weapons of war . . . and take them not again" (Mormon 7:4). "Man shall not judge, neither shall he smite" (Mormon 8:20). This in accordance with what I call the Great General Order: "For the Lord worketh not in secret combinations, neither doth he will that man should shed blood, but in all things hath forbidden it, from the beginning of man" (Ether 8:19). This rule was actually observed by the Saints during Johnston's War, and it reads now like the epitaph of the modern world. We now know the fate of all those who set their hearts on riches. We know that God esteems all flesh in one. We discover that the powerful appeal of the Book of Mormon is a deep, warm, personal affection miraculously conveyed to the reader personally from the writers. We know that this is not our real existence—even the Gentiles feel that and resent the madness of it all. Here we are nothing, but here we want everything, because we think this is our only chance. And it is indeed our only chance in a sense. Our great day of probation in which we show how we can adjust ourselves to eternity—here is where we do it.

Notes

1. Yigael Yadin, *Bar-Kochba* (New York: Random House, 1971), 247-48.

2. Nahman Avigad, *Hebrew Bullae from the Time of Jeremiah* (Jerusalem: Israel Exploration Society, 1986), 133-36.

3. John L. Hilton, "Book of Mormon 'Wordprint' Measurements Using 'Wrap-Around' Block Counting" (Provo: F.A.R.M.S., 1988).

4. H. Haertel, "Buddha," in *Die Religion in Geschichte und Gegenwart* (Tübingen: Mohr, 1957), 1:1469-73.

5. Ibid.

6. Erik Hornung, *Grundzüge der ägyptischen Geschichte* (Darmstadt: Wissenschaftlich Buchgesellschaft, 1978), 2.

7. Ibid., 4.

8. James G. Frazer, *The Golden Bough*, 12 vols. (New York: Macmillan, 1935), 11:285-86.

9. Hugh W. Nibley, *An Approach to the Book of Mormon* (Salt Lake City: Deseret Book, 1957), 178-89; reprinted in *CWHN* 6:209-21.

10. Friedrich Jeremias, "Semitische Völker in Vorderasien," in A. Bertholet and E. Lehmann, *Lehrbuch der Religionsgeschichte* (Tübingen: Mohr, 1925), 1:620, 641; Izebel is a goddess named "na" in a Phoenician inscription from Cyprus, world center of the love-cult; also in Palestine.

11. The intermarriage of these people is discussed in Nibley, *An Approach to the Book of Mormon*, 58-69; in *CWHN* 6:71-83.

12. Hornung, *Grundzüge*, 5.

13. S. C. Northrop Filmer, *The Meeting of East and West* (New York: Macmillan, 1946), cited in R. Buckminster Fuller, *Earth Inc.* (Garden City, New York: Anchor, 1973), 391.

14. Sophocles, *Oedipus Rex*, lines 1186-89.

15. These topics are also discussed in Nibley, *An Approach to the Book of Mormon*, 336-65; in *CWHN* 6:400-43; Hugh W. Nibley, *Since Cumorah* (Salt Lake City: Deseret Book, 1970), 373-435; in *CWHN* 7:337-97.

16. Karl R. Popper, "Science: Problems, Aims, Responsibilities," *Federation of American Societies for Experimental Biology* 22 (1963): 963-64.

17. William Shakespeare, *Timon of Athens*, Act 4, Scene 3, line 43.

18. Joseph Smith, *Teachings of the Prophet Joseph Smith*, selected by Joseph Fielding Smith (Salt Lake City: Deseret Book, 1938), 349.

19. John G. Taylor, *Black Holes* (New York: Avon, 1975), 187-88.

Scripture References

572

Index

Abinadi, 285-86, 487-88;
likened to Teacher of
Righteousness in Dead Sea
Scrolls, 303-9
Abraham: lost history of, 108;
as "psychanodic" hero, 499
Adams, Charles Francis, 172
Aeneid, the, 504
Akish, 440
Allegro, John, 385
Alma, name of, 281-82, 310
Alma the Elder: wilderness
church founded by, 252,
285-86, 311-12, 317-25; wrote
Abinadi's words, 285, 310;
flees with righteous
followers, 502
Alma the Younger: book of,
224; confrontation of, with
Korihor, 342-43; forsook
office to bear testimony,
354-55, 361, 466-67, 514; duel
of, with Amlici, 491, 523-24
Amalickiah, 331-34, 358, 437-
38, 510-11
Amalickiahites, 282-83, 356-57
Amaron, 484
America: elephants in, 111-12;
ancient ruins in, 255;
ancient, lack of knowledge
about, 499; ethnic mix in,
544-46

Amiet, Pierre, 110
Amlici, 491, 523-24
Ammon: missionary labors of,
355-56, 465-66, 486-87, 524;
defends flocks at waters of
Sebus, 539-40
Ammonites, 356, 466, 487, 502,
514, 517
Ammoron, 353
Amulek, 562-63
Andrews, E.W., 373
Angel Moroni, 234, 549
Angels, ministering of, 548,
549-50
Anselm (St.), 174
Anthon Transcript, 136, 386
Anticipation, church of, 76-83,
250-51, 308
Apocalypses of major
prophets, 391-92, 470
Apocalyptic writings, 89-90,
411-12, 470, 499-500
Apocrypha: corruption of, 74;
apocalyptic themes in, 89-90;
stereotyped imagery in, 92;
arbitrary classification of,
213. *See also* Forty-day
writings
Arabs, 103-4
Arbaugh, George B., 140-41
Archaeology: inconclusiveness
of, 265-66; parallels in, on